T0178643

Lecture Notes in Computer Science 14358

The series Lecture Notes in Computer Science (LNCS), including its subseries Lecture Notes in Artificial Intelligence (LNAI) and Lecture Notes in Bioinformatics (LNBI), has established itself as a medium for the publication of new developments in computer science and information technology research, teaching, and education.

LNCS enjoys close cooperation with the computer science R & D community, the series counts many renowned academics among its volume editors and paper authors, and collaborates with prestigious societies. Its mission is to serve this international community by providing an invaluable service, mainly focused on the publication of conference and workshop proceedings and postproceedings. LNCS commenced publication in 1973.

Huchuan Lu · Wanli Ouyang · Hui Huang ·
Jiwen Lu · Risheng Liu · Jing Dong · Min Xu
Editors

Image
and Graphics

12th International Conference, ICIG 2023
Nanjing, China, September 22–24, 2023
Proceedings, Part IV

Springer

Editors
Huchuan Lu ⓘ
Dalian University of Technology
Dalian, China

Hui Huang ⓘ
Shenzhen University
Shenzhen, China

Risheng Liu ⓘ
Dalian University of Technology
Dalian, China

Min Xu ⓘ
University of Technology Sydney
Sydney, NSW, Australia

Wanli Ouyang ⓘ
University of Sydney
Sydney, NSW, Australia

Jiwen Lu ⓘ
Tsinghua University
Beijing, China

Jing Dong ⓘ
Institute of Automation, CAS
Beijing, China

ISSN 0302-9743   ISSN 1611-3349 (electronic)
Lecture Notes in Computer Science
ISBN 978-3-031-46313-6   ISBN 978-3-031-46314-3 (eBook)
https://doi.org/10.1007/978-3-031-46314-3

This Springer imprint is published by the registered company Springer Nature Switzerland AG
The registered company address is: Gewerbestrasse 11, 6330 Cham, Switzerland

Paper in this product is recyclable.

Preface

These are the proceedings of the 12th International Conference on Image and Graphics (ICIG 2023), which was held in Nanjing, China, on September 22–24, 2023. The Conference was hosted by China Society of Image and Graphics (CSIG), organized by Nanjing University of Posts & Telecommunications, co-organized by Nanjing University of Science & Technology and Nanjing University of Information Science and Technology, supported by Springer.

ICIG is a biennial conference that focuses on innovative technologies of image, video, and graphics processing and fostering innovation, entrepreneurship, and networking. ICIG 2023 featured world-class plenary speakers, exhibits, and high-quality peer-reviewed oral and poster presentations.

CSIG has hosted the series of ICIG conference since 2000. Details about the past conferences are as follows:

Conference	Place	Date	Submitted	Proceedings
First (ICIG 2000)	Tianjin, China	August 16–18	220	156
Second (ICIG 2002)	Hefei, China	August 15–18	280	166
Third (ICIG 2004)	Hong Kong, China	December 17–19	460	140
4th (ICIG 2007)	Chengdu, China	August 22–24	525	184
5th (ICIG 2009)	Xi'an, China	September 20–23	362	179
6th (ICIG 2011)	Hefei, China	August 12–15	329	183
7th (ICIG 2013)	Qingdao, China	July 26–28	346	181
8th (ICIG 2015)	Tianjin, China	August 13–16	345	170
9th (ICIG 2017)	Shanghai, China	September 13–15	370	172
10th (ICIG 2019)	Beijing, China	August 23–25	384	183
11th (ICIG 2021)	Haikou, China	December 26–28	421	198

For ICIG 2023, 409 submissions were received and 166 papers were accepted. To ease the search for a required paper in these proceedings, the accepted papers have been arranged into different sections according to their topic.

We sincerely thank all the contributors, who came from around the world to present their advanced work at this event. We would also like to thank all the reviewers, who carefully reviewed all submissions and made their valuable comments for improving the accepted papers. The proceedings could not have been produced without the invaluable efforts of the members of the Organizing Committee, and a number of active members of CSIG.

September 2023

Huchuan Lu
Wanli Ouyang
Hui Huang
Jiwen Lu
Risheng Liu
Jing Dong
Min Xu

Organization

Organizing Committee

General Chairs

Yaonan Wang   Hunan University, China
Qingshan Liu   Nanjing University of Posts &
     Telecommunications, China
Ramesh Jain   University of California, Irvine, USA
Alberto Del Bimbo   University of Florence, Italy

Technical Program Chairs

Huchuan Lu   Dalian University of Technology, China
Wanli Ouyang   University of Sydney, Australia
Hui Huang   Shenzhen University, China
Jiwen Lu   Tsinghua University, China

Organizing Committee Chairs

Yuxin Peng   Peking University, China
Xucheng Yin   University of Science and Technology Beijing,
     China
Bo Du   Wuhan University, China
Bingkun Bao   Nanjing University of Posts &
     Telecommunications, China

Publicity Chairs

Abdulmotaleb El Saddik   University of Ottawa, Canada
Phoebe Chen   La Trobe University, Australia
Kun Zhou   Zhejiang University, China
Xiaojun Wu   Jiangnan University, China

Award Chairs

Changsheng Xu	Institute of Automation, CAS, China
Shiguang Shan	Institute of Computing Technology, CAS, China
Mohan Kankanhalli	National University of Singapore, Singapore

Publication Chairs

Risheng Liu	Dalian University of Technology, China
Jing Dong	Institute of Automation, CAS, China
Min Xu	University of Technology Sydney, Australia

Workshop Chairs

Yugang Jiang	Fudan University, China
Kai Xu	National University of Defense Technology, China
Zhu Li	University of Missouri, USA
Oliver Deussen	Universität Konstanz, Germany

Exhibits Chairs

Qi Tian	Huawei Cloud, China
Wu Liu	JD.COM, China
Weishi Zheng	Sun Yat-sen University, China
Kun Xu	Tsinghua University, China

Tutorial Chairs

Weiwei Xu	Zhejiang University, China
Nannan Wang	Xidian University, China
Shengsheng Qian	Institute of Automation, CAS, China
Klaus Schöffmann	Klagenfurt University, Austria

Sponsorship Chairs

Xiang Bai	Huazhong University of Science and Technology, China
Mingming Cheng	Nankai University, China

Finance Chairs

Lifang Wu	Beijing University of Technology, China
Yubao Sun	Nanjing University of Information Science & Technology, China
Miao Hong	CSIG, China

Social Media Chairs

Zhenwei Shi	Beihang University, China
Wei Jia	Hefei University of Technology, China
Feifei Zhang	Tianjin University of Technology, China

Local Chairs

Jian Cheng	Institute of Automation, CAS, China
Xiaotong Yuan	Nanjing University of Information Science & Technology, China
Yifan Jiao	Nanjing University of Posts & Telecommunications, China

Website Chairs

Rui Huang	Chinese University of Hong Kong, Shenzhen, China
Jie Wang	Nanjing University of Posts & Telecommunications, China

Area Chairs

Yuchao Dai	Xi Peng	Yong Xia
Yulan Guo	Boxin Shi	Shiqing Xin
Xiaoguang Han	Dong Wang	Feng Xu
Tong He	Lijun Wang	Jia Xu
Gao Huang	Limin Wang	Kun Xu
Meina Kan	Nannan Wang	Yongchao Xu
Yu-Kun Lai	Xinchao Wang	Junchi Yan
Li Liu	Xinggang Wang	Shiqi Yu
Huimin Lu	Yunhai Wang	Jian Zhang
Jinshan Pan	Baoyuan Wu	Pingping Zhang
Houwen Peng	Jiazhi Xia	Shanshan Zhang

Additional Reviewers

Bingkun Bao
Yulong Bian
Chunjuan Bo
Zi-Hao Bo
JIntong Cai
Zhanchuan Cai
Mingwei Cao
Jianhui Chang
Yakun Chang
Bin Chen
Guang Chen
Hongrui Chen
Jianchuan Chen
Junsong Chen
Siming Chen
Xiang Chen
Xin Chen
Ziyang Chen
Jinghao Cheng
Lechao Cheng
Ming-Ming Cheng
Jiaming Chu
Hainan Cui
Yutao Cui
Enyan Dai
Tao Dai
Jisheng Dang
Sagnik Das
Xinhao Deng
Haiwen Diao
Jian Ding
Wenhui Dong
Xiaoyu Dong
Shuguang Dou
Zheng-Jun Du
Peiqi Duan
Qingnan Fan
Yongxian Fan
Zhenfeng Fan
Gongfan Fang
Kun Fang
Sheng Fang
Xianyong Fang

Zhiheng Fu
Wei Gai
Ziliang Gan
Changxin Gao
Qing Gao
Shang Gao
Zhifan Gao
Tong Ge
Shenjian Gong
Guanghua Gu
Yuliang Gu
Shihui Guo
Yahong Han
Yizeng Han
Yufei Han
Junwen He
Mengqi He
Xiaowei He
Yulia Hicks
Yuchen Hong
Ruibing Hou
Shouming Hou
Donghui Hu
Fuyuan Hu
Lanqing Hu
Qiming Hu
Ruimin Hu
Yang Hu
Yupeng Hu
Bao Hua
Guanjie Huang
Le Hui
Chengtao Ji
Naye Ji
Xiaosong Jia
Xu Jia
Chaohui Jiang
Haoyi Jiang
Peng Jiang
Runqing Jiang
Zhiying Jiang
Leyang Jin
Yongcheng Jing

Hao Ju
Yongzhen Ke
Lingshun Kong
Jian-Huang Lai
Yu-Kun Lai
Xingyu Lan
Yang Lang
Wentao Lei
Yang Lei
Baohua Li
Bocen Li
Boyang Li
Chao Li
Chenghong Li
Dachong Li
Feng Li
Gang Li
Guanbin Li
Guorong Li
Guozheng Li
Hao Li
Hongjun Li
Kunhong Li
Li Li
Manyi Li
Ming Li
Mingjia Li
Qifeng Li
Shifeng Li
Shutao Li
Siheng Li
Xiaoyan Li
Yanchun Li
Yang Li
Yi Li
Ying Li
Yue Li
Yunhao Li
Zihan Li
Dongze Lian
Jinxiu Liang
Junhao Liang
Tian Liang

Zhengyu Liang
Zhifang Liang
Bencheng Liao
Zehui Liao
Chuan Lin
Feng Lin
Qifeng Lin
Weilin Lin
Wenbin Lin
Xiaotian Lin
Yiqun Lin
Jingwang Ling
Qiu Lingteng
Aohan Liu
Chang Liu
Cheng-Lin Liu
Haolin Liu
Jingxin Liu
Jinyuan Liu
Kenkun Liu
Lei Liu
Long Liu
Meng Liu
Min Liu
Qingshan Liu
Risheng Liu
Shengli Liu
Shiguang Liu
Shuaiqi Liu
Songhua Liu
Wei Liu
Wenrui Liu
Wenyu Liu
Xuehu Liu
Yiguang Liu
Yijing Liu
Yipeng Liu
Yong Liu
Yu Liu
Yunan Liu
Zhenguang Liu
Zilin Lu
Weiqi Luo
Yong Luo
Zhaofan Luo

Zhongjin Luo
Yunqiu Lv
Junfeng Lyu
Youwei Lyu
Chunyan Ma
Fengji Ma
Huimin Ma
Tianlei Ma
Xinke Ma
Qirong Mao
Yuxin Mao
Wei Miao
Yongwei Miao
Weidong Min
Jiawen Ming
Weihua Ou
Jinshan Pan
Yun Pei
Zongju Peng
Hongxing Qin
Liangdong Qiu
Xinkuan Qiu
Yuda Qiu
Zhong Qu
Weisong Ren
Nong Sang
Guangcun Shan
Linlin Shen
Zhiqiang Shen
Jiamu Sheng
Jun Shi
Zhenghao Shi
Zhenwei Shi
Chengfang Song
Jiechong Song
Jifei Song
Yong Song
Zhengyao Song
Qingtang Su
Jiande Sun
Long Sun
Xuran Sun
Zhixing Sun
Gary Tam
Hongchen Tan

Jing Tan
Jiajun Tang
Jin Tang
Shiyu Tang
Minggui Teng
Yao Teng
Yanling Tian
Zhigang Tu
Matthew Vowels
Bo Wang
Dong Wang
Dongsheng Wang
Haiting Wang
Hao Wang
Jingyi Wang
Jinjia Wang
Jinting Wang
Jinwei Wang
Junyu Wang
Lijun Wang
Longguang Wang
Meng Wang
Miao Wang
Peizhen Wang
Pengjie Wang
Rui Wang
Ruiqi Wang
Ruotong Wang
Shengjin Wang
Shijie Wang
Tao Wang
Xiaoxing Wang
Xin Wang
Xingce Wang
Yili Wang
Yingquan Wang
Yongfang Wang
Yue Wang
Yun Wang
Zi Wang
Hongjiang Wei
Shaokui Wei
Xiu-Shen Wei
Ziyu Wei
Shuchen Weng

Zhi Weng
Qian Wenhua
Jianlong Wu
Lianjun Wu
Tao Wu
Yadong Wu
Yanmin Wu
Ye Wu
Yu Wu
Yushuang Wu
Di Xiao
Yuxuan Xiao
Jin Xie
Jingfen Xie
Jiu-Cheng Xie
Yutong Xie
Jiankai Xing
Bo Xu
Hongming Xu
Jie Xu
Xiaowei Xu
Yi Xu
Mingliang Xue
Xiangyang Xue
Difei Yan
Xin Yan
Yichao Yan
Zizheng Yan
Bin Yang
Cheng Yang
Jialin Yang
Kang Yang
Min Yang

Shuo Yang
Shuzhou Yang
Xingyi Yang
Xue Yang
Yang Yang
Yiqian Yang
Zhongbao Yang
Chao Yao
Chengtang Yao
Jingfeng Yao
Chongjie Ye
Dingqiang Ye
Jingwen Ye
Yiwen Ye
Xinyu Yi
Xinyi Ying
Di You
Bohan Yu
Chenyang Yu
Jiwen Yu
Runpeng Yu
Songsong Yu
Danni Yuan
Yang Yue
Lin Yushun
Qingjie Zeng
Qiong Zeng
Yaopei Zeng
Yinwei Zhan
Dawei Zhang
Guozhen Zhang
Jianpeng Zhang
Jiawan Zhang

Jing Zhang
Mingda Zhang
Pengyu Zhang
Pingping Zhang
Xiao-Yong Zhang
Xinpeng Zhang
Xuanyu Zhang
Yanan Zhang
Yang Zhang
Ye Zhang
Yuanhang Zhang
Zaibin Zhang
ZhiHao Zhang
Jie Zhao
Sicheng Zhao
Yuchao Zheng
Shuaifeng Zhi
Fan Zhong
Chu Zhou
Feng Zhou
JiaYuan Zhou
Jingyi Zhou
Tao Zhou
Yang Zhou
Zhanping Zhou
Minfeng Zhu
Mingli Zhu
Mingrui Zhu
Xu Zhu
Zihao Zhu
Shinan Zou

Contents – Part IV

Artificial Intelligence

Artificial Intelligence

Deep Discriminative Hashing for Cross-Modal Hashing Based Computer-Aided Diagnosis

ChongShen Yang[1] and YuFeng Shi[2(✉)]

[1] School of Software, Hefei University of Technology, Hefei 230009, China
prometheus@mail.hfut.edu.cn
[2] School of Electronic Information and Communications, Huazhong University of Science and Technology, Wuhan 430074, China
YufengShi17@hust.edu.cn

Abstract. Massive medical data in multi-modalities emerges with the development of modern medicine, which facilitates the construction of computer-aided diagnosis (CAD) methods. However, most existing CAD methods diagnose diseases only based on the relevant single-modal data, and thus their applications are limited in single modality. To reveal intrinsic connections between heterogeneous modalities and further build multi-modal CAD methods, a novel cross-modal hashing model named Deep Discriminative Hashing (DDH) is proposed. Specifically, semantic labels are encoded to obtain a fixed classifier for the preservation of semantic similarity. Furthermore, benefiting from the classifier, the optimization of hash functions for different modalities is regarded as a classification task that aims to further consider the improvement of discriminability with angular softmax loss. Therefore, DDH projects medical multi-modal data into the common hamming space, and performs multi-modal CAD via cross-modal retrieval. Moreover, since the encoding procedure of different modalities is decoupled, DDH can also execute single-modal CAD based on the medical image retrieval. Experimental results demonstrate the superior accuracy of DDH compared with state-of-the-arts in both medical image retrieval and cross-modal medical data retrieval tasks.

Keywords: Computer aided diagnosis (CAD) · Multi-modal medical data · Biomedical image retrieval · Hashing · Representation learning

1 Introduction

Nowadays, medical detection technologies offer access to a systematic and complete characterization about patients. For physicians, based on the inspection results such as distinct X-ray images and radiology reports, manual diagnosis becomes effective. On the other side, massive medical data is accumulated over time, which also provides materials for computer-aided diagnosis (CAD) methods [1,14,34].

H. Lu et al. (Eds.): ICIG 2023, LNCS 14358, pp. 3–20, 2023.
https://doi.org/10.1007/978-3-031-46314-3_1

Existing CAD methods can be roughly divided into two categories: classifier-based approaches [2,16,45] and retrieval-based approaches [11,17,48]. The former regard CAD as a classification problem and classify medical data according to the contained disease. For example, Andre et al. [13] trains a convolutional neural network in an end-to-end manner to classify skin lesions. Later, Jian-peng et al. [46] adopt attention mechanism and residual learning to train a CNN model for skin lesion classification in dermoscopy images. Recently, Jordi et al. [25] design a diabetic retinopathy deep learning interpretable classifier to classify retina images into different levels of severity. Since its interpretability is empowered by assigning a score for each point without relevant medical profiles as support, there is still room for the interpretability of outcomes.

On the other side, given a query profile, retrieval-based approaches locate relevant medical profiles and return the corresponding diagnosis. As a representative work, Erfankhah et al. [12] utilize homogeneity and the second moment of local neighborhoods to capture the polymorphism in histopathology images, which facilitates the matching between profiles. In the process of retrieving large-scale medical data, query speed and memory usage should be also considered. Therefore, Jingjing et al. [31] introduce hashing to handle large-scale clinical images, and therefore extend Anchor Graph Hashing with iterative quantization to capture the visual similarities between mammographic images. To surmount semantic block, Xiaoshuang et al. [36] design a supervised graph-based hashing model and apply matrix factorization for medical image retrieval. Although medical images such as X-ray are fully explored by retrieval-based CAD, the multi-modal attribute of current medical data is ignored. As a result, a CAD method that owns strong interpretability and handles medical multi-modal data should be built.

To build interpretable multi-modal CAD methods, cross-modal hashing (CMH) [19,23,26] that projects multi-modal data into the common hamming space and further performs cross-modal retrieval, is introduced to build a CMH-based CAD method. The reasons for the choice can be summarized into three points. Firstly, since CMH retrieves relevant medical profiles in heterogeneous modalities to diagnose profiles, its interpretability is guaranteed. Secondly, unlike existing retrieval-based approaches that only handle medical data in the single modality, intrinsic connections between heterogeneous modalities are revealed by CMH. Therefore, the sces of knowledge have increased and thus improves the reliability of CAD methods. Finally, CMH utilizes binary codes to represent medical data and further performs retrieval with hamming distance. Since binary codes save storage and hamming distance is accelerated with XOR calculation, CMH can handle massive medical data with low hardware cost. Moreover, there exists an extra demand for CMH-based CAD method. Since histopathology image plays an irreplaceable role in early disease detection and grading [24,35,41], CMH-based CAD method should also be able to medical image retrieval. To achieve this goal, its training procedure of image representation modules needs to be independent of information from other modalities.

The suitable CMH methods for CAD are supervised CMH methods [22, 26,37], which can utilize manual annotations during training procedure to model inter-class or intra-class relations. Owing to the participation of high-level semantic information, current supervised hashing approaches can approximate pair-wise or triplet-wise correlations with distances in common Hamming space and thus obtain semantic similarity preserving hash codes. The most well-known semantic similarity preserving method is Semantic Correlation Maximization (SCM) [44]. It aims to maximize the correlation between hash code and semantic similarity matrix. Despite the consideration of semantic similarity by the semantic similarity matrix, the neglect of the discriminative property severely deteriorate its retrieval performance. Therefore, discriminative approaches [32,39,42] are proposed. As a representative discriminative method, Multimodal Discriminative Binary Embedding (MDBE) [39] formulates the hash function learning in terms of classification to produce similar binary codes in the same class. Although intra-class packed hash codes are obtained, this kind of methods including MDBE fails to take into consideration the relations between different classes especially in the multi-label scenario where a class possesses various categories.

In this paper, a novel CMH-based CAD method named Deep Discriminative Hashing (DDH) is proposed. To preserve inter-class relations and push intra-class data aggregated simultaneously, DDH trains a common classifier using semantic labels and apply it with the angular-softmax loss [33] to optimize hash functions in classification procedure. Specifically, the classifier aims to preserve inter-class semantic similarity and constitute common hamming space, whereas the classification process intends to increase discriminability for intra-class aggregation. Since the encoding procedure of different modalities is decoupled, DDH can also directly perform medical image retrieval.

To summarize, main contributions are threefold:

- A novel CMH-based CAD method named DDH, which cooperates hashing-based retrieval with classification preserve inter-class relations and push intra-class data aggregated, is proposed.
- A-softmax loss is elegantly incorporated into DDH to flexibly deal with discriminability. Moreover, as a modality-decoupled method, DDH can perform single-modal and cross-modal retrieval concurrently, which meets the needs of current multimodal clinical data.
- Experiments on large-scale multimodal medical dataset MIMIC-CXR show that DDH can model inter-class and intra-class relations more effectively than other methods, thus boosting the retrieval accuracy.

The rest of this paper is organized as follows. Section 2 introduces related studies and basic knowledge on A-softmax loss. Section 3 presents the proposed DDH method and its optimization. The experimental results and analysis are reported in Sect. 4. Finally, Sect. 5 concludes this paper.

2   Related Work

In this section, representative supervised CMH methods are briefly reviewed. To make readers easier to understand work, some knowledge of A-softmax loss is also introduced.

2.1   CMH

Supervised CMH methods including semantic similarity preserving methods and discriminative methods are thereafter proposed to model inter-class or intra-class relations. Similarity preserving methods encode data points to express semantic mutual similarity such as pair-wise [3,5], triplet-wise [8,20] or multi-wise similarity relations [4,22]. One of the most well-known supervised methods is Cross-Modal Similarity Sensitive Hashing (CMSSH) [3], which approximates the pair-wise similarity with hash codes from different modalities. For triplet-wise, Triplet-based Deep Hashing (TDH) [8] utilizes the triplet labels, which describe the relative relationships among three samples as supervision to capture more semantic correlations. Semantics-Preserving Hashing (SePH) [30] minimizes the KL-divergence between distributions of semantic labels and hash codes to cover multi-wise similarity. As an early attempt with deep learning, Deep Cross-modal Hashing (DCMH) [22] directly encodes origin data points by minimizing the negative log likelihood of the cross-modal similarities. To discover high-level semantic information, self-supervised adversarial hashing (SSAH) [26] harnesses a self-supervised semantic network to preserve the pair-wise relationships. Due to the consideration of inter-class relations, the performance is significantly improved. However, their neglect of intra-class relations limits higher retrieval accuracy.

Different from similarity preserving methods, discriminative methods [32,37,43] aim to make intra-class data points aggregated. As the earliest discriminative method, Multimodal Discriminative Binary Embedding (MDBE) [39] attempts to learn hash functions based on classification to produce similar binary codes in the same class. As another representative method, Discriminative Cross-View Hashing (DCVH) [32] utilizes CNN based multi-label classification to explore the discriminative information. Recently, Category Supervised Cross-Modal Hashing (CSCMH) [47] builds hash code for categories, and utilizes the category hash code as supervised information. Compared with the former type, discriminative approaches push intra-class data points close to each other. However, the aforementioned algorithms forget to handle inter-class and intra-class relations in a joint manner.

Consequently, there remains a need for a hashing method which can preserve semantic similarity and strengthen discriminability simultaneously for CMH-based CAD. Furthermore, the representation modules should also be decoupled to perform medical image retrieval.

2.2   A-Softmax Loss

Despite great efforts to handle the big intra-class variance of medical data, the discriminability of hash codes still needs to be strengthened. To alleviate such limitation, a promising solution is A-softmax loss that has been proved to constrain maximal intra-class distance smaller than minimal inter-class distance theoretically and practically [9,21]. Before elaborating on solution, we introduce basic knowledge on A-softmax loss below.

A-softmax originally aims to learn discriminative face feature h_i^a for face recognition. It constrains features on a hypersphere, where h_i^a has intrinsic angular distribution and an angular margin is incorporated. Analysis starts from the normalized posterior probability of h_i^a, which is obtained by softmax:

$$p_i = \frac{\exp\left(w_i^T h_i^a\right)}{\sum_l \exp\left(w_l^T h_i^a\right)}, \tag{1}$$

where w_l is the class anchor of class y_l. To analyze the cosine relations between vectors, the inner products of vectors are expanded as:

$$p_i = \frac{\exp\left(\|w_i\|\|h_i^a\|\cos\left(\theta_{w_i,h_i^a}\right)\right)}{\sum_l \exp\left(\|w_l\|\|h_i^a\|\cos\left(\theta_{w_l,h_i^a}\right)\right)}. \tag{2}$$

To normalize the class anchor and embed the feature to a unit sphere, we set $\|w_i\| = 1$. Hence, the softmax function becomes the modified softmax loss:

$$L_{modified} = \sum_i -\log\left(\frac{e^{\|h_i^a\|\cos\left(\theta_{w_i,h_i^a}\right)}}{\sum_l e^{\|h_i^a\|\cos\left(\theta_{w_l,h_i^a}\right)}}\right). \tag{3}$$

This indicates that cosine metric determines the classification result. To enhance discrimination, the authors manipulate decision boundaries to produce angular margin. Specifically, a multiplier m is applied to the angle between h_i^a and its corresponding class anchor w_i in Eq. (2), which leads decision boundaries to produce an angular margin in:

$$L_A = \sum_i -\log\left(\frac{e^{\|h_i^a\|\cos\left(m\theta_{w_i,h_i^a}\right)}}{e^{\|h_i^a\|\cos\left(m\theta_{w_i,h_i^a}\right)} + \sum_{l\neq i}e^{\|h_i^a\|\cos\left(\theta_{w_l,h_i^a}\right)}}\right), \tag{4}$$

where the value of θ_{w_i,h_i^a} should be within $\left[0,\frac{\pi}{m}\right]$. To make it optimizable in neural networks, the definition range of $\cos\left(\theta_{w_i,h_i^a}\right)$ is expanded by generalizing it to a monotonically decreasing angle function $\psi\left(\theta_{w_i,h_i^a}\right)$, which is equal to $\cos\left(\theta_{y_i,i}\right)$ in $\left[0,\frac{\pi}{m}\right]$. Consequently, the A-softmax loss is:

$$L_A = \sum_i -\log\left(\frac{e^{\|h_i^a\|\psi\left(\theta_{w_i,h_i^a}\right)}}{e^{\|h_i^a\|\psi\left(\theta_{w_i,h_i^a}\right)} + \sum_{l\neq i}e^{\|h_i^a\|\cos\left(\theta_{w_l,h_i^a}\right)}}\right), \tag{5}$$

where $\psi\left(\theta_{w_i,h_i^a}\right) = (-1)^k \cos\left(m\theta_{w_i,h_i^a}\right) - 2k$, $\theta_{w_i,h_i^a} \in \left[\frac{k\pi}{m}, \frac{(k+1)\pi}{m}\right]$ and $k \in [0, m-1]$.

By optimizing A-Softmax loss, the decision regions become more separated, simultaneously enlarging the inter-class margin and compressing the intra-class distribution. Obviously, the motivation of A-softmax loss coincides with the reinforcement of discriminability.

3   Method

For illustration purposes, DDH preforms retrieval among X-ray images and radiology reports.

3.1   Problem Definition

Let $\boldsymbol{X}^1 = \left\{\boldsymbol{x}_i^1\right\}_{i=1}^{N_1}$ and $\boldsymbol{X}^2 = \left\{\boldsymbol{x}_j^2\right\}_{j=1}^{N_2}$ symbolize X-ray images and radiology reports of training set, where $\boldsymbol{x}_i^1 \in \mathbb{R}^{d_1}$, $\boldsymbol{x}_j^2 \in \mathbb{R}^{d_2}$. And their semantic labels that indicate the existence of pathology are represented by $\boldsymbol{Y} = \left\{\boldsymbol{y}_l\right\}_{l=1}^{N_3}$, where $\boldsymbol{y}_l = \left\{y_{l1}, y_{l2}, ..., y_{ld_3}\right\} \in \mathbb{R}^{d_3}$. Following [5, 22, 30], we define the semantic affinities $\boldsymbol{S}_{N_1 \times N_2}$ between $\boldsymbol{x}_i^1$ and $\boldsymbol{x}_j^2$ using semantic labels. If $\boldsymbol{x}_i^1$ and $\boldsymbol{x}_j^2$ share at least one category label, they are similar and $\boldsymbol{S}_{ij} = 1$. Otherwise, they are dissimilar and thus $\boldsymbol{S}_{ij} = 0$.

DDH aims to learn hash functions $f^1\left(\theta_1; \boldsymbol{X}^1\right) : \mathbb{R}^{d_1} \to \mathbb{R}^{d_c}$ and $f^2\left(\theta_2; \boldsymbol{X}^2\right) : \mathbb{R}^{d_2} \to \mathbb{R}^{d_c}$, which can map X-ray images and radiology reports as approximate binary features $\boldsymbol{H}^1$ and $\boldsymbol{H}^2$ in the same continuous space respectively. Later, binary codes $\boldsymbol{B}^{1,2}$ can be generated by applying a sign function to $\boldsymbol{H}^{1,2}$:

$$\boldsymbol{B}^{1,2} = sign(\boldsymbol{H}^{1,2}) \tag{6}$$

Hash codes indicate fixed length (c-bits) binary vectors, whose elements are $\{-1,1\}^c$ like most existing hashing methods [22, 26]. Meanwhile, Hamming distance $D\left(\boldsymbol{b}_i^1, \boldsymbol{b}_j^2\right)$ between hash codes $\boldsymbol{b}_i^1$ and $\boldsymbol{b}_j^2$ needs to indicate the semantic similarity $\boldsymbol{S}_{ij}$ between $\boldsymbol{x}_i^1$ and $\boldsymbol{x}_j^2$, which can be formulated as below:

$$\boldsymbol{S}_{ij} \propto -D\left(\boldsymbol{b}_i^1, \boldsymbol{b}_j^2\right). \tag{7}$$

3.2   The Overall Architecture of Deep Discriminative Hashing

As shown in Fig. 1, DDH consists of two parts. Firstly, labNet f^y is built to learn the semantic similarity preserving classifier $\boldsymbol{W}$. After processing of labNet, hash codes of non-redundant semantic labels are employed to compose $\boldsymbol{W}$ for the following classification. Then, binary feature extractors imgNet f^1 and txtNet f^2 are utilized as hash functions to extract features which are easily classified by $\boldsymbol{W}$. To verify the contribution of the DDH method, modules in DDH is formed by basic structures. The labNet is a fully-connected network with one 4096-node hidden layer. Following existing works [22, 26], The imgNet is modified from the CNN-F [7]. Moreover, the txtNet is the same as the txtNet in SSAH [26] for fair comparisons. To reduce quantization error, the activation function of the last layer is $tanh\left(\cdot\right)$.

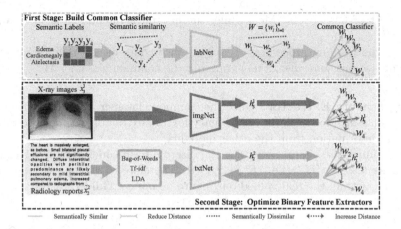

Fig. 1. The architecture of Deep Discriminative Hashing (DDH) framework. Firstly, labNet encodes semantic labels as hash codes to compose common classifier W with similarity preservation. Later, imgNet (or txtNet) are guided to extract features that are easily classified by W.

Common Classifier. To preserve semantic similarity among different classes, w in the common classifier is encoded as binary codes that represent their corresponding d_3-dimensional semantic labels.

To concentrate on inter-class relations, repetitive semantic labels are eliminated and the rest are transformed into N_3 multi-class annotations $Y = \{y_l\}_{l=1}^{N_3}$ ($y_l = \{y_{l1}, y_{l2}, ..., y_{ld_3}\}$). Then, Y are encoded as hash codes based on semantic similarity, and the corresponding loss function of labNet is:

$$\min_{W,\theta_y} L^y = L_1^y + \alpha L_2^y + \beta L_3^y$$

$$= \sum_{l,j}^{N_3} \|S_{lj} - f^y(\theta_y; y_l)^T f^y(\theta_y; y_j)\|^2$$

$$+ \alpha \sum_{l=1}^{N_3} (\|w_l - f^y(\theta_y; y_l)\|^2)$$

$$+ \beta \|\sum_{l=1}^{N_3} f^y(\theta_y; y_l)\|^2,$$

$$s.t. W = \{w_l\}_{l=1}^{N_3} \in \{-1, 1\}^c \tag{8}$$

where $f^y(\theta_y; y_l)$ indicates the continues output of labNet, w_l is the hash codes of y_l, and α, β are hyper-parameters.

The first term of Eq. (8) utilizes the L_2 norm to make hash codes preserve the semantic similarity. In Hamming space, vectors in the classifier should also comply with binarization and fire each bit with 50% probability [22,40]. Therefore, the second term restricts the output of labNet to approximate binary as the request of hash codes. Meanwhile, the last term intends to keep -1 and 1 balance.

After the training procedure of labNet, hash codes of non-redundant multi-label annotations $\{w_1; w_2; ...; w_l\}$ compose the common classifier W.

Binary Feature Extractor. Once the common classifier W is built, the next step is a classification task for each binary feature extractor without the participation of information from the other modality.

To optimize the neural networks, the discrete hash codes B^n are relaxed to continuous features H^n (i.e., $f^n(\theta_n; X^n)$). Therefore, the binarization loss is added to constrain the real-valued outputs to be binary. Guided by the common classifier, the loss function of imgNet (or txtNet) is as follows:

$$\min_{\theta_n} L^n = L_1^n + \gamma L_2^n$$

$$= \sum_{i=1}^{N_n} -\log\left(\frac{e^{\|\bar{h}_i^n\|\psi\left(\theta_{\bar{w}_i,h_i^n}\right)}}{e^{\|\bar{h}_i^n\|\psi\left(\theta_{\bar{w}_i,h_i^n}\right)} + \Sigma_{l\neq i}e^{\|\bar{h}_i^n\|\cos\left(\theta_{\bar{w}_l,h_i^n}\right)}}\right)$$

$$+ \gamma\sum_{i=1}^{N_n}\left(\|w_i - h_i^n\|^2\right), \tag{9}$$

where $\bar{w}_i$ and $\bar{h}_i^n$ are normalized vectors, $\psi\left(\theta_{\bar{w}_i,h_i^n}\right) = (-1)^k\cos\left(m\theta_{\bar{w}_i,h_i^n}\right) - 2k, \theta_{\bar{w}_i,h_i^n} \in \left[\frac{k\pi}{m}, \frac{(k+1)\pi}{m}\right]$, $k \in [0, m-1]$, $\{w_l\}_{l=1}^{N_3} \in \{-1,1\}^c$ are consisted of hash codes corresponding to semantic labels, and γ is a hyper-parameter. Following original A-softmax loss [33], we also set m as 4 and generalize $\cos\left(\theta_{\bar{w}_i,h_i^n}\right)$ as the monotonically decreasing angle function $\psi\left(\theta_{\bar{w}_i,h_i^n}\right)$.

The second term is binarization loss, which leads outputs of extractors H^n to approximate binary codes B^n. To utilize the discriminability brought by classification, the remaining work is to make features easily classified by W and thus the first term of Eq. (9) is the A-softmax loss.

Integrating the loss function of labNet L^y and the loss function of imgNet (or txtNet) L^n, the whole objective function of DDH is obtained:

$$\min_{\theta_y, W, \theta_1, \theta_2} L = L^y + L^1 + L^2, \tag{10}$$

3.3   Optimization

In DDH, the common classifier W should be built firstly, and then the binary feature extractors $f^n(\theta_n; x_i^n)$ need to be optimized respectively. Moreover, to obtain W, the parameters of labNet θ_y should be also updated. The whole optimization procedure is summarized in Algorithm 1.

For θ_y of labNet, Eq. (8) is derivable. Therefore, Back-propagation algorithm (BP) with mini-batch stochastic gradient descent (mini-batch SGD) method is applied to update it. As for w_l, the $sign(\cdot)$ function is directly utilized:

$$w_l = sign\left(f^y\left(\theta_y; y_l\right)\right). \tag{11}$$

For parameters in binary feature extractors, θ_1 and θ_2 are updated with the BP with mini-batch SGD method.

During the testing stage, the out-of-sample profiles are encoded by the optimized imgNet or txtNet with $sign(\cdot)$:

$$b_i^n = sign\left(h_i^n\right), \tag{12}$$

where $h_i^n = f^n\left(\theta_n; x_i^n\right)$.

4 Experiments

In this section, Sect. 4.1 first introduces the experimental setting. Then, Sect. 4.2 and Sect. 4.3 evaluate the performance of DDH in CMH-based CAD and medical image retrieval respectively. Finally, Sect. 4.4 conducts sensitivity analysis to the hyper-parameters of DDH.

4.1 Experimental Setting

DDH is evaluated on the large-scale chest X-ray and radiology report dataset MIMIC-CXR [24]. Every X-ray image corresponds to more than one radiology report. And each profile is labeled with a 14-dimensional label that indicates whether symptoms exist or not. During experiments, original X-ray images are directly adopted. Radiology reports are represented as 617-dimensional bag-of-word vectors. Following [47], 73876 image-report pairs is utilized for assessment. During the testing stage, 762 image-report pairs are randomly sampled as the query set and the rest are used as the retrieval set. To optimize models, 14000 pairs from the retrieval set are used as training set.

Ten state-of-the-art CMH methods including CCA [18], CMSSH [3], SCM [44], STMH [38], CMFH [10], SePH [29], DCMH [22], SSAH [26], EGDH [37] and CSCMH [47]. Based on whether utilizes semantic labels, CCA, STMH and CMFH are unsupervised approaches, and the rest are supervised approaches. Moreover, based on whether adopts nerual networks as backbones, DCMH, SSAH, EGDH and CSCMH are deep methods, and the others are shallow methods. To verify the performance of DDH in medical image retrieval, six generic hashing methods including SH [40], ITQ [15], DPSH [28], DHN [49], DSDH [27] and HashNet [6] are also used for comparison. They can be divided into two types. SH and ITQ are unsupervised shallow methods while the remaining methods are deep supervised methods that directly learn hash codes from original images to preserve semantic similarity.

Algorithm 1: The Optimization Procedure of DDH

Input : X-ray images X^1, radiology reports X^2, semantic labels Y, learning rates $\lambda_y, \lambda_1, \lambda_2$, and iteration numbers T_y, T_1, T_2.

Output: Parameters θ_1 and θ_2 of imgNet and txtNet

Initialization: Randomly initialize θ_y, θ_1, θ_2 and $\boldsymbol{w}_l$.

repeat

    for *iter=1 to T_y* **do**

        Update θ_y by BP algorithm:

            $\theta_y \leftarrow \theta_y - \lambda_y \cdot \nabla_{\theta_y} L^y$

        Update $\boldsymbol{W}$ by Eq. (11);

    for *iter=1 to T_1* **do**

        Update θ_1 by BP algorithm:

            $\theta_1 \leftarrow \theta_1 - \lambda_1 \cdot \nabla_{\theta_1} L^1$

    for *iter=1 to T_2* **do**

        Update θ_2 by BP algorithm:

            $\theta_2 \leftarrow \theta_2 - \lambda_2 \cdot \nabla_{\theta_2} L^2$

until *Convergence*;

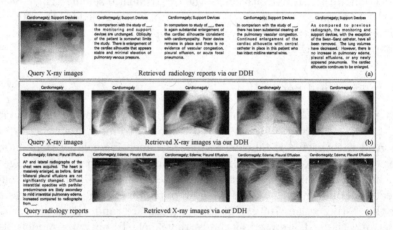

Fig. 2. The top 4 profiles retrieved by DDH via X-ray images to radiology reports retrieval (a), X-ray images to X-ray images retrieval (b) and radiology reports to X-ray images retrieval (c) on the MIMIC-CXR dataset with 128 bits.

Source codes of all comparison algorithms are kindly provided by their authors and performances are evaluated on a server with four NVIDIA 1080ti GPUs. For fair comparison with shallow baselines, the pretrained CNN-F network is utilized to extract 4096-dimensional features to represent X-ray images. Since CNN-F requires its inputs to be $224 \times 224 \times 3$, all X-ray images are resized to $224 \times 224 \times 3$ before possessing. The hyper-parameters in DDH are empirically set as $\alpha = 0.01$, $\beta = 1$ and $\gamma = 1$. More detailed discussions about hyper-parameters are exhibited in Sect. 4.4. To make results more convincing, all experiments are repeated five times to prevent random interference and the averaged results are reported.

To evaluate performance in CMH-based CAD and hashing-based medical image retrieval, Hamming ranking and hash lookup are used as retrieval criterion. Hamming ranking is to sort data points in retrieval set based on their Hamming distances to the given query point. For comparison, we adopt mean average precision (MAP) and TopN-precision curve to measure it. To reflect the overall property of rankings, the size of database set is used as the retrieval radius when MAP is calculated. Meanwhile, TopN-precision curve are plotted according to the relation of the precision with the number of retrieved instances. Hash lookup aims to return correlated data points in radius of a certain Hamming distance to the given query point. We use Precision-Recall (PR) curve to assess its accuracy. PR curve is plotted by varying hamming radius from 0 to 128, which reflects the precision at different recall levels.

4.2   The Efficacy of DDH in CMH-Based CAD

CMH-based CAD stresses on two retrieval directions: using X-ray images to query radiology reports ($X \rightarrow R$) and using radiology reports to query X-ray images ($R \rightarrow X$). For evaluation, bit length is set as 16 bits, 32 bits, 64 bits, and 128 bits respectively.

Hamming Ranking in CMH-Based CAD. The MAP results of CMH-based CAD on the MIMIC-CXR dataset are reported in Table 1. From Table 1, three phenomenons can be observed. Firstly, among competitors, CCA achieves the worst performance. Different from others, CCA models the cross-modal connections from statistical views. It indicates that the semantics also plays an important role in medical data. Moreover, since the MAP results of unsupervised methods are generally lower than the MAP results of supervised methods, the reliable semantics from the manual annotations can further boost the retrieval accuracy. Secondly, the MAP results of deep methods are higher than the MAP results of shallow methods on the whole. This phenomenon demonstrates that neural networks are feasible to handle medical multi-modal data. Finally, DDH outperforms all competitors. The reason for this phenomenon is that DDH utilizes the nerual networks to simultaneously grasp the inter-class and intra-class semantics. Specifically, compared with the deep hashing baseline SSAH by MAP, DDH achieves average absolute increases of 2.42%/1.81%.

On the other hand, the TopN-precision curves on MIMIC-CXR dataset are shown in Fig. 3 (a) and Fig. 3 (b). The relative altitude positions of top-N curves also prove that DDH achieves the state-of-the-art accuracy in Hamming ranking. Meanwhile, the top 4 retrieved medical profiles by DDH on $X \rightarrow R$ and $R \rightarrow X$ directions are visualized in Fig. 2 (a) and Fig. 2 (c). These results confirm concern that DDH can retrieval much more user-desired heterogeneous data again.

Table 1. Comparison with baselines in terms of MAP in CMH-based CAD. The best results are marked with **bold**.

Task	Method	MIMIC-CXR			
		16 bits	32 bits	64 bits	128 bits
$X \rightarrow R$	CCA [3]	0.3468	0.3354	0.3273	0.3215
	CMSSH [3]	0.4224	0.4020	0.3935	0.3896
	SCM [44]	0.4581	0.4648	0.4675	0.4684
	STMH [38]	0.3623	0.3927	0.4211	0.4387
	CMFH [10]	0.3649	0.3673	0.3736	0.3760
	SePH [29]	0.4684	0.4776	0.4844	0.4903
	DCMH [22]	0.4834	0.4878	0.4885	0.4839
	SSAH [26]	0.4894	0.4999	0.4787	0.4624
	EGDH [37]	0.4821	0.5010	0.4996	0.5096
	CSCMH [47]	0.4870	0.4850	0.4900	0.4980
	DDH	**0.5013**	**0.5023**	**0.5081**	**0.5158**
$R \rightarrow X$	CCA [3]	0.3483	0.3368	0.3288	0.3230
	CMSSH [3]	0.3899	0.3967	0.3646	0.3643
	SCM [44]	0.4516	0.4574	0.4604	0.4611
	STMH [38]	0.3980	0.4183	0.4392	0.4453
	CMFH [10]	0.4130	0.4156	0.4303	0.4309
	SePH [30]	0.4475	0.4555	0.4601	0.4658
	DCMH [22]	0.4366	0.4513	0.4561	0.4830
	SSAH [26]	0.4688	0.4806	0.4832	0.4833
	EGDH [37]	0.4821	0.4943	0.4982	0.5041
	CSCMH [47]	0.4420	0.4560	0.4730	0.4850
	DDH	**0.4837**	**0.4963**	**0.5025**	**0.5058**

Hash Lookup in CMH-Based CAD. Figure 3 (c) and Fig. 3 (d) present the PR curves on MIMIC-CXR dataset for all CMH methods. With the change of precision, the curves of DDH still locate higher than all competitors. These evaluation results are consistent with the ranking in Hamming ranking task. From above observations, based on large-scale multi-modal medical data, DDH can perform more accurate CMH-based CAD.

4.3 The Efficacy of DDH in Medical Image Retrieval

As medical image retrieval plays a crucial role in CAD, the performance of DDH in medical image retrieval is further evaluated. Since DDH is a modality-decoupled method that trains the imgNet without the participation of radiology reports information, following the experimental setting in CMH-based CAD, the corresponding experimental results are summarized in Table 2 and Fig. 4.

Table 2. Comparison with baselines in terms of MAP in medical image retrieval. The best results are marked with **bold**.

Method	MIMIC-CXR			
	16 bits	32 bits	64 bits	128 bits
SH [40]	0.3282	0.3237	0.3158	0.3067
ITQ [15]	0.3840	0.3789	0.3791	0.3840
DPSH [28]	0.4358	0.4375	0.4443	0.4224
DHN [49]	0.4431	0.4486	0.4472	0.4534
DSDH [27]	0.4394	0.4552	0.4599	0.4603
HashNet [6]	0.4327	0.4408	0.4420	0.4643
DDH	**0.4574**	**0.4649**	**0.4707**	**0.4729**

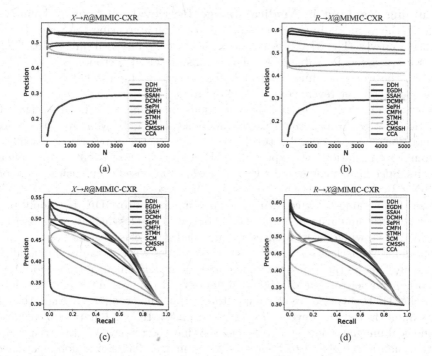

Fig. 3. Top$N$-precision curves and Precision-Recall curves using CNN-F feature with 128 bits in CMH-based CAD.

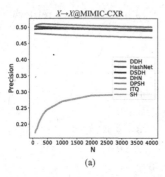
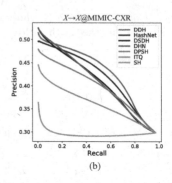

(a)   (b)

Fig. 4. TopN-precision curves and Precision-Recall curves using CNN-F feature with 128 bits in medical image retrieval.

Hamming Ranking in Medical Image Retrieval. In terms of hamming ranking, the medical image retrieval task is also evaluated using MAP and TopN-precision curves. The MAP results of medical image retrieval on MIMIC-CXR dataset are listed in Table 2. As shown, unsupervised methods SH and ITQ perform the worst in almost all cases. The reason to interpret it is that their hash codes can not reveal semantic information. Owing to the consideration of semantic similarity, supervised deep methods including DPSH, DHN, DSDH, and HashNet perform better than unsupervised methods. Moreover, they also benefit from the deep neural networks that can extract features from scratch and fit complex correlations. As expected, DDH obtains the best results across different bits. Specifically, compared with the recently proposed deep hashing method HashNet by MAP, DDH achieves absolute increases of 2.15% on MIMIC-CXR dataset from Table 2. By comparing deep competitors to DDH, they only preserve semantic similarity in hash code learning and pay less attention to discriminability. Meanwhile, DDH reduces the maximal intra-class distance and enlarge the minimal inter-class distance to equip hash codes with extra discriminability.

Figure 4 shows the TopN-precision curves of medical image retrieval for DDH and other competitors on MIMIC-CXR dataset. The curves in these figures illustrate that DDH outperforms all competitors in Hamming ranking. In Fig. 2 (b), we also exhibit the top 4 retrieved X-ray images from MIMIC-CXR dataset by method on medical image retrieval task. We can see that the retrieved X-ray images are quite semantic correlated to the query X-ray image. Therefore, aforementioned evaluations on MAP, TopN-precision curve, and Top-4 visualization jointly reveal that DDH can achieve superior performance in terms of Hamming ranking.

Hash Lookup in Medical Image Retrieval. To further analyze the Hash lookup performance in medical image retrieval, the results of PR curves for all methods are shown in Fig. 4. We can observe clearly that the curves corresponding to DDH are always higher than all other competitors. One reason accounts for this phenomenon is that DDH further emphasizes discriminability, which makes intra-class data points more aggregated. Therefore, the precision is improved and the best performance of Hash lookup is achieved by DDH. Consequently, based on large amounts of x-ray images, DDH can also perform more accurate medical image retrieval.

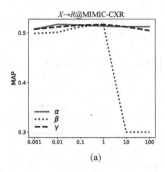
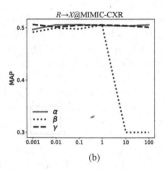

| (a) | (b) |

Fig. 5. Influence of hyper-parameters

4.4 Parameter Sensitivity

Finally, the retrieval accuracy of DDH on MIMIC-CXR dataset at 128 bits with different hyper-parameter values is evaluated. Figure 5 shows the MAP with different hyper-parameters (i.e., α and β in Eq. 8, and γ in Eq. 9). When the effect of one hyper-parameter is tested, others are set to default values (i.e., $\alpha = 0.01$, $\beta = 1$ and $\gamma = 1$). From the results shown in Fig. 5, the performance of DDH is robust to its parameters in a reasonable range, which is a nice property that can benefit real applications. Specifically, Fig. 5 indicates that DDH can achieve satisfying retrieval accuracy when hyper-parameters are within 0.001–1. However, when the value of β is out of this range, the performance of method deteriorates dramatically. For this reason, cross validation is recommended to determine the value of β in different applications.

5 Conclusion

In this paper, a novel Deep Discriminative Hashing (DDH) for multi-modal based computer-aided diagnosis (CAD) is proposed. Each semantic label is firstly encoded as hash codes to form a common classifier with the preservation of inter-class similarity. Then, the optimization of hash functions is viewed as a classification task for intra-class aggregation. Since the optimization procedure of different hash functions is separate, medical image retrieval can be performed without any changes. Extensive experiments are conducted on the large-scale medical dataset MIMIC-CXR. Compared with other state-of-the art methods, DDH can preserve semantic similarity and improve discriminability, which thus simultaneously model inter-class and intra-class relations in CMH-based CAD. Moreover, DDH also shows superior retrieval accuracy against all competitors in terms of single-modal CAD based on the medical image retrieval.

References

1. Altaf, F., Islam, S.M.S., Akhtar, N., Janjua, N.K.: Going deep in medical image analysis: concepts, methods, challenges, and future directions. IEEE Access **7**, 99540–99572 (2019). https://doi.org/10.1109/ACCESS.2019.2929365

2. Azizi, S., et al.: Big self-supervised models advance medical image classification. In: Proceedings of the IEEE/CVF International Conference on Computer Vision (ICCV), pp. 3478–3488, October 2021

3. Bronstein, M.M., Bronstein, A.M., Michel, F., Paragios, N.: Data fusion through cross-modality metric learning using similarity-sensitive hashing. In: 2010 IEEE Computer Society Conference on Computer Vision and Pattern Recognition, pp. 3594–3601. IEEE (2010)

4. Cao, Y., Long, M., Wang, J., Liu, S.: Collective deep quantization for efficient cross-modal retrieval. In: Thirty-First AAAI Conference on Artificial Intelligence (2017)

5. Cao, Y., Long, M., Wang, J., Zhu, H.: Correlation autoencoder hashing for supervised cross-modal search. In: Proceedings of the 2016 ACM on International Conference on Multimedia Retrieval, pp. 197–204. ACM (2016)

6. Cao, Z., Long, M., Wang, J., Yu, P.S.: HashNet: deep learning to hash by continuation. In: Proceedings of the IEEE International Conference on Computer Vision, pp. 5608–5617 (2017)

7. Chatfield, K., Simonyan, K., Vedaldi, A., Zisserman, A.: Return of the devil in the details: delving deep into convolutional nets. arXiv preprint arXiv:1405.3531 (2014)

8. Deng, C., Chen, Z., Liu, X., Gao, X., Tao, D.: Triplet-based deep hashing network for cross-modal retrieval. IEEE Trans. Image Process. **27**(8), 3893–3903 (2018)

9. Deng, J., Guo, J., Xue, N., Zafeiriou, S.: ArcFace: additive angular margin loss for deep face recognition. In: Proceedings of the IEEE Conference on Computer Vision and Pattern Recognition, pp. 4690–4699 (2019)

10. Ding, G., Guo, Y., Zhou, J., Gao, Y.: Large-scale cross-modality search via collective matrix factorization hashing. IEEE Trans. Image Process. **25**(11), 5427–5440 (2016)

11. Erfankhah, H., Yazdi, M., Babaie, M., Tizhoosh, H.R.: Heterogeneity-aware local binary patterns for retrieval of histopathology images. IEEE Access **7**, 18354–18367 (2019). https://doi.org/10.1109/ACCESS.2019.2897281

12. Erfankhah, H., Yazdi, M., Babaie, M., Tizhoosh, H.R.: Heterogeneity-aware local binary patterns for retrieval of histopathology images. IEEE Access **7**, 18354–18367 (2019)

13. Esteva, A., et al.: Dermatologist-level classification of skin cancer with deep neural networks. Nature **542**(7639), 115–118 (2017)

14. Fourcade, A., Khonsari, R.: Deep learning in medical image analysis: a third eye for doctors. J. Stomatol. Oral Maxillofac. Surg. **120**(4), 279–288 (2019) https://doi.org/10.1016/j.jormas.2019.06.002, https://www.sciencedirect.com/science/article/pii/S2468785519301582, 55th SFSCMFCO Congress

15. Gong, Y., Lazebnik, S., Gordo, A., Perronnin, F.: Iterative quantization: a procrustean approach to learning binary codes for large-scale image retrieval. IEEE Trans. Pattern Anal. Mach. Intell. **35**(12), 2916–2929 (2012)

16. Guo, Z., Shen, Y., Wan, S., Shang, W.L., Yu, K.: Hybrid intelligence-driven medical image recognition for remote patient diagnosis in Internet of Medical Things. IEEE J. Biomed. Health Inform. **26**(12), 5817–5828 (2022). https://doi.org/10.1109/JBHI.2021.3139541

17. Hashimoto, N., et al.: Case-based similar image retrieval for weakly annotated large histopathological images of malignant lymphoma using deep metric learning. Med. Image Anal. **85**, 102752 (2023)

18. Hotelling, H.: Relations between two sets of variates. In: Kotz, S., Johnson, N.L. (eds.) Breakthroughs in Statistics, pp. 162–190. Springer, New York (1992). https://doi.org/10.1007/978-1-4612-4380-9_14

19. Hu, P., Zhu, H., Lin, J., Peng, D., Zhao, Y.P., Peng, X.: Unsupervised contrastive cross-modal hashing. IEEE Trans. Pattern Anal. Mach. Intell. **45**(3), 3877–3889 (2023). https://doi.org/10.1109/TPAMI.2022.3177356

20. Hu, Z., Liu, X., Wang, X., Cheung, Y.M., Wang, N., Chen, Y.: Triplet fusion network hashing for unpaired cross-modal retrieval. In: Proceedings of the 2019 on International Conference on Multimedia Retrieval, pp. 141–149 (2019)

21. Huang, Z., Wang, S., Yu, K.: Angular softmax for short-duration text-independent speaker verification. In: Interspeech, pp. 3623–3627 (2018)

22. Jiang, Q.Y., Li, W.J.: Deep cross-modal hashing. In: Proceedings of the IEEE Conference on Computer Vision and Pattern Recognition, pp. 3232–3240 (2017)

23. Jiang, Q.Y., Li, W.J.: Discrete latent factor model for cross-modal hashing. IEEE Trans. Image Process. **28**(7), 3490–3501 (2019). https://doi.org/10.1109/TIP.2019.2897944

24. Johnson, A.E., et al.: MIMIC-CXR-JPG, a large publicly available database of labeled chest radiographs. arXiv preprint arXiv:1901.07042 (2019)

25. de La Torre, J., Valls, A., Puig, D.: A deep learning interpretable classifier for diabetic retinopathy disease grading. Neurocomputing **396**, 465–476 (2020)

26. Li, C., Deng, C., Li, N., Liu, W., Gao, X., Tao, D.: Self-supervised adversarial hashing networks for cross-modal retrieval. In: Proceedings of the IEEE Conference on Computer Vision and Pattern Recognition, pp. 4242–4251 (2018)

27. Li, Q., Sun, Z., He, R., Tan, T.: Deep supervised discrete hashing. In: Advances in Neural Information Processing Systems, pp. 2482–2491 (2017)

28. Li, W.J., Wang, S., Kang, W.C.: Feature learning based deep supervised hashing with pairwise labels. In: Twenty-Fifth International Joint Conference on Artificial Intelligence (2016)

29. Lin, Z., Ding, G., Han, J., Wang, J.: Cross-view retrieval via probability-based semantics-preserving hashing. IEEE Trans. Cybern. **47**(12), 4342–4355 (2016)

30. Lin, Z., Ding, G., Hu, M., Wang, J.: Semantics-preserving hashing for cross-view retrieval. In: Proceedings of the IEEE Conference on Computer Vision and Pattern Recognition, pp. 3864–3872 (2015)

31. Liu, J., Zhang, S., Liu, W., Deng, C., Zheng, Y., Metaxas, D.N.: Scalable mammogram retrieval using composite anchor graph hashing with iterative quantization. IEEE Trans. Circuits Syst. Video Technol. **27**(11), 2450–2460 (2016)

32. Liu, L., Qi, H.: Discriminative cross-view binary representation learning. In: 2018 IEEE Winter Conference on Applications of Computer Vision (WACV), pp. 1736–1744. IEEE (2018)

33. Liu, W., Wen, Y., Yu, Z., Li, M., Raj, B., Song, L.: SphereFace: deep hypersphere embedding for face recognition. In: Proceedings of the IEEE Conference on Computer Vision and Pattern Recognition, pp. 212–220 (2017)

34. Maier, A., Syben, C., Lasser, T., Riess, C.: A gentle introduction to deep learning in medical image processing. Z. Med. Phys. **29**(2), 86–101 (2019). https://doi.org/10.1016/j.zemedi.2018.12.003, https://www.sciencedirect.com/science/article/pii/S093938891830120X, Special Issue: Deep Learning in Medical Physics

35. Segovia, F., et al.: Multivariate analysis of dual-point amyloid pet intended to assist the diagnosis of Alzheimer's disease. Neurocomputing **417**, 1–9 (2020)

36. Shi, X., Sapkota, M., Xing, F., Liu, F., Cui, L., Yang, L.: Pairwise based deep ranking hashing for histopathology image classification and retrieval. Pattern Recogn. **81**, 14–22 (2018)

37. Shi, Y., You, X., Zheng, F., Wang, S., Peng, Q.: Equally-guided discriminative hashing for cross-modal retrieval. In: Proceedings of the 28th International Joint Conference on Artificial Intelligence, pp. 4767–4773. AAAI Press (2019)
38. Wang, D., Gao, X., Wang, X., He, L.: Semantic topic multimodal hashing for cross-media retrieval. In: Twenty-Fourth International Joint Conference on Artificial Intelligence (2015)
39. Wang, D., Gao, X., Wang, X., He, L., Yuan, B.: Multimodal discriminative binary embedding for large-scale cross-modal retrieval. IEEE Trans. Image Process. **25**(10), 4540–4554 (2016)
40. Weiss, Y., Torralba, A., Fergus, R.: Spectral hashing. In: Advances in Neural Information Processing Systems, pp. 1753–1760 (2009)
41. Xing, F., Yang, L.: Robust nucleus/cell detection and segmentation in digital pathology and microscopy images: a comprehensive review. IEEE Rev. Biomed. Eng. **9**, 234–263 (2016)
42. Xu, X., Shen, F., Yang, Y., Shen, H.T.: Discriminant cross-modal hashing. In: Proceedings of the 2016 ACM on International Conference on Multimedia Retrieval, pp. 305–308. ACM (2016)
43. Yu, J., Wu, X.J., Kittler, J.: Discriminative supervised hashing for cross-modal similarity search. Image Vis. Comput. **89**, 50–56 (2019)
44. Zhang, D., Li, W.J.: Large-scale supervised multimodal hashing with semantic correlation maximization. In: Twenty-Eighth AAAI Conference on Artificial Intelligence (2014)
45. Zhang, J., Xie, Y., Wu, Q., Xia, Y.: Medical image classification using synergic deep learning. Med. Image Anal. **54**, 10–19 (2019)
46. Zhang, J., Xie, Y., Xia, Y., Shen, C.: Attention residual learning for skin lesion classification. IEEE Trans. Med. Imaging **38**(9), 2092–2103 (2019)
47. Zhang, Y., Ou, W., Zhang, J., Deng, J.: Category supervised cross-modal hashing retrieval for chest X-ray and radiology reports. Comput. Electr. Eng. **98**, 107673 (2022). https://doi.org/10.1016/j.compeleceng.2021.107673, https://www.sciencedirect.com/science/article/pii/S0045790621005942
48. Zheng, Y., et al.: Encoding histopathology whole slide images with location-aware graphs for diagnostically relevant regions retrieval. Med. Image Anal. **76**, 102308 (2022)
49. Zhu, H., Long, M., Wang, J., Cao, Y.: Deep hashing network for efficient similarity retrieval. In: Thirtieth AAAI Conference on Artificial Intelligence (2016)

Image Super-Resolution via Deep Dictionary Learning

Yi Huang[1,2], Weixin Bian[1,2(✉)], Biao Jie[1,2], Zhiqiang Zhu[1,2], and Wenhu Li[1,2]

[1] School of Computer and Information, Anhui Normal University,
Wuhu 241002, Anhui, China
bwx2353@ahnu.edu.cn
[2] Anhui Provincial Key Laboratory of Network and Information Security,
Wuhu 241002, Anhui, China

Abstract. The method of image super-resolution reconstruction through a dictionary usually only uses a single-layer dictionary, which not only fails to extract the deep features of the image, but also the trained dictionary may be relatively large. This paper proposes a new deep dictionary learning model. First, after preprocessing the images of the training set, the dictionary is trained by the deep dictionary learning method, and the super-resolution reconstruction is performed by adjusting the anchored neighborhood regression method. The proposed algorithm is compared with several classical algorithms on the Set5 data set and Set14 data set. The visualization and quantification results show that the proposed algorithm has a good improvement in PSNR and SSIM compared with the traditional super-resolution algorithm, and effectively reduces the dictionary size and saves reconstruction time.

Keywords: deep dictionary learning · image super-resolution · anchored neighborhood regression · sparse representation

1 Introduction

Image super-resolution (SR) reconstruction technology refers to the process of reconstructing a high-resolution image of a corresponding scene from a low-resolution image of a given scene. The single-image super-resolution problem focuses on how to generate believable, visually pleasing high-resolution (HR) output images from low-resolution (LR) input images.

The method of sparse representation provides a feasible way for SR. Yang et al. [12] constructed a dictionary that can sparsely represent image blocks through dictionary learning, and then based on the input LR image, by solving the dictionary as the sparse representation coefficient of the input image, and

Supported by Natural Science Foundation of Anhui Provincial (Grant No. 2108085MF206) and National Natural Science Foundation of China (Grant No. 61976006).

H. Lu et al. (Eds.): ICIG 2023, LNCS 14358, pp. 21–32, 2023.
https://doi.org/10.1007/978-3-031-46314-3_2

the linear combination of the sparse representation coefficients obtained by the linear programming solution to obtain the reconstructed image. On the basis of Yang, Zeyde et al. [13] used K-SVD to train the dictionary, which improved the learning efficiency and the reconstruction effect. Afterwards, Timtet et al. [10] performed manifold learning on the dictionary obtained through dictionary sparse training, which accelerated the image reconstruction time and ensured the image reconstruction effect. They then proposed an improved A+ algorithm [11] that speeds up training time and improves reconstruction quality. But these works are all based on a single-layer training dictionary, resulting in a relatively large size of the training dictionary if the reconstruction effect is expected to be good, and these methods do not pay attention to the deep features of the image.

TARIYAL et al. [9] proposed the method of Deep Dictionary Learning (DDL). In shallow dictionary learning, a dictionary is learned to synthesize data from learned coefficients. DDL generalizes this concept to multiple layers. Instead of single-layer dictionaries, multi-layer dictionaries are learned so that the coefficients of the deepest layers can be used to synthesize data. Mahdizade-haghdam et al. [5] introduce a new model that attempts to learn a deep dictionary hierarchy for image classification tasks. Tang et al. [8] proposed a new deep-to-point encoding network for image multi-classification to solve the classification problem. Thereafter, Montazeri et al. [6] proposed a multi-layer K-SVD method, which was also used to solve classification problems. However, image super-resolution reconstruction using deep dictionary learning is relatively rare. Inspired by these research results, this paper will propose an improved image super-resolution reconstruction method through dictionary learning to address the limitations of image super-resolution reconstruction methods. In the training part, this paper uses the deep dictionary learning method to learn the deep dictionary, and then uses the A+ method to complete the super-resolution reconstruction of the image. Experimental results show that with the same dictionary size, the proposed algorithm has a significant improvement in PSNR and structural similarity, and effectively reduces the dictionary size.

The rest of the paper is organized as follows. Section 2 outlines the relevant technologies and concepts used in our approach. Section 3 introduces the detailed process of the method. In Sect. 4, we conducted an experimental evaluation of the proposed scheme, and in Sect. 5, we summarized our work.

2   Related Work

2.1   Deep Dictionary Learning

The shallow dictionary learning model is:

$$X = DZ \tag{1}$$

where X is the training data, D represents the dictionary, and Z is the sparse coefficient. Deep dictionary learning draws on the idea of deep learning, and further extracts more abstract deep features by extending shallow dictionary learning to multiple layers. Figure 1 shows a schematic diagram of two-layer dictionary learning. Mathematically, it can be modeled as:

$$\boldsymbol{X} = \boldsymbol{D}_1 \varphi (\boldsymbol{D}_2 \boldsymbol{Z}_2) \tag{2}$$

here φ is a nonlinear activation function. Extending this idea, the problem of multi-level dictionary learning can be expressed as:

$$\boldsymbol{X} = \boldsymbol{D}_1 \varphi (\boldsymbol{D}_2 \varphi (\cdots \varphi (\boldsymbol{D}_N \boldsymbol{Z}_N))) \tag{3}$$

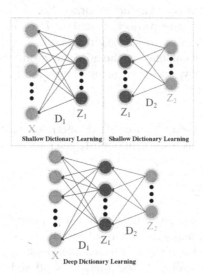

Fig. 1. Schematic diagram of two-layer deep dictionary learning.

2.2 Adjust Anchored Neighborhood Regression (A+)

In the image super-resolution problem, most of the neighborhood embedding (NE) and sparse coding (SC) methods use the l_1 norm of coefficients to constrain or regularize the least squares (LS) problem, causing the algorithm to computational power requirements are high. Therefore, this paper uses Adjust Anchored Neighborhood Regression (A+) [11] to transform the problem into solving the following optimization problems:

$$\min_{\delta} \|\boldsymbol{x} - \boldsymbol{S}_l \boldsymbol{\beta}\|_2^2 + \lambda \|\boldsymbol{\beta}\|_2 \tag{4}$$

here, $\boldsymbol{x}$ represents the input LR patches feature, the matrix $\boldsymbol{S}_l$ represents the neighborhood of LR dictionary space, which represents K training samples closest to the dictionary atom matched by the input patches $\boldsymbol{x}$, $\boldsymbol{\beta}$ represents the sparse coefficient, λ is the regularization coefficient. The algebraic solution of the optimization problem can be expressed as:

$$\beta = \left(S_l^T S_l + \lambda I\right)^{-1} S_l^T x \tag{5}$$

Based on the fact that LR dictionary and HR dictionary share the same sparse coefficient, HR patches reconstruction can be expressed as follows:

$$y = S_h \beta \tag{6}$$

where y is the reconstructed HR patches, and S_h is the neighborhood of the HR dictionary space corresponding to S_l.

For each atom in the dictionary, select its K nearest neighbor atoms, and define these neighbor atoms as the neighborhood of the atom. Once the neighborhood is defined, a separate projection matrix P_j can be calculated for each dictionary atom d_j according to its neighborhood. Then, the super-resolution problem can be solved by calculating the adjacent atom dj of each input patches feature y in the dictionary, and then using the stored projection matrix P_j to map it to the HR space:

$$y = P_j x \tag{7}$$

This method is an approximation of NE method with low complexity, so it can greatly reduce the execution time and time complexity of the algorithm.

3   Proposed Scheme

In this section, we introduce the details of the proposed scheme. The method learns the corresponding high- and low-resolution dictionary from the training set through deep dictionary learning, and selects dictionary atomic pairs to calculate the projection matrix. Finally, the test image is read and reconstructed through the dictionary and projection matrix. The symbols involved are shown in Table 1.

3.1   Pretreatment

In this paper, the same features as Zeyde et al. [13] are used to extract the first-order and second-order features of image patches, and PCA is applied to reduce the dimensionality. We subtract the bicubic interpolated LR image from the HR image to create normalized HR patches. The patches generated from the SR process are added to the bicubic interpolated LR input image (overlaps are averaged) to reconstruct the output.

3.2   Dictionary Construction

In the dictionary construction process of this paper, the same set of training samples are used as those used by Zeyde et al. [13] and Yang et al. [12]. For the dictionary learning method, this paper improves on the deep dictionary learning method proposed by TARIYAL et al. [9].

Table 1. The notations used in this paper.

Notations	Description
X	LR training data
Y	HR training data
x	LR testing data
y	HR reconstruction data
D	learned dictionary
Z	sparse coefficient
D_1	the first layer dictionary
Z_1	the first layer coefficients
λ	regularization factor
I	regularization term
φ	activation function
D_2	the second layer dictionary
D_2	the second layer coefficients
Z_{N-1}	the (N−1)th layer coefficients
D_N	the Nth layer dictionary
Z_N	the Nth layer coefficients
D_l	LR dictionary
D_h	HR dictionary
S_l	neighborhood of LR dictionary atoms
S_h	neighborhood of HR dictionary atoms
β	sparse coefficients when reconstructing
P_j	projection matrix

For single-layer dictionary, D and Z are obtained by solving the following optimization problems:

$$\min_{D,Z} \|X - DZ\|_F^2 \tag{8}$$

For the problem of sparse representation, the purpose is to learn the basis that can represent samples in a sparse way, that is, Z is required to be sparse. K-SVD is the most commonly used algorithm to solve this problem. Fundamentally, it solves the following optimization problems:

$$\min_{D,Z} \|X - DZ\|_F^2 \quad s.t. \|Z\|_0 < \varepsilon \tag{9}$$

For deep dictionary learning, as shown in Eq. (3), this paper uses the greedy learning method to learn one layer at a time, that is, first learn the dictionaries and coefficients of the first layer:

$$\min_{D_1,Z_1} \|X - D_1 Z_1\|_F^2 \tag{10}$$

Z_1 is not required to be sparse, except for the coefficients of the last layer, the rest do not require sparseness.

The above optimization problems can be solved by alternately solving D_1 and Z_1:

$$Z_1 = \left(D_1^T D_1 + \lambda I\right)^{-1} D_1^T X \tag{11}$$

$$D_1 = Z_1 X^T \left(Z_1 Z_1^T + \lambda I\right)^{-1} \tag{12}$$

alternate the above two processes to solve the problem.

For the second layer, we need to solve the following problems:

$$\min_{D_2, Z_2} \left\|\varphi^{-1}(Z_1) - D_2 Z_2\right\|_F^2 \tag{13}$$

it can also be solved by alternately solution:

$$Z_2 = \left(D_2^T D_2 + \lambda I\right)^{-1} D_2^T \varphi^{-1}(Z_1) \tag{14}$$

$$D_2 = Z_2 \varphi^{-1}\left(Z_1^T\right)\left(Z_2 Z_2^T + \lambda I\right)^{-1} \tag{15}$$

solve alternately until the last layer:

$$\min_{D_N, Z_N} \left\|\varphi(Z_{N-1})^{-1} - D_N Z_N\right\|_F^2 + \lambda \|Z_N\|_0 \tag{16}$$

Adding a regularization term requires the last layer coefficient Z_N to be sparse. The last layer can be solved using K-SVD method.

Use deep dictionary learning to learn the final LR dictionary through LR image patches, and the resulting final LR dictionary can be expressed as:

$$D_l = D_1 \varphi\left(D_2 \varphi\left(\cdots \varphi\left(D_N\right)\right)\right) \tag{17}$$

its corresponding D_h is then reconstructed by forcing the coefficients in the HR patch decomposition on D_h to be the same as those in the corresponding LR patch decomposition on D_l, which can be calculated by the following expression:

$$D_h = Y \varphi Z_N^T \left(\varphi Z_N \varphi Z_N^T\right)^{-1} \tag{18}$$

where Y represents the feature of the HR image patch, and Z_N is the sparse coefficient learned by the last layer of dictionary learning. The process of dictionary construction is shown in Fig. 2.

3.3   Super-Resolution Reconstruction

We adopt the A+ [11] method, input the LR image to be processed, and segment it with the same block size as the dictionary training stage, and then perform feature extraction on all LR image segmented blocks. For each LR feature block X finding which class it is closest to in the neighborhood of LR dictionary atoms, which can be expressed as an optimization problem in Eq. (4), solve the optimization problem to get the coefficient β. Directly use the projection matrix

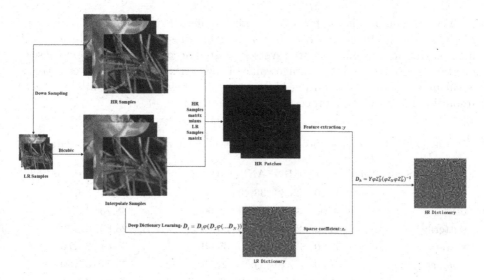

Fig. 2. Dictionary construction.

to which this class belongs to obtain the corresponding HR block Y, as shown in Eq. (5). Then according to Eq. (6), y can be expressed as:

$$y = S_h \left(S_l^T S_l + \lambda I \right)^{-1} S_l^T x \tag{19}$$

according to Eq. (7), the projection matrix can be expressed as:

$$P_j = S_h \left(S_l^T S_l + \lambda I \right)^{-1} S_l^T \tag{20}$$

After the LR neighborhood and the HR neighborhood are sampled, the projection matrix can be directly computed.

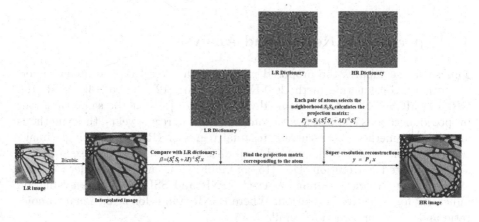

Fig. 3. Super-resolution reconstruction.

The calculation is performed on all input image blocks until all low-resolution image blocks have corresponding high-resolution image blocks. All high-resolution image blocks are reversely pasted according to the previous segmentation coordinates (the average value of the overlapping area between blocks is calculated), and the resulting high-resolution image is obtained. The super-resolution reconstruction process is shown in Fig. 3.

Table 2. PSNR of each algorithm with different zoom scales on the Set5 dataset.

Images	Scale	Yang	Zeyde	GR	ANR	NE+LLE	MCSR	A+	our method
baby		–	38.20	38.30	38.40	38.30	–	38.13	**38.50**
bird		–	39.90	39.00	40.00	40.00	–	38.76	**41.22**
butterfly	x2	–	30.60	29.10	30.40	30.40	–	28.83	**32.03**
head		–	35.60	35.60	35.60	35.60	–	35.51	**35.75**
woman		–	34.50	33.70	34.50	34.50	–	33.57	**35.30**
average		–	35.76	35.14	35.82	35.76	–	34.96	**36.56**
baby		34.30	35.10	34.90	35.10	35.10	35.00	34.59	**35.10**
bird		34.10	34.60	33.90	34.60	34.60	**35.40**	33.49	35.38
butterfly	x3	25.60	25.90	25.00	25.90	25.70	**28.80**	24.77	27.14
head		33.20	33.60	33.50	33.60	33.60	33.60	33.30	**33.73**
woman		29.90	30.40	29.70	30.30	30.20	**31.40**	29.36	31.12
average		31.42	31.92	31.40	31.90	31.84	**32.80**	31.10	32.49
baby		–	33.10	32.80	33.00	33.00	**32.90**	32.55	33.24
bird		–	31.70	31.30	31.80	31.70	32.40	31.03	**32.58**
butterfly	x4	–	23.60	23.10	23.50	23.40	**25.90**	22.82	24.34
head		–	32.20	32.10	32.30	32.20	32.30	31.98	**32.51**
woman		–	27.90	27.40	27.80	27.70	**28.80**	27.17	28.64
average		–	29.70	29.34	29.68	29.60	**30.50**	29.11	30.26

4   Experimental Results and Analysis

This section compares the proposed method with several typical image super-resolution reconstruction methods NE+LLE, Yang [12], Zeyde [13], ANR [10], GR [10], MCSR [3] and A+ (same dictionary size) [11]. At the same time, our proposed method is compared with some methods in recent years, these methods are Huang's method [2], recurrent residual regressor (RRR) [14], single image super-resolution (SISR) [1], coupled deep dictionary learning [7], based on deep learning-dilated convolution (DC) [15] and multi-scale encoder decoder (MSED) [4]. By using the most commonly used PSNR and SSIM in image evaluation indicators for objective evaluation. Where PSNR stands for peak signal-to-noise ratio and SSIM for structural similarity.

Table 3. SSIM of each algorithm at different zoom scales on the Set5 dataset.

Images	Scale	Yang	Zeyde	GR	ANR	NE+LLE	MCSR	A+	our method
baby		–	0.9362	**0.9648**	0.9645	0.9631	–	0.9628	0.9647
bird		–	0.9837	0.9812	0.9844	0.9834	–	0.9804	**0.9866**
butterfly	x2	–	0.9532	0.9297	0.9514	0.9509	–	0.9290	**0.9647**
head		–	0.8818	0.8848	0.8838	0.8829	–	0.8813	**0.8849**
woman		–	0.9647	0.9604	0.9656	0.9648	–	0.9595	**0.9693**
average		–	0.9493	0.9442	0.9499	0.9490	–	0.9426	**0.9540**
baby		0.9043	0.9211	0.9216	**0.9225**	0.9210	0.9191	0.9155	0.9218
bird		0.9391	0.9477	0.9404	0.9488	0.9477	0.9518	0.9330	**0.9543**
butterfly	x3	0.8611	0.8770	0.8316	0.8717	0.8705	**0.9213**	0.8250	0.9076
head		0.8024	0.8204	0.8223	0.8239	0.8226	0.8230	0.8166	**0.8262**
woman		0.9037	0.9176	0.9048	0.9168	0.9161	0.9280	0.8969	**0.9282**
average		0.8821	0.8968	0.8841	0.8968	0.8956	**0.9080**	0.8774	0.9076
baby		–	0.8797	0.8782	0.8811	0.8797	0.8716	0.8722	**0.8835**
bird		–	0.8999	0.8908	0.9018	0.9004	0.9051	0.8842	**0.9136**
butterfly	x4	–	0.7965	0.7483	0.7887	0.7850	**0.8641**	0.7395	0.8365
head		–	0.7736	0.7734	0.7762	0.7751	0.7774	0.7685	**0.7825**
woman		–	0.8643	0.8459	0.8619	0.8608	**0.8913**	0.8390	0.8836
average		–	0.8428	0.8237	0.8419	0.8402	**0.8628**	0.8207	0.8599

Table 4. Comparison with recent methods.

Images	PSNR							SSIM					
	RRR	SISR	Huang	DC	MSED	CDDL	our method	RRR	SISR	DC	MSED	CDDL	our method
set5													
baby	36.47	37.16	38.21	38.38	38.34	38.38	**38.50**	0.84	0.86	0.96	0.96	0.96	**0.96**
bird	36.86	37.46	39.12	38.76	38.76	40.60	**41.22**	0.91	0.98	0.98	0.96	0.98	**0.99**
butterfly	26.85	30.14	29.17	32.50	31.99	**32.88**	32.03	0.84	0.85	0.96	0.93	**0.97**	0.96
head	33.55	34.67	35.53	35.74	35.61	**35.78**	35.75	0.81	0.80	0.87	0.87	0.88	**0.88**
woman	32.16	34.01	33.85	35.26	35.17	**35.60**	35.30	0.86	0.97	0.97	0.96	**0.98**	0.97
average	33.18	34.69	35.18	36.13	35.98	**36.65**	36.56	0.85	0.89	0.95	0.94	0.95	**0.95**
set14													
baboon	23.28	24.07	–	25.16	25.29	25.24	**25.62**	0.67	0.68	0.74	0.75	0.76	**0.76**
barbara	26.19	28.02	–	28.23	28.57	28.53	**28.69**	0.79	0.78	0.86	0.87	0.88	**0.88**
brigde	26.14	27.11	–	27.63	27.40	27.66	**27.75**	0.75	0.74	0.84	0.84	0.85	**0.85**
coastguard	28.30	29.19	–	30.51	30.43	**30.69**	30.56	0.75	0.75	0.84	0.85	**0.86**	0.84
comic	26.33	27.05	–	28.30	27.53	**28.74**	28.24	0.81	0.81	0.91	0.89	**0.92**	0.91
face	34.04	34.65	–	35.77	35.69	**35.79**	35.72	0.80	0.80	0.88	0.88	0.88	**0.88**
flower	30.41	31.10	–	33.38	33.75	**33.78**	33.02	0.85	0.84	0.93	0.92	**0.95**	0.93
foreman	31.71	31.88	–	34.59	34.50	34.58	**37.03**	0.81	0.85	0.96	0.95	0.96	**0.97**
lena	33.47	34.55	–	36.59	36.56	**36.99**	36.58	0.82	0.83	0.93	0.93	**0.94**	0.93
man	29.50	30.23	–	30.99	30.28	**31.25**	30.85	0.79	0.78	0.87	0.87	0.89	**0.89**
monarch	33.40	35.22	–	37.64	36.51	**37.90**	37.00	0.87	0.87	0.97	0.97	0.98	**0.98**
pepper	33.37	34.10	–	35.52	34.98	35.74	**37.00**	0.81	0.82	0.92	0.91	**0.93**	0.92
ppt3	26.38	28.04	–	**30.45**	30.30	30.26	30.08	0.80	0.80	0.97	0.95	0.97	**0.98**
zebra	30.74	31.32	–	33.44	33.45	33.44	**33.66**	0.83	0.94	0.94	0.92	0.94	**0.94**
average	29.52	30.47	–	32.01	31.80	32.19	**32.27**	0.80	0.81	0.90	0.89	**0.91**	0.90

The datasets used in the experiment are set5 and set14. Set5 and Set14 datasets are low-complexity single image super-resolution data sets based on non-negative neighborhood embedding. These two training sets are used for single image super-resolution reconstruction, that is, to reconstruct HR images based on LR images to obtain more details.

4.1 Experimental Parameters

The experimental platform is Intel Core i7-11800H@2.30 GHz, the operating system is 64 bit Windows10 Professional Edition, Matlab R2019a. The dictionaries used in this experiment are two-layer dictionaries. When the magnification is 2, 3 and 4, the size of the deep dictionaries are $2048 \times 1024 \times 512$, $4096 \times 2048 \times 1024 \times 512$, and $8192 \times 4096 \times 2048 \times 1024$, respectively. The neighborhood size $K = 2048$.

4.2 Experimental Results and Analysis

Table 2 and Table 3 give the quantitative experimental results on the set5 dataset. Figure 4 shows the experimental results of the proposed method on the set14 dataset when the scale is 3. Through the experimental results, it is not difficult to find that compared with some classic methods, the algorithm in this paper has obvious improvements in PSNR and SSIM. Table 4 shows the results of the comparison with the methods in recent years. It can be seen that compared with some methods in recent years, our method is also very competitive in PSNR, and in terms of SSIM, our method has achieved good results on most of the test pictures. Figure 5 and Fig. 6 show the visualization experimental results

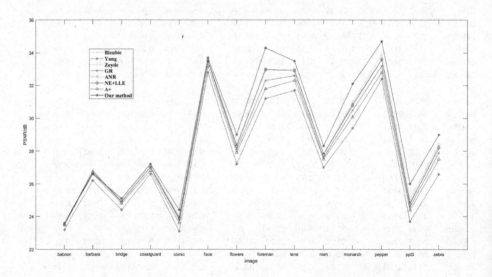

Fig. 4. PSNR at scale 3 on set14 dataset.

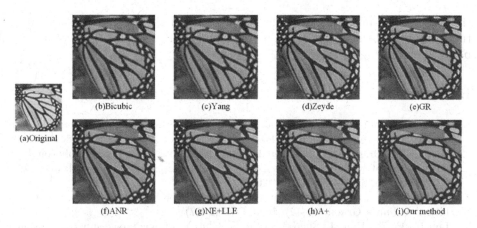

Fig. 5. Reconstruction effect of each algorithm of butterfly when the zoom scale is 3.

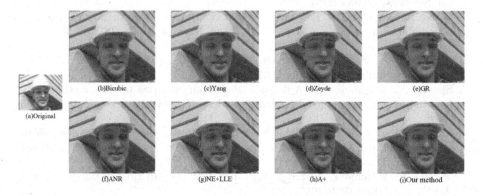

Fig. 6. Reconstruction effect of each algorithm of foreman when the zoom scale is 3.

of the super-resolution reconstructed part of the image. It can be seen from the figure that the proposed method combines A+ and deep dictionary learning to reconstruct the image, so that the edge of the reconstructed image is clear, and the visual effect is better than the previous method.

5   Conclusion

Aiming at the reason why the image super-resolution reconstruction algorithm ignores the image depth, this paper proposes a deep dictionary model for image super-resolution, extracts the features of the image to train the depth dictionary, and then performs super-resolution by adjusting the anchored neighborhood regression method. Resolution reconstruction. The algorithm in this paper effectively reduces the size of the dictionary. The experimental results show that the reconstruction results of the algorithm in this paper are more ideal than those of various image super-resolution methods in the case of the same dictionary size, and the objective evaluation standard PSNR and SSIM got a nice boost.

References

1. Chen, Y., et al.: Single-image super-resolution algorithm based on structural self-similarity and deformation block features. IEEE Access **7**(11), 58791–58801 (2019)
2. Huang, J.J., Dragotti, P.L.: A deep dictionary model for image super-resolution. In: 2018 IEEE International Conference on Acoustics, Speech and Signal Processing (ICASSP), pp. 6777–6781. IEEE (2018)
3. Li, Y., Fu, R., Jin, W., Ji, N.: Image super-resolution using multi-channel convolution. J. Image Graph. **22**(12), 1690–1700 (2017)
4. Liu, H., Fu, Z., Han, J., Shao, L., Hou, S., Chu, Y.: Single image super-resolution using multi-scale deep encoder-decoder with phase congruency edge map guidance. Inf. Sci. **473**, 44–58 (2019)
5. Mahdizadehaghdam, S., Panahi, A., Krim, H., Dai, L.: Deep dictionary learning: a parametric network approach. IEEE Trans. Image Process. **28**(10), 4790–4802 (2019)
6. Montazeri, A., Shamsi, M., Dianat, R.: MLK-SVD, the new approach in deep dictionary learning. Vis. Comput. **37**, 707–715 (2021)
7. Singhal, V., Majumdar, A.: A domain adaptation approach to solve inverse problems in imaging via coupled deep dictionary learning. Pattern Recogn. **100**, 107163 (2020)
8. Tang, H., Liu, H., Xiao, W., Sebe, N.: When dictionary learning meets deep learning: deep dictionary learning and coding network for image recognition with limited data. IEEE Trans. Neural Netw. Learn. Syst. **32**(5), 2129–2141 (2020)
9. Tariyal, S., Majumdar, A., Singh, R., Vatsa, M.: Deep dictionary learning. IEEE Access **4**, 10096–10109 (2016)
10. Timofte, R., De Smet, V., Van Gool, L.: Anchored neighborhood regression for fast example-based super-resolution. In: Proceedings of the IEEE International Conference on Computer Vision, pp. 1920–1927 (2013)
11. Timofte, R., De Smet, V., Van Gool, L.: A+: adjusted anchored neighborhood regression for fast super-resolution. In: Cremers, D., Reid, I., Saito, H., Yang, M.H. (eds.) Computer Vision-ACCV 2014: 12th Asian Conference on Computer Vision, Singapore, Singapore, 1–5 November 2014, Revised Selected Papers, Part IV 12, vol. 9006, pp. 111–126. Springer, Cham (2015). https://doi.org/10.1007/978-3-319-16817-3_8
12. Yang, J., Wright, J., Huang, T.S., Ma, Y.: Image super-resolution via sparse representation. IEEE Trans. Image Process. **19**(11), 2861–2873 (2010)
13. Zeyde, R., Elad, M., Protter, M.: On single image scale-up using sparse-representations. In: Boissonnat, J.D., et al. (eds.) Curves and Surfaces: 7th International Conference, Avignon, France, 24–30 June 2010, Revised Selected Papers 7, pp. 711–730. Springer, Cham (2012). https://doi.org/10.1007/978-3-642-27413-8_47
14. Zhang, K., Wang, Z., Li, J., Gao, X., Xiong, Z.: Learning recurrent residual regressors for single image super-resolution. Signal Process. **154**, 324–337 (2019)
15. Zhang, Z., Wang, X., Jung, C.: DCSR: dilated convolutions for single image super-resolution. IEEE Trans. Image Process. **28**(4), 1625–1635 (2018)

ACLM: Adaptive Compensatory Label Mining for Facial Expression Recognition

Chengguang Liu[1] , Shanmin Wang[2] , Hui Shuai[1] ,
and Qingshan Liu[1,3(✉)]

[1] Nanjing University of Information Science and Technology, Nanjing 210044, China
qsliu@nuist.edu.cn
[2] Nanjing University of Aeronautics and Astronautics, Nanjing 210016, China
smwang1994@nuaa.edu.cn
[3] Nanjing University of Posts and Telecommunications, Nanjing 210023, China

Abstract. Label ambiguity is one of the key issues in Facial Expression Recognition (FER). Previous works tackle this issue by modifying the original annotations to another one or characterizing them with soft labels, but this is often insufficient or redundant. Different from these methods, we analyze ambiguous samples from the perspective of label compensation with the subjectivity of FER into consideration. To this end, we propose an **A**daptive **C**ompensatory **L**abel **M**ining model (ACLM), which adaptively learns compensatory labels for ambiguous samples while remaining original labels. The Compensated Label Mining (CLM) module is used to evaluate the confidence and importance of the learned compensatory labels. Qualitative and quantitative experiments have demonstrated the superiority of using an adaptive combination of original labels and compensatory labels to guide FER models.

Keywords: Facial Expression Recognition · Ambiguous Samples · Compound Label Mining

1 Introduction

Facial expression is one of the most direct ways to convey emotional information [1]. Automatic Facial Expression Recognition (FER) has a wide range of applications in human-computer interaction, psychological counseling, driver fatigue monitoring, and other fields [2]. In recent years, with the emergence of large-scale databases, such as RAF-DB [3] and AffectNet [4], methods based on deep learning technology have boosted the performance of FER a lot. However, unlike other classification tasks (e.g., face recognition), some expressions have a similar appearance, resulting in the issue of label ambiguity. As shown in Fig. 1, we pick some samples from the RAF-DB database, where Fig. 1(a) and Fig. 1(c) are angry and fear samples, respectively. Both of them have explicit expressions. Samples in Fig. 1(b) have ambiguous labels, and they have similar expressions with samples in both Fig. 1(a) and Fig. 1(c). It is these ambiguous samples that

H. Lu et al. (Eds.): ICIG 2023, LNCS 14358, pp. 33–46, 2023.
https://doi.org/10.1007/978-3-031-46314-3_3

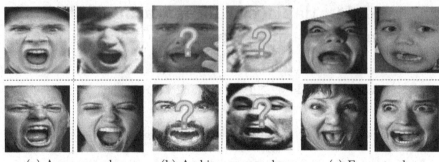

(a) Angry samples.   (b) Ambiguous samples.   (c) Fear samples.

Fig. 1. Demonstration of ambiguous samples in the dataset RAF-DB.

hinder the FER model from focusing on effective features, and affect the FER performance seriously.

Some works try to alleviate the issue of label ambiguity by relabeling ambiguous samples [5,6], selecting confidence examples [7,8], designing robust loss functions [9,10]. Such kind of methods regards ambiguous samples as noisy ones. However, due to label ambiguity, methods using a single label are not sufficient to accurately describe ambiguous samples, such as samples in Fig. 1(b). Another popular solution to ambiguous samples is soft labels [11], which characterize samples by the probability of each class. However, It is a huge challenge to design a reliable algorithm to obtain accurate soft labels. Besides, soft labels are often redundant as these ambiguous samples tend to be confused between a few expressions. In fact, [12] demonstrates that facial expressions in the real world are often presented in the form of compound expressions. In most cases, two expressions are involved in faces [3]. Inspired by this, in this paper, we propose to add compensatory descriptions to ambiguous samples, so as to characterize them sufficiently and accurately.

To this end, we propose an Adaptive Compensatory Label Mining model (ACLM), which adaptively learns additional compensatory labels for ambiguous samples while remaining original labels. Based on the original annotations, ACLM regards the FER model as another annotator and is to add compensatory labels for those samples if their predictive labels are not consistent with the original ones. Moreover, ACLM designs a Class Feature Modulation (CFM) module in the FER model to improve the qualities of its predicted labels. To further ensure the quality of the learned compensatory labels, ACLM designs a compensatory label mining (CLM) module, which evaluates the confidence and importance of the learned compensatory labels in steps. Thus, ACLM adaptively distinguishes good samples and ambiguous samples, and mines compensatory labels and corresponding importance for ambiguous ones. To verify the effectiveness of ACLM, we conduct experiments on popular databases. Both qualitative and quantitative results have demonstrated the rationality and superiority of ACLM. Overall, the main contributions of our work are summarized as follows:

- We propose an Adaptive Compensatory Label Mining model (ACLM) to address the issue of label ambiguity in FER, which adaptively learns compensatory labels for ambiguous samples while remaining original labels for good samples.
- To improve the quality of the learned compensatory labels, we propose a Class Feature Modulation module to obtain class discriminative features.
- We design a Compensatory Label Mining module to evaluate the confidence and the importance of the learned compensatory labels, so as to sufficiently and accurately.

2   Related Work

2.1   Noisy Label

Some works deal with ambiguous samples in a similar way to noise samples, because the ambiguity of expressions and the subjectivity of annotation are the key factors that cause these problems. Li. et al. [7] proposes to deal with noisy labels by building trusted data pairs. Contrastive learning with trusted data pairs to obtaining robust representations. Zeng et al. [13] proposed to mine latent true labels from inconsistent labels to solve the noisy problem. Wang et al. [9] proposes a classic self-cure network (SCN), which suppresses uncertain samples from participating in model training by designing a robust loss function.

Although such research has made some progress in dealing with ambiguous expressions, expressions have inherent inter-class similarities [7,14]. For these ambiguous samples, the original labels reflect part of the expression information, so it is unreasonable to directly discard them, which may cause the model to under-fit. Furthermore, even if the samples are accurately relabeled, a single label is still insufficient to describe ambiguous samples.

2.2   Soft Label

Due to the insufficient capability of a single label to accurately describe ambiguous samples, some works advocate the use of soft labels in order to mine the latent expression information. Soft labels describe facial expressions by using the probability of each class. Early work was inspired by knowledge distillation [15] to learn soft labels from pre-trained FER models. [11] builds class-level soft labels by computing the average of each class to avoid the uncertainty of instance-level soft labels. [16] proposes a potential label mining method and an uncertainty evaluation method between samples.

Although soft labels are more comprehensive in describing facial expressions, they are often redundant. By analyzing the training process of [16,17], it can be found that the vast majority of samples have only one class with large probability values, and the rest of the samples basically have only two classes with large probability values. This shows that most of the samples are good samples with only one basic expression, and the remaining ambiguous samples mainly combine two basic expressions. This finding validates the compound expression view in the real world [3,12]. Different from previous methods, we selectively mine potential compensatory labels and confidences of corresponding labels for ambiguous samples based on the provided single label to describe facial expressions more accurately.

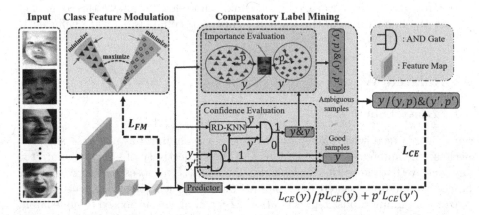

Fig. 2. The pipeline of the Adaptive compensatory Label Mining model (ACLM). ACLM contains two modules, Class Feature Modulation (CFM) and Compensatory Label Mining (CLM). The CFM module proposes a feature modulation loss (L_{FM}) to obtain a more discriminative feature. The CLM module evaluates the confidence and importance of compensatory labels. y is the original label. y' is the compensatory label. p and p' are corresponding label weight ratios. y and y' jointly supervise network learning according to the ratio p and p'.

3   Method

ACLM aims at adaptively learning compensatory labels for ambiguous samples while retaining their original labels. To this end, ACLM designs two modules: Class Feature Modulation (CFM) and Compensatory Label Mining (CLM), as shown in Fig. 2. Given a batch of samples, ACLM first extracts feature with the backbone networks. Then, the CFM module modulates the feature by enlarging the inter-class distance and narrowing the intra-class distance. With the modulated feature, the FER model can initially learn compensatory labels for ambiguous samples when the predicted labels are inconsistent with the original annotations. After obtaining the compensatory labels initially, ACLM proposes a Compensatory Label Mining module, which evaluates the confidence and importance of the compensatory in steps. The innovative Relative Density K-Nearest Neighbor (RD-KNN) algorithm is used to evaluate the confidence of the compensatory. Specifically, RD-KNN filters the nearest k good samples of ambiguous samples according to the relative density, so as to perform label prediction.

The labels will be regarded as compensatory descriptions if the outputs of the FER model reach agreements with RD-KNN. ACLM evaluates the importance of both original labels and compensatory labels by calculating the average distance to the corresponding classes. With the modulated labels and corresponding importance, ACLM designed an objective function to guide the learning of the FER model.

3.1   Class Feature Modulation

To mine compensatory labels accurately, we design a Class Feature Module (CFM), and the key of CFM is the feature modulation loss L_{FM}. L_{FM} expands the inter-class distance while reducing the intra-class distance, which can be written as follows:

$$L_{FM} = 1 + \frac{1}{2N} \sum_{i=1}^{N} (\frac{1}{N_{\widetilde{y_i}}} \sum_{j=1,y_j \neq y_i}^{N_{\widetilde{y_i}}} cs(f_i, f_j) - \frac{1}{N_{y_i}} \sum_{j=1,y_j=y_i}^{N_{y_i}} cs(f_i, f_j)) \quad (1)$$

where $cs(f_i, f_j)$ is the cosine similarity of samples (x_i, y_i) and (x_j, y_j), and f_i and f_j are their features. N is the number of batch samples, N_{y_i} is the number of samples belonging to y_i class, and $N_{\widetilde{y_i}}$ is the number of samples belonging to the remaining classes, satisfying $N_{y_i} + N_{\widetilde{y_i}} = N$. i, j are indices. L_{FM} can make the predictor better perceive the ambiguous samples at the edge of the class, which will be proved in the experimental section.

3.2   Compensatory Label Mining

To accurately describe ambiguous samples, ACLM proposes the Compensatory Label Mining (CLM) module evaluating the confidence and the importance of the compensatory label.

Confidence Evaluation. With the predicted results y' of the FER model, ACLM designs a dual AND Gate to decide whether y' is to be the compensatory label. In the first step, the predicted label y' is compared with the original label y to decide if it is ambiguous sample. In the second step, y' is compared with the output of RD-KNN to decide if it is confident to work as the compensatory label. For clarity, the process is divided into three parts: Label Comparison, Relative Density K-Nearest Neighbor (RD-KNN), and Prediction Matching.

(1) Label Comparison: We initially filter out ambiguous samples by judging whether the predicted label $Y' = \{y'_1, \cdots, y'_i, \cdots, y'_N\}$ of the predictor is consistent with the original label $Y = \{y_1, \cdots, y_2, \cdots, y_N\}$, the given samples $X = \{(x_1, y_1), \cdots, (x_i, y_i), \cdots, (x_N, y_N)\}$ are divided into a good sample set X^g and a ambiguous sample set X^a, which is,

$$X \Rightarrow \begin{cases} X^g = \{(x_1^g, y_1^g), \cdots, (x_j^g, y_j^g), \cdots, (x_Q^g, y_Q^g)\} \\ X^a = \{(x_1^a, y_1^a), \cdots, (x_i^a, y_i^a), \cdots, (x_P^a, y_P^a)\} \end{cases} \quad (2)$$

where $P + Q = N$. y_j^g and y_i^a are both predictor predicted labels of the sample. $y_j^g \in Y^g, Y^g = Y \cap Y'$. $y_i^a \in Y^a, Y^a = Y' - (Y \cap Y')$.

(2) RD-KNN: The predicted outputs are to be worked as compensatory labels if they are not consistent with original annotations. To ensure the exactness of the learned compensatory labels, ACLM proposes an RD-KNN algorithm. RD-KNN a predicts label for each ambiguous sample. Specifically, RD-KNN finds the K good samples that are closest to the current ambiguous sample to form the nearest neighbor set N, and then filters each good sample in the neighbor set N forming a filter set $\tilde{N}, \tilde{N} \subset N$. The label that appears most frequently in the filters set $\tilde{N}$ is used as the RD-KNN prediction label. Among them, We compare the density to filter the nearest neighbor set N.

For the ambiguous samples x_i^a, all good samples are arranged in ascending order according to the cosine distance. We define $N(x_i^a, k)$ to represent the K nearest neighbor set of the ambiguous sample x_i^a, which is presented as follows:

$$N(x_i^a, k) = \{(m_1^g, y_1^g), \cdots, (m_j^g, y_j^g), \cdots, (m_k^g, y_k^g)\} \tag{3}$$

where $|N(x_i^a, k)| = k$, $N(x_i^a, k) \subset X^g$. Then filter $N(x_i^a, k)$. We define $O(x_i^a, m_j^g)$ to represent the nearest neighbor rank of the sample m_j^g in x_i^a. For example, $O(x_i^a, m_1^g) = 1$, $O(x_i^a, m_j^g) = j$, $O(x_i^a, m_k^g) = k$. In the same way, $O(m_j^g, x_i^a)$ represents the nearest neighbor rank of the sample x_i^a in m_j^g, and the optional nearest neighbor samples of m_j^g include good samples Set X^g and ambiguous samples x_i^a. Then, the relative density difference between the samples x_i^a and m_j^g can be expressed as $O(x_i^a, m_j^g) - O(m_j^g, x_i^a)$.

We set that when $O(x_i^a, m_j^g) - O(m_j^g, x_i^a)$ is negative, x_i^a's nearest neighbor set N removes m_j^g, otherwise keeps m_j^g. Traverse the nearest neighbor set N of x_i^a to form a filter set $\tilde{N}$. The label category that appears most frequently in the filter set is selected as the RD-KNN predicted label, i.e.

$$\bar{y}_i^a = \arg\max_c \left| \{(m_s^g, y_s^g) \in \tilde{N} | y_s^g = c\} \right| \tag{4}$$

The meaning of the screening process in RD-KNN is to use two samples as the center of the sphere and their distance as the radius to compare the number of other good samples within their respective ranges. This comparison of the number of samples in the same range is a manifestation of density comparison, so this method is called relative density. Replacing the traditional distance measurement method with relative density can deal with the situation of data imbalance and density imbalance. Using the RD-KNN algorithm, we can generate a prediction label for each ambiguous sample, thus forming an RD-KNN predicted label set $\bar{Y}^a$.

(3) Prediction Matching: To verify the confidence of the predictor and ensure that the compensatory labels are reliable, we use the RD-KNN prediction results to match the predictor prediction results to further filter the ambiguous samples. When the predicted label of RD-KNN is consistent with the predicted label of the predictor, the label is selected as the compensatory label of the sample; if it is inconsistent, the predictor may be unreliable, and the ambiguous sample is

mixed into the good sample set and treated with caution. Re-form X^g and X^a, which is,

$$
\begin{cases}
X^g = \{\cdots, (x_j^g, y_j^g), \cdots\} & j \in [1, S] \\
X^a = \{\cdots, (x_i^a, (y_i^a, y_i^{'})), \cdots\} & i \in [1, M]
\end{cases}
\tag{5}
$$

where $S + M = N$, $S >= Q, M <= P$. y_j^g, y_i^a is the original label of the sample, $y_j^g \in Y$, $y_i^a \in Y$. $y_i^{'}$ is the compensatory label of the sample, $y_i^{'} \in Y^{'}$, $Y^{'} = Y^a \cap \bar{Y}^a$.

Importance Evaluation. To accurately characterize ambiguous samples, we evaluate the importance of the original labels and the compensatory labels. The label importance weights of M ambiguous samples are P, $P = [..., (p_i, p_i^{'}), ...]$. Where $p_i^{'} = 1 - p_i$. i is the index. The calculation formula of p_i is as follows:

$$
p_i = \frac{1}{2} + \frac{1}{2N_{y_i}} \sum_{j=1, y_i = y_j}^{N_{y_i}} \frac{<f_i, f_j>}{\|f_i\| \|f_j\|} \in [0, 1]
\tag{6}
$$

where f_i, f_j are the feature representations of the samples, all of which belong to the same category y_i. $\|\cdot\|$ is the modulus of the feature, N_{y_i} is the number of samples of class y_i, and j is the index. If p_i is low, it means that the expression information of the original label is insufficient, and it is necessary to focus on using the compensatory label, and vice versa.

3.3   Loss Function

ACLM uses the CLM module to divide the samples into good samples and ambiguous samples. Meanwhile, each ambiguous sample is annotated with both compensatory labels and the corresponding importance. The importance of the label represents the extent of corresponding expression involved in the sample. Thus, we utilize both original and compensatory labels to supervise the training of the FER model, and the importance corresponds to the weights of labels. The classification loss function is as follows:

$$
\begin{aligned}
L_{CL} &= L_{CL}(X^g) + L_{CL}(X^a) \\
&= -\frac{1}{S} \sum_{i=1}^{S} L_{CE}(x_i^g, y_i^g) - \frac{1}{M} \sum_{i=1}^{M} [p_i * L_{CE}(x_i^a, y_i^a) + p_i^{'} * L_{CE}(x_i^a, y_i^{'})]
\end{aligned}
\tag{7}
$$

where $p_i^{'} = 1 - p_i$. L_{CE} is Cross-Entropy Loss. Apparently, L_{CL} is related to p_i. For ambiguous samples with weaker confidence of the original label, the smaller the p_i, the more the model learns from the potential compensatory labels mined.

Combined with feature modulation loss and classification loss, the unified loss function can be summarized as follows:

$$
L_{total} = L_{CL} + \lambda L_{FM}
\tag{8}
$$

where λ is the hyperparameter.

4 Experiments

4.1 Datasets

RAF-DB [3] contains 30,000 facial expression images with basic or composite annotations. In the experiments, to be fair, we only use seven basic expressions in the dataset, which include six discrete basic expressions and one neutral expression, involving 12,271 training samples and 3,068 test samples.

AffectNet [4] is currently the largest publicly available FER dataset, with over 1 million images collected from the Internet by querying sentiment-related keywords in search engines. Among them, more than 440,000 images were manually annotated with eight expressions (seven basic expressions + contempt). In our experiments, we use 280K training samples and 40K test samples to conduct experiments on seven basic expressions and eight expressions including contempt, respectively.

SFEW [18] is collected from a movie and annotated for seven basic emotions. Including 958 images for training and 436 images for testing.

CAER-S [19] is a dataset obtained by selecting video still frames from CAER. The dataset is independently annotated into seven basic expressions, and contains 65,083 images, of which 44,996 images are used for training and 20,987 images are used for testing.

4.2 Implementation Details

Pre-processing and Facial Features. In our ACLM, face images are detected and aligned by the [20] method, and further resized to 224×224 pixels by data preprocessing. ACLM is implemented by Pytorch, the backbone network is ResNet18 [21], and 512-dimensional features are extracted from the last pooling layer of the backbone network. Before using the CLM module, we preheat the training with original labels and feature modulation loss in the first few stages to obtain discriminative and reliable representations of sample features. The backbone network ResNet-18 is pre-trained on the MS-Celeb-1M face recognition dataset when compared with various state-of-the-art methods.

Training. We train our ACLM in an end-to-end fashion using 1 Nvidia Titan 2080s GPU and set the batch size to 128. The hyperparameter K of the RD-KNN method in the CLM module is set to 10 by default, and can also be designed as other learnable parameters. The setting of the K value will be discussed in detail in the following experiments. The entire network is jointly optimized by L_{CL} and L_{FM}. As a rule of thumb, λ is set to 1.

4.3 Ablation Studies

We designed an ablation study to evaluate the effect of different designs in ACLM. As shown in Table 1, it includes Class Feature Modulation (CFM) module and the Confidence Evaluation (CLM-ce) and Importance Evaluation (CLM-ie) for Compensatory Label Mining Module. The effects of different combinations

Table 1. Evaluation of the two modules in ACLM.

CFM	CLM-ce	CLM-ie	RAF-DB	AffectNet-7
✗	✗	✗	86.47	63.13
✓	✗	✗	87.81	64.22
✗	✓	✗	87.71	64.18
✗	✓	✓	87.84	64.38
✓	✓	✗	87.91	64.44
✓	✓	✓	88.1	64.52

on RAF-DB are analyzed to demonstrate the effectiveness of the model design. It is important to note that CLM-ie cannot be used independently of CLM-ce, but CLM-ce can be used independently of CLM-ie. When CLM-ce is used independently, the weights of the original labels and compensated labels of the ambiguous samples are both set to 0.5. To better demonstrate the experimental effect, the backbone network we use is not pre-trained but trained from scratch.

It can be intuitively observed that using the CFM module greatly improves the network performance. Using only the CFM module improves the results from 86.47% of the baseline to 87.81%. Using the CLM-ce while using CFM resulted in a 0.2% improvement over using the CLM-ce alone and a 0.07% improvement over using both the CLM-ce and CLM-ie. This also proves from the perspective of experimental results that L_{FM} can make the network extract more discriminative class features, so that the predictor can better perceive the ambiguous samples at the class edge and improve the quality of learning compensatory labels. Furthermore, combining the CLM-ie and CLM-ce considerably improves the effect of the CLM-ce alone under the same conditions. This demonstrates that CLM-ie evaluates the importance of labels and adaptively utilizes original labels and compensatory labels, which can accurately describe ambiguous samples. Finally, we achieve 88.1% accuracy on the RAF-DB dataset without pretraining.

4.4 Visualization Results

Visualization of Compensatory Label and Label Weight. To further explore the reasonableness of the compensatory labels and labels weights obtained by the CLM module, we randomly visualized some ambiguous samples with original labels and compensatory labels according to the training results of ACLM on RAF-DB, as shown in the Fig. 3. The first row below the image is the original label of the data, the second row below the image is the compensatory label obtained by the CLM module, and the weight of the label is in parentheses, which is intuitively consistent with the "ground truth". The weight of the compensatory label represents the ambiguity of the expression. The larger the weight, the more the model learns from the "hidden expressions".

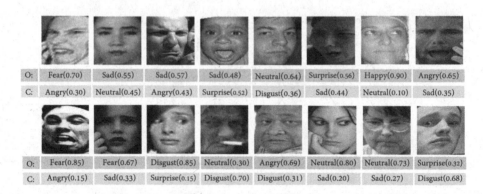

O:	Fear(0.70)	Sad(0.55)	Sad(0.57)	Sad(0.48)	Neutral(0.64)	Surprise(0.56)	Happy(0.90)	Angry(0.65)
C:	Angry(0.30)	Neutral(0.45)	Angry(0.43)	Surprise(0.52)	Disgust(0.36)	Sad(0.44)	Neutral(0.10)	Sad(0.35)

O:	Fear(0.85)	Fear(0.67)	Disgust(0.85)	Neutral(0.30)	Angry(0.69)	Neutral(0.80)	Neutral(0.73)	Surprise(0.32)
C:	Angry(0.15)	Sad(0.33)	Surprise(0.15)	Disgust(0.70)	Disgust(0.31)	Sad(0.20)	Sad(0.27)	Disgust(0.68)

Fig. 3. Visualization of the compensatory label and weights. O and C represent original and compensatory labels, respectively.

Visualization of the Effect of the CFM Module. We use the T-SNE [22] method to analyze the effect of the CFM module. To be fair, we uniformly use the ResNet-18 pre-trained on the dataset MS-Celeb-1M as the backbone network. The feature visual comparison results on the RAF-DB dataset are shown in Fig. 4.

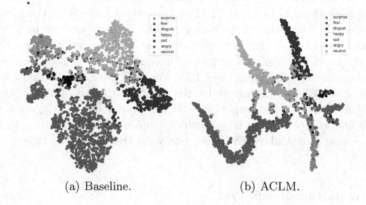

(a) Baseline.   (b) ACLM.

Fig. 4. The t-SNE visualization comparison w/o the CFM module.

Figure 4(a) shows the feature distribution results using only the cross-entropy classification loss as a training constraint. Figure 4(b) shows the result of the feature distribution as a constraint with the CFM module added in addition to the classification loss. The visualization results intuitively show that by adding L_{FM} loss, the network can learn more discriminative expression features. Using different directions as the basis for separability relieves the data scaling problem based on Euclidean distance and increases the separability of classes with small sample size.

Table 2. Comparison with state-of-the-art.

(a) RAF-DB

Method	Acc.
SCN*[23]	88.14
EfficientFace[24]	88.36
RUL [25]	88.98
ADDL [26]	89.34
DAN [27]	89.37
DMEU[16]	89.42
ACLM	**89.60**

(b) SFEW

Method	Acc.
DAN [27]	50.92
Island loss[28]	52.52
Icept-ResV1[29]	51.90
RAN[4]	56.40
DMEU[16]	58.34
ADDL [26]	**62.16**
ACLM	60.55

(c) CAER-S

Method	Acc.
CAERNet[19]	73.51
MobileNetV2[30]	79.23
DAN [27]	84.48
ResNet18[21]	85.28
Res2Net50[31]	85.35
EfficientFace	85.87
ACLM	**87.34**

Table 3. Comparison with state-of-the-art on AffectNet.

(a) AffectNet-7

Method	Acc.
DMEU(Res-50) [16]	63.11
EfficientFace [24]	63.70
KTN [32]	63.97
DAN [27]	64.83
DACL [33]	65.20
EfficientNet-B0 [34]	**65.74**
ACLM	65.42

(b) AffectNet-8

Method	Acc.
RAN [4]	59.50
EfficientFace [24]	59.89
SCN [23]	60.23
PSR [35]	60.68
DAN [27]	61.25
EfficientNet-B0 [34]	61.32
ACLM	**61.39**

4.5   Comparison with State of the Art

We compare ACLM with several state-of-the-art methods on RAF-DB, SFEW, CAER-S, and AffecNet, such as RAN [4], ADDL [26], and DAN [27]. RAN utilizes a cascaded attention network to focus on facial region features. ADDL utilizes additional data for multi-task learning and adversarial transfer learning to remove various irrelevant interference factors. DAN sets up multiple attention blocks to simultaneously focus on multiple regions of the face. Since code for some methods is readily available, we reimplement the results of the algorithm on various datasets with the same settings. We found that the reimplemented results and the reported results have certain gaps, which may be due to different data processing procedures and training techniques. ADDL is pre-trained on Multi-Pie [36] and EfficientFace, SCN, and DMEU are pre-trained on MS-Celeb-1M. We use the same MS-Celeb-1M pre-training method as most algorithms.

Table 2 presents the quantitative comparison results between ACLM and other methods in RAF-DB, SFEW, and CAER-S. As shown in Table 2(a) and Table 2(c), ACLM achieved the best results, with 88.6% and 87.34%, respectively. Since the CAER-S dataset is relatively novel and there are few studies on this dataset, the results of MobileNet-V2 and Res2Net-50 are provided by recurrence. On the CAER-S dataset, ACLM outperforms the next best by 1.47%. Such as Table 2(b), ACLM achieved the next best results. Table 3(a) and Table 3(b) give the comparison results on AffecNet-7 and AffectNet-8. ACLM also achieves good performance in these benchmarks.

5   Conclusion

We analyze the issue of label ambiguity in FER and propose to solve this issue by mining compensatory labels for ambiguous samples adaptively. Thus, we propose an Adaptive Compensatory Label Mining (ACLM) Model, which mines compensatory labels for ambiguous samples and keeps original labels for good samples. The proposed ACLM selects ambiguous samples by comparing the original annotations and predicted labels of the FER model. It regards the predicted labels as the compensatory ones for ambiguous samples and evaluates the confidence and importance of compensatory labels, so as to characterize ambiguous samples exactly. Moreover, ACLM designs a novel objective function to guide the FER network with the learned compensatory labels and corresponding weights. Experiments on four public datasets have validated the effectiveness and superiority of the proposed ACLM.

References

1. Tian, Y., Kanade, T.: Recognizing action units for facial expression analysis. IEEE Trans. Pattern Anal. Mach. Intell. **23**(2), 97–115 (2001)
2. Shan, L., Deng, W.: Deep facial expression recognition: a survey. IEEE Trans. Affect. Comput. **13**(3), 1195–1215 (2018)
3. Li, S., Deng, W., Du, J.: Reliable crowdsourcing and deep locality-preserving learning for expression recognition in the wild. In: Proceedings of the IEEE Conference on Computer Vision and Pattern Recognition, pp. 2852–2861 (2017)
4. Mollahosseini, A., Hasani, B., Mahoor, M.H.: Affectnet: a database for facial expression, valence, and arousal computing in the wild. IEEE Trans. Affect. Comput. **10**(1), 18–31 (2017)
5. Chen, S., Wang, J., Chen, Y., Shi, Z., Geng, X., Rui, Y.: Label distribution learning on auxiliary label space graphs for facial expression recognition. In: Proceedings of the IEEE/CVF Conference on Computer Vision and Pattern Recognition, pp. 13984–13993 (2020)
6. Zhang, S., Huang, Z., Paudel, D.P., Van Gool, L.: Facial emotion recognition with noisy multi-task annotations. In: Proceedings of the IEEE/CVF Winter Conference on Applications of Computer Vision, pp. 21–31 (2021)
7. Li, S., Xia, X., Ge, S., Liu, T.: Selective-supervised contrastive learning with noisy labels. arXiv preprint arXiv:2203.04181 (2022)
8. Chen, L.H., Li, H., Yang, W.: Anomman: detect anomaly on multi-view attributed networks (2022)
9. Wang, K., Peng, X., Yang, J., Lu, S., Qiao, Y.: Suppressing uncertainties for large-scale facial expression recognition. IEEE (2020)
10. Zhang, Z., Sabuncu, M.: Generalized cross entropy loss for training deep neural networks with noisy labels. In: Advances in Neural Information Processing Systems, vol. 31 (2018)

11. Gan, Y., Chen, J., Xu, L.: Facial expression recognition boosted by soft label with a diverse ensemble. Pattern Recogn. Lett. **125**, 105–112 (2019)

12. Du, S., Tao, Y., Martinez, A.M.: Compound facial expressions of emotion. Proc. Natl. Acad. Sci. **111**(15), E1454–E1462 (2014)

13. Zeng, J., Shan, S., Chen, X.: Facial expression recognition with inconsistently annotated datasets. In: Proceedings of the European Conference on Computer Vision (ECCV), pp. 222–237 (2018)

14. Yi, L., Liu, S., She, Q., Mcleod, A.I., Wang, B.: On learning contrastive representations for learning with noisy labels. arXiv e-prints (2022)

15. Hinton, G., Vinyals, O., Dean, J.: Distilling the knowledge in a neural network. arXiv preprint arXiv:1503.02531 (2015)

16. She, J., Hu, Y., Shi, H., Wang, J., Shen, Q., Mei, T.: Dive into ambiguity: latent distribution mining and pairwise uncertainty estimation for facial expression recognition. In: Proceedings of the IEEE/CVF Conference on Computer Vision and Pattern Recognition, pp. 6248–6257 (2021)

17. Goldberger, J., Ben-Reuven, E.: Training deep neural-networks using a noise adaptation layer (2016)

18. Dhall, A., Goecke, R., Lucey, S., Gedeon, T.: Static facial expression analysis in tough conditions: data, evaluation protocol and benchmark. In: 2011 IEEE International Conference on Computer Vision Workshops (ICCV Workshops), pp. 2106–2112. IEEE (2011)

19. Lee, J., Kim, S., Kim, S., Park, J., Sohn, K.: Context-aware emotion recognition networks. In: Proceedings of the IEEE/CVF International Conference on Computer Vision, pp. 10143–10152 (2019)

20. Deng, J., Guo, J., Zhou, Y., Yu, J., Kotsia, I., Zafeiriou, S.: Retinaface: single-stage dense face localisation in the wild. arXiv preprint arXiv:1905.00641 (2019)

21. He, K., Zhang, X., Ren, S., Sun, J.: Deep residual learning for image recognition. In: Proceedings of the IEEE Conference on Computer Vision and Pattern Recognition, pp. 770–778 (2016)

22. Van der Maaten, L., Hinton, G.: Visualizing data using t-SNE. J. Mach. Learn. Res. **9**(11) (2008)

23. Wang, K., Peng, X., Yang, J., Lu, S., Qiao, Y.: Suppressing uncertainties for large-scale facial expression recognition. In: Proceedings of the IEEE/CVF Conference on Computer Vision and Pattern Recognition, pp. 6897–6906 (2020)

24. Zhao, Z., Liu, Q., Zhou, F.: Robust lightweight facial expression recognition network with label distribution training. In: Proceedings of the AAAI Conference on Artificial Intelligence, vol. 35, pp. 3510–3519 (2021)

25. Zhang, Y., Wang, C., Deng, W.: Relative uncertainty learning for facial expression recognition. Adv. Neural. Inf. Process. Syst. **34**, 17616–17627 (2021)

26. Ruan, D., Mo, R., Yan, Y., Chen, S., Xue, J.H., Wang, H.: Adaptive deep disturbance-disentangled learning for facial expression recognition. Int. J. Comput. Vis. **130**, 1–23 (2022)

27. Wen, Z., Lin, W., Wang, T., Xu, G.: Distract your attention: multi-head cross attention network for facial expression recognition. arXiv preprint arXiv:2109.07270 (2021)

28. Cai, J., Meng, Z., Khan, A.S., Li, Z., O'Reilly, J., Tong, Y.: Island loss for learning discriminative features in facial expression recognition. In: 2018 13th IEEE International Conference on Automatic Face & Gesture Recognition (FG 2018), pp. 302–309. IEEE (2018)

29. Acharya, D., Huang, Z., Pani Paudel, D., Van Gool, L.: Covariance pooling for facial expression recognition. In: Proceedings of the IEEE Conference on Computer Vision and Pattern Recognition Workshops, pp. 367–374 (2018)
30. Sandler, M., Howard, A., Zhu, M., Zhmoginov, A., Chen, L.C.: Mobilenetv 2: inverted residuals and linear bottlenecks. In: Proceedings of the IEEE Conference on Computer Vision and Pattern Recognition, pp. 4510–4520 (2018)
31. Gao, S., Cheng, M.M., Zhao, K., Zhang, X.Y., Yang, M.H., Torr, P.H.: Res2net: a new multi-scale backbone architecture. IEEE Trans. Pattern Anal. Mach. Intell. **43**(2), 652–662 (2019)
32. Li, H., Wang, N., Ding, X., Yang, X., Gao, X.: Adaptively learning facial expression representation via CF labels and distillation. IEEE Trans. Image Process. **30**, 2016–2028 (2021)
33. Farzaneh, A.H., Qi, X.: Facial expression recognition in the wild via deep attentive center loss. In: Proceedings of the IEEE/CVF Winter Conference on Applications of Computer Vision, pp. 2402–2411 (2021)
34. Savchenko, A.V.: Facial expression and attributes recognition based on multi-task learning of lightweight neural networks. In: 2021 IEEE 19th International Symposium on Intelligent Systems and Informatics (SISY), pp. 119–124. IEEE (2021)
35. Vo, T.H., Lee, G.S., Yang, H.J., Kim, S.H.: Pyramid with super resolution for in-the-wild facial expression recognition. IEEE Access **8**, 131988–132001 (2020)
36. Gross, R., Matthews, I., Cohn, J., Kanade, T., Baker, S.: Multi-pie. Image Vis. Comput. **28**(5), 807–813 (2010)

Semantic-Guided Multi-feature Fusion for Accurate Video Captioning

Yunjie Zhang[1], Tianyang Xu[1]([✉]), Xiaoning Song[1], Zhenghua Feng[2], and Xiao-Jun Wu[1]

[1] Jiangnan University, Wuxi 214122, China
6213113148@stu.jiangnan.edu.cn, {tianyang.xu,x.song,
wu_xiaojun}@jiangnan.edu.cn
[2] University of Surrey, Guildford GU2 7XH, UK
z.feng@surrey.ac.uk

Abstract. In recent years, pre-trained visual language models (PVLMs) have achieved superior performance in many downstream tasks by extracting comprehensive cross-modal relevance from billions of pieces of data. Video captioning is a typical topic that aims to generate semantic texts from video clips, which also benefits from the advances in PVLMs. However, existing PVLMs only extract holistic features from still images, neglecting the local and temporal changes in the video appearance, which impedes fine-grained video understanding. Drawing on this, we propose to add explicit spatio-temporal semantics to the existing video captioning system by wrapping the detected salient objects over sampled frames, reflecting thematic events within a video. In particular, an auxiliary detection branch is designed to collaborate with PVLMs, achieving fine-grained object awareness. To achieve efficient temporal aggregation, we further employ the Gated Recurrent Unit (GRU) to extract temporally ordered cues, compensating for the limited temporal appearance capacity of PVLMs. The experimental results obtained on several benchmark datasets demonstrate the effectiveness of the proposed solution, with superior performance compared to the state-of-the-art approaches.

Keywords: Video Captioning · Object Detection · Gated Recurrent Unit

1 Introduction

Video captioning aims to understand the events in a video, with the ability to automatically predict captions, which has many practical applications in pattern recognition and computer vision, *e.g.*, video summary, video key detection,

This work is supported in part by the National Natural Science Foundation of China (Grant No.62106089, 62020106012); National Social Science Fundation of China(21&ZD166); Natural Science Foundation of Jiangsu Province, China (BK20221535).

H. Lu et al. (Eds.): ICIG 2023, LNCS 14358, pp. 47–58, 2023.
https://doi.org/10.1007/978-3-031-46314-3_4

and blind navigation. A traditional video captioning framework typically first extracts hand-crafted visual features from a given video clip. After obtaining feature representations, the video subtitle generation system generates sentences using predefined templates. The effectiveness of this framework is highly dependent on the predefined templates, while fixed templates always result in fixed syntactic structures in the generated caption sentences [16]. In recent years, deep learning has become the mainstream technique for video captioning, similar to the development of other visual or language tasks. In general, many sequential learning networks adopt the encoder-decoder architecture to flexibly generate caption output. The seminal encoder-decoder model is Sequence to Sequence Video to Text (S2VT) [9] which has two stacked Long Short Term Memories (LSTMs).

S2VT is the initial deep learning-based framework for the video description task and it is the first to introduce the encoder-decoder structure to the video description task, which has inspired many subsequent models. For example, Spatio-Temporal Attention Long Short Term Memory (SA-LSTM) [10] presents an attention method that combines local and global temporal structures of video features and considers different motion patterns, which can effectively generate accurate video captions. Reconstruction Network (RecNet) [24], on the other hand, is a novel video caption reconstruction network, which not only adopts video-to-text generation but also explores text-to-video mapping, unifying the semantic space between the two modalities [5].

Almost all of the above approaches use Convolutional Neural Networks as video encoders. However, since CNNs are experts in processing visual features, but lack the power of textual semantic extraction, it is not optimal to implement video captioning using pure CNNs. To solve this problem, Transformer methods [1], which construct inter-dependencies between vision and language, are proposed to provide improved generation capabilities over CNN approaches. Nevertheless, the task is still far from being solved due to the inconsistency between video appearance and language cues.

The PVLM has received considerable attention in recent years for bridging the complex semantic gap between images and texts. It learns large and sophisticated patterns in a Transformer-like network and has achieved superior performance in a number of well-known benchmarks [2,3] and competitions. In principle, the success of PVLM lies in its transferability to the downstream tasks in terms of preserving the intrinsic discrimination and perception between the two modalities involved. Despite its power in bridging images and texts, PVLM is not tailored for video captioning, as it focuses on extracting holistic features from still images and text [19]. Therefore, the essential issues that need to be addressed for PVLM-based video captioning are two-fold: firstly, how to explore the local spatial semantics rather than holistic representations; secondly, how to perceive temporally ordered appearance variations in videos.

To mitigate the first issue, additional spatial modelling techniques have been studied accordingly. Yu et al. [20] propose to use a spatial attention mechanism to focus on local spatial semantics. However, this approach performs poorly when detecting overlapping objects. With the development of target detectors, some methods attempt to extract local spatial semantics using target detectors. For instance, Zheng et al. [14] use a target detector to detect multiple object targets and further focus on the interactions between targets to generate high-quality predicates and verb subtitles. Therefore, we inherit the previous research methodology, using powerful object detection modules to explore the comprehensive capacity between holistic and local spatial semantics. To address the second issue, various designs have been proposed to reflect temporal cues from input videos. Cho et al. [4] use the GRU model to obtain a temporal representation of the cross-frame motion patterns. Zhang et al. [21] further use bi-directional temporal maps to capture the temporal trajectory of each salient object as a way to obtain motion relevance cues between video frames. Considering the absence of temporal representation within video features, in our work, we utilise a lightweight Gated Recurrent Unit (GRU) to perceive temporally ordered appearance variations in videos.

To summarise, the main contributions of the proposed method include:

- Local semantics are highlighted by an object detection module. This provides complementary visual cues for accurate video captioning. A dedicated multi-feature fusion module is employed to balance the saliency between object semantics and scenario overview.
- Temporally ordered cues are moderately aggregated via GRU, eliminating information redundancy among video frames. The temporal order can also be reflected by GRU, highlighting the potential causality of video data.
- State-of-the-art results are obtained on the MSVD [2] and MSR-VTT [3] datasets, demonstrating the effectiveness and robustness of the proposed approach.

2   Related Work

Video Captioning Based on CNN and RNN. In the early days, there are many traditional approaches used to formulate the video captioning task. In the beginning, Kojima et al. [8] propose a template-based method that predicts the words represented by specific objects and actions in video frames. Although straightforward, this approach suffers from the obvious disadvantage of not being able to generate diverse and flexible video descriptions. To alleviate this limitation, encoder-decoder architecture is adopted for video captioning to simultaneously predict the sequential output. Venugopalan et al. [9] are the first to explore the encoder-decoder structure for video captioning. They use CNN to extract video features from each frame and perform pooling operations to obtain a global video representation, and then generate the output captions with an LSTM module. Although this structure can extract descriptive visual features, it cannot interact visual features with textual features, so it lacks support from textual semantics. To remedy this shortcoming, Transformer-based methods are now widely used.

Transformer Techniques in Video Captioning. The success of Transformer models in natural language processing tasks has been transferred to the computer vision field in recent years. Due to the powerful attention mechanism, Transformer architectures are also widely used in the video captioning field. As LSTM cannot address the long-term dependency in the process of video encoding, Zhou *et al.* [1] proposed to use a Transformer instead of LSTM to extract relevant video features. Furthermore, to highlight the multi-modal property, Ging *et al.* [17] proposed a multi-layer Transformer structure that facilitates the semantic alignment of visual and textual features in a common embedding space. The Transformer-based encoder-decoder structure dominates the current designs, which is also our baseline structure. However, fine-tuning a Transformer model in the training stage often requires huge computational expenses, which impedes its practical applications. In order to reduce the computational burden, the use of PVLMs has become the most popular method, with promising transferability to downstream multi-modal tasks.

Pre-trained Visual-Language Models. PVLMs establish powerful multimodal interactions by training on large-volume image-text pairs, bridging the semantic gap between the vision and language data. In particular, the CLIP model proposed by Radford *et al.* uses contrast learning to perform unsupervised training of images with massive texts. For downstream extensions, Li *et al.* propose ALBEF [18], which uses a detector-free image encoder and a text encoder to encode images and text independently. Specifically, we use the CLIP4Clip model to extract high-performance visual representations. Although PVLMs provide relevant connections between visual and language pairs, they tend to focus on holistic spatial semantics at the expense of neglecting local spatial semantics [23]. Therefore, it is necessary to explore the target local semantics in order to obtain enhanced perceptions that can promote accuracy and concentration during video-text alignment.

Utilising Local Semantics. Local target details play an important role in generating high-quality headlines. In order to perceive local semantics, pre-trained object detection models, *e.g.*, YOLO [12] and Faster-RCNN [6], have been widely studied in general computer vision field. In terms of video captioning, there have also been existing attempts to exploit the detected semantic information. In the work proposed by Aafaq *et al.* [13], the pre-trained YOLO object detector is used to extract the locations and scales of objects. Similarly, Ye *et al.* [22] used a pre-trained Faster-RCNN object detector to extract salient objects, with a multi-level modular network being constructed to effectively analyse the relationship among these objects, delivering accurate video captioning [26]. Consistent with the above development, we also aim to balance the local and holistic semantics of individual detection and PVLMs, respectively.

3   The Proposed Approach

In order to introduce local semantics and temporal information into the current captioning model, our model uses a target detector and a GRU model to extract local spatial semantics and temporally ordered cues, respectively. Then, the fusion module is used to fuse the holistic spatial pattern, local semantic information, and temporal clue. Finally, the Symmetric Cross Entropy (SCE) Loss [7] is used to guide the training of the model. The details of the overall structure of the method are shown in Fig. 1.

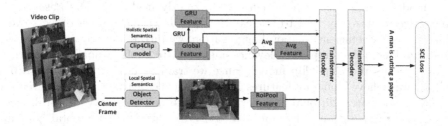

Fig. 1. Illustration of the proposed network structure that integrates multi-frame global features and local detection cues, compensating for the incomplete perception of local and holistic semantics. The fused features are input to the encoder-decoder Transformer blocks with Symmetric Cross Entropy (SCE) Loss for video captioning.

3.1   Spatial Semantics

To reflect comprehensive spatial appearance, both the holistic and local semantics of a video should be explicitly represented. In our method, twelve frames are extracted from each video sequence. The holistic spatial semantics of all twelve frames is obtained by the powerful CLIP4Clip model [25] with freezing parameters, while the object detection module is applied for extracting the local spatial semantics from the centre frame. In particular, the object detection module is used to store the locations of local entities in the video frame. Then the features are extracted from these local spatial regions using the convolutional layers of ResNet50. Finally, a Multi-layer Perceptron (MLP) module is used to further strengthen the features and unify the dimensions, so that they can be projected into the same feature space with other features.

In view of the superior universality, robustness and better performance of the Faster-RCNN object detector, we use it as our target detector. In this paper, the Faster-RCNN object detector with freezing parameters is used to detect the objects in each centre frame. By using the Faster-RCNN, the local spatial semantics obtained is $N \times 1024$, where N is the number of detected targets, 1024 is the candidate feature dimension on the convolutional layer output. Since we prefer to obtain more local spatial semantics, the classification threshold of Faster-RCNN is set to 0.3. Using a lower classification threshold allows the detector to obtain more objects in a video frame. Even if the lower classification threshold results in inaccurate classification results, we can still obtain effective spatial local semantics. Because we value the spatial local semantics within the prediction box, we focus on the accuracy of the prediction box rather than the accuracy of the classification results. By paying attention to both local and holistic spatial semantics, a more comprehensive representation of video features can be obtained.

3.2 Temporally Ordered Representations

Despite the holistic and local spatial semantics provided by the above appearance model, temporally ordered cues are currently neglected. The absence of time-ordered cues may lead to unclear changes of action between objects over time. To achieve efficient temporal aggregation, we further employ a GRU module to emphasise the temporal relevance of text-related holistic spatial semantics extracted from the Clip4Clip model. Since we train with features extracted by PVLM, we believe that our features have sufficiently learned the video representation, so that additional complex models are not necessary to obtain the temporal representation. Therefore, we use GRU to obtain temporal cues in features, taking into account the parsimony of the GRU structure.

In this module, the size of the holistic spatial semantics is set to 12×512, where 12 is the number of frames and 512 is the feature dimension. To unify the feature dimensions and extract the inter-frame relationship from the 12 video frames, the size of the temporally ordered representations is 1×512 after the GRU module. Effective temporal series representation can compensate for the lack of temporal cues in the features and enrich the video feature representation.

3.3 Feature Fusion Method

After obtaining the holistic spatial semantics, the local spatial semantics, and the temporally ordered representations, it is essential to effectively integrate these features.

In our design, since the size of the local spatial semantics is $N \times 1024$, which does not match the dimension of the holistic spatial semantics, a linear projection layer is used to reduce its dimensionality to $N \times 512$. Then, we cascade the holistic spatial semantics, the local spatial semantics, and the temporally ordered representations in the feature dimension to obtain the fused features. The plus sign indicates that the individual features are combined by concatenation. The characteristic dimension of the fusion is $(13+N) \times 512$. Where N is the number of objects detected by the target detector. The 13 dimensions contain 12 dimensional frame features and 1 dimensional temporally ordered features.

Next, the global average pooling is applied to obtain the global average features with the size of 1×512. Last, the global average features are merged with the fused features, and the final size of the Transformer input is $(14+N) \times 512$. The 14 dimensions contain 12 dimensional frame features, 1 dimensional global average features, and 1 dimensional temporally ordered features.

The fusion of multiple feature representations as described above allows for a comprehensive consideration of global and detailed features, holistic and partial features, and the incorporation of temporal cues. The complementarity between multiple features is exploited to obtain a video representation that is more semantic, less noisy and contains more critical information. To make a long story short, good features are the key to improving the effectiveness of the model.

3.4 The SCE Loss

Since the video labels are generally noisy and blurred, we use the SCE Loss instead of the original Cross Entropy (CE) Loss to relieve over-fitting and against noise with a regular term. The specific approach is to use the SCE Loss to relax the original strict binary label. We slightly decrease the value of the correct label from 1 and increase the values of the other categories from 0 to relax the strict constraint of cross entropy. SCE Loss is a combination of Cross Entropy (CE) Loss and Reverse Cross Entropy (RCE) Loss. CE Loss and RCE Loss are defined as follows:

$$\mathbf{L}_{ce} = -\sum_{t=1}^{L} P(t) \log Q(t) \tag{1}$$

$$\mathbf{L}_{rce} = -\sum_{t=1}^{L} Q(t) \log P(t) \tag{2}$$

where P and Q are the predictions and real outputs respectively. $\mathbf{L}_{ce}$ is the normal cross entropy loss, $\mathbf{L}_{rce}$ is cross entropy loss of switched labels. The SCE Loss is defined as:

$$\mathbf{L}_{sl} = \lambda_1 \mathbf{L}_{ce} + \lambda_2 \mathbf{L}_{rce}, \tag{3}$$

where λ_1 and λ_2 are two hyper-parameters.

By smoothing the labels in this way, we relax the original strict classification prediction results, so that the predicted captions can be some synonyms of the ground truth captions, improving the universality and rationality of the predicted captions.

4   Experimental Results

We evaluate the proposed method on two publicly available data sets, *i.e.*, MSVD and MSR-VTT. The used evaluation metrics of MSVD and MSR-VTT are BLUE@4(B@4), METEOR(M), ROUGE-L(R) and CIDEr(C).

Table 1. Ablation studies on MSVD and MSR-VTT

	MSVD					MSR-VTT				
Methods	B@4↑	M↑	R↑	C↑	Params↓	B@4	M	R	C	Params
Baseline	57.1	40.0	76.8	114.0	81MB	46.8	31.3	64.8	60.1	81MB
Baseline+OD	58.7	40.8	77.7	117.9	81MB	48.0	31.7	65.2	60.7	81MB
Baseline+OD+GRU	59.1	41.0	77.6	119.4	85MB	48.4	31.7	65.5	61.1	85MB

4.1 Ablation Study

In order to verify the effectiveness of the proposed method, we first report the corresponding ablation analysis. Table 1 reports the performance on MSVD and MSV-VTT datasets. In general, OD represents the object detection module, GRU represents the GRU module. Our baseline is the CLIP4Clip model equipped with holistic spatial semantics. We then test the baseline model with local spatial semantic features. Finally, we experiment with models with additional temporal sequence cues.

The impact of the OD module. Compared to the baseline, the use of local spatial semantics increases the performance in terms of CIDEr by 3.9 and 0.6 on the two data sets. The exploration of local spatial semantics can compensate for the shortcomings of PVLM in extracting only holistic features from images, which is the main reason for the improvement of our evaluation metrics.

The impact of the GRU module. By integrating the temporally ordered cues through GRU, we can further improve the performance by 5.4 and 1.0 in terms of CIDEr on the two datasets. Due to the particularity of the video task, the temporal feature transformation in the video is extremely important compared to the static image feature. Therefore, the GRU module can be used to sense the appearance change of the temporal sequence in the video, which can further improve the evaluation index.

In addition, although there are more variables involved in our design, the increase in parameters is less than 10%. This is mainly due to the fact that the lightweight GRU module we use does not increase the number of parameters by a large amount. Given that our baseline is already able to extract valid global spatial transformations, it is perfectly adequate to use the lightweight GRU module to compensate for the lack of temporal cues.

We also test two methods to reduce the dimension of local spatial semantics, Linear and Transformer, respectively. For transformer, we use a layer of transformer encoder structure and change the size of its output dimensions. According to the experimental results in Table 2, leading results can be obtained by directly using linear projection. Based on this, we believe that the Transformer, which focuses on strong relationships between features, can support improved visual semantics. However, the loss of superficial feature details undermines the valid feature relationships extracted in PVLM. Based on this, the use of the Transformer to convert dimensions yields poor results in this paper.

Table 2. Different methods of dimensionality reduction on MSVD

Methods	B@4	M	R	C
Linear	58.7	40.8	77.7	117.9
Transformer	53.8	38.8	75.5	104.1

4.2 Comparison to State-of-The-Art

To demonstrate our modelling merits, we compare the proposed method with 15 state-of-the-art approaches on MSVD and MSR-VTT benchmarks. The results are reported in Table 3. As can be seen from the table, on the MSVD dataset, the performance of the proposed method is only 0.1 lower than that of HMN in the BLEU@4 evaluation index, while the performance of METEOR, ROUGE-L and CIDEr is higher than that of the previous optimal methods respectively. On the MSR-VTT dataset, our method outperforms all other methods on all evaluation indices.

This is mainly due to the fact that we exploit the sufficient prior knowledge in PVLM and the use of the target detector and the temporal model to compensate for the lack of local semantic features and temporal cues in PVLM. By fully integrating multi-scale and multi-angle features, our method is more comprehensive and versatile. Its excellent performance in each evaluation index also confirms the advantages and superiority of the method over other approaches.

Table 3. Comparison with 15 state-of-the-art MSVD and MSR-VTT benchmark methods. The best results are shown in bold.

Methods	Backbone	Features Motion	Object	MSVD				MSR-VTT			
				B@4	M	R	C	B@4	M	R	C
M3 (CVPR-18)	VGG	C3D	-	51.8	32.5	-	-	38.1	26,6	-	-
RecNet (CVPR-18)	Inception-V4	-	-	52.3	34.1	69.8	80.3	39.1	26.6	59.3	42.7
PickNet (ECCV-18)	ResNet-152	-	-	52.3	33.3	69.6	76.5	41.3	27.7	59.8	44.1
MARN (CVPR-19)	ResNet-101	C3D	-	48.6	35.1	71.9	92.2	40.4	28.1	60.7	47.1
OA-BTG (CVPR-19)	ResNet-200	-	Mask-RCNN	56.9	36.2	-	90.6	41.4	28.2	-	46.9
POS-GG (ICCV-19)	InceptionResnetV2	OpticalFlow	-	52.5	34.1	71.3	88.7	42.0	28.2	61.6	48.7
MGSA (AAAI-19)	InceptionResnetV2	C3D	-	53.4	35.0	-	86.7	42.4	27.6	-	47.5
GRU-EVE (CVPR-19)	InceptionResnetV2	C3D	YOLO	47.9	35.0	71.5	78.1	38.3	28.4	60.7	48.1
STG-KD (CVPR-20)	ResNet-101	I3D	Faster-RCNN	52.2	36.9	73.9	93.0	40.5	28.3	60.9	47.1
SAAT (CVPR-20)	InceptionResnetV2	C3D	Faster-RCNN	46.5	33.5	69.4	81.0	40.5	28.2	60.9	49.1
ORG-TRL (CVPR-20)	InceptionResnetV2	C3D	Faster-RCNN	54.3	36.4	73.9	95.2	43.6	28.8	62.1	50.9
SGN (AAAI-21)	ResNet-101	C3D	-	52.8	35.5	72.9	94.3	40.8	28.3	60.8	49.5
MGRMP (ICCV-21)	InceptionResnetV2	C3D	-	55.8	36.9	74.5	98.5	41.7	28.9	62.1	51.4
HMN (CVPR-22)	InceptionResnetV2	C3D	Faster-RCNN	**59.2**	37.7	75.1	104.0	43.5	29.0	62.7	51.5
CLIP4Caption (CVPR-21)	CLIP4Clip	-		-	-	-	-	46.1	30.7	63.7	57.7
Ours	CLIP4Clip		Faster-RCNN	59.1	**41.0**	**77.6**	**119.4**	**48.4**	**31.7**	**65.5**	**61.1**

4.3 Qualitative Results

We present qualitative results in Fig. 2, from which we can see that the proposed method can generate high-quality captions. The old method often produced wrong subtitles, see Wrong in Fig. 2, and the wrong place is usually the

Fig. 2. Qualitative results on MSVD. The images are the sampled frames of two videos. The image on the right is the feature attention map of the features extracted from the CLIP4Clip model. The text "GT" represents the ground truth video captions, "Wrong" represents the wrong video captions generated by the baseline model, and "Ours" represents our generated captions respectively.

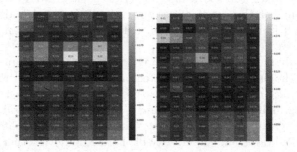

Fig. 3. The heat map relationship matrix between video captions and video features. The abscissa represents our predicted video captions, where SEP represents the end character of the predicted captions. The ordinate represents the video frame extracted from the video. If the text is closely related to the video features, the corresponding values are large and the colours are bright.

subject, object or verb. Therefore, in our approach, we use different models to further focus on area objects and the action relationships between objects. These practices often lead to more accurate subject, object or verb predictions. See Ours in Fig. 2. In addition, based on the attention heat maps obtained from our transformer decoder on the right side of Fig. 2, the region of salient objects can be correctly selected by the proposed method, indicating that the proposed method can distinguish the objects from their surroundings. More importantly, our model can also ignore some redundant frames. In the second example, the proposed method only focuses on the man and the motorbike, rather than the tire that appears in the first frame.

We also show the heat map relationship matrix between video captions and video features, as shown in Fig. 3. We choose two examples that match those shown in Fig. 2. As can be seen in Fig. 3, nouns and verbs are closely related to video features. This is mainly due to the addition of a target detection model and a GRU model of perceptual temporal cues to our approach, which focuses more on regional objects and actions. And, since not all video frames are relevant to the caption, some are redundant and our method is able to focus on the key video frames and ignore the irrelevant ones. The closest relationship tends to focus on certain key frames.

5 Conclusion

This paper presents a semantic-guided multi-feature fusion approach for accurate and robust video captioning. The proposed method harmonises holistic spatial semantics, local spatial semantics, and temporally ordered representations for high-performance video captioning. By constructing an effective feature fusion method, the proposed approach fuses the above features via attention operations, to obtain comprehensive visual representations of captions. Meanwhile, the SCE Loss is advocated for training the Transformer model with relaxed supervision. The proposed method achieves state-of-the-art performance on both the MSVD and MSR-VTT benchmarks, validating the merits of the method.

References

1. Zhou, L., Zhou, Y., Corso, J.J., Socher, R., Xiong, C.,: End-to-end dense video captioning with masked transformer. In: Proceedings of the IEEE Conference on Computer Vision and Pattern Recognition, pp. 8739–8748 (2018)
2. Guadarrama, S., Krishnamoorthy.: YouTube2Text: recognizing and describing arbitrary activities using semantic hierarchies and zero-shot recognition. In: Proceedings of the IEEE International Conference on Computer Vision, pp. 2712–2719 (2013)
3. Xu, J., Mei, T., Yao, T., Rui, Y.: MSR-VTT: a large video description dataset for bridging video and language. In: Proceedings of the IEEE Conference on Computer Vision and Pattern Recognition, pp. 5288–5296 (2016)
4. Cho, K., et al.: Learning phrase representations using RNN encoder-decoder for statistical machine translation. arXiv preprint arXiv:1406.1078(2014)
5. Xu, T., Wu, X.J., Kittler, J.: Non-negative subspace representation learning scheme for correlation filter based tracking. In: 2018 24th International Conference on Pattern Recognition, pp. 1888–1893 (2018)
6. Girshick, R.: Fast R-CNN. In: Proceedings of the IEEE International Conference on Computer Vision, pp. 1440–1448 (2015)
7. Wang, Y., Ma, X., Chen, Z., Luo, Y., Yi, J., Bailey, J.: Symmetric cross entropy for robust learning with noisy labels. In: Proceedings of the IEEE/CVF International Conference on Computer Vision, pp. 322–330 (2019)
8. Kojima, A., Tamura, T., Fukunaga, K.: Natural language description of human activities from video images based on concept hierarchy of actions. Int. J. Comput. Vision **50**, 171–184 (2002). https://doi.org/10.1023/A:1020346032608
9. Venugopalan, S ., et al.: Sequence to sequence-video to text. In: Proceedings of the IEEE International Conference on Computer Vision, pp. 4534–4542 (2015)
10. Yao, L., et al.: Describing videos by exploiting temporal structure. In: Proceedings of the IEEE International Conference on Computer Vision, pp. 4507–4515 (2015)
11. Hori, C., et al.: Attention-based multimodal fusion for video description. In: Proceedings of the IEEE International Conference on Computer Vision, pp. 4193–4202 (2017)

12. Redmon, J., Farhadi, A.: YOLO9000: better, faster, stronger. In: Proceedings of the IEEE Conference on Computer Vision and Pattern Recognition, pp. 7263–7271 (2017)

13. Aafaq, N., Akhtar, N., Liu, W., Gilani, S.Z., Mian, A.: Spatio-temporal dynamics and semantic attribute enriched visual encoding for video captioning. In: Proceedings of the IEEE/CVF Conference on Computer Vision and Pattern Recognition, pp. 12487–12496 (2019)

14. Zheng, Q., Wang, C., Tao, D.: Syntax-aware action targeting for video captioning. In: Proceedings of the IEEE/CVF Conference on Computer Vision and Pattern Recognition, pp. 13096–13105 (2020)

15. Pan, B., et al.: Spatio-temporal graph for video captioning with knowledge distillation. In: Proceedings of the IEEE/CVF Conference on Computer Vision and Pattern Recognition, pp. 10870–10879 (2020)

16. Xu, T., Feng, Z.H., Wu, X.J., Kittler, J.: An accelerated correlation filter tracker. Pattern Recogn. **102**, 107172 (2020)

17. Ging, S., Zolfaghari, M., Pirsiavash, H., Brox, T.: COOT: cooperative hierarchical transformer for video-text representation learning. In: Advances in Neural Information Processing Systems (2020)

18. Li, J., Selvaraju, R., Gotmare, A., Joty, S., Xiong, C., Hoi, S.C.H.: Align before fuse: vision and language representation learning with momentum distillation. In: Advances in Neural Information Processing Systems (2021)

19. Xu, T., Feng, Z., Wu, X.J., Kittler, J.: Toward robust visual object tracking with independent target-agnostic detection and effective siamese cross-task interaction. IEEE Transactions on Image Processing, pp. 1541–1554 (2023)

20. Yu, H., Wang, J., Huang, Z., Yang, Y., Xu, W.: Video paragraph captioning using hierarchical recurrent neural networks. In: Proceedings of the IEEE Conference on Computer Vision and Pattern Recognition, pp. 4584–4593 (2016)

21. Zhang, J., Peng, Y.: Object-aware aggregation with bidirectional temporal graph for video captioning. In: Proceedings of the IEEE/CVF Conference on Computer Vision and Pattern Recognition, pp. 8327–8336 (2019)

22. Ye, H., Li, G., Qi, Y., Wang, S., Huang, Q., Yang, M.H.: Hierarchical modular network for video captioning. In: Proceedings of the IEEE/CVF Conference on Computer Vision and Pattern Recognition, pp. 17939–17948 (2022)

23. Xu, T., Zhu, X.-F., Wu, X.-J.: Learning spatio-temporal discriminative model for affine subspace based visual object tracking. Visual Intell. **1**(1) (2023). https://doi.org/10.1007/s44267-023-00002-1

24. Wang, B., Ma, L., Zhang, W., Liu, W.: Reconstruction network for video captioning. In: Proceedings of the IEEE Conference on Computer Vision and Pattern Recognition, pp. 7622–7631 (2018)

25. Luo, H., et al.: CLIP4Clip: An empirical study of CLIP for end to end video clip retrieval and captioning. Neurocomputing **508**, 293–304 (2022)

26. Xu, T., Feng, Z., Wu, X.-J., Kittler, J.: Adaptive channel selection for robust visual object tracking with discriminative correlation filters. Int. J. Comput. Vision **129**(5), 1359–1375 (2021). https://doi.org/10.1007/s11263-021-01435-1

Scale-Adaptive Multi-area Representation for Instance Segmentation

Huiyong Zhang, Lichun Wang[✉], Shuang Li, Kai Xu, and Baocai Yin

Beijing Key Laboratory of Multimedia and Intelligent Software Technology, Beijing
Artificial Intelligence Institute, Beijing University of Technology, Beijing 100124,
China
{zhyzhy,shuangli,xukai}@emails.bjut.edu.cn, {wanglc,ybc}@bjut.edu.cn

Abstract. For the instance segmentation task, instance representation
directly determines the quality of generated masks, so achieving efficient
and accurate instance representation is crucial. Grid-based or box-based
instance representation contains redundant information from background
or other instances, activation-based instance representation includes a
small part of the instance. The instance representation based on current
methods is not accurate enough. In order to represent more information of an instance under the condition of excluding irrelevant information, this paper proposes multi-area representation (MAR), which is in
the form of a scale-adaptive multi-area activation map generated by a
multi-branch structure. MAR can adapt to the structure and pose of an
instance, thereby representing the shape and size of the instance. Experiments show that, compared with SparseInst, MARInst can improve the
performance of instance segmentation and keep the inference speed and
training memory almost unchanged. In particular, MARInst achieved
30.3% AP on the MS COCO 2017 val, and 1.6% AP higher than Sparse-
Inst when using the same ResNet-50 backbone, proving the effectiveness
of the proposed method.

Keywords: Instance Segmentation · Instance Representation ·
Scale-Adaptive · Multi-Area

1 Introduction

Instance segmentation is one of the most challenging tasks in the field of computer vision. From the initial two-stage to the current single-stage, from anchor-
base to anchor-free, the instance segmentation model becomes simpler and more
efficient. As shown in Fig. 1, the direct-segmentation method represented by
SOLO and SparseInst has greatly improved the speed and accuracy of instance
segmentation. The model consists of two main branches and uses dynamic convolution as a link. The instance branch is responsible for instance representation
and predicts instance category. The mask branch is responsible for generating
the instance mask corresponding to the instance representation. Because a set of

H. Lu et al. (Eds.): ICIG 2023, LNCS 14358, pp. 59–71, 2023.
https://doi.org/10.1007/978-3-031-46314-3_5

instance representations and decoder features are used as two inputs of dynamic convolution to generate the final mask, one instance representations will correspond to one generated mask. Therefore, the quality of the instance representation directly determines the quality of the generated mask. But for the instances in the actual scene, it is difficult to express them in a unified paradigm due to their different shapes and sizes, which puts forward high requirements for the accurate representation of instances.

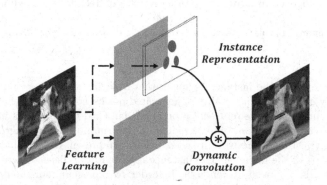

Fig. 1. The direct segmentation framework consists of two branches which are linked through dynamic convolutions ⊛. The instance representation branch is responsible for expressing instances and predicting instance category. The lower branch is responsible for generating the mask corresponding to the prediction out by the instance branch.

Existing instance segmentation models have explored different forms of instance representation including grid-basd, box-based and instance activation map, as shown in Fig. 2a. SOLO [20] divides an image into a certain number of grids. The grid which contains the center of an object is responsible for predicting the mask of the object. The density of the grid determines the accuracy of instance location, while the density of the grid also affects the calculation speed. So, manually setting grid division rules is necessary, and it is difficult to give a rule that applies to images having different contents. CondInst [18] extracts rough features for an object contained in the predicted box output by an object detection model. The form of rectangular is simple for expression and calculation, but the background and other objects included in the box will generate noise, as shown in Fig. 2b. So, the location and size of the box output by the object detector have great effect on the performance of mask prediction. The above two forms of introducing external information does not give full play to the end-to-end advantages of the network, which also indirectly affects the generalization ability of the model. SparseInst [2] represents an instance in the form of an instance activation map (IAM) and distinguishes different instances by focusing on instance locations, as shown in Fig. 2c. Usually, the coverage of the generated points in different instance activation maps changes little even if the sizes of instances are different, which is not benefit for expressing of the instance because the instance activation map is used for extracting instance-aware features. The low richness of IAM does not sufficiently represent the differences between instances. A natural idea is that there are more positions activated for instance activation maps corresponding to larger objects.

This paper explores a representation form that can adapt to instance shape and size, which is conductive to improving the quality of instance representation and further improves the accuracy of instance segmentation in complex scenes. Different from the single activation of SparseInst, the proposed model in this paper learns multiple mutually exclusive activation areas. Each activation area adaptively locates on an appropriate position of an instance and the union of the learned activation areas is used to represent the instance. The outer boundary of the merged activation areas can encode the size information of the instance, and the coverage of the merged activation areas can assist in locating the instance, as shown in Fig. 2d. In summary, multi-area based instance activation representation (MAR) has the following advantages: (1) without resorting to object detector or manual design; (2) adaptively perceiving shape and size of object; (3) lightweight model and efficient inference.

By employing scale-adaptive multi-area activations for instance representation, we design an efficient instance segmentation model that achieves 30.3 AP on the COCO dataset. The proposed model not only outperforms the baseline[1] by 1.6%, but also reaches a competitive level.

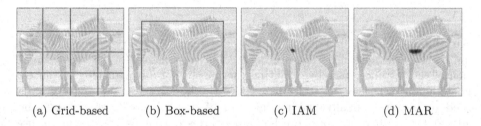

    (a) Grid-based   (b) Box-based   (c) IAM   (d) MAR

Fig. 2. Different representations of object. (a) Grid-based representation may fail to hit the instance; (b) Box-based representation contains features from other instances and background; (c) IAM primarily characterizes instance location, lacking a reasonable estimation for object size; (d) MAR varies with object size.

2 Related Works

2.1 Instance Segmentation

According to the presentation form of instances, instance segmentation methods can be divided into Contour-Based and Mask-Based. Contour-Based models,

---

[1] baseline means that SparseInst does not employ G-IAM and data augmentation.

such as PolarMask [23] and E2EC [27], regard instance segmentation as a regression task and have an absolute advantage in speed. The Mask-Based models can be divided into top-down and bottom-up according to the way of distinguishing instances. The top-down methods [1,7,13] rely on object detectors to detect objects and then segment instances within the detection boxes. The segmentation results are distinguished according to the detection results. The bottom-up methods [5,12] generate dense per-pixel embedding features and use some grouping strategies [3,14] to group them, thus distinguishing different instances. In addition to the above methods, there is another mask-based method that is direct segmentation, which does not require anchors and bounding boxes. It decouples mask prediction into instance representation and feature learning, such as SOLO [20], SparseInst [2]. As the predicted kernel is generated dynamically conditioned on the instance representation, it benefits from the flexibility and adaptive nature [21]. This paradigm can generate instance segmentation masks in an efficient way.

2.2 Instance Representation

For models based on direct segmentation, the instance representation is the innovation of the whole network. According to whether external factors are used for instance representation, the direct segmentation methods can be divided into two categories: auxiliary-base and auxiliary-free.

Auxiliary-base. SOLO [20,21] divides an image into grids, and the grid unit where the instance center is located is responsible for the representation of the instance, thereby achieving the purpose of distinguishing instances. For different scenarios, in order to achieve the best results, the division grids need to be set manually and the number of divided grids also needs to be adjusted. CondInst [18] uses the bounding boxes output by a detector to distinguish instances, and generates corresponding controllers (instance representation) according to the box information. Although the method based on bounding box is convenient for calculation, the encoding process neglects the shape and pose of object. In addition, redundant information such as the background or other objects in the bounding box will cause over-expression of the instance, thus affecting the quality of instance features.

Auxiliary-free. SparseInst [2] highlights the instance area based on the instance activation map, and the location of the activation area is learned by the network. However, the activation area roughly locates object, and the activation area is usually small, resulting in that the instance representation based on activation area is under-expressed. Insufficient instance representation will directly affect the quality of instance segmentation result.

3 Proposed Approach

Fig. 3 shows the proposed model architecture, which is single-stage, and anchor-free. Similar with SparseInst [2] and SOLO [20,21], the proposed model decouples instance segmentation into instance representation and feature learning, and uses dynamic convolution to link the two parts. In Fig. 3, the encoder is responsible for feature learning, the decoder is responsible for segmenting instances which first generates instance representation and then performs dynamic convolution on the feature map with the instance representation.

Following, we first analyze the role of instance representation in the direct segmentation approach and the characteristics of different representations, and then describe the proposed multi-area activation approach.

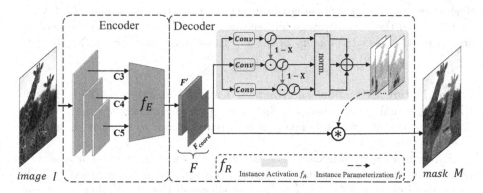

Fig. 3. The overall pipeline of MARInst. f_E is the feature extraction process. The instance representation f_R consists of instance activation f_A and instance parameterization f_P ⊛ denotes dynamic convolution. *norm* means normalization

3.1 Instance Representation

For an input image $I \in \mathbb{R}^{H \times W \times 3}$, the final instance mask is generated by performing dynamic convolution on the feature map $F \in \mathbb{R}^{\frac{H}{8} \times \frac{W}{8} \times (C+2)}$ with the instance representation $IR \in \mathbb{R}^{N \times C}$ as parameter, as shown in Eq. (1):

$$F = Concat(F'; F_{coord})$$
$$M = IR \circledast F, \tag{1}$$
$$Q(M) \propto Q(IR|F) \cdot Q(F),$$

where $Concat$ denotes concatenation, F' is feature output by encoder, $F_{coord} \in \mathbb{R}^{\frac{H}{8} \times \frac{W}{8} \times 2}$ is coordinate feature which consists of normalized absolute (x; y) coordinates of spatial locations, and ⊛ denotes dynamic convolution. Therefore, the quality of the mask $Q(M)$ depends on the instance representation quality $Q(IR|F)$ and the feature quality $Q(F)$. The main component of feature F is the output of the encoder f_E which acts on the backbone features $C3, C4, C5$, so its quality depends on f_E without considering the performance of backbone, as shown in Eq. (2):

$$F \approx f_E(C3, C4, C5),$$
$$Q(F) \propto f_E. \tag{2}$$

The input of the instance representation module $f_R(\cdot)$ is the feature F, and the quality of the instance representation result depends on them, as shown in Eq. (3):

$$IR = f_R(F),$$
$$Q(IR|F) \propto f_R(\cdot)Q(F). \tag{3}$$

Therefore, for the models using the direct segmentation paradigm, the feature extraction in the encoder stage and the instance representation in the decoder stage directly affect the quality of the generated mask, as shown in Eq. (4):

$$Q(M) \propto f_R \cdot f_E. \tag{4}$$

For feature extraction f_E, common feature extraction methods include FPN [10], visual transformer [19]. SparseInst proposes an efficient single-output encoding structure, which is acceptable in our opinion, so this part is not discussed in this paper.

For instance representation modules f_R, box-based instance representation usually takes the form of simple rectangular boxes, but can be disturbed by background and other instance information, as shown in Fig. 2b. While the instance representation in the form of activation maps have incomplete information due to the lack of adaptive adjustment to the size, as shown in Fig. 2c. Since the grid-based method(Fig. 2a) is manually set, the above two situations may occur during instance representation process. Therefore, a feasible idea is to consider the size of the instance fully.

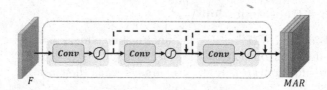

Fig. 4. Multi-area activation in cascaded form.

3.2   Multi-area Representation

The instance representation modules f_R consists of two parts: instance activation f_A and instance parameterization f_P. In order to obtain multiple activation areas without interfering with each other at the same time, we resolve the instance activation f_A into multiple simultaneous activations $f_{A_{b_i}}$, each branch b_i is responsible for activating one area corresponding to an instance, which can be expressed as Eq. (5):

$$f_R = f_P \circ f_A,$$
$$f_A = \bigcup_{i=1}^{N} f_{A_{b_i}},$$
$$f_{A_{b_i}}(F) = \sigma(Conv(F)),$$
(5)

where $\circ$ represent composition of functions, σ is the sigmoid function and N represents the number of branches.

In addition, the activated areas need to be as non-overlapping as possible to make the instance representation more sufficient. When learning the representation, the activation result of branch b_i is used as prompt information to assist another branch b_{i+1} to find the areas not activated by branch b_i, which can be expressed as Eq. (6):

$$A_{b_i} = f_{A_{b_i}}(F),$$
$$A_{b_{i+1}} = \sigma(Conv(F) \cdot (1 - A_{b_i})).$$
(6)

In order to represent multiple activation areas of the same instance as a whole, the activation results output by different branches need to be fused together through function $f(\cdot)$, as shown in Eq. (7).

$$A = f(A_{b_1}, \ldots, A_{b_i}),$$
$$\mathbf{A} = f_m(A)$$
(7)

The mapping function $f_m(\cdot)$ consists of a 3×3 convolution, which maps the activation maps $A \in \mathbb{R}^{D \times \frac{H}{8} \times \frac{W}{8}}$ into a new space from D dimensions to 100 dimensions, as shown in Eq. (7). The final instance activation map $\mathbf{A} \in \mathbb{R}^{100 \times \frac{H}{8} \times \frac{W}{8}}$ can represent the shape information of the instance.

Normalization. When the activation map of some branch acts as prompt information, the multiplication of the activation map and feature map conducts to decrease of the values in feature map. The decrease may cause inconsistent activation weights among different branches. To alleviate this problem, we normalized the activation map of each branch before fusing them, as shown in Fig. 3, to ensure that the activation map values output by different branches remain at the same level.

Cascade Structure. Except for the multi-branch method, the cascade structure can also achieve multi-area activation, as shown in Fig. 4. And shortcuts could be added in the cascade structure to ensure that the result of each activation can be passed forward to the output. The specific experimental details will be discussed in Sect. 4.2.

4 Experiments

In this section, we verify the effectiveness of the proposed method with extensive experiments and quantitatively analyze the performance of the model through ablation experiments. Further, the rationality of the multi-area activation method is proved by visualization experiments. Details as follow.

Dataset and Evaluation Metrics. MS COCO [11] is a large-scale dataset that can be used for a variety of vision tasks. It contains 80 different categories and different annotation forms, and is one of the most challenging datasets. Specifically, all our experiments are trained on train2017 (118k images), evaluated on val2017 (5k images), and AP is used as the main evaluation indicator.

Implementation Details. Unless specifically emphasized, the training process of MARInst follows the SparseInst training scheme, and uses the model (ResNet-50 [8]) pre-trained on ImageNet [4] as the backbone. Based on the Detectron2 [22] framework, we adopt AdamW [15] optimizer to carry out 90k iterations. The initial learning rate is 0.0001. The learning rate is divided by 10 at 60k and 80k iterations respectively, and the weight decay is 0.05. The training batch size is 48. Xavier initialization [6] is applied to initialize newly defined network layers. During the inference stage, when an image is input, the model outputs the predicted masks and corresponding confidence scores.

Table 1. Instance segmentation performance comparison of different models on MS COCO val (%). * means the G-IAM and data augmentation are removed. † means the two deformation modules are removed.

Methods	Backbone	Epochs	AP	AP_{50}	AP_{75}	AP_S	AP_M	AP_L
MEInst [26]	ResNet-50	12	32.2	53.9	33.0	13.9	34.4	48.7
CenterMask-Lite [9]	ResNet-50	48	32.9	-	-	12.9	34.7	48.7
DeepSnake [16]	DLA-34	160	30.5	-	-	-	-	-
PolarMask [23]	ResNet-50	12	29.1	49.5	29.7	12.6	31.8	42.3
YOLACT-550 [1]	ResNet-50	12	28.2	46.6	29.2	9.2	29.3	44.8
PointINS [17]	ResNet-50	12	32.2	51.6	33.4	13.4	34.4	48.4
E2EC† [27]	DLA-34	140	31.7	52.2	32.8	-	-	-
BorderPointsMask [25]	ResNet-50	12	31.4	52.0	32.8	16.3	34.4	42.8
PolarMask++ [24]	ResNet-50	12	30.2	52.6	30.8	14.4	32.5	43.1
SparseInst* [2]	ResNet-50	12	28.7	47.7	29.7	10.7	30.4	44.5
MARInst	ResNet-50	12	30.3	49.3	31.5	11.3	31.9	46.8

4.1 Main Result

We compared MARInst with some mainstream instance segmentation models, as shown in Table 1. The experimental results demonstrate the superiority of the proposed method on the COCO dataset. Specifically, with the same ResNet-50 backbone, our method achieves a gain of 1.6% AP over SparseInst.

4.2 Ablation Study

In this section, we separately conduct multiple ablation experiments to verify the effect of different structures. Unless otherwise specified, the setting of ablation experiments uses ResNet-50 as Backbone and 1× as the training schedule.

Number of Branch. The number of branches directly determines the number of activation areas. We verified the impact of number of branches on the accuracy through ablation experiments. It can be seen from Table 2a that as the number of branches increases, the accuracy presents an upward trend. This means that multiple activation areas contribute to the efficient representation of instances. When the number of activation areas reaches four, the accuracy starts to drop. Therefore, three activation areas are sufficient for instance expression.

Effect of Channel Dimension. The information contained in the low dimensional activation map may be incomplete, while high-dimensional representations may consume a lot of training resources. So, the trade-off between accuracy and resource consumption should be considered. Therefore, we design an ablation experiment on the channel dimension during activation to explore the most suitable representation dimension. As can be seen from Table 2b, increasing from 100 dimensions to 256 dimensions brings 0.4% gain in accuracy due to richer information representation. When the dimension equals 300, the improvement becomes limited, and the training time becomes longer.

Comparison of Fusion Methods. For the fusion process of multiple activation maps, different methods may produce different effects. We evaluated two fusion methods for add and concat, and the results are shown in Table 2c. There is little difference in the accuracy of the two methods.

Contributions of Different Structure Component. In order to generate multiple non-overlapping activation areas, we designed a multi-branch structure and an operation to perform subtraction between branches. We analyze the contributions of different components through ablation experiments, which can be seen from Table 2d. Specifically, when adopting single-branch structure, the accuracy is 29.4%, which is 0.7% higher than SparseInst due to the increase in dimension from 100 to 256. The application of multiple branches brings 0.4% improvement in accuracy. The performance improvement of MAR is more pronounced for large objects (+0.7 AP) than for small objects (+0.1 AP), which also shows that the richness of IAM is not enough. Continue to add subtraction

Table 2. Ablation experiments on different components of MARInst on MS COCO val.

(a) Number of Branches.

N	AP	AP_S	AP_M	AP_L
1	29.4	11.5	31.0	44.9
2	29.6	**12.3**	30.9	**45.5**
3	**29.8**	12.1	**31.6**	45.3
4	29.5	11.6	31.1	44.5

(b) Channel Dimension (N=3).

D	AP	AP_S	AP_M	AP_L
100	29.4	11.4	31.0	44.8
256	**29.8**	**12.1**	**31.6**	**45.3**
300	29.8	12.1	31.6	45.0

(c) Fusion Methods.

Fusion	AP	AP_S	AP_M	AP_L
add	**29.8**	**12.1**	31.6	**45.3**
concat	29.8	11.6	**31.7**	44.9

(d) Effect of Component.($N = 3, D = 256$)

Parallel	Subtract	Norm.	AP	AP_S	AP_M	AP_L
			29.4	11.5	31.0	44.9
✓			29.8	11.6	31.1	45.6
✓	✓		29.8	**12.1**	31.6	45.3
✓	✓	✓	**30.3**	11.3	**31.9**	**46.8**

(e) Effect of Cascade Structures.($N = 3, D = 256$)

Cascade	Shortcut	AP	AP_S	AP_M	AP_L
		29.4	11.5	31.0	44.9
✓		**29.8**	11.8	**31.8**	**45.1**
✓	✓	29.5	**12.3**	30.9	44.5

Fig. 5. Comparison of activation maps generated by different instance representations. The upper row shows the results of SparseInst, and the lower row shows the results of MARInst.

Table 3. The Comparison of our proposed method and baseline on training time and inference efficiency.

Method	Train time	Inference Speed	AP
Baseline	36 h (1.44 s/iter)	40 FPS	28.7
MARInst	44 h (1.76 s/iter)	36 FPS	30.3

operation on the basis of multi-branch, the accuracy of AP_S is further improved by 0.5%. Normalization bring 0.5% gain to increase the accuracy to 30.3%. This demonstrates that each component is valid.

Effect of Cascade Structure. The activation map of the cascade structure could be activated multiple times, and then the intermediate result can be passed to the end with the help of shortcuts. It can be seen from Table 2e that the shortcut havs a certain negative impact on the result.

4.3   Further Analysis

The multi-branch method inevitably introduces additional computational overhead. We compared the training time and inference efficiency of our proposed method and the baseline method, and the results are shown in Table 3. Under the same experimental condition, MARInst has better performance but is associated by longer training time and slightly slower inference speed.

4.4   Visualizations

The comparison of activation maps between MARInst and SparseInst is shown in Fig. 5. There are three instances with different sizes in the input image, the upper row shows activation results of SparseInst and the lower row shows activation results of MARInst. Comparing the three activation areas in each row, there are few changes in the upper row, but the activation areas in the lower row have different sizes and each is proportional to the size of the instance. So, MAR is more adaptive to the size of the instance. In Fig. 6, MARInst shows better performance in complex backgrounds, occlusive and dense scenes, which proves that MAR is more robust.

Fig. 6. Comparison of segmentation result generated by SparseInst(upper) and MARInst(lower).

5 Conclusion

In this paper, we propose a new instance representation (MAR) that can adaptively adjust the instance activation area according to the size of the instance. Using the proposed instance representation, the accuracy of instance segmentation is improved to 30.3%, demonstrating its effectiveness. In future research, we will further explore more efficient instance representations for the decoder of model.

Acknowledgment. This work is supported by The National Key R&D Program of China (No. 2021ZD0111902), NSFC (U21B2038, 61876012), Foundation for China university Industry-university Research Innovation (No. 2021JQR023).

References

1. Bolya, D., Zhou, C., Xiao, F., Lee, Y.J.: YOLACT: real-time instance segmentation. In: CVPR (2019)
2. Cheng, T., et al.: Sparse instance activation for real-time instance segmentation. In: CVPR (2022)
3. De Brabandere, B., Neven, D., Van Gool, L.: Semantic instance segmentation with a discriminative loss function. arXiv preprint arXiv:1708.02551 (2017)
4. Deng, J., Dong, W., Socher, R., Li, L.J., Li, K., Fei-Fei, L.: ImageNet: a large-scale hierarchical image database. In: CVPR (2009)
5. Gao, N., et al.: SSAP: single-shot instance segmentation with affinity pyramid. In: ICCV (2019)
6. Glorot, X., Bengio, Y.: Understanding the difficulty of training deep feedforward neural networks. In: AISTATS (2010)
7. He, K., Gkioxari, G., Dollár, P., Girshick, R.: Mask r-cnn. In: ICCV (2017)
8. He, K., Zhang, X., Ren, S., Sun, J.: Deep residual learning for image recognition. In: CVPR (2016)
9. Lee, Y., Park, J.: CenterMask: real-time anchor-free instance segmentation. In: CVPR (2020)
10. Lin, T.Y., Dollár, P., Girshick, R., He, K., Hariharan, B., Belongie, S.: Feature pyramid networks for object detection. In: CVPR (2017)
11. Lin, T.-Y., et al.: Microsoft COCO: Common Objects in Context. In: Fleet, D., Pajdla, T., Schiele, B., Tuytelaars, T. (eds.) ECCV 2014. LNCS, vol. 8693, pp. 740–755. Springer, Cham (2014). https://doi.org/10.1007/978-3-319-10602-1_48
12. Liu, S., Jia, J., Fidler, S., Urtasun, R.: SGN: sequential grouping networks for instance segmentation. In: ICCV (2017)
13. Liu, S., Qi, L., Qin, H., Shi, J., Jia, J.: Path aggregation network for instance segmentation. In: CVPR (2018)
14. Liu, Y., et al.: Affinity Derivation and Graph Merge for Instance Segmentation. In: Ferrari, V., Hebert, M., Sminchisescu, C., Weiss, Y. (eds.) ECCV 2018. LNCS, vol. 11207, pp. 708–724. Springer, Cham (2018). https://doi.org/10.1007/978-3-030-01219-9_42
15. Loshchilov, I., Hutter, F.: Decoupled weight decay regularization. In: ICLR (2019)
16. Peng, S., Jiang, W., Pi, H., Li, X., Bao, H., Zhou, X.: Deep snake for real-time instance segmentation. In: CVPR (2020)

17. Qi, L., et al.: Pointins: point-based instance segmentation. IEEE Trans. Pattern Anal. Mach. Intell. **44**(10), 6377–6392 (2021)

18. Tian, Z., Shen, C., Chen, H.: Conditional Convolutions for Instance Segmentation. In: Vedaldi, A., Bischof, H., Brox, T., Frahm, J.-M. (eds.) ECCV 2020. LNCS, vol. 12346, pp. 282–298. Springer, Cham (2020). https://doi.org/10.1007/978-3-030-58452-8_17

19. Vaswani, A., et al.: Attention is all you need. In: NeurIPS (2017)

20. Wang, X., Kong, T., Shen, C., Jiang, Y., Li, L.: SOLO: Segmenting Objects by Locations. In: Vedaldi, A., Bischof, H., Brox, T., Frahm, J.-M. (eds.) ECCV 2020. LNCS, vol. 12363, pp. 649–665. Springer, Cham (2020). https://doi.org/10.1007/978-3-030-58523-5_38

21. Wang, X., Zhang, R., Kong, T., Li, L., Shen, C.: Solov2: dynamic and fast instance segmentation. In: NIPS (2020)

22. Wu, Y., Kirillov, A., Massa, F., Lo, W.Y., Girshick, R.: Detectron2. https://github.com/facebookresearch/detectron2 (2019)

23. Xie, E., et al.: PolarMask: single shot instance segmentation with polar representation. In: CVPR (2020)

24. Xie, E., Wang, W., Ding, M., Zhang, R., Luo, P.: Polarmask++: enhanced polar representation for single-shot instance segmentation and beyond. IEEE Trans. Pattern Anal. Mach. Intell. **44**(9), 5385–5400 (2021)

25. Yang, H., Zheng, L., Barzegar, S.G., Zhang, Y., Xu, B.: BorderPointsMask: one-stage instance segmentation with boundary points representation. Neurocomputing **467**, 348–359 (2022)

26. Zhang, R., Tian, Z., Shen, C., You, M., Yan, Y.: Mask encoding for single shot instance segmentation. In: CVPR (2020)

27. Zhang, T., Wei, S., Ji, S.: E2ec: an end-to-end contour-based method for high-quality high-speed instance segmentation. In: CVPR (2022)

Multi-level Semantic Extraction Using Graph Pooling Network for Text Representation

Tiankui Fu, Bing-Kun Bao, and Xi Shao[✉]

School of Telecommunications and Information Engineering, Nanjing University of Posts and Telecommunications, Nanjing, China
shaoxi@njupt.edu.cn

Abstract. Graph Neural Networks (GNNs) have achieved remarkable results in several areas of pattern recognition, since GNNs handle complex structures well. Recently, GNNs have been used to learn text representation. However, the existing GNNs-based methods ignore the structure of graphs when generating graph representations from node representations, which limits their ability to learn hierarchical representations of graphs and capture hierarchical semantics. In this paper, we propose Multi-Level Semantic Graph Pooling Network (MLSGPool), a novel hierarchical graph pooling for text representation. MLSGPool consists of two parts: the local pooling layer and the semantic interaction layer. The local pooling layer utilizes GNNs to get a score for each node and then selects nodes with higher scores to form a smaller subgraph. We treat the representation of each subgraph as a semantic level. By stacking multiple local pooling layers, we can learn the hierarchical graph structure and extract multi-level semantics. In addition, we design a multi-head attention-based semantic interaction layer to capture the interaction between selected nodes and the nodes before the local pooling layer, which addresses the difficulty of interaction between a word and its distant neighbours. We apply our proposed model to text classification tasks, and experimental results on several benchmark datasets showed that the proposed method outperformed the baseline methods.

Keywords: Text representation · Graph pooling network · Graph Neural Networks

1 Introduction

Text representation is the basis for many real-world applications, including retrieval systems [25], text recognition [24] and community detection [17]. A superior text representation should be able to capture the semantics of the text, enabling the machine to approach the human cognitive system in terms of text understanding. Conventional methods obtain text representation with hand-crafted features, e.g., bag-of-words (BOW), term frequency-inverse document frequency (TF-IDF), and skip-gram [11]. However, they lack efficiency and

H. Lu et al. (Eds.): ICIG 2023, LNCS 14358, pp. 72–83, 2023.
https://doi.org/10.1007/978-3-031-46314-3_6

have difficulty capturing semantic connections. With the development of deep learning, Convolutional Neural Network (CNN) [9] and Recurrent Neural Network (RNN) [14] are widely applied to learn text sequences. These deep learning models based on text sequence prioritise locality and sequentiality, which can capture consecutive semantics well but ignore non-consecutive word dependencies.

Recently, graph-based methods have attracted increasing attention in text representation, showing superior performance over sequence-based models. These methods model the text sequence as a graph, and then use GNNs to learn text graph representations. Due to their great power in processing graph-structured data, GNNs can capture co-occurrence relationships between words and non-consecutive semantics. In these approaches, TextGCN [22] constructs a heterogeneous corpus-level text graph containing word nodes and document nodes based on word co-occurrence and document-word relations, turning the text classification task into a semi-supervised node classification task. TextING [26] and AGGNN [1] construct an individual graph for each document based on word co-occurrence. They then apply Gated Graph Neural Networks (GGNN) [13] to realize inductive text classification.

Despite the promising early results of these models, two drawbacks hinder their performance. First, the hierarchical structures of text graphs are neglected in graph representation learning. These methods generate word embeddings in text graphs via GNNs and then globally pool (e.g., use a simple summation [5] or a readout function [26]) all these embeddings together to generate the graph representation. These global pooling methods are not aware of the hierarchical structure of text graphs, and cannot aggregate node information in a hierarchical way, thus it is difficult to capture the hierarchical semantic information of the text. Second, most graph-based models perform best with two layers of GNNs, which means that they cannot aggregate information from more than two-hop neighbor nodes. Although we can stack more layers of GNNs to aggregate more distant neighbor nodes, the model performance will be severely degraded due to severe over-smoothing problems. This drawback makes the model unable to capture long-distance dependency relations between words.

To overcome the above limitations, in this work, we apply a hierarchical graph pooling based on the node dropping method to learn the graph representation. Unlike global pooling, hierarchical pooling stacks multiple local pooling layers and drops unimportant nodes at each pooling layer, which can capture the hierarchical structure of the graph. Furthermore, in order to capture the long-range word interactions and extract the semantic interactions, we design a semantic interaction layer based on multi-head attention. In this layer, nodes after pooling and nodes before pooling can feature interaction, even if they are far apart on the text graph.

To summarize, the main contributions of our work are as follows:

- Our proposed model applies hierarchical graph pooling to learn accurate graph representations, which can capture the structure of text graphs and mine the hierarchical semantics.

– We propose a semantic interaction layer based on multi-head attention to capture hierarchical semantic interaction, which can overcome the limitation that GNNs cannot extract the information of neighbor node with more than two hops.
– Extensive experiments on a series of benchmark datasets demonstrate that our method outperforms existing methods.

2   Related Work

2.1   Deep Learning for Text Classification

Deep learning models such as CNN and RNN can learn high-dimensional features of text and demonstrate superior performance over traditional methods in text classification tasks. TextCNN [7] applies convolutional layers with multiple filter widths and feature maps, then learns text representations via max pooling. [14] proposes three information-sharing mechanisms based on long short-term memory (LSTM) to model text. These methods model texts as sequences, focusing on locality and sequentiality, but lacking the ability to model non-consecutive word dependencies.

2.2   Graph Neural Networks

GNNs are efficient deep neural networks for graph representation learning, which are widely used in various graph learning tasks. GNNs learn node representations via message passing among neighbor nodes in the graph. There are different forms of GNNs, where Graph Convolutional Network (GCN) [10] utilizes mean pooling to aggregate node information, while GraphSAGE [4], GAT [19], and GGNN [13] use more sophisticated methods to aggregate nodes.

Recently, some GNNs-based methods have been used for text representation and have achieved superior performance. TextGCN [22] builds a heterogeneous text graph containing document nodes and word nodes and then applies GCN to learn document node representations. Text-level GNN [5] applies message-passing mechanism-based GNNs to learn text graphs. TextING [26] constructs an individual graph for each document and applies GGNN to learn node representations. After obtaining node representation vectors, these methods use the sum over all node features or a readout function to obtain graph representations. However, these global pooling methods take all nodes equally without considering the graph structure.

2.3   Hierarchical Graph Pooling

Global pooling method is inherently flat, treats all nodes equally, and cannot learn the hierarchical representation and the structural information of graphs. In contrast, hierarchical graph pooling can overcome this drawback by node clustering or node dropping. Diffpool [23] and EigenPool [15] are hierarchical pooling models based on node clustering. These models map nodes to a set of clusters and build a multi-layer network to learn the graph representation, which is computationally expensive. The node dropping methods are less computationally expensive and more efficient. gPool [3] and SAGpool [12] design learnable scoring functions to drop nodes with lower scores and build a hierarchical pooling framework. In this paper, we will learn the text graph structure using the scoring function and hierarchical architecture of SAGpool.

3   Proposed Method

MLSGPool consists of three key components: text graph construction, hierarchical graph pooling network, and graph representation. Learning the embeddings of the word nodes in the initial graph via GGNN. In the hierarchical graph pooling network, each local pooling layer drops nodes, forming a smaller subgraph. We regard the node representations of the subgraph as a semantic level. The semantic interaction layer captures the interaction between the subgraph node features and the initial graph node features to update the representation of the subgraph nodes. We stack local pooling layers and semantic interaction layers to learn text graph structure and multi-level semantics. Finally, we sum the outputs of each local pooling layer and feed this sum into a classifier. The overall architecture is illustrated in Fig. 1.

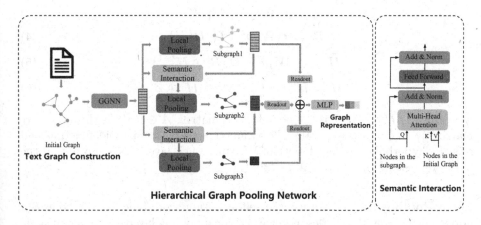

Fig. 1. The architecture of MLSGPool.

3.1   Text Graph Construction

Modeling text sequences as graphs is the initial step of our method. We denote a text as a graph $\mathcal{G} = (\mathcal{V}, \mathcal{E})$, where $\mathcal{V} = \{v_1, v_2, \cdots, v_n\}$ represents the set of the word nodes of the graph, and $\mathcal{E} = \{e_{11}, e_{12}, \cdots, e_{nn}\}$ represents the set of edges formed between nodes. In set $\mathcal{V}$, all word nodes are unique. Each edge starts at a node and ends at the l-hop neighbors of the node, where the maximum value of l is p, which is formulized as $e_{i,j}, j \in [i - p, i + p]$. To get edge weights, we apply a sliding window strategy, create a sliding window of size $2p + 1$, set the center of the window as v_i, and count the number of word pairs (v_i, v_j). The formula for the weight $a_{i,j}$ of $e_{i,j}$ is as follows:

$$a_{i,j} = \frac{\#W(i,j)}{\#W} \tag{1}$$

where $\#W(i, j)$ is the number of word pairs (v_i, v_j) and $\#W$ is the number of all word pairs in the document. $a_{i,j}$ is the normalized result value.

3.2   Hierarchical Graph Pooling Network

Gated Graph Neural Networks. Due to the high computational efficiency of Gated Graph Neural Networks [13], we apply GGNN to learn the embeddings of the word nodes in the initial graph. GGNN utilizes gated recurrent units to aggregate neighbor node features. Node v_i is initialized with a d-dimensional vector, denoted as $h_{v_i}^0 \in \mathbb{R}^{1 \times d}$. The formula from time step $t - 1$ to time step t is as follows:

$$a^t = AH^{t-1}W_1 + b \tag{2}$$
$$Z^t = \sigma\left(W_2 a^t + U_1 H^{t-1}\right) \tag{3}$$
$$R^t = \sigma\left(W_3 a^t + U_2 H^{t-1}\right) \tag{4}$$
$$\widehat{H}^t = \rho\left(W_4 a^t + U_3 R^t \odot H^{t-1}\right) \tag{5}$$
$$H^t = h^{t-1} \odot \left(1 - Z^t\right) + \widehat{H}^t \odot Z^t \tag{6}$$

where H^{t-1}, $H^t \in \mathbb{R}^{n \times d}$ is the node feature matrix, $A \in \mathbb{R}^{n \times n}$ is the adjacency matrix, W, U and b are trainable parameters, σ is the sigmoid function and ρ is the hyperbolic tangent function. We stack such layer twice and obtain the initial representation matrix $X_0 \in \mathbb{R}^{n \times d}$.

Local Pooling Layer. We use the self-attention score function [12] to assign importance scores S to nodes. For the t-th local pooling layer, let the input node representation matrix be X_t and the input adjacency matrix be A_t:

$$S = \sigma\left(\widetilde{D}^{-\frac{1}{2}} \widetilde{A}_t \widetilde{D}^{\frac{1}{2}} X_t W_s\right) \tag{7}$$

where $S \in \mathbb{R}^{n \times 1}$, $\widetilde{A}_t = A_t + I_n$, $\widetilde{D} \in \mathbb{R}^{n \times n}$ is the degree matrix of $\widetilde{A}_t$, $W_s \in \mathbb{R}^{n \times 1}$ is trainable parameter.

We drop nodes with low scores and get the top-k nodes and a new adjacency matrix as the output of the local pooling layer. The pooling rate $k \in (0, 1]$ is a hyperparameter that determines the number of nodes to be retained in each text graph. The top kn nodes and the edges between them will be selected to form a subgraph $\mathcal{G}_t$, which can be presented as follows:

$$X_{t_k} = topk\left(X_t'\right) \tag{8}$$
$$A_{t_k} = topk\_idx\left(A_t\right) \tag{9}$$

where $X_{t_k} \in \mathbb{R}^{kn \times d}$ is the node representation matrix and $A_{t_k} \in \mathbb{R}^{kn \times kn}$ is the adjacency matrix of the subgraph $\mathcal{G}_t$.

Readout Layer. A readout layer aggregates the node features of the $\mathcal{G}_t$ to make a graph-level representation R_t. The readout layer is a concatenation of sum pooling and maximum pooling. The formula is as follows:

$$R_t = \frac{1}{n_t} \sum_{i=1}^{n_t} x_i \| \max_{i=1}^{n_t} x_i \tag{10}$$

where n_t is the number of nodes of $\mathcal{G}_t$, x_i is the row vector of X_{t_k} and $\|$ denotes concatenation.

Each pooling layer gets a subgraph and a fixed size graph-level representation. We consider each graph-level representation as a semantic level. By stacking multiple local pooling layers and readout layers, we can obtain multiple subgraph representations and thus multiple semantic levels.

Semantic Interaction Layer. After the pooling layer, we design a semantic interaction layer based on the multi-head attention mechanism [18] to capture the interaction between nodes in the subgraph and nodes in the initial text graph. The formulas of the t-th semantic interaction layer are as follows:

$$Q = \sigma\left(X_{t_k} W_q + b_q\right), K = V = \sigma\left(X_0 W_k + b_k\right) \tag{11}$$
$$Att_i = Attention\left(QW_i^Q, KW_i^K, VW_i^V\right) \tag{12}$$
$$O = \left[\|_{i=1}^I Att_i\right] W_o \tag{13}$$
$$M = LayerNorm\left(O + Q\right) \tag{14}$$
$$X_{t+1} = LayerNorm\left(FFN\left(M\right) + M\right) \tag{15}$$

where X_{t_k} is the subgraph node feature matrix and X_0 is the initial graph node feature matrix. We construct X_{t_k} as query, X_0 as key and value by using linear layers, where W_q, $W_k \in \mathbb{R}^{d \times d}$, $b_q \in \mathbb{R}^{kn \times d}$, $b_k \in \mathbb{R}^{n \times d}$ are the training weights and biases of linear layers. *Attention* is a multi-head attention function that consider interactions between Q and K, V, which can be presented as follows:

$$Q_i = QW_i^Q, K_i = KW_i^K, V_i = VW_i^V \tag{16}$$
$$Attention\left(Q_i, K_i, V_i\right) = softmax(\frac{Q_i K_i^T}{\sqrt{d}})V_i \tag{17}$$

where $\boldsymbol{W}_i^Q, \boldsymbol{W}_i^K, \boldsymbol{W}_i^V \in \mathbb{R}^{d \times d}$ are the projection matrices for the i-th head. $\boldsymbol{W}_o \in \mathbb{R}^{Id \times kn}$ is the output projection matrix. $\boldsymbol{O}$ is the output of multi-head attention and shares the same dimension as $\boldsymbol{Q}$. *LayerNorm* is a layer normalization and *FFN* is a fully connected feed-forward network consisting of two linear layers. Finally, we obtain a new subgraph node representation matrix $\boldsymbol{X}_{t+1}$.

Our model is quite different from the classical graph pooling architectures [3,12,15,23], which use GNNs to update node representations after a local pooling layer. GNNs can only aggregate features of low-hop neighbor nodes in the subgraph, while the semantic interaction layer considers interactions between nodes in the subgraph $\mathcal{G}_t$ and nodes in the initial text graph $\mathcal{G}$. In other words, the semantic interaction layer captures long-range word interactions in a hierarchical ways.

3.3   Graph Representation

We add up the outputs of each readout layer and feed the sum into a linear layer for a graph representation.

$$G = \text{MLP} \left(\sum_{t=1}^{T} \boldsymbol{R}_t \right) \tag{18}$$

We feed the graph representation vector G into a softmax layer and use the cross-entropy function as training loss:

$$\hat{\boldsymbol{y}} = \text{softmax} \left(\boldsymbol{W} \boldsymbol{G} + \boldsymbol{b} \right) \tag{19}$$

$$\mathcal{L} = - \sum_i \boldsymbol{y}_i \log \left(\hat{\boldsymbol{y}}_i \right) \tag{20}$$

where $\boldsymbol{W}$ and $\boldsymbol{b}$ are trainable parameters, $\hat{\boldsymbol{y}}_i$ denotes the i-th element of predicted lable $\hat{\boldsymbol{y}}$, and $\boldsymbol{y}_i$ is the i-th element of the ground truth one-hot label $\boldsymbol{y}$.

4   Experiments

In this section, we describe the experimental setup and report our experimental results.

4.1   Datasets

For a comprehensive evaluation, we run experiments on five benchmark datasets including MR, R8, R52, SST-2 and 20NG. These datasets are widely used to evaluate text classification methods. The statistics of the preprocessed datasets are listed in Table 1.

- MR[1] is a movie review dataset consisting of 5331 positive and 5331 negative reviews, which is used for binary text classification.

---

[1] https://github.com/mnqu/PTE/tree/master/data/mr.

– R8 and R52[2] are subsets of Reuters-21578, a multiclass classification news corpus. R8 has 8 categories and R52 has 52 categories.
– SST-2[3] is a binary sentiment analysis dataset. Its documents are classified as positive or negative.
– 20NG[4] is a collection of 18846 newsgroup documents categorised into 20 different categories.

Table 1. The summary statistics of the datasets, **Avg Length** represents the average length of documents. There are there long corpora R8, R52 and 20NG and two short corpora MR and SST-2.

Dataset	#Docus	#Training	#Test	#Classes	Avg Length
MR	10,662	7,108	3,554	2	20.39
R8	7,674	5,485	2,189	8	65.72
R52	9,100	6,532	2,568	52	69.82
SST-2	9,613	7,792	1,821	2	20.32
20NG	18,846	11,314	7,532	20	221.26

4.2 Baselines

We compare MLSGPool with multiple text classification methods, which can be divided into three categories: (i)fast and efficient word embedding-based methods including, fastText [8], and LEAM [20]; (ii) sequence-based deep learning methods including CNN [9], LSTM [14] and Bi-LSTM [6]; (iii) graph-based methods including TextGCN [22], SGC [21], Text-level GNN [5], TextING [26], Hyper-GAT [2] and AGGNN [1].

4.3 Implementation Details

For our model and baselines that need to use pre-trained word embeddings, we use 300-dimensional GloVe[5] word embedding as initial word vectors. We randomly select 10% of training set as validation set. We use the Adam optimizer with an initial learning rate of 0.01. L2 weight decay is set to 10^{-4}, pooling rate of local pooling layers is set to 0.8 and the dropout rate of the linear layer is set to 0.5.

We set $p = 1$, $k = 0.8$ and stack three local pooling layers. In the parameter sensitivity subsection, we will set different p, k and the number of local pooling layers.

---

[2] https://www.cs.umb.edu/~smimarog/textmining/datasets/.
[3] https://nlp.stanford.edu/sentiment/.
[4] http://qwone.com/jason/20Newsgroups/.
[5] http://nlp.stanford.edu/data/glove.6B.zip.

Table 2. The results of test accuracy(%) on text classification with different models. For each model, the mean of results is reported according to 10 times run. Some baseline results stem from AGGNN [1] and HyperGAT [2]. The best results are indicated in bold, and the second-best results are underlined.

Categories	Model	MR	R8	R52	SST-2	20NG
word embedding-based	fastText	75.14	96.13	92.81	81.45	79.38
	LEAM	76.95	93.31	91.84	80.52	81.91
sequence-based	CNN	77.75	95.71	87.59	80.07	82.15
	LSTM	77.33	96.09	90.48	79.52	75.43
	Bi-LSTM	77.68	96.31	90.54	80.56	73.18
graph-based	TextGCN	76.74	97.07	93.56	81.02	86.34
	SGC	75.91	97.21	94.02	75.95	-
	Text-level GNN	75.96	97.07	94.60	81.75	84.16
	HyperGAT	78.32	97.97	<u>94.98</u>	81.26	**86.62**
	TextING	78.93	97.34	93.73	<u>83.64</u>	-
	AGGNN	<u>80.03</u>	<u>98.18</u>	94.72	-	85.26
	MLSGPool(ours)	**80.73**	**98.54**	**95.56**	**84.68**	<u>86.56</u>

Table 3. The results of ablation studies on our model, *w/i global pooling* is a model that replaces the hierarchical graph pooling network with a concatenation of max-pooling and mean-pooling, and *w/o semantic interaction layer* is a variant that replaces the semantic interaction layers with GGNN.

Model	MR	R8	R52	SST-2	20NG
w/i global pooling	78.90	97.63	95.10	83.82	85.94
w/o semantic interaction layer	80.03	97.81	95.25	83.96	86.30
MLSGPool(ours)	**80.73**	**98.54**	**95.56**	**84.68**	**86.56**

4.4   Experimental Results

Table 2 shows the performance comparison of our models and baselines on five benchmark datasets. We observe that our model outperforms all baselines on four datasets. In addition, we also perform the following analyses:

- We can see that graph-based methods generally outperform word embedding-based methods and sequence-based methods, indicating that modeling text into graphs and capturing non-consecutive word interactions benefit document classification.
- It is noteworthy that even simple word embedding-based methods can reach or exceed sequence-based methods on long corpora. For example, fastText [8] simply sums all word vectors to represent a text, completely ignoring the order of the text, but achieves better results than CNN [9] and LSTM [14] on

the long corpora, R8, R52 and 20NG, suggesting that sequentiality may not be a critical factor for text classification tasks, especially for long texts.
- Among all graph-based models, our model achieves the best results in most datasets. In particular, our models, TextING [26] and AGGNN [1] both use GGNN to learn node embeddings, suggesting that our hierarchical graph pooling is superior to the global graph pooling of TextING and AGGNN. The reasons for the improved performance of our model are that we consider the hierarchical structure of the text graph and focus on multi-level semantic extraction, while other graph-based methods ignore the structure of the text graph and only interact word features once on the initial text graph. There exists a node-subgraph-graph hierarchical structure of the text graph, and our method mines this structure to extract multi-level features of the text graph. It is clear that our hierarchical graph pooling network is able to produce more powerful graph representations than the baselines.

4.5 Ablation Study

To investigate the contribution of each module in MLSGPool, we perform a series of ablation experiments, and the results are shown in Table 3. From the reported results we can learn that hierarchical graph pooling can achieve better performance than global pooling (concatenation of max pooling and average pooling). Furthermore, replacing the semantic interaction layer with GGNN degrades the performance, which shows that the semantic interaction layer can significantly improve the performance of MLSGPool since it captures long-range node interactions between the subgraph and the initial graph, while GGNN can only aggregate features of low-hop nodes in a single subgraph.

4.6 Parameter Sensitivity

We investigate the impact of the number of stacked local pooling layers and pooling rates on model performance on the text set. Test accuracy is reported in Fig. 2. We observe that the model achieves the best performance when stacking three local pooling layers. Too few pooling layers may not mine enough semantic levels, while too many local pooling layers may be redundant, fail to improve model performance and cost more training time. The test accuracy of the model tends to decrease at pooling rates greater than 0.85 or less than 0.6. The pooling rate affects the size of the subgraphs generated by each local pooling layer. Neither too large or too small subgraphs are not conducive to the extraction of multi-level semantics.

Figure 2 also illustrates the performance of our model with different p. We find that our model achieves the best performance when $p = 1$, which means that only one-hop neighbor nodes are connected when building the text graph. The previous methods [5,16] achieve the best results when p is 2 or 3. The p of our method is smaller, so there are fewer edges in the text graph, which means the text graph is sparser. Although the text graph only connects one-hop neighbors, the model can still aggregate multi-hop node information because the semantic interaction layer can interact with distant words.

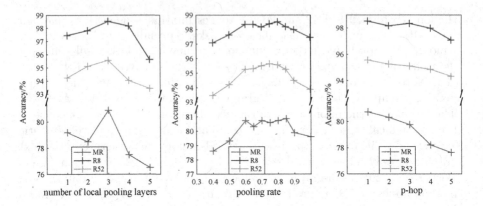

Fig. 2. Test accuracy with different numbers of local pooing layers, pooling rate and p.

5 Conclusion

In this work, we propose a new hierarchical graph pooling network, named MLS-GPool, for text classification. Our model extracts the multi-level semantics of text graphs using hierarchical graph pooling. Extensive experiments show that our model achieves better results than other competitive methods. Furthermore, our method not only provides an efficient method for text classification but can also be applied to other tasks requiring text representation.

Acknowledgment. This work was supported by National Key Research and Development Project (No.2020AAA0106200), the National Nature Science Foundation of China under Grants (No.61936005, 61872424, 61872199), and the Natural Science Foundation of Jiangsu Province (Grants No. BK20200037 and BK20210595).

References

1. Deng, Z., Sun, C., Zhong, G., Mao, Y.: Text classification with attention gated graph neural network. Cogn. Comput. **14**(4), 1464–1473 (2022)
2. Ding, K., Wang, J., Li, J., Li, D., Liu, H.: Be more with less: Hypergraph attention networks for inductive text classification. In: Proceedings of the 2020 Conference on Empirical Methods in Natural Language Processing (EMNLP), pp. 4927–4936 (2020)
3. Gao, H., Ji, S.: Graph u-nets. In: international conference on machine learning, pp. 2083–2092. PMLR (2019)
4. Hamilton, W., Ying, Z., Leskovec, J.: Inductive representation learning on large graphs. In: Advances in Neural Information Processing Systems 30 (2017)
5. Huang, L., Ma, D., Li, S., Zhang, X., Wang, H.: Text level graph neural network for text classification. arXiv preprint arXiv:1910.02356 (2019)
6. Huang, Z., Xu, W., Yu, K.: Bidirectional lstm-crf models for sequence tagging. arXiv preprint arXiv:1508.01991 (2015)
7. Johnson, R., Zhang, T.: Deep pyramid convolutional neural networks for text categorization. In: Proceedings of the 55th Annual Meeting of the Association for Computational Linguistics (Volume 1: Long Papers), pp. 562–570 (2017)

8. Joulin, A., Grave, E., Bojanowski, P., Mikolov, T.: Bag of tricks for efficient text classification. arXiv preprint arXiv:1607.01759 (2016)
9. Kim, Y.: Convolutional neural networks for sentence classification. arXiv preprint arXiv:1408.5882 (2014)
10. Kipf, T.N., Welling, M.: Semi-supervised classification with graph convolutional networks. arXiv preprint arXiv:1609.02907 (2016)
11. Kusner, M., Sun, Y., Kolkin, N., Weinberger, K.: From word embeddings to document distances. In: International Conference on Machine Learning, pp. 957–966. PMLR (2015)
12. Lee, J., Lee, I., Kang, J.: Self-attention graph pooling. In: International Conference on Machine learning, pp. 3734–3743. PMLR (2019)
13. Li, Y., Tarlow, D., Brockschmidt, M., Zemel, R.: Gated graph sequence neural networks. arXiv preprint arXiv:1511.05493 (2015)
14. Liu, P., Qiu, X., Huang, X.: Recurrent neural network for text classification with multi task learning. arXiv preprint arXiv:1605.05101 (2016)
15. Ma, Y., Wang, S., Aggarwal, C.C., Tang, J.: Graph convolutional networks with eigenpooling. In: Proceedings of the 25th ACM SIGKDD International Conference on Knowledge Discovery and Data Mining, pp. 723–731 (2019)
16. Piao, Y., Lee, S., Lee, D., Kim, S.: Sparse structure learning via graph neural networks for inductive document classification. In: Proceedings of the AAAI Conference on Artificial Intelligence. vol. 36, pp. 11165–11173 (2022)
17. Su, X., et al.: A comprehensive survey on community detection with deep learning. IEEE Transactions on Neural Networks and Learning Systems (2022)
18. Vaswani, A., et al.: Attention is all you need. In: Advances in Neural Information Processing Systems 30 (2017)
19. Veličković, P., Cucurull, G., Casanova, A., Romero, A., Lio, P., Bengio, Y.: Graph attention networks. arXiv preprint arXiv:1710.10903 (2017)
20. Wang, G., et al.: Joint embedding of words and labels for text classification. In: Proceedings of the 56th Annual Meeting of the Association for Computational Linguistics (Volume 1: Long Papers), pp. 2321–2331 (2018)
21. Wu, F., Souza, A., Zhang, T., Fifty, C., Yu, T., Weinberger, K.: Simplifying graph convolutional networks. In: International Conference on Machine Learning, pp. 6861–6871. PMLR (2019)
22. Yao, L., Mao, C., Luo, Y.: Graph convolutional networks for text classification. In: Proceedings of the AAAI Conference on Artificial Intelligence. vol. 33, pp. 7370–7377 (2019)
23. Ying, Z., You, J., Morris, C., Ren, X., Hamilton, W., Leskovec, J.: Hierarchical graph representation learning with differentiable pooling. In: Advances in Neural Information Processing Systems 31 (2018)
24. Yun, X.L., Zhang, Y.M., Yin, F., Liu, C.L.: Instance gnn: a learning framework for joint symbol segmentation and recognition in online handwritten diagrams. IEEE Trans. Multimedia **24**, 2580–2594 (2021)
25. Zhang, Q., Lei, Z., Zhang, Z., Li, S.Z.: Context-aware attention network for image-text retrieval. In: Proceedings of the IEEE/CVF Conference on Computer Vision and Pattern Recognition, pp. 3536–3545 (2020)
26. Zhang, Y., Yu, X., Cui, Z., Wu, S., Wen, Z., Wang, L.: Every document owns its structure: Inductive text classification via graph neural networks. In: Proceedings of the 58th Annual Meeting of the Association for Computational Linguistics, pp. 334–339 (2020)

Research on Strategies for Tripeaks Variant with Various Layouts

Yijie Gao[1], Shuchang Xu[1(✉)], and Shunpeng Du[2]

[1] Hangzhou Normal University, Hangzhou, Zhejiang 311121, China
xusc@hznu.edu.cn
[2] Beijing DAILYBREAD CO., LTD, Beijing 100192, China

Abstract. A Tripeaks variant game, derived from the classic card game Tripeaks, is gaining popularity among players. In order to evaluate the difficulty of Tripeaks variant games and assist in level design, this paper investigates the playing strategies for Tripeaks variant games. Firstly, three heuristic strategies based on player experience are proposed. Then, reinforcement learning agents are trained and tested on different datasets to evaluate their generalization performance. The experiments demonstrate that Tripeaks variant games have a high degree of randomness and also possess certain strategies. The reinforcement learning agents have some generalization ability, but cannot handle the rich layouts of Tripeaks variant games. Heuristic strategies have stable and efficient performance, and are more suitable for difficulty detection and level design assistance in Tripeaks variant games.

Keywords: tripeaks · game strategy · DQN

1 Introduction

Tripeaks is a single-player card game with simple but challenging gameplay. Figure 1 shows Microsoft's Tripeaks game, which can be divided into three main areas: the red box is the playing area, the blue box is the stock area, and the yellow box is the waste pile. The game consists of 52 cards, with 28 cards forming the playing area and the remaining 24 cards forming the stock area. At the beginning of the game, a card is taken from the stock area and placed face-up in the waste pile (which is initially empty). The player then has two ways to play: 1) select a card from the playing area that is adjacent in rank to the card in the waste pile (according to the adjacent rule Q-K-A-2-3-......-Q-K-A) and move it to the waste pile; 2) draw a card from the stock area and place it in the waste pile. As shown in Fig. 1, the current possible moves include: 1) selecting either 10♢ or 10♣ from the playing area, 2) flipping a card from the stock area and placing it in the waste pile. The player continues to take either of these actions until neither can be taken. If all the cards in the playing area are cleared, the game is won. Otherwise, the game is lost.

This work was supported in part by the Hangzhou Normal University under Grant 1115B20500409.

Fig. 1. Microsoft's Tripeaks game.

Tripeaks became popular after being included in Microsoft Solitaire Collection. In recent years, various Tripeaks variant games have appeared on mobile platforms, which maintain the basic rules while having a diverse range of layouts. As shown in Fig. 2, the variant game Solitaire Grand Harvest has a different layout for each level.

Fig. 2. Puzzles with different layouts in "Solitaire Grand Harvest".

Tripeaks variant games, like traditional Tripeaks games, also have a large number of face-down cards and a high degree of randomness. However, there are also some playing strategies, and players who master these strategies are more likely to win the game. By analyzing player strategies, the difficulty of Tripeaks puzzles can be understood and evaluated, which can assist in the design of Tripeaks game levels.

In order to improve the user experience, game designers will try to understand user strategies, such as using reinforcement learning to obtain optimal strategies for different puzzles. Currently, game AI agents based on reinforcement learning have reached a high level of proficiency, as demonstrated by Atari

[1], AlphaGo [2], Libratus [3], OpenAI Five [4], and AlphaStar [5]. However, more and more evidence shows that intelligent agents are prone to overfitting their specific training environment, which leads to strategies that cannot be well generalized to related problems [6]. There is too much structure in Tripeaks variant games, and the training environment cannot cover all possible scenarios, which poses a challenge to the generalization ability of reinforcement learning.

This paper explores the optimal strategies and generalization ability of reinforcement learning in Tripeaks variants. First, several heuristic strategies for Tripeaks variants are proposed based on game experience. Then, we used the RLcard reinforcement learning toolkit [7] to construct the training environment for the Tripeaks variant game. During the training process, program content generation (PCG) was introduced, and an RL-based strategy model was eventually obtained. Finally, we compared the performance of the heuristic strategy and the reinforcement learning strategy, and summarized the optimal battle strategy for the Tripeaks variant game.

2   Related Work

In recent years, decision intelligence technologies represented by reinforcement learning have achieved a series of remarkable achievements in the game field, and intelligent agents that can defeat human players have appeared in various types of games.

2.1   Typical Game Agents

Chess games are classic turn-based and perfect information games. In Go, AlphaGo [2] was the first AI to defeat a human professional Go player. AlphaZero [8] can learn Go, chess, and shogi from scratch and defeat champion-level AI agents. MuZero [9] can demonstrate superhuman performance in Go, chess, and shogi without prior knowledge of the game rules.

Real-time strategy (RTS) games are a classic electronic game with a complex environment. In Dota 2, OpenAI Five [4] was the first AI to defeat world champions in an e-sports event. AlphaStar [5] uses a general learning algorithm to learn how to play StarCraft II, and its performance ranks in the top 99.8% of official human player rankings.

Atari games are often used to evaluate the performance of reinforcement learning because they are diverse and interesting. Go-explore [10] avoids the detachment and derailment problems in exploration of reinforcement learning and has strong performance in Atari platform games, surpassing the previous algorithm's highest level in 11 game competition tests.

2.2   Agents in Card Games

Card games are a type of classic casual games. When Microsoft's Windows operating system is released, it often comes with card games, making card games widely popular around the world. In recent years, as research on reinforcement learning continues to deepen, many studies have applied reinforcement learning to card games.

1. No-Limit Texas Hold'em Poker: No-Limit Texas Hold'em is an imperfect information game. The emergence of DeepStack [11] and Libratus [3] has successfully enabled artificial intelligence to defeat professional players in imperfect information games [12].
2. DouDiZhu: DouDiZhu has two characteristics, one is the existence of cooperation and competition in the game, and the other is a huge action space. Jiang et al. [13] achieved results beyond human level, but the training cost was high and highly dependent on abstract human knowledge. Zha et al. [14] proposed Douzero, which enhances traditional Monte Carlo methods with deep neural networks and action encoding, and is currently the strongest artificial intelligence for playing DouDiZhu.
3. Cego: Cego is a German card game with high randomness and is an imperfect information game. Philipp Oeschger [15] applied reinforcement learning to Cego, training specific subgame models using deep Q-learning (DQN), neural fictitious self-play (NFSP), and deep Monte Carlo (DMC) algorithms. After comparison, deep Monte Carlo showed the highest performance.
4. Tripeaks: He Yi [16] studied the efficiency of Q-learning and Monte Carlo methods in Tripeaks and found that Q-learning outperformed Monte Carlo and exceeded the average human level. Building on this research, this paper aims to use reinforcement learning to obtain the optimal strategy for Tripeaks.

3   Strategies Based on Reinforcement Learning

The action space of the Tripeaks game is discrete, so we chose to use deep Q-network (DQN) [17] for reinforcement learning training. The Q-Learning algorithm maintains a Q-table, which stores the Q-values for each state-action pair in a table. The update of Q-values depends on the current state s, the chosen action a, the reward received r, and the next state s''. The update rule for Q-values is as follows:

$$Q(s,a) \leftarrow Q(s,a) + \alpha \left(r + \gamma \max_{a'} Q(s'',a') - Q(s,a) \right) \tag{1}$$

In the above equation, α represents the learning rate, and γ represents the discount factor. DQN uses a deep neural network to approximate the Q-values directly instead of using a Q-table, which is suitable for situations where there are many states and actions. In our experiments, we use Double DQN [18], which trains two Q-networks simultaneously to reduce overestimation errors.

We represent state-action pairs as afterstates [19], which refer to the state after the agent has made its decision but before the environment responds. The afterstate representation can be much more succinct than the state-action pair representation when multiple state-action pairs are leading to an identical afterstate. In Fig. 3, moving a card from the playing area to the waste pile enters the afterstate. Then, the environment responds by flipping a card in the playing area to enter the next state.

The afterstate needs to be encoded as a binary sequence to be input into the neural network. The encoding method is as follows:

1) Encode the information of each card. Each position of a card has three states: face-up, face-down, and removed. We use 19 binary digits to store the state information of each card. As the suit of a card does not affect the choice of action during gameplay, only the rank of the card is encoded. The first 13 binary digits correspond to "A, 2, 3, ..., Q, K". The first 13 binary digits correspond to "A, 2, 3, ..., Q, K". The 14th to 17th binary digits represent the number of cards covering the current encoded card, with a range of 1–4 corresponding to the 14th to 17th binary digits. The 18th binary digit indicates whether the card is facing down. The 19th binary digit indicates whether the card has been removed. Table 1 shows the encoding of the cards. For example, the encoding of the 2♠ card is 01000...00. The encoding of a card that is facing down and covered by three cards is 00000...001010. The encoding of a card that has been removed is 00000...01.

Table 1. Code of card

Indices	Description
1–13	rank of the card
14–17	Number of cards covered
18	Face-down card
19	Card removed

2) Combine all card information. To begin with, we need to assign a unique number to each card, starting with the face-up cards, and then assigning numbers in a breadth-first search manner to each card. The cards in the stock area are numbered after the cards in the playing area, and the cards in the waste pile are always assigned the number 51. Figure 4 shows an example of numbering the cards using the aforementioned method. Once each card has been assigned a number, the codes for each card are concatenated in numerical order, resulting in an input code of length 52*19.

The binary sequence of the afterstate is inputted into the neural network to output the corresponding Q value. The reinforcement learning agent selects an action and enters the next state based on the Q value of the afterstate.

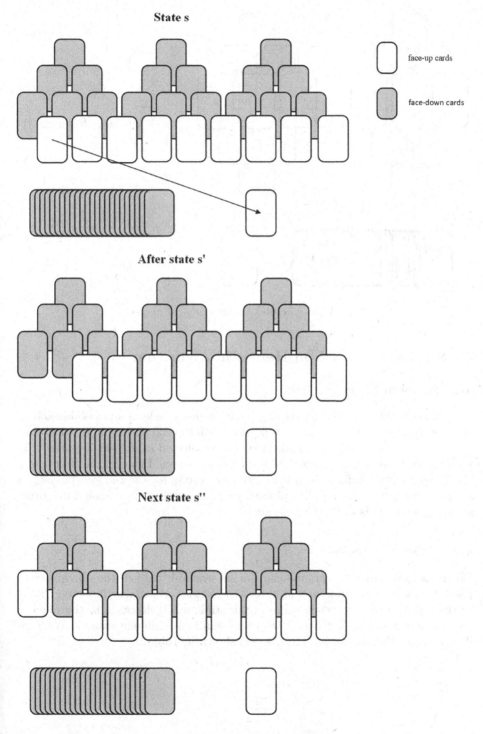

Fig. 3. The process from the current state s to the next state s''.

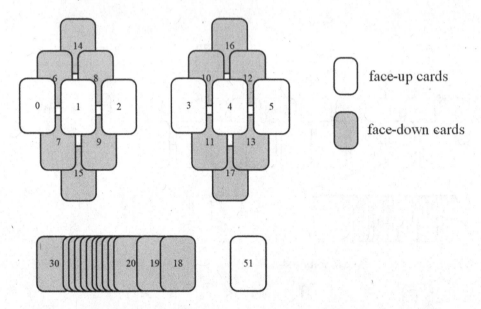

Fig. 4. an example of numbering the cards.

4   Strategies Based on Heuristic Algorithm

4.1   Random Strategy

Random policy is the simplest strategy that randomly selects an available action at the current state and repeats this process until the end of the game. According to the rules, even if there are cards that can be selected in the playing area, it is possible to choose to flip a new card from the stock area. However, in most cases, this is not a wise choice, which leads to poor results for the random policy. To improve the performance of the random policy, we specify that it should prioritize selecting legal cards in the playing area.

4.2   Other Strategies

When there is only one available card or no available card in the playing area, there is only one possible action and all strategies will make the same choice in that state. However, when there are multiple available cards in the playing area, as shown in Fig. 5, different strategies will make different choices. We have designed three strategies for Tripeaks, as shown in Table 2.

Table 2. Introduction of various strategies based on Fig. 5

Strategy	Characteristic	Action
A	Let more cards flip	Card 7
B	Let more cards flip in the future	Select randomly from 7 and 9
C	Select cards continuously	Card 9

Fig. 5. Status when there are multiple cards available. The puzzle comes from our website(http://47.111.89.175:5000/).

We refer to the face-up cards on the playing area that can be selected as candidate cards C. The cards covered by one or more candidate cards are referred to as sub-cards S. $C_i\{S_m, S_n\}$ represents that sub-cards S_m and S_n are covered by candidate card C_i, as shown in Fig. 6(a). $S_m\{C_i, C_j\}$ represents that sub-card S_m is covered by two candidate cards C_i and C_j, as shown in Fig. 6(b). Here, i, j, m and $n \in [1,51]$.

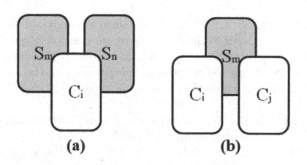

Fig. 6. Example description of candidate cards C and sub-cards S.

The strategy selection is related to the sub-cards, and to quantify the strategy selection, we have designed the following scoring rules: When a candidate card is removed, all the sub-cards that have a covering relationship with it are denoted as S_1, S_2,..., S_n. The numbers of other candidate cards that have a covering relationship with these sub-cards are denoted as SN_1, SN_2, ..., SN_n, respectively. $n \in [1,52]$.$SN_n \in [0,3]$. The score can be expressed as:

$$score = 10^{3-SN_1} + 10^{3-SN_2} + ... + 10^{3-SN_n} \tag{2}$$

Strategy A. Strategy A chooses among multiple candidate cards based on the score obtained from the scoring rule for each candidate card. The card with the highest score will be selected. If multiple cards have the same highest score, a random selection will be made. The purpose of this strategy is to choose a card that can reveal as many cards as possible, thereby increasing the range of the next selection.

In the example given in Fig. 5, the candidate cards are 7 and 9. According to the scoring rule, the card with the rank of 7 has a score of $1000 + 100 = 1100$, while the card with the rank of 9 has a score of 100. Therefore, Strategy A will select the card with the rank of 7.

Strategy B. Compared with strategy A, strategy B considers not only the candidate card and its sub-cards, but also the sequence of candidate cards that can be continuously selected in the current situation. As shown in the above Fig. 5, the available sequences are (7, 7-6, 9, 9-10, 9-10-J). The score of each sequence is evaluated as a whole, and the first card of the sequence with the highest score is selected. If there are multiple sequences with the same highest score, a random one is chosen. Compared with strategy A, this strategy considers more long-term factors, taking into account both the possibility of revealing more cards and the situation of available sequences in the current state.

In the above Fig. 5, there are two sequences starting with candidate card 7: 7 and 7-6, with scores 1100 and 2100, respectively. There are three sequences starting with candidate card 9: 9, 9-10, and 9-10-J, with scores 100, 1100, and 2100, respectively. The sequences 7-6 and 9-10-J have the same maximum score, so one of the two first candidate cards will be randomly selected.

Strategy C. In strategy C, when facing multiple candidate cards, the first card of the longest sequence is chosen. If there are multiple sequences with the same maximum length, one of them is randomly selected. This strategy does not consider the cards that may be revealed in the future, with the aim of selecting the maximum number of cards that can be taken consecutively in the current state.

As shown in Fig. 5, the longest sequence starting with candidate card 7 is 7-6, and the longest sequence starting with candidate card 9 is 9-10-J. Therefore, strategy C selects the first candidate card of the longest sequence, which is 9 in this case.

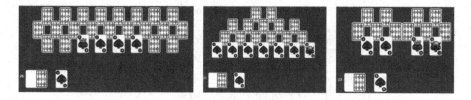

Fig. 7. Puzzles with different layouts in "Solitaire Grand Harvest".

5   Experiment

5.1   Experimental Dataset and Evaluation Criteria

Tripeaks variants have diverse structures, and it is very difficult to train all of them. Therefore, we have prepared the following two datasets to test the generalization performance of reinforcement learning.

1) Generated data (Dataset A): This dataset contains 31 puzzle layouts generated by the program, as shown in Fig. 7.

2) Mobile game data (Dataset B): This dataset contains 40 different layouts of puzzles, which come from real data of different levels in "Solitaire Grand Harvest", as shown in Fig. 2. During the collection process, we ignored various rewards, Wild cards and other special situations that may exist in the actual game.

Based on the above two datasets, an infinite number of puzzles of varying difficulty can be generated by shuffling a deck of cards randomly. Reinforcement learning will be trained on dataset A and then tested for its generalization performance on dataset B.

This experiment uses win rate to evaluate the performance of different algorithms. For the datasets, a random layout is selected from the dataset, then shuffled and played using a certain algorithm, repeated 10,000 times. The win rate of the algorithm on that dataset is the number of wins divided by the total number of games played. For a specific layout, it is shuffled and played using a certain algorithm, repeated 10,000 times. The win rate of the algorithm on that layout is the number of wins divided by the total number of games played.

5.2   Training

During the training process, we used experience replay [20]. We randomly sampled data using a greedy strategy and added it to the memory buffer, allowing the neural network to randomly select samples from the memory buffer for learning. In terms of rewards, winning a game was rewarded with 1 point and losing a game was rewarded with -1 point. To obtain better training results, we conducted experiments using different hyperparameters, compared the learning curves under different hyperparameters, and then selected the best-performing parameters as shown in Table 3.

Table 3. Hyperparameters

Hyperparameter	Value
Replay memory size	500000
Replay memory init size	50000
Update target estimator every	1000
Discount factor	0.96
Epsilon start	1
Epsilon end	0.1
Epsilon decay steps	100000
Batch size	32
Optimizer	SGD
Learning rate	10^{-2}
MLP layers	[512,512,512,512]

During the training process, the DQN agent played 100,000 games. Every 1,000 games played, the training results were evaluated by having the agent play 10,000 different puzzles and obtaining the win rate. We selected the best-performing model based on the evaluation results and plotted the learning curve.

5.3 Results

The learning curve in Fig. 8 was obtained by training the model using the parameters in Table 3. During training, we stipulated that the agent should prioritize selecting legal cards from the playing area. The "Train line" in Fig. 8 represents the training process of the agent on dataset A. After the start of training, the agent's winning rate on dataset A quickly increased and then stabilized. The "Test Line" represents the process of testing the generalization ability of the agent on dataset B. After the start of training, the agent's winning rate on dataset B quickly increased and then stabilized. "Train Baseline" and "Test Baseline" represent the winning rates on dataset A and dataset B, respectively, using a random strategy.

We tested and evaluated four heuristic strategies and DQN on each layout of the puzzles in datasets A and B, and obtained the win rates for each layout of the puzzles. The specific test data can be found in the appendix.

6   Discussion

Based on the above experiments, we found that:

The Tripeaks Variant Has a Certain Degree of Strategy, and the Optimal Strategy Depends on the Layout of the Puzzle. The testing results

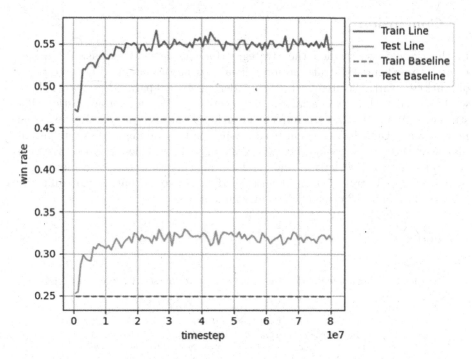

Fig. 8. learning curve. The x-axis represents the total number of steps executed in the environment. The y-axis is the algorithm's win rate on the dataset.

show that strategy A, strategy B, and DQN have relatively high win rates and perform well across different layouts. While Tripeaks variant has a high degree of randomness, it still requires certain skills. Perhaps this is one of the reasons why Tripeaks game is popular, as experienced players have higher win rates than novices, but still face the risk of failure due to randomness. Even novice players can win the game without any strategy.

Reinforcement Learning Has a Certain Degree of Generalization Ability in the Environment of Tripeaks Variants. The reinforcement learning algorithm trained on dataset A has learned a certain strategy with good performance, and has the best performance in some layouts of puzzles. Although it is slightly inferior to strategies A and B in dataset B, it can still adapt to new environments. We randomly select layouts and shuffle them to generate new puzzles to prevent overfitting and improve generalization ability. In addition, we also tried to increase the number of layouts in the dataset to improve generalization ability, but when the dataset increased to a certain number, increasing the number of layouts did not improve generalization ability (Tables 4 and 5).

7   Conclusion

In this article, we studied the strategies for Tripeaks variations. We implemented three heuristic strategies for Tripeaks variations and used DQN to try to obtain the optimal strategy. Through experiments comparing these algorithms, we found that Tripeaks variations have certain strategic characteristics. The strategies A and B that we implemented have relatively stable and excellent performance. DQN has excellent performance on the training set, but its performance on the test set is slightly worse than that of strategies A and B. Tripeaks variations have a rich layout, and reinforcement learning cannot achieve complete learning. Therefore, using heuristic strategies to evaluate puzzle difficulty is more stable and efficient in this environment.

Appendix

Table 4. Performance of different algorithms in dataset A (across 5 seeds)

Index	Rand/%	Strategy A/%	Strategy B/%	Strategy C/%	DQN/%
1	39.206 ± 0.414	51.728 ± 0.435	53.904 ± 0.475	41.522 ± 0.453	47.634 ± 0.316
2	75.042 ± 0.695	85.738 ± 0.294	86.046 ± 0.373	76.05 ± 0.408	84.058 ± 0.461
3	29.116 ± 0.372	41.618 ± 0.298	41.372 ± 0.428	29.95 ± 0.411	40.112 ± 0.401
4	84.41 ± 0.408	92.746 ± 0.225	92.736 ± 0.112	84.864 ± 0.221	91.606 ± 0.356
5	81.328 ± 0.337	85.704 ± 0.364	85.806 ± 0.238	81.648 ± 0.363	86.806 ± 0.477
6	36.358 ± 0.413	43.452 ± 0.61	43.068 ± 0.63	36.498 ± 0.334	43.14 ± 0.63
7	37.226 ± 0.143	49.432 ± 0.308	49.514 ± 0.307	37.842 ± 0.282	49.316 ± 0.317
8	57.034 ± 0.555	70.142 ± 0.546	70.416 ± 0.365	57.702 ± 0.515	69.482 ± 0.368
9	47.456 ± 0.432	59.6 ± 0.262	59.452 ± 0.374	47.97 ± 0.177	58.056 ± 0.408
10	66.522 ± 0.176	75.594 ± 0.328	75.274 ± 0.241	66.804 ± 0.471	75.188 ± 0.247
11	55.726 ± 0.46	63.39 ± 0.295	63.224 ± 0.213	55.342 ± 0.32	62.914 ± 0.43
12	49.45 ± 0.378	61.648 ± 0.251	61.152 ± 0.52	49.652 ± 0.378	60.702 ± 0.42
13	68.996 ± 0.215	73.648 ± 0.272	73.594 ± 0.374	68.492 ± 0.125	73.376 ± 0.325
14	71.562 ± 0.342	79.596 ± 0.37	79.818 ± 0.483	71.006 ± 0.553	78.632 ± 0.324
15	48.538 ± 0.113	54.14 ± 0.336	53.942 ± 0.473	48.358 ± 0.301	53.454 ± 0.418
16	0.374 ± 0.044	0.666 ± 0.061	0.718 ± 0.07	0.432 ± 0.064	0.65 ± 0.081
17	48.59 ± 0.459	58.458 ± 0.415	58.458 ± 0.692	48.664 ± 0.546	59.134 ± 0.518
18	23.298 ± 0.195	33.022 ± 0.454	33.144 ± 0.407	23.794 ± 0.375	32.938 ± 0.438
19	12.064 ± 0.428	20.554 ± 0.378	20.736 ± 0.382	13.032 ± 0.519	22.644 ± 0.726
20	17.432 ± 0.454	30.018 ± 0.329	31.316 ± 0.528	19.21 ± 0.171	27.494 ± 0.217
21	56.4 ± 0.29	68.642 ± 0.145	68.566 ± 0.267	57.388 ± 0.29	69.204 ± 0.32
22	91.06 ± 0.216	96.122 ± 0.074	96.07 ± 0.087	91.304 ± 0.342	95.442 ± 0.123
23	66.744 ± 0.42	80.706 ± 0.429	80.148 ± 0.286	67.212 ± 0.327	80.572 ± 0.183
24	91.642 ± 0.067	96.08 ± 0.163	96.102 ± 0.174	91.608 ± 0.238	95.086 ± 0.205
25	52.692 ± 0.515	61.644 ± 0.328	62.042 ± 0.621	53.298 ± 0.388	63.684 ± 0.177
26	12.046 ± 0.296	22.658 ± 0.291	23.602 ± 0.273	13.738 ± 0.219	20.478 ± 0.3
27	53.26 ± 0.431	76.11 ± 0.377	77.266 ± 0.526	56.74 ± 0.556	75.254 ± 0.227
28	4.85 ± 0.297	7.696 ± 0.169	8.57 ± 0.336	5.968 ± 0.082	7.564 ± 0.164
29	4.232 ± 0.142	10.7 ± 0.266	10.802 ± 0.248	5.424 ± 0.185	10.198 ± 0.13
30	11.02 ± 0.453	21.546 ± 0.295	24.068 ± 0.439	14.254 ± 0.2	18.802 ± 0.246
31	29.37 ± 0.576	47.072 ± 0.471	51.902 ± 0.619	36.012 ± 0.561	47.708 ± 0.781

Table 5. Performance of different algorithms in dataset B (across 5 seeds)

Index	Rand/%	Strategy A/%	Strategy B/%	Strategy C/%	DQN/%
1	20.626 ± 0.288	30.166 ± 0.293	32.092 ± 0.457	22.51 ± 0.273	27.498 ± 0.379
2	13.444 ± 0.347	16.906 ± 0.31	17.114 ± 0.303	13.778 ± 0.461	15.964 ± 0.471
3	48.426 ± 0.109	59.004 ± 0.306	59.022 ± 0.275	48.82 ± 0.322	56.592 ± 0.341
4	72.378 ± 0.156	83.352 ± 0.244	84.266 ± 0.102	72.73 ± 0.221	83.168 ± 0.332
5	55.272 ± 0.413	68.736 ± 0.442	69.064 ± 0.121	56.22 ± 0.338	63.912 ± 0.431
6	22.612 ± 0.47	28.834 ± 0.22	29.824 ± 0.616	23.946 ± 0.378	25.878 ± 0.368
7	11.22 ± 0.325	17.646 ± 0.321	18.044 ± 0.283	12.278 ± 0.154	16.872 ± 0.33
8	2.194 ± 0.095	5.918 ± 0.331	6.676 ± 0.205	3.274 ± 0.113	4.86 ± 0.177
9	37.722 ± 0.457	49.462 ± 0.176	50.086 ± 0.314	38.57 ± 0.597	48.28 ± 0.347
10	50.008 ± 0.673	59.73 ± 0.336	59.886 ± 0.207	50.418 ± 0.539	58.226 ± 0.477
11	48.75 ± 0.16	59.318 ± 0.411	61.3 ± 0.224	51.508 ± 0.187	56.514 ± 0.318
12	49.812 ± 0.521	65.094 ± 0.648	65.632 ± 0.465	51.544 ± 0.652	62.442 ± 0.451
13	47.464 ± 0.343	59.324 ± 0.439	59.128 ± 0.392	47.958 ± 0.518	57.736 ± 0.298
14	42.82 ± 0.319	52.734 ± 0.282	55.33 ± 0.356	45.778 ± 0.419	50.522 ± 0.336
15	13.334 ± 0.416	19.022 ± 0.448	19.276 ± 0.417	13.724 ± 0.349	17.676 ± 0.26
16	50.792 ± 0.274	68.8 ± 0.362	70.904 ± 0.523	53.804 ± 0.134	66.756 ± 0.521
17	2.43 ± 0.121	3.762 ± 0.109	3.976 ± 0.199	2.504 ± 0.125	3.316 ± 0.141
18	20.598 ± 0.351	33.898 ± 0.133	36.436 ± 0.453	24.062 ± 0.54	28.794 ± 0.536
19	21.842 ± 0.145	28.73 ± 0.388	28.946 ± 0.306	22.356 ± 0.418	27.888 ± 0.484
20	27.084 ± 0.273	44.32 ± 0.285	46.338 ± 0.354	31.426 ± 0.642	40.764 ± 0.259
21	19.632 ± 0.441	30.766 ± 0.455	32.128 ± 0.279	22.482 ± 0.121	28.792 ± 0.206
22	13.616 ± 0.348	18.33 ± 0.298	19.116 ± 0.182	14.754 ± 0.377	18.084 ± 0.17
23	15.818 ± 0.224	26.602 ± 0.46	30.132 ± 0.333	19.67 ± 0.511	24.292 ± 0.421
24	27.038 ± 0.32	38.124 ± 0.557	39.624 ± 0.361	29.908 ± 0.789	36.15 ± 0.356
25	19.522 ± 0.098	23.612 ± 0.235	24.532 ± 0.23	20.472 ± 0.333	25.34 ± 0.311
26	1.606 ± 0.145	2.786 ± 0.035	4.96 ± 0.197	3.38 ± 0.14	2.938 ± 0.19
27	18.304 ± 0.611	28.226 ± 0.523	31.792 ± 0.269	22.896 ± 0.448	24.7 ± 0.287
28	22.496 ± 0.363	29.746 ± 0.369	32.864 ± 0.215	26.066 ± 0.433	27.156 ± 0.612
29	3.276 ± 0.131	7.246 ± 0.268	7.368 ± 0.215	3.9 ± 0.198	6.126 ± 0.371
30	6.254 ± 0.142	12.928 ± 0.169	12.678 ± 0.33	7.274 ± 0.179	11.354 ± 0.32
31	0.468 ± 0.087	1.216 ± 0.049	1.196 ± 0.095	0.626 ± 0.029	1.006 ± 0.044
32	1.564 ± 0.096	2.226 ± 0.089	2.284 ± 0.113	1.628 ± 0.141	1.896 ± 0.059
33	59.254 ± 0.577	75.418 ± 0.213	75.576 ± 0.406	61.068 ± 0.368	73.466 ± 0.364
34	29.29 ± 0.336	44.968 ± 0.474	45.248 ± 0.322	31.166 ± 0.48	43.566 ± 0.524
35	36.396 ± 0.387	53.87 ± 0.414	55.748 ± 0.495	39.478 ± 0.402	47.264 ± 0.671
36	7.664 ± 0.104	12.926 ± 0.225	16.234 ± 0.311	11.148 ± 0.279	10.024 ± 0.197
37	3.282 ± 0.17	4.768 ± 0.201	4.986 ± 0.18	3.57 ± 0.227	4.436 ± 0.099
38	2.074 ± 0.141	3.072 ± 0.103	3.708 ± 0.159	2.724 ± 0.109	2.734 ± 0.035
39	11.842 ± 0.452	19.462 ± 0.389	21.532 ± 0.481	14.296 ± 0.497	17.328 ± 0.298
40	37.544 ± 0.419	56.446 ± 0.22	58.752 ± 0.243	41.362 ± 0.413	53.898 ± 0.207

References

1. Mnih, V., et al.: Human-level control through deep reinforcement learning. Nature **518**(7540), 529–533 (2015)
2. Silver, D., et al.: Mastering the game of go with deep neural networks and tree search. Nature **529**(7587), 484–489 (2016)
3. Brown, N., Sandholm, T.: Superhuman AI for heads-up no-limit poker: Libratus beats top professionals. Science **359**(6374), 418–424 (2018)
4. Berner, C.,et al.: Dota 2 with large scale deep reinforcement learning. arXiv preprint arXiv:1912.06680 (2019)

5. Vinyals, O., et al.: Grandmaster level in starcraft ii using multi-agent reinforcement learning. Nature **575**(7782), 350–354 (2019)
6. Justesen, N., Torrado, R.R., Bontrager, P., Khalifa, A., Togelius, J., Risi, S.: Illuminating generalization in deep reinforcement learning through procedural level generation. arXiv preprint arXiv:1806.10729 (2018)
7. Zha, D., Lai, K.H., Cao, Y., Huang, S., Wei, R., Guo, J., Hu, X.: Rlcard: A toolkit for reinforcement learning in card games. arXiv preprint arXiv:1910.04376 (2019)
8. Silver, D., et al.: A general reinforcement learning algorithm that masters chess, shogi, and go through self-play. Science **362**(6419), 1140–1144 (2018)
9. Schrittwieser, J., et al.: Mastering atari, go, chess and shogi by planning with a learned model. Nature **588**(7839), 604–609 (2020)
10. Ecoffet, A., Huizinga, J., Lehman, J., Stanley, K.O., Clune, J.: First return, then explore. Nature **590**(7847), 580–586 (2021)
11. Moravčík, M., et al.: Deepstack: Expert-level artificial intelligence in heads-up no-limit poker. Science **356**(6337), 508–513 (2017)
12. Yin, Q., Yang, J., Ni, W., Liang, B., Huang, K.: Ai in games: techniques, challenges and opportunities. arXiv preprint arXiv:2111.07631 (2021)
13. Jiang, Q., Li, K., Du, B., Chen, H., Fang, H.: Deltadou: Expert-level Doudizhu AI through self-play. In: IJCAI, pp. 1265–1271 (2019)
14. Zha, D., et al.: Douzero: Mastering doudizhu with self-play deep reinforcement learning. In: International Conference on Machine Learning, pp. 12333–12344. PMLR (2021)
15. Oeschger, P.: Applying deep reinforcement learning to the card game cego. informatik J. **13**, 91–99 (2022)
16. Yi, H.: Some case studies on the efficiency of reinforcement learning in card game solitaire with uncertainty (2021)
17. Mnih, V., Kavukcuoglu, K., Silver, D., Graves, A., Antonoglou, I., Wierstra, D., Riedmiller, M.: Playing atari with deep reinforcement learning. arXiv preprint arXiv:1312.5602 (2013)
18. Van Hasselt, H., Guez, A., Silver, D.: Deep reinforcement learning with double q-learning. In: Proceedings of the AAAI Conference on Artificial Intelligence, vol. 30 (2016)
19. Sutton, R.S., Barto, A.G.: Reinforcement learning: An introduction. MIT press (2018)
20. Lin, L.J.: Reinforcement learning for robots using neural networks. Carnegie Mellon University (1992)

A Neural Network Model with the Ringed Residual Block and Attention Mechanism for Image Forgery Localization

Ying Guo[✉] and Shan Jiang

North China University of Technology, Beijing, China
guoying@ncut.edu.cn

Abstract. In recent years, significant progress has been made in image forgery localization technology, but there are still shortcomings in accuracy and robustness, especially for different types of forgeries. Currently, convolutional neural networks are the mainstream forgery localization technology, but the local receptive field of convolutional operations limits the accuracy of the model. In this paper, an image forgery localization neural network model is proposed, which uses the ringed residual structure to extract features better and multiple attention mechanisms to focus on important features better. The method can effectively handle various common forgeries types, such as copy-paste, region replacement, and local modification, and can also overcome the problem of the local receptive field of convolutional operations to achieve long-distance feature dependencies. The authors conducted experiments on multiple datasets to verify and compare the proposed method with existing methods. The experimental results show that the method achieved excellent performance on different datasets, demonstrating its effectiveness and robustness.

Keywords: Deep Learning · Image forgery localization · Attention mechanism

1 Introduction

Digital images have become a primary means of conveying information on social media due to their convenience and rich expressiveness. They are also frequently used as evidential content in resolving civil disputes and criminal proceedings due to their wealth of information. However, as information technology continues to advance at a rapid pace, it has become easier to capture and acquire digital images, while also becoming faster to modify and edit them. Professional program for image processing, such as Photoshop, has made it easy for users to modify images to suit their needs.

The use of tampered photographs has generated much discussion in the military, political, and social arenas, leading to misleading perceptions and social unrest. As a result, it has become necessary to determine the authenticity of

H. Lu et al. (Eds.): ICIG 2023, LNCS 14358, pp. 99–110, 2023.
https://doi.org/10.1007/978-3-031-46314-3_8

images and whether they have been modified using image processing software. In certain situations, such as forensics, it is not enough to know whether an image has been tampered with - one must also determine which area of the image has been tampered with. For this reason, more focus has been placed on image forgery location than on image forgery detection.

In the area of image forgery localization, research can be categorized into two main types: traditional methods and deep learning methods. Traditional methods involve researchers designing manual features and filtering images based on those features. However, these methods place high demands on researchers' ability to design features and have limitations, which can result in varying performance on different images. Therefore, deep learning methods have become the mainstream of current research. These methods attempt to create an end-to-end neural network. For image forgery localization tasks, researchers typically use target detection networks and fully convolutional semantic segmentation networks to identify tampered areas. Although both methods have their advantages, more research is focused on semantic segmentation due to its higher localization accuracy. Numerous researchers have contributed to the field of semantic segmentation, including D-Net [1], RRU-Net [2], PSCC-Net [3], and CAT-Net [4].

Despite their effectiveness, existing methods for image forgery localization still have some limitations. One key issue is that these models do not fully consider the local receptive fields of the convolutional operation when extracting image features. As a result, the convolutional operation may not be effective in capturing global information, which can affect the generalizability of the network.

To address these limitations, this paper proposes an attention mechanism-based model. Building upon the successful U-shaped structure and the ringed residual blocks of RRU-Net, this paper improves and fine-tunes this classical work. Specifically, the proposed model employs the ringed residual block in the Encoder and incorporates various attention mechanisms to better extract and utilize features that are more aligned with the target. This allows the network to focus on both local and global features simultaneously.

This paper makes the following main contributions:

- Proposing an novel Encoder module with ringed residual blocks that incorporates channel and spatial attention mechanisms, enhancing the model's capability for feature extraction.
- Conducting extensive experiments on the classical datasets CASIA1.0 [5] and Columbia [6]. The experimental results demonstrate the superiority of the proposed approach over previous methods.

The rest of the paper is structured as follows. Section 2 describes some related work. In Sect. 3, the proposed attention mechanism-based ringed residual UNet model aimed at the forgery localization is introduced. The related experiments and the results are shown in Sect. 4. Finally, Sect. 5 gives the conclusion of this paper.

2 Related Work

2.1 Image Forgery Localization Techniques

Image forgery localization techniques can be broadly classified into two categories: traditional methods and methods based on deep learning. Traditional methods rely on manually designed features to locate the tampered regions. However, in recent years, more researchers have shifted their focus towards using deep learning techniques for forgery localization in images.

Deep learning is a model-building method that uses neural networks to learn from data by modifying their parameters through backpropagation. Computer vision tasks are typically processed using deep learning networks that can be categorized into classification, detection, and segmentation networks. While detection networks output bounding box information for a target in an input image, segmentation networks are better suited for image forgery localization tasks since they perform pixel-level classification and output an image that has the same size as the input image, with each pixel indicating the category to which it belongs. In the past few years, many excellent works have been done in segmentation networks for image forgery localization.

Salloum [7] was a pioneer in using the fully convolutional network (FCN) proposed in the literature [8] for image forgery localization. Liu and Pun [9] enhanced the method by combining FCN and proposing a number of FCNs with different scales for image forgery localization. Bi [2] proposed the RRU-Net for image forgery based on U-Net, a classical semantic segmentation network, while Zhang [10] proposed a densely connected U-shaped network to locate the tampered part of the image. Shi [11] designed a Dual-Domain convolutional network using convolution and SRM filtering to locate the tampered region in the image. Similarly, Kwon [4] used information from dual streams and proposed a convolutional network based on RGB domain and DCT streams to locate the tampered parts of the image.

2.2 RRU-Net

Convolutional neural networks have proven to be highly effective in various computer vision tasks. However, as the size of the data increases, researchers have explored deeper and wider network architectures to improve model accuracy. Unfortunately, as the number of layers in these networks surpasses 50, the model's effectiveness tends to decrease, which is known as the "degradation of the network." This issue has led to a bottleneck in the development of neural networks. To overcome this, Kaiming proposed the Residual Network (ResNet) in 2015 [12], which addresses the degradation problem by introducing residual connections. By allowing certain network layers to skip the next layer and connect to every other layer by residual connections, ResNet weakens the tight connection between each layer. The residual structure of the network can be expressed as follows:

$$y = F(x) + x \qquad (1)$$

The input image is denoted by x, and the output of the model is denoted by y. With this residual block, the neural network exceeds 100 layers for the first time. Not only does the residual structure perform well in deep networks, but it also shows better feature extraction ability in shallow networks. In 2017, Zheng [13] incorporated the residual structure into UNet [14] to create ResUNet, a semantic segmentation network. The results of comparison experiments show the ResUNet significantly outperforms the original UNet. Inspired by this, Bi [2] proposed to feed the output of the residual block back to the residual block based on the human "learning-forgotten-review" mechanism, which constitutes a ringed residual structure as shown in Fig. 1. The whole ringed residual block includes residual propagation and residual feedback parts. The authors think that such a ringed residual block can better extract the differences between features, and the comparison experiment confirms this point. RRU-Net is constructed based on such a ringed residual block and UNet by the authors.

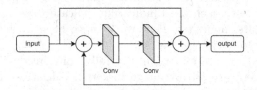

Fig. 1. The ringed residual block proposed in RRU-Net.

2.3 Attention Mechanism

The structure of neural networks takes inspiration from the information exchange between neurons in the human brain, while attention mechanisms are influenced by the human nervous system. Studies have shown that humans allocate varying degrees of attention to different parts of objects, focusing more on key parts which usually represent the essential features. The attention mechanism helps in filtering important information, and researchers have introduced this concept into the neural network by selecting the features extracted by the network. This enhances the network's overall performance by prioritizing important parts of the features. In computer vision, attention mechanisms can be broadly classified into channel attention, spatial attention, and mixed attention. Channel attention selects the importance level between different channels of features like SENet and SKNet, while spatial attention focuses on the network paying attention to the spatial information of images represented by Self-Attention and Coordinate Attention. Mixed attention is a combination of both channel attention and spatial attention, which prioritizes both channel-wise and spatial-wise information such as CBAM and DANet. The attention mechanism improves network accuracy without a huge increase in the number of parameters, making it widely used by researchers.

3   Methods

The task of image forgery localization involves semantic segmentation, where the model is a function that outputs an identical-sized single-channel image to the input. The output image, denoted as Y, contains pixel values of 0 or 1, where 0 denotes an untampered pixel and 1 denotes a tampered pixel.

We have developed a model called CSRUNet, which stands for CA_SE_RRUNet. The model structure consists of Encoder and Decoder, and a diagram of the entire model is presented in Fig. 2.

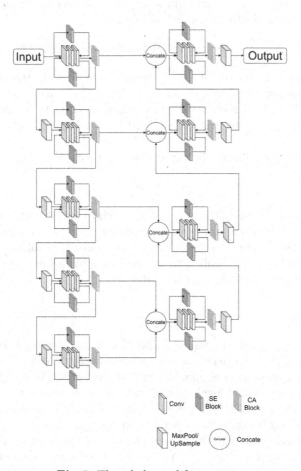

Fig. 2. The whole model structure.

The model takes a multi-channel image as input, typically in RGB format. The Encoder part of the model extracts feature information from the input image in a layer-by-layer manner, using a ringed residual block, SE block, and CA block. In the Decoder part, the shallow features extracted by the Encoder module are fed into the Decoder module through a skip connection. The other input of the Decoder module is the deep feature information recovered by the previous Decoder layer. The shallow and deep features are then combined by concatenation, and this fused feature is used as the input of the subsequent Decoder layer until the final output is obtained.

3.1   Ringed Residual Block

In 2019, Bi [2] introduced the ringed residual block, as depicted in Fig. 1. This block comprises two parts: residual propagation and residual feedback. The former can be mathematically expressed as follows:

$$y_f = F(x, \{W\}) + W_s * x \tag{2}$$

In the equation, x refers to the input image, y_f represents the output of the residual propagation operation, W refers to the weight matrix of this layer, and function $F(x, W)$ indicates the residual mapping that is to be learned. Additionally, W_s is solely the weight matrix employed in the shortcut connection to align the dimensions.

For the residual feedback, the expression can be expressed as:

$$y_b = (s(G(y_f)) + 1) * x \tag{3}$$

where the input of the module is denoted by x, which is the original input image. The output of the residual propagation operation, y_f, is calculated using Eq. 2. The output of the residual feedback, y_b, is also part of the block. The sigmoid function, denoted by s, is applied to y_b. Additionally, a linear projection G is used to adjust the dimension of y_f to match x.

3.2   SE Block

In 2019, Jie Hu proposed the Squeeze-and-Excitation Networks [16] as a novel approach to improve the performance of convolutional neural networks. The SE Block, which employs a channel attention mechanism to assign weights to the features at the channel level, was introduced by the authors and proved to be effective in the IMAGENET competition that year. Figure 3 illustrates the structure of the SE Block, which operates on a feature map $x \in \mathbb{R}^{H \times W \times C}$. To express the relative importance of each channel of the feature, the SE Block creates a weight matrix $t \in \mathbb{R}^{1 \times 1 \times C}$. The construction process of this weight matrix involves three functions: Squeeze, Excitation, and Scale, denoted by F_{sq}, F_{ex}, and F_{scale}, respectively. Specifically, F_{sq} compresses the feature map along the channel dimension, F_{ex} applies a nonlinear transformation to the squeezed feature, and F_{scale} rescales the feature map using the learned weights. The SE Block can be mathematically formulated as follows:

$$y_{se} = F_{scale}(F_{ex}(F_{sq}(y_{res}), W), y_{res}) \tag{4}$$

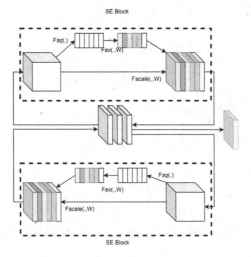

Fig. 3. The SE block used in our model.

where y_{res} refers to the output of residual propagation and residual feedback operations, in our model, is y_f and y_b, and the y_{se} means the output of our SE block, this block uses global average pooling to squeeze global spatial information into a channel descriptor in each channel, and generates the weight map $t \in \mathbb{R}^{1 \times 1 \times C}$, and then we use this weight map to multiply with the original feature map to complete the filtering of the original feature map. The F_{sq}, F_{ex}, and F_{scale} can be formulated as follows:

$$z = F_{sq}(u) = \frac{1}{H \times W} \sum_{i=1}^{H} \sum_{j=1}^{W} u(i, j) \tag{5}$$

$$t = F_{ex}(z, W) = \sigma(g(z, W)) = \sigma(W_2 \delta(W_1 z)) \tag{6}$$

where σ refers to the ReLU function, W_1 and W_2 denote the weight matrices of the two fully connected layers, respectively. The number of feature channels is reduced and then increased by the two fully connected layers, and then activated by the sigmoid function to obtain the final weight matrix s. This matrix is multiplied by the input, to generate the output feature map by the SE block.

3.3   CA Block

The CA Block [17] is an adaptation of the Coordinate Attention method introduced by Hou in 2021. Unlike the SE Block, which attends to channel dimension, the CA Block directs attention towards the spatial dimension. The architecture of the CA Block is illustrated in Fig. 4. Given an input x, the CA Block initially encodes each channel separately along the horizontal and vertical coordinates,

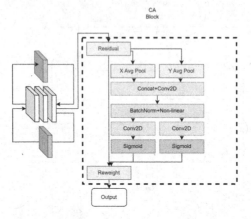

Fig. 4. The CA block used in our model.

using $(H, 1)$ and $(1, W)$ pooling kernels, respectively. This allows the output of the c-th channel at height h and width w to be formulated separately as:

$$z_c^h(h) = \frac{1}{W} \sum_{i=1}^{W} x_c(h, i), z_c^w(w) = \frac{1}{H} \sum_{j=1}^{H} x_c(j, w) \tag{7}$$

Once the information is encoded, we combine the aforementioned features by concatenating them, followed by passing them through a 1×1 convolution operation denoted as F_1. This is then followed by non-linear activation, resulting in:

$$f = \delta(F_1([z^h, z^w])) \tag{8}$$

where the $[,]$ indicates concatenation, while the letter f refers to the intermediate feature map that captures spatial information in both horizontal and vertical directions. To further analyze f, we split it along the spatial dimension, resulting in two distinct tensors: f_h and f_w. To match the input tensor of the CA block, we apply two separate 1×1 convolution operations, denoted by F_h and F_w, to adjust the channel of f_h and f_w accordingly. And then we can get:

$$g^h = \sigma(F_h(f^h)), g^w = \sigma(F_w(f^w)) \tag{9}$$

where the σ refers to the sigmoid function, g_h and g_w represent the attention weight matrices along two directions of the input feature. The final output of CA block y_{ca} can be described as follows:

$$y_c(i, j) = x_c(i, j) \times g_c^h(i) \times g_c^w(j) \tag{10}$$

4   Experiments

In this section, we conduct experiments using well-established public datasets for image forgery localization. By performing comparative analyses, we show that our model surpasses previous works in terms of performance on these datasets.

Fig. 5. The outputs of compared models on test dataset. From left to right, each column is the input image, the ground truth, UNet, ResUNet, AttentionUNet, RRUNet, SE_RRUNet, CA_RRUNet, CA_SE_RRUNet (ours).

Dataset. We found that the currently available public datasets do not provide sufficient data for model training. Therefore, we opted to use the SF-Data [18] dataset, which we utilized for pre-training our model. This dataset was introduced by Yang Wei in 2022 and is composed of 82,608 JPEG color images generated by a GAN-based method known as the SAN network. The authors used CASIA2.0 and Forensics datasets for training the network. We chose this dataset due to its substantial size, which enabled us to perform effective pre-training. Having completed pre-training with the SF-Data dataset, we then proceed to use established public benchmark datasets to fine-tune and test our model, such as CASIA1.0 and Columbia (Fig. 5).

- **CASIA 1.0**: This dataset comprises 921 color images that have been tampered through splicing and copy-moving techniques. The dataset also provides corresponding ground truth for various objects. For our experiment, we only use the splice parts of the images.
- **Columbia**: This dataset consists of 180 JPEG color images that have been tampered using splicing techniques, making it distinct from CASIA 1.0. However, the dataset is relatively small in size.

4.1 Evaluation Metrics

The localization of image forgery falls under the category of image semantic segmentation, which involves the task of classifying pixels at a granular level. This research utilizes the metrics of Precision, Recall, and F1-Score to evaluate the performance of various models. The evaluation metrics are calculated as follows:

$$Precision = \frac{TP}{TP + FP} \tag{11}$$

$$Recall = \frac{TP}{TP + FN} \tag{12}$$

$$F1 = \frac{2 \times Precision \times Recall}{Precision + Recall} \tag{13}$$

where TP refers to true positive, FP means false negative, and FN represents false negative.

4.2 Implementation Details

In this study, PyTorch was utilized to implement all the neural network models. The optimizer employed was Adam, with an initial learning rate of 0.001. During training, the learning rate was reduced using the cosine decay method. All experiments were conducted on an NVIDIA RTX3060 GPU.

4.3 Baseline Models

Our proposed method is compared to several classic approaches in the area of image forgery localization.

- UNet [14]: A U-shaped model proposed for completing image segmentation tasks that is also utilized for image forgery localization.
- AttentionUNet [15]: An attention-based UNet model that includes an attention gate to improve the extraction of shallow and deep features.
- ResUNet [13]: A U-shaped model that incorporates residual blocks for improved feature extraction.
- RRUNet [2]: A U-shaped model that introduces the ringed residual block to further enhance feature extraction capabilities.

4.4 Experimental Results and Analysis

Comparison Experiments. This section provides a comprehensive evaluation of our proposed image forgery localization model and its performance in comparison to baseline models, using some benchmark datasets. Table 1 displays the experimental results of different methods on two distinct datasets. Our work exhibits substantial improvements in most metrics compared to the previous research, as demonstrated by the comparison.

Ablation Study. To assess the individual effects of each module, we conducted a series of experiments to evaluate the metrics of the proposed model under varying settings by incrementally incorporating components. The models were trained using identical settings and datasets for consistency.

Table 2 presents the performance of various models, including UNet with ringed residual block (RRUNet), RRUNet with Squeeze-and-Excitation (SE) block, and RRUNet with Coordinate Attention (CA) block. The results indicate that the ringed residual block enhances the feature extraction capability, leading to better model performance. Additionally, the attention blocks (SE and CA) are effective in identifying and emphasizing the significant features, as evidenced by the considerable improvements in the evaluation metrics in the table.

Table 1. Comparision of different methods

Method	CASIA1.0			Columbia		
	Precision	*Recall*	*F1*	*Precision*	*Recall*	*F1*
UNet	39.27	**73.18**	51.11	84.23	87.09	85.64
ResUNet	68.10	58.09	62.70	93.40	83.56	88.21
AttentionUNet	70.89	60.27	65.15	94.08	89.43	91.70
RRUNet	65.04	66.15	65.59	94.25	**91.96**	93.09
Ours	**76.95**	69.77	**73.18**	**95.23**	91.35	**93.24**

Table 2. Ablation Study

Method	CASIA1.0			Columbia		
	Precision	*Recall*	*F1*	*Precision*	*Recall*	*F1*
RRUNet	65.04	66.15	65.59	94.25	91.96	93.09
SE_RRUNet	70.99	71.36	71.17	97.58	89.07	93.13
CA_RRUNet	76.92	68.09	72.24	94.86	91.68	93.24
CA_SE_RRUNet	76.95	69.77	73.18	95.23	91.35	93.24

5   Conclusion

This study proposes a novel model for image forgery localization, to extract more relevant information from the input image and build deeper networks, we utilize a ringed residual block to extract features. Additionally, various attention blocks are incorporated into the model to highlight the most important parts of the features. Our proposed method is evaluated on various datasets and yields promising results, indicating its effectiveness.

References

1. Liu, B., et al.: D-UNet: a dual-encoder U-Net for image splicing forgery detection and localization. arXiv preprint arXiv:2012.01821 (2020)
2. Bi, X., Wei, Y., Xiao, B., et al.: RRU-Net: the ringed residual U-Net for image splicing forgery detection. In: Proceedings of the IEEE/CVF Conference on Computer Vision and Pattern Recognition Workshops (2019)
3. Liu, X., Liu, Y., Chen, J., et al.: PSCC-Net: progressive spatio-channel correlation network for image manipulation detection and localization. IEEE Trans. Circuits Syst. Video Technol. **32**(11), 7505–7517 (2022)
4. Kwon, M.J., Yu, I.J., Nam, S. H., et al. Cat-net: Compression artifact tracing network for detection and localization of image splicing. In: Proceedings of the IEEE/CVF Winter Conference on Applications of Computer Vision, pp. 375–384 (2021)
5. Dong, J., Wang, W., Tan, T.: CASIA image tampering detection evaluation database. In: 2013 IEEE China Summit and International Conference on Signal and Information Processing. IEEE, pp. 422–426 (2013)

6. Hsu, Y.F., Chang, S.F.: Detecting image splicing using geometry invariants and camera characteristics consistency. In: 2006 IEEE International Conference on Multimedia and Expo, IEEE, pp. 549–552 (2006)
7. Salloum, R., Ren, Y., Kuo, C.C.J.: Image splicing localization using a multi-task fully convolutional network (MFCN). J. Visual Commun. Image Represent. **51**, 201–209 (2018)
8. Long, J., Shelhamer, E., Darrell, T.: Fully convolutional networks for semantic segmentation. In: Proceedings of the IEEE Conference on Computer Vision and Pattern Recognition, pp. 3431–3440 (2015)
9. Liu, B., Pun, C.M.: Locating splicing forgery by fully convolutional networks and conditional random field. Signal Process.: Image Commun. **66**, 103–112 (2018)
10. Zhang, R., Ni, J.: A dense u-net with cross-layer intersection for detection and localization of image forgery. In: ICASSP 2020–2020 IEEE International Conference on Acoustics, Speech and Signal Processing (icassp). IEEE, pp. 2982–2986 (2020)
11. Shi, Z., Shen, X., Kang, H., et al.: Image manipulation detection and localization based on the dual-domain convolutional neural networks. IEEE Access **6**, 76437–76453 (2018)
12. He, K., Zhang, X., Ren, S., et al.: Deep residual learning for image recognition. In: Proceedings of the IEEE Conference on Computer Vision and Pattern Recognition, pp. 770–778 (2016)
13. Zhang, Z., Liu, Q., Wang, Y.: Road extraction by deep residual u-net. IEEE Geosci. Remote Sens. Lett. **15**(5), 749–753 (2018)
14. Ronneberger, O., Fischer, P., Brox, T.: U-Net: convolutional networks for biomedical image segmentation. In: Navab, N., Hornegger, J., Wells, W.M., Frangi, A.F. (eds.) MICCAI 2015. LNCS, vol. 9351, pp. 234–241. Springer, Cham (2015). https://doi.org/10.1007/978-3-319-24574-4_28
15. Oktay, O., Schlemper, J., Folgoc, L.L., et al.: Attention u-net: Learning where to look for the pancreas[J]. arXiv preprint arXiv:1804.03999 (2018)
16. Hu, J., Shen, L., Sun, G.: Squeeze-and-excitation networks. In: Proceedings of the IEEE Conference on Computer Vision and Pattern Recognition, pp. 7132–7141 (2018)
17. Hou, Q., Zhou, D., Feng, J.: Coordinate attention for efficient mobile network design. In: Proceedings of the IEEE/CVF Conference on Computer Vision and Pattern Recognition, pp. 13713–13722 (2021)
18. Wei, Y., Ma, J., Wang, Z., et al.: Image splicing forgery detection by combining synthetic adversarial networks and hybrid dense U-net based on multiple spaces. Int. J. Intell. Syst. **37**(11), 8291–8308 (2022)

ACMA-GAN: Adaptive Cross-Modal Attention for Text-to-Image Generation

Longlong Zhou, Xiao-Jun Wu$^{(\boxtimes)}$, and Tianyang Xu

The School of Artificial Intelligence and Computer Science, Jiangnan University,
Wuxi 214122, People's Republic of China
{wu_xiaojun,tianyang.xu}@jiangnan.edu.cn

Abstract. Automatically generating realistic and natural high resolution images from text descriptions is a complicated problem in the cross-modal research field. Recently, multi-stage conditional generative adversarial networks based on word attention are the mainstream of Text-to-Image generation. A close examination of these methods reveals two fundamental issues. Firstly, the granularity difference between the words and local image features makes the words cannot accurately express the local image features. Second, the discriminators cannot extract enough image information, which will result in poor discrimination effect. In this paper, we address these issues by proposing an adaptive cross-modal attention generative adversarial network (ACMA-GAN). Specifically, we design (1) an adaptive word attention module, which can reform the granularity of words and mine the context information of words; (2) a feature alignment module, which uses the pre-trained CNN model to improve the feature extraction ability of discriminator. Extensive experiments on CUB-200 and MS-COCO datasets demonstrate that our method is superior to the existing methods.

Keywords: cGAN · adaptive word attention · feature alignment

1 Introduction

In recent years, adversarial discriminant techniques are widely used in various fields [1,2,7,8,17–19], especially Text-to-Image generation (T2I) [4,6,9,10,14, 16,20–23]. T2I is based on conditional generation adversarial network (cGANs) [7,8], which is a variant of generative adversarial networks (GANs) [2]. At present, T2I methods are mostly based on multi-stage network structure. Each stage contains a generator and a discriminator to control the generation of images of a specific size.

It is undeniable that AttnGAN [16] has an inestimable place in the field of Text-to-Image generation, it is the basis for the vast majority of three-stage generative models. AttnGAN [16] introduces word attention at both 64 and 128

This work is supported in part by the National Natural Science Foundation of China (Grant No. 62020106012, 62106089).

H. Lu et al. (Eds.): ICIG 2023, LNCS 14358, pp. 111–123, 2023.
https://doi.org/10.1007/978-3-031-46314-3_9

resolutions, which is essential to improve the details of the generated images. A significant problem also arises: whether the word features are at an identical granularity to the local image features at different resolutions. It is well known that local image features are pixel-level, whereas the granularity of word features is significantly higher than pixel-level local image features, and usually a word corresponds to a set of local feature vectors. Therefore, it is important to effectively reduce the granularity difference between words and local Image features before using word attention. DM-GAN [23] uses the image features after global pooling on the intermediate image features as modulation information, then the word features and image features are weighted and summed through a gating mechanism to obtain a new word representation, which will be used in word attention. We believe that the design of DM-GAN [23] still has some shortcomings. Firstly, the global image feature vector and sentence vector should have similar semantics and granularity. DM-GAN [23] does not explore the possibility of using sentence vector as modulation information. Secondly, whether the weighted sum of word feature vector and global feature vector will affect the context information between words. To alleviate these shortcomings, we designed an Adaptive Word Attention Module (AWAM). In AWAM, we concatenate the sentence feature vector and global image feature vector to the word feature vectors, and then use a self-attention module to obtain the new words. The new words constructed by our method can be regarded as a weighted sum of words, sentence and image features, and we not only consider the granularity relationship between word and local image features, but also take into account the context information of words.

As we all know, the discriminant ability of discriminator is based on its ability to extract features, if the discriminator can not extract enough effective information, it will be difficult to make a good discrimination. However, the discriminators in AttnGAN [16] and DM-GAN [23] are composed of few convolution and activation operations, so the feature extraction ability is poor. In order to improve the feature extraction ability of discriminators, we designed a Feature Alignment Module (FAM). In FAM, We use the excellent image classification network Inception-v3 model [13] as our feature extraction template, and then align the image features extracted by discriminator and pre-trained Inception-v3 model [13] at local and global levels. Specifically, we design a feature alignment loss to gradually reduce the distance of discriminator and Inception-v3 model [13] during training (Fig. 1).

In summary, the key contributions of our paper are as follows:

- We propose a novel model ACMA-GAN with adaptive cross-modal attention to generate realistic images.
- We design an adaptive word attention module (AWAM) to reform the granularity of words. The new words constructed by AWAM preserve the context information between words.
- A feature alignment loss is proposed to improve the feature extraction ability of discriminator. To be specific, We use a pre-trained CNN model to force the discriminator to extract more similar features.

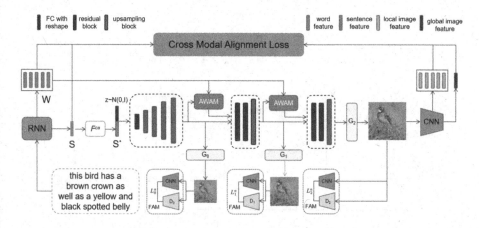

Fig. 1. The structure of our ACMA-GAN.

- Extensive experiments confirm that our ACMA-GAN outperforms most advanced methods.

2 Methodology

In this section, we first illustrate the overall structure of our ACMA-GAN, then analyze the Adaptive Word Attention Module (AWAM) and Feature Alignment Module (FAM), finally we analyze the loss function of generator and discriminator in detail.

2.1 Model Overview

Our ACMA-GAN contains a text encoder, an image encoder, a three-stage generator, and three discriminators. The text encoder and the image encoder are the pre-trained Bi-LSTM [12] and Inception-v3 [13] models, respectively.

The generator takes random noise, sentence vector and word vectors as input. Sentence vector is concatenated with noise after a conditioning augmentation module F^{ca} as the input of the first stage. The output of the previous stage and AWAM are the inputs for the second and third stages. We use the pre-trained RNN and CNN models to calculate a cross-modal alignment loss to optimize the training of generator.

The discriminator contains a feature alignment loss L^a in addition to the adversarial loss, and we use the Inception-v3 model [13] to optimize the feature extraction capability of our discriminator by narrowing the distance of local features and global features in two CNN models.

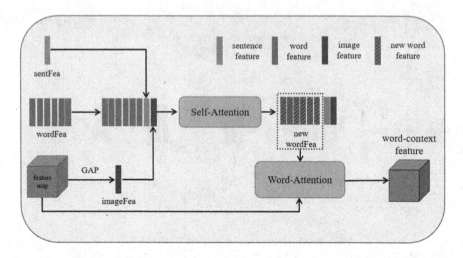

Fig. 2. The pipeline of Adaptive Word Attention Module (AWAM).

2.2 Adaptive Word Attention Module

The previous methods AttnGAN [16] and DM-GAN [23] fail to reduce the granularity difference between words and local image features, and DM-GAN [23] neglects the context of words when it rewrite the word embeddings. To address these problem, we propose an Adaptive Word Attention Module (AWAM). As shown in Fig. 2, we use global average pooling on the image features to obtain an image feature vector with the same dimension as the sentence and word vectors, then we concatenate the image vector, sentence vector and word vectors together, finally input them into a self-attention Module for rewriting word embeddings. The self-attention is as follows:

$$
\begin{aligned}
o_j &= v(\sum_{i=1}^{N} \beta_{j,i} h(x_i)), \\
h(x) &= W_h x, \\
v(x) &= W_v x.
\end{aligned}
\tag{1}
$$

where x_i represents the content vector before self-attention and o_j represents the content vector after self-attention, $\beta_{j,i}$ represents the attention score between the jth and ith content vectors, and W_h and W_v are the weights of the fully connected layer. $\beta_{j,i}$ is calculated as follows:

$$\beta_{j,i} = \frac{exp(s_{i,j})}{\sum_{i=1}^{N} exp(s_{i,j})},$$
$$s_{i,j} = f(x_i)^T g(x_j),$$
$$f(x) = W_f x,$$
$$g(x) = W_g x.$$

(2)

where x_i and x_j represent the ith and jth content vectors, and W_f and W_g are the weights of the fully connected layer.

The new words after self-attention not only retain the context information between words, but also reduce the granularity difference between words and local image features. The new word features and image feature are input into the word attention module to calculate the word-content feature. Finally, the original image feature and the word-content feature are used as the input of the next stage. The word-content feature are computed as follows:

$$c_j = \sum_{i=0}^{T-1} \beta_{j,i} e_i,$$
$$\beta_{j,i} = \frac{exp(s_{j,i})}{\sum_{k=0}^{T-1} exp(s_{j,k})},$$
$$s_{j,i} = v_j \cdot e_i.$$

(3)

where c_j represents the word-content feature vector at the jth pixel position, $\beta_{j,i}$ represents the attention score between the local feature at the jth pixel position and the ith word, v_j represents the jth sub-region of the image, and e_i represents the ith word.

In our adaptive word attention module, the new words constructed from the words, sentence and image information can better play the ability of word attention. The sentence feature vector and image feature vector constructed by the self-attention module are discarded in the word attention module, because their granularity is higher than the local features of the image, using them will not be conducive to the construction of word-content feature.

2.3   Feature Alignment Module

In order to improve the feature extraction ability of the discriminator and promote the better performance of the discriminative network, we design a Feature Alignment Module (FAM). In FAM, we design a feature alignment loss between the discriminator and the pretrained Inception-v3 model [13] at both local and global levels. Before the feature alignment, we use convolution operation to adjust the dimension of local and global features in discriminator, aiming to project the features of Inception-v3 model [13] and discriminator into a common space. The feature alignment loss in FAM is calculated as follows:

$$L_{D_i}^{FA} = -[\sum_{i=1}^{N} log \frac{exp(\gamma R(x_i^G, y_i^G))}{\sum_{j=1}^{N} exp(\gamma R(x_i^G, y_j^G))}$$
$$+ \sum_{i=1}^{N} log \frac{exp(\gamma R(x_i^G, y_i^G))}{\sum_{j=1}^{N} exp(\gamma R(x_j^G, y_i^G))}$$
$$+ \sum_{i=1}^{N} log \frac{exp(\gamma R(x_i^R, y_i^R))}{\sum_{j=1}^{N} exp(\gamma R(x_i^R, y_j^R))}$$
$$+ \sum_{i=1}^{N} log \frac{exp(\gamma R(x_i^R, y_i^R))}{\sum_{j=1}^{N} exp(\gamma R(x_j^R, y_i)^R)}] \tag{4}$$

where x_i^G and x_i^R represent the global and local image features extracted from discriminator, y_i^G and y_i^R represent the global and local image features extracted from pretrained Inception-v3 model, $R(\cdot)$ represents the matching function, and γ is a smoothing factor.

2.4   Objective Function

Adversarial Loss. As with our baseline AttnGAN [16], we use the cross-entropy loss as our adversarial loss. The adversarial loss of discriminator is defined as:

$$L_{D_i}^{adv} = -\frac{1}{2}[\mathbb{E}_{x \sim p_{data}} log D_i(x) + \mathbb{E}_{\hat{x} \sim p_{G_i}} log(1 - D_i(\hat{x}))$$
$$+ \mathbb{E}_{x \sim p_{data}} log D_i(x, s) + \mathbb{E}_{\hat{x} \sim p_{G_i}} log(1 - D_i(\hat{x}, s))] \tag{5}$$

where x and $\hat{x}$ represent the real and generated images and s represents the text condition. The adversarial loss of generator is defined as:

$$L_{G_i}^{adv} = -\frac{1}{2}[\mathbb{E}_{\hat{x} \sim p_{G_i}} log D_i(\hat{x}) + \mathbb{E}_{\hat{x} \sim p_{G_i}} log D_i(\hat{x}, s)] \tag{6}$$

Cross-Modal Alignment Loss. The cross-modal alignment loss used on generator has the same functional template as the feature alignment loss on discriminator, which can motivates the generator to generate semantically consistent images. It is defined as:

$$L_{CMA} = -[\sum_{i=1}^{N} log \frac{exp(\gamma R(x_i, y_i))}{\sum_{j=1}^{N} exp(\gamma R(x_i, y_j))}$$
$$+ \sum_{i=1}^{N} log \frac{exp(\gamma R(x_i, y_i))}{\sum_{j=1}^{N} exp(\gamma R(x_j, y_i))}] \tag{7}$$

where (x_i, y_i) is the image-text pair, $R(\cdot)$ represents the matching function between image and text, γ is a smoothing factor. The cross-modal alignment loss contains two components, x_i represents the global image feature when y_i represents the sentence feature, and x_i represents the local image feature when y_i represents the word feature.

Generator Loss. Based on the adversarial loss $L_{G_i}^{adv}$, we add the cross-modal alignment loss L_{CMA}, thus the whole generator loss is defined as:

$$L_G = \sum_{i=0}^{N} L_{G_i}^{adv} + \lambda_1 L_{CMA} \tag{8}$$

Discriminator Loss. Based on the adversarial loss $L_{D_i}^{adv}$, we add the feature alignment loss $L_{D_i}^{FA}$, thus the whole discriminator loss is defined as:

$$L_D = \sum_{i=0}^{N} (L_{D_i}^{adv} + \lambda_2 L_{D_i}^{FA}) \tag{9}$$

3   Experiments

In this section, we will demonstrate the feasibility and effectiveness of our proposed innovations through comprehensive and rigorous experiments. Firstly, we introduce the datasets and metrics. Then, we quantitatively and qualitatively analyzed the superiority of our method. Finally, we verify the generalization performance of our method through ablation experiments.

3.1   Datasets and Metrics

To demonstrate the capability of our proposed ACMA-GAN, we conduct experiments on CUB [15] and COCO [5] datasets. The CUB dataset contains 200 bird categories with 11,788 images, where 150 categories with 8,855 images are used for training while the remaining 50 categories with 2,933 images for testing. There are ten text descriptions for each image in CUB dataset. The COCO dataset includes a training set with 80k images and a test set with 40k images. Each image in the COCO dataset has five text descriptions. We quantify the performance of ACMA-GAN in terms of Inception Score (IS) [11], Fréchet Inception Distance (FID) [3], and R-precision [16]. In the testing phase, 30 000 images are randomly generated.

3.2   Quantitative Results

In this subsection we will analyze the effect of our innovation points in terms of three metrics: Inception Score [11], FID [3] and R-Precision [16]. As shown in Table 1, ACMA-GAN obtains the second highest Inception Score and FID on CUB dataset, slightly behind TIME [6], but obtains the best R-precision. ACMA-GAN obtains the state-of-the-art results on all metrics for COCO dataset.

Compared with our baseline AttnGAN [16] on CUB and COCO datasets, ACMA-GAN improves 11.47% and 24.26% on Inception Score, improves 38.62% and 28.97% on FID, and improves 11.53% and 9.97% on R-Precision.

Table 1. Comparing the results of our ACMA-GAN with other advanced methods. AttnGAN [16] is our baseline model. The bold is best.

Methods	Inception Score↑		FID↓		R-Precision↑	
	CUB	COCO	CUB	COCO	CUB	COCO
StackGAN [21]	3.70	8.45	51.89	74.05	N/A	N/A
StackGAN++ [22]	4.04	8.30	15.30	81.59	N/A	N/A
AttnGAN [16]	4.36	25.89	23.98	35.49	67.82	83.53
ControlGAN [4]	4.58	24.06	N/A	N/A	69.33	82.43
SEGAN [14]	4.67	27.86	18.17	32.28	N/A	N/A
DM-GAN [23]	4.75	30.49	16.09	32.64	72.31	88.56
TIME [6]	**4.91**	30.85	**14.30**	31.14	71.57	89.57
ACMA-GAN	4.86	**32.17**	14.72	**25.21**	**75.64**	**91.86**

The quantitative results show that our ACMA-GAN model has significant advantages over other state-of-the-art methods in generating high-quality images and improving image diversity, as well as in maintaining semantic consistency, especially for COCO dataset of complex scenes (Fig. 3).

3.3 Qualitative Results

By comparing the images generated by ACMA-GAN with those generated by AttnGAN [16] and DM-GAN [23], qualitative results will indicate the validity of the generated images from a visual perspective.

As shown in Fig. 4. The text in column 2 gives "This bird is brown and white", however the abdomen of the bird generated by AttnGAN [16] is hardly noticeable as brown, and the abdomen of the bird generated by DM-GAN [23] is completely white, whereas the bird generated by our method is perfectly consistent with the semantic of the given text and has good morphology. The text in column 4 contains a description of "a large crowd", which is not reflected in the images generated by AttnGAN [16] and DM-GAN [23], while The images generated by our method reflect the concept of "a large crowd".

In summary, compared with the mainstream AttnGAN [16] and DM-GAN [23] our method can better understand the semantics of text descriptions and then synthesize images with consistent content, and the images generated by our method contain more well-posed objects and have higher image diversity.

3.4 Ablation Study

In this section, we first quantitatively analyze the use of added information in AWAM, then quantitatively analyze the proposed Adaptive Word Attention Module (AWAM) and Feature Alignment Module (FAM), and qualitatively analyze the differences of word attention between ACMA-GAN and AttnGAN [16]. Finally, we qualitatively analyze the generalization performance of ACMA-GAN.

Fig. 3. Examples (CUB: 1st–3rd columns), COCO: (4th–6th columns) are generated by AttnGAN [16], DM-GAN [23] and our proposed ACMA-GAN.

Table 2. The results of using different added information in AWAM.

ID	Components		IS↑	FID↓	R-Precision↑
	SentFea	ImageFea			
0	-	-	4.57 ± 0.05	21.41	70.66 ± 0.69
1	✓	-	4.69 ± 0.05	16.85	73.12 ± 0.73
2	-	✓	4.76 ± 0.06	16.56	75.16 ± 0.76
3	✓	✓	4.81 ± 0.04	15.78	75.64 ± 0.54

Added Information. We fine-tune the AttnGAN [16] model and obtain a better baseline model. We analyzed in the introduction that DM-GAN [23] only uses the image features after the global average pooling as the modulation information to optimize the semantics of words, which can obtain better word attention results, but whether the sentence information also has this ability has not been explored. So we explored the effect of using sentence features and image features to obtain new words in the adaptive word attention module. As shown in Tables 2, when we used sentence features, both Inception Score, FID and R-Precision were improved, which indicates that the way to optimize the semantics of words with sentence features. When we use both sentence features and image features as modulation information to optimize the word semantics, our model can obtain the best results, which indicates that it is necessary to automatically optimize the word semantics according to the current image features and sentence features before using word attention, and then we can get the best attention results.

Table 3. The performance of AWAM and FAM on CUB dataset.

Architecture	Inception Score	FID	R-Precision
baseline	4.57	21.41	70.66
+AWAM	4.81	15.78	74.78
+FAM	4.83	16.96	74.20
+AWAM+FAM	4.86	14.72	75.64

Effectiveness of AWAM and FAM. As shown in Table 3, when we replace the word attention module of our baseline model with AWAM, the Inception Score, FID, and R-Precision are improved by 5.25%, 26.30%, and 5.83%, when we add the FAM to our baseline, the Inception Score, FID and R-Precision are improved by 5.69%, 20.78% and 5.01%, these results indicate that both the AWAM and FAM are effective. The best results are obtained by using both the AWAM and FAM on our baseline model, which indicates the proposed AWAM and FAM are mutually beneficial and not in conflict.

Attention Results. Qualitative analysis of word attention is shown in Fig. 4, where we show the top five words with the highest attention score and mark them with different colors in the text, and highlight the areas attentioned by each word in the image. The given text contains three descriptions: "long black legs," "brown feathers" and "black beak," but AttnGAN [16] mistakenly makes the brown feathers blue, but the generated image by our method is completely consistent with these three descriptions. The attention areas in AttnGAN [16] are not match the semantics of the words, which disturbs the generation of the image. In our method, "leg" and "beak" are accurately matched to the corresponding area, and the word "have" is the public description of "leg", "feather" and "beak", which should be related to the three words in the context of text. In our attention results, the word "have" noticed two areas "leg" and "beak", although not perfectly noticed all the relevant regions, it is also enough to show that our adaptive word attention can accurately focus on the word-related areas while maintaining the word context semantics.

Generalisation Ability. As shown in Fig. 5, when we change the partial description of the bird in the text, our ACMA-GAN can generates the images of the bird with the corresponding semantics. These results indicate that our ACMA-GAN is sensitive to the input text, and has good generalisation performance.

this bird has long black legs, brown feathers, and a black beak.

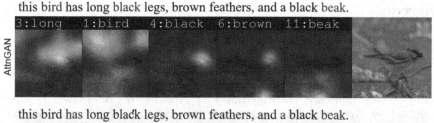

this bird has long black legs, brown feathers, and a black beak.

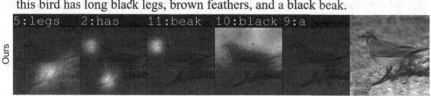

Fig. 4. Attention results for AttnGAN [16] and our ACMA-GAN at 128 resolution.

(1)This bird is red with white and has a very short beak.
(2)This bird is red with white and has a very black beak.
(3)This bird is red with white and has a very white beak.
(4)This bird is blue with white and has a very long beak.
(5)This bird is blue with white and has a very short beak.

body color: red   body color: red   body color: red   body color: blue   body color: blue
  beak: short   beak: black   beak: white   beak: long   beak: short

Fig. 5. Experiment of text sensitivity.

4   Conclusion

In this paper, we propose a novel Text-to-Image generation model ACMA-GAN. We design an Adaptive Word Attention Module (AWAM), which uses both image features and sentence features to modify the word embeddings. The updated words can better play the role of cross-modal attention. In addition, a feature alignment loss is designed to use the pre-trained image classification model to encourage the discriminator to extract more image features, so as to improve the feature extraction ability of the discriminator. Extensive experiments on two common datasets confirm that ACMA-GAN significantly outperforms other state-of-the-art methods.

References

1. Frolov, S., Hinz, T., Raue, F., Hees, J., Dengel, A.: Adversarial text-to-image synthesis: a review. Neural Netw. **144**, 187–209 (2021)
2. Goodfellow, I., et al.: Generative adversarial nets. In: Advances in Neural Information Processing Systems, vol. 27 (2014)
3. Heusel, M., Ramsauer, H., Unterthiner, T., Nessler, B., Hochreiter, S.: GANs trained by a two time-scale update rule converge to a local Nash equilibrium. In: Advances in Neural Information Processing Systems, vol. 30 (2017)
4. Lee, M., Seok, J.: Controllable generative adversarial network. IEEE Access **7**, 28158–28169 (2019)
5. Lin, T.-Y., et al.: Microsoft COCO: common objects in context. In: Fleet, D., Pajdla, T., Schiele, B., Tuytelaars, T. (eds.) ECCV 2014. LNCS, vol. 8693, pp. 740–755. Springer, Cham (2014). https://doi.org/10.1007/978-3-319-10602-1_48
6. Liu, B., Song, K., Zhu, Y., de Melo, G., Elgammal, A.: Time: text and image mutual-translation adversarial networks. In: Proceedings of the AAAI Conference on Artificial Intelligence, vol. 35, pp. 2082–2090 (2021)
7. Mirza, M., Osindero, S.: Conditional generative adversarial nets. Computer Science, pp. 2672–2680 (2014)
8. Miyato, T., Koyama, M.: cGANs with projection discriminator. arXiv preprint arXiv:1802.05637 (2018)
9. Qiao, T., Zhang, J., Xu, D., Tao, D.: MirrorGAN: learning text-to-image generation by redescription. In: Proceedings of the IEEE/CVF Conference on Computer Vision and Pattern Recognition, pp. 1505–1514 (2019)
10. Reed, S., Akata, Z., Yan, X., Logeswaran, L., Schiele, B., Lee, H.: Generative adversarial text to image synthesis. In: International Conference on Machine Learning, pp. 1060–1069. PMLR (2016)
11. Salimans, T., Goodfellow, I., Zaremba, W., Cheung, V., Radford, A., Chen, X.: Improved techniques for training GANs. Adv. Neural. Inf. Process. Syst. **29**, 2234–2242 (2016)
12. Schuster, M., Paliwal, K.K.: Bidirectional recurrent neural networks. IEEE Trans. Sig. Process. **45**(11), 2673–2681 (1997)
13. Szegedy, C., Vanhoucke, V., Ioffe, S., Shlens, J., Wojna, Z.: Rethinking the inception architecture for computer vision. In: Proceedings of the IEEE Conference on Computer Vision and Pattern Recognition, pp. 2818–2826 (2016)
14. Tan, H., Liu, X., Li, X., Zhang, Y., Yin, B.: Semantics-enhanced adversarial nets for text-to-image synthesis. In: Proceedings of the IEEE/CVF International Conference on Computer Vision, pp. 10501–10510 (2019)
15. Wah, C., Branson, S., Welinder, P., Perona, P., Belongie, S.: The Caltech-UCSD Birds-200-2011 dataset (2011)
16. Xu, T., et al.: AttnGAN: fine-grained text to image generation with attentional generative adversarial networks. In: Proceedings of the IEEE Conference on Computer Vision and Pattern Recognition, pp. 1316–1324 (2018)
17. Xu, T., Feng, Z., Wu, X.J., Kittler, J.: Adaptive channel selection for robust visual object tracking with discriminative correlation filters. Int. J. Comput. Vis. **129**, 1359–1375 (2021)
18. Xu, T., Feng, Z., Wu, X.J., Kittler, J.: Toward robust visual object tracking with independent target-agnostic detection and effective Siamese cross-task interaction. IEEE Trans. Image Process. **32**, 1541–1554 (2023)

19. Xu, T., Zhu, X.F., Wu, X.J.: Learning spatio-temporal discriminative model for affine subspace based visual object tracking. Vis. Intell. **1**(1), 4 (2023)
20. Yin, G., Liu, B., Sheng, L., Yu, N., Wang, X., Shao, J.: Semantics disentangling for text-to-image generation. In: Proceedings of the IEEE/CVF Conference on Computer Vision and Pattern Recognition, pp. 2327–2336 (2019)
21. Zhang, H., et al.: StackGAN: text to photo-realistic image synthesis with stacked generative adversarial networks. In: Proceedings of the IEEE International Conference on Computer Vision, pp. 5907–5915 (2017)
22. Zhang, H., et al.: StackGAN++: realistic image synthesis with stacked generative adversarial networks. IEEE Trans. Pattern Anal. Mach. Intell. **41**(8), 1947–1962 (2018)
23. Zhu, M., Pan, P., Chen, W., Yang, Y.: DM-GAN: dynamic memory generative adversarial networks for text-to-image synthesis. In: Proceedings of the IEEE/CVF Conference on Computer Vision and Pattern Recognition, pp. 5802–5810 (2019)

Registration-Propagated Liver Tumor Segmentation for Non-enhanced CT-Based Interventions

Pengju Lyu[1,2], Cheng Wang[2], Wei Fang[2,3], Junchen Xiong[2], Xuan Li[2,3], Hao Luo[2], Wenjian Liu[1(✉)], and Jianjun Zhu[2,4(✉)]

[1] City University of Macau, Macau, China
andylau@cityu.mo
[2] Hanglok-Tech Co. Ltd., Hengqin 519000, China
[3] Macau University of Science and Technology, Macau, China
[4] Center of Interventional Radiology and Vascular Surgery, Department of Radiology, Zhongda Hospital, Medical School, Southeast University, Nanjing 210009, China
jj.zhu@hanglok-tech.cn

Abstract. Intra-operative non-enhanced computed tomography (CT) has grown as a prominent tool in interventional surgeries for liver tumor by offering a real-time, more precise imaging guidance over its pre-operative enhanced counterpart as well as intra-operative ultrasound. Though deep learning has demonstrated promising performance in various medical image tasks, the challenges for liver tumor segmentation in the context of intra-operative non-enhanced CT remain due to the scarcity of accurate pixel-level-labeled tumor data and low visibility of tumor without contrast enhancement. In this paper, based on a pre-assumption of consistent relative spatial relation between liver and liver tumor at pre- and intra-surgical stages, we propose a two-step (segmentation - registration) framework to propagate liver tumor segmentation mask from pre-operative enhanced CT to corresponding intra-operative non-enhanced CT via nonrigid registration. A Multi-scale Bridged spatial attention block embedded in the popular "U-shaped" network architecture termed MsBs-Unet is introduced to better accommodate variations of tumor during segmentation. We show that MsBs-Unet uniformly achieves superior performances against other baselines on liver and liver tumor segmentation task in terms of Dice score and HD95 metrics on our in-house data containing a cohort of intra-operative non-enhanced CT scans and Medical Segmentation Decathlon task03 liver tumor dataset respectively. Final registration results were evaluated via tumor landmarks matching on 20 in-house intra-subject paired CT scans for both intensity and feature-based methods. Specifically for the latter, mean target registration error is 3.3 mm, and the overall intra-operative process takes around 48 s per case. The resulting tumor segmentation show gratifying promise of applying our framework for non-enhanced CT-based liver intervention.

Keywords: Intra-operative non-enhanced CT · Multi-scale bridged spatial attention · Liver tumor segmentation · Nonrigid Registration

H. Lu et al. (Eds.): ICIG 2023, LNCS 14358, pp. 124–136, 2023.
https://doi.org/10.1007/978-3-031-46314-3_10

1   Introduction

Liver tumors pose a significant threat to human health, the malignancies were reported to have accounted for an alarming figure of 8.3% of cancer-related deaths worldwide [17]. In recent years, it has become the norm in many medical fields for generating pre- and intra-operative imaging to perform minimally or non-invasive image-guided surgical interventions. Conventionally, under liver tumor interventional procedures, pre-surgical advanced imaging, such as computed tomography (CT) or magnetic resonance imaging (MRI), is employed for surgical planning. Because of tissue deformations such as pneumoperitoneum often complicating the anatomical alignment with the pre-operative images and patient's anatomy during surgery, surgeons rely on intra-operative ultrasound (iUS) for timely guidance. However, the iUS's poor resolution and operator dependence with a cumbersome reconstruction of the navigation view impede its wide application [1]. Intra-operative CT represents a valuable tool for liver surgery, offering higher resolution images, real-time feedback, and a more comprehensive assessment of the liver than iUS [4].

As deep learning technique has achieved revolutionary successes in Computer-Aided Diagnosis (CAD), the seminal work Unet [14] based on convolutional neural network (CNN) has emerged as the fundamental framework in the realm of medical image segmentation which is deemed an essential prerequisite in therapy planning support and intra-operative assistance. Non-enhanced CT scans without the need for contrast agents (CAs) or other preparations means the high risk caused by potential toxicity of CAs and allergic reaction could therefore be avoided [4], which makes them a convenient option during the course of surgery where time and patients' safeties are often at stake. However, most of the existing liver tumor segmentation networks are trained only on pre-operative enhanced CT. Due to the absence of accurate pixel-level tumor label and low visibility of tumor without contrast enhancement, the problem of liver tumor segmentation on intra-operative non-enhanced CT remain unsolved. *We indicate in the remaining sections pre-operative enhanced CT and intra-operative non-enhanced CT as preCT and iCT respectively.*

In this work, based on our hypothesis that the relative spatial relationship of liver and liver tumor largely maintains at pre/intra-surgical phases, we propose a fully automated framework for iCT liver tumor segmentation which is propagated from preCT via nonrigid liver mask registration for spatial mapping. Specifically, Our main contributions are three-fold:

- We introduce a two-step framework for eventual tumor segmentation derivation in iCT, which incorporates a deep learning-based segmentation step for the acquisition of liver tumor and liver segmentation mask from preCT and iCT respectively. And a registration step to transfer tumor masks from preCT to iCT using liver mask as a guiding frame.
- We propose a Multi-scale Bridged spatial attention (MsBs) block to enhance Unet architecture for tumors detection. We validate its effectiveness against other baseline models on MSD task03 liver tumor-labeled public dataset and

our in-house iCT liver-labeled dataset, in which MsBs-Unet readily yields exceeding performance.
- We compare the intensity-based and feature-based registration on crop liver (mask) regions. Final mean Target Registration Error (mTRE) with reference to the liver tumor central point in iCT suggests feature-based method produces finer tumor mask propagation from preCT.

2   Related Work

2.1   Segmentation with Unets

The primary value of Unet lies in its modular design rendering it an optimal choice for extensive customization and seamless integration with a variety of plug-and-play modules to enhance its performance. We review diverse enhancements on four perspectives that hold special contributions to liver tumor segmentation and also shed enlightenment on our design of MsBs-Unet.

Skip Connection Enhancement. Oktay et al. [13] introduced attention gates mechanism to the skip connections to implicitly learn to suppress irrelevant regions in the input image while highlighting the feature in regions of task specific interest. The Unet++ [19] used nested and dense skip connections across different layers such that features of different semantic scales can be aggregated while the number of parameters increase exponentially.

Multi-scale Block. Capturing the complex and heterogeneous nature of tumors can be partly achieved by leveraging the benefits of multi-scale receptive fields. Huang et al. [7] introduced the ISA-Net with inception-like blocks characterized by varying convolutional kernel sizes in parallel to obtain perceptions at different scales in their PET-CT liver tumor segmentation. Ibtehaz et al. [8] proposed an efficient MultiRes block, tactfully formulating the large kernels (5 × 5 and 7 × 7) convolutions as consecutive small kernel (3 × 3) convolutions to capture more fine-grained features without increasing the model complexity.

Attention Mechanism. The attention mechanism is capable of enhancing the assignment of the most informative feature representations while suppressing the less useful ones, thus allowing the model to focus on the important regions in the context adaptively. The sSE [15] (spatial Squeeze-and-Excitation) block, a modification of the original SE-Net [15] architecture, instead "squeezes" along the channel dimension and "excites" spatially, therefore learns space-specific descriptors to recalibrate the feature maps to highlight useful spatial information that is more critical for medical segmentation tasks.

Transformer. While ConvNets enjoy inductive biases in a multitude of segmentation tasks, the Vision Transformer (ViT) [3] model based on self-attention mechanism was later introduced to alleviate the deficiency of CNNs in capturing the long-range semantic dependencies to achieve on par or even better performance than CNNs. UNETR [6] employs ViT exclusively at the encoder stage to capture global contextual information in a 3D volumetric style. SwinUNETR [5] incorporates the hierarchical Transformer architecture of Swin Transformer that utilizes shifted windowing scheme to efficient extracted multi-scale features.

2.2 Pre- and Intra-operative Images Registration

Intra-operative and pre-operative image registration has witnessed a wide range of applications in the field of image-guided surgery for enhancing surgical precision and accuracy. The registration process involves the identification of corresponding features in both images acquired prior to and during surgery and create a transformation matrix that aligns pre-operative images in the same coordinate system as its intra-operative counterparts. Registration algorithms for pre-operative and intra-operative images fusion can be categorized into intensity-based and feature-based. Image-based algorithms use image intensity to establish correspondences while feature-based methods find corresponding points (landmarks) or delineated target structures (segmentation mask) in both images. Oguro et al. [12] validated the feasibility of intensity-based nonrigid registration between pre- and intra-operative MR for MRI-guided brachytherapy of the prostate. Nitsch et al. [11] proposed a pMR-iUS registration method, in which the structures in the iUS are segmented using a random forest classifier, which

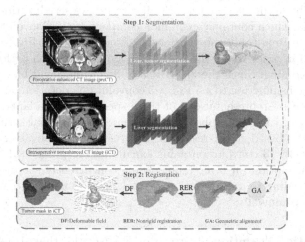

Fig. 1. Overview of proposed framework for liver tumor segmentation in iCT scans. Segmentation masks of liver and tumor in preCT as well as liver in iCT are obtained via Unet in step 1. Tumor mask in preCT are then transformation to the coordinate system of iCT in step 2 by registration between these two resultant liver masks.

are further utilized as additional spatial information for the registration to enable an alignment of selected structures. Museyko et al. [10] showed that registering images acquired from the same subject at different times based on binary bone VOI (volume of interest) masks is superior to that using gray value VOIs in the scenarios of mono-modality CT - CT and multimodality μCT - μMR.

3   Methodology

In this section, we detail the framework to achieve iCT liver tumor segmentation, which is constituted by a segmentation step followed by registration step as depicted in Fig. 1.

3.1   Segmentation Step

Since the anatomical structure of liver is relatively fixed and its annotation requires less manual effort than that for tumor, with the presence of additional liver labeled iCT data we performed a liver and liver tumor segmentation in iCT and preCT respectively using the classic Unet to generate masks in a fully supervised setting. To capture the high inter-patient variations in terms of shape and size of liver tumors, we innovatively designed a Multi-scale Bridged spatial attention block (MsBs) for Unet architecture (MsBs-Unet) to enhance segmentation performance as shown in Fig. 2. The MsBs block is mainly comprised of two functional parts: Multi-Scale and Bridged Spatial Attention (BSA) module.

Multi-scale. We obtain multi-scale features from the outputs of convolution operations with varying kernel sizes. Similar to [8], we serialize three ConvNormAct subblocks which contains a common compound: 3D Convolution + Batch normalization + Relu (only convolution blocks are shown in Fig. 2). The kernel sizes are 1, 3, 3 in order where the first $1 \times 1 \times 1$ Convolution performs channel dimension scheduling. Since the 3rd $3 \times 3 \times 3$ convolutional blocks effectively perform analogous function to a $5 \times 5 \times 5$ convolution operation on layer inputs, fusing these feature representations of three specific scales adaptively captures the irregularity of tumor morphology. The chose of sequential kernel size (1, 3, 3) over (3, 3, 3) is based on the resultant discovery that in the latter case, output of the 3rd $3 \times 3 \times 3$ convolution gains expanding reception field resembling a $7 \times 7 \times 7$ convolution on layer input) while concurrently sacrifices details of small tumors leading to a degradation of model performance and an increase of computational complexity.

Bridged Spatial Attention. Inspired by BA-Net [18] that straightforwardly bridges features from previous neighboring convolution layers into cSE Net [15] to obtain better channel attention. Considering the shape and location of tumors carrying more weight than their texture or color during segmentation, we derived multiple spatial-wise relevant information from feature compression in spatial attention sSE on previously learned multi-scale features. The integration of these

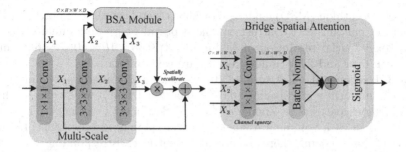

Fig. 2. Illustration of the detailed composition of MsBs block.

multi-scale mutual-supplemented relevance results in a more robust spatial attention weight. Concretely, the spatial attention $F_{BSA}(\cdot)$ mainly includes channel
squeeze and spatial excitation. For a certain layer, let the output of each Con-
vNormAct subblock be $X_i \in \mathbb{R}^{C \times H \times W \times D}, i = 1, 2, 3$, where C, H, W, D represent channel, height, width, and depth of output feature maps. The squeeze along
the channel is achieved through a convolution with weight $W_{sq} \in \mathbb{R}^{1 \times 1 \times 1 \times C \times 1}$.
The final bridged weight is obtained through direct element wise addition after
batch Normalization $BN(\cdot)$ is applied to ensure similar distribution across three
output features that is conducive to network training. A sigmoid layer $\sigma(\cdot)$ ultimately scale the weight to in between 0 and 1. The position-wise multiplication
of attention weight with its most adjacent layer output (i.e., X_3) concludes spatial excitation. Residual connection is added to smooth gradient flow preventing
training instability.

$$F_{BSA}(X_1, X_2, X_3) = \sigma \left(\sum_i^3 BN \left(W_{sq} X_i \right) \right) X_3 \tag{1}$$

3.2 Registrations Step

We conduct registration within liver region of interest. Thus, two bounding
boxes defined by resulting pair-wise, individual level liver masks are selected
in both phases, which are cropped to reduce the perturbation of irrelevant background information and speed up the optimization process. An initial transform
is applied to align the geometric central points of preCT liver mask to that of
iCT in case of interpolation failure during registration process. After rigid and
nonrigid registration are successively carried out, the resultant deformation field
is applied to map preCT tumor mask onto iCT.

4 Experiments

4.1 Dataset

We conducted experiments on two datasets for volumetric segmentation. For
preCT segmentation, the models were trained and evaluated on Medical Seg-

mentation Decathlon (MSD) challenge task03 (Liver Tumors segmentation) [16]. The dataset contains 131 contrast-enhanced portal phase abdominal CT scans with a voxel spatial resolution of ($[0.55 - 1] \times [0.55 - 1] \times [0.45 - 6.0]$) mm^3 where both liver and liver tumors regions are well annotated.

For iCT segmentation, A total of 100 in-house abdominal non-enhanced CT scans with uniform voxel spacing ($0.67 \times 0.67 \times 5.0$ mm^3) were collected from 100 anonymous patients in Zhongda Hospital Southeast University. The entire liver regions in each volume are labeled by an experienced radiologist. In addition, out of the 100 scans, there are also 20 patient-level corresponding contrasted enhanced CT scans in which pairs of landmarks (tumor central points) are provided as the test set for final registration result evaluation.

4.2 Implementation Details

1) Segmentation

Data Processing. We followed a general data processing step on both datasets. Preprocessing: firstly, we applied intensity clipping (min: -20, max: 200) to remove irrelevant regions followed by histogram normalization to enhance the contrast of soft tissues. Z-score normalization was further performed on clipped volume according to non-zero voxels. All previous steps were implemented per volume. We then randomly cropped sub-volumes with size $96 \times 96 \times 96$ in which foreground (liver region) and background were sampled at ratio 2 : 1 during training, and resampled to a $1 \times 1 \times 1$ mm isotropic resolution. All the patches finally underwent randomly operation of flip, elastic deformation intensity shifting, and scaling (scaling factor: 0.1) as data augmentation. Postprocessing: Finding the largest connected component on liver worked as the final postprocess step to remove false positive outside liver region.

Loss Function. We employed a combination of two loss functions, namely Combo loss $\mathcal{L}_{combo}$ (Cross entropy loss and Dice loss) [6] and Weighted Normalized Boundary loss $\mathcal{L}_{wnbl}$ [2] so as to directly optimize Dice score and Hausdorff distance (HD) [6] . The overall loss function $\mathcal{L}_{total}$ is given by:

$$\mathcal{L}_{combo} = 1 - \frac{2}{C} \sum_{k=1}^{C} \frac{\sum_{i=1}^{N} G_{i,k} P_{i,k}}{\sum_{i=1}^{N} G_{i,k}^2 + \sum_{i=1}^{N} P_{i,k}^2}$$
$$- \frac{1}{N} \sum_{k=1}^{C} \sum_{i=1}^{N} G_{i,k} \log P_{i,k} \tag{2}$$

$$\mathcal{L}_{wnbl} = 1 - \frac{\sum_{k=1}^{C} w_k \sum_{i=1}^{N} \left(D_{i,k} \left((1 - G_{j,k})^2 - P_{i,k} \right) \right)^2}{\sum_{k=1}^{C} w_k \sum_{i=1}^{N} \left(D_{i,k} \left((1 - G_{j,k})^2 - G_{i,k} \right) \right)^2} \tag{3}$$

$$\mathcal{L}_{total} = \alpha \mathcal{L}_{combo} + (1 - \alpha) \mathcal{L}_{wnbl} \tag{4}$$

$P_{i,k}$ and $G_{i,k}$ denote the probability output and one-hot encoded ground truth for class k at voxel i, w_k respectively, $D_{i,k}$ is the i-th voxel in the Distance Transform Maps (DTM) for the k-th class in the ground truth. w_k represents segmentation weights for k-th class precalculated as the inverse of percentage of each class per volume. Loss scheduler α decreases linearly with training epochs.

Model Training and Evaluation. For segmentation, we adopted PyTorch[1] and MONAI[2] frameworks to carry out model implementation on a 4 GPU RTX 3090 equipped System. The batch size per GPU was set to 1. All models were trained with randomly initialized weights until convergence. we use the SGD optimizer with a cosine annealing learning rate scheduler, the initial learning rate of which was set as $1e-3$. For inference, we utilized a sliding window approach with an overlapping of 0.5 for neighboring voxels. 5-fold cross-validation technique was implemented on both datasets for respective segmentation evaluation measured by 95% Hausdorff Distance (HD95) and Dice score (DSC).

2) Registration

Data Processing. Prior to registration, the obtained segmentation masks for any intra-subject preCT and iCT images were resampled to the same isotropic voxel size of $1\,mm$. For preCT, we converted the original label value of tumor mask into that of liver mask by means of thresholding method. In this way that we were able to obtain cropped binary volumes of interest from segmentation masks (mask VOIs) and the gray value VOIs from CT image (image VOIs) with respect to the entire liver regions in pre/intra-operative phases.

Registration Realization. We conducted for comparison intensity-based (image) registration with image VOIs and feature-based (mask) registration with mask VOIs. Both methods were implemented using SimpleElastix[3] package through a sequence of rigid and B-spline transform with preconfigured default parameter maps e.g., multiresolution strategy with four levels of image smoothing, adaptive stochastic gradient descent (ASGD) optimizer, sum of squared differences (SSD) for feature-based registration and Mattes mutual information (MMI) for intensity-based registration and transform bending energy Penalty to encourage anatomical plausibility. Mean Target Registration Error (mTRE) were chosen for registration evaluation which measures the distance between corresponding landmarks that are tumor centers in this case.

---

[1] http://pytorch.org/.
[2] https://monai.io/.
[3] http://simpleelastix.github.io/.

4.3 Results Analysis

Table 1. The average of 5-fold cross validation evaluation results are shown. MsBs-Unet achieves state-of-the-art performance compared to prior baselines.

Methods	MSD Task03 (preCT)				In-house Data (iCT)	
	Liver		Tumor		Liver	
	Dice (%)↑	HD95 (mm)↓	Dice (%)↑	HD95 (mm)↓	Dice (%)↑	HD95 (mm)↓
UNETR [6]	93.94	21.67	76.88	26.48	94.17	7.84
SwinUNETR [5]	94.63	23.14	78.35	27.23	95.34	6.22
Unet++ [19]	95.76	10.15	82.43	13.92	95.22	4.91
nnUnet [9]	96.42	3.16	84.69	23.3	96.37	6.22
AttentionUnet [13]	96.67	2.43	86.42	5.13	95.64	5.92
MsBs-Unet	**97.36**	**2.01**	**89.36**	**3.54**	**97.25**	**3.91**

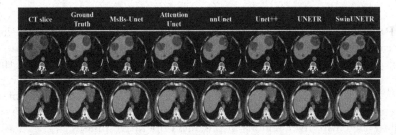

Fig. 3. Qualitative comparisons of representative segmentation on liver tumor in preCT (first row) and liver in iCT (second row). MsBs-Unet shows distinct improvement on the tumor (green) and liver (red) segmentation against baselines. (Color figure online)

Segmentation. We conducted extensive comparisons among CNN or transformer-based Unet variants as shown in Table 1. All models adopt hierarchical architecture of 5 stages with 64 feature maps at the top layer and the number of channels doubles as the resolution reduces per layer. In the case of liver segmentation in preCT and iCT, MsBs-Unet demonstrates superior performance in terms of Dice score (< 96%) and HD95 (> 7 mm) than widely used baselines with slight improvement over AttentionUnet and current versatile SOTA model of nnUnet [9]. With respects to preCT tumor segmentation, MsBs module can significantly boost Unet performance reaching a 89.4% Dice score which surpasses nnUnet by a large margin of 5%, which leads to a concomitantly reduction on HD95 (< 8 mm), almost twice less than that of nnUnet. It is worth noting that there is a distinctive performance gap between transformer-based model namely UNETR and SwinUNETR comparing to their CNN counterparts, which could be attributed to the inherent data-hungry characteristic of transformer and ignorance of local spatial information especially for small tumors inside patches.

Qualitative PreCT liver tumor segmentation comparisons are presented in first row of Fig. 3. MsBs-Unet demonstrates consistency with quantitative evaluation on its capability in capturing the fine-grained details of tumor structures. It shows evident improvement in detecting tumor of various morphologies, which validates the effectiveness of MsBs module while nnUnet and UNETR suffer severe tumor under-segmentation and SwinUNETR fails to differentiate normal liver tissue and tumor. As illustrated in the second row of Fig. 3, MsBs-Unet for iCT liver segmentaiton presents higher liver boundary segmentation accuracy against neighboring organs, which indicate its ability of identifying heterogeneous organs by capturing better spatial context where the rest of models confuse the liver/heart tissues as indicated by small yellow circles.

Table 2. Overview of results of two registration approaches

Metric	Intensity-based registration	Feature-based registration
mTRE (mm) ↓	9.5	3.3

Registration. By relying on the automatically generated liver masks in the segmentation step, we compared two registration methods namely intensity-based (image) registration, feature-based (liver binary segmentation masks) registration. The computed deformation fields were applied to the landmarks provided in the registration test set. The mean Target Registration Error (mTRE) namely average tumor central points distance (mm) of the two registrations methods are displayed in Table 2, which suggests feature-based method could generate more precise alignment whose mTRE score is only 3.3 mm.

Figure 4 illustrates the final registration results with feature-based registration, 2 cases of iCT along with the overlay of its ground truth and transformed tumor from preCT segmentation are shown. Both of the tumor central point errors are below 5mm, and the delineated contours and 3D volume are great indicators of the success of our method in locating the tumor region of interest.

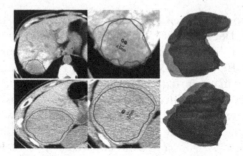

Fig. 4. Qualitative results of registered tumor (red) comparing with manually labeled tumor (green) in iCT. Two cases are shown in terms of central tumor point deviation (first column and zoom-in view in second column) and overlap of tumor 3D volume and ground truth delineation in third column. (Color figure online)

5 Discussion and Conclusion

In the work, we target the critical problem on liver tumor segmentation in iCT for lacking of pixel-level tumor labels. Our proposed framework addresses this with a segmentation-registration pipeline. To better accommodate the variance of liver tumors, we compared several state of the arts Unet models, and introduced a novel Multi-Scale Bridged Spatial Attention as a basic building block for each layer of Unet. MsBs-Unet achieved consistently exceeding performance with Dice score 97% and 89.4% for preCT liver and tumor segmentation respectively as well as 96% for iCT liver segmentation. The visualization segmentation results further validated model's capability in capturing better spatial information for detecting the fine-grained details of tumor structures. The combination of resultant liver segmentation masks acted as guiding-frame for a subsequent feature-based registration approach to get reliable tumor propagation. Target Registration Error (Central point matching) were as low as 3.3 mm, which well supports our pre-assumption of unchanged positional correlation for liver and liver tumors.

Table 3. Intra-operative time consumption showcase

Image size (Spacing)	Process time (s)	
$512 \times 512 \times 316$ ($0.67 \times 0.67 \times 0.5 \, \text{mm}^3$)	Liver segmentation in iCT	Registration
	8	40

Although our method delivers iCT liver tumor segmentation, there are still further improvements that deserve our continued attentions. 1. Since Registration purely depends on liver segmentation results, segmentation with other organs could add external constraints in case liver segmentation fails. 2. As traditional registration methods execute iterative optimization in the intra-operative phase, The overall intra-operative procedure concerned including iCT liver segmentation and registration process for a CT image with a typical 3D volume 512 × 512 × 316 takes 48 s as shown in Table 3. Instead, This can be alleviated by taking advantage of deep learning approach, which can also be weakly supervised by anatomical segmentation, such that we are able to obtain the deformation field beforehand which can be apply directly on tumor during registration as one single forward process.

In conclusion, our proposed framework represents a promising avenue for liver tumor segmentation in iCT. We hope our method has the potential and applicability for improving the safety and efficacy of liver interventions.

Acknowledgment. The study was supported by National Natural Science Foundation of China (81827805, 82130060, 61821002, 92148205), National Key Research and Development Program (2018YFA0704100, 2018YFA0704104). The project was funded by China Postdoctoral Science Foundation (2021M700772), Zhuhai Industry-University-Research Collaboration Program (ZH22017002210011PWC), Jiangsu Provincial Medical Innovation Center (CXZX202219), Collaborative Innovation Center of Radiation Medicine of Jiangsu Higher Education Institutions, and Nanjing Life Health Science and Technology Project (202205045). The funding sources had no role in the writing of the report, or decision to submit the paper for publication.

References

1. Bozinov, O., Burkhardt, J.K., Fischer, C.M., Kockro, R.A., Bernays, R.L., Bertalanffy, H.: Advantages and limitations of intraoperative 3D ultrasound in neurosurgery. Technical note. In: Pamir, M., Seifert, V., Kiris, T. (eds.) Intraoperative Imaging. Acta Neurochirurgica Supplementum, vol. 109. Springer, Vienna (2011). https://doi.org/10.1007/978-3-211-99651-5_30 (2011)
2. Celaya, A., Diaz, A., Balsells, A., Riviere, B., Fuentes, D.: A weighted normalized boundary loss for reducing the Hausdorff distance in medical imaging segmentation. arXiv preprint arXiv:2302.03868 (2023)
3. Dosovitskiy, A., et al.: An image is worth 16x16 words: transformers for image recognition at scale. arXiv preprint arXiv:2010.11929 (2020)
4. Fang, H.Y., et al.: Efficacy and safety of preoperative vs intraoperative computed tomography-guided lung tumor localization: a randomized controlled trial. Front. Surg. **8**, 809908 (2022)
5. Hatamizadeh, A., Nath, V., Tang, Y., Yang, D., Roth, H.R., Xu, D.: Swin UNETR: Swin transformers for semantic segmentation of brain tumors in MRI images. In: Crimi, A., Bakas, S. (eds.) Brainlesion: Glioma, Multiple Sclerosis, Stroke and Traumatic Brain Injuries. BrainLes 2021. LNCS, vol. 12962. Springer, Cham (2022). https://doi.org/10.1007/978-3-031-08999-2_22
6. Hatamizadeh, A., et al.: UNETR: transformers for 3d medical image segmentation. In: Proceedings of the IEEE/CVF Winter Conference on Applications of Computer Vision, pp. 574–584 (2022)
7. Huang, Z., et al.: ISA-Net: improved spatial attention network for PET-CT tumor segmentation. Comput. Methods Programs Biomed. **226**, 107129 (2022)
8. Ibtehaz, N., Rahman, M.S.: MultiResUNet: rethinking the u-net architecture for multimodal biomedical image segmentation. Neural Netw. **121**, 74–87 (2020)

9. Isensee, F., Jaeger, P.F., Kohl, S.A., Petersen, J., Maier-Hein, K.H.: nnU-Net: a self-configuring method for deep learning-based biomedical image segmentation. Nat. Methods **18**(2), 203–211 (2021)
10. Museyko, O., Eisa, F., Hess, A., Schett, G., Kalender, W.A., Engelke, K.: Binary segmentation masks can improve intrasubject registration accuracy of bone structures in CT images. Ann. Biomed. Eng. **38**, 2464–2472 (2010)
11. Nitsch, J., et al.: Automatic and efficient MRI-US segmentations for improving intraoperative image fusion in image-guided neurosurgery. NeuroImage: Clin. **22**, 101766 (2019)
12. Oguro, S., et al.: MRI signal intensity based B-spline nonrigid registration for pre- and intraoperative imaging during prostate brachytherapy. J. Magn. Reson. Imag. **30**(5), 1052–1058 (2009)
13. Oktay, O., et al.: Attention U-Net: learning where to look for the pancreas. arXiv preprint arXiv:1804.03999 (2018)
14. Ronneberger, O., Fischer, P., Brox, T.: U-Net: convolutional networks for biomedical image segmentation. In: Navab, N., Hornegger, J., Wells, W.M., Frangi, A.F. (eds.) MICCAI 2015. LNCS, vol. 9351, pp. 234–241. Springer, Cham (2015). https://doi.org/10.1007/978-3-319-24574-4_28
15. Roy, A.G., Navab, N., Wachinger, C.: Concurrent spatial and channel 'squeeze & excitation' in fully convolutional networks. In: Frangi, A.F., Schnabel, J.A., Davatzikos, C., Alberola-López, C., Fichtinger, G. (eds.) MICCAI 2018. LNCS, vol. 11070, pp. 421–429. Springer, Cham (2018). https://doi.org/10.1007/978-3-030-00928-1_48
16. Simpson, A.L., et al.: A large annotated medical image dataset for the development and evaluation of segmentation algorithms. arXiv preprint arXiv:1902.09063 (2019)
17. Sung, H., et al.: Global cancer statistics 2020: Globocan estimates of incidence and mortality worldwide for 36 cancers in 185 countries. CA: Cancer J. Clin. **71**(3), 209–249 (2021)
18. Zhao, Y., Chen, J., Zhang, Z., Zhang, R.: BA-Net: bridge attention for deep convolutional neural networks. In: Avidan, S., Brostow, G., Cissé, M., Farinella, G.M., Hassner, T. (eds.) Computer Vision – ECCV 2022. ECCV 2022. LNCS, vol. 13681. Springer, Cham (2022). https://doi.org/10.1007/978-3-031-19803-8_18
19. Zhou, Z., Siddiquee, M.M.R., Tajbakhsh, N., Liang, J.: UNet++: redesigning skip connections to exploit multiscale features in image segmentation. IEEE Trans. Med. Imaging **39**(6), 1856–1867 (2019)

FML-MIS: A Scheme of Privacy Protection and Model Generalization for Medical Images Segmentation via Federated Meta-learning

Mohan Yu and Heng Liu[✉]

Anhui University of Technology, Ma'anshan, Anhui, China
{hengliusky,hengliusky}@aliyun.com

Abstract. Federated learning enables diverse distributed medical institutions to learn a global prediction model collaboratively while preserving data privacy. However, in practical clinical deployment, the global model may suffer from degraded generalization performance due to the high heterogeneity of medical data from different sites. In this paper, we propose and implement a robust framework for medical image segmentation (FML-MIS) via a federated meta-learning scheme, which can achieve effective privacy preservation and model generalization. Our scheme consists of three components: (1) a federated domain image generation mechanism that synthesizes diverse and realistic images across domains; (2) a meta-learning strategy that leverages the generated images to enhance the model's adaptability to new domains; and (3) a differential privacy mechanism that protects the model's security and resists inference attacks during federated training. We evaluate our scheme in a federated learning setting on three public datasets. Extensive experiments and comparison results show that our scheme can effectively utilize rich multi-source data and improve the generalization ability of the model while preserving data privacy. The project code is available at https://github.com/yuwxl/FML-MIS.

Keywords: meta-learning · federated learning · medical image segmentation · differential privacy

1 Introduction

Deep learning algorithms have advanced the analysis of complex medical data. However, medical data are privacy-sensitive and can only be stored and trained locally at each site. This leads to the problem of model locality, which means that the trained model is only suitable for local data and cannot be generalized to other scenarios.

Federated learning (FL) was proposed as a solution for data interaction across isolated regions. The main idea is to keep the private raw data locally and

H. Lu et al. (Eds.): ICIG 2023, LNCS 14358, pp. 137–150, 2023.
https://doi.org/10.1007/978-3-031-46314-3_11

only upload the model parameters to a central server for aggregation after local training. The mechanism of FL can be applied in the medical field, however, most of the existing work only focuses on improving the model performance within the domain, while ignoring the generalization ability across domains. In actual scenarios, especially in medical image segmentation scenarios, the data collected by different sites is highly heterogeneous due to different environments and equipment. Therefore, the model aggregation strategy of federated learning alone is insufficient to solve the cross-domain medical image segmentation task effectively.

To improve the cross-domain generalization ability of medical image segmentation models, we apply a meta-learning scheme which can achieve better domain generalization effects while preserving the privacy of medical images. We mitigate the privacy risk of gradient leakage in FL by adopting a differential privacy mechanism during model parameter upload. We enhance local client data security through gradient clipping and Gaussian noise. Our approach is applicable to diverse medical image processing tasks, not limited to medical image segmentation.

To summarize, this paper's contributions are as follows:

(1) We propose a mechanism for generating federated domain images. Specifically, we transfer the image amplitude spectrum across clients and generate the federated domain image by performing an inverse Fourier transform with the local phase spectrum. These federated domain images carry the distribution information of multiple source domains but keep the core semantics unchanged, and will be used for downstream training tasks.
(2) We design a meta-learning scheme based on federated domain images. Through meta-learning we can learn domain-shift knowledge from original images and federated domain images, helping to improve the model's ability to adapt to unseen domains.
(3) We implement the first complete prototype system FML-MIS for medical image segmentation via federated meta-learning. Our scheme can utilize multi-source medical data without compromising privacy protection. In addition to improving the model's generalization performance, we also incorporate a model privacy protection mechanism to further safeguard the security of user data.

The rest of the paper is organized as follows. We present the background and related work in Sect. 2. Section 3 gives the system overview of FML-MIS and the key techniques we design and implement. Section 4 presents the implementation details and the experimental results. Finally, we conclude our paper in Sect. 5.

2   Related Works

2.1   Federated Domain Medical Image Processing

Federated learning (FL) has been applied to the medical field in some research [16]. Since the training data in FL are often non-independent and identically distributed (Non-IID) and unlabeled, directly applying various deep learning methods to federated domains poses challenges. New technologies are needed to address the issues of FL. FSSL proposed in [7] established a consistency-based semisupervised learning model under FL framework. The work in [13] studied the adaptation of unsupervised schemes to FL. However, these methods still require target data to fine-tune the model when deployed. In some situations, it is challenging to collect medical data in a short time, so the domain generalization ability of the federated model is crucial for clinical deployment applications.

2.2 Model Generalization

Domain generalization is a commonly used technique to enhance the generalization ability of deep models. Domain generalization (DG) aims to learn from multiple tasks and quickly adapt to new data by leveraging multi-source data. Existing DG methods usually rely on accessing multi-source distributions. Li et al. [9] used data samples from multiple sites to train a domain discriminator. Dou et al. [3] constructed meta-test and meta-train sets from multi-source data. These methods required a centralized data source for learning, which violates data privacy. Some DG methods do not need to access multi-source data but directly manipulate local data or design network structures. For instance, Zhang et al. [21]augmented the images by applying various transformations on the images. Zhou et al. [22] proposed a novel DG method based on depth-domain adversarial image generation (DDAIG). These methods do preserve data privacy but fail to exploit the rich data distribution.

2.3 Federated Model Privacy Protection

Zhu et al. [23] showed that a malicious attacker can infer the original data from the gradient information. There are also other threats such as Byzantine attacks, and membership inference attacks, that try to compromise the model and mine privacy. Therefore, federated learning is often combined with other privacy-preserving techniques to achieve higher levels of security. Currently, the technologies related to privacy protection in FL mainly include encryption, perturbation, and trusted hardware.

3   Methodology

3.1   FML-MIS Scheme Overview

In this section, we provide an overview of FML-MIS, the proposed federated meta-learning scheme for enabling privacy preservation and model generalization. FML-MIS designs a federated-domain image generation mechanism that enables each client to access multi-source distributed information without compromising their privacy. Figure 1 presents an overview of FML-MIS.

The experiments in [14] suggest that the amplitude spectrum and phase spectrum in the frequency domain of an image represent its low-level distribution and high-level semantics, respectively. Hence, we design a scheme to transmit the local amplitude spectrum across clients. The client can interact with these shared amplitude spectra to acquire multi-source distributions, and generate federated domain images with varying distributions but preserving the same semantics. These images can be utilized in the training task of the downstream medical segmentation network. We will elaborate on this in Sect. 3.2.

In the local federated training, a meta-learning strategy is applied to use the local original image as the training set and the federated domain image as the testing set and enhance the generalization capability of the model by learning domain shift knowledge in the original image and the federated domain image. Segmentation loss and contrastive loss are used to devise loss functions to guide the optimization of boundary regions for medical segmentation.

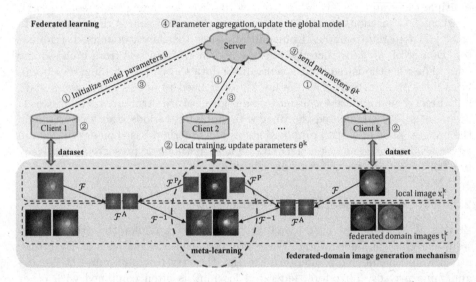

Fig. 1. An overview of our scheme. The local client employs the federated domain image generation mechanism to acquire diverse multi-source distributions. Based on this, a meta-learning scheme is devised to enhance the model's generalization capability, and finally, parameters are aggregated under the federated learning framework.

3.2   Proposed Method

Meta-learning Based on Federated Domain. Meta-learning is the concept of learning to learn. Its aim is to address the bottleneck of deep learning, which is limited generalization performance and poor adaptability to new tasks. The basic objective is to learn a model that can rapidly learn and adapt to new tasks. In deep learning, the performance of the model will be influenced by the choice of hyperparameters and the setting of the learning rate. These all need to be manually set up with experience. In meta-learning, the goal is not to learn a specific model to solve a certain problem but to learn from a large number of different tasks, and eventually be able to quickly adapt to new tasks by fine-tuning on few samples.

Among the current research methods, the learning to initialize based on strong generalization has made the most remarkable progress, represented by MAML [4]. Literature [8] used meta-learning for domain generalization for the first time and proposed the MLDG method under the framework of MAML. In each iteration, the meta-train set and meta-test set are divided from the source domain data to simulate domain shift. Based on its method, we devise a meta-learning algorithm (see Algorithm 1).

Based on Algorithm.1, the model can learn domain-shift knowledge from multi-source data to enhance its generalization capability. We enable each client to access multi-source distributed information in a privacy-preserving manner. Specifically, we denote the i-th original medical image of the k-th client as $x_i^k \in R^{H \times W \times 3}$, and its frequency-space signal is obtained by Fourier transform $\mathcal{F}$:

$$\mathcal{F}\left(x_i^k\right)(m,n) = \sum_{h,w} x_i^k(h,w) e^{-j2\pi\left(\frac{h}{H}m + \frac{w}{W}n\right)}, j^2 = -1 \tag{1}$$

The amplitude spectrum $\mathcal{F}^A$ and phase spectrum $\mathcal{F}^P$ of the image are further separated from $\mathcal{F}(.)$, which reflect the low-level distribution and high-level semantics of the image respectively.The amplitude spectrum of the local client interacts $\mathcal{F}^{A}{}_i^k$ with the amplitude spectrum transmitted across clients $\mathcal{F}^{A}{}_j^n$:

$$\mathcal{F}^{A}{}_{i,\lambda}^{k \to n} = (1-\lambda)\mathcal{F}^{A}{}_i^k + \lambda \mathcal{F}^{A}{}_j^n \tag{2}$$

Local images acquire other domain distribution information through the interaction of amplitude spectrum, where λ is the balance parameter of the interaction degree. Finally, we use $\mathcal{F}^A$ and $\mathcal{F}^P$ as input to perform inverse Fourier transform $\mathcal{F}^{-1}$to generate a federated domain image(see Fig. 2).

$$t_{i,\lambda}^{k \to n} = \mathcal{F}^{-1}\left(\mathcal{F}^{A}{}_{i,\lambda}^{k \to n}, \mathcal{F}^{A}{}_i^k\right) \tag{3}$$

The final federated domain image can be expressed as t_i^k. Clients interacting with these amplitude spectra can generate federated images with different distribution information but maintain the same semantics [10]. According to the literature [18], the federated domain image will not affect the recognition of its core semantics.

Our meta-learning scheme is divided into three steps. The local original medical images are used as the meta-train set, and the federated domain images generated interactively are used as the meta-test set. In the meta-train stage, the model parameters $\theta^k$are updated with the segmentation loss L_{seg} (see Algorithm 1 line 3) and α is the meta-train learning rate (see Algorithm 1 line 4):

$$\hat{\theta}^k = \theta^k - \alpha \nabla_{\theta^k} L_{seg}\left(x_i^k; \theta^k\right) \tag{4}$$

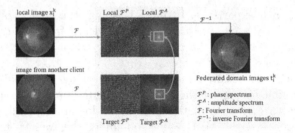

Fig. 2. Spectral transfers across clients. Local images can interact with amplitude spectra from other domains, and they are then mapped to target "styles" without changing the semantic content. This federated-domain image shows perceptually smaller domain gaps.

Algorithm 1. Meta-Learning Domain Generalization

Input:
    Domains S.
Output:
    Init: Model parameters θ. Hyperparameters α, β, γ
1: for ite in iterations do
2: split: $\bar{S}$ and $\widetilde{S} \longleftarrow S$
3: meta-train: $\nabla \theta = \mathcal{F}'_\theta\left(\bar{S}; \theta\right); Updated\ parameters\ \theta' = \theta - \alpha \nabla_\theta$
4: meta-test: $Loss\ is\ \mathcal{G}\left(\widetilde{S}; \theta'\right)$
5: meta-optimization: $Update\ \theta; \theta = \theta - \gamma \dfrac{\partial \mathcal{F}\left(\bar{S};\theta\right) + \beta \mathcal{G}\left(\widetilde{S};\theta - \alpha\nabla_\theta\right)}{\partial\theta}$
6: end for
7: return θ

In meta-test stage, based on the fast weights generated by meta-train, the next update direction follows the direction of the fast weights to converge rapidly. We use loss L_{cont} to update the model parameters $\hat{\theta}^k$. In meta-optimization stage, both the L_{seg} and L_{cont} will be optimized together with respect to the original parameter θ^k, and γ is the balancing hyper-parameter, the overall loss is $L_{all}(x_i^k; t_i^k; \hat{\theta}^k) = L_{seg}(x_i^k; \theta^k) + \gamma L_{cont}(x_i^k; t_i^k; \hat{\theta}^k)$. After the clients finish local training, they upload the model parameters to the server.

Contrastive Loss. We adopt contrastive learning of boundary features in medical image segmentation based on SimCLR proposed by literature [2]. SimCLR constructs positive and negative samples through data augmentation and trains the encoder by maximizing the similarity of positive samples. The aim of introducing contrastive learning is to extract boundary features through the guidance of contrastive loss and enhance the ability of the medical segmentation network to distinguish boundaries and backgrounds. The implementation is divided into 3 steps:

Step 1. Random data augmentation. Perform morphological operations on sample data to generate two related views.

Step 2. Encoding (to obtain features). The segmentation boundary and background feature information output by the network are respectively denoted as z_{bg} and z_{bd}.

Step 3. Compute loss. Use NT-Xent loss for optimization, and use cosine similarity to compute the similarity between z_{bg} and z_{bd}:

$$l_{cont} = -\log \frac{\exp\left(\text{sim}\left(\mathbf{z}_{bg}, \mathbf{z}_{bd}\right)/\tau\right)}{\sum_{k=1}^{2N} 1_{[k \neq i]} \exp\left(\text{sim}\left(\mathbf{z}_{bg}, \mathbf{z}_{bd}\right)/\tau\right)} \tag{5}$$

where $1_{[k \neq i]} \in \{0, 1\}$is an indicator function evaluating to 1 iff $k \neq i$ and τ denotes a temperature parameter.

Differential Privacy for Federated Learning. In the field of deep learning security, the most prevalent differential privacy algorithm is DPSGD proposed by Abadi et al. [1]. The core idea of this algorithm is to add Gaussian noise to the updated gradient value in the process of neural network backpropagation. In addition, the process of applying homomorphic encryption and secure multiparty computation to network training is also a common privacy protection method. However, considering the limitations of communication and computation costs, we use a differential privacy mechanism to perform gradient clipping during local client training and add Gaussian noise before uploading to the server to safeguard data privacy (see Algorithm 2).

Algorithm 2. Differential Privacy for FL Based on Gaussian Mechanism

---

Input:

    Gradient norm bound C, privacy budget ϵ gradient g, local data set D; loss function l.

    Init: Latest model parameters $\theta$from server.

    Client k receives θ and starts local training:

1: Compute and clip the gradient $g_i = \frac{g_i}{\max\left(1, |g_i|/C\right)}, g = \frac{1}{|D|}\Sigma g_i = \frac{1}{|D|}\sum argmin$ $l(D_i, \theta)$

2: Descent $\theta^k = \theta - \alpha g$

3: Add noise $\theta^k = \theta^k + Gauss(\Delta f/\epsilon)$

Output:

    Output θ^k and upload it to the server.

---

4   Experiments

4.1   Dataset

The experimental datasets come from three public fundus datasets, Drishti-GS [17], RIM-ONE-r3 [5] and REFUGE [12]. Among them, REFUGE contains two different data sources. We divide these fundus image data into four sites (see Fig. 3). Fundus image segmentation is divided into the optic cup (OC) and optic disc (OD) segmentation and the segmentation results are quantitatively evaluated by the Dice coefficient (Dice) and Hausdorff distance (HD).

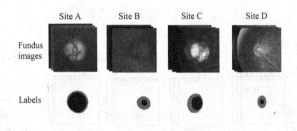

Fig. 3. Fundus Image Dataset

4.2   Implementation Details

We employ horizontal federated learning. We implement the construction of federated learning based on a lightweight federated learning framework fedlab [20]. The modules of fedlab are highly decoupled and can be flexibly configured according to different application scenarios.

The communication strategy of federated learning adopts synchronous mode. Specifically, each federation round t is initiated by the server, the server randomly selects clients to join the federated domain, sends the latest global model θ to each client, and the client receives it for local training. Our federated learning involves one server and three clients. In our experiments, we follow the practice to adopt the leave-one-domain-out strategy in domain generalization literature, i.e., training on K-1 distributed source domains and testing on the one left-out unseen target domain (i.e., site A). Once the server receives all the parameters, it updates the global model and enters the next round of federation t. This process is repeated until the model converges (see Fig. 4).

In the federated training, the batch_size is set to 5, the meta-learning rate α is $1e^{-3}$, the hyperparameter γ is set to 0.1, and the federated training setting for 100 rounds. The experiments are conducted in PyTorch 1.10.0, Python 3.8, and Cuda 11.3 using an RTX 3090 24 GB and Intel®Xeon®Silver 4210R CPU @ 2.40 GHz. We train on Linux ubuntu and use TensorBoard to visualize the training process, U-net architecture [15] is adopted as the backbone network. In the experiment, the server and the client communicate with the local loopback address, ip 127.0.0.1, port 3002.

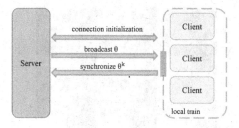

Fig. 4. Federated Learning Communication Process

4.3   Experimental Result

Comparison Results. According to the experimental settings, we compared our scheme with the classic FedAvg [11] benchmark, as shown in Fig. 5. During local training, to generate federated domain images, we transfer the amplitude spectrum across clients and design a new meta-learning scheme based on it. From the experimental results, our scheme significantly improves the segmentation accuracy of unknown domains, demonstrating the effectiveness of our proposed meta-learning strategy based on federated-domain images.

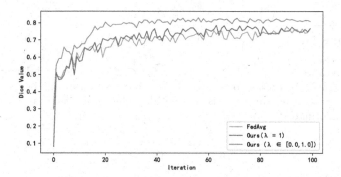

Fig. 5. Curves of generalization performance on unseen fundus datasets as the number of iterations increases, using our proposed scheme and FedAvg. And the comparison of the curves of different λ on the segmentation accuracy.

Effect of Parameter λ. Literature [19] shows, the size of the domain λ will affect the quality of the converted image.Experimentally, it can be concluded that increasing λ will decrease the domain gap but introduce artifacts (see Fig. 6). We use t-SNE [6] to visualize the distribution information of fundus image datasets from different sites, as shown in Fig. 7. Points of different colors in the figure represent the distribution of fundus datasets of different clients. Figure 7(a) is the original image data distribution of the four sites. Figure 7(b,c) is the image distribution information of the federal domain under different λ parameters. Inspired by literature [10], when we choose λ to randomly sample from [0.0,1.0],

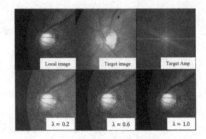

Fig. 6. Effect of parameter λ, the choice of λ has an impact on federated domain image.

it can be seen intuitively from the Fig. 7(c) that the local image can obtain richer continuous multi-source distribution information. We conduct experiments under different values of λ, and the results show that λ will affect the accuracy of image segmentation (see Fig. 5). In general, the random sampling method works better.

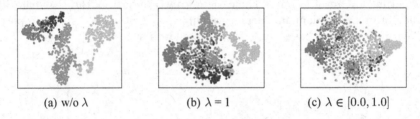

(a) w/o λ　　　　　　(b) $\lambda = 1$　　　　　　(c) $\lambda \in [0.0, 1.0]$

Fig. 7. Different values of λ will generate different "style" of federated-domain images, as shown in Fig. 6. According to the distribution information in this figure, when the value of λ is more randomized, it is obvious that the local client can obtain richer distribution information.

Effect of DP. We explore the effects of differential privacy on model performance in federated learning. Clipping and adding Gaussian noise to model parameters before uploading them can potentially decrease model accuracy. As shown in Fig. 8, The model with Gaussian noise initially performs worse than the non-DP model, but quickly converges to a similar segmentation quality as training progresses. This acceptable trade-off between privacy protection and model quality sacrifices only a small amount of performance. Additionally, adding noise in deep learning training helps prevent overfitting.

Segmentation Result Analysis. Figure 9 shows the segmentation results from unseen domains under different settings. Our scheme consistently outperforms FedAvg in fundus segmentation (Table 1). It achieves an overall improvement of 2.51% in Dice and 3.34 in HD across all unseen domain settings. Adding moderate noise has minimal impact on performance but enhances security against inference attacks. Our scheme improves generalization in the unseen domain, resulting in more balanced and higher-quality segmentation results (Fig. 9(b)). In conclusion, FML-MIS provides a robust and efficient federated meta-learning system for medical image segmentation.

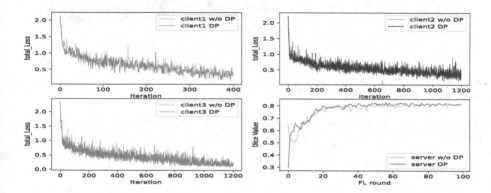

Fig. 8. Comparison curve of training effect with and without DP..

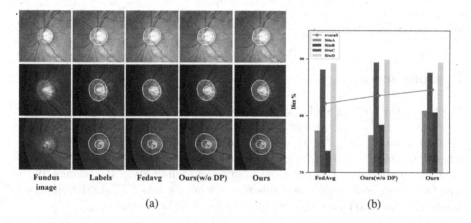

(a)   (b)

Fig. 9. Comparison on the results of different settings in fundus image segmentation.

Ablation Study. Our scheme employs two key techniques for model training: boundary contrastive loss and meta-learning with federated domain images. We perform ablation experiments to evaluate the contribution of each technique. Under the same experimental settings, we remove either boundary contrast loss or meta-learning from the 100 rounds of federated training. Figure 10(a) demonstrates the impact of each technique on the model performance, and Fig. 10(b) displays the segmentation results. The results confirm the validity of our technique design.

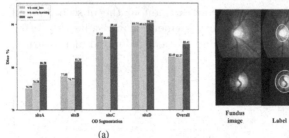
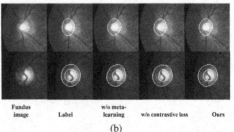

(a)   (b)

Fig. 10. Ablation results to analyze the effect of the two techniques (i.e. cont_loss and meta-learning) in our scheme.

Table 1. Comparison of results on fundus images OD/OC segmentation from different sites.

Task	OD Segmentation					OC Segmentation					
Unseen Site	A	B	C	D	Avg.	A	B	C	D	Avg.	Overall
Hausdorff Distance (HD) ↓											
Fedavg	25.56	18.00	8.98	6.96	14.88	32.30	18.03	8.82	6.72	16.47	15.67
Ours (w/o DP)	19.71	14.39	**8.18**	**6.31**	12.14	24.45	14.46	**8.31**	6.11	13.33	12.74
Ours	**16.84**	**12.86**	9.19	6.86	**11.44**	**23.77**	**13.46**	9.56	**6.08**	**13.22**	**12.33**
Dice Coefficient (Dice) ↑											
Fedavg	75.86%	74.05%	89.20%	90.47%	82.39%	78.95%	73.60%	87.07%	88.06%	81.92%	82.16%
Ours (w/o DP)	75.22%	78.25%	**90.61%**	**91.23%**	83.83%	78.03%	78.59%	**88.19%**	**88.63%**	83.36%	83.59%
Ours	**80.58%**	**81.35%**	89.44%	90.28%	**85.41%**	**81.31%**	**79.96%**	85.81%	88.60%	**83.92%**	**84.67%**

5   Conclusion

We employ the technique of amplitude spectrum exchange to generate federated domain images and devise our meta-learning algorithm based on this. Experimental results on public datasets demonstrate that our scheme can effectively enhance the model's adaptability in unseen domains. Moreover, we apply differential privacy to further increase the security and reliability of the scheme. In the near future, we will develop self-supervised learning based FML-MIS approach to address the scarcity of high-quality labeled data in practice.

Acknowledgements. This work is supported in part by the National Natural Science Foundation of China under Grant No. 61971004, the Natural Science Foundation of Anhui Province, China (Grant No. 2008085MF190), the Equipment Advanced Research Project (Sharing Technology), China (Grant No. 80912020104), and the University Synergy Innovation Program of Anhui Province, China (NO. GXXT-2022-044).

References

1. Abadi, M., et al.: Deep learning with differential privacy. In: Proceedings of the 2016 ACM SIGSAC Conference on Computer and Communications Security, pp. 308–318 (2016)

2. Chen, T., Kornblith, S., Norouzi, M., Hinton, G.: A simple framework for contrastive learning of visual representations. In: International Conference on Machine Learning, pp. 1597–1607. PMLR (2020)

3. Dou, Q., Coelho de Castro, D., Kamnitsas, K., Glocker, B.: Domain generalization via model-agnostic learning of semantic features. In: Advances in Neural Information Processing Systems, vol. 32 (2019)

4. Finn, C., Abbeel, P., Levine, S.: Model-agnostic meta-learning for fast adaptation of deep networks. In: International Conference on Machine Learning, pp. 1126–1135. PMLR (2017)

5. Fumero, F., Alayón, S., Sanchez, J.L., Sigut, J., Gonzalez-Hernandez, M.: Rimone: an open retinal image database for optic nerve evaluation. In: 2011 24th International Symposium on Computer-Based Medical Systems (CBMS), pp. 1–6. IEEE (2011)

6. Hinton, G., van der Maaten, L.: Visualizing data using t-SNE. J. Mach. Learn. Res. **9**, 2579–2605 (2008)

7. Jeong, W., Yoon, J., Yang, E., Hwang, S.J.: Federated semi-supervised learning with inter-client consistency & disjoint learning. arXiv preprint arXiv:2006.12097 (2020)

8. Li, D., Yang, Y., Song, Y.Z., Hospedales, T.: Learning to generalize: meta-learning for domain generalization. In: Proceedings of the AAAI Conference on Artificial Intelligence, vol. 32 (2018)

9. Li, H., Pan, S.J., Wang, S., Kot, A.C.: Domain generalization with adversarial feature learning. In: Proceedings of the IEEE Conference on Computer Vision and Pattern Recognition, pp. 5400–5409 (2018)

10. Liu, Q., Chen, C., Qin, J., Dou, Q., Heng, P.A.: Feddg: federated domain generalization on medical image segmentation via episodic learning in continuous frequency space. In: Proceedings of the IEEE/CVF Conference on Computer Vision and Pattern Recognition, pp. 1013–1023 (2021)

11. McMahan, B., Moore, E., Ramage, D., Hampson, S., y Arcas, B.A.: Communication-efficient learning of deep networks from decentralized data. In: Artificial Intelligence and Statistics, pp. 1273–1282. PMLR (2017)

12. Orlando, J.I., et al.: Refuge challenge: a unified framework for evaluating automated methods for glaucoma assessment from fundus photographs. Med. Image Anal. **59**, 101570 (2020)

13. Peng, X., Huang, Z., Zhu, Y., Saenko, K.: Federated adversarial domain adaptation. arXiv preprint arXiv:1911.02054 (2019)

14. Piotrowski, L.N., Campbell, F.W.: A demonstration of the visual importance and flexibility of spatial-frequency amplitude and phase. Perception **11**(3), 337–346 (1982)

15. Ronneberger, O., Fischer, P., Brox, T.: U-net: convolutional networks for biomedical image segmentation. In: Navab, N., Hornegger, J., Wells, W.M., Frangi, A.F. (eds.) MICCAI 2015, Part III. LNCS, vol. 9351, pp. 234–241. Springer, Cham (2015). https://doi.org/10.1007/978-3-319-24574-4_28

16. Silva, S., Gutman, B.A., Romero, E., Thompson, P.M., Altmann, A., Lorenzi, M.: Federated learning in distributed medical databases: meta-analysis of large-scale subcortical brain data. In: 2019 IEEE 16th International Symposium on Biomedical Imaging (ISBI 2019), pp. 270–274. IEEE (2019)

17. Sivaswamy, J., Krishnadas, S., Chakravarty, A., Joshi, G., Tabish, A.S., et al.: A comprehensive retinal image dataset for the assessment of glaucoma from the optic nerve head analysis. JSM Biomed. Imaging Data Papers **2**(1), 1004 (2015)

18. Yang, .Y., Lao, D., Sundaramoorthi, G., Soatto, S.: Phase consistent ecological domain adaptation. In: Proceedings of the IEEE/CVF Conference on Computer Vision and Pattern Recognition, pp. 9011–9020 (2020)
19. Yang, Y., Soatto, S.: Fda: fourier domain adaptation for semantic segmentation. In: Proceedings of the IEEE/CVF Conference on Computer Vision and Pattern Recognition, pp. 4085–4095 (2020)
20. Zeng, D., Liang, S., Hu, X., Wang, H., Xu, Z.: Fedlab: a flexible federated learning framework. arXiv preprint arXiv:2107.11621 (2021)
21. Zhang, L., et al.: Generalizing deep learning for medical image segmentation to unseen domains via deep stacked transformation. IEEE Trans. Med. Imaging **39**(7), 2531–2540 (2020)
22. Zhou, K., Yang, Y., Hospedales, T., Xiang, T.: Deep domain-adversarial image generation for domain generalisation. In: Proceedings of the AAAI Conference on Artificial Intelligence, vol. 34, pp. 13025–13032 (2020)
23. Zhu, L., Liu, Z., Han, S.: Deep leakage from gradients. In: Advances in Neural Information Processing Systems, vol. 32 (2019)

RoICLIP: Text-Enhanced UAV-Based Video Object Detection

Peiyi Zhang, Yali Li$^{(\boxtimes)}$, and Shengjin Wang

Beijing National Research Center for Information Science and Technology (BNRist), Department of Electronic Engineering, Tsinghua University, Beijing 100086, China
zhangpy20@tsinghua.org.cn, {liyali13,wgsgj}@tsinghua.edu.cn

Abstract. In recent years, Unmanned Aerial Vehicles (UAV)-based video object detection algorithms have attracted a lot of attention due to their widespread applications in real life. However, due to the lack of visual features such as few pixels, motion blur, and defocus objects in the video, the accuracy improvement of existing video object detection methods on UAV-based videos is very limited. In this paper, we propose a novel video object detection framework **RoICLIP**, by transferring the knowledge from pre-trained CLIP models to the downstream video object detection task. Richer information can be obtained from text for frames in UAV videos with insufficient visual features. Specifically, a **Cross-Modal Feature Enhancement(CMFE)** module is designed to improve the transfer of pre-trained knowledge by establishing multi-modal correlations at different detection stages. It minimizes the gap between downstream and pre-training tasks, allowing the model to learn more comprehensive visual representations with text supervision. To further exploit temporal information within videos, we design an **Attention-guided Frame-level Feature Aggregation(AFFA)** module. Extensive experiments demonstrate the superior performance of our method on the task of UAV-based video object detection.

Keywords: Video object detection · Multi-modal · Prompt learning

1 Introduction

With the development of aerial technology, general UAVs are being deployed in many commercial and government applications, including remote monitoring, power inspection, etc. UAV-based video object detection is a challenging task in computer vision, which aims to classify and localize objects in each frame of video captured by UAVs. However, processing UAV-captured videos to extract meaningful information is hampered by many challenges such as small objects, occlusions and changes in scene lighting. Traditional video object detection methods are mostly based on static object detectors and fuse temporal information in various ways. However, due to insufficient visual-only information of objects in video frames captured by UAVs, the performances of previous video object detectors are limited.

H. Lu et al. (Eds.): ICIG 2023, LNCS 14358, pp. 151–163, 2023.
https://doi.org/10.1007/978-3-031-46314-3_12

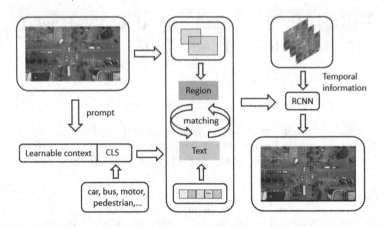

Fig. 1. Illustration for the proposed RoICLIP.

The pre-trained CLIP [10] model has been proposed recently, which leverages contrastive learning on 400 million image-text pairs to align the features of two modalities in the embedding space. Benefiting from the popularity of prompt engineering in the NLP field, the prompt learning method has gradually been adopted to transfer the knowledge from the pre-trained CLIP models to downstream computer vision tasks. Prompt learning mimics the original tasks of the pre-training process by modifying downstream tasks. Due to the proximity of the objective, there has been many works applying CLIP to classification task that requires instance-level features, while the video object detection task requires more fine-grained representations at region-level. DenseCLIP [11] provides a good example for fine-tuning CLIP to downstream dense prediction tasks by converting image-text matching into pixel-text matching, but there is still a gap between video object detection tasks which requires region-level matching.

In this paper, we introduce a novel framework named **RoICLIP** to transfer the knowledge from the pre-trained CLIP models to downstream UAV-based video object detection task. Specifically, a Cross-Modal Feature Enhancement(**CMFE**) module is proposed to enhance cross-modal association and feature enhancement at different stages of detection. It utilizes the text to perceive the visual context information and transforms the image-text matching task in original CLIP [10] model into a more suitable region-text matching task. The video has a distinct advantage over static images due to its rich temporal context. To further enhance the features of a single frame, we develop an Attention-guided Frame-level Feature Aggregation(**AFFA**) module to leverage this temporal information.

Our work proposes a novel approach to fine-tune pre-trained CLIP models and transfer the knowledge from CLIP to UAV-based video object detection task. Experiments on the VisDrone-VID2019 dataset show that compared with Faster R-CNN baseline, the mAP is increased by 6.3%, and the performance is significantly improved compared with other video object detection methods while having a comparable fps.

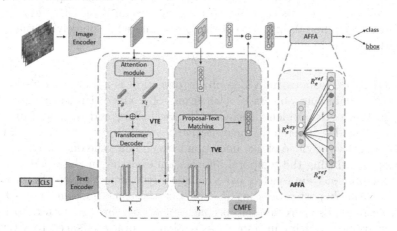

Fig. 2. Architecture of our proposed RoICLIP. We adopt the CLIP framework consists of an image encoder and an text encoder to extract features for image and text. The CMFE module facilitates feature enhancement and cross-association between two modalities. And the AFFA module is utilized to integrate temporal information from different frames.

2 Related Work

Vision-Language Pretraining. In recent years, there has been significant advancement in pre-training visual language models using contrastive learning methods, such as CLIP [10] and ALIGN [6]. By learning the joint visual-text or visual representation with language supervision from web-scale data, these models show great transferability in various downstream tasks such as visual question answering, image classification, and so on. A great deal of work is proposed to utilize pre-trained models for downstream tasks. Among them, CoOp [17] improves at the data level to transfer the knowledge of the CLIP model to downstream tasks by learning appropriate prompts, while CLIP-Adapter [4] and Tip-Adapter [15] improve at the model level to make the pre-training knowledge more suitable for downstream tasks by inserting an additional adapter into the network.

There have been attempts to use the CLIP model for dense prediction tasks. The CPT [14] model is capable of color-filling images and text at the same time, while performing cloze tasks on both visual and text. PointCLIP [16] utilizes the knowledge from the pre-trained model to achieve point cloud understanding by introducing an inter-view adapter to preform feature interaction among multiple views. Denseclip [11] transfers the knowledge of the pre-trained model to the dense prediction tasks by converting the image-text matching in the pre-training task into pixel-text matching, and prompting the language model through the image context, which is mostly related to ours. Although DenseCLIP performs well on segmentation task, the improvements on detection are not significant, and we believe that the reason is that object detection tasks require local constraints. We propose a cross-modality feature enhancement module and a region-text matching module to introduce local constraints while perceiving the global information of the image.

Video Object Detection. Video object detection is a challenge visual task that involves detecting objects in each frame of a video. Unlike image object detection, there are problems such as blur, occlusion, and defocus caused by motion in the video. Therefore, the objective of video object detection is. Therefore, the objective of video object detection is to enhance the detection accuracy and speed by utilizing the temporal information exsisting in the video.

Several previous approaches have enhanced the detection results of static detectors through post-processing [5,7,8], but these methods are not end-to-end. Other methods aggregate and propagate features through optical flow [19–21] across frames, which can improve detection accuracy or speed to a certain extent, but the results depend on the accuracy of optical flow estimation, which is not robust enough for objects appearance changes and raises suboptimization problems. An alternative way to improve detection performance is to aggregate features at the semantic level [3,13]. Employing more sophisticated techniques such as incorporating extra memory networks [1,2] or attention mechanisms can further boost the performance of detectors.

Although the methods used for improving video performance are generally effective, they do not yield significant improvements for drone-captured videos. These videos often contain numerous small objects, resulting in limited visual information. Furthermore, when the neural network becomes deeper, the visual features of objects tend to be lost. Consequently, it is essential to first enhance the visual features before fusing them across frames.

3   Method

The model's overall structure is presented in Fig. 2. It begins with a pre-trained CLIP model that utilizes an image encoder and a text encoder for feature extraction. Then, a Cross-Modal Feature Enhancement (CMFE) module is introduced to provide visual supplemental information from text supervision. The CMFE module is composed of two sub-modules, the vision-to-text enhancement module and the text-to-vision enhancement module, which allows the model to learn from both modalities and leverage the pre-trained model's knowledge effectively. Finally, an Attention-guided Frame-level Feature Aggregation module is utilized to further exploit the temporal information within videos and improve the detection performance.

3.1   Preliminary: Feature Extraction

The feature extraction module is based on the CLIP framework. The original CLIP network adds an attention pool layer to the backbone network, leaving only the global feature of the image as the output of the image encoder for subsequent processing and ignoring other feature maps. However, we believe that although the global feature contains the global semantic information of the image, it lacks the more fine-grained representation required for detection, and the ignored feature map fully retains the spatial information of the image and can be used for subsequent detection. Therefore, unlike the original design of CLIP, the output of our image encoder contains the global feature and retains the remaining features as the local feature for detection. Specifically, we pass a single-frame input image through the image encoder to obtain the feature maps X, and we select one feature map $x_i \in X$ through an attention module to obtain the image global feature map x_g and the image local feature map x_l by:

$$(x_g, x_l) = AttentionModule(x_i) \tag{1}$$

In order to provide richer visual features for UAV-based video object detection, we design two methods to obtain the global and local features of the image, as shown in Fig. 3. The first choice we consider is simple linear layers, in which the feature map x_i from the backbone network is passed through the global average pooling layer and the fully connected layer to obtain the global feature x_g, and the local feature x_l is obtained by x_i through the fully connected layer. Inspired by the BAM [9], the second option is to use a spatial encoder by applying the channel attention to obtain the global feature x_g and the spatial attention to obtain the local feature x_l on the feature map x_i extracted by backbone. In order to fully perceive visual information, the global feature x_g and the local feature x_l are concatenated as the visual context representation f_c by:

$$f_c = Concatenate(x_g, x_l) \tag{2}$$

3.2   Cross-Modal Feature Enhancement

We consider learning visual representations from text supervision for objects in UAV-based video frames with insufficient visual information. The design of using a fixed template like "A photo of [CLS]" in original CLIP is not optimal and has poor scalability for downstream tasks. To strengthen the multimodal association between the visual and textual context and improve the transfer of pre-training knowledge to the downstream task, we are inspired by CoOp [17] and construct a learnable text embedding denoted by $T = \{V, e_k\}_{k=1}^{K}$ to serve as the input to the text encoder. The V represents the learnable context, while e_k denotes the embedding of k-th class names. By combining these, we produce the context of K class names. A 12-layer transformer is adopted as the text encoder and we can extract the text feature $t \in R^{K \times C}$ by:

$$t = TextEncoder(T) \tag{3}$$

To make full use of the knowledge from text supervision, a module called Cross-Modal Feature Enhancement(CMFE) was developed. This module is designed to enhance multi-modal features from different detection stages and is comprised of two sub-modules: Vision-to-Text Enhancement (VTE) and Text-to-Vision Enhancement (TVE). The VTE sub-module helps the text embeddings to improve the understanding of shallow visual context information. On the other hand, the TVE sub-module integrates text and shallow visual information to improve visual representations, resulting in better detection performance.

Vision-to-Text Enhancement Module. Since objects with insufficient visual information in UAV-based videos tend to lose features as the network deepens, we develop a method that involves incorporating text to help maintain more visual features from the shallow network. Specifically, our approach utilize the text feature t as query, the visual context feature f_c as key and value, and applies a transformer decoder for multi-modal interaction. The resulting visual-enhanced text feature t_e is obtained using the following formula:

$$t_e = t + \alpha TransformerDecoder(t, f_c) \tag{4}$$

where the α is a learnable temperature coefficient. According to prompt the language model by visual information, the text feature can perceive both global and local context of the image in the spatial dimension, while also aligning the two modalities more closely in feature space.

Text-to-Vision Enhancement Module. We pass the local feature x_l through the RPN(Region Proposal Network) to generate region proposals and extract region features R by the RoIAlign (Region of Interest Align) network. In order to obtain visual complementary information from the shallow network while making better use of knowledge from pre-trained CLIP models, we design a TVE module.

$$R = RoIAlign(RPN(x_l)) \tag{5}$$

The module begins by calculating matching maps between vision-enhanced text features and region features, as is shown in Eq. 6, which helps to measure the degree of matching between text and region. This transformation of the image-text matching task in pre-training into a region-text matching task that is more suitable for video object detection, and we eliminate the gap between the pre-training and downstream detection task. Then, the text-enhanced region feature Re is obtained by concatenate these matching maps along the channel dimension into region feature R.

$$M = R{t_e}^T \tag{6}$$

$$R_e = Concatenate(R, M) \tag{7}$$

According to this module, the visual model can explicitly incorporate the language prior, while supplementing the region feature with visual information from the shallow layer.

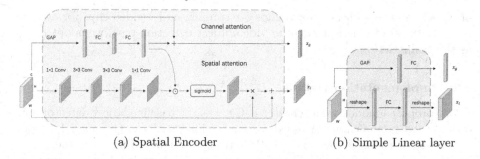

(a) Spatial Encoder   (b) Simple Linear layer

Fig. 3. Two different strategies to get image context.

3.3 Attention-Guided Frame-Level Feature Aggregation

Compared to images, videos can present more challenges for static detection algorithms due to motion blur, occlusion, etc., caused by objects moving between frames. This makes it harder for the algorithms to accurately detect objects in each frame. Object detection in videos can be improved by utilizing temporal information and aggregate features across multiple frames to compensate for low-quality frames, so an important question is to choose the proper frames for reference. Adjacent video frames have great similarity, and there is a lot of redundant information, while frames far apart have too much appearance variation, which cannot be a good reference for low-quality objects. Considering the above factors, by using the frame to be detected as a key frame and randomly selecting reference frames from within a temporal window, we can utilize an attention-guided approach to more accurately detect low-quality objects by aggregating more comprehensive features at frame-level.

We denote the text-enhanced region feature for the key frame as $R_e{}^{key}$, and the text-enhanced region features for the reference frames as $R_e{}^{ref}$. The relevance between the text-enhanced region features of the key frame and the reference frames are measured by computing an attention score:

$$S = softmax(R_e{}^{key}(R_e{}^{ref})^T/\sqrt{d}) \tag{8}$$

where d is a scaling factor. We use this score as a guidance to weight the aggregation of the text-enhanced region features of the reference frame to the key frame, a residual connection is also applied:

$$R_e{}^{key} = R_e{}^{key} + SR_e{}^{ref} \tag{9}$$

4 Experiments

4.1 Datasets and Evaluation Protocol

VisDrone-VID2019 [18] is a large-scale benchmark of video object detection which was captured by unmanned aerial vehicles (UAVs). It contains 10 classes of objects and provides 56 video clips for training and 7 video clips for evaluation. As the traditional protocol in video object detection task, we adopt mAP as the evaluation metric.

4.2   Implementation Details

In our proposed model, we use Faster R-CNN as the baseline object detector and our method is implemented based on mmtracking toolbox. Our model adopts ResNet-50 as the backbone and CLIP pretrained weights to initialize the image and text encoders. The weights of the text encoder are fixed in the training process to ensure that the model can effectively utilize the pre-trained knowledge. For the text prompt, we set up 8 learnable token embeddings to perceive the context. And we utilize a transformer decoder with 3 layers and 4 heads for multimodal association in CMFE module, which can prompt the language model to perceive the visual context in spatial dimension. During the training process, we utilize the AdamW optimizer and the image encoder's learning rate is set to 1/10 of the other parameters. For training, the current frame is used as a key frame and two random frames from the same video are sampled as reference frames. During inference, 14 frames from the same video are sampled alongside the inference frame. Both training and inference require the images to be resized to 1333×800 pixels.

Table 1. Performance comparison with strong video object detection models on VisDrone-VID2019 *val*.

Model	mAP	AP_S	AP_M	AP_L	FPS
DFF	18.8	2.0	7.0	21.1	59.3
FGFA	32.6	4.7	14.1	28.7	3.4
SELSA	33.4	5.1	14.8	30.5	4.6
Ours	**37.7**	4.7	16.8	29.3	4.1

Table 2. Effectiveness of each module in our framework on VisDrone-VID2019 *val*.

Model	TVE	VTE	AFFA	mAP	AP_S	AP_M	AP_L
Baseline				31.4	3.6	14.0	29.1
	✓			35.9	4.6	16.8	30.7
	✓	✓		36.4	4.9	16.1	31.2
Ours	✓	✓	✓	**37.7**	4.7	16.8	29.3

4.3   Ablation Study

Main Results. We compare our method with several excellent video object detection methods. Table 1 shows a comparison of precision and frames-per-second(fps) performance. Our approach provides superior performance compared to these strong video object detection methods while maintaining a comparable frame rate. Compared to DFF [21] and FGFA [20], two optical flow-based methods, our RoICLIP improves the mAP by 18.9% and 5.1%, separately. Our proposed method offers a unique combination of accuracy and speed, surpassing the two optical flow-based methods in detection accuracy while providing a detection rate that lies in between the two. This is achieved by randomly sampling reference frames in the same video, which reduces invalid calculations while still providing enough inter-frame information. When compared to SELSA [13], a video object detector that aggregates features at the semantic level, our method is superior. This is because we integrate textual knowledge to enhance the region features, which leads to a better understanding of the visual context. As a result, our method is more robust to changes in the appearance of objects in videos. Our method outperforms SELSA [13] by achieving a 4.3% improvement in mAP while maintaining the comparable fps.

Effectiveness of Each Module in Our Framework. We conduct several experiments to demonstrate the effectiveness of each module in our framework as is shown in Table 2. We adopt general Faster R-CNN as our baseline, the method proposed by us provides a 6.3% mAP gain over the baseline detector, with a final mAP of 37.7%. The addition of the TVE module yielded the highest increase in mAP, with an improvement of 4.5%, highlighting the significance of converting the pre-trained image-text matching task to the downstream region-text matching task for effectively transferring the knowledge from pre-trained models. Furthermore, the VTE module provided an additional 0.5% mAP improvement, demonstrating the benefit of cross-modal interaction through feature alignment between the visual and text modalities. Finally, the AFFA module was used to aggregate features at the frame-level, resulting in a 1.3% mAP improvement, confirming the importance of incorporating temporal information in the video for improving the accuracy of the video object detection task.

Table 3. Comparison of three attention methods in backbone on VisDrone-VID2019 *val*. wht: with temporal information, atp: attention pool, sln: simple linear, spe: spatial encoder.

Dataset		VisDrone VID				ImageNet VID
attn_type	wht	mAP	AP_S	AP_M	AP_L	mAP
atp		35.4	5.0	15.9	30.2	–
sln		36.4	4.9	16.1	31.2	–
spe		**36.9**	5.4	16.3	30.0	–
atp	✓	35.9	6.3	16.3	27.7	69.0
sln	✓	**37.7**	4.7	16.8	29.3	68.3
spe	✓	34.5	5.1	15.3	27.2	**69.2**

Table 4. Compare with DenseCLIP on two datasets.

Dataset		VisDrone-VID2019				ImageNet VID
Model	wht	mAP	AP_S	AP_M	AP_L	mAP
DenseCLIP		35.4	5.6	15.9	28.8	–
Ours		**36.9**	5.4	16.3	30.0	–
DenseCLIP	✓	35.7	6.1	16.5	24.7	44.9
Ours	✓	**37.7**	4.7	16.8	29.3	**69.2**

Comparison of Three Attention Methods in Backbone. We experiment with three different attention methods to obtain global features and local features. Table 3 shows the comparison of three attention methods on the VisDrone-VID2019 dataset based on static image detectors and video detectors. The static image detector without the AFFA module achieved the best results when using a spatial encoder, scoring 36.9% mAP. The video detector with a simple linear layer had the highest performance, reaching 37.7% mAP. In order to further verify the effectiveness of the module, we also conducted experiments on the large video object detection dataset ImageNet VID [12]. As is shown in Table 3, the video detector with the spatial encoder was able to attain the best result of 69.2% mAP.

Comparison with the Related Method. Table 4 shows the comparison of our framework and related work DenseCLIP [11] on two video datasets. The results show that based on the static detector, our method can reach 36.9% mAP on the VisDrone-VID2019 dataset, surpassing DenseCLIP 1.5% mAP based on Faster R-CNN. For fair comparison based on video detectors, we add AFFA module to DenseCLIP for cross-frame feature aggregation. It can be achieved on the VisDrone-VID2019 dataset 35.7% mAP, which is 0.3% mAP higher than static DenseCLIP, which suggests that our AFFA module is a reliable plug-and-play solution for improving the performance of static detectors. On the VisDrone-VID2019 dataset, the method achieves 37.7% mAP, which is 2.0% mAP higher than DenseCLIP. Similarly, on the ImageNet VID dataset, our method achieves 69.2% AP50, surpassing DenseCLIP 24.3% AP50. It appears that the region-text matching in our TVE module is more effective for downstream detection tasks than the pixel-text matching used by DenseCLIP, which explains the improved performance compared to that of DenseCLIP.

4.4 Visualization

Figure 4 shows several detection results with scores greater than 0.8 obtained by RoICLIP and we compared them with baseline. Figure 4 demonstrates that our method significantly enhances the detection of small objects compared to the baseline approach. Moreover, in situations where there is insufficient visual information such as occlusion and lighting changes, our method exhibits a remarkable improvement in performance over the baseline method. These findings suggest that our method is more appropriate for detecting small objects and more robust in dealing with challenging scenarios, potentially enhancing the accuracy and robustness of object detection in various contexts.

(a) Baseline   (b) Ours

Fig. 4. Visualization of our methods.

5   Conclusion

We present a new UAV-based video object detection framework RoICLIP by transferring the knowledge from pre-trained CLIP models to the downstream UAV-based video object detection task. RoICLIP is a novel framework that can use learnable prompts to perceive image spatial context and use knowledge in a way that is more suitable for pre-training tasks, while also utilizing rich temporal information in videos to improve the quality of object features. We have conducted massive experiments to prove that our method can improve the object detection accuracy of both static images and videos.

Acknowledgements. This work was supported by the National Key Research and Development Program of China in the 14th Five-Year (Nos. 2021YFFO602103 and 2021YFF0602102).

References

1. Chen, Y., Cao, Y., Hu, H., Wang, L.: Memory enhanced global-local aggregation for video object detection. In: Proceedings of the IEEE/CVF Conference on Computer Vision and Pattern Recognition, pp. 10337–10346 (2020)
2. Deng, H., et al.: Object guided external memory network for video object detection. In: Proceedings of the IEEE/CVF International Conference on Computer Vision, pp. 6678–6687 (2019)
3. Deng, J., Pan, Y., Yao, T., Zhou, W., Li, H., Mei, T.: Relation distillation networks for video object detection. In: Proceedings of the IEEE/CVF International Conference on Computer Vision, pp. 7023–7032 (2019)
4. Gao, P., et al.: Clip-adapter: better vision-language models with feature adapters. arXiv preprint arXiv:2110.04544 (2021)
5. Han, W., et al.: Seq-NMS for video object detection. arXiv preprint arXiv:1602.08465 (2016)
6. Jia, C., et al.: Scaling up visual and vision-language representation learning with noisy text supervision. In: International Conference on Machine Learning, pp. 4904–4916. PMLR (2021)
7. Kang, K., et al.: T-cnn: Tubelets with convolutional neural networks for object detection from videos. IEEE Trans. Circuits Syst. Video Technol. **28**(10), 2896–2907 (2017)
8. Kang, K., Ouyang, W., Li, H., Wang, X.: Object detection from video tubelets with convolutional neural networks. In: Proceedings of the IEEE Conference on Computer Vision and Pattern Recognition, pp. 817–825 (2016)
9. Park, J., Woo, S., Lee, J.Y., Kweon, I.S.: Bam: bottleneck attention module. arXiv preprint arXiv:1807.06514 (2018)
10. Radford, A., et al.: Learning transferable visual models from natural language supervision. In: International Conference on Machine Learning, pp. 8748–8763. PMLR (2021)
11. Rao, Y., et al.: DenseCLIP: language-guided dense prediction with context-aware prompting. In: Proceedings of the IEEE/CVF Conference on Computer Vision and Pattern Recognition, pp. 18082–18091 (2022)
12. Russakovsky, O., et al.: ImageNet large scale visual recognition challenge. Int. J. Comput. Vision **115**, 211–252 (2014)
13. Wu, H., Chen, Y., Wang, N., Zhang, Z.: Sequence level semantics aggregation for video object detection. In: Proceedings of the IEEE/CVF International Conference on Computer Vision, pp. 9217–9225 (2019)
14. Yao, Y., Zhang, A., Zhang, Z., Liu, Z., Chua, T.S., Sun, M.: Cpt: colorful prompt tuning for pre-trained vision-language models. arXiv preprint arXiv:2109.11797 (2021)
15. Zhang, R., et al.: Tip-adapter: training-free clip-adapter for better vision-language modeling. arXiv preprint arXiv:2111.03930 (2021)
16. Zhang, R., et al.: PointCLIP: point cloud understanding by clip. In: Proceedings of the IEEE/CVF Conference on Computer Vision and Pattern Recognition, pp. 8552–8562 (2022)
17. Zhou, K., Yang, J., Loy, C.C., Liu, Z.: Learning to prompt for vision-language models. Int. J. Comput. Vision **130**(9), 2337–2348 (2022)
18. Zhu, P., et al.: Visdrone-vid2019: the vision meets drone object detection in video challenge results. In: 2019 IEEE/CVF International Conference on Computer Vision Workshop (ICCVW), pp. 227–235 (2019). https://doi.org/10.1109/ICCVW.2019.00031

19. Zhu, X., Dai, J., Yuan, L., Wei, Y.: Towards high performance video object detection. In: Proceedings of the IEEE Conference on Computer Vision and Pattern Recognition, pp. 7210–7218 (2018)
20. Zhu, X., Wang, Y., Dai, J., Yuan, L., Wei, Y.: Flow-guided feature aggregation for video object detection. In: Proceedings of the IEEE International Conference on Computer Vision, pp. 408–417 (2017)
21. Zhu, X., Xiong, Y., Dai, J., Yuan, L., Wei, Y.: Deep feature flow for video recognition. In: Proceedings of the IEEE Conference on Computer Vision and Pattern Recognition, pp. 2349–2358 (2017)

Class Incremental Learning
with Important and Diverse Memory

Mei Li, Zeyu Yan, and Changsheng Li[✉]

School of Computer Science and Technology, Beijing Institute of Technology,
Beijing, China
{lcs,yzy}@bit.edu.cn, limei_siner@163.com

Abstract. Class incremental learning (CIL) has been attracting increasing attention in computer vision and machine learning communities, where a well-known issue is catastrophic forgetting. To mitigate this issue, a popular approach is to utilize the replay-based strategy, which stores a small portion of past data and replays it when learning new tasks. However, selecting valuable samples from previous classes for replaying remains an open problem in class incremental learning. In this paper, we propose a novel sample selection strategy aimed at maintaining effective samples from old classes to address the catastrophic forgetting issue. Specifically, we employ the influence function to evaluate the impact of each sample on model performance, and then select important samples for replay. However, given the potential redundancy among selected samples when only considering importance, we also develop a diversity strategy to select not only important but also diverse samples from old classes. We conduct extensive empirical validations on the CIFAR10 and CIFAR100 datasets and the results demonstrate that our proposed method outperforms the baselines, effectively alleviating the catastrophic forgetting issue in class incremental learning.

Keywords: Class incremental learning · Catastrophic forgetting · Influence function · Diversity

1 Introduction

Class incremental learning has recently gained significant attention as it allows for continuous learning of new knowledge from streaming data and gradually incorporates this knowledge into the model, building a common model for all tasks and classes [1,2]. However, this approach is known to suffer from catastrophic forgetting [3–5], where training on subsequent tasks may potentially erase information in the model parameters pertaining to previous tasks, mainly due to the inaccessibility of data for classes in previous tasks.

To mitigate knowledge forgetting while sequentially updating the model on a stream of tasks, various approaches have been proposed, including regularization-based methods (e.g., [4,6]), architecture-based methods (e.g., [7,8]) and replay-based methods [9–11]. Among these methods, replay-based methods are representative, which maintains a memory to store a small portion of the old data for

© The Author(s), under exclusive license to Springer Nature Switzerland AG 2023
H. Lu et al. (Eds.): ICIG 2023, LNCS 14358, pp. 164–175, 2023.
https://doi.org/10.1007/978-3-031-46314-3_13

each task or class, and jointly optimizes the model on the samples from both the memory and new task [12,13]. These methods recognize that the unavailability of old data is the root cause of performance degradation. With just 1% of saved old data using random sampling, a significant improvement can be achieved over other approaches in continual learning [13].

However, the replay-based method naturally raises another important question: *what is the optimal strategies to manage the memory?*. As the number of stored samples is much smaller than the entire old data, it is crucial to select representative samples that cover the structure of the old data as much as possible, or the biased samples would either incur overfitting or be ignored during training due to their small amount. However, previous studies have largely relied on random or simpler herding exemplar selection, resulting in redundant or non-representative samples. Thus, it is necessary to develop more effective approaches for maintaining sufficient information of old classes, especially when only a small number of samples are available.

To tackle this challenge, we propose a new strategy focused on selecting samples that are both important and diverse—a perspective not previously explored. We put forward a memory management approach based on influence function that measures the per-sample impact on model predictions to identify highly significant and varied samples to be stored in the memory buffer. As there may be redundancy among the selected samples when only considering importance, we have also developed a diversity strategy. This strategy enables the selection of not only important but also diverse samples from old classes. We evaluate our method on the CIFAR10 and CIFAR100 datasets, demonstrating its effectiveness in mitigating catastrophic forgetting compared to the baselines.

2   Related Work

We will briefly review three kinds of related works related to class incremental learning [2]:

Architecture-Based Methods: The work in [14] involves isolating specific parameters and gradually expanding the model's parameters and architectures as new tasks arise [15]. Conversely, other methods select a task-specific sub-network for each new task [16–18]. While some dynamic architecture methods, such as CNDPM [19], do not require a task-ID.IWR [20] suggests utilizing a dependency-preserving hypernetwork to produce weights for the target network. Nevertheless, these approaches have limitations, either because of memory consumption or effectiveness.

Regularization-Based Methods: This method aims to prevent catastrophic forgetting by avoiding large changes in model parameters compared to previous iterations [13]. This is achieved usually by adding additional regularization terms to the loss function [21] or modifying the gradient of the parameters during backpropagation [22]. LwF [23] preserves knowledge learned from past tasks via knowledge distillation [24] in the multi-head setting. Other works use selective synaptic plasticity [25], attention map distillation [26], and variational inference framework [27] for model regularization in continual learning. However, these methods perform poorly in longer task sequences and online CIL setup considered in this paper [12].

Replay-Based Methods: These methods tackle catastrophic forgetting by either storing a subset of previous examples in an additional, relatively small memory [9], or by synthesizing past data using generative models and replaying them in the subsequent tasks [3,10]. GEM [11] restrict parameter updates using the samples in the memory buffer. MIR [28] selects replay samples based on loss increases following estimated parameter updates. MER [29] combines episodic memory with meta-learning, DER++ [30] enhances ER with logits distillation on memory samples, HAL [31] adds an objective term on the meta-learned anchor data points, and RRR [32] stores saliency maps with images and applies a saliency-based regularization objective for less drift on past tasks. However, all replay-based methods have a common challenge of sample selection, which some previous works address through proper memory management strategies to improve sample representativeness [12,31,33]. ER [9] applies random sampling to replay samples in the next task, ensuring each sample has an equal probability of selection, but its impact on performance can be accidental. ICaRL [34] attempts to select the central samples per class, but is limited to its specific classifier. OTGNet [35] implements a method of selecting both important and diverse sample sets, however, it is designed for the graph neural networks. In contrast, we propose a universal and improved approach that focuses on per-sample importance and diversity for replay-based methods, resulting in enhanced performance.

3   Preliminary and Problem Formulation

We define class incremental learning as a series of tasks $\{T_1, T_2, ..., T_t\} = T$, where each task T_i consists of independent classes of samples and labels, represented by

$$\mathcal{D}_i = \left\{ x_i^k, y_i^k \right\}_{k=1}^{N_i} \sim \mathcal{X}_i \times \mathcal{Y}_i$$

where N_i denotes the total number of training data in the i-th task, while $\mathcal{X}_i$ and $\mathcal{Y}_i$ represent the corresponding training data sets and label sets, respectively. Additionally, for any two tasks T_a and T_b, their label sets $\mathcal{Y}_a$ and $\mathcal{Y}_b$ are non-intersecting, as denoted by

$$\mathcal{Y}_a \cap \mathcal{Y}_b = \emptyset, \forall a \neq b$$

The classifier model's parameters are denoted by θ, and the output obtained by feeding an input x into the model is represented as $f_\theta(x)$. For a given task T_i, we define the training objective as follows:

$$\underset{\theta}{\text{argmin}} \sum_{(x,y) \in D_i} l\left(y, f_\theta(x)\right) \tag{1}$$

We use the cross-entropy loss function (represented by l) as our chosen loss function.

To mitigate the issue of catastrophic forgetting, a replay-based approach to class incremental learning has been employed. Specifically, this approach involves preserving the exemplars of each prior task within the task T_i, as denoted by

$$\mathcal{M}_j = \left\{x_j^k, y_j^k\right\}_{k=1}^M \sim \mathcal{D}_j, \forall j < i$$

where M represents the number of exemplars per class, $M \ll N_i$. For the sake of brevity, we omit the subscript of $\mathcal{M}_j$ in the following text and use $\mathcal{M}$ to refer to it. It's worth noting that the total number of exemplars stored in all previous tasks is limited to a fixed upper bound, denoted by K.

4   Proposed Methodology

To maximize the value of stored limited exemplars and mitigate the problem of catastrophic forgetting, we propose a novel sample selection strategy to preserve effective samples of old classes. First, we use the influence function to assess the impact of each sample on the model's performance. Based on this analysis, we select the most important samples for retention and replaying. Second, to avoid selecting redundant samples when focusing only on important ones, we implement a diversity strategy that enables us to choose not only important but also diverse samples from old classes.

4.1   Important Sample Selection

In order to determine the significance of a sample, we assess the impact it has on the model's performance if it were to be removed. The more influential a sample is, the more informative it is deemed to be, and the more critical it becomes to retain. One direct way to evaluate this is to iteratively remove individual training points and retrain the model. However, this approach can be highly time-consuming, presenting a significant challenge. Drawing inspiration from the concept of influence function [36, 37], we propose an extension to estimate the potential change in model parameters resulting from upweighting a given sample by a small amount ϵ. Specifically, for any training sample z_c^k, where c denotes its class and k represents its index within the class, we estimate its impact on model parameters as follows:

$$\mathcal{L}_{params}\left(z_c^k\right) = \left.\frac{d\theta_{\epsilon, z_c^k}}{d\epsilon}\right|_{\epsilon=0} = -H_\theta^{-1} \nabla_\theta L\left(z_c^k, \theta\right) \tag{2}$$

where L represents the loss function, H_θ is the Hessian matrix, and θ_{ϵ, z_c^k} denotes the parameters of a retrained model if the sample z_c^k were upweighted by a small amount ϵ. To evaluate the influence of sample z_c^k, we apply the chain rule by computing the change in the model loss, denoted as:

$$\mathcal{L}_{loss}(z_c^k, \theta) = \frac{dL(S_c, \theta_{\epsilon, z_c^k})}{d\epsilon}\bigg|_{\epsilon=0} \tag{3}$$

$$= \nabla_\theta L(S_c, \theta)^\top \frac{d\theta_{\epsilon, z_c^k}}{d\epsilon}\bigg|_{\epsilon=0}$$

$$= -\nabla_\theta L(S_c, \theta)^\top H_\theta^{-1} \nabla_\theta L(z_c^k, \theta)$$

where S_c refers to the data set of class c. The notations $\nabla_\theta L(S_c, \theta)$ and $\nabla_\theta L(z_c^k, \theta)$ represent the gradients of the loss with respect to S_c and z_c^k, respectively. We evaluate the significance of training data using $\mathcal{L}_{loss}(z_c^k, \theta)$ as the criterion. A more negative $\mathcal{L}_{loss}(z_c^k, \theta)$ indicates that the sample z_c^k has a greater positive impact on model performance, meaning that it is more important for training.

Given limited memory resources, our goal is to retain the most important past samples to better preserve prior knowledge. To achieve this, we compute influence values for each sample in every class c for a given task, and subsequently rank all training samples based on their influence. We prioritize the most influential samples to construct the candidate set $\mathcal{R}_c$. Our objective function is defined as follows:

$$\mathcal{R}_c = \underset{\{z_{c,1}, z_{c,2}, \dots, z_{c,3M}\}}{\arg\min} \sum_{i=1}^{3M} \mathcal{L}_{loss}(z_{c,i}, \theta) \tag{4}$$

4.2   Diverse Sample Selection

We acknowledge that the complexity of real-world data means that selecting only important samples may result in a high level of redundancy among the selected samples, which could negatively impact performance. As a solution, we aim to replace redundant samples with diverse ones so that our selected sample set $\mathcal{R}_c$ is not only important but also diverse. To determine the similarity between two samples, we calculate the distance between their respective features using the following formula:

$$\mathcal{P}(z_{c,i}) = \{z_{c,j} | \|h(z_{c,j}) - h(z_{c,i})\|_2 \le \eta, z_{c,j} \in \mathcal{R}_c\} \tag{5}$$

where $h(z_{c,j})$ represents the features of $z_{c,j}$, and η represents a similar radius. $\mathcal{P}(z_{c,i})$ denotes the set of similar samples to $z_{c,i}$. To select samples, we use $\mathcal{P}(z_{c,i})$ to exclude those that are similar.

4.3   Important and Diverse Sample Selection

We propose an approach that combines the two methods described above to perform important and diverse sample selection, as outlined in Algorithm 1.

To begin with, we use the influence function to estimate the importance of each sample and obtain a candidate set. Next, we assess the similarity between samples in the candidate set to generate a set of similar samples for each individual sample. We prioritize important samples and mark their similar samples. Next time, when encountering a sample that has been marked, we will skip them directly to avoid selecting similar samples, resulting in a set of samples that are both important and diverse.

Algorithm 1: Important and Diverse Sample Selection

Input: all training data $\mathcal{D}_i^c$ for class c in task $\mathcal{T}_i$; M that is the memory size of each class;

Output: important and diverse samples G_c for class c;

1 Initialize $G_c = \Phi$ and the influence function list as empty; Let $R_c = \Phi$, which represents the candidate set sorted by importance;

2 **for** $x \in \mathcal{D}_i^c$ **do**

3   Obtain the importance of x by calculating the influence function using Equation 3: $v = \mathcal{L}_{loss}(x, \theta)$;

4   Add v to the influence function list;

5 Obtain the candidate set R_c according to Equation 4;

6 **for** $x \in R_c$ **do**

7   Calculate the similar sample set $\mathcal{P}(x)$ according to Equation 5;

8 **for** $x \in R_c, |G_c| < M$ **do**

9   If x is not marked as a similar sample, append x to G_c and then mark the similar samples according to $\mathcal{P}(x)$;

10   If x is marked as a similar sample, skip it;

11 **return** G_c;

---

5   Experiments

Based on the theory presented above, we conduct extensive experiments on the CIFAR-100 [13] and CIFAR-10 [13] datasets to demonstrate the feasibility and effectiveness of our method. Our approach is evaluated using widely used benchmark protocols for each dataset, and we also conduct ablation experiments to investigate the impact of different components of our approach.

5.1   Experiment Setup and Implementation Details

Datasets. We employ two widely-used image classification datasets: CIFAR-100 and CIFAR-10. Each dataset consists of 60,000 color images with a resolution of 32×32 pixels, which are split into 50,000 training images and 10,000 test images. However, CIFAR-10 has only 10 categories, with 5,000 training images and 1,000 test images for each category, while CIFAR-100 has 100 categories, with 500 training images and 100 test images for each category.

Table 1. Comparison of average accuracy (%) across all tasks on CIFAR-100 and CIFAR-10. Our experiments are conducted under three different settings on CIFAR-100: 5, 10 and 20 steps, and under 5-step setting on CIFAR-10. The best results are highlighted in bold.

Method	CIFAR-100(K = 2,000)			CIFAR-10(K = 500)
	5 steps	10 steps	20 steps	5 steps
iCaRL [34]	55.64	51.19	47.82	53.16
DMC [38]	47.23	37.02	23.67	–
BiC [39]	56.69	51.32	57.16	57.24
BiC-random	55.55	55.42	56.32	59.78
Ours	**61.24**	**61.32**	**60.16**	**72.28**

Testing Protocols. Our experiments adhere to widely used benchmark protocols. To evaluate our method on CIFAR-100, we split the 100 classes into 5, 10, and 20 increments, with each step adding 20, 10, and 5 new classes, respectively. As for CIFAR-10, which has fewer classes, we divided it into 5 increments, with 2 new classes added in each increment. In order to make a fair comparison, we use the same memory size of 2,000 exemplars for CIFAR-100, and set the memory size to 500 for CIFAR-10.

Implementation Details. We implement all experiments using Pytorch. For CIFAR-100, we adopt the ResNet-32 network used in previous works [34]. The training hyperparameters are consistent with BiC, with 250 epochs per incremental training. The learning rate is initially set to 0.1 and decreases to 0.01, 0.001, and 0.0001 after 100, 150, and 200 epochs, respectively. Weight decay is 0.0002, and the batch size is 128. For CIFAR-10, we employ ResNet-18 [13] as our backbone network. BiC uses herding-based exemplar selection to identify the sample that has the closest mean value to the real sample. In order to assess the efficacy of our approach, we replace BiC's sample selection strategy with random sampling and conduct a comparative analysis.

Metrics. We adopt two commonly used metrics from the CIL literature [40] to assess the effectiveness of our approach.

1. Average Accuracy (AA): indicates the average test accuracy of all previous tasks, including the current one, after completing incremental learning for a task. The formula is as follows: $AA = \frac{1}{t} \sum_{i=1}^{t} aa_i$, where aa_i is the test accuracy of task $\mathcal{T}_i$, and t is the total number of tasks completed thus far.
2. Average Forgetting (AF): is the mean difference between the highest accuracy achieved on a set of previously learned tasks and the accuracy obtained for the final task after all incremental learning tasks have been completed. The formula is as follows: $AF = \frac{1}{t-1} \sum_{i=1}^{t-1} \max_{j \in \{1,...,t-1\}} (a_{j,i} - a_{t,i})$, where $a_{j,i}$ represents the test accuracy of task $\mathcal{T}_j$ on the newly added class in task $\mathcal{T}_i$.

Table 2. Comparison with the average forgetting (%) metric (lower values are preferable) for CIFAR-100 and CIFAR-10 datasets across all tasks. The best results are highlighted in bold.

Method	CIFAR-100(K = 2,000)			CIFAR-10(K = 500)
	5 steps	10 steps	20 steps	5 steps
iCaRL [34]	24.05	30.61	38.36	47.40
BiC [39]	13.64	12.91	16.99	0.28
BiC-random	15.51	14.90	17.14	3.63
Ours	**9.95**	**8.69**	**13.22**	**−0.20**

5.2 Results

We conduct a comparison of our approach to other works in class incremental learning, as summarized in Table 1. Our work is centered around sample selection strategies. To demonstrate the benefits of our approach, we use BiC as a baseline and compare several variations in its sample selection strategy. Specifically, we compare BiC's original herding sample selection approach, random selection, and our proposed strategy. Our strategy selects samples that have a significant impact on the results while also aiming for diversity. We conduct comparative experiments to evaluate the effect of incorporating diversity into the selection process.

Table 1 shows that our method outperforms other sample selection strategies for CIFAR-100 across all experimental settings. Specifically, in the 5-step incremental learning setting, our method achieves a final average classification accuracy of 61.24%, which is 5.69% and 4.55% higher than the random selection method and herding selection method [34], respectively. Our sample selection strategy consistently outperforms other methods, demonstrating its effectiveness across various settings. Notably, our approach performs equally well on both the CIFAR-10 and CIFAR-100 datasets, indicating that it is more useful than currently used strategies in mitigating catastrophic forgetting.

Table 2 presents the average forgetting metric (AF) for CIFAR-100 and CIFAR-10, which demonstrates that our method exhibits less forgetting of old knowledge compared to other replay-based methods. This is also the reason for the improvement in average accuracy. Our experiments indicate that our method outperforms other baselines not only in terms of average accuracy but also in its ability to resist forgetting of old knowledge.

5.3 Ablation Studies

We also conduct ablation experiments to evaluate our proposed method, as shown in Table 3. When selecting only the most important samples for analysis, there is a risk that these samples may be too similar to accurately represent the entire data distribution. To address this issue, we compare our method with and without adding diversity. The experimental results demonstrate that the method with added diversity outperforms the method without diversity. This could be due to the redundancy of highly similar samples among the important samples. Adding diversity helps ensure more uniform sampling, which aids the model in retaining discriminative boundaries for each category.

Table 3. Conduct ablation studies using different settings on two datasets to compare the impact of considering diversity versus not considering diversity, while focusing on important samples. The best results are highlighted in bold.

Method	CIFAR-100(K = 2,000)			CIFAR-10(K = 500)
	5 steps	10 steps	20 steps	5 steps
Ours w/o Diversity	59.04	57.74	58.38	66.50
Ours	**61.24**	**61.32**	**60.16**	**72.28**

Table 4. The average accuracy (%) of class incremental learning results for CIFAR-100 and CIFAR-10, using 5 steps where each step comprises 20 classes per increment for CIFAR-100 and 2 classes per increment for CIFAR-10.

	Method	step 1	step 2	step 3	step 4	step 5
CIFAR-100	iCaRL [34]	78.50	69.55	64.13	59.50	55.64
	BiC [39]	84.00	74.69	67.93	61.25	56.69
	BiC-random	85.20	74.59	66.76	60.14	55.55
	Ours w/o Diversity	82.90	75.65	69.07	64.25	59.04
	Ours	82.90	75.35	70.30	65.35	61.24
CIFAR-10	iCaRL [34]	98.50	77.60	68.63	60.05	53.16
	BiC [39]	96.80	82.45	72.03	62.35	57.24
	BiC-random	96.80	77.15	71.77	65.18	59.78
	Ours w/o Diversity	98.90	85.60	77.53	71.48	66.50
	Ours	98.90	91.95	83.30	77.15	72.28

Table 4 presents a detailed overview of the incremental learning steps, while Fig. 1 displays the corresponding results in a more intuitive manner by showing the performance curve of the entire class incremental learning process. The plot clearly demonstrates the change in performance for different methods with each new task. Notably, our method shows a smoother curve, indicating its strong anti-forgetting performance.

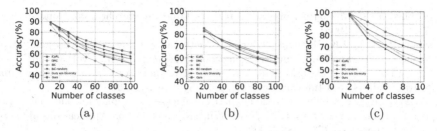

Fig. 1. The classification accuracy of different methods on CIFAR-100 and CIFAR-10 for each incremental task. In particular, (a) corresponds to 10 new classes added per task on CIFAR-100, (b) corresponds to 20 new classes added per task on CIFAR-100 and (c) corresponds to 2 new classes added per task on CIFAR-10.

6 Conclusion

This paper proposes a sample selection strategy that can choose important and diverse samples. The strategy is combined with a replay-based class incremental learning method to better utilize training data, retain old knowledge to a greater extent, and mitigate forgetting. We conduct experiments on two widely-used datasets in class incremental learning, and our results demonstrate the effectiveness of our approach.

Acknowledgements. This work was supported by the NSFC under Grants 62122013, U2001211. This work was also supported by the Innovative Development Joint Fund Key Projects of Shandong NSF under Grants ZR2022LZH007.

References

1. Li, X.: Referencing unlabelled world data to prevent catastrophic forgetting in class-incremental learning, Ph.D. thesis, Virginia Tech (2022)
2. Mai, Z., Li, R., Jeong, J., Quispe, D., Kim, H., Sanner, S.: Online continual learning in image classification: an empirical survey. Neurocomputing **469**, 28–51 (2022)
3. Tang, Y.M., Peng, Y.X., Zheng, W.S.: Learning to imagine: diversify memory for incremental learning using unlabeled data. In: Proceedings of the IEEE/CVF Conference on Computer Vision and Pattern Recognition, pp. 9549–9558 (2022)
4. Leo, J., Kalita, J.: Incremental deep neural network learning using classification confidence thresholding. IEEE Trans. Neural Networks Learn. Syst. **33**(12), 7706–7716 (2021)
5. Feng, K., Li, C., Zhang, X., Zhou, J.: Towards open temporal graph neural networks. arXiv preprint arXiv:2303.15015 (2023)
6. Li, Z., Hoiem, D.: Learning without forgetting. IEEE Trans. Pattern Anal. Mach. Intell. **40**(12), 2935–2947 (2017)
7. Yoon, J., Yang, E., Lee, J., Hwang, S.J.: Lifelong learning with dynamically expandable networks. arXiv preprint arXiv:1708.01547 (2017)
8. Aljundi, R., Chakravarty, P., Tuytelaars, T.: Expert gate: lifelong learning with a network of experts. In: Proceedings of the IEEE Conference on Computer Vision and Pattern Recognition, pp. 3366–3375 (2017)

9. Robins, A.: Catastrophic forgetting, rehearsal and pseudorehearsal. Connect. Sci. **7**(2), 123–146 (1995)
10. Shin, H., Lee, J.K., Kim, J., Kim, J.: Continual learning with deep generative replay. In: Advances in Neural Information Processing Systems, vol. 30 (2017)
11. Lopez-Paz, D., Ranzato, M.: Gradient episodic memory for continual learning. In: Advances in Neural Information Processing Systems, vol. 30 (2017)
12. Saha, G., Roy, K.: Saliency guided experience packing for replay in continual learning. In: Proceedings of the IEEE/CVF Winter Conference on Applications of Computer Vision, pp. 5273–5283 (2023)
13. Tiwari, R., Killamsetty, K., Iyer, R., Shenoy, P.: GCR: gradient coreset based replay buffer selection for continual learning. In: Proceedings of the IEEE/CVF Conference on Computer Vision and Pattern Recognition, pp. 99–108 (2022)
14. Hao, Y., Fu, Y., Jiang, Y.G., Tian, Q.: An end-to-end architecture for class-incremental object detection with knowledge distillation. In: 2019 IEEE International Conference on Multimedia and Expo (ICME), pp. 1–6. IEEE (2019)
15. Rusu, A.A., et al.: Progressive neural networks. arXiv preprint arXiv:1606.04671 (2016)
16. Mallya, A., Lazebnik, S.: PackNet: adding multiple tasks to a single network by iterative pruning. In: Proceedings of the IEEE conference on Computer Vision and Pattern Recognition, pp. 7765–7773 (2018)
17. Saha, G., Garg, I., Ankit, A., Roy, K.: Space: structured compression and sharing of representational space for continual learning. IEEE Access **9**, 150480–150494 (2021)
18. Serra, J., Suris, D., Miron, M., Karatzoglou, A.: Overcoming catastrophic forgetting with hard attention to the task. In: International Conference on Machine Learning, pp. 4548–4557. PMLR (2018)
19. Lee, S., Ha, J., Zhang, D., Kim, G.: A neural dirichlet process mixture model for task-free continual learning. arXiv preprint arXiv:2001.00689 (2020)
20. Chandra, D.S., Varshney, S., Srijith, P., Gupta, S.: Continual learning with dependency preserving hypernetworks. In: Proceedings of the IEEE/CVF Winter Conference on Applications of Computer Vision, pp. 2339–2348 (2023)
21. Lee, S.W., Kim, J.H., Jun, J., Ha, J.W., Zhang, B.T.: Overcoming catastrophic forgetting by incremental moment matching. In: Advances in Neural Information Processing Systems, vol. 30 (2017)
22. Chaudhry, A., Ranzato, M., Rohrbach, M., Elhoseiny, M.: Efficient lifelong learning with a-gem. arXiv preprint arXiv:1812.00420 (2018)
23. Li, Z., Hoiem, D.: Learning without forgetting. IEEE Trans. Pattern Anal. Mach. Intell. **40**(12), 2935–2947 (2017)
24. Feng, K., Li, C., Yuan, Y., Wang, G.: FreeKD: free-direction knowledge distillation for graph neural networks. In: Proceedings of the 28th ACM SIGKDD Conference on Knowledge Discovery and Data Mining, pp. 357–366 (2022)
25. Zenke, F., Poole, B., Ganguli, S.: Continual learning through synaptic intelligence. In: International Conference on Machine Learning, pp. 3987–3995. PMLR (2017)
26. Dhar, P., Singh, R.V., Peng, K.C., Wu, Z., Chellappa, R.: Learning without memorizing. In: Proceedings of the IEEE/CVF Conference on Computer Vision and Pattern Recognition, pp. 5138–5146 (2019)
27. Nguyen, C.V., Li, Y., Bui, T.D., Turner, R.E.: Variational continual learning. arXiv preprint arXiv:1710.10628 (2017)
28. Aljundi, R., Caccia, L., Belilovsky, E., Caccia, M., Lin, M., Charlin, L., Tuytelaars, T.: Online continual learning with maximally interfered retrieval. CoRR abs/1908.04742 (2019), http://arxiv.org/abs/1908.04742

29. Riemer, M., et al.: Learning to learn without forgetting by maximizing transfer and minimizing interference. arXiv preprint arXiv:1810.11910 (2018)

30. Buzzega, P., Boschini, M., Porrello, A., Abati, D., Calderara, S.: Dark experience for general continual learning: a strong, simple baseline. Adv. Neural. Inf. Process. Syst. **33**, 15920–15930 (2020)

31. Chaudhry, A., Gordo, A., Dokania, P., Torr, P., Lopez-Paz, D.: Using hindsight to anchor past knowledge in continual learning. In: Proceedings of the AAAI Conference on Artificial Intelligence, vol. 35, pp. 6993–7001 (2021)

32. Ebrahimi, S., et al.: Remembering for the right reasons: explanations reduce catastrophic forgetting. Appl. AI Lett. **2**(4), e44 (2021)

33. Chaudhry, A., et al.: Continual learning with tiny episodic memories. arXiv:1902.10486 (2019)

34. Rebuffi, S.A., Kolesnikov, A., Sperl, G., Lampert, C.H.: ICaRL: incremental classifier and representation learning. In: Proceedings of the IEEE conference on Computer Vision and Pattern Recognition, pp. 2001–2010 (2017)

35. Feng, K., Li, C., Zhang, X., Zhou, J.: Towards open temporal graph neural networks. In: The Eleventh International Conference on Learning Representations (2023). https://openreview.net/forum?id=N9Pk5iSCzAn

36. Lapedriza, À., Pirsiavash, H., Bylinskii, Z., Torralba, A.: Are all training examples equally valuable? CoRR abs/1311.6510 (2013), http://arxiv.org/abs/1311.6510

37. Koh, P.W., Liang, P.: Understanding black-box predictions via influence functions (2020)

38. Zhang, J., et al.: Class-incremental learning via deep model consolidation. In: Proceedings of the IEEE/CVF Winter Conference on Applications of Computer Vision, pp. 1131–1140 (2020)

39. Wu, Y., et al.: Large scale incremental learning. In: Proceedings of the IEEE/CVF Conference on Computer Vision and Pattern Recognition, pp. 374–382 (2019)

40. Yoon, J., Madaan, D., Yang, E., Hwang, S.J.: Online coreset selection for rehearsal-based continual learning. arXiv preprint arXiv:2106.01085 (2021)

41. Castro, F.M., Marín-Jiménez, M.J., Guil, N., Schmid, C., Alahari, K.: End-to-end incremental learning. In: Proceedings of the European Conference on Computer Vision (ECCV), pp. 233–248 (2018)

42. Liu, Z., Ding, H., Zhong, H., Li, W., Dai, J., He, C.: Influence selection for active learning. CoRR abs/2108.09331 (2021), https://arxiv.org/abs/2108.09331

Core Issues and Key Arguments of ChatGPT: Topic Mining and Sentiment Analysis Based on U.S. News Reports

Shuyi Wang⬡, Da Ren⬡, and Xin Lyu(✉)

Communication University of China, Beijing 100024, People's Republic of China
{shuyiwang,renda}@cuc.edu.cn, lvxincuc@163.com

Abstract. The large language model ChatGPT developed by the American artificial intelligence company OpenAI has quickly become a hot topic in the global media as soon as it is launched. The "Pseudo-Environment" and "discourse field" formed by these media reports have profound implications for governments, industries, and the public. By exploring the core issues and key debates in media coverage of ChatGPT, it is possible to effectively map media attitudes, industry perceptions, and public sentiment. In this study, text mining methods such as sentiment analysis and Latent Dirichlet Allocation (LDA) topic modeling were employed to analyze 2,829 valid news data obtained from the LexisNexis news database. The research results reveal that the news coverage of ChatGPT primarily involves areas such as technological development, functional applications, and social impact. Sentiment analysis indicates that the media generally hold a positive attitude towards ChatGPT, albeit with some negative evaluations. Topic mining results demonstrate that the core issues and key debates include "new challenges of intelligent automation for human labor," "novel human-machine collaboration paradigms," "a new milestone in artificial intelligence," and "new tests for AI ethics and societal issues."

Keywords: ChatGPT · Word Frequency Analysis · Sentiment Analysis · LDA Topic Model

1 Introduction

Recently, a notable artificial intelligence model known as ChatGPT has garnered considerable attention. ChatGPT (Chat Generative Pre-trained Transformer) is a publicly accessible tool derived from GPT language model technology [1], developed by the renowned artificial intelligence laboratory OpenAI in the United States. This advanced model is capable of executing text-based requests, encompassing both simple question-answering tasks and more sophisticated assignments [2]. Furthermore, the generated response text closely resembles natural human language [3]. Launched on November 30, 2022, ChatGPT has been swiftly integrated into a diverse array of domains, including media, education, healthcare, marketing, and entertainment.

H. Lu et al. (Eds.): ICIG 2023, LNCS 14358, pp. 176–185, 2023.
https://doi.org/10.1007/978-3-031-46314-3_14

As of January 2023, ChatGPT boasts over 100 million users, rendering it the fastest growing consumer application to date [4]. As the utilization of ChatGPT becomes increasingly pervasive, its potential societal ramifications become more significant. Evidently, ChatGPT can effectively enhance productivity through various means, such as writing and debugging computer programs, intelligently generating news articles, novels, screenplays, poems, music, academic papers, and more, as well as functioning as translators and intelligent customer service agents. Additionally, it can provide entertainment experiences, including but not limited to real-time chatting and playing games like Tic-Tac-Toe. These functionalities have profoundly impacted modern lifestyles, work dynamics, and social interactions.

Nevertheless, the employment of ChatGPT also raises concerns regarding potential negative consequences, encompassing information leakage, variable factual accuracy, technological fears, algorithmic biases, and ethical and moral questions surrounding its usage. Consequently, ChatGPT has faced criticism from various stakeholders, including educators, journalists, artists, ethicists, academics, and public advocates.

Upon the emergence of technologies, events, or issues with significant societal impact, news media frequently become inundated with relevant stories, creating a mimetic environment that profoundly influences potential consumers [5]. It is evident that media outlets, through their selection of topics and construction of discourse and imagery, shape consumers' comprehension, cognition, attitudes, and judgments. The pivotal role of media in facilitating information dissemination and fostering an understanding of innovation has been well-documented [6]. In light of these considerations, this study endeavors to elucidate the progression of social discourse, core issues, and key debates instigated by ChatGPT by analyzing media news reports readily accessible to the public. This approach aims to accurately depict media attitudes, industry perceptions, and public sentiments associated with ChatGPT.

2 Methodology

2.1 Data Collection and Pre-processing

The United States, as a frontrunner and catalyst in AI technology [7], has played a crucial role in the development and application of ChatGPT, resulting in extensive news coverage about the AI model. For instance, Kevin Rose, in a New York Times review, referred to ChatGPT as "the best artificial intelligence chatbot ever released to the general public" [8]. Derek Thompson perceives the advent of ChatGPT as "an explosion of generative AI," postulating that it will alter our understanding of work, cognition, and the essence of human creativity [9]. Elon Musk expressed more directly that "ChatGPT is scary good; We are not far from dangerously strong AI" [10]. Concurrently, the U.S. has encountered challenges and controversies while promoting ChatGPT, such as Mike Pearl's test revealing incorrect answers generated by the AI model [11], as well as concerns regarding the balance of benefits and drawbacks, data privacy, and consumer rights protection.

Studying U.S. media coverage and attitudes towards ChatGPT enables a more comprehensive understanding and assessment of the AI model's social impact and development prospects. This study selects article titles about ChatGPT in U.S. coverage as the analysis text data for two reasons: first, news headlines provide concise summaries of news content, encapsulating the most critical information; second, the "previewability" of article titles effectively represents media's agenda-setting trends.

The U.S. media news headline data utilized in this study were sourced from the LexisNexis news database. To collect relevant headlines, "ChatGPT" was employed as the keyword, and all news headlines in the U.S. coverage that included "ChatGPT" within the title or content were gathered. The search was restricted to the English language, and short news items and duplicate articles were excluded. An initial dataset of 4,984 news headlines was obtained, which, after the removal of irrelevant and redundant data, resulted in a final sample of 2,829 headlines for analysis. It should be noted that in the data preprocessing phase, we ensured the ethical considerations of data privacy and anonymization by not collecting any personally identifiable information from the news reports.

Given that the data collected in this study consists of text-based unstructured data, preprocessing is necessary before topic extraction and sentiment analysis can be conducted. The preprocessing workflow is as follows: first, remove punctuation marks and special symbols present in the text data, followed by performing word frequency statistics and lexical tagging on all text data. Second, based on lexical markers, extract only meaningful and functional nouns, adjectives, and verbs while adding other lexical properties (e.g., pronouns, prepositions, conjunctions) to the stopword list. Third, consolidate synonyms by replacing abbreviations (e.g., "Artificial Intelligence" and "AI" with "AI"), singular and plural nouns (e.g., "Students" and "Student"), and verb tenses (e.g., "asked" and "ask") with a single representative term. Finally, designate specific phrases (e.g., "Social Media", "Tech Giants", "Wall Street") as a custom lexicon. This systematic preprocessing approach ensures that the data is accurately represented and prepared for subsequent analysis.

2.2 Analysis Method

In this study, pre-processed U.S. media headline data obtained from the LexisNexis news database undergoes analysis through keyword frequency analysis, sentiment analysis, and LDA (Latent Dirichlet Allocation) topic modeling, employing text mining techniques. The objective of this analysis is to investigate the core issues and key debates associated with ChatGPT as they are presented in the media, providing insight into the predominant narratives and discussions surrounding the AI model.

This study employs keyword frequency analysis and sentiment analysis on pre-processed news text data to discern the primary topics and media attitudes related to ChatGPT in coverage. Keyword frequency analysis involves counting and examining the most frequently occurring words or phrases in text data, enabling the identification of prevalent or significant keywords within a given field or topic. This, in turn, assists researchers in obtaining a deeper understanding of the subjects and trends relevant to the topic or field [12]. Sentiment analysis is a natural language processing technique used to detect sentiment, attitudes, and emotional polarity within textual data by extracting, analyzing, processing, generalizing, and reasoning about text containing emotional nuances [13]. In this study, sentiment analysis is conducted using the Natural Language Toolkit (NLTK), a Python library that supports text processing, classification, and tokenization, among other features. Within NLTK, we utilize VADER (Valence Aware Dictionary for Sentiment Reasoning), a lexicon and rule-based sentiment analysis tool that is adept at gauging the sentiment in English language. VADER's strength lies in its ability to understand both the polarity (positive/negative) and the intensity (strength) of the emotion. It makes use of grammatical and syntactical conventions, along with word order, degree modifiers, punctuation, and capitalization to produce finely grained sentiment scores [14]. This makes it particularly effective in capturing sentiment in various contexts, including the journalistic language employed in news headlines. This approach allows us to effectively identify and measure positive and negative sentiment as expressed in the media headlines related to ChatGPT, with the overall goal of illuminating the predominant sentiments towards ChatGPT as portrayed by the media.

The significance of keyword frequency analysis lies in its ability to deduce the main keywords within a target text; however, it falls short in determining the relationships between these keywords, necessitating further analysis using topic modeling. Topic modeling is a widely employed text mining tool for discovering hidden semantic structures within text [15]. Among the various topic modeling methods, Latent Dirichlet Allocation (LDA) is the most easily interpretable model and is capable of extracting a range of topics from large datasets by addressing the issue of overfitting [16].

3 Data Analysis

3.1 Keyword Frequency Analysis

By conducting keyword frequency analysis on the collected news headlines, the top twenty keywords related to ChatGPT in U.S. news media coverage are presented in Table 1. It can be observed that the top three most frequently mentioned keywords are "AI," "ChatGPT," and "Technology," indicating that news media coverage extensively discusses the artificial intelligence technology underpinning ChatGPT. Additionally, prominent AI technology companies such as "Google," "Microsoft," and "OpenAI" (the developer of ChatGPT) occupy leading positions, representing the focus of news media attention. Moreover, AI products related to ChatGPT, such as "Chatbot" and "Robot," as well as functional keywords like "Write," "Tool," "Search," and "Human (Humanlike)" are also focal points in media discourse. Finally, the frequent occurrence of terms like "Student," "Jobs," "Schools," and "Business" suggests that ChatGPT has permeated various aspects of public work, education, and daily life. The prominence of keywords such as "Future," "Change," and "World" further reflects the high level of media discussion regarding the impact of ChatGPT on the world and its future development.

Following the sentiment analysis of U.S. media news headlines, the top 10 positive and negative sentiment words were identified and summarized, as shown in Table 2. Firstly, positive sentiment words such as "New," "Innovation," and "Create" appear frequently, suggesting that U.S. news media coverage positions ChatGPT as a novel, innovative, and creative product. Simultaneously, words like "Good," "Like," "Help," and "Smart" reveal that media outlets hold a positive view of ChatGPT's service capabilities, believing it can provide effective assistance in real-life situations. Furthermore, terms such as "Share," "Challenge," and "Value" indicate that media coverage is filled with anticipation for the continuous development of ChatGPT.

Table 1. Keyword word frequency statistics of Top20 in US news reports

	Words	Freq		Words	Freq
1	AI	825	11	Schools	82
2	ChatGPT	778	12	World	80
3	Technology	226	13	OpenAI	66
4	Google	198	14	Change	64
5	Microsoft	194	15	Search	62
6	Chatbot	181	16	Future	61
7	Write	160	17	Human	59
8	Tool	87	18	Robot	54
9	Student	86	19	Business	53
10	Jobs	83	20	BigDate	50

In the negative sentiment word statistics table, terms such as "Cannot," "Cheat," and "Ban" are prominent, indicating that numerous news media outlets express concerns about the incompleteness and complexity of ChatGPT's functionality. Furthermore, words like "Fear," "Threat," "Worry," and "Scary" evidently convey media apprehension and fear regarding the social issues and negative impacts resulting from ChatGPT. Simultaneously, it is observed that potentially hazardous sentiment words, such as "War," "Warn," and "Crime," have been mentioned, reflecting some media outlets' concerns about the uncertainty and potential threats posed by emerging technologies.

Table 2. Statistics of Top 10 positive emotion keywords and negative emotion keywords in US news reports

	Positive Words	Freq.	Negative Words	Freq.
1	New	213	Cannot	97
2	Good	62	Cheat	41
3	Create	51	Ban	30
4	Like	47	Fear	24
5	Help	42	Threat	22
6	Smart	27	Worry	24
7	Challenge	22	War	16
8	Share	18	Warn	20
9	Value	15	Crime	13
10	Innovation	13	Scary	11

3.2 LDA Theme Modeling Analysis

To further identify the core issues and latent topics related to ChatGPT in media news, the pre-processed news text data is analyzed using the LDA algorithm.

First, the number of topics for the LDA model is determined. When the number of topics is excessive, the LDA model often overfits, producing overly specific topics that are not conducive to analysis. Consequently, based on the volume of pre-processed text data, the maximum number of topics is limited to 10. Further, topic coherence and perplexity evaluations are conducted, resulting in coherence and perplexity indicator charts, as shown in Fig. 1.

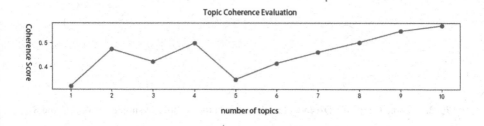

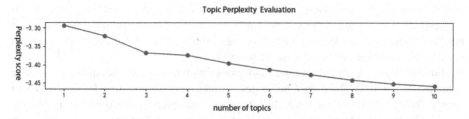

Fig. 1. LDA Coherence Score and Perplexity score

In addition, observing the topic coherence indicator reveals a noticeable increase in coherence scores when the number of topics is 4. Simultaneously, perplexity is relatively low when the number of topics is 6, 7, or 8. Further analysis is conducted on the LDA topic model with 4, 6, 7, and 8 topics, and bubble charts are generated using pyLDAvis (as shown in Fig. 2).

In the bubble chart, each circle represents a topic, the size of the circle's area indicates the importance of each topic, and the distance between the centers of the circles indicates the similarity between the topics. Based on experience, a good topic model should have large, non-overlapping bubbles, which leads to the exclusion of models with 6 and 7 topics. Further examination of the keywords ultimately determines that the optimal number of topics is 4. By filtering the keywords for these four topics and retaining those that more accurately summarize each topic, the LDA model results are obtained, as shown in Table 3.

From the table, it can be observed that the LDA model extracts four topics from U.S. media news, with each topic's name determined through discussion among researchers

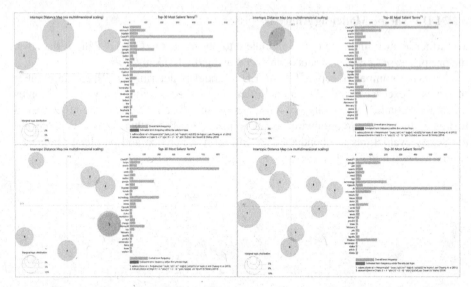

Fig. 2. Bubble Chart of LDA model analysis when the number of subjects is 4, 6, 7 and 8

based on the keywords of that topic. It is noteworthy that the keywords "ChatGPT," "AI," "Technology," and "New" appear in each topic, suggesting that the emergence of artificial intelligence technology, represented by ChatGPT, brings about new changes in human society. This underlying theme serves as the foundation for each topic and will not be elaborated further in subsequent descriptions.

Firstly, Topic 1 derived from the LDA model analysis of U.S. media news coverage is named "ChatGPT: The New Challenges of Intelligent Automation for the Future of Human Work." In this theme, intelligent automation refers to the process of utilizing artificial intelligence technology to automate ("Automation") and make work processes more intelligent ("Intelligent"). This topic includes both "the changes in human work in the future" (e.g., keywords "Future," "Job," "Change," "Work," "Robot") and "the potential impacts" (e.g., keywords "Layoff," "Threat," "Money," "Expert," "Engineer," etc.).

As an artificial intelligence robot, ChatGPT excels in natural language processing, machine translation, text creation, and dialogue generation. This enables it to replace humans in executing repetitive and tedious tasks in various work scenarios, thereby improving work efficiency and quality and generating higher returns. In this transformative process, technical research and development roles, such as experts and engineers, need to play a more significant role, such as writing and debugging artificial intelligence algorithms and software and addressing emerging technical and data ethics issues. However, at the same time, some jobs may be replaced by intelligent automation technologies, represented by ChatGPT, resulting in layoffs and unemployment.

Therefore, how to balance the division of labor and collaboration between machines and humans in the workplace, and how to safeguard the value and rights of human work in the future, are evidently new challenges brought by innovative technologies like ChatGPT. These challenges are also issues that need to be considered and resolved.

Table 3. LDA model results

Topic 1	Topic 2	Topic 3	Topic 4
ChatGPT: The New Challenges of Intelligent Automation for the Future of Human Work	ChatGPT: A New Paradigm for Human-Machine Collaboration	ChatGPT: A New Milestone in Artificial Intelligence	ChatGPT: A New Test for AI Ethics and Social Issues
ChatGPT	AI	AI	AI
AI	ChatGPT	ChatGPT	Google
New	Technology	Google	New
Google	New	BigDate	ChatGPT
Technology	Writer	Technology	Microsoft
Robot	Student	New	Technology
Future	Bot	Chatbot	World
Job	Business	Easy	Apple
Intelligent	School	Twitter	Amazon
World	Revolution	Algorithm	Wall street
Layoff	Service	Ask	Facebook
Think	Program	Answer	Texas
Business	Bot	Write	Race
Change	Trend	Help	Security
Expert	Change	Terminator	CEO
Money	Tool	Question	Tech Giants
Automation	Coming	Replace	China
Work	Human	Use	Privacy
Threat	Assitance	Article	Fight
Engineer	Company	Vision	Robot

Secondly, Topic 2 is named "ChatGPT: A New Paradigm for Human-Machine Collaboration." Under this theme, there is a set of keywords related to specific application scenarios of ChatGPT (e.g., "Assistance," "Bot," "Writer," "Business," "Company," "School," "Service," "Student," etc.) and their impacts (e.g., "Trend," "Change," "Revolution," "Coming," etc.). ChatGPT can interact and collaborate with humans through natural language, bringing human-machine collaboration to a new stage. In application fields such as healthcare, education, and business, ChatGPT can serve as an intelligent assistant, customer service representative, and even perform intelligent writing tasks. The emergence of ChatGPT provides a new paradigm for human-machine collaboration, bringing transformative changes and opportunities to many industries and fields.

Topic 3 is named "ChatGPT: A New Milestone in Artificial Intelligence." This theme primarily includes discussions on ChatGPT's technology (e.g., "Big Data," "Chatbot," "Algorithm," etc.) and functional use (e.g., "Ask," "Answer," "Write," "Help," "Question," "Use," "Easy," etc.). ChatGPT adopts the most advanced natural language processing technology, and its emergence signifies a new milestone in artificial intelligence. ChatGPT has achieved remarkable results in areas such as question-answering, conversation, and text generation, which hold significant implications for the future of natural language processing and intelligent interaction.

Lastly, Topic 4 is named "ChatGPT: A New Test for AI Ethics and Social Issues." This topic discusses ChatGPT from a macro perspective, including the technology hegemony battle among tech giants ("Google," "Microsoft," "Amazon," "Facebook," "Apple," "Texas (a Texas-based AI company)," "Tech Giants," "Fight," etc.); and potential ethical and social issues arising after ChatGPT's emergence ("Security," "Privacy"), such as whether the text generated by ChatGPT contains ethical and moral problems, the risk of misinformation, and how to protect consumer privacy and data security during use. These are new challenges posed to contemporary society. Furthermore, the appearance of "China" in this topic demonstrates that the U.S. media consistently pays close attention to and monitors the development of artificial intelligence in China.

4 Conclusion

This study, through a topic mining and sentiment analysis based on U.S. news articles, aims to identify the main agenda and emotional attitudes towards ChatGPT within the mimetic environment constructed by news media. Specifically, the research begins by conducting a keyword frequency analysis on news headlines, revealing that the topics and focal points of media discussions mainly involve technological development, functional applications, and social impacts. Subsequently, a sentiment analysis is performed, which shows that the overall attitude of news media towards ChatGPT is positive, considering it a novel, innovative, and useful service, and holding expectations for its development. However, some media outlets express negative evaluations regarding the potential social issues that ChatGPT might bring.

Finally, to more accurately determine the primary topics in ChatGPT's media coverage, we employ Latent Dirichlet Allocation (LDA) topic modeling analysis and ultimately identify four main topics: "ChatGPT: A New Challenge for Human Work in Intelligent Automation," "ChatGPT: A New Paradigm for Human-Machine Collaboration," "ChatGPT: A New Milestone in Artificial Intelligence," and "ChatGPT: A New Test for AI Ethics and Social Issues."

According to Habermas (1991), "media coverage, as a social discourse in the form of public forums, can create and coordinate various public agendas" [17]. It is evident that the results of this study contribute to a deeper understanding of the public agenda and social discourse surrounding ChatGPT, addressing the limitations of existing research and providing assistance for subsequent related studies.

Moreover, to avoid misunderstandings and guide future research investigations, it is crucial to consider the limitations of this study. Firstly, the analysis was conducted solely on news headlines, without considering the content of the news articles. In future research, it is necessary to analyze the entirety of the news content to provide a more comprehensive interpretation of the study. Secondly, while conducting sentiment analysis, this study directly matched keywords with words from a sentiment dictionary to determine the emotional inclination of the text, without considering the context in which the vocabulary appeared. This approach may potentially introduce biases into the analysis results.

Acknowledgments. This work is supported in part by the Communication University of China School-level Research Project, 'Research on Design Strategies for Enhancing Viewer Acceptance of Artificial Intelligence-Powered Announcers', under project number CUC23GP004.

References

1. OpenAI: ChatGPT: Optimizing Language Models for Dialogue [EB/OL]. 17 Feb 2022. https://openai.com/blog/chatgpt/
2. Lund, B.D., Wang, T.: Chatting about ChatGPT: How may AI and GPT impact academia and libraries? Library Hi Tech News (2023)
3. Dale, R.: GPT-3: What's it good for? Nat. Lang. Eng. **27**(1), 113–118 (2021)
4. Dan, M.: ChatGPT reaches 100 million users two months after launch. The Guardian, 2 Feb 2023
5. Turing, A.M.: Computing Machinery and Intelligence, 2nd edn. Springer Netherlands (2009)
6. Lippmann, W.: Public opinion 1922. (1965). http://infomotions.com/etexts/gutenberg/dirs/etext04/pbpnn10.htm
7. Brossard, D.: New media landscapes and the science information consumer. Proc. Nat. Acad. Sci. **110**(supplement_3), 14096–14101 (2013)
8. Popescu, I.I.: Word Frequency Studies. Walter de Gruyter (2009)
9. Roose, K.: The brilliance and weirdness of ChatGPT. The New York Times (2022)
10. Thompson, D.: Breakthroughs of the year. The Atlantic (2022)
11. Kay, G.: Elon Musk founded — and has since criticized — the company behind the buzzy new AI chatbot ChatGPT. Here's everything we know about OpenAI. Business Insider (2022)
12. Pearl, M.: The ChatGPT chatbot from OpenAI is amazing, creative, and totally wrong. Mashable (2022)
13. Chaffar, S., Inkpen, D.: Using a heterogeneous dataset for emotion analysis in text. In: Advances in Artificial Intelligence: 24th Canadian Conference on Artificial Intelligence, Canadian AI 2011, St. John's, Canada, May 25–27, 2011. Proceedings 24, pp. 62–67. Springer, Berlin, Heidelberg (2011)
14. Hutto, C.J., Gilbert, E.E.: VADER: a parsimonious rule-based model for sentiment analysis of social media text. In: Proceedings of the Eighth International Conference on Weblogs and Social Media (ICWSM-14). The AAAI Press, Ann Arbor, MI (2014)
15. Blei, D.M., Ng, A.Y., Jordan, M.I.: Latent Dirichlet allocation. J. Mach. Learn. Res. 3(Jan), 993–1022 (2003)
16. Blei, D.M.: Probabilistic topic models. Commun. ACM **55**(4), 77–84 (2012)
17. Habermas, J.: The Structural Transformation of the Public Sphere: An Inquiry into a Category of Bourgeois Society. MIT Press (1991)

Joint Memory Propagation and Rectification for Video Object Segmentation

Jiale Wang[1], Hongli Xu[1(✉)], Hui yin[2], Jin Wan[2], and Jianhuan Chen[1]

[1] Key Laboratory of Beijing for Railway Engineering, Beijing Jiaotong University, Beijing, China
hlxu@bjtu.edu.cn
[2] Beijing Key Lab of Traffic Data Analysis and Mining, Beijing Jiaotong University, Beijing, China

Abstract. Spatio-temporal memory matching-based methods have achieved significant breakthroughs in the task of video object segmentation. Nevertheless, they are deficient in exploiting the long-term temporal correlation of frames by performing pixel-wise memory matching with limited reference frames, and tend to segment similar objects incorrectly. In this paper, we propose two novel modules, memory propagation and rectification modules, that are able to execute the memory reading in all proceeding frames while leveraging long-term temporal smoothness. Specifically, the memory propagation module employs the lightweight ConvGRU architecture to integrate abundant temporal cues from the reference frame sequence. Afterwards, the memory rectification module guided by the similarity between frames is proposed to increase the inter-frame consistency constraint to retrieve reliable memory and transfer them to the current frame. Additionally, we adopt a tiny-capacity spatio-temporal matching module to model the pixel relationship with only two reference frames. The experimental results on DAVIS and YouTube-VOS datasets demonstrate that combining memory propagation and rectification can achieve considerable performance gain and maintain constant inference time and memory usage in the sequence segmentation. To facilitate research in this direction, we release the project code at https://github.com/GDPUCJH/MPRNet.

Keywords: Video object segmentation · Time memorization · Memory propagation · Memory rectification · Spatio-temporal matching

1 Introduction

Video object segmentation (VOS) is a fundamental task in the community of computer vision, which is widely utilised in 3D reconstruction [7], video edit-

This work is supported by National Nature Science Foundation of China (51827813), National Key R&D Program "Transportation Infrastructure" "Reveal the List and Take Command" Project (2022YFB2603302) and R&D Program of Beijing Municipal Education Commission (KJZD20191000402).

ing [7], automatic driving [23]. This paper focuses on semi-supervised video object segmentation that aims to segment the target objects from a video sequence according to the given mask of the first frame (reference frame). Due to occlusion, large-scale change and morphological change of objects, and there may be one or more objects in a video, VOS is thus extremely challenging to perform accurate segmentation.

In the task of semi-supervised VOS, there are two mainstream branches: propa-gation-based methods [5,10,13,22] and matching-based methods [4,6,14, 17,20]. In recent years, the methods based on spatio-temporal memory matching have achieved remarkable results via sampling segmented frames to build the memory pool and calculating the pixel-level correspondence between the current frame and the selected reference frames. However, they make insufficient use of the long-term temporal correlation from the sequence, which leads to segmentation results that are difficult to maintain inter-frame consistency and tend to mis-match with similar objects. To capture the temporal cues, [4] and [20] track the target regions from the perspective of increasing spatial constraints and employing the optical flow priors. Although these methods perform promising predictive results, long-term temporal information remains under-explored and the performance is highly directed by the accuracy of the estimated flows.

To address this problem, we propose a novel framework, termed MPRNet (see Fig. 1), which exploits memory propagation and rectification modules to efficiently facilitate memory reading for video object segmentation. Concretely, inspired by the fact that RNN [2] can model the long-term dependence on historical information, we develop a new memory propagation paradigm that incorporates lightweight ConvGRU to smoothly memorize the reference frame sequence in the temporal dimension, which can cast the long-term temporal information sufficiently. To construct reliable memory information, we design a novel memory rectification scheme to correct the propagated memory and integrate the long-term temporal cues into the subsequent frames. This is achieved by employing the guidance of the similarity between the current frame and the previous adjacent frame. Besides, benefiting from the effective long-term temporal correlation modelling, we only use a tiny-capacity spatio-temporal matching module to build the pixel relationship with only two reference frames. For evaluation, we conduct extensive experiments on two widely used benchmark datasets and the results show that our method obtains a significant performance gain margin and follows a stable inference time and memory usage manner. The contributions of this work are summarized as follows:

- We propose a new memory propagation (MP) module that memorizes reference frame features in the temporal dimension and learns continuous appearance information to track target objects.
- We propose a novel memory rectification (MR) module that corrects propagated memory which is guided by the appearance similarity between the current frame and the previous adjacent frame, transferring reliable memory information to the current frame to predict consistent segmentation results in the video sequence.

– Experimental results on the DAVIS and YouTube VOS datasets demonstrate that our proposed method has a considerable influence on semi-supervised VOS performance, and achieves constant segmentation time and memory consumption in the segmentation prediction.

2 Related Works

In this section, we introduce the methods of the two major mainstream categories.

2.1 Propagation Methods

Propagation-based methods refine object segmentation masks in a manner that propagates in the temporal dimension. Given an arbitrary object instance, OSMN [22] employs a meta neural network called modulator to adjust the intermediate layers of the generic segmentation network. RGMP [13] constructs a Siamese encoder-decoder network that propagates the previous mask to the current frame and detects the target objects according to the given reference frame. AGSS-VOS [10] uses an attention mechanism to fuse the output of instance-agnostic module and instance-specific module to segment object instances. DIP-Net [5] utilises a novel identity representation to adaptively propagate objects' reference information over time, which enhances the robustness to videos' temporal variations.

2.2 Matching Methods

Matching-based methods perform pixel-level matching between reference frames and the current frame. VideoMatch [6] calculates soft matching with the foreground and background of the first frame respectively. FEELVOS [17] performs global matching with the initial frame and local matching with the previous adjacent frame, generating distance maps. The STMNet [14] series methods sample the segmented frames to build a memory pool, and then perform spatio-temporal retrieval on the memory frames, which have achieved remarkable results in the field of VOS, but pixel-level matching can easily lead to wrong segmentation of similar pixels. To solve this problem, LCM [4] tracks the target regions from the perspective of increasing spatial constraints and RMNet [20] employs the optical flow priors.

The propagation based methods can effectively track the temporal continuity of the target when it changes smoothly. Accordingly, we innovatively combine propagation to track the target object, using RNN method to remember the video in the temporal dimension, which learns the long-term evolution of objects to reduce the wrong segmentation caused by pixel level matching.

3   Method

Firstly, a temporal description of semi-supervised VOS is given. $X = (x_1, \ldots, x_T)$ is an RGB video sequence with T frames input, and x_t represents the tth frame, which is the current frame to be segmented. The real masks for the sequence X is defined as $Y = (Y_1, \ldots, Y_T)$. The goal is to estimate the masks $\widehat{Y}$ of subsequent video frames, $\widehat{Y} = \left(\widehat{Y}_2, \ldots, \widehat{Y}_T\right)$, $\widehat{Y}_t$ represents the prediction mask for the tth video frame. As the video frame segmentation proceeds, the initial frame and the segmented frames $(x_1, \ldots, x_{t-1})$ are used as reference frames, and the prediction masks of the segmented frames can assist in the segmentation of subsequent frames.

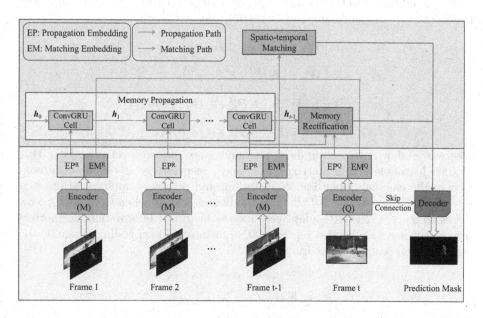

Fig. 1. The network structure diagram of joint memory propagation and rectification for video object segmentation.

The network framework is shown in Fig. 1, and the MPRNet is a typical encoder-decoder structure. Firstly, the reference frame with mask and the current frame x_t are sent to the encoder (ResNet50 [3]) for feature encoding, and using two 3×3 convolutions on the 4th stage output $res4$ to generate matching embedding and propagation embedding, define the propagation embeddings of the reference frame and the current frame as EP^R and EP^Q, and the matching embeddings are EM^R and EM^Q respectively, all feature dimensions are $\mathbb{R}^{H \times W \times C}$, where H and W represent $\frac{1}{16}$ of the video frame input size, and C denotes 512 channels. The MP module memorizes the reference features frame by frame, and the MR module transfers the memory to the current frame. The

STM module learns the pixel-level correlation between the current frame and the memory frames.

Finally, the outputs of the two parts are merged into decoder [14] to generate the final segmentation mask. Skip connection is used to combine low-level features. The convolution weights of the reference frame and the current frame in MPRNet are not shared.

3.1   Memory Propagation Module

The MP module can learn long-term, rich continuous changes of reference frames to generate memory features, ConvGRU is used to memorize the reference frames, EP^R is sent to the ConvGRU unit, and the hidden state h_0 of ConvGRU is initialized to **0**. Taking the previous adjacent frame as an example, the process of memory updating and forgetting can be described as:

$$
\begin{aligned}
z_{t-1} &= \sigma\left(W_z * \left(EP^R_{t-1} \oplus h_{t-2}\right)\right), \\
r_{t-1} &= \sigma\left(W_r * \left(EP^R_{t-1} \oplus h_{t-2}\right)\right), \\
\tilde{h}_{t-1} &= \tanh\left(W_o * \left(EP^R_{t-1} \oplus (h_{t-2} \circ r_{t-1})\right)\right), \\
h_{t-1} &= (1 - z_{t-1}) \circ h_{t-2} + z_{t-1} \circ \tilde{h}_{t-1},
\end{aligned}
\tag{1}
$$

where z and r represent update gate and reset gate respectively, W_z, W_r, W_o are learnable weight matrixes, $\oplus$, $*$ and $\circ$ respectively represent concatenation in the channel dimension, convolution, and pixel-wise multiplication, σ is sigmoid function, $h_{t-1} \in \mathbb{R}^{H \times W \times C}$ is the hidden feature when ConvGRU memorizes to x_{t-1}. ConvGRU adaptively forgets historical information, memorizes new features, and generates representative memory hidden codings to guide the segmentation of subsequent frames.

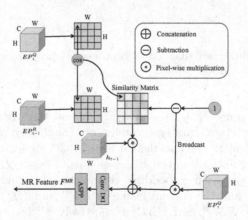

Fig. 2. The network structure diagram of memory rectification module.

3.2 Memory Rectification Module

Figure 2 is the network structure of the MR module, which transfers the mask information in the memory to the current frame without mask information. There are pixel changes in the current frame compared with the previous adjacent frame, including the conversion between some foreground and background pixels, then the memory contains outdated information, so we propose a rectification strategy to correct the memory according to the degree of difference between adjacent frames, forget the outdated features, and update the changed pixel features.

This module rectifies the memory using the similarity between x_{t-1} and x_t. In the propagation features EP_{t-1}^R and EP_t^Q, each pixel feature can be regarded as a vector of length C, and the number of pixels is $H \times W$. Accordingly, calculating the similarity matrix, using the C dimensional feature vector on the same position to calculate the cosine similarity, and perform an exponential operation to make it positive, then normalize the value to $0{\sim}1$ by dividing the maximum value of all pixels. The calculation process can be described as:

$$S_P(i) = \frac{\exp\left(\cos\left(EP_{t-1}^R(i), EP_t^Q(i)\right)\right)}{\max\left(\exp\left(\cos\left(EP_{t-1}^R(i), EP_t^Q(i)\right)\right)\right)}, \tag{2}$$

where i is the pixel index, $S_P \in \mathbb{R}^{H \times W}$. Then, according to this similarity matrix, guiding the memory rectification:

$$F^R = \mathrm{Conv}\left((S_P \circ h_{t-1}) \oplus \left((1 - S_P) \circ EP_t^Q\right)\right), \tag{3}$$

where Conv means 1×1 convolution. $F^R \in \mathbb{R}^{H \times W \times C}$ is the rectified memory feature. The greater the difference between x_t and x_{t-1}, the greater the weight of memory rectification.

The memory rectification process is performed at the pixel level, F^R is a weighted combination of memory features (including mask information) and current frame features (excluding mask information), which is an unaligned feature, so the rectified feature F^R is sent to the ASPP [1] module that uses multiple parallel convolution layers with different dilated ratios for multi-scale feature

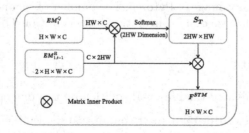

Fig. 3. The network structure diagram of spatio-temporal matching module.

fusion to align feature and learn space context information. The output feature is defined as $\boldsymbol{F}^{MR} \in \mathbb{R}^{H \times W \times C}$.

3.3   Spatio-Temporal Matching Module

The STM module uses the initial frame and the previous adjacent frame to build a memory pool, because the initial frame contains an accurate object mask, and the previous adjacent frame has a similar appearance to the current frame.

The STM module is shown in Fig. 3, the matching features of the initial frame $\boldsymbol{EM}_1^R$ and the previous adjacent frame $\boldsymbol{EM}_{t-1}^R$ are concatenated in the time dimension, the concatenated features are expressed as $\boldsymbol{EM}_{1,t-1}^R \in \mathbb{R}^{2 \times H \times W \times C}$. Then the correlation calculation with $\boldsymbol{EM}_t^Q$ following by the Softmax normalization in the pixel dimension of the reference frames is conducted, this progress can be described as:

$$S_T(i,j) = \frac{\exp\left(\boldsymbol{EM}_{1,t-1}^R(i) \odot \boldsymbol{EM}_t^Q(j)^\top\right)}{\sum_i \exp\left(\boldsymbol{EM}_{1,t-1}^R(i) \odot \boldsymbol{EM}_t^Q(j)^\top\right)}, \tag{4}$$

where Softmax can determine the location of the pixel in the memory pool that is most similar to the pixel in the current frame. $\boldsymbol{S}_T \in \mathbb{R}^{2HW \times HW}$, the spatio-temporal feature retrieval can be described as:

$$F^{STM}(j) = \sum_i S_T(i,j) \circ \boldsymbol{EM}_{1,t-1}^R(i). \tag{5}$$

In Eq. (4) and Eq.(5), i and j are pixel indexes, $\odot$ represents vector inner product, $\boldsymbol{F}^{STM} \in \mathbb{R}^{H \times W \times C}$ is the spatio-temporal matching feature. The STM module retrieves appearance features that are highly similar to the current frame pixels, which can increase the recall rate of the target pixels.

3.4   Multi-object Segmentation Method and Parameter Setting

We treat multiple objects in the video sequence as multiple single objects for processing, and use soft aggregation [14] to merge the segmentation results. During training, we calculate the cross entropy loss of multi-classification, which is due to the batch advantage of Pytorch. The number of channels C in MPRNet is set to 512, and the size of all convolution kernels in ConvGRU is 5×5.

4   Experiments

We trained and evaluated the proposed solution on two different datasets.

DAVIS. The DAVIS 2016 [15] dataset contains 50 single-object videos. Considering its limited size and versatility, it was soon added to the DAVIS 2017 [16] dataset, including 150 sequences, one of which contains one or more objects.

According to the standard of the DAVIS dataset, we use $\mathcal{J}$ score to calculate the average Intersection over Union (IoU) between the prediction and the ground truth, use $\mathcal{F}$ score to calculate the average boundary similarity, $\mathcal{J}\&\mathcal{F}$ is the average of $\mathcal{J}$ and $\mathcal{F}$. In addition, the Frames Per Second (FPS) is used to measure the segmentation speed.

YouTube-VOS. YouTube-VOS [21] includes 4453 videos with multiple object annotations. Its validation set has 474 sequences covering 91 object classes, 26 of which are not seen in the training set. On YouTube-VOS, we report the total score $\mathcal{J}\&\mathcal{F}$, which is the index average of object classes that have be seen and have not be seen in the training set.

We first used affine transformations on the static image dataset MS COCO [11] to generate 4-frames pseudo video sequences and pre-trained on this dataset for a total of 250K iterations, then randomly sampled 4 frames each time on DAVIS 2017 and YouTube-VOS for formal training, with a total of 450K iterations. The input size during training was 384×384, all training and testing were conducted on 1 NVIDIA GeForce RTX 2080 Ti GPU, and the batch size was set to 4 by manual accumulation.

4.1 Ablation Study

All experiments are verified on the DAVIS 2017 Validation dataset.

Ablation Study for Network Modules. Table 1 shows the results. (1) Remove the MP and MR modules, $\mathcal{J}\&\mathcal{F}$ drops to 80.3% (–2.5%). (2) Replace the MP module with short-term memory, that is, do not memorize through ConvGRU, but directly use $\boldsymbol{EP}_{t-1}^{R}$ for the subsequent rectification process. At this time, $\mathcal{J}\&\mathcal{F}$ drops to 82.3% (–0.5%), indicating long-term information is more effective as it remains unaffected by the fault segmentation results of the previous frame, making it more reliable than short-term information. (3) Remove the STM module, $\mathcal{J}\&\mathcal{F}$ drops to 77.2% (-5.6%). Figure 4 shows the visualization results, removing the MP and MR modules will lead to a large degree of wrong matching. The STM module has a great contribution to the overall network, removing it will easily lead to incomplete segmentation.

Table 1. Ablation experimental results for network modules.

MP	MR	STM	$\mathcal{J}\&\mathcal{F}\uparrow$ (%)	$\mathcal{J}\uparrow$ (%)	$\mathcal{F}\uparrow$ (%)
–	–	✓	80.3	77.8	82.8
–	✓	✓	82.3	79.7	84.9
✓	✓	-	77.2	74.2	80.3
✓	✓	✓	**82.8**	**80.3**	**85.2**

Ablation Study for MR Module Structure. Table 2 shows the results, which are divided into the following three parts:

(1) Replace 1×1 convolution with addition, $\mathcal{J}\&\mathcal{F}$ drops to 82.1% (-0.7%). (2) Remove the ASPP module, $\mathcal{J}\&\mathcal{F}$ drops to 82.0% (-0.8%), indicating multi-scale feature learning helps to learn spatial context information and obtain more consistent intra-frame feature representation. (3) Replace the feature weighted combination guided by adjacent frames with 3×3 convolution, $\mathcal{J}\&\mathcal{F}$ drops to 81.2% (-1.6%), indicating the proposed memory rectification strategy can effectively forget the memory features according to the degree of difference between frames, and fuse the new pixel features in the current frame.

Table 2. Ablation experimental results for memory rectification module.

FWC	1×1 convolution	ASPP	$\mathcal{J}\&\mathcal{F} \uparrow$ (%)	$\mathcal{J} \uparrow$ (%)	$\mathcal{F} \uparrow$ (%)
✓	(addition)	✓	82.1	79.6	84.6
✓	✓	(remove)	82.0	79.7	84.3
(convolution)	✓	✓	81.2	78.6	83.8
✓	✓	✓	**82.8**	**80.3**	**85.2**

FWC: Feature weighted combination

Table 3. Ablation experimental results for training strategy.

pre-training	formal training	$\mathcal{J}\&\mathcal{F} \uparrow$ (%)	$\mathcal{J} \uparrow$ (%)	$\mathcal{F} \uparrow$ (%)
✓	–	75.2	72.9	77.5
–	✓	81.2	78.8	83.6
✓	✓	**82.8**	**80.3**	**85.2**

Fig. 4. Visual comparison of ablation study of network modules.

Ablation Study for Training Strategy. Table 3 shows the results. When only the image dataset is used for pre-training, $\mathcal{J}\&\mathcal{F}$ reaches 75.2%, which shows the effectiveness of the pre-training method, when the two training processes are combined, $\mathcal{J}\&\mathcal{F}$ reaches the optimum of 82.8%.

5   Comparative Experiment

DAVIS 2017. As shown in Table 4, the $\mathcal{J}\&\mathcal{F}$ of MPRNet reaches 82.8% on the DAVIS 2017 Validation dataset, slightly lower than the LCM [4] and RMNet [20] models which scored 83.5. This difference in performance is attributed to our method has constant segmentation time and memory usage during testing. In this case, $\mathcal{J}\&\mathcal{F}$ still exceeds STMNet by 1%. AFB URR [9], GC [8] and Swift-Net [18] all effectively alleviate this problem of STMNet, AFB URR constructs an adaptively updated feature pool, GC uses a fixed-size feature representation, and SwiftNet is a pixel adaptive memory update method. The $\mathcal{J}\&\mathcal{F}$ of MPR-Net (without using YouTube-VOS for training) is 3.4% higher than AFB URR, 6.6% higher than GC, and 1.7% higher than SwiftNet (using YouTube-VOS for training).

The results on the DAVIS 2017 Test-dev dataset are also reported in Table 4, the $\mathcal{J}\&\mathcal{F}$ also achieves the best result of 75.2%, significantly exceeding STMNet (+3%).

Table 4. Comparison of quantitative results on DAVIS 2017 dataset.

Method	Validation Set			Test-dev Set		
	$\mathcal{J}\&\mathcal{F}\uparrow$ (%)	$\mathcal{J}\uparrow$ (%)	$\mathcal{F}\uparrow$ (%)	$\mathcal{J}\&\mathcal{F}\uparrow$ (%)	$\mathcal{J}\uparrow$ (%)	$\mathcal{F}\uparrow$ (%)
OSMN [22]	54.8	52.5	57.1	41.3	37.7	44.9
VideoMatch [6]	62.4	56.5	68.2	–	–	–
RGMP [13]	66.7	64.8	68.6	52.9	51.3	54.4
FEELVOS [17] (+YV)	71.5	69.1	74.0	57.8	55.2	60.5
STMNet [14] (+YV)	81.8	79.2	84.3	72.2	69.3	75.2
GC [8]	71.4	69.3	73.5	-	-	-
AFB URR [9]	74.6	73.0	76.1	–	–	–
GraphMem [12] (+YV)	82.8	80.2	85.2	–	-	-
SSM [24]	77.6	75.3	79.9	62.0	60.2	63.8
SwiftNet [18] (+YV)	81.1	78.3	83.9	–	–	–
LCM [4] (+YV)	**83.5**	80.5	**86.5**	**78.1**	**74.4**	**81.8**
RMNet [20] (+YV)	**83.5**	**81.0**	86.0	-	-	-
MPRNet (Ours)	78.0	75.1	80.9	-	–	–
MPRNet (Ours) (+YV)	82.8	80.3	85.2	75.2	71.7	78.7

Note: (+YV) indicates DAVIS 2017 and YouTube-VOS are used for training

DAVIS 2016. DAVIS 2016 is a single-object dataset, and its evaluation is not affected by the interaction of multiple objects, so its performance largely depends on the accuracy of segmentation details. As shown in Table 5, the $\mathcal{J}\&\mathcal{F}$ of MPR-Net reaches 89.3%. When YouTube-VOS is not added for training, the $\mathcal{J}\&\mathcal{F}$ exceeds STMNet by 1%. When YouTube-VOS is used for training, MPRNet and STMNet reach the same effect, but the latter achieves a faster speed.

YouTube-VOS. As shown in the Table 6, the $\mathcal{J}\&\mathcal{F}$ of MPRNet reaches 80.1% on the YouTube-VOS dataset, which exceeds STMNet by 0.7%. Compared with the optimal method GraphMem [12], the $\mathcal{J}\&\mathcal{F}$ is 0.1% lower, but for the objects that have not appeared in the training set (unseen), the $\mathcal{J}$ is 0.4% higher, the $\mathcal{F}$ is 0.7% higher, which proves our method has good generalization performance.

Table 5. Comparison of quantitative results on DAVIS 2016 Validation dataset.

Method	$\mathcal{J}\&\mathcal{F}$ ↑ (%)	$\mathcal{J}$ ↑ (%)	$\mathcal{F}$ ↑ (%)	FPS ↑ (frame/s)
RGMP [13]	81.8	81.5	82.0	7.7
FEELVOS [17] (+YV)	81.7	81.1	82.2	2.22
STMNet [14]	86.5	84.8	88.1	8.93
RANet+ [19]	87.1	86.6	87.6	0.25
STMNet [14] (+YV)	89.3	88.7	89.9	8.93
GC [8]	86.6	87.6	85.7	25
SSM [24]	85.9	86.2	85.6	**37**
LCM [4]	**90.7**	**89.9**	**91.4**	–
RMNet [20] (+YV)	88.8	88.9	88.7	–
MPRNet (Ours)	87.5	86.3	88.6	9.78
MPRNet (Ours) (+YV)	89.3	88.9	89.7	9.78

Note: (+YV) indicates DAVIS 2017 and YouTube-VOS are used for training

Qualitative Results Fig. 5 shows the visualization results compared with the matching-based methods STMNet [14], SSM [24] and GraphMem [12] on the DAVIS 2017 Validation dataset, all three methods have different degrees of wrong matching, including the confusion of similar objects and incorrect segmentation caused by close interaction between objects. However, our method can reduce wrong matching and achieve more accurate segmentation results.

Figure 6 shows the qualitative results on the YouTube-VOS dataset, our method can distinguish multiple objects well when there are multiple similar objects in the video, achieving excellent segmentation results.

Table 6. Comparison of quantitative results on YouTube-VOS Validation dataset.

Method	$\mathcal{J}\&\mathcal{F} \uparrow$ (%)	Seen		Unseen	
		$\mathcal{J} \uparrow$ (%)	$\mathcal{F} \uparrow$ (%)	$\mathcal{J} \uparrow$ (%)	$\mathcal{F} \uparrow$ (%)
OSMN [22]	51.2	60.0	60.1	40.6	44.0
RGMP [13]	53.8	59.5	–	45.2	–
STMNet [14]	79.4	79.7	84.2	72.8	80.9
AFB URR [9]	79.6	78.8	83.1	74.1	82.6
GraphMem [12]	80.2	80.7	85.1	74.0	80.9
SSM [24]	66.5	72.3	57.8	73.3	62.6
SwiftNet [18]	77.8	77.8	81.8	72.3	79.5
LCM [4]	**82.0**	**82.2**	**86.7**	**75.7**	**83.4**
RMNet [20]	81.5	82.1	85.7	75.5	82.4
MPRNet (Ours)	80.1	80.3	84.2	74.4	81.6

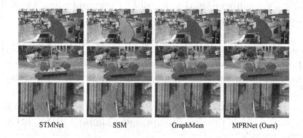

STMNet   SSM   GraphMem   MPRNet (Ours)

Fig. 5. Comparison of qualitative results on DAVIS 2017 Validation dataset.

Fig. 6. Demonstration of qualitative results on YouTube-VOS dataset.

6   Conclusion

This paper studies semi-supervised video object segmentation and proposes a novel method that joint memory propagation and rectification to address the problem that existing spatio-temporal matching based methods are prone to similar pixels' wrong matching. We introduce the memory propagation module to integrate abundant temporal cues from the reference frame sequence and memory rectification module guided by the similarity between frames to increase the inter-frame consistency constraint to retrieve reliable memory. Our method maintains constant inference time and memory usage in the sequence segmentation, experimental results verify that it can effectively reduce wrong matching and achieve good segmentation results in sequences with multiple similar objects.

References

1. Chen, L.C., Papandreou, G., Kokkinos, I., Murphy, K., Yuille, A.L.: Deeplab: semantic image segmentation with deep convolutional nets, atrous convolution, and fully connected crfs. IEEE Trans. Pattern Anal. Mach. Intell. **40**(4), 834–848 (2018)
2. Elman, J.L.: Finding structure in time. Cognitive Sci. **14**(2), 179–211 (1990). https://www.sciencedirect.com/science/article/pii/036402139090002E
3. He, K., Zhang, X., Ren, S., Sun, J.: Deep residual learning for image recognition. In: 2016 IEEE Conference on Computer Vision and Pattern Recognition (CVPR), pp. 770–778 (2016)
4. Hu, L., Zhang, P., Zhang, B., Pan, P., Xu, Y., Jin, R.: Learning position and target consistency for memory-based video object segmentation. In: 2021 IEEE/CVF Conference on Computer Vision and Pattern Recognition (CVPR), pp. 4142–4152 (2021)
5. Hu, P., Liu, J., Wang, G., Ablavsky, V., Saenko, K., Sclaroff, S.: Dipnet: Dynamic identity propagation network for video object segmentation. In: 2020 IEEE Winter Conference on Applications of Computer Vision (WACV). pp. 1893–1902 (2020)
6. Hu, Y.-T., Huang, J.-B., Schwing, A.G.: VideoMatch: matching based video object segmentation. In: Ferrari, V., Hebert, M., Sminchisescu, C., Weiss, Y. (eds.) ECCV 2018. LNCS, vol. 11212, pp. 56–73. Springer, Cham (2018). https://doi.org/10.1007/978-3-030-01237-3_4
7. Jiang, H., Zhang, G., Wang, H., Bao, H.: Spatio-temporal video segmentation of static scenes and its applications. IEEE Trans. Multimedia **17**(1), 3–15 (2015)
8. Li, Yu., Shen, Z., Shan, Y.: Fast video object segmentation using the global context module. In: Vedaldi, A., Bischof, H., Brox, T., Frahm, J.-M. (eds.) ECCV 2020. LNCS, vol. 12355, pp. 735–750. Springer, Cham (2020). https://doi.org/10.1007/978-3-030-58607-2_43
9. Liang, Y., Li, X., Jafari, N.H., Chen, J.: Video object segmentation with adaptive feature bank and uncertain-region refinement. In: Advances in Neural Information Processing Systems 33: Annual Conference on Neural Information Processing Systems 2020 (2020)
10. Lin, H., Qi, X., Jia, J.: Agss-vos: attention guided single-shot video object segmentation. In: 2019 IEEE/CVF International Conference on Computer Vision (ICCV), pp. 3948–3956 (2019)
11. Lin, T.-Y., et al.: Microsoft COCO: common objects in context. In: Fleet, D., Pajdla, T., Schiele, B., Tuytelaars, T. (eds.) ECCV 2014. LNCS, vol. 8693, pp. 740–755. Springer, Cham (2014). https://doi.org/10.1007/978-3-319-10602-1_48
12. Lu, X., Wang, W., Danelljan, M., Zhou, T., Shen, J., Van Gool, L.: Video object segmentation with episodic graph memory networks. In: Vedaldi, A., Bischof, H., Brox, T., Frahm, J.-M. (eds.) ECCV 2020. LNCS, vol. 12348, pp. 661–679. Springer, Cham (2020). https://doi.org/10.1007/978-3-030-58580-8_39
13. Oh, S.W., Lee, J.Y., Sunkavalli, K., Kim, S.J.: Fast video object segmentation by reference-guided mask propagation. In: 2018 IEEE/CVF Conference on Computer Vision and Pattern Recognition, pp. 7376–7385 (2018)

14. Oh, S.W., Lee, J.Y., Xu, N., Kim, S.J.: Video object segmentation using space-time memory networks. In: 2019 IEEE/CVF International Conference on Computer Vision (ICCV), pp. 9225–9234 (2019)

15. Perazzi, F., Pont-Tuset, J., McWilliams, B., Van Gool, L., Gross, M., Sorkine-Hornung, A.: A benchmark dataset and evaluation methodology for video object segmentation. In: 2016 IEEE Conference on Computer Vision and Pattern Recognition (CVPR), pp. 724–732 (2016)

16. Pont-Tuset, J., Perazzi, F., Caelles, S., Arbeláez, P., Sorkine-Hornung, A., Van Gool, L.: The 2017 davis challenge on video object segmentation. arXiv preprint arXiv:1704.00675 (2017)

17. Voigtlaender, P., Chai, Y., Schroff, F., Adam, H., Leibe, B., Chen, L.C.: Feelvos: fast end-to-end embedding learning for video object segmentation. In: 2019 IEEE/CVF Conference on Computer Vision and Pattern Recognition (CVPR), pp. 9473–9482 (2019)

18. Wang, H., Jiang, X., Ren, H., Hu, Y., Bai, S.: Swiftnet: real-time video object segmentation. In: 2021 IEEE/CVF Conference on Computer Vision and Pattern Recognition (CVPR), pp. 1296–1305 (2021)

19. Wang, Z., Xu, J., Liu, L., Zhu, F., Shao, L.: Ranet: ranking attention network for fast video object segmentation. In: 2019 IEEE/CVF International Conference on Computer Vision (ICCV), pp. 3977–3986 (2019)

20. Xie, H., Yao, H., Zhou, S., Zhang, S., Sun, W.: Efficient regional memory network for video object segmentation. In: 2021 IEEE/CVF Conference on Computer Vision and Pattern Recognition (CVPR), pp. 1286–1295 (2021)

21. Xu, N., et al.: YouTube-VOS: sequence-to-sequence video object segmentation. In: Ferrari, V., Hebert, M., Sminchisescu, C., Weiss, Y. (eds.) ECCV 2018. LNCS, vol. 11209, pp. 603–619. Springer, Cham (2018). https://doi.org/10.1007/978-3-030-01228-1_36

22. Yang, L., Wang, Y., Xiong, X., Yang, J., Katsaggelos, A.K.: Efficient video object segmentation via network modulation. In: 2018 IEEE/CVF Conference on Computer Vision and Pattern Recognition, pp. 6499–6507 (2018)

23. Zhang, Z., Fidler, S., Urtasun, R.: Instance-level segmentation for autonomous driving with deep densely connected mrfs. In: 2016 IEEE Conference on Computer Vision and Pattern Recognition (CVPR), pp. 669–677 (2016)

24. Zhu, W., Li, J., Lu, J., Zhou, J.: Separable structure modeling for semi-supervised video object segmentation. IEEE Trans. Circuits Syst. Video Technol. **32**(1), 330–344 (2022)

A Novel Intelligent Assessment Based on Audio-Visual Data for Chinese Zither Fingerings

Wenting Zhao, Shigang Wang[✉], Yan Zhao, Jian Wei, and Tianshu Li

College of Communication Engineering, Jilin University, Changchun, China
wangshigang@vip.sina.com

Abstract. In this paper, we make a novel study on the intelligent assessment for Chinese zither (Zheng) fingerings in the cross field of art AI. Due to the gaps between science and art, there is a lack of deep combination of musical instrument expertise with computer aided technology. This paper attempts to explore the inheritance and innovation of Chinese classical musical instrument in this interdisciplinary study. We integrate video understanding, audio analysis with zither professional knowledge to design a pipeline for Zheng intelligent evaluation. Firstly, we establish a Zheng fingering Dataset based on video and audio (ZF-VA-Dataset). Then, according to zither teaching experience and accumulated research on machine perception, we formulate a Zheng fingering assessment scale, which is served as a bridge between Zheng knowledge and audio-visual technology. Finally, an intelligent evaluation method based on dual modes is put forward for Chinese zither fingerings. The experimental results show that the proposed scheme is feasible and effective in achieving intelligent assessment of Zheng fingerings.

Keywords: Chinese zither · video understanding · audio analysis · fingering assessment · dataset

1 Introduction

Basic fingerings are the foundation for learning musical instruments. As is well known, basic skills are the top priority in acquiring any skill. Performers express the emotions of composers and individuals through musical instruments and the music expression requires many performance techniques, so skills are the foundation and support for emotional expression. In the process of Zheng teaching and learning, timely feedback and intelligent evaluation of fingerings can greatly help beginners correct fingering deviations, thereby improving the efficiency of Zheng practice.

This paper proposes an intelligent assessment method for Chinese zither fingerings, which aims to bridge the gap between music and computer science. The proposed approach integrates image recognition, video understanding, audio analysis and professional knowledge of Zheng performance in a framework designed for Chinese zither intelligent evaluation. To facilitate this research, we first establish a Zheng fingering dataset based on audio and video. This dataset includes various recordings of experienced zither players performing specific fingerings, allowing for a diverse set of data to be utilized in recognizing and assessing proper Zheng fingerings. We also formulate a comprehensive Zheng fingering assessment scale based on zither teaching experience and machine vision technique. This scale includes multiple criteria for evaluating finger selection, string selection, intonation and so on, enabling a detailed analysis of player performance. An intelligent evaluation method based on dual modes is proposed, which integrates both visual and audio data for a more accurate and reliable assessment of Zheng fingerings. Specifically, the proposed method uses advanced machine learning algorithms to process and analyze audio and video data separately before combining the outputs of both branches for a final evaluation result. The proposed scheme is not only feasible but also highly effective in promoting the inheritance and innovation of Chinese classical music. The intelligent assessment method not only enables objective and unbiased evaluation of player performance but also provides valuable insights for both zither players and music educators in improving their skills and teaching approaches.

In the aspect of musical instrument AI, most of the study focus on the electronic music, such as music retrieval [1–3], audio transcription [4–6], artificial intelligence composition [7–10], etc. The research on musical instruments mainly focuses on electronic keyboard and other musical instruments with MIDI interface [11–14]. The majority of research on musical instrument AI also focuses on the piano [15–20], which is inevitably related to the highest popularity of the piano worldwide. In addition, there is research on western musical instruments such as violin [21, 22], guitar [23, 24], and drum. Relatively speaking, there is relatively less study on traditional Chinese ethnic musical instruments. The relevant work we retrieved is also aimed at Guqin [25, 26], which is easier to get started with. Furthermore, due to the extremely high professional barriers in art and technology, there is a lack of professional knowledge and relevant technology integration in this interdisciplinary research at present, resulting in the inability of most current research to effectively provide both intelligent and professional fingering assessment of musical instruments.

The primary objective of this paper is to develop an approach for predicting intelligent assessment of Zheng fingerings. The proposed method combines traditional Chinese art with video comprehension in computer vision, which offers a special view of video comprehension. In order to address the existing gap, we formulate an assessment scale and establish the ZF-VA-Dataset which comprises video and audio data samples. A multimodal evaluation method based on audio-visual perception is proposed for Zheng fingerings and experimentally validated. The rest of this paper is structured as follows: Sect. 2 elaborates the overall architecture. Datasets are introduced in Sect. 3. In Sect. 4, we describe the proposed method. The results of experiments are provided in Sect. 5. At last, we conclude the whole work in Sect. 6.

2 Framework

In this paper, we propose an intelligent assessment based on audio-visual data for Chinese zither fingerings. The general scheme not only conforms to the basic rules of Zheng but also realizes the computer-aided automatic evaluation, which is of professionalism and intelligence. The framework of our proposed method is shown in Fig. 1.

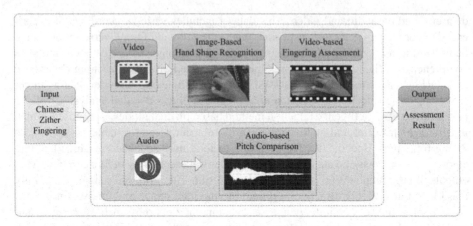

Fig. 1. Framework of Zheng fingering assessment based on bimodal

2.1 Video Assessment

Zheng professional knowledge:
To learn the zither, it is required to master the proper hand shape, and then learn the five basic right hand fingerings, including Tuo, Mo, Gou, Da Cuo, Xiao Cuo, with the interpretation shown in Table 1.

Table 1. Zheng fingering symbol

Symbol	Interpretation	Name
	Thumb outward pluck	Tuo
	Middle finger inward pluck	Gou
	Index finger inward pluck	Mo
	Thumb and middle finger combination	Da Cuo
	Thumb and index finger combination	Xiao Cuo

Video understanding technology:
Image based hand shape recognition: Images are extracted from the fingering video at the beginning and the end. A self-designed deep neural network is used to evaluate the basic hand shape of Chinese zither [27, 28].Video based fingering assessment: Mediapipe [30] is used to detect and track hand key points in fingering videos. Joint point information is combined with Zheng fingering prior knowledge to conduct visual based Zheng fingering evaluation.

2.2 Audio Assessment

Zheng expertise:

Chinese zither is a traditional Chinese pentatonic musical instrument (excluding the chromatic scale), namely, do, re, mi, sol, and la. The chromatic scale fa and si are produced by pressing the left string of the Zheng code with the left hand and simultaneously plucking this string with the right hand, as shown in Fig. 2. The zither has a total of 21 strings. It is easy to pluck the wrong string for beginners. Therefore, it is necessary to judge whether the string plucked is correct and whether the chromatic scale is accurate from an audio perspective.

Fig. 2. Example of chromatic scale

Audio Analysis Technology:

Audio based pitch comparison: Audio is extracted from the input. Fourier transform is used to obtain frequency domain information. The fundamental frequency is compared with the standard pitch to determine whether the pitch and string selection are correct or not.

3 Dataset

The datasets involved in this paper are shown in Fig. 3. CZ-Dataset V3 [28] is a hand shape recognition dataset for Chinese zither, which is established by us. It is used to evaluate hand shape images from the beginning and the end frames of fingering video. Mediapipe Dataset [30] is a dataset used to track hand key points in video, obtain motion information of fingering key points and provide the required data for video based fingering evaluation. ZF-Dataset [29] is a Zheng fingering video dataset constructed in our previous work to evaluate the basic fingerings from a visual perspective.

ZF-VA-Dataset is a Zheng fingering dataset based on audio and video dual modes, which is constructed in this paper. ZF-VA-Dataset collects 600 examples from 22 volunteers in total. There are 5 subsets included and the number of subsets is shown in Table 2. Each subset contains correct and common errors in fingerings, as well as accurate and biased pitch.

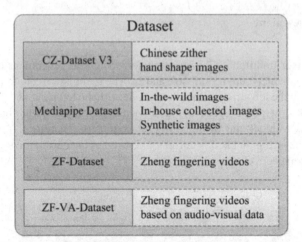

Fig. 3. Dataset

Table 2. Number of ZF-VA-Dataset

Subset	Gou	Tuo	Mo	Da Cuo	Xiao Cuo
Number	120	156	145	86	93

4 Method

We formulate an assessment scale for Zheng fingering, as shown in Table 3, which not only meets the key points of Zheng knowledge, but also can be characterized and calculated by machines. The video based evaluation method for Zheng fingering has been completed in our previous work. This section will elaborate on audio based intonation comparison.

Zheng is usually set in D major and the corresponding relationship between musical scale and frequency is shown in Table 4. The audio is extracted from the input and converted the time domain to the frequency domain to obtain its frequency.

The temporal expression of sound is:

$$Y_k = \sum_{i=0}^{\infty} A_i cos(2\pi f_i k t_s + \varphi_i), k = 0, 1, 2, \cdots \tag{1}$$

where Y_k is a discrete acoustic wave function, A_i is the amplitude, f_i is the frequency, t_s is the sampling time interval, and φ_i is the phase.

After discrete Fourier transform (DFT), the frequency domain expression of sound is:

$$Z_k = \sum_{n=0}^{N-1} Y_n e^{-i\frac{2\pi}{N}kn}, 0 \leq k \leq N - 1 \tag{2}$$

Table 3. Assessment Scale for Zheng Fingering based on Audio and Video

Result	Description	Suggestion
Video Correct	Gou	----
	Tuo	----
	Mo	----
	Da Cuo	----
	Xiao Cuo	----
Video Error	Wrong hand shape	Refer to the assessment scale of Zheng hand shape
	Fingering selected error	Check fingering symbol
	Wrong direction of plucking	Pluck the string towards the centre of the palm
	Hand joint collapse	Make a hollow fist with all knuckles bulged
	Hand instability	Keep the hand stable
	Crooked joints	Relax the finger, bent it in a natural way
Audio Correct	Correct intonation	----
Audio Error	Wrong string selection	Pluck the right string
	Chromatic scale inaccurate	Adjust the strength of the left hand against the string

Table 4. Musical scale and frequency correspondence chart (D major; Middle register)

Pentatonic scale	Roll call	Musical alphabet	Frequency(Hz)
1	Do	D	587
2	Re	E	659
3	Mi	#F	740
5	Sol	A	880
6	La	B	988
Chromatic scale	Roll call	Musical alphabet	Frequency(Hz)
4	Fa	G	784
7	Si	#C	1109

Z_k is a complex sequence:

$$Z_k = a_k + b_k i, 0 \le k \le N - 1 \tag{3}$$

The mode and phase angle of Z_k can directly reflect the amplitude A_k and phase φ_k of sound waves.

$$A_k = \frac{\sqrt{a_k^2 + b_k^2}}{N} \times 2, 1 \le k \le N-1 \tag{4}$$

$$\varphi_k = tan^{-1}\frac{b_k}{a_k} \tag{5}$$

(1) Judgement of string selection

The obtained frequency is compared with the frequency of each pentatonic scale. We take the tone level P corresponding to the minimum absolute value. If it is the same as the specified tone level Q, then the string played is correct. If it is different, then it is an error.

$$O = min|f - f(i)|, i = D, E, \#F, A, B \tag{6}$$

Judgement:

$$\begin{cases} P = Q, \text{Correct} \\ P \ne Q, \text{Error} \end{cases} \tag{7}$$

(2) Judgement of chromatic accuracy

The resulting frequency is compared to the standard frequency of the chromatic scale. If it is greater than the threshold δ, it is higher, and the left hand pressing force on the string needs to be reduced. If it is less than $-\delta$, it is low, and the left hand needs to press the string harder. If the absolute value is less than or equal to the threshold value, it is correct.

$$\begin{cases} f - f(i) > \delta, & \text{Higher} \\ -\delta \le f - f(i) \le \delta, & \text{Correct} \\ f - f(i) < -\delta, & \text{Lower} \end{cases} \tag{8}$$

5   Experiments

5.1   Results of Video Assessment

The hand joint tracking of Zheng fingering is realized by using MediaPipe Hands method. Take the thumb outward pluck (Tuo) as an example, part of the results for Zheng fingering key point tracking is shown in Fig. 4. (a) is the 1st frame, (b) is the 20th frame, (c) is the 30th frame, (d) is the 40th frame, and (e) is the 50th frame.

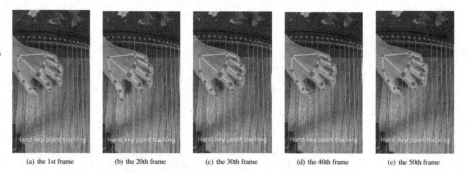

(a) the 1st frame   (b) the 20th frame   (c) the 30th frame   (d) the 40th frame   (e) the 50th frame

Fig. 4. Results of Zheng fingering joint tracking (Thumb)

For the constructed ZF-VA-Dataset, results of the video evaluation are shown in Table 5, which provides the detection and recognition accuracy. Each fingering subset includes the following audio samples: correct fingering, wrong hand shape, fingering selected error, wrong direction of plucking, hand joint collapse, hand instability, crooked joints.

Table 5. Results of video assessment (%)

Subset	Gou	Tuo	Mo	Da Cuo	Xiao Cuo
Accuracy	72.50	73.72	74.48	67.44	62.37

The experimental results show that the accuracy of Da Cuo and Xiao Cuo is lower than that of the other three subsets. Because the fingering Cuo involves two fingers simultaneously plucking strings, while Gou, Tuo and Mo are all completed by a single finger, which increases the difficulty of detecting and tracking hand key points and affects the final accuracy.

5.2 Results of Audio Assessment

Taking the chromatic scale 'fa' as an example, its time-domain waveform is shown in Fig. 5 and frequency domain is shown in Fig. 6. (a) contains harmonic information. (b) clearly displays its fundamental frequency.

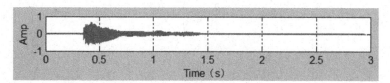

Fig. 5. Time domain of chromatic scale (fa)

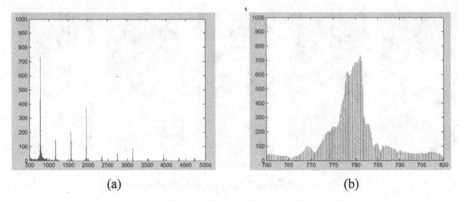

(a)   (b)

Fig. 6. Frequency domain of chromatic scale (fa)

Using the ZF-VA-Dataset we established for testing, results of the audio assessment are shown in Table 6. Each fingering subset includes the following audio samples: correct intonation, wrong string selection, chromatic scale inaccurate.

Table 6. Results of audio assessment (%)

Subset	Gou	Tuo	Mo	Da Cuo	Xiao Cuo
Accuracy	98.33	99.35	97.93	95.34	96.77

5.3 Examples of Zheng Fingering Assessment

Examples of an intelligent evaluation of Chinese zither fingering in Fig. 7. (a) is an example of video error with correct audio; (b) is an example of correct video with bias audio. For the input of Zheng fingering, intelligent assessment results and improvement suggestions are given.

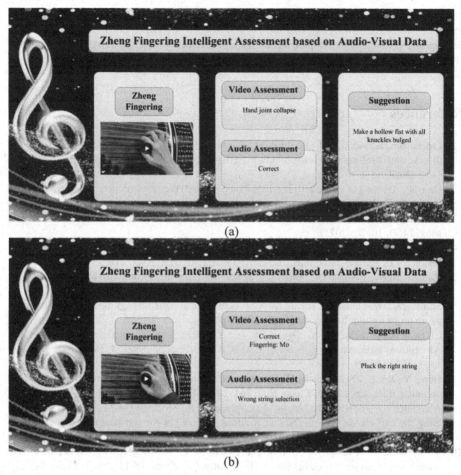

Fig. 7. Examples of Zheng fingering assessment

6 Conclusion

This paper attempts to explore the intelligent evaluation of Zheng fingerings in the cross field of art AI. We integrate professional knowledge, video understanding and audio analysis to provide a cognitive solution so that technology empowers the inheritance and innovation of Chinese traditional musical instruments. An audio-visual dataset of Zheng fingerings is constructed. We formulate a fingering evaluation scale that combines knowledge and technology. A bimodal Zheng fingering assessment method is proposed in this paper. This scheme converts professional musical instrument knowledge into computer-representable and computable digital information through audio-visual data, making intelligent professional learning possible. The design idea we put forward can be transplanted to intelligent fingering evaluation of other musical instruments, which reflects the extensibility and wide application of this interdisciplinary exploration.

Acknowledgment. This work is supported by Science and Technology Development Plan of Jilin Province (No.20210201027GX); National Natural Science Foundation of China (No.61901187); Science and Technology Development Plan of Jilin Province (No.20220101104JC); Fundamental Research Funds for the Central Universities (No.415010300076).

References

1. Ostermann, F., Vatolkin, I., Ebeling, M.: AAM: a dataset of artificial audio multitracks for diverse music information retrieval tasks. EURASIP J. Audio, Speech, Music Proc. **2023**(1), 1–12 (2023)
2. Bao, N.: Analysis of music retrieval based on emotional tags environment. J. Environ. Public Health **2022**, 4670963 (2022)
3. Olivieri, M., et al.: Audio information retrieval and musical acoustics. IEEE Instrum. Meas. Mag. **24**(7), 10–20 (2021)
4. Alfaro-Contreras, M., Valero-Mas, J.J., Iñesta, J.M., Calvo-Zaragoza, J.: Late multimodal fusion for image and audio music transcription. Expert Syst. Appl. **216**, 119491 (2023)
5. Román, M.A., Pertusa, A., Calvo-Zaragoza, J.: Data representations for audio-to-score monophonic music transcription. Expert Syst. Appl. **162**, 113769 (2020)
6. Shibata, K., Nakamura, E., Yoshii, K.: Non-local musical statistics as guides for audio-to-score piano transcription. Inf. Sci. **566**, 262–280 (2021)
7. Li, H., Sakai, T., Tanaka, A., Ogura, M., Lee, C., Yamaguchi, S., Imazato, S.: Interpretable AI explores effective components of CAD/CAM resin composites. J. Dent. Res. **101**(11), 1363–1371 (2022)
8. Deng, Y., Xu, Z., Zhou, L., Liu, H., Huang, A.: Research on AI composition recognition based on music rules. Lect. Notes Electr. Eng. **761**, 187–197 (2021)
9. Alabduljabbar, H., Khan, K., Awan, H.H., Alyousef, R., Mohamed, A.M., Eldin, S.M.: Modeling the capacity of engineered cementitious composites for self-healing using AI-based ensemble techniques. Case Stud. Constr. Mater. **18**, e01805 (2023)
10. Vallejos, S., Da Rocha, L., Araujo, G.R., Berdun, L., Toscani, R.: Preference-based AI planning for web service composition. IEEE Latin Am. Trans. **18**(11), 1987–1995 (2020)
11. Yang, R.: Extended QUALIFLEX method for electronic music acoustic quality evaluation based on the picture fuzzy multiple attribute group decision making. J. Intell. Fuzzy Syst. **44**(3), 5021–5032 (2023)
12. Guo, T.: Evaluation of the emotion model in electronic music based on PSO-BP. Comput. Intell. Neurosci. **2022**(1), 1–9 (2022)
13. de Marques Andrade, T.G.: Free robotics and the teaching of physics and programming developing an electronic music keyboard (Article). Texto Livre **11**(3), 317–330 (2018)
14. Hanson, A.: Music Keyboard Based on Flexible Hybrid Electronics (2018)
15. Sparkes, M.: Being graded by an AI could improve your piano playing. New Scientist **249**(3319), 15 (2021)
16. Chen, Y., Zheng, N.: AI based research on exploration and innovation of development direction of piano performance teaching in university. J. Intell. Fuzzy Syst. 1–7 (2020)
17. Guo, R., Cui, J., Zhao, W., Li, S.: AI and AR based interface for piano training. In: 2020 International Conference on Virtual Reality and Visualization (ICVRV) (2020)
18. Parmar, P., Reddy, J., Morris, B.: Piano skills assessment. In: 2021 IEEE 23rd International Workshop on Multimedia Signal Processing (MMSP) (2021)
19. Arthur, P., McPhee, E., Blom, D.: Determining what expert piano sight-readers have in common. Music Educ. Res. **22**(4), 447–456 (2020)

20. Zheng, Y.D., Tian, T., Zhang, A.: Training strategy of music expression in piano teaching and performance by intelligent multimedia technology. Int. Trans. Electr. Energy Syst. **2022**, 1–14 (2022)
21. Giraldo, S., et al.: Automatic assessment of tone quality in violin music performance. Front. Psychol. **10**, 334 (2019)
22. Nauncef, A.M., et al.: 14. Interdisciplinary approach to assessing the acoustic quality of violins. Rev. Artistic Educ. **23**(1), 111–119 (2022)
23. Giampiccolo, R., Bernardini, A., Sarti, A.: Virtualization of guitar pickups through circuit inversion. IEEE Signal Process. Lett. **30**, 1–5 (2023)
24. Ferretti, S.: Clustering of musical pieces through complex networks: an assessment over guitar solos. IEEE Multimedia **25**, 57–67 (2018)
25. Shen, D.: Sound design of guqin culture: interactive art promotes the sustainable development of traditional culture. Sustainability **14**(4), 2356 (2022)
26. Zhang, M., Zhang, J.: A gesturally controlled virtual musical instruments for Chinese Guqin. In: International Conference on Intelligent Computing and Human-Computer Interaction (ICHCI) (2020)
27. Zhao, W., et al.: CZ-Base: a database for hand gesture recognition in Chinese zither intelligence education. In: Zhai, G., Zhou, J., Yang, H., An, P., Yang, X. (eds.) Digital TV and Wireless Multimedia Communication: 17th International Forum, IFTC 2020, Shanghai, China, December 2, 2020, Revised Selected Papers, pp. 282–292. Springer Singapore, Singapore (2021). https://doi.org/10.1007/978-981-16-1194-0_25
28. Zhao, W., Wang, S., Zhao, Y., Wei, J., Li, T., Zhang, R.: Self-designed hierarchical network based hand shape intelligent recognition and evaluation for Chinese zither performing. Displays **76**, 102291 (2023)
29. Zhao, W., Wang, S., Zhao, Y., Wei, J., Li, T.: Knowledge and data co-driven intelligent assessment of Chinese zither fingerings. Displays **78**, 102442 (2023)
30. Zhang, F., Bazarevsky, V., et al.: Mediapipe hands: on-device real-time hand tracking. CVPR (2020)

A Full-Level Based Network to Detect Every Aircraft in Airport Scene

Xinzhi Li[1], Xiang Zhang[1,2(✉)], Juncong Meng[1], and Lanjie Jiang[1]

[1] University of Electronic Science and Technology of China (UESTC), Chengdu 611731, Sichuan, China
uestchero@uestc.edu.cn, 202052012112@std.uestc.edu.cn

[2] Yangtze Delta Region Institute (Quzhou), University of Electronic Science and Technology of China, Quzhou 324000, Zhejiang, China

Abstract. The rapid development of civil aviation has led to increasingly crowded airports. The complex airport environment and large number of aircraft make airport object detection a difficult task. Due to the large extension of the fuselage and wings, close-range aircraft objects have scattered features, making it difficult for prediction boxes to accurately locate them. Objects at far distances are too small in scale, and their features are easily lost during network feature extraction and fusion processes, resulting in frequent missed detections. Lower-level signals in the network contain more object positioning information and small object detection information, but existing networks usually do not fully utilize low-level signals. Therefore, this paper focuses more on utilizing lower-level signals and designs an object detection network for airport scenarios with several advantages as follows: (1) We designed a fusion module to incorporate low-level network signals into the neck, reducing the network's missed detection rate for small objects and improving its ability to locate objects. (2) We add a detection head on the low-level network for detecting small and medium objects in airports, improving the network's versatility in detection scale. (3) The anchor-free improvement of the network greatly not only reduces the computational complexity during training, but also improves the network's full-scale accuracy. We validate our experimental method on the AGVS (Airport Ground Video Surveillance) airport scene detection dataset.

Keywords: Airport Scene · CBAM · TiC Module · Detection Head · Anchor-free

1 Introduction

Airport scene monitoring is of great significance in preventing runway intrusion and airway conflicts. Currently, Global is in the process of transitioning from manual monitoring to automated monitoring. Due to the fact that most of the surveillance cameras in airports are fixed, and different planes have different distances from the cameras, there is a large difference in scale between aircrafts. The large number of distant aircrafts from the cameras results in a higher proportion of small-scale aircrafts. In addition, the similarity between the color of most aircrafts and the airport ground also increases the difficulty of network detection. Therefore, how to correctly and robustly identify aircraft in airport is an important and difficult issue.

Fig. 1. Examples of aircraft object in AGVS dataset, Including different monitoring perspectives, lighting conditions, and occlusion situations.

During the process of collecting the dataset, we noticed that airport scene images have significant variations due to different camera angles, lighting conditions, and obstruction situations. As shown in Fig. 1, the dataset covers scenes of airports during day and night time with different camera focal lengths and various building obstructions, resulting in extremely complex scenes in the dataset images. Secondly, due to the long length of aircraft wings, features of aircraft objects are relatively scattered under certain angles making it difficult to achieve perfect regression for detection boxes. Thirdly, most aircraft objects have paint colors similar to those on airport grounds which increases difficulty for networks to extract features from aircrafts. More information about object positioning and small object detection exists at lower-level networks while higher-level networks focus more on object characteristics themselves. Existing networks utilize lower-level features relatively less often and tend to only focus on higher-level features; thus still facing difficulties when predicting box regressions for objects with dispersed features or detecting small objects. Due to these reasons mentioned above, existing object detection networks are not entirely suitable for detecting aircraft objects in airport scenes. The goal of this paper is to design an object detection network for airport scenarios, in order to replace the manual visual monitoring of airport scenes.

In conclusion, the main contributions of this paper are:

- We integrate attention mechanism into the network to help it find the regions of interest in scene images with large coverage.
- We designed TiC(Tri-directional Concatenation) module. Through the TiC module, the neck integrates additional signals from lower-level networks at each layer during the signal fusion process, thereby improving the network's ability to locate objects.
- An additional small object detection head was designed specifically for small object detection, forming a prediction network with four detection heads.
- When designing the network, decoupling was applied to the detection head and an anchor-free approach was used, which reduced the complexity of the network during computation and improved overall detection accuracy.

The remaining parts of this paper are as follows: In Sect. 2, we briefly review the research related to our work. Then, details of the proposed detection network are given in Sect. 3. In Sect. 4, we introduce our datasets and evaluation metrics. Finally, in Sect. 5, we summarize our methods and provide perspectives for future work.

2   Related Work

In this task, the goal of the network is to extract features of aircrafts in the airport and perform object detection based on these features. Traditional object detection networks usually extract features manually, which can be summarized into several steps: region selection, feature extraction, and classifier classification. Among them, feature extraction is the core step. In 2001, the VJ detector [1, 2] was proposed, which used sliding windows to detect objects. In 2005, Dalal proposed the HOG [3] detector, which extracted feature histograms of image pixel blocks as features and achieved good results in combination with support vector machines. However, traditional methods have always faced shortcomings such as poor recognition performance, high computational complexity leading to slow operation speed, and non-unique correct recognition results. They are gradually being replaced by convolutional neural networks.

After entering the field of deep learning, many paper focus on researching network design for aircraft aviation image recognition, but few paper pay attention to the recognition networks for aircraft themselves. Traditional airports usually use radar [4] or ADS-B [5] to locate aircraft, which is accurate but visually poor. The earliest deep learning-based object recognition used a two-stage calculation with a CNN [6]. Firstly, the region proposal network creates candidate regions and feature maps for the object, and then the ROI pooling layer is used to crop and detect the object from the candidate regions. However, this method is only suitable for simple scenes and performs poorly in complex scenes. YOLO [7–10] considers classification and regression as one task and completes detection with one calculation. YOLO divides the input image into S*S cells, and the cell that contains the center of an object is responsible for object detection. YOLOv3 uses Darknet53 as backbone and obtains three different-sized feature maps through a series of convolutional and residual operations, responsible for detecting objects of different scales. In recent years, more and more networks have abandoned anchor-based and chosen to use the anchor-free concept for network design. The three-stage network structure proposed by YOLO has great potential in both academia and industry. Various improved versions based on it have been widely used in various fields.

3   The Proposed Method

This paper focuses on the detection of aircraft objects in airport scenes, especially the problem of small-scale aircraft object detection and the fit of the prediction box to the object. We used a three-stage network structure (backbone, neck and prediction network) and designed an object detection network suitable for airport scenes. We will introduce the network in the order of the network structure.

3.1   Backbone with CBAM

CBAM [11] is a simple yet effective attention module. It is a lightweight module that can be easily integrated into CNN architectures and trained end-to-end. Given a feature map, CBAM sequentially infers attention maps along both channel and spatial dimensions independently, and then multiplies the attention maps with the input feature map to perform adaptive feature refinement. Figure 2 is the Overview of CBAM module. In the airport scene images captured by surveillance cameras, there are many confusing elements. Using CBAM can help the network eliminate interference and extract key feature, improving the network's detection accuracy for full-scale objects.

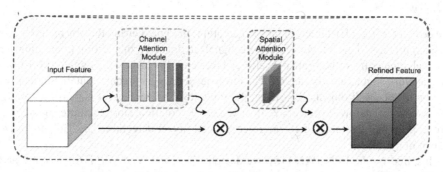

Fig. 2. Overview of CBAM module.

Figure 3 shows the detailed structure of our backbone. After conducting comparative experiments by splitting the attention module into multiple locations, we chose to insert it into the backbone network to achieve maximum network performance improvement. All four layers of the C2-C5 network have signal input to the neck network.

We choose ACON [12] as the activation function on the basic convolution block. The ACON activation function unifies the ReLU [13] and Swish [14] activations with better non-linear performance. The combination of blocks named CBA results in a convolutional block. We use two types of convolution modules with different kernel sizes and strides: 3×3 kernels with a stride length of 2, and 3×3 kernels with a stride length of 1. Two types of convolutional modules are alternately used to downsample the feature map while achieving better feature extraction.

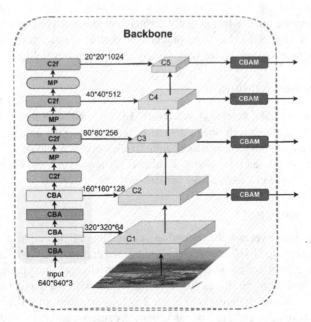

Fig. 3. Detail Structure of Backbone.

3.2 TiC-FPN

We design the TiC (Tri-directional Concatenation) module. During the downward transmission process of each layer of network signals in the neck, in addition to merging the original signals from the higher-level P_{i+1} layer and this layer's C_i signal, lower-level C_{i-1} network signals are also added. The lower-level network signals contain more information about small objects. By fusing the three levels of signals, it is possible to take into account both low-level signals, then effectively combine strong feature signals and strong positioning signals, achieving better small object detection. The TiC module is shown in Fig. 4.

Inspired by the FPN-PAN [15], we designs TiC-FPN. The SPP [16] structure and RepBlock [17] are added to the design of the neck. In the process of downward transmission of features from layer P5 to P3, we added TiC modules for three-way signal fusion. The neck designed called TiC-PAN, which outputs four signals corresponding to four different sizes of detection heads. Figure 5 shows the structure of TiC-PAN.

3.3 Additional Detection Head

The AGVS [18] dataset contains many small objects at long distances, so we have added an additional prediction head for detecting these small objects. The four detection heads work together to achieve high-performance detection of full-scale objects. Since the additional detection head is located in a shallow position in the network, it not only enhances the network's ability to detect small objects but also improves its ability to locate objects. This comes at a certain computational cost but results in significant

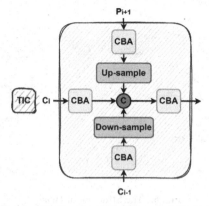

Fig. 4. Tri-directional Concatenation Module

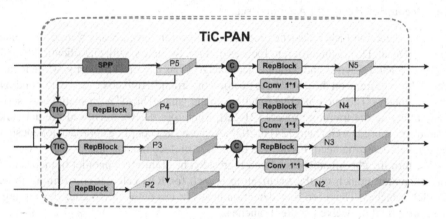

Fig. 5. The Structure of TiC-PAN

improvements in small object detection performance. The structure of the network's detection head is shown in Fig. 6. The four detection heads range in size from small to large, measuring 20×20, 40×40, 80×80, and 160×160 respectively. Since this paper decouples the detection head and calculates the classification and regression tasks separately, each detection head has two big branches.

We chose ms-testing as the strategy for inference and trained four models to obtain model ensembles. The ms-testing in this paper includes two steps: scaling the images by 1x, 0.83x, and 0.67x respectively; flipping the images horizontally. We input the four images into the network and perform combination testing using NMS [19] method. The results of different models are fused through WBF [20] to obtain the final prediction result.

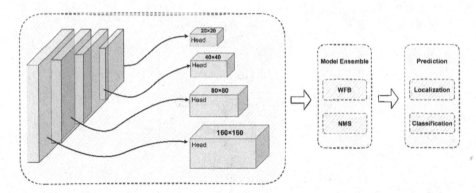

Fig. 6. The Structure of Head

3.4 Decoupled Head and Anchor-Free

In object detection tasks, classification and localization have always shared the same detection head. Due to the different focuses of these two tasks, with classification focusing on extracted features and which object category has a higher similarity, while localization focuses more on the coordinate position of Ground Truth box to correct bounding box parameters. The two objective functions in the "shared head" have spatial bias, seriously affecting the training process [21–23]. Therefore, So we borrowed the network structure proposed by Gezheng [24] in 2021. And used a decoupling approach to redesign the original detection head. Figure 7 is the design of decoupled head.

We turn the classification head and regression head into two parallel branches and add a separate branch on the localization branch for IOU calculation, forming three parallel branches. There are four detection heads in our network, so after decoupling, there are a total of twelve parallel branches.

We reduced the number of candidate boxes at each position from three to one, and directly predicted the four values of w, h, x, and y to complete the transformation of anchor-free. By setting the center position of an object as a positive sample, and predefining a scale range for each object, we can quickly confirm objects in the layer where FPN is located.

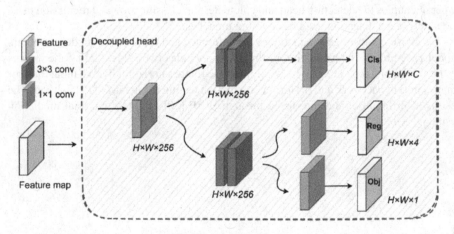

Fig. 7. Decoupled head

The label assignment is a method of assigning labels between predicted boxes and true boxes. Good label assignment has four characteristics: 1. loss/quality aware, 2. center prior, 3. dynamic number of positive anchors for each ground-truth, 4. Global view. In this paper, we choose SimOTA [25] as the tag assignment method. SimOTA calculates the matching degree of pairs and represents the matching degree of each predicted-true value with cost or quality, which is an network with very low computational complexity. Through the above improvements, the overall performance of the network can have a qualitative improvement.

4 Experiments

We evaluate the model on the AGVS dataset. Since there is only one classification for this dataset, which is aircraft, so we only report AP and FPS.

4.1 Implementation Details

We implement the network in Pytorch 1.8 and train and test all models on NVIDIA RTX2080ti. Due to the relatively small size of the AGVS training set, we trained for 80 epochs on it. We chose Adam optimizer with an initial learning rate of 3e-4 combined with cosine lr decay. The input image size is 3840×2160, so we set the batchsize to 4.

When developing neural network models for computer vision tasks, data augmentation is a commonly employed strategy to enhance performance and reduce generalization errors. Additionally, image data augmentation can be applied to the test dataset when making predictions using the model, allowing it to make predictions on several variations of the same image. The predictions made on these augmented images can be averaged to improve prediction accuracy.

To elaborate, during the testing process, we rescale the test images to three distinct sizes and also flip them horizontally, resulting in a total of six images. We then use the model to make predictions on each of the six images and combine the results to obtain the final test outcome.

4.2 Comparisons with SOTA

We compared our network with some previous networks including SOTA on the AGVS dataset. The experimental data is shown in Table 1. Our method achieved a score of 82.1% in AP.

4.3 Ablation Studies

The final model in this paper was obtained by combining four trained models through model ensemble. Results of ablation experiments on each key component are shown in Table 2. 'w/o' is an abbreviation for 'without', indicating that the network has removed that module.

Table 1. The comparisons of the performance in AGVS.

Network	AP
Faster RCNN	63.2
Cascade-RCNN [26]	68.9
CenterNet [27]	67.1
YOLOv5s	78.6
RRNet [28]	80.1
SMPNet [29]	78.7
PP-YOLOE-s	79.2
DESTR	79.8
DPNetV3	81.3
YOLOX-s	80.2
Ours	82.1

Table 2. Ablation Study on AGVS.

Network	AP	FPS
Baseline	82.1	73
Baseline w/o CBAM	80.9	72
Baseline w/o TiC module	80.3	70
Baseline w/o extra prediction head	79.2	68

Effect of CBAM Block. After adding the CBAM module separately behind the backbone, and FPS did not decrease significantly. The addition of CBAM after the backbone can improve AP value without affecting detection speed and almost no impact on the size of the network. It plays a role in full-scale aircraft detection in dense scenes and close-range aircraft detection.

Effect of TiC-FPN. The main function module of TiC-FPN is the TiC module. The 4 channels are mainly used to receive signals from additional detection heads and do not directly affect network performance. The addition of the TiC module has greatly improved the network AP value, mainly due to the network's improvement in object positioning ability and increased detection rate for small objects.

Effect of Extra Prediction Head. An additional detection head was added to the network for small object detection, increasing GFLOPS from 18.6 to 22.1. Although this led to an increase in parameter volume, and a corresponding decrease in detection speed, the improvement in AP is very significant. Increasing the computational complexity of the network to improve detection performance is definitely worth it.

Figure 8 shows some detection results of the algorithm in this paper on the AGVS dataset. We have selected representative scenes for display, including daytime and night-time apron and runway scenes, as well as scenes with different aircraft densities. We can see that our network has good detection performance both during the day and at night. Even in dense scenes, it basically does not miss any objects, and the predicted frame also fits the aircraft object well.

Fig. 8. Detection results of AGVS

5 Conclusion

In this work, we have designed a new object detection method for airport scenes, which focuses on the use of low-level signals in the network. There are four advantages: First, we added the CBAM attention module separately after the backbone of the network to improve its ability to capture key features. Second, we added a detection head for small object detection to improve the accuracy of detecting small objects. Thirdly, we designed TiC-FPN neck network to add signals at a lower level during feature fusion process, which improves the network's ability in object regression. Fouthly, we decoupled the detection head and improved the network with anchor-free approach. Through extensive experiments, our network achieved leading performance on AGVS dataset and performed well in different situations in airport scenes. In the future, we will further study the fusion methods between different levels of signals in the network and improve the algorithm in an end-to-end manner. We hope this paper can help researchers in airport scene detection.

Acknowledgements. This work was supported by the National Natural Science Foundation of China under grants U1733111 and U19A2052, and partly by the Project of Quzhou Municipal Government (2022D034).

References

1. Viola, P., Jones, M.: Rapid object detection using a boosted cascade of simple features. In: Proceedings of the 2001 IEEE computer society conference on computer vision and pattern recognition, CVPR 2001, vol. 1. Ieee (2001)
2. Viola, P., Jones, M.J.: Robust real-time face detection. Int. J. Comput. Vision **57**, 137–154 (2004)
3. Dalal, N., Triggs, B.: Histograms of oriented gradients for human detection. In: 2005 IEEE Computer Society Conference on Computer Vision and Pattern Recognition (CVPR'05), vol. 1. Ieee (2005)
4. Wilson, J.W., et al.: Microburst wind structure and evaluation of Doppler radar for airport wind shear detection. J. Appl. Meteorol. Climatol. **23**(6), 898–915 (1984)
5. Costin, A., Francillon, A.: Ghost in the air (traffic): on insecurity of ADS-B protocol and practical attacks on ADS-B devices. black hat USA 1, 1–12 (2012)
6. Ren, S., et al.: Faster r-cnn: Towards real-time object detection with region proposal networks. Adv. Neural Inf. Proc Syst. **28** (2015)
7. Bochkovskiy, L., Wang, C.-Y., Mark Liao, H.Y.: Yolov4: optimal speed and accuracy of object detection. arXiv preprint arXiv:2004.10934 (2020)
8. Redmon, J., Divvala, S., Girshick, R., Farhadi, A.: You only look once: unified, real-time object detection. In: Proceedings of the IEEE conference on computer vision and pattern recognition, pp. 779–788 (2016)
9. Redmon, J., Farhadi, A.: Yolo9000: better, faster, stronger. In: Proceedings of the IEEE conference on computer vision and pattern recognition, pp. 7263–7271 (2017)
10. Redmon, J., Farhadi, A.: Yolov3: an incremental improvement. arXiv preprint arXiv:1804.02767 (2018)
11. Woo, S., et al.: Cbam: Convolutional block attention module. In: Proceedings of the European Conference on Computer Vision (ECCV) (2018)
12. Ma, N., et al.: Activate or not: Learning customized activation. In: Proceedings of the IEEE/CVF Conference on Computer Vision and Pattern Recognition (2021)
13. Glorot, X., Bordes, A., Bengio, Y.: Deep sparse rectifier neural networks. In: Proceedings of the fourteenth international conference on artificial intelligence and statistics. JMLR Workshop and Conference Proceedings (2011)
14. Ramachandran, P., Zoph, B., Le, Q.V.: Swish: a self-gated activation function. arXiv preprint arXiv:1710.05941 7.1, 5 (2017)
15. Liu, S., et al.: Path aggregation network for instance segmentation. In: Proceedings of the IEEE Conference on Computer Vision and Pattern Recognition (2018)
16. He, K., et al.: Spatial pyramid pooling in deep convolutional networks for visual recognition. IEEE Trans. Pattern Anal. Mach. Intell. **37**(9), 1904–1916 (2015)
17. Li, C., et al.: YOLOv6: a single-stage object detection framework for industrial applications. arXiv preprint arXiv:2209.02976 (2022)
18. Zhang, X., et al.: Extended motion diffusion-based change detection for airport ground surveillance. IEEE Trans. Image Process. **29**, 5677–5686 (2020)
19. Neubeck, A., Van Gool, L.: Efficient nonmaximum suppression. In: 18th International Conference on Pattern Recognition (ICPR'06), vol. 3, pp. 850–855. IEEE (2006)

20. Solovyev, R., Wang, W., Gabruseva, T.: Weighted boxes fusion: ensembling boxes from different object detection models. Image Vis. Comput. **107**, 104117 (2021)

21. Jie, F., et al.: Atrous spatial pyramid convolution for object detection with encoder-decoder. Neurocomputing **464**, 107–118 (2021)

22. Song, G., Liu, Y., Wang, X.: Revisiting the sibling head in object detector. In: Proceedings of the IEEE/CVF Conference on Computer Vision and Pattern Recognition (2020)

23. Wu, Y., Chen, Y., Yuan, L., et al.: Rethinking classification and localization for object detection. In: Proceedings of the IEEE/CVF Conference on Computer Vision and Pattern Recognition 10186–10195 (2020)

24. Ge, Z., et al.: Yolox: Exceeding yolo series in 2021. arXiv preprint arXiv:2107.08430 (2021)

25. Ge, Z., et al.: Ota: Optimal transport assignment for object detection. In: Proceedings of the IEEE/CVF Conference on Computer Vision and Pattern Recognition (2021)

26. Cai, Z., Vasconcelos, N.: Cascade r-cnn: delving into high quality object detection. In: Proceedings of the IEEE conference on computer vision and pattern recognition (2018)

27. Duan, K., et al.: Centernet: Keypoint triplets for object detection. In: Proceedings of the IEEE/CVF international conference on computer vision (2019)

28. Chen, C., et al.: Rrnet: a hybrid detector for object detection in drone-captured images. In: Proceedings of the IEEE/CVF International Conference on Computer Vision Workshops (2019)

29. Ding, S., et al.: Noncontact multiphysiological signals estimation via visible and infrared facial features fusion. IEEE Trans. Instrum. Meas. **71**, 1–13 (2022)

Fusing Multi-scale Residual Network for Skeleton Detection

Qingqing Fan, Zhenglin Li[✉], and Zhiwen Wang

School of Automation, Guangxi University of Science and Technology, Liuzhou 545616, China
59545980@qq.com

Abstract. The skeleton is an important topological description of the object's geometric form. As an advanced feature, the object skeleton information constitutes an abstract representation of the original shape. Skeleton detection helps further understanding of the object detection and recognition tasks. When processing natural images with complex backgrounds, which often blurred skeleton pixel scale or inaccurate classification. In this paper, we propose a Fusing Multi-scale Residual Network (FMRN) to improve the accuracy of skeleton detection, driven by pre-training the backbone network and adding multi-scale side output in its different stages, we also add the residual module to solve the computational redundancy problem. The atrous spatial pyramid pooling (ASPP) to robustly segment objects at multiple scales and ensure good resolution in feature maps. The experiments were conducted on five open datasets, where the datasets SK-LARGE, SK-SMALL (SK506), and WH-SYMMAX are commonly used for the skeleton detection task. The F-measure score obtained for these three datasets are 0.789, 0.751, and 0.865, respectively. The effectiveness of the method in this paper can be verified by ablation study, and the evaluation protocol are represented by F-measure and P-R curve. The test results showed that our approach has positive extraction accuracy and generalization ability.

Keywords: Skeleton Detection · Multi-scale · Feature Fusion · ASPP

1 Introduction

The object skeleton can better understand the shape information form natural image. The concept of skeleton was proposed by Blum [1] for the first time in 1967.The skeleton is a stable description with the original object topology information, object skeleton detection from the natural images, as shown in Fig. 1. In fact, skeleton detection has unique advantages over contour extraction in some application areas. For example, there is a lot of room to play in field that focus on object shape and require strict data volume. It has a wide range of applications in object recognition and retrieval, image retrieval, pose estimation, gesture recognition, scene text detection, road detection, and medical diagnosis [2, 4–6, 21].

- Early skeleton detection, also known as symmetry detection, was mainly through a hand-designed with an algorithmic framework, such as median axis transformation, mathematical morphology and index table algorithm [1, 3, 7]. The input image must be

H. Lu et al. (Eds.): ICIG 2023, LNCS 14358, pp. 224–236, 2023.
https://doi.org/10.1007/978-3-031-46314-3_18

Fig. 1. Object skeleton detection in natural images, and the skeletons with yellow line.

a pre-processed binary image, skeleton detection cannot be performed on color images. Applications are mostly seen in fingerprint recognition and handwriting fonts, etc. With the development of deep learning, the accuracy of object detection and recognition has been significantly improved. Classical frameworks such as RCNN [8] series, YOLO [9] series, and SSD [10] series have appeared in the field of object detection. The skeleton is a favorable cue in object detection, which complements the contour of the object. Object skeleton is concise and effective expression of shape, especially for variable objects. This is because the object skeleton information can express the topological information of the object while retaining the original object shape information. In some cases when dealing with, for example, variable or occlusion-like objects, skeleton-based methods are more effective than contour-based methods.

In recent years, some deep learning-based skeleton detection approaches have been proposed, essentially, the object skeleton detection is viewed as a problem of pixels with classification or regression. Because skeleton detection is highly dependent on spatial location, the combination of local and global background information of the image is required in the extraction. By Fusing Scale-associated Deep Side Outputs (FSDS) [11] can effectively localize skeleton pixels with multi-scale, however, it needs to labeling each skeleton point, which will consume more computational resources. Although feature fusion is one of the methods for pixel-level prediction as well as effective feature representation, there is the problem of low feature resolution, which can adversely affect the final detection results. Skeleton detection with Hierarchical Feature Integration (Hi-Fi) [12] enriches the semantic information of shallow features and enhances the resolution of deep features. This approach requires a large amount of prior knowledge to support supervised learning. Skeleton detection is different from the general object detection, which is often subject to complex background and noise interference. Because the skeleton pixels occupy only a small fraction of the global pixels, this makes supervised learning difficult. To address the above problems, we have developed a Fusing Multi-scale Feature Residual network (FMRN) to implement the object skeleton detection perfectly. As shown in Fig. 2, the ASPP [26] (Atrous Spatial Pyramid Pooling) module is added to the network structure to expand the receptive field while avoiding excessive down-sampling and ensuring constant feature resolution. Implemented scale quantization and classification for skeleton pixels, and side outputs with multi-scale features are fused after residual unit processing and ASPP. The contributions of this paper are summarized include:

- we proposed a fusing multi-scale residual network for skeleton detection, use stage side output with residual units (RU) and a hierarchical refinement of the feature class map.
- The network can effectively improve the problem of partial missing as well as low-resolution features of existing methods in extracting object skeletons in complex backgrounds.
- The FMRN shows excellent test results with good generalization ability in all five commonly used skeleton detection benchmark datasets.

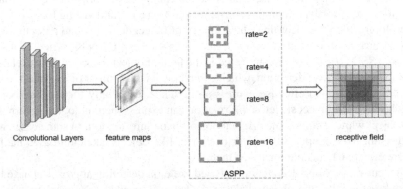

Fig. 2. Scale feature detection module with ASPP

2 Related Works

Before learning-based methods, mostly the object skeleton was extracted by means of geometric constraints [13, 24], which compute the gradient intensity. For example, symmetry is used to perform shape segmentation of the image and identify its symmetry axis and localize the object skeleton [7, 14]. By defining a pseudo distance map (PDM) [15], no region segmentation or edge detection is required to extract the object skeleton in the binary map. Extraction of road grids in remotely sensed images using centerline detection and line width estimation [2], and localization of object areas by scale size and median axis [16]. Zero-sum self-symmetric skeleton filters [17] have been proposed to obtain the skeleton in the high-noise case in recent years, and based on probability masks and vector routers [18] for object skeleton detection. Inspired by holistic nested edge detection (HED) [19], fusing scale-associated deep side outputs (FSDS) [11] for object skeleton detection use ground-truth supervised side outputs of different scales and fuse the side outputs according to weight layers of different sizes, then obtain a skeleton map of the corresponding scale. Training by back propagation using richer convolutional features (RCF) [20] can make full use of the multi-scale and multi-level information of the object for skeleton prediction.

Deep learning-based skeleton detection methods have shown groundbreaking results in processing natural images with complex backgrounds. According to the adaptive linear span network for skeleton detection (AdaLSN) [21] proposed by linear span theory, which is materialized by defining a mixed unit-pyramid search space. However, the model is complex to build and difficult to train. Side-output residual network (SRN) [22] proposes a benchmark for object symmetry detection in complex backgrounds, to fit the errors between the object symmetry ground-truth and the outputs of residual unit, and stacking side output residual units in a deep to shallow manner can suppress complex background interference. The rich side output residual network (RSRN) [23] takes the advantages of SRN and RCF to enrich the features using a multi-scale combination strategy. Hierarchical feature integration (HiFi) [12] is obtained by integrating different feature layers and adding a bi-directional guidance mechanism to obtain refinement of features at different levels. Geometry-aware [24]is a geometric approach based on HED improved to learn to detect skeleton information in an end-to-end.

The subject of multi-scale convergence is constantly discussed, meanwhile, balancing detection accuracy and model lightweighting to reduce the computational burden has been a major issue in the academic community. Our approach seeks to find optimal solutions and more practicable possibilities for skeleton detection tasks.

3 Methodology

With the rapid development of deep learning, the application of pre-trained deep neural networks for skeleton detection has become increasingly widespread and effective. The method in this paper is obtained based on the improvement and optimization of the overall nested network structure and multi-scale side output fusion aspects to better obtain the effectiveness of the object skeleton detection and extraction.

3.1 Network Architecture

For skeleton detection, it is important to understand the information at different scales. In this paper, the FMRN we propose is converted from Inception-v4/Inception-ResNet [25] by adding additional side output and fuse layer. According to [25], the Stem consists of convolutions, filter contact and Max-pool layer. Additionally, both Stage-A and Stage-B contain inception/inception-resnet and reduction sections, but Stage-C does not contain reduction section. The input, after passing through the Stem module, gives a reduced output size and an increased number of channels. Due to the Stem module has the same size and the same number of channels as the Stage-A module output, the Stem module can be used as a pre-processing layer for the input. Therefore, no side outputs are connected at the filter connection layer of Stem, the other three stages are connected to different side outputs and set stride to 2, 4, and 8, respectively. In that order, adjust to produce different sizes of side output receptive field depending on the addition of the ASPP [26] module. When there are fewer features, up-sampling is performed first, normal convolution is performed second, then down-sampling is performed. Operate with ASPP when there are more features. The side outputs obtained at each stage are SO-A, SO-B, and SO-C, the residual units (RU) are stacked sequentially, while the skeleton Ground-Truth (GT) are added as supervised training to better predict the skeleton pixels. The overall structure of the network is shown in Fig. 3.

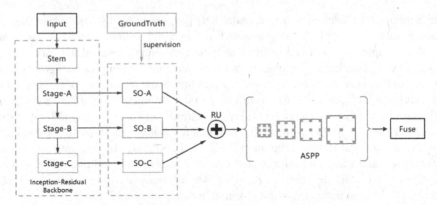

Fig. 3. The proposed network architecture for skeleton detection, which is converted from Inception-v4/Inception-ResNet. It has 3 stages with additional side-output layers, those sections in this backbone are composed of multiple convolutional kernels of multi-sizes and pooling layers. The RU makes the network easier to optimize, ASPP ensures high resolution of dense feature to fuse.

3.2   Fusing Multi-scale Feature and Residual Unit

Skeleton scale assisted skeleton pixel localization is important for skeleton detection, therefore, in this paper classifies it explicitly. Furthermore, to make the method more effective, we convert skeleton detection into a pixel classification task with segment quantization. Consider the object skeleton detection as a single-pixel classification problem, given an original input image $X = \{x_i, i = 1, \ldots, |X|\}$, The object skeleton is extracted as $\hat{Y} = \{\hat{y}_i, i = 1, \ldots, |X|\}$. If pixel x_i is detected as a skeleton pixel, $\hat{y}_i = 1$; otherwise $\hat{y}_i = 0$, expressed as a set in the form of $\hat{y}_i \in \{0, 1\}$. There are two tasks in our new network structure, one is the classification of skeletal and non-skeletal pixels, and the other is the calculation of the skeletal scale. We define the scale of the skeleton pixel as $S = \{s_i, i = 1, \ldots, |X|\}$, also specify that the scale of non-skeleton pixels is zero. Due to the existence of different scale features in the image, different convolutional layers at different stages require different sizes of receptive field. To ensure that the complete features can be captured, the receptive field size should be larger than the skeleton pixel scale. According to the real skeleton pixel should be single pixel width, the quantized value of scale S quantization value Q is defined as follows:

$$Q = \begin{cases} arg\ min_{i=1,\ldots,N}\ s > 0 \\ 0 \qquad\qquad\ s = 0 \end{cases} \tag{1}$$

The size of each layer of the receptive field is recorded as $RF_i(i = 1, \ldots, N)$ and specify $RF_i > 1$. The detection of skeletal pixels and feature computation at different stages can be better assisted by scale quantization of skeletal pixels. In general, the distribution of skeletal pixels and non-skeletal pixels in the image at different scales is unbalanced. Therefore, a weighted loss function is defined to balance the loss between multiple classifications:

$$\mathcal{L}(W, w) = \sum_i \left[-\lambda \sum_{k \neq 0} \log(p_i, k) 1(g_i = k) - (1 - \lambda) \log(p_i, 0) 1(g_i = 0) \right] \quad (2)$$

where W is the layer parameter of the network, w is the stage classifier parameter, λ is the loss weight, (p_i, k) denotes the probability that pixel x_i belongs to the k th class, and g_i denotes the ground truth of pixel x_i.

As can be seen from the network architecture, the residual unit is added after the side output of each stage, given the skeleton ground truth for supervised learning. Where the residual unit computes the output to the next layer, which will be denoted as $\mathcal{F}_i(x)$. According to Fig. 4, we refer to the residual module in [27] and the residual output is defined as follows:

$$\mathcal{F}_i(x) = w_1 * s(x_i) + (w_1 w_2 - 1) * r_i \quad (3)$$

where w_1, w_2 are both the convolution weights of the connected layers, $s(x_i)$ is the ith side output, and r_i is the i th RU input.

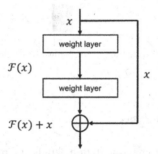

Fig. 4. The side-output Residual Unit (RU), learning by supervision both on the input and output of RU, the additional mapping $\mathcal{F}(x)$ estimates the residual of x.

3.3 Multi-scale Combination

Generally, multi-scale feature fusion is used in object detection and segmentation tasks to improve the accuracy of the results. The first thing about multi-scale can be associated with the image pyramid in digital image processing, which means that the input image is scaled down to multiple scales, and each scale calculates the feature map separately and performs subsequent processing operations. This approach can improve the detection accuracy, but it consumes more computational resources, so the residual unit is added to improve the training speed for this situation. The specific implementation of feature fusion at different scales in this paper is the inclusion of the ASPP [25] module in the feedforward network, which is explained in the introduction section.

According to the skeleton scale quantization rule, it is known that for any one pixel of the input x_i, the networks all give their corresponding predicted probabilities about the quantified results of the scales. The input image is processed by the backbone network to obtain different stages of the side output result in a certain number of scale-specific pixel sets, and the multi-scale feature fusion equation is defined as follows:

$$F = \alpha_1 * f_1 + \alpha_2 * f_2 + \cdots + \alpha_n * f_n \tag{4}$$

where α_n denotes the nth stage normalized weight, $\sum_n^\alpha = 1$, and f_n denotes the feature quantization value of the nth stage, and the feature fusion operation can be performed in the network model using 1×1 convolution kernel. As shown in Fig. 5, the skeleton map with good resolution is obtained by different scale adjustment and fusion.

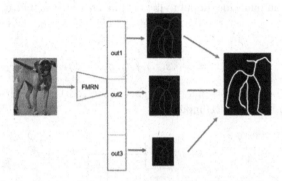

Fig. 5. Multi-scale feature combination for skeleton detection.

4 Experiment and Analysis

In this section, we discuss the implementation details and report the performance of the proposed method on several open datasets. The Inception-v4/ResNet network model is first pre-trained.

4.1 Implementation Details

Datasets: Several datasets commonly used for skeleton detection, namely SK-LARGE, SK-SMALL (SK506), WH-SYMMAX, SYM-PASCAL, and SYMMAX were used to evaluate the performance of FMRN. Among them, SK-LAGRE contains about 16 categories, 746 training images, 500 test images, and 245 validation images; SK-SMALL contains 298 training images and 206 test images; WH-SYMMAX contains 227 training images and 100 test images; SYM-PASCAL contains 648 training images and 788 test images; SYMMAX contains 197 training images and 100 test images.

Data augmentation: Deep learning cannot be obtained without rich and complete dataset which can often train a better performing network model. However, in many practical projects it is difficult to have sufficient data with labeled specifications. Therefore, in order to obtain more data to enrich the dataset, we need to perform simple data augmentation. In this paper, the images are rotated at (45°, 90°, 135°, 180°, 225°, 270°,

315°), and then flipped with different axes, such as vertical flipping, horizontal flipping, and no flipping. Since the true value of single pixel width is affected by the resizing of the original image, operations such as scaling or cropping, i.e., multi-scale enhancement, are not used in this paper.

4.2 Implementation Setting

Parameter Setting: In this paper, we choose to build the newly proposed network model (FMRN) within the PyTorch framework, running on Intel Core i5-12500H (3.1GHz) CPU model, NVIDIA GeForce RTX 3060Ti GPU with 32GB memory. The backbone network is pre-trained and the initial learning rate is set to 1e-6 using Adam optimizer, the momentum factor is (0.9, 0.9999) and the weight decay factor is 0.0005. The network parameters are updated every 10 forward propagations with a minimum batch size of 1 and a maximum number of iterations of 50,000.

Evaluation Protocol: Evaluating the performance of a detector requires reasonable rules to evaluate its good or bad performance. In object skeleton detection and extraction task, P-R curve (Precision and Recall curve) and F-measure are often used as evaluation metrics. Among them, the F-measure evaluation metric is usually formulated as:

$$F = 2PR/(P + R) \tag{5}$$

To obtain the P-R curve, the extracted skeleton feature maps are first converted into binary maps with threshold values, which are then matched with the skeleton true values. By setting different thresholds, a series of precision and recall values can be obtained, which are then combined to generate the P-R curve. The F-measure then provides a single performance metric that weights the precision and recall.

4.3 Performance Comparison

The F-measure for comparing the skeleton detection results of different methods in the experiment is shown in Table 1. The performance and operation results of different network models on the dataset SK-LARGE are shown in Table 2. The FMRN performs better than the other three network models in terms of both F-measure and running time. The P-R curve obtained on the four datasets are able to show that the method of this paper surpasses other methods, as shown in Fig. 6. The comparison of the skeleton detection results of different methods shows that FMRN further refines the extracted skeleton pixels and maintains good topology and connectivity. As shown in Fig. 7.

Table 1. Comparison of test F-measure of different methods in five datasets.

Methods	SK-LARGE	SK506	WH-SYMMAX	SYM-PASCAL	SYMMAX
MIL [29]	0.353	0.392	0.365	0.174	0.362
HED [20]	0.497	0.541	0.732	0.369	0.427
FSDS [12]	0.633	0.623	0.769	0.418	0.467
SRN [23]	0.678	0.632	0.780	0.443	0.446
HiFi [13]	0.724	0.681	0.805	0.454	-
Deep-Flux [28]	0.732	0.695	0.840	0.502	0.491
Geo. Net [25]	0.757	0.727	0.849	0.520	0.501
AdaLSN [22]	0.786	0.740	0.851	0.497	0.495
FMRN(Ours)	**0.789**	**0.751**	**0.865**	0.508	0.489

Table 2. Performance and runtime of different network models on dataset SK-LARGE.

Methods	F-measure	Runtime(s)
FSDS	0.633	0.017
Hi-Fi	0.724	0.030
DeepFlux	0.732	0.017
FMRN	**0.789**	**0.015**

4.4 Ablation Study

To verify the effectiveness of the added modules in the network, ablation experiments are performed on the datasets SK-LARGE and WH-SYMMAX. The network performance after adding or removing the RUs and ASPP modules is further analyzed and discussed. As shown in Table 3, among the four cases of choosing not to add RU and ASPP, adding only RU, adding only ASPP, and adding RU and ASPP, either tested in the dataset SK-LARGE or WH-SYMMAX, the network performance of adding RU and ASPP modules is the best way as shown by the obtained F-measure. In a single experiment where only the ASPP module was added to the network after increasing the perceptual field to improve detection, it was found that the performance was improved by 1.6% and 1.5% on the datasets SK-LARGE and WH-SYMMAX, respectively. Similarly, adding RU and ASPP modules to the network improved the performance by 5% and 4.7% on the data sets SK-LARGE and WH-SYMMAX, respectively. Regarding the new method in solving the multi-scale and feature fusion problem, by comparing different feature fusion methods. Such as FSDS, SRN, HiFi and other methods, the experimental results on the dataset SK-LARGE are shown in Table 4.

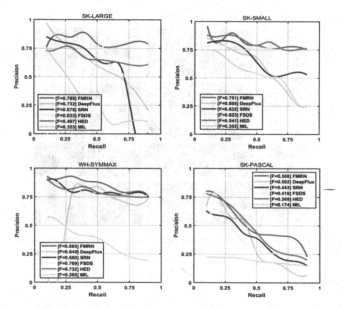

Fig. 6. Precision-Recall curve under the four datasets.

Table 3. Impact of the RU and ASPP module on network performance.

Dataset	RU	ASPP	F-measure
SK-LARGE			0.673
	√		0.686
		√	0.701
	√	√	**0.789**
WH-SYMMAX			0.715
	√		0.729
		√	0.786
	√	√	**0.865**

Table 4. Comparison of different feature fusion methods.

Method	FSDS	SRN	HiFi	FMRN
F-measure	0.633	0.678	0.724	**0.789**

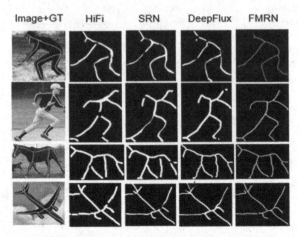

Fig. 7. Comparison of the effect of skeleton detection by various methods.

5 Conclusion

In this paper, we introduce a deep learning-based method for extracting skeletons from natural images, and propose a residual network with multi-scale feature fusion, which quantifies the skeleton pixel scale and performs multi-scale feature fusion, finally regression classification to obtain the object skeleton. Although the Inception-v4/ResNet has a large number of parameters and is a relatively large network model, compared with other common backbone networks, Inception-v4 has a longitudinal and horizontal network structure, which also makes its model accuracy improved, and the inclusion of the residual module will improve the training speed. Experiments show that the method in this paper not only solves the problem of breakage at topological connections better than FSDS, HiFi, SRN and other methods, but also makes the skeleton pixels further refined. The method can effectively improve the completeness and accuracy of skeleton detection, while the model has good generalization ability. In the future, we would like to explore more theoretical methods and implementations on object skeleton detection, and will strive to enrich the datasets and expand from two dimensional images to higher-dimensional object processing.

Acknowledgement. This work is supported by the National Natural Science Foundation of China (NSFC) under Grant 61962007 and in part by the HET of Guangxi Province of China under Grant 2020JGB238.

References

1. Blum, H.: A transformation for extracting new descriptors of shape. Models for the Preception of Speech & Visual Form **19**, 362–380 (1967)
2. Saha, P.K., et al.: A survey on skeletonization algorithms and their applications. Pattern Recognit. Lett. **76**, 3–12 (2016)

3. Zhu, S.C., Yuille, A.L.: FORMS: a flexible object recognition and modelling system. Int. J. Comp. Visi. **20**, 187–212 (1995)
4. Felzenszwalb, P.F., Huttenlocher, D.P.: Pictorial structures for object recognition. Int. J. Comput. Vision **61**(1), 55–79 (2005)
5. Shotton, J., et al.: Real-time human pose recognition in parts from single depth images. In: IEEE Conference on Computer Vision and Pattern Recognition, pp. 1297–1304 (2011)
6. Zhang, Z., Shen, W., Yao, C., Bai, X.: Symmetry-based text line detection in natural scenes. In: IEEE Conference on Computer Vision and Pattern Recognition, pp. 2558–2567 (2015)
7. Widynski, N., et al.: Local symmetry detection in natural images using a particle filtering approach. IEEE Transactions on Image Processing **23**, 5309–5322 (2014)
8. Girshick, R.B., et al.: Rich feature hierarchies for accurate object detection and semantic segmentation. In: IEEE Conference on Computer Vision and Pattern Recognition, pp. 580–587 (2014)
9. Redmon, J., et al.: You Only Look Once: Unified, Real-Time Object Detection. In: IEEE Conference on Computer Vision and Pattern Recognition, pp. 779–788 (2015)
10. Liu, W., et al.: SSD: Single Shot MultiBox Detector. In: European Conference on Computer Vision (2015)
11. Shen, W., et al.: Object skeleton detection in natural images by fusing scale-associated deep side outputs. In: IEEE Conference on Computer Vision and Pattern Recognition, pp. 222–230 (2016)
12. Zhao, K., et al.: Hi-Fi: hierarchical feature integration for skeleton detection. In: International Joint Conference on Artificial Intelligence (2018)
13. Lindeberg, T.: Edge detection and ridge detection with automatic scale selection. Int. J. Comp. Visi. **30**, 117–156 (1996)
14. Liu, T.-L., et al.: Segmenting by seeking the symmetry axis. Proceedings. In: International Conference on Pattern Recognition, vol.2, p. 2, 994–998 (1998)
15. Jang, J.H., Ki, S.H.: A pseudo-distance map for the segmentation-free skeletonization of gray-scale images. In: IEEE International Conference on Computer Vision, pp. 18–23 (2001)
16. Postolski, M., et al.: Scale filtered euclidean medial axis and its hierarchy. Comp. Visi. Ima. Underst. **129**, 89–102 (2014)
17. Bai, X., et al.: Skeleton filter: a self-symmetric filter for skeletonization in noisy text images. IEEE Transactions on Image Processing **29**, 1815–1826 (2020)
18. Bai, X., et al.: ProMask: Probability Mask for Skeleton Detection. Neural Networks 162, (2022)
19. Xie, S., Tu, Z.: Holistically-nested edge detection. Int. J. Comp. Visi. **125**, 3–18 (2015)
20. Liu, Y., et al.: Richer convolutional features for edge detection. In: IEEE Conference on Computer Vision and Pattern Recognition, pp. 5872–5881 (2016)
21. Liu, C., et al.: Adaptive linear span network for object skeleton detection. IEEE Transactions on Image Processing **30**, 5096–5108 (2021)
22. Ke, W., et al.: SRN: side-output residual network for object symmetry detection in the wild. In: IEEE Conference on Computer Vision and Pattern Recognition, pp. 302–310 (2017)
23. Liu, C., et al.: RSRN: rich side-output residual network for medial axis detection. In: IEEE International Conference on Computer Vision Workshops, pp. 1739–1743 (2017)
24. Xu, W., et al.: Geometry-aware end-to-end skeleton detection. British Machine Vision Conference (2019)
25. Szegedy, C., et al.: Inception-v4, Inception-ResNet and the Impact of Residual Connections on Learning. ArXiv abs/1602.07261 (2016)
26. Chen, L.,-C., et al.: DeepLab: Semantic Image Segmentation with Deep Convolutional Nets, Atrous Convolution, and Fully Connected CRFs. IEEE Trans. Pattern Anal. Machi. Intelli. **40**, 834–848 (2016)

27. He, K., et al.: Deep residual learning for image recognition. In: IEEE Conference on Computer Vision and Pattern Recognition, pp. 770–778 (2015)
28. Wang, Y., et al.: DeepFlux for skeletons in the wild. In: IEEE Conference on Computer Vision and Pattern Recognition, pp. 5282–5291 (2018)
29. Tsogkas, S., Kokkinos, I.: Learning-based symmetry detection in natural images. In: European Conference on Computer Vision (2012)

LogoNet: A Fine-Grained Network for Instance-Level Logo Sketch Retrieval

Binbin Feng, Jun Li[✉], and Jianhua Xu

School of Computer and Electronic Information, Nanjing Normal University,
Nanjing 210023, China
{202243020,lijuncst,xujianhua}@njnu.edu.cn

Abstract. Sketch-based image retrieval, which aims to use sketches as queries to retrieve images containing the same query instance, receives increasing attention in recent years. Although dramatic progress has been made in sketch retrieval, few efforts are devoted to logo sketch retrieval which is still hindered by the following challenges: Firstly, logo sketch retrieval is more difficult than typical sketch retrieval problem, since a logo sketch usually contains much less visual contents with only irregular strokes and lines. Secondly, instance-specific sketches demonstrate dramatic appearance variances, making them less identifiable when querying the same logo instance. Thirdly, there exist several sketch retrieval benchmarking datasets nowadays, whereas an instance-level logo sketch dataset is still publicly unavailable. To address the above-mentioned limitations, we make twofold contributions in this study for instance-level logo sketch retrieval. To begin with, we construct an instance-level logo sketch dataset containing 2k logo instances and exceeding 9k sketches. To our knowledge, this is the first publicly available instance-level logo sketch dataset. Next, we develop a fine-grained triple-branch CNN architecture based on hybrid attention mechanism termed LogoNet for accurate logo sketch retrieval. More specifically, we embed the hybrid attention mechanism into the triple-branch architecture for capturing the key query-specific information from the limited visual cues in the logo sketches. Experimental evaluations both on our assembled dataset and public benchmark datasets demonstrate the effectiveness of our proposed network.

Keywords: sketch-based image retrieval · logo retrieval · hybrid attention mechanism · triple-branch CNN architecture

1 Introduction

With the development of the Internet and the increasing popularity of touch screen devices nowadays, the availability of a sketch makes it as common as

---

Supported by the Natural Science Foundation of China (NSFC) under grants 62173186 and 62076134.

H. Lu et al. (Eds.): ICIG 2023, LNCS 14358, pp. 237–249, 2023.
https://doi.org/10.1007/978-3-031-46314-3_19

an image which is usually captured by an exquisite camera. This significantly facilitates the research on sketches in recent years, leading to a wide variety of sketch applications including sketch recognition [6,15], sketch-based image retrieval [4,12], sketch-based 3D model retrieval [8,13] and sketch analysis [2, 11]. Among them, sketch retrieval, which uses sketches as queries to retrieve images containing the same query instance, has received special attention due to its potentials in practical applications. Different from a traditional image retrieval task, sketch retrieval needs to perform visual comparisons and matching cross sketch-image domain. This dramatic domain gap usually results in serious misalignment with the candidate images, since a sketch is highly abstract and iconic due to the lack of visual clues such as color and texture. Therefore, sketch retrieval is a more difficult task.

In image retrieval, logo retrieval plays a critical role in commercial applications and has been extensively applied to the business of intellectual property, copyright infringement prevention and industrial product design. In particular, sketch-based logo retrieval, which can help users or designers to find similar logo images given a query logo sketch, demonstrates a bright prospect for the aforementioned commercial applications. Although significant progress has been made in sketch retrieval, few efforts are devoted to sketch-based logo retrieval which is still hindered by the following challenges: 1) logo sketch retrieval is more difficult than a typical sketch retrieval task, since a logo sketch usually contains much less visual cues with only irregular strokes and lines. 2) Depending on personal painting levels and styles, instance-specific sketches demonstrate dramatic appearance variances, making them less distinguishable when querying the same logo instance. 3) Although there exist several sketch retrieval benchmarking datasets nowadays, a fine-grained instance-level logo sketch dataset is still publicly unavailable. Compared with the existing category-level datasets, an instance-level one is more difficult to obtain and should be fine-grained, such that the learned models can capture large domain differences and variability of human painting styles.

To address the above challenges, we make twofold contributions in this study for fine-grained instance-level logo sketch retrieval. Firstly, we construct an instance-level logo sketch dataset comprising 2k logo instances, the corresponding 9k sketches along with 2000 text labels. Each logo has at least three corresponding sketches, reflecting the diversity of the drawing styles. According to the retrieval difficulty level, the whole dataset is divided into easy, medium and hard three subsets. Furthermore, our dataset allows cross-modal sketch retrieval with text labels. To our knowledge, this is the first instance-level sketch-based logo retrieval dataset publicly available thus far. Secondly, we develop a triple-branch Convolutional Neural Network (CNN) architecture based on hybrid attention mechanism for fine-grained instance-level logo sketch retrieval. More specifically, we introduce hybrid attention mechanism into the triple-branch network such that the model has spatial and channel perception capability for characterizing the fine-grained logo features. In addition, due to the lack of texture information in the sketch, a larger filter is used in the convolution layer for enhancing the representation capability. Furthermore, text labels are used as auxiliary information for sketches to improve the model accuracy while reducing the requirements for painting ability.

The rest of the paper is organized as follows. After introducing our constructed instance-level logo dataset in Sect. 2, we elaborate on our framework in details in Sect. 3. Next, we present the experimental evaluations in Sect. 4. Finally, our work is concluded and summarized in Sect. 5.

2   Our Instance-Level Logo Sketch Dataset

We have collected an instance-level logo sketch dataset, which contains a total of 2,000 logo instances. We have also collected three or more corresponding sketches for each logo to capture the variability of painting ability and style, leading to a total of 9,347 sketches. In addition, we also provide 2,000 text labels for each instance, such that the dataset allows cross-modal retrieval. Next, we will briefly introduce how the sketches are collected. Besides, we will also compare our newly collected logo sketch dataset with the other existing sketch datasets. Our dataset is available at https://github.com/abin333/logoNet.

2.1   Logo Collection

Since our dataset is built for instance-level retrieval, the logos should cover instance-level variability of visual appearance. To this end, we have exhausted major websites including Edge, Google, Baidu, Firefox, 360 explorers to collect logos in daily life scenes. All the logos come from all walks of life and can be divided into three categories: transportation, life service and enterprise business. Since a logo sketch does not contain color information, logos with the same shape but different colors are filtered out, and duplicate logos are removed with only one remained. Thus, a total of 2,000 logo images are obtained. We perform standard preprocessing strategies such as clipping and denoising on the collected images, such that the logo images have the same white background, allowing the model to focus on learning the fine-grained visual information for logo sketch retrieval. In terms of the sketch collection, we employ the collected logo images to generate corresponding sketches. To reflect the real-world application scenarios along with the variability of painting ability and style, we use different input devices to collect sketches and generate multiple sketches for each logo image.

2.2   Sketch Generation

Given a logo, multiple corresponding sketches need to be painted and collected. Considering the diversity of sketch painting, the volunteers collecting the logo sketches are divided into three groups. The first group of volunteers have professional drawing ability and they drew sketches on a tablet PC. With general painting ability, the second group of volunteers make use a variety of equipment including mobile phones, white paper and drawing boards to draw sketches.

Transportation	Life Service	Enterprise Business

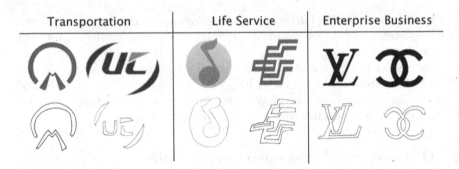

Fig. 1. Representative examples of our collected logos (the first row) and the corresponding hand-drawn sketches (the second row).

Lacking sufficient drawing skills, the third group of volunteers draw incomplete or simple strokes of logo sketches using different input devices. For a given logo instance, three or more sketches are obtained by different volunteers under different settings, leading to a total of 9,347 sketches. Some representative logo examples and the corresponding sketches drawn are shown in Fig. 1. The logo sketches exhibiting diverse drawing qualities under different settings indicate different difficulty levels of sketch retrieval. We divide the whole sketch dataset into easy, medium and hard three subsets accordingly. In general, the sketches in the easy subset are well-drawn with substantial similarity to the original logo image. In contrast, the sketches in the medium and hard subsets are poorly drawn due to limited conditions. Table 1 summarizes the three logo sketch subsets. We impose data augmentation such as random cropping and horizontal flipping on the collected sketches for alleviating the scarcity of datasets.

Table 1. A summary of the three subsets in our logo sketch dataset.

	Easy	Medium	Hard
Logo sketches	1321	5016	3010
Input devices	tablet PCs	mobile phones & paper	mobile phones & paper

2.3 Text Labeling for Cross-Modal Retrieval

In addition to sketch-photo paired labels, we also collect 2,000 text annotations as auxiliary information for sketches, allowing cross-modal logo sketch retrieval. The labeled texts mainly characterize the key attributes of logos in terms of color, shape, quantity to supplement the logo description. They not only reduce the requirements for human sketch painting ability but also improve the retrieval accuracy of the model.

2.4   Comparison of Different Public Sketch Datasets

To summarize, we compare our assembled logo sketch dataset with the existing public sketch benchmark datasets. Table 2 presents the comparison of different popular sketch datasets in terms of dataset size, categorization and data modalities. The complete comparison is available at our project homepage. To our knowledge, our collected dataset is the first instance-level logo sketch dataset which lends itself to fine-grained and cross-model logo sketch retrieval.

Table 2. Comparison of assembled logo sketch dataset and the other public sketch datasets. To our knowledge, our collected dataset is the first instance-level logo sketch dataset for fine-grained and cross-model logo sketch retrieval.

Datasets	Size	Type	Modalities
QMUL-Shoe [17]	419 sketches, 419 images	instance-level	sketch-image
QMUL-Chair [17]	297 sketches, 297 images	instance-level	sketch-image
QMUL-Handbag [12]	568 sketches, 568 images	instance-level	sketch-image
QMUL-ShoeV2 [18]	6730 sketches, 2000 images	instance-level	sketch-image
QMUL-ChairV2 [18]	1275 sketches, 400 images	instance-level	sketch-image
TU-Berlin [3]	20k sketches	category-level	sketch
QuickDraw [5]	50M+ sketches	category-level	sketch
Sketchy [9]	75k sketches, 12k images	instance-level	sketch-image
Ours	9374 sketches, 2000 images	instance-level	sketch-image-text

3   LogoNet: A Fine-Grained Triple-Branch Network for Logo Sketch Retrieval

In this study, we develop a triple-branch network based on hybrid attention mechanism termed logoNet for fine-grained logo sketch retrieval. Figure 2 illustrates the overall framework of LogoNet. In the triple-branch network, large-kernel convolutions are followed by CNN backbone with hybrid attention mechanism embedded, which will be discussed in details as follows.

3.1   Large-Kernel Convolutions

Among CNN architecture, the size of the filter in the first convolution layer may be the most crucial and sensitive parameter, since all subsequent modules depend on the output of the first layer. Recent research suggests large kernel convolution is conducive to capturing more crucial visual cues with larger receptive fields. In addition, considering that logo sketches with simple strokes and irregular outlines lack texture, color and other visual information, we assume that larger filters from scratch are indispensable for sketch modeling and helps to capture more structured contents. Therefore, a larger filter helps to capture more structured

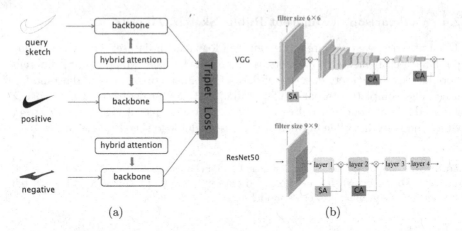

Fig. 2. The triple-branch framework of our LogoNet (Fig. 2a) and two different backbones with hybrid attention mechanism within LogoNet (Fig. 2b). SA and CA denote spatial and channel attention modules respectively.

context rather than information such as texture. Consequently, we employ large-kernel convolutions in the first place within the respective three branches of our LogoNet. We will discuss the impact of kernel size on the model performance in the section of experiments.

3.2   Hybrid Attention Mechanism

To capture the fine-grained visual cues of logo sketches, we incorporate a hybrid attention mechanism [14] into the triple-branch network. More specifically, channel attention module adaptively re-calibrates the weight of each channel, which plays an important role in emphasizing important channels while suppressing noise. In addition, spatial attention focuses on local discriminative visual information of the logo sketches, which helps to improve the representation ability of the network. To be specific, a hybrid attention module is added to each branch of logoNet, and the spatial attention mechanism is imposed on the larger feature maps, whilst the channel attention mechanism is embedded following the larger feature map. After calculating the channel attention mask and spatial attention mask, the enhanced feature map is obtained by multiplying the attention mask and the input feature map accordingly. Despite different architectures of VGG and ResNet50, the hybrid attention is embedded into the respective backbone networks following the principle that spatial attention aims to capture fine-grained clues from larger feature map, while the channel attention helps to identify the channel-aware feature importance as the network goes deeper with increased channels.

Table 3. Performance of the proposed LogoNet in our logo sketch dataset (%).

backbone	acc@1	acc@5	acc@10
VGG	86.33	95.26	97.68
ResNet50	85.78	95.81	97.57

Table 4. Performance of our LogoNet on the three subsets (%).

Subset	VGG			ResNet50		
	acc@1	acc@5	acc@10	acc@1	acc@5	acc@10
easy	99.02	100.00	100.00	97.20	99.77	99.92
medium	93.32	99.58	99.96	89.43	99.02	99.54
hard	78.54	94.72	96.98	74.45	93.75	96.81

3.3 Loss Function

Given a triplet (s, p^+, p^-) where s, p^+, p^- respectively denote the query sketch, the positive and the negative sample, the triplet loss function adopted in our LogoNet is formulated as:

$$L_t = max(0, \Delta + D(f_\theta(s), f_\theta(p^+)) - D(f_\theta(s), f_\theta(p^-))) \quad (1)$$

where $f_\theta(\cdot)$ is the feature embedding, while $D(\cdot)$ quantifies the pairwise Euclidean distance. Besides, Δ suggests the pre-defined margin between the positive and negative example distance. As seen in Eq. (1), the triplet loss function aims to minimize the distance between the query sketch and the positive sample while maximize the distance between the sketch and the negative sample.

4 Experiments

4.1 Datasets and Evaluation Metrics

In addition to our collected logo sketch dataset, we have also evaluated the proposed LogoNet on the public QMUL benchmark datasets [18]. The evaluation metric is commonly used acc@k for the application scenario where an user can retrieve a specific image in the first returned shortlist. More specifically, we report acc@1, acc@5 and acc@10 scores which indicate the proportion of positive samples in the top 1, top 5 and top 10 search results. They are obtained by calculating the cumulative matching accuracy under different rankings.

4.2 Experimental Setting

All the experiments are carried out on a server equipped with a single NVIDIA RTX 3090 GPU and 24 GB memory using PyTorch framework under the Linux

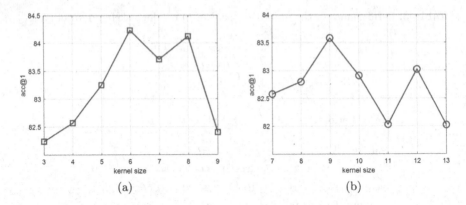

Fig. 3. The effect of convolutional kernel size when using VGG (Fig. 3a) and ResNet50 (Fig. 3b) as backbones.

operating system. The learning rate and margin Δ are set to 0.0001 and 0.2, respectively. The Adam algorithm is used as the optimizer. During the training process, we use random clipping and horizontal flipping for data augmentation, and triplet labels are used for supervision.

4.3 Results

As shown in Table 3, our LogoNet reports 86.33% and 85.78% acc@1 scores with VGG and ResNet50 used as the respective backbones, indicating that LogoNet can find ground truth image within the first returned shortlist.

In addition to the overall performance, we also provide results on the three subsets with varying difficulty levels. As shown in Table 4, with two different backbones, highest acc@1 accuracies of 99.02% and 97.20% are reported. However, when evaluating LogoNet on hard subset, considerable performance drops of exceeding 20% are observed, achieving only 78.54% and 74.45% acc@1 scores. This implies that it is still challenging to identify the sketches with simple or incomplete strokes and weak human painting ability may be detrimental to accurate logo sketch retrieval.

4.4 Ablation Studies

The Effect of Convolutional Kernel Size. We first explore the impact of the convolutional kernel size on our LogoNet. Since logo sketches lack texture, color and other information, we assume larger-kernel convolutions in the first place help capture more structured context with larger receptive field, and thus are beneficial for sketch modeling. To verify the beneficial effect of large-kernel convolutions, we have carried out a series of experiments for respective VGG and ResNet50 backbones. Figure 3 illustrates the performance of our model with varying kernel. It can be shown that the best results are obtained when the

Table 5. Ablation studies using VGG as backbone (%). CA and SA denote channel and spatial attention mechanism respectively.

Baseline	CA	SA	large-kernel convolutions	acc@1	acc@5	acc@10
✔				82.24	92.17	95.48
✔	✔			83.35	95.41	97.57
✔		✔		82.57	93.32	96.03
✔			✔	84.23	95.56	96.69
✔	✔	✔		83.79	96.71	97.57
✔	✔		✔	84.34	96.45	96.69
✔		✔	✔	85.56	94.17	95.70
✔	✔	✔	✔	**87.21**	**96.82**	**97.80**

Table 6. Ablation studies using ResNet50 as backbone (%).

Baseline	CA	SA	large-kernel convolutions	acc@1	acc@5	acc@10
✔				82.58	93.24	96.69
✔	✔			83.79	96.01	97.35
✔		✔		84.01	95.63	**98.24**
✔			✔	83.68	96.55	97.79
✔	✔	✔		84.67	95.11	97.46
✔	✔		✔	85.00	97.67	98.02
✔		✔	✔	85.34	**97.99**	98.02
✔	✔	✔	✔	**85.78**	97.26	97.57

kernel sizes is set as 6 and 9 respectively for VGG and ResNet50 backbones, suggesting that larger convolutional kernel size is conducive to capturing the discriminative visual cues of logo sketches.

Analysis of Hybrid Attention Mechanism. To gain a deep insight into the beneficial effect of the hybrid attention mechanism, we have conducted comprehensive ablation experiments to explore the individual attention module on the model performance. As shown in Table 5 and 6, hybrid attention mechanism combining spatial and channel attention can capture discriminative visual cues from the limited strokes and line of logo sketch, such that our model enjoys sufficient spatial and channel perception capabilities. When combined with the large-kernel convolutions, additional performance gains are reported when using both backbones.

In addition to the above quantitative results, we also qualitatively explore the effect of the hybrid attention within our LogoNet. As shown in Fig. 4, although the sketches lack sufficient visual contents, our LogoNet tends to focus on local cues (such as edges) with the help of the hybrid attention, which is considerably beneficial for accurate sketch retrieval.

Fig. 4. Example sketches (the first row) and the corresponding feature maps w/o attention (the second row) and the counterparts w/ attention (the third row). It is clearly shown hybrid attention mechanism within our network can capture local cues (such as edges) from the sketches with limited and irregular strokes, which contributes to fine-grained sketch retrieval.

a red parrot with a red circle outside

three green circles of different sizes surrounded by each other

a pink ribbon of love

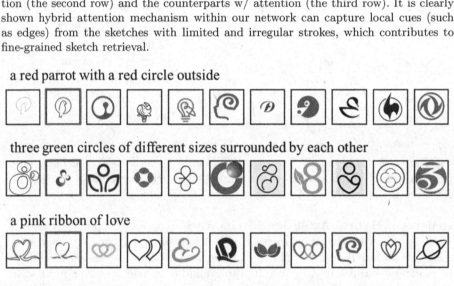

Fig. 5. Qualitative examples for cross-modal retrieval. The first image is the query sketch followed by top returned 10 images. Query-related ground truth is annotated in a red box. (Color figure online)

Table 7. Comparison of our LogoNet with other state-of-the-art methods on public QMUL datasets.

Method	QMUL-ShoeV2		QMUL-ChairV2	
hand-crafted based methods	acc@1	acc@10	acc@1	acc@10
Dense-HOG + rankSVM [18]	11.63	48.01	29.32	75.31
CNN-based methods	acc@1	acc@10	acc@1	acc@10
ISNDeep+rankSVM [18]	7.21	34.02	11.73	57.40
InceptionV3+rankSVM [18]	30.78	78.35	48.15	86.73
Triplet-SN [17]	30.93	72.02	45.06	86.42
Triplet-RL [1]	36.91	78.32	54.18	**95.51**
Jigsaw [7]	36.50	**85.90**	56.10	88.70
SketchAA [16]	32.33	79.63	52.89	94.88
LogoNet-ResNet50 (Ours)	27.17	69.36	59.65	93.40
LogoNet-VGG (Ours)	**36.93**	76.27	**60.28**	94.77

4.5 Results of Cross-Modal Retrieval

Using the labeled texts as auxiliary information to supplement the sketch query, our assembled dataset allows model to perform cross-modal retrieval. Since text labels provide abundant semantic information that is either implicitly encoded or incapable of being characterized in sketches, the two input modalities are complementary to each other for cross-model retrieval. In our experiments, we directly utilize the TASK-former model pre-trained with large-scale training data [10], and acc@1, acc@5 and acc@10 scores of 89.1%, 95.79% and 99.2% are reported respectively. As shown in Fig. 5, additional input texts can greatly improve the model accuracy, sufficiently suggesting the complementarity between sketches and the corresponding text descriptions.

4.6 Comparison with Other State-of-the-Art Methods

To further demonstrate the effectiveness of our method, we compare our LogoNet with other state-of-the-art methods on public QMUL-ShoeV2 and QMUL-ChairV2 benchmark datasets. More specifically, both traditional hand-crafted based methods and recent deep learning based approaches are involved in our comparative studies. As shown in Table 7, our LogoNet achieves competitive performance compared with the state-of-the-arts. In particular, LogoNet reports the highest acc@1 scores of 36.93% and 60.28% on QMUL-ShoeV2 and QMUL-ChinaV2, which demonstrates the efficacy of our network.

5   Conclusion

Current research on logo sketch retrieval is mainly challenged by the scarcity of public logo sketch dataset and insufficient representation capability of logo sketches with limited visual cues. To address the problems, we first assemble an instance-level logo sketch dataset. It is not only suitable for fine-grained logo sketch retrieval but also allows cross-modal retrieval with the help of supplementary labeled texts. In addition, we develop a triple-branch network based on hybrid attention mechanism termed LogoNet. It can characterize crucial and discriminative query-specific information from the limited visual cues in the logo sketches. Experiments on our collected dataset and the public benchmark datasets demonstrate the efficacy of our proposed LogoNet.

References

1. Bhunia, A.K., Yang, Y., Hospedales, T.M., Xiang, T., Song, Y.Z.: Sketch less for more: on-the-fly fine-grained sketch-based image retrieval. In: CVPR, pp. 9776–9785 (2020)
2. Browne, J., Lee, B., Carpendale, S., Riche, N., Sherwood, T.: Data analysis on interactive whiteboards through sketch-based interaction. In: SCM ISS, pp. 154–157 (2011)
3. Eitz, M., Hays, J., Alexa, M.: How do humans sketch objects? ACM Trans. Graph. (TOG), 1–10 (2012)
4. Eitz, M., Hildebrand, K., Boubekeur, T., Alexa, M.: Sketch-based image retrieval: benchmark and bag-of-features descriptors. IEEE Trans. Visualiz. Comput. Graph. (TVCG), 1624–1636 (2010)
5. Ha, D., Eck, D.: A neural representation of sketch drawings, pp. 1–15 . arXiv preprint arXiv:1704.03477 (2017)
6. Li, Y., Song, Y.Z., Gong, S., et al.: Sketch recognition by ensemble matching of structured features. In: BMVC, pp. 1–11 (2013)
7. Pang, K., Yang, Y., Hospedales, T.M., Xiang, T., Song, Y.Z.: Solving mixed-modal jigsaw puzzle for fine-grained sketch-based image retrieval. In: CVPR, pp. 10344–10352 (2020)
8. Qi, A., et al.: Toward fine-grained sketch-based 3D shape retrieval. IEEE Trans. image Process. (TIP), 8595–8606 (2021)
9. Sangkloy, P., Burnell, N., Ham, C., Hays, J.: The sketchy database: learning to retrieve badly drawn bunnies. ACM Trans. Graph. (TOG), 1–12 (2016)
10. Sangkloy, P., Jitkrittum, W., Yang, D., Hays, J.: A sketch is worth a thousand words: image retrieval with text and sketch. In: ECCV, pp. 251–267 (2022). https://doi.org/10.1007/978-3-031-19839-7_15
11. Schneider, R.G., Tuytelaars, T.: Sketch classification and classification-driven analysis using fisher vectors. ACM Trans. Graph. (TOG), 1–9 (2014)
12. Song, J., Yu, Q., Song, Y.Z., Xiang, T., Hospedales, T.M.: Deep spatial-semantic attention for fine-grained sketch-based image retrieval. In: ICCV, pp. 5551–5560 (2017)
13. Wang, F., Kang, L., Li, Y.: Sketch-based 3d shape retrieval using convolutional neural networks. In: CVPR, pp. 1875–1883 (2015)
14. Woo, S., Park, J., Lee, J.-Y., Kweon, I.S.: CBAM: convolutional block attention module. In: Ferrari, V., Hebert, M., Sminchisescu, C., Weiss, Y. (eds.) ECCV 2018. LNCS, vol. 11211, pp. 3–19. Springer, Cham (2018). https://doi.org/10.1007/978-3-030-01234-2_1
15. Xu, P., Joshi, C.K., Bresson, X.: Multigraph transformer for free-hand sketch recognition. IEEE Trans. Neural Netw. Learn. Syst. (TNNLS), 5150–5161 (2021)

16. Yang, L., Pang, K., Zhang, H., Song, Y.Z.: SketchAA: abstract representation for abstract sketches. In: ICCV, pp. 10077–10086 (2021)
17. Yu, Q., Liu, F., Song, Y.Z., Xiang, T., Hospedales, T.M., Loy, C.C.: Sketch me that shoe. In: CVPR, pp. 799–807 (2016)
18. Yu, Q., Song, J., Song, Y.Z., Xiang, T., Hospedales, T.M.: Fine-grained instance-level sketch-based image retrieval. Inter. J. Comput. Vis. (IJCV), pp. 484–500 (2021)

NCCNet: Arbitrary Neural Style Transfer with Multi-channel Conversion

Jin Xiang[1], Huihuang Zhao[1,2(✉)], Mugang Lin[1], and Qingyun Liu[1]

[1] College of Computer Science and Technology, Hengyang Normal University,
Hengyang 421002, China
happyday.huihuang@gmail.com
[2] Hunan Provincial Key Laboratory of Intelligent Information Processing
and Application, Hengyang 421002, China

Abstract. Arbitrary style transfer aims to create a novel image from a content image and a style image, stylizing the content image with the style of the style image. However, recent algorithms are prone to unnatural output due to focusing on the statistical distribution of deep features and ignoring the relationship between channels in feature maps. In this paper, we devise a novel Arbitrary Neural Style Transfer Network called NCCNet, which is useful for artistic style transfer. Specifically, NCCNet creates good visual effects by fusing different layers of textures. Moreover, we design an Effective Channel Conversion Modules (ECCM) which uses a multi-channel matrix to rearrange style feature maps to the appropriate range by analyzing the relationship between channels. Then, we can obtain a covariance based on the rearranged style feature map. At the same time, we design a decoder named Self-Adaptive Decoder (SA-Decoder) that conforms to our algorithm. Moreover, we apply our algorithm to the video style transfer and get good results. Qualitative and quantitative evaluations demonstrate that NCCNet performs well in arbitrary video and image style transfer tasks.

Keywords: Image style transfer · Video style transfer · Image-to-image translation

1 Introduction

Art style transfer is a technique for generating images, which is widely used in commercial products [8,19]. Based on the given content image and style image, the migration algorithm generates a new image by applying style patterns of a style image onto a content image while preserving content structure (Fig. 1).

In 2016, Gatys et al. [5] discovered that the deep neural network can extract the underlying texture information and high-level semantic information of the

This work was supported by the National Natural Science Foundation of China (61772179), Hunan Provincial Natural Science Foundation of China (2020JJ4152, 2022JJ50016, 2023JJ50095), and Scientific Research Fund of Hunan Provincial Education Department (21B0649).

H. Lu et al. (Eds.): ICIG 2023, LNCS 14358, pp. 250–261, 2023.
https://doi.org/10.1007/978-3-031-46314-3_20

Fig. 1. Illustration of our results. From left to right are examples of artistic image/video style transfer.

image at the same time, introduced this technology into the field of style transfer, and took the lead in developing a neural style based on the VGG (Visual Geometry Group) network. The work of Gatys et al. [4–6] has attracted a lot of attention from academia and the arts and initiated a huge technological innovation. After that, subsequent algorithms have been improved for shortcomings of Gatys et al.'s algorithm. These algorithms will be described in detail in Part II.

In recent years, image transfer algorithms have emerged in an endless stream, but they still cannot balance image style and content well. The local distortions produced by image style transfer still exist. Taking the paper CCPL published on ECCV in 2022 as an example, we randomly select one image for style transfer and point out its defects (see Fig. 2).

Therefore, in order to alleviate the local distortion of the image, and balance the flexibility and quality of the style, we propose a novel Arbitrary Neural Style Transfer Network called NCCNet. To summarize, our contributions are threefold:

1. We propose a new network NCCNet, which can flexibly and efficiently transfer styles from style features onto content features.
2. We design an Effective Channel Conversion Module (ECCM) and a Self-Adaptive Decoder (SA-Decoder), which performs well on the channel mapping transformation between content feature maps and style feature maps.
3. Our experiments show that our algorithm is balanced in local and global styles and can generate high-quality images.

2   Related Work

Image Style Transfer. Recently some algorithms [7,11,16] simply adjust the features of content images to match the second-order statistics of style images to achieve the purpose of stylization. Dumoulin et al. put forward conditional instance normalization (CIN), which allows multiple styles to be learned in a

Style   Content   CCPL   Ours

Fig. 2. Problems with existing SOTA algorithms. There is the effect of comparison between CCPL and our algorithm.

model by reducing a style image to a single point in an embedded space. Fifei et al. proposed a real-time style transfer approach that deals with a particular style in a model. Huang et al. proposed an arbitrary style transfer method using adaptive instance normalization (AdaIN) [7], which used means and variables to normalize content features. However, because the too-simple network architecture, the images generated by AdaIN [7] are often of low quality, which is just a simple mixture of content and style. WCT [11] utilized singular value decomposition to whiten and then recolor images.

Video Style Transfer. Ruder et al. [15] first proposed introducing timing constraints in the loss function directly through optical flow mapping in 2016. Both Lai [9] and Gao [3] embed long-short-term memory units into CNN, which has better temporal modeling ability than RNN. Chen et al. [1] added an optical flow sub-network and a mask sub-network outside the main network, and input two frames of images to get their optical flow and motion masks. Li et al. [10] utilized the linear transformation of content features to make the content structure more convergent. Wang at all. [17] enhanced the robustness of the network to motion changes through regularization over compound time. But they still don't guarantee fast processing and good perceived style quality. Compared with these methods, our proposed NCCNet is relatively simple. Not only does it produce satisfyingly stylized images, but more importantly, its video quality exceeds SOTA.

3   Methods

3.1   Network Architecture NCCNet

Inspired by fusing multi-layer feature maps, we propose a new style transfer network NCCNet. In order to utilize feature fusion to achieve better style transfer results, we design ECCM. Besides, SA-Decoder is designed to decode the output of ECCM. Generally, NCCNet includes feature fusion, ECCM, and SA-Decoder. Specifically, we formulate feature fusion as:

$$f_c, f_s = E\left(I_c, I_s\right), \tag{1}$$

$$S_*^x = C\left(f_*^0\right) \oplus C\left(f_*^1\right) \oplus \ldots \oplus C\left(f_*^x\right). \tag{2}$$

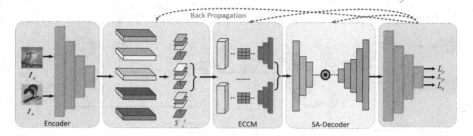

Fig. 3. Overview of the full framework, where the Encoder is fixed while three ECCM modules and SA-decoder are trainable. SA-Decoder transforms the combined ECCM output features to I_{cs}.

Here E refers to the encoding (VGG-19) operation. The feature list $(f_c,\ f_s)$ is obtained by encoding the content image and style image. $*$ represents c or s. And the x-layer feature map is represented by f_*^x. We employ dimensional transformation function C to change the feature map size for adapting the linear addition operation ($\oplus$ blending the feature map relying on channels). The front x layer of fusion is characterized by S_*^x (S_*^2, S_*^3, S_*^4).

The preliminary composite feature map gF^x (gF^2, gF^3, gF^4) is obtained by the ECCM group. Then we want to get the final image I_{cs} by decoding gF^x. The mathematical formula is as follows:

$$I_{cs} = De(gF^2, gF^3, gF^4). \tag{3}$$

The De (see Fig. 3) represents the entire decoding operation processing the three inputs. Therefore, loss calculation is essential, when training the network. After performing the VGG coding operation again, the feature map of each layer is obtained, and the loss can be calculated according to the loss function. In this article, three loss functions are employed. As shown in Fig. 3, L_c calculate based on I_{cs} and I_c, L_s on I_{cs} and I_s, and L_p on I_{cs} and I_c. The specific implementation details of loss and the detailed steps of the decoding operation De will be described in detail in the following content.

3.2 Effective Channel Conversion Module

The consideration of the inevitable correlation between features prompted us to design ECCM (see Fig. 4), which first analyzes the relationship between content features and style features, and then performs effective style transfer on content features.

Specifically, we first calculate the multi-channel attention matrix A^x (A^2, A^3, A^4), a distribution matrix, which describes the structural similarity between the content and the style image. Tt is formulated as:

$$A^x = \zeta(S_c^x) \otimes \psi(S_s^x). \tag{4}$$

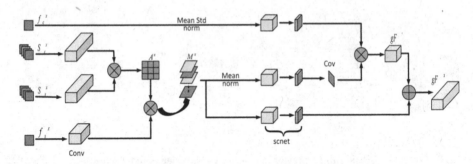

Fig. 4. Details of the ECCM. There Conv and scnet represent, separately, a convolutional layer and three convolutional layers. Besides, the std norm represents normalizing features by the means and standard deviations of its channels, while the mean norm normalizes features by the means of its channels.

where ζ and ψ denote nonlinear constraint function, $\otimes$ denotes matrix multiplication.

Then we spatially rearrange style image features using A^x to get the style-mean matrix M^x, which is intended to achieve a better balance between style pattern transfer and content structure preservation. M^x is a description of the deeper relationship between I_s and A^x. Simply put, it is the output of style-structured preprocessing combined with I_s and A^x. It is formulated as:

$$M^x = A^x \otimes \vartheta(f_s^x). \tag{5}$$

where ϑ refers to the nonlinear constraint function, which constrains the features of the x-layer of the style image. The result M^x is obtained by multiplying the output of ϑ by the multi-channel attention matrix A^x.

After that, the content features are normalized to make the local feature statistics the same as the reconstructed style feature statistics. Specifically, it is required that the content feature map f_c be preprocessed first by a nonlinear function and then by a multi-layer network (scnet, it is used for key feature extraction). Then the obtained value is multiplied by the covariance (Cov) calculated by M^x to get gF'. Finally, we add gF' directly to M^x getting gF^x, which is formulated as:

$$Cov = scnet(norm(M^x)), \tag{6}$$

$$gF' = Cov \otimes scnet(norm(\varsigma(f_c^x))), \tag{7}$$

$$gF^x = gF' \oplus M^x. \tag{8}$$

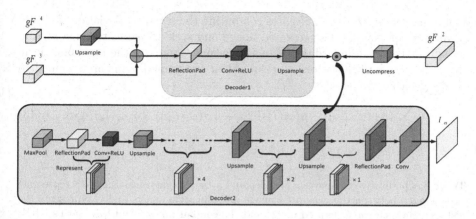

Fig. 5. Details of the SA-Decoder. There, $\odot$ means addition by channels.

3.3 SA-Decoder

Moreover, due to the application of multi-layer features and ECCM modules, we design a new Decoder (SA-Decoder) to correspond to the output in ECCM, making our feature distribution fusion more global, smoother, and more reasonable.

After three ECCM, the corresponding output we got is gF^2, gF^3, and gF^4. The overall decoding operation is shown in Formula 3. The detailed formula is as follows:

$$I_{cs} = D(gF^2 \odot Df(gF^3 \oplus gF^4)). \tag{9}$$

A feature map fusion with Deconder that is sent to Df for initial decoding is performed between gF^3 and gF^4. As shown in Fig. 5. Df output is needed to get a channel plus operation ($\odot$). After that, I_{cs} will be got by decoding secondly.

3.4 Loss Function

We apply Contrastive Coherence Preserving Loss (CCPL [18]) in the training to further constrain artifacts of images. The CCPL loss L_p constrains inter-domain differences via the InfoNCE loss [13]:

$$L_p = \sum_{m=1}^{8 \times N} -log[\frac{exp(d_g^m \cdot d_c^m / \tau)}{exp(d_g^m \cdot d_c^m / \tau) + \sum_{n=1, n \neq m}^{8 \times N} exp(d_g^m \cdot d_c^n / \tau)}]. \tag{10}$$

In addition to the loss CCPL [18], we employ two commonly used style transfer losses. The weighted sum of these losses constitutes the total training loss:

$$L_t = \lambda_p \cdot L_p + \lambda_c \cdot L_c + \lambda_s \cdot L_s. \tag{11}$$

Compute the content loss L_c using the Frobenius norm:

$$L_c = \parallel \phi_l(I_{cs}) - \phi_l(I_c) \parallel_F, \tag{12}$$

Obtaining the style loss L_s requires computing the standard deviation $\mu(\bullet)$ and mean $\sigma(\bullet)$ of each layer's generated image and style image feature maps. And we subtract their standard deviations or means. Computes the Frobenius norm from the standard deviation or mean. Their Frobenius norms are summed to finally get the style loss:

$$L_s = \sum_l (\| \mu(\phi_l(I_{cs})) - \mu(\phi_l(I_s)) \|_F + \| \sigma(\phi_l(I_{cs})) - \sigma(\phi_l(I_s)) \|_F), \quad (13)$$

Table 1. Qualitative comparison of video and artistic style transfer. Here S represents the distance between the generated image and the style image, and C represents the distance between the generated image and the content image. And I&V means NIQE measurement for images or videos. We show the first-place score in bold and the last-place score with underlining.

Methods	LPIPS ($\downarrow$)	SSIM($\uparrow$)	PSNR($\uparrow$)	NIQE($\downarrow$)
	S&C	S&C	S&C	I&V
AdaIN [7]	**0.657** 0.650	0.208 <u>0.306</u>	10.89 <u>11.11</u>	4.785 4.400
Linear [10]	<u>0.771</u> <u>0.713</u>	**0.231** 0.316	11.10 11.25	<u>5.413</u> 4.532
MCCNet [2]	0.669 0.631	0.224 0.413	**11.14** 11.40	4.935 5.955
AdaAttN [12]	0.683 0.604	<u>0.159</u> 0.457	<u>10.29</u> 12.34	4.294 <u>7.712</u>
CCPL [18]	0.692 0.590	0.208 0.461	10.77 11.59	4.621 4.245
Ours	0.691 **0.572**	0.196 **0.533**	10.54 **11.84**	**3.866 3.196**

4   Experiments

4.1   Comparison with Former Methods

Artistic Style Transfer. Compared with SOTAs (CCPL, MCCNet, Linear, SANet and AdaIN), it can be clearly seen that the irregular texture and local color distortion are significantly reduced in our results (see Fig. 6). Our algorithm apply multi-layer features for migration, uses covariance-based transformation, and has the most suitable Decoder structure for this network, which allows the final migrated features to be sufficiently local and global during decoding. Our algorithm performs well for any style, which is the best proof of its effectiveness.

Moreover, in order to further prove that our algorithm better balances stylization and content retention, and achieves higher quality results, we use a total of four measurement indicators (LPIPS, SSIM, PSNR and NIQE) to compare with SOTAs. Simply put, LPIPS, SSIM, PSNR, these three indicators are used to describe the similarity between two images. We use them to compute the similarity between the generated image and the style image or between the generated image and the content image. NIQE is a no-reference image evaluation index, which is used by us to directly judge the quality of generated images.

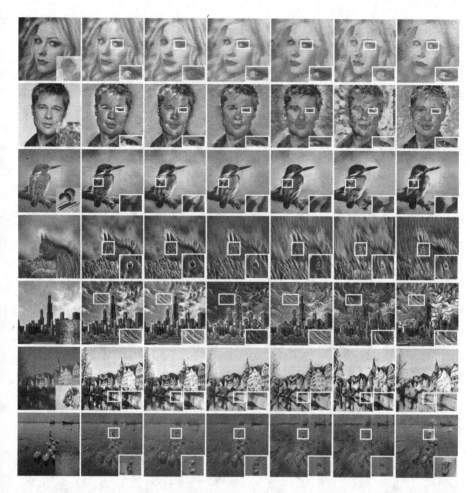

Fig. 6. Comparison of image style transfer results. The first column shows content images, and the second column shows style images. The remaining columns are style sized results of different methods (from left to right: Ours, CCPL [18], MCCNet [2], Linear [10], SANet [14], and AdaIN [7]).

As shown in Table 1, our generated image has the highest similarity to the content image, proving that the details are preserved more completely. The similarity between the generated image and the style image is between SOTAs, because in the network we discard the styles that are less integrated with the content image according to the relationship between content features and style features. More importantly, we have the best performance in NIQE values, which shows that the quality of our generated images is better than SOTAs, and it also reflects that we have a better balance between stylization and content structure preservation.

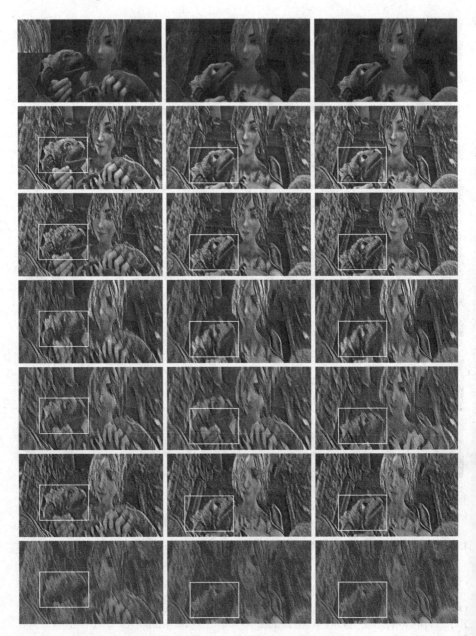

Fig. 7. Comparison of video style transfer results (3 frames). The first row shows content video frames. The remaining rows are stylized results of different methods (from top to bottom: Ours, CCPL [18], AdaAttN [12], MCCNet [2], Linear [10] and AdaIN [7]).

Video Style Transfer. In order to better demonstrate the effect of our algorithm on video style transfer, we compare the first three frames of a stylized video with other 5 methods (see Fig. 7). It can be clearly seen that the visual quality of our generated results is significantly better than other algorithms without reducing the stylization effect. Moreover, for continuous multi-frame video formatting, our NIQE is lower than all other SOTAs, which indicates that our video quality is optimal (see Table 1). All these further validate the effectiveness of our NCCNet.

4.2 Ablation Studies

As shown in Fig. 8, the top diagram represents the content and style of the image. And the left column indicates the number of ECCM in use and whether multi-layer fusion is used (for example, if one ECCM and no multi-layer fusion is used, it is shown as 1-1; using an ECCM with multiple layers of fusion is 1-n). In addition, the horizon shows which Relu layer in VGG is used. By embedding features at multiple levels (looking at the last image, which is the final choice), we can enrich the local and global patterns for the stylized images.

To better illustrate the effectiveness of three ECCM and applying fused multi-layer features, we design one, two, and three ECCM, respectively, and conduct experiments on whether to apply fused multi-layer features (14 models will be obtained). Color distortion can be seen in the results obtained by using only one ECCM without blending multi-layer features (1-1 row), whereas the model obtained by using layer 5_1 of VGG will also produce content structure loss

Fig. 8. Multi-level feature embedding.

(1-1, 5-1 columns). However, even if multiple ECCM is used, the results are not good (1-2, 1-3 rows) as long as they do not incorporate multiple features. The results of the fusion of multi-layer features are shown on the right, with a single ECCM result (1-n row) significantly improved over the previous single ECCM result (1-1 row). It is clear from the comparison that the three ECCM and the application of multi-layer feature fusion work best for balancing content structure and style textures.

5   Conclusions

In this work, we propose a simple and effective network NCCNet to alleviate the distortion caused by image stylization and balance the flexibility of arbitrary style transfer with the quality of the generated image. We design an Effective Channel Conversion Module (ECCM) and a Self-Adaptive Decoder (SA-Decoder), which performs well on channel mapping transformation.

The trained NCCNet achieves a good trade-off between time consistency and style effect while generating a satisfactory image. Moreover, we apply our algorithm to the video style transfer and get good results. Experimental results show that both images and videos synthesized by this method are superior to other most advanced arbitrary style transmission algorithms.

However, we still cannot completely solve the local distortion problem, and the image quality can still be improved. Therefore, in future work, we will further analyze the algorithm and strive for further improvement of the effect. In the meantime, we will try to combine the GAN network to construct the model and add a text drive at the same time to propose an effective multi-modal stylized network.

References

1. Chen, D., Liao, J., Yuan, L., Yu, N., Hua, G.: Coherent online video style transfer. In: Proceedings of the IEEE International Conference on Computer Vision, pp. 1105–1114 (2017)
2. Deng, Y., Tang, F., Dong, W., Sun, W., Huang, F., Xu, C.: Arbitrary style transfer via multi-adaptation network. In: Proceedings of the 28th ACM International Conference on Multimedia, pp. 2719–2727 (2020)
3. Gao, W., Li, Y., Yin, Y., Yang, M.H.: Fast video multi-style transfer. In: Proceedings of the IEEE/CVF Winter Conference on Applications of Computer Vision, pp. 3222–3230 (2020)
4. Gatys, L., Ecker, A.S., Bethge, M.: Texture synthesis using convolutional neural networks. In: Advances in Neural Information Processing Systems, vol. 28 (2015)
5. Gatys, L.A., Ecker, A.S., Bethge, M.: A neural algorithm of artistic style. arXiv preprint arXiv:1508.06576 (2015)
6. Gatys, L.A., Ecker, A.S., Bethge, M.: Image style transfer using convolutional neural networks. In: Proceedings of the IEEE Conference on Computer Vision and Pattern Recognition, pp. 2414–2423 (2016)

7. Huang, X., Belongie, S.: Arbitrary style transfer in real-time with adaptive instance normalization. In: Proceedings of the IEEE International Conference on Computer Vision, pp. 1501–1510 (2017)
8. Kwon, G., Ye, J.C.: Clipstyler: Image style transfer with a single text condition. In: Proceedings of the IEEE/CVF Conference on Computer Vision and Pattern Recognition, pp. 18062–18071 (2022)
9. Lai, W.S., Huang, J.B., Wang, O., Shechtman, E., Yumer, E., Yang, M.H.: Learning blind video temporal consistency. In: Proceedings of the European Conference on Computer Vision (ECCV), pp. 170–185 (2018)
10. Li, X., Liu, S., Kautz, J., Yang, M.H.: Learning linear transformations for fast image and video style transfer. In: Proceedings of the IEEE/CVF Conference on Computer Vision and Pattern Recognition, pp. 3809–3817 (2019)
11. Li, Y., Fang, C., Yang, J., Wang, Z., Lu, X., Yang, M.H.: Universal style transfer via feature transforms. In: Advances in Neural Information Processing Systems, vol. 30 (2017)
12. Liu, S., et al.: Adaattn: revisit attention mechanism in arbitrary neural style transfer. In: Proceedings of the IEEE/CVF International Conference on Computer Vision, pp. 6649–6658 (2021)
13. Oord, A.v.d., Li, Y., Vinyals, O.: Representation learning with contrastive predictive coding. arXiv preprint arXiv:1807.03748 (2018)
14. Park, D.Y., Lee, K.H.: Arbitrary style transfer with style-attentional networks. In: Proceedings of the IEEE/CVF Conference on Computer Vision and Pattern Recognition, pp. 5880–5888 (2019)
15. Ruder, M., Dosovitskiy, A., Brox, T.: Artistic style transfer for videos. In: Rosenhahn, B., Andres, B. (eds.) GCPR 2016. LNCS, vol. 9796, pp. 26–36. Springer, Cham (2016). https://doi.org/10.1007/978-3-319-45886-1_3
16. Sheng, L., Lin, Z., Shao, J., Wang, X.: Avatar-net: multi-scale zero-shot style transfer by feature decoration. In: Proceedings of the IEEE Conference on Computer Vision and Pattern Recognition, pp. 8242–8250 (2018)
17. Wang, W., Yang, S., Xu, J., Liu, J.: Consistent video style transfer via relaxation and regularization. IEEE Trans. Image Process. 29, 9125–9139 (2020)
18. Wu, Z., Zhu, Z., Du, J., Bai, X.: CCPL: contrastive coherence preserving loss for versatile style transfer. In: Avidan, S., Brostow, G., Cissé, M., Farinella, G.M., Hassner, T. (eds.) ECCV 2022, Part XVI. LNCS, vol. 13676, pp. 189–206. Springer, Cham (2022). https://doi.org/10.1007/978-3-031-19787-1_11
19. Yang, J., Guo, F., Chen, S., Li, J., Yang, J.: Industrial style transfer with large-scale geometric warping and content preservation. In: Proceedings of the IEEE/CVF Conference on Computer Vision and Pattern Recognition, pp. 7834–7843 (2022)

BRMR: TAL Based on Boundary Refinement and Multi-scale Regression

Jing Jiang, Jiankun Zhu, Lining Wang, and Hongxun Yao[✉]

Harbin Institute of Technology, Harbin, China
h.yao@hit.edu.cn

Abstract. Transformer based networks have been widely used in Temporal Action Localization (TAL). An example of this is the previous state of the art method ActionFormer. By analyzing the predicted results of these transformer based models, we find that though these models are lightweight and powerful, they still have two drawbacks: inaccurate boundary predictions and unreliable confidence in results. Therefore, we propose the **B**oundary **R**efinement and **M**ulti-scale **R**egression (BRMR) model to solve these two weaknesses and improve model performance. The core of BRMR is the RCE Head and MTDR Module. The RCE Head supervises the quality of the predicted boundaries of the action segments during training, allowing the model to have objective evaluation indicators for the quality of the action segments during testing. The MTDR Module synthesizes and extracts the information of Encoders to obtain aggregated feature pyramids with different temporal scales, which is beneficial for the model to perceive the information of actions at different scales. BRMR achieves state of the art on THUMOS14 and EPIC-Kitchens 100. Besides, BRMR has comparable performance on ActivityNet 1.3.

Keywords: Temporal action localization · Regression confidence · Multi-scale features

1 Introduction

Video understanding has proposed the task of temporal action localization, which both localizes the temporal boundaries and classifies the action of instances in untrimmed long videos. So far, deep neural network models in TAL have made significant progress. Most of the approaches used the "proposal-generation" method [1–3], which used sliding windows, boundary probability prediction, and other proposal generation methods. Later approaches used convolutional [20,27], transformer [4,28], and graph neural networks [23,25].

Recently, a lightweight and efficient model, ActionFormer [5], has been proposed in TAL. The model uses a minimalistic Transformer [6] that applies local self-attention to the temporal context of the input video, then extracting a feature pyramid, where each position represents a moment in the video. The model

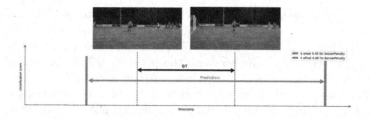

Fig. 1. Example diagram of inaccurate boundary prediction.

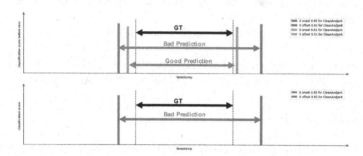

Fig. 2. Example of unreliability of confidence.

classifies each of the predefined moments and regresses the action boundaries. It establishes a new state of the art across several major TAL benchmarks, surpassing previous works by a large margin.

Our work is to address two drawbacks in this model. By analyzing the results of ActionFormer on the test set, we found that the model has two weaknesses: (1) Inaccurate prediction of boundaries. Classification and regression of Action-Former are independent processes, which leads to unreliable confidence in the results. As shown in Fig. 1, it can be seen that the predicted boundary is far from the starting and end of its corresponding ground truth, indicating that some boundaries predicted by ActionFormer are inaccurate. (2) The confidence of the results is unreliable. It is found that after soft-NMS [7], some of the better action segments may be suppressed due to lower classification confidence. As in Fig. 2, the quality of the prediction with a confidence of 0.61 is significantly better than that of the prediction with a confidence of 0.65, but after soft-NMS, the better prediction is suppressed.

To deal with the above two weaknesses of ActionFormer, we propose the Regression Confidence Estimation (RCE) Head and Multi-scale Transformer Decoder Regression (MTDR) Module. RCE head extracts the video features aligned with the predicted segments. It predicts the value of t-IoU between the segment and its corresponding ground truth based on the features. To further improve the performance, we propose MTDR module, which is a stack of downsampling Transformer decoders. It synthesizes and extracts the context of multi-scale Transformer encoder, facilitating the model to perceive the information of different scales of actions.

We found that the model performance was further improved after proposing these two modules. Our model achieves state of the art on several major TAL benchmarks. For example, it achieves 79.2% mAP when tIoU $= 0.4$ in THU-MOS14 [8], which is 1.4% higher than the previous SOTA ActionFormer; In addition, our model achieves 36.6% average mAP on ActivityNet-1.3 [9], which is comparable with ActionFormer; Our work also significantly outperforms Action-Former on EPIC-Kitchens 100 [10], with 1.2% average mAP improvement on the noun subset. Our main contributions are summarized as follows:

(1) We found two weaknesses in ActionFormer, and to alleviate them, we proposed RCE head.
(2) We proposed MTDR module to further improve the performance of Action-Former.
(3) Our model achieves state-of-the-art results on THUMOS14 and EPIC-Kitchens 100 and is comparable to TCANet [20] on ActivityNet-1.3.

2   Related Works

Action Recognition. Action recognition is a fundamental task in computer vision, which identifies classes of actions throughout a video. Action recognition have been studied for decades, and it remains a trendy topic due to its widespread use in the real world, including video retrieval [11] and visual surveillance [12,13]. Moreover, with the rise of convolutional neural networks, there has been a breakthrough in the performance of action recognition since 2014. In this paper, we use I3D [14], R(2+1)D [15], and SlowFast [16] for video feature extraction.

Temporal Action Localization. There are two main frameworks of TAL: "two-stage TAL" and "single-stage TAL". Specifically, the former is based on "proposal-classification", in which a proposal is first proposed based on the model to obtain several possible starting and end of actions. Then the proposed proposal is classified to obtain action labels. Previous work focused on temporal action proposal generation by classifying the anchor window and locating the action boundaries [1–3]. But some recent work used graph convolutional neural networks or Transformer, which can generate proposal and classify segments simultaneously. It is therefore called single-stage TAL.

RoI Align. K He et al. proposed RoIAlign [21], which removes the harsh quantization of RoIPool [17] and precisely aligns the extracted features of the input. RoI Align avoids any quantization of RoI boundaries or spatial bins. It uses bilinear interpolation to compute the exact values of the input features at the four regularly sampled locations in each RoI and aggregate the results using maximum pooling.

3   Boundary Refinement and Multi-scale Regression

In this section, we will introduce the two proposed modules: Regression Confidence Estimation(RCE) Head and Multi-scale Transformer Decoder Regression (MTDR) Module. An overview of the model structure is in Fig. 3.

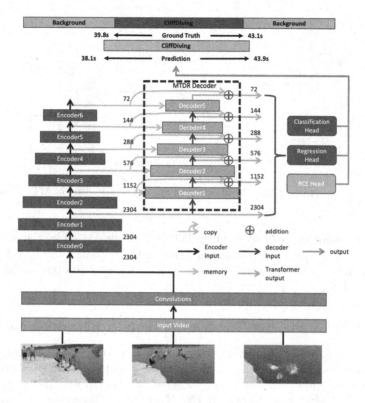

Fig. 3. Overview of model structure.

3.1 Preliminar

Given an input video X, suppose X can be represented by a set of feature vectors $X = \{x_1, x_2, ..., x_T\}$. These feature vectors take values on the discrete timestamp $t = \{1, 2, ..., T\}$, where T changes with the video time, and x_t can be the feature vector of the segment corresponding to time t extracted from a 3D convolutional network.

3.2 RCE: Regression Confidence Estimation Head

The structure of RCE head is shown in Fig. 4. Given the feature sequence $X_E \in \mathbb{R}^{T_S \times C}$ output by the Transformer encoder g and predicted fragments $\hat{s}_i = (\hat{t}_i^s, \hat{t}_i^e)$. To include contextual information around the boundary, it is necessary to extend the time dimension of the predicted segment $\hat{s}_i$ to obtain $\hat{s}_i^{expand} = (\hat{t}_i^s - \eta L, \hat{t}_i^e + \eta L)$, where η is the expansion rate, and L is the length of the predicted segment. Afterwards, we use RoIAlign [21] with temporal dimension on X_E to obtain the expanded predicted segment $\hat{s}_i^{expand}$ aligned feature $X_{\hat{s}_i} \in \mathbb{R}^{T_R \times C}$, which is the dimension of the RoIAlign feature extracted from the segment. Then, the feedforward network takes $X_{\hat{s}_i}$ as input to predict the

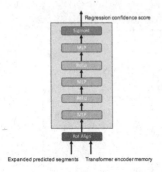

Fig. 4. The structure of RCE head.

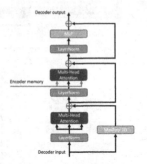

Fig. 5. The structure of MTDR module.

regression confidence $\hat{g}_i$ of segment $\hat{s}_i$, Where $\hat{g}_i$ is supervised by the maximum t-IoU g_i between $\hat{s}_i$ and all ground truth during the training process. With RCE head, the detector will be more sensitive to local features and the boundaries of actions.

3.3   MTDR: Multi-scale Transformer Decoder Regression Module

The structure of MTDR Module is shown in Fig. 5. We take X as the input of the Transformer encoder g and obtain the features $Z = \{Z_1, Z_2, ..., Z_L\}$ outputted by all L layers. Afterward, the features are fed into MTDR module to obtain the aggregated multi-scale features $U = \{U_1, U2, ..., U_L\}$. The specific process is as follows.

Take MTDR module Layer f_I where $I \geq 1$ as an example, f_I takes the output $Z_I \in \mathbb{R}^{T_I \times D}$ of Transformer encoder of layer I and the output $Z_{I+1} \in \mathbb{R}^{T_{I+1} \times D}$ of Transformer encoder of layer $I + 1$ as input.

The overall calculation process of f_I is as follows:

$$U_I^0 = D_1(MSA(LN(Z_I), LN(Z_I), LN(Z_I))) + D_2(Z_I) \tag{1}$$

$$U_I^1 = MSA(Z_{I+1}, LN(U_I^0), Z_{I+1}) + U_I^0 \tag{2}$$

$$U_I^2 = MLP(LN(U_I^1)) + U_I^1 \tag{3}$$

$$U_I = U_I^2 + Z_{I+1} \tag{4}$$

where $U_I^0, U_I^1, U_I^2, U_I \in \mathbb{R}^{T_{I+1} \times D}$. $MSA(K, Q, V)$ represents multi-head self-attention operation, $\frac{T_I}{T_{I+1}}$ is the downsampling rate, which is set to 2 in this paper. To improve efficiency, downsampling D_1 uses depth-wise 1D convolution with a step size of 1 and downsampling D_2 uses a 1D maximum pooling with a step size of 2 and kernel size of 3. Due to f_I takes g_I and g_{I+1} as input, $I \leq L - 1$. To maintain the same number of the output layers as encoder g, Z_1 is added to the final output of f. Therefore, the aggregated multi-scale features $U = \{U_1, U_2, ..., U_{L-1}, Z_1\}$ are ultimately obtained, denoted as $U = \{U_1, U_2, ..., U_L\}$.

3.4 Implementation Details

Training. The loss function of the model includes three parts: (1) classification loss L_{cls} is Focal loss [18]; (2) Regression loss L_{reg} is DIoU loss [19]; (3) Regression confidence loss L_{act} is L1 Loss. The loss of each video X is defined as:

$$L = \sum_t (L_{cls} + \lambda_{reg}\mathbb{I}_{c_t}L_{reg} + \lambda_{act}\mathbb{I}_{c_t}L_{act})/T_+ \tag{5}$$

where T_+ is the total number of positive samples. $\mathbb{I}_{c_t}$ is an indicator function indicating whether time t is within an action. If it is 1, it indicates that the sample at time t is positive. λ_{reg} is the weight coefficient of the regression loss, λ_{act} is the weight coefficient of the regression confidence loss. Only when the current time t is within the positive sample will there be L_{reg} and L_{act}.

Inference. Due to the addition of RCE head, we can get the classification score $p(a_t)$ and regression confidence $q(a_t)$. They can be fused during inference to obtain the fusion score $s(a_t)$, and we take it as the confidence for each action segment. The score fusion adopts linear fusion as follows:

$$s(a_t) = p(a_t) + \alpha * q(a_t) \tag{6}$$

where α is a hyperparameter.

4 Experiments

In this section, we will present our experimental results. Our model obtained results on three datasets, including THUMOS14 [8], ActivityNet-1.3 [9], and EPIC-Kitchens 100 [10]. In addition, we conducted extensive ablation experiments on our model and visualized a series of results. **Evaluation Metric.** We report the standard mean average precision (mAP) for all datasets at different temporal intersections over union (tIoU) thresholds, widely used to evaluate TAL methods.

4.1 Results on THUMOS14

Dataset. THUMOS14 comes from the 2014 THUMOS Challenge. This dataset includes two tasks: action recognition and temporal action localization. Most papers are evaluated in this dataset. The THUMOS dataset has video-level category annotations for 101 action classes in its training, validation, and testing sets. In contrast, only a portion of the 20 class in validation and testing sets have TAL annotations.

Experiment Setup. We use two-stream I3D [14] pre-trained on Kinetics [14] to extract the video features on THUMOS14. mAP@[0.3:0.1:0.7] is used to evaluate our model.

Result. The experimental results on the THUMOS14 dataset are shown in Table 1. As we can see, the average mAP of BRMR is the best, reaching 67.6%, 0.8% higher than ActionFormer. As a result, the two modules proposed in this paper can be fused well and perform better, reaching the current SOTA.

Table 1. Results on THUMOS14 and ActivityNet-1.3.

model	THUMOS14						ActivityNet-1.3			
	0.3	0.4	0.5	0.6	0.7	avg	0.5	0.75	0.95	avg
BMN [2]	56.0	47.4	38.8	29.7	20.5	38.5	50.1	34.8	8.3	33.9
G-TAD [23]	54.5	47.6	40.3	30.8	23.4	39.3	50.4	34.6	**9.0**	34.1
MUSES [24]	68.9	64.0	56.9	46.3	31.0	—	50.0	35.0	6.6	34.0
TCANet [20]	60.6	53.2	44.6	36.8	26.7	44.3	54.3	**39.1**	8.4	**37.6**
ContextLoc [25]	68.3	63.8	54.3	41.8	26.2	50.9	**56.0**	35.2	3.6	34.2
RTD-Net [4]	68.3	62.3	51.9	38.8	23.7	49.0	47.2	30.7	8.6	30.8
GTAN [26]	57.8	47.2	38.8	—	—	—	52.6	34.1	8.9	34.3
AFSD [27]	67.3	62.4	55.5	43.7	31.1	52.0	52.4	35.3	6.5	34.4
TadTR [28]	62.4	57.4	49.2	37.8	26.3	46.6	49.1	32.6	8.5	32.3
ActionFormer [5]	82.1	77.8	71.0	59.4	43.9	66.8	54.7	37.8	8.4	36.6
RCE Head (Ours)	82.5	78.7	71.6	**60.2**	44.7	67.5	54.8	37.8	8.2	36.6
MTDR Decoder (Ours)	82.5	78.7	**71.7**	59.6	**45.4**	67.6	54.5	37.5	8.5	36.4
BRMR (Ours)	**82.9**	**79.2**	**71.7**	59.5	44.7	67.6	54.9	38.0	8.4	36.6

4.2 Results on ActivityNet-1.3

Dataset. ActivityNet-1.3 is the largest dataset in TAL and can be used for action recognition and temporal action localization. The total duration of the video is 648 h. ActivityNet-1.3 contains only 1.5 action occurrences per video on average, most videos contain only one action, and an average of 36% of the time is background.

Experiment Setup. The features are extracted from the R(2+1)D-34 model [15] pre-trained with TSP [22] on ActivityNet. We used mAP@[0.5:0.05:0.95] for evaluation and reported the average mAP.

Result. The experimental results on ActivityNet-1.3 are shown in Table 1. It can be seen that the average mAP of the RCE head and BRMR are both comparable with ActionFormer, reaching 36.6%. Although our model performs less than current SOTA TCANet [20], it achieves comparable results in ActivityNet-1.3.

4.3 Results on EPIC-Kitchens 100

Dataset. EPIC-Kitchens 100 contains videos up to 100 h, 20 million frames, and 90k actions. EPIC-Kitchens 100 is challenging because the average video contains 128 action instances, much more than the average of 1.5 action instances in ActivityNet-1.3.

Experiment Setup. We use the SlowFast [16] network pre-trained on EPIC-Kitchens for feature extraction. mAP@[0.1:0.1:0.5] is used to evaluate our model.

Result. The experimental results on the EPIC Kitchens 100 dataset, in Table 2 and Table 3, show that the average mAP of MTDR is the best, reaching 23.6% on

Table 2. results on EPIC-Verb.

model	0.1	0.2	0.3	0.4	0.5	avg
BMN [2]	10.8	9.8	8.4	7.1	5.6	8.4
G-TAD [23]	12.1	11.0	9.4	8.1	6.5	9.4
ActionFormer [5]	26.6	25.4	24.2	22.3	19.1	23.5
RCE Head (Ours)	26.6	25.8	24.2	22.2	**19.2**	**23.6**
MTDR Decoder (Ours)	26.7	25.9	24.2	**22.4**	19.0	**23.6**
BRMR (Ours)	**27.0**	**26.0**	**24.4**	22.3	18.0	23.5

Table 3. results on EPIC-Noun.

model	0.1	0.2	0.3	0.4	0.5	avg
BMN [2]	10.3	8.3	6.2	4.5	3.4	6.5
G-TAD [23]	11.0	10.0	8.6	7.0	5.4	8.4
ActionFormer [5]	25.2	24.1	22.7	20.5	17.0	21.9
RCE Head (Ours)	25.5	24.4	22.8	20.3	16.3	21.9
MTDR Decoder (Ours)	**26.6**	**25.6**	**23.9**	21.4	**17.9**	**23.1**
BRMR (Ours)	26.2	25.3	23.5	21.4	17.7	22.8

the verb subset. The average mAP of MTDR reaches 23.1% on the noun subset, 1.2% higher than ActionFormer. BRMR also achieves 22.8% mAP in the noun subset, 0.9% higher than ActionFormer. In conclusion, Our approach achieves SOTA in EPIC.

4.4 Ablation Experiments

In this section, we conduct ablation experiments on the proposed model using THUMOS14 as the dataset.

Table 4. Position Encoding.

model	0.5	0.7	avg
RCE	71.6	44.7	67.5
RCE+PE	70.7	43.7	66.6
MTDR	**71.7**	**45.4**	**67.6**
MTDR-PE	71.3	44.1	66.8
BRMR	**71.7**	44.7	**67.6**
BRMR+PE	71.0	43.2	67.0

Table 5. Skip Connection.

model	0.5	0.7	avg
MTDR	**71.7**	**45.4**	**67.6**
MTDR+skip	71.1	44.2	67.0
BRMR	**71.7**	44.7	**67.6**
BRMR-skip	70.9	43.7	66.7

Position Encoding. The position encoding used in this paper is sin-cosine encoding. As shown in Table 4, PE has different gains for different models, so it is necessary to use PE according to model performance.

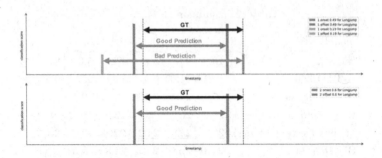

Fig. 6. Example figure of score fusion.

Skip Connection. When adding the Transformer decoder, considering that ActionFormer can achieve good results only by using the Transformer encoder, and to avoid the problem of gradient disappearance caused by increasing the number of network layers, a skip connection is added between the encoder and decoder. As shown in Table 5, MTDR with skip connection reduce average mAP by 0.6 %. Conversely, when skip connection is added to BRMR, the average mAP increases by 0.9 %. We think the Transformer decoder can fuse the features of the Transformer encoder further, improving the model performance significantly but increasing the number of parameters a little. So the skip connection is not required to feed the features of the Transformer encoder into the following head. Because the number of model parameters that fuse the two models increases greatly, model training is more difficult and time-consuming. Adding a skip connection can reduce the difficulty of model training and improve model performance.

Table 6. Loss Weight Factor.

model	0.5	0.7	avg
RCE $\lambda_{act} = 200$	71.4	44.5	<u>67.5</u>
RCE $\lambda_{act} = 250$	<u>71.6</u>	<u>44.7</u>	<u>67.5</u>
RCE $\lambda_{act} = 300$	71.0	<u>44.7</u>	67.3
BRMR $\lambda_{act} = 150$	71.1	44.6	67.1
BRMR $\lambda_{act} = 200$	**71.7**	<u>44.7</u>	**67.6**
BRMR $\lambda_{act} = 250$	70.9	**44.9**	67.2
BRMR $\lambda_{act} = 300$	70.2	44.0	66.4

Table 7. Score Fusion.

model	0.5	0.7	avg
RCE $\alpha = 0.0$	71.3	**44.8**	<u>67.4</u>
RCE $\alpha = 0.1$	71.4	**44.8**	67.5
RCE $\alpha = 0.3$	<u>71.5</u>	**44.8**	67.5
RCE $\alpha = 0.5$	**71.6**	<u>44.7</u>	67.5
RCE $\alpha = 0.7$	**71.6**	44.6	67.5
RCE $\alpha = 0.9$	<u>71.5</u>	44.5	67.5
RCE $\alpha = 1.5$	71.2	44.0	67.2

Weight Factor for Loss Function of RCE Head. A new loss has been introduced due to the addition of the RCE head. The weight factor ablation results of the loss function of the RCE head are shown in Table 6. When training RCE head model, selecting $\lambda_{act} = 250$ or 200 gives the best results, with average mAP reaching 67.5%; When training BRMR, choosing $\lambda_{act} = 200$ gives the best results, with average mAP reaching 67.6%.

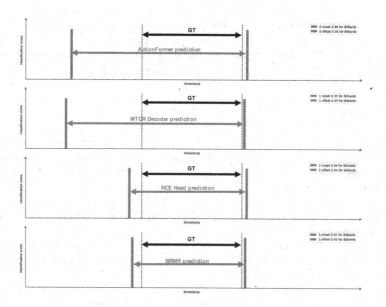

Fig. 7. Example figure for boundary refinement. The top-down result model is Action-Former, MTDR decoder, RCE head, and BRMR.

Score Fusion. The fusion coefficient is α. As shown in Table 7, the ablation results show that when α is between 0.1 and 0.9, mAP is the highest.

4.5 Result Visualization

As is shown in Fig. 6, on the top of the graph is the model without fusing RCE head scores, and on the bottom is the model with fusing RCE head scores. When RCE head score fusion is added, some poor predictions have lower scores and even be discarded if it is below the predicted result threshold. Better predictions have higher confidence, such as the confidence of the best results in Fig. 6 increased from 0.49 to 0.60. Therefore, the RCE head alleviates the problem of unreliable prediction confidence.

As is shown in Fig. 7, compared with the predictions of the ActionFormer, the predictions of RCE head are significantly better, and the confidence is improved. Therefore, it is known that the RCE head alleviates the inaccurate boundary prediction weakness of ActionFormer. RCE head can further alleviate the weakness of inaccurate boundary prediction by fusing the MTDR module.

5 Conclusion

The main contribution of this paper is to study and analyze the weaknesses of ActionFormer and propose two modules for the TAL task to solve the above weaknesses and improve the model performance. The superior results on three public datasets demonstrate the effectiveness of our method and provide a new solution for the community to address the TAL task. The limitation of our method is that the model still generates many redundant prediction segments and uses the traditional post-processing method like soft-NMS.

References

1. Lin, T., Zhao, X., Su, H., Wang, C., Yang, M.: BSN: boundary sensitive network for temporal action proposal generation. In: Ferrari, V., Hebert, M., Sminchisescu, C., Weiss, Y. (eds.) ECCV 2018. LNCS, vol. 11208, pp. 3–21. Springer, Cham (2018). https://doi.org/10.1007/978-3-030-01225-0_1
2. Lin, T., Liu, X., Li, X., Ding, E., Wen, S.: BMN: Boundary-matching network for temporal action proposal generation. In: International Conference on Computer Vision, pp. 3889–3898 (2019)
3. Liu, Y., Ma, L., Zhang, Y., Liu, W., Chang, S.F.: Multi-granularity generator for temporal action proposal. In: IEEE Conference on Computer Vision Pattern Recognition, pp. 3604–3613 (2019)
4. Tan, J., Tang, J., Wang, L., Wu, G.: Relaxed transformer decoders for direct action proposal generation. In: International Conference Computer Vision, pp. 13526–13535 (2021)
5. Zhang, C., Wu, J., Li, Y.: ActionFormer: localizing moments of actions with transformers. arXiv preprint arXiv:2202.07925 (2022)
6. Vaswani, A., et al.: Attention is all you need. In: Advances in Neural Information Processing Systems, vol. 30 (2017)
7. Bodla, N., et al.: Soft-NMS-improving object detection with one line of code. In: Proceedings of the IEEE International Conference on Computer Vision (2017)
8. Idrees, H., et al.: The THUMOS challenge on action recognition for videos "in the wild". Comput. Vis. and Image Under. 155, 1–23 (2017)
9. Caba Heilbron, F., Escorcia, V., Ghanem, B., Carlos Niebles, J.: ActivityNet: a large-scale video benchmark for human activity understanding. In: IEEE Conference on Computing Vision Pattern Recognition, pp. 961–970 (2015)
10. Damen, D., et al.: Rescaling egocentric vision. arXiv preprint arXiv:2006.13256 (2020)
11. Ciptadi, A., Goodwin, M.S., Rehg, J.M.: Movement pattern histogram for action recognition and retrieval. In: Fleet, D., Pajdla, T., Schiele, B., Tuytelaars, T. (eds.) ECCV 2014. LNCS, vol. 8690, pp. 695–710. Springer, Cham (2014). https://doi.org/10.1007/978-3-319-10605-2_45
12. Hu, W., Xie, D., Fu, Z., Zeng, W., Maybank, S.: Semantic-based surveillance video retrieval. IEEE Trans. Image Process. 16(4), 1168–1181 (2007)
13. Singh, S., Velastin, S.A., Ragheb, H.: Muhavi: a multicamera human action video dataset for the evaluation of action recognition methods. In: 2010 Seventh IEEE International Conference on Advanced Video and Signal Based Surveillance (AVSS), pp. 48–55. IEEE (2010)
14. Carreira, J., Zisserman, A.: Quo vadis, action recognition? A new model and the kinetics dataset. In: Proceedings of the IEEE Conference on Computer Vision and Pattern Recognition, pp. 6299–6308 (2017)
15. Tran, D., et al.: A closer look at spatiotemporal convolutions for action recognition. In: Proceedings of the IEEE Conference on Computer Vision and Pattern Recognition, pp. 6450–6459 (2018)

16. Feichtenhofer, C., Fan, H., Malik, J., et al.: Slowfast networks for video recognition. In: Proceedings of the IEEE/CVF International Conference on Computer Vision, pp. 6202–6211 (2019)
17. Girshick, R.: Fast R-CNN. In: Proceedings of the IEEE International Conference on Computer Vision (2015)
18. Lin, T.Y., Goyal, P., Girshick, R., He, K., Doll'ar, P.: Focal loss for dense object detection. In: International Conference on Computing Vision, pp. 2980–2988 (2017)
19. Zheng, Z., Wang, P., Liu, W., Li, J., Ye, R., Ren, D.: Distance-IoU loss: faster and better learning for bounding box regression. In: AAAI (2020)
20. Qing, Z., et al.: Temporal context aggregation network for temporal action proposal refinement. In: IEEE Conference Computer Vision Pattern Recognition, pp. 485–494 (2021)
21. He, K., et al.: Mask R-CNN. In: Proceedings of the IEEE International Conference on Computer Vision (2017)
22. Alwassel, H., Giancola, S., Ghanem, B.: TSP: temporally-sensitive pretraining of video encoders for localization tasks. In: Proceedings of the IEEE/CVF International Conference on Computer Vision (2021)
23. Xu, M., Zhao, C., Rojas, D.S., Thabet, A., Ghanem, B.: G-TAD: sub-graph localization for temporal action detection. In: IEEE Conference Computing Vision Pattern Recognition, pp. 10156–10165 (2020)
24. Liu, X., Hu, Y., Bai, S., Ding, F., Bai, X., Torr, P.H.: Multi-shot temporal event localization: a benchmark. In: IEEE Conference Computer Vision Pattern Recognition, pp. 12596–12606 (2021)
25. Zhu, Z., Tang, W., Wang, L., Zheng, N., Hua, G.: Enriching local and global contexts for temporal action localization. In: International Conference Computer Vision, pp. 13516–13525 (2021)
26. Long, F., Yao, T., Qiu, Z., Tian, X., Luo, J., Mei, T.: Gaussian temporal awareness networks for action localization. In: IEEE Conference Computer Vision Pattern Recognition, pp. 344–353 (2019)
27. Lin, C., et al.: Learning salient boundary feature for anchor-free temporal action localization. In: IEEE Conference on Vision Pattern Recognition, pp. 3320–3329 (2021)
28. Liu, X., Wang, Q., Hu, Y., Tang, X., Bai, S., Bai, X.: End-to-end temporal action detection with transformer. arXiv preprint arXiv:2106.10271 (2021)

AE-Reorient: Active Exploration Based Reorientation for Robotic Pick-and-Place

Hao Luo, Zhenyu Wu, and Haibin Yan$^{(\boxtimes)}$

Beijing University of Posts and Telecommunications, Beijing, China
{haroll_luo,wuzhenyu,eyanhaibin}@bupt.edu.cn

Abstract. Finding objects in dense clutter and placing them in specific poses play an important role in robot manipulation in fields like warehousing and logistics, and have a significant influence on the automation of these fields. However, most methods that perform well in simple clutter do not hold up well in dense clutter because of severe stacking and occlusion between objects, which prevents the target objects from grasping successfully. In this paper, we propose an interactive exploration framework called AE-Reorient based on reinforcement learning to let robots learn the interactive exploration autonomously. AE-Reorient enables robots to actively find the target objects and accomplish the pick-and-place task. Our AE-Reorient generates iterative and interactive actions to improve the visibility of the target objects which is an important factor affecting the success of grasping. Specifically, we first collect the scene information through an RGB-D camera. Then, using the point cloud reconstruction and pose estimation methods to obtain the height map of the clutter, through which we generate the grasp pose or predict the position. We apply interaction to change the state of the scene by pushing if the grasp is unsuccessful. The generated push action is applied to disrupt and recreate a new state of the clutter with the target objects more exposed, which greatly improves the probability of grasp success. Robots can successfully perform pick-and-place tasks in dense clutter by applying our proposed framework. We test our AE-Reorient in 130 dense clutters and it enhances the success rate and the visibility of the target object by 7.60% and 4.10% compared with the baseline method.

Keywords: Active Exploration · Interaction · Reorientation · Robotic · Pick-and-place Tasks

1 Introduction

In recent years, vision-based robotic manipulation has become mainstream due to the gradual maturity of computer vision technologies [4,14,17], which enhances the robot's ability to adapt autonomously in complex environments. However, in fields such as warehousing and logistics, finding target objects from dense clutter and placing them in specific poses remains a complex task for robots. Compared with traditional robotic pick-and-place tasks, the robot needs

H. Lu et al. (Eds.): ICIG 2023, LNCS 14358, pp. 274–286, 2023.
https://doi.org/10.1007/978-3-031-46314-3_22

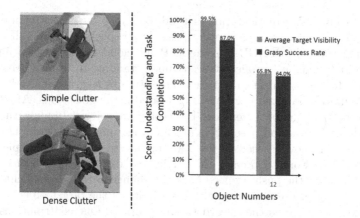

Fig. 1. Relationship between visibility and grasp success. Two scenes with an average of 6 objects and 12 objects. In the dense clutter with more occlusion, the decreased visibility of the target object led to a decrease in the success rate of the grasp.

to perform higher-level scene understanding to locate the target object and consider its placement pose.

Because of the limitations of the structure or workspace, robots are not always capable of placing objects successfully in one attempt. Motivated by that a supermarket staff turns the product label outward before putting it on the shelf, reorientation methods have been introduced to robot pick-and-place tasks by using intermediate poses to solve the problem of the inability to reach the final pose in one step. The reorientation method has been studied as one of the basic operations in lots of robotic tasks. Traditional reorientation methods have applied pre-designed poses of reorientation for continuous attempts, which requires multiple steps to complete the entire reorientation process. Due to the complexity of robotic tasks, multi-step reorientation methods are not efficient enough and the intermediate state is difficult to understand, which leads to the randomness in task completion. Some researchers have optimized multi-step reorientation by employing models to predict or sample abstract geometric features to find stable reorientation poses. The reorientation poses obtained from these methods have more interpretability, but sacrifice efficiency to a certain extent. Other studies have selected unstable reorientation poses as intermediate states and the released object tends to stabilize on its own, which could improve the efficiency. For the single-step reorientation methods, they are limited by the complexity of the scene and perform poorly in complex scenes due to severe stacking and occlusion. Figure 1 illustrates that as the complexity of the scene increases, the performance of robots in completing the pick-and-place task decreases significantly.

In this paper, we propose a framework named AE-Reorient to actively explore the scene, which allows the robot to autonomously learn scene interaction strategies through reinforcement learning to search for target objects in clutter.

We apply a single-step reorientation method to regrasp the object in an unstable state and finally place it in a specific pose. More specifically, we collect scene information through an RGB-D camera. Point cloud reconstruction and pose estimation methods are applied in scene understanding to form a height map. We detect the target object in the scene and attempt to grasp it. Active exploration around the target object will be initiated if the grasp fails. AE-Reorient executes the push action to explore the scene and aims at finding the target object. Meanwhile, we propose a reinforcement learning framework. The height map mentioned above is used as the state of the framework. We apply a fully convolutional network to predict the origin and direction of the push in the height map. After the push, we feed back the change of the scene, including the value evaluation of the push action, the visibility of the target object, and the success rate of grasp, as the reward to AE-Reorient. Our contributions are as follows:

1) We propose AE-Reorient for a robotic pick-and-place system that is capable of autonomously exploring complex scenes, searching for and grasping target objects, and placing them in specific poses.
2) We also propose a reinforcement learning framework for robotic scene interaction and active exploration. Our proposed AE-Reorient employs RGB-D information to predict the position for pushing interaction.
3) We train and test our AE-Reorient extensively in simulated complex scenes to verify the significant improvement in the robot's ability to complete target searching and specific pose placement tasks.

2   Related Works

In this section, we briefly introduce the previous work from two aspects of reorientation and regrasping and active interaction exploration.

Reorientation and Regrasping: Object reorientation and regrasping is an important link for the robot to find an intermediate state to transport objects from the initial state to the final state during the pick-and-place task. The existing reorientation and regrasping methods are mainly based on planning. Cheng et al. [2] proposed a robot system for planning a series of picking and placing operations. Xu et al. [16] applied deep neural networks to generate diverse placements of objects on the plane to find a stable intermediate state for reorientation. These two works and some other research such as [8] used planning methods to find stable poses to regrasp and reorient objects, which sacrificed the motion efficiency. Raessa et al. [7] proposed a motion planning method that constructs a regrasp graph to describe robot manipulation planning. It is limited to specific scenarios and the target objects. Wermelinger et al. [13] uses a physics engine to search for stable attitudes for grasp planning and object manipulation to reorient highly irregular objects. Although the results are reliable, a lot of computing resources are required. Wada et al. [9] applied a learned model to predict the probability of a collision-free path between a pair of waypoints, improving object reorientation planning efficiency. In addition, some research such as [19] has been conducted on the basis of in-hand manipulation. However, these methods are limited to the size of objects and specific tasks. In this work, we use a general suction gripper and unstable intermediate poses for the reorientation to ensure the generalization of the method and operation efficiency.

Active and Interactive Exploration: Active exploration as part of active learning is already widely applied in a number of other fields [10–12]. Recently, there has been a lot of research on active vision, especially in the field of robotics, which aims to make robots explore scene information more actively. Wu *et al.* [15] proposed an active exploration framework named Smart Explorer to accurately recognize objects in dense clutter scenes. Liu *et al.* [5] proposed GE-Grasp framework to improve the success rate of object grasping in dense scenes with active interaction. Ye *et al.* [18] applied an intrinsic-extrinsic reward setting to train a model for object searching. Novkovic *et al.* [6] proposed an interactive perception system based on reinforcement learning to perform physical interaction. In this work, we use active physical exploration to interact with the scene to help the robot to find the target object in dense clutter.

3 Approach

In this section, we first briefly introduce the pipeline overview of our AE-Reorient and then introduce the mathematical description of the active interaction problem. After that, we detail the process of push action generation and provide details of training.

3.1 Pipeline Overview

Our basic task is to find the target object in dense clutter and arrange it in a specific position. However, it is usually difficult to find the appropriate grasp position in dense clutter because of the severe stacking and occlusion. We use physical interaction to disturb the clutter to make the target object more exposed, which is confirmed to have a strong correlation with the success of grasp.

Figure 2 shows the overall pipeline of our AE-Reorient. The RGB-D image is collected to generate a depth map and a color map for the robot to understand the scene. Through the depth map, we use a fully convolutional network (FCN) to predict the position and direction of the push. After the interaction, we put the change of target visibility, push success, and grasp success as rewards into the FCN. When the grasp is successful, the reorient and place planner plans collision-free paths for reorientation and placement, and then the robot executes. We apply push as the action of our active scene interaction, accomplished by moving the end-effector perpendicular to the desktop in a direction parallel to the desktop. Through the method of reinforcement learning, the robot can gradually learn the best pushing position and direction in the process of each execution, to maximize the exposure of the target object, which can improve the possibility of grasping success.

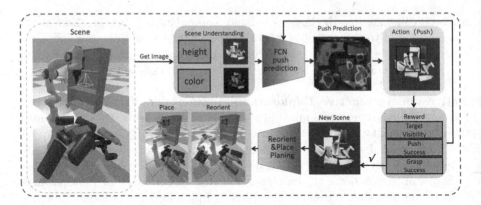

Fig. 2. Pipeline Overview of AE-Reorient. The scene point cloud reconstructed by the RGB-D camera of the top-down view will be sent to the agent to generate iterative and interactive actions. When the visibility of the object is large enough to grasp the object successfully, the robot performs the subsequent operation.

3.2 Problem Formulation and Learning Policy

We formulate the task of active interaction as a Markov decision process: at a certain state s_t at a given moment t, the robot takes certain actions a_t according to the strategy π, gets the new state s_{t+1} at the next time $t+1$, and obtains the current reward $R_{a_t}(s_t, s_{t+1})$. The expected reward is as follows:

$$R(s_t, a_t) = \Sigma_{t=0}^{\infty} \gamma^t R_{a_t}(s_t, s_{t+1}) \tag{1}$$

where γ represents the attenuation factor, indicating that with the continuous progress of the decision, the reward will continue to decline.

The relationship between decision and reward is described as a cumulative reward by the following functions:

$$V^{\pi}(s) = R(s_0) + \gamma \sum_{s_1} V^{\pi}(s) \tag{2}$$

In this equation, $R(s_0)$ is the current reward of the decision taken in the current state, and the second part is the expected reward in the future state.

Once the mathematical relationship between the decision and the reward is confirmed, the goal is to maximize the cumulative reward function $V^{\pi}(s)$ from any state:

$$V^*(s) = \max_{\pi} V^{\pi}(s) = R(s) + \max_{\pi} V^{\pi}(s_1) \tag{3}$$

Our actions are generated by the strategy function $a = \pi(s)$. In the cumulative reward functions, the strategy function is the variation we need to optimize. It can be seen from the above function that the decision function corresponding to the maximized cumulative reward is the optimal decision, and the cumulative reward corresponding to the optimal decision is also the largest, so the optimal decision is as follows:

$$\pi^*(s) = \arg\max_{a \in A} \sum_{s_i \in S} V^*(s, a) \tag{4}$$

where A is the set of all actions and S is all available states.

In this work, our state is the height map generated by the input RGB-D image. Since it requires physical interaction to change the scene, we collect image information again after each interaction and then update the state information. As shown in Fig. 2, our action is the starting point and direction of the push action generated by the FCN, so the adjustment of our policy function is to adjust the network parameters of the FCN. We calculate the loss for each prediction based on the reward of each interaction as follows:

$$L = \begin{cases} \frac{1}{2}(Q_i(s_i, a_i) - v_i)^2, & if |Q_i(s_i, a_i) - v_i| < 1 \\ |Q_i(s_i, a_i) - v_i| - \frac{1}{2}, otherwise \end{cases} \tag{5}$$

Our goal is to help the robot successfully find and grasp the target object in the clutter. Therefore, the goal of strategy selection is to make the interaction more effective. Based on experimental results, we have found that the visibility of target objects has a significant impact on the success of the grasping task, so we designed a reinforcement learning reward scheme to restrict the robot from finding the most effective push action to improve the visibility of target objects. We use the mask map before and after each interaction to calculate the visibility of the target object in $Vis_{imp} = targetvisibility_{(new)} - targetvisibility_{(pre)}$ and set a series of thresholds to judge the visibility improvement and assign a reward value, which is calculated as follows:

$$V_{(s_t, s_{t+1})} = \begin{cases} -0.1, & Vis_{imp} < 0 \\ 0.1, & 0 < Vis_{imp} < 0.1 \\ 0.3, & 0.1 < Vis_{imp} < 0.3 \\ 0.5, & Vis_{imp} > 0.3 \end{cases} \tag{6}$$

In addition, the robot may have some interactions that lead to changes in the scene but do not improve the visibility of the object, so we calculate the difference of the height maps before and after the interaction. When the difference is greater than the threshold, we add 0.2 to the reward. When the grasp is successful, which means the task can be accomplished, we add 1 to the reward.

3.3 Push Generation

Inspired by [20], we use FCN to predict the starting position and direction of our push action. The network predicts the score of push actions in 16 discrete directions at each pixel point. We control the end-effector perpendicular to the tabletop and move it in a direction parallel to the tabletop to push objects. The end-effector we use is a suction gripper that is widely used in common scenarios.

Figure 3 shows the process of generating and executing push actions. First, the height map is fed into the FCN to predict the start point and direction of the push. As shown in Fig. 3(a), we rotate the height map 16 times and predict the value evaluation of push actions in the same direction. Figure 3(b) shows the

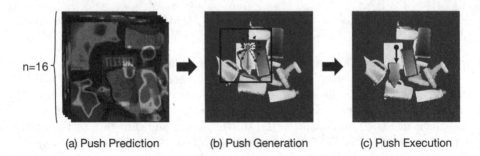

(a) Push Prediction   (b) Push Generation   (c) Push Execution

Fig. 3. Process of the push generation and execution. (a) shows the input when we use the FCN to predict the push action, which is 16 height maps in different directions; (b) shows the motion generation and the region of interest (ROI) we set; (c) shows the height map formed after the execution of the interactive action.

evaluation of the 16 directions on a pixel. The length of the line indicates the score rating. Then, we select the one with the highest score to generate the push action through a coordinate transformation. The robot places the end-effector at the starting point and pushes a fixed distance(20cm) in the direction we selected. When the end-effector cannot reach the position, we re-select the starting point.

As shown in Fig. 3(b), to reduce searching cost, we limit the prediction of push point to the area around the target object and intercept a 224×224 pixel window as the region of interest (ROI) on the original 448×448 pixel image with the target as the center. The specific method is as follows: first, we find all the pixels occupied by the target object in the mask map, calculate the central coordinates of the target object, and then move 112 pixels from this point along the negative direction of the x and y axes. Depending on this point, we intercept 224 pixels forward along the x and y axes to form the ROI window. When the captured window is out of the original image, we limit the ROI window to the edge of the original image. Note that the coordinate transformation is required when giving the position to the robot for push action.

The interactive action is designed to better complete the pick-and-place task. Only when the grasp fails, the robot will start active interaction to expose and find the target objects. In the training process, we set the exit conditions of interactive actions: (1) Exit the interaction when the grasp is successful, (2) Exit the interaction when the visibility of the target object is greater than 90% but still cannot be grasped successfully or the number of interactions is greater than 10. In this case, the grasp is not successful due to other factors such as the robot's joint angle limitation. (3) Other situations, such as when the robot pushes the target object out of sight so that the grasping task is no longer possible.

4   Experiment

In this section, we conduct extensive experiments in a PyBullet [3] simulation environment to validate our proposed AE-Reorient. The main goal of the exper-

Fig. 4. The objects selected in our experiments in the simulation environment.

iments is to verify that (1) our active interaction method can effectively improve the grasping success rate in heavily occluded scenes, and (2) the reinforcement learning-based interaction generation method outperforms random generation.

4.1 Implementation Details

In the simulation scene, the workspace is a rectangular region with 0.896 m × 0.896 m to ensure that the robot arm can work properly. The whole scene is perceived by a top-down view RGB-D camera with the resolution set to 640 × 480 pixels. In the world coordinate system, we set the height map voxelization resolution to 2 mm and discretize the robot arm XY plane workspace into a grid of 448 pixels. To further improve the effectiveness of the interaction and reduce the computational cost, we crop the 224 × 224 pixels region in the height map centered on the target and feed it into the agent to generate the push action. In our experiments, we set an upper limit of 10 for the number of interactions in order to avoid numerous ineffective interactions.

The objects of the dense clutter scenes constructed in the experiments are from the YCB [1] dataset, which contains 79 3D models of everyday objects with high-resolution textured RGB images. To ensure the validity of the constructed scenes, we apply the following two rules to filter the objects: (1) the selected objects require good visibility in the depth map in order to reconstruct the scene point cloud, and (2) the selected objects could be grasped by the robot arm employed. We finally select 7 objects for the experiments, as shown in Fig. 4. All experiments are conducted on one NVIDIA GTX 2080Ti GPU.

4.2 Evaluation Metrics

We evaluate our proposed AE-Reorient in terms of overall execution success and efficiency of executive actions. In the first regard, we leverage the overall success rate of pick and place (including reorient and place) to demonstrate the performance improvement of the proposed framework on dense clutter scenes. Second, we verify the effectiveness of the interaction actions with the visibility of the final grasp. Finally, the efficiency of action execution is measured by the robot arm execution time, which is employed to illustrate the balance between the success rate and time cost of AE-Reorient.

Fig. 5. Visualization of randomly generated scenes. Red boxes mark the target objects for each scene. (Color figure online)

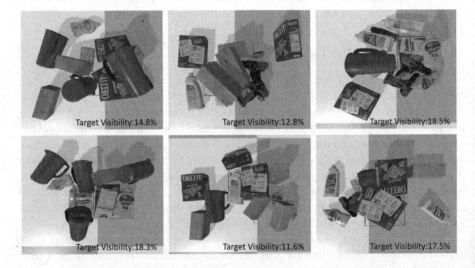

Fig. 6. Challenging scene visualization. The objects in each scene are manually adjusted to expect a higher degree of occlusion. The visibility of the target objects in each scene is less than 20%.

4.3   Results and Discussions

We perform interactive actions on a Franka Emika Panda robot equipped with a suction gripper, where the solution of the kinematic equations for each joint of the robot is implemented by a Pybullet built-in module. To verify the effectiveness of AE-Reorient interaction generation, we compare our approach with ReorientBot and the random interaction ReorientBot framework. The average execution time of each scene is also reported to demonstrate the efficiency-success trade-off. In the test scenes, only cases with unsuccessful grasp or target visibility less than 90% will be explored interactively. To facilitate comparison with the selected baseline, we only count the robot-specific operation time, excluding the inference time.

Table 1. Comparison on randomly generated and challenging scenes. We report the average of the three measures of overall execution success, final grasp visibility, and execution time, where the success rate and time are only calculated for the scene with successful manipulation.

Setting	Method	Success(%)	Visibility(%)	Time(s)
Random	ReorientBot	23.10	84.60	19.20
	ReorientBot+Random	27.70	85.90	24.88
	AE-Reorient	30.70	88.70	30.52
Challenging	ReorientBot	0.00	15.58	–
	ReorientBot+Random	0.00	37.92	–
	AE-Reorient	16.67	49.68	32.61

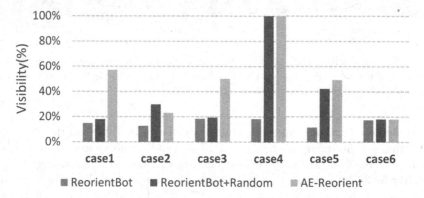

Fig. 7. Visibility comparison results with challenging scenes, AE-Reorient has significant improvement compared to other methods.

Random Clutters: Objects fall into a set workspace in a random order in free fall, where the initial pose and position of each object is random. Since the difficulty of grasping is positively correlated with the object clutter density, we increase the ReorientBot experiment setting of 6 objects to 12, which significantly reduces the visibility of the target objects as shown in Fig. 5. The experimental results of random clutters are shown in Table 1 in the row with the setting as *Random*, where our proposed AE-Reorient significantly enhances the success rate and visibility by 7.60% (30.70% vs. 23.10%) and 4.10% (88.70% vs. 84.60%), compared with the baseline method without active interaction by only increasing the 11.32s execution time. It demonstrates the effectiveness of our proposed AE-Reorient, which further indicates the effectiveness of the reward mechanism based on the degree of visibility and push interaction.

Challenging Clutters: To further validate the effectiveness of AE-Reorient in dense clutter scenes, we evaluated the proposed framework in 6 challenging scenes with less than 20% visibility of the target object as shown in Fig. 6. The

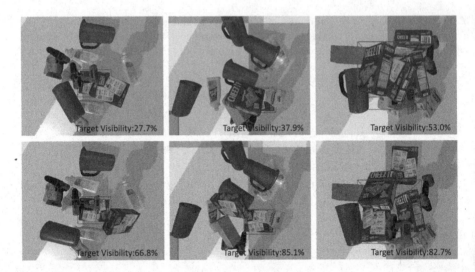

Fig. 8. Visualization of the results of the interaction manipulations, with each row representing the execution sequence of AE-Reorient. As the interaction continues, the visibility of the target object increases significantly.

experimental results of challenging clutter are shown in Table 1 in the row with the setting as *Challenging*, where our AE-Reorient enhances success rate 16.67% (16.67% vs. 0.00%) compared with the baseline and increases the average target visibility by 34.10%. Since ReorientBot failed to grasp the challenging scene, we cannot count the execution time. Meanwhile, due to the increased complexity of clutter, random interactions increase negligible success rates. Figure 7 demonstrates the comparative results of visibility for each challenging scene. Due to the overly complex nature of challenging scenes, randomly generated interactions have the potential to enhance the visibility of target objects and achieve higher boosts in a collision-intense manner. In contrast, our AE-Reorient is constrained by the spatial geometry information during interaction and still outperforms the randomly generated approach in general and shows a significant improvement in success rate and visibility, further illustrating the effectiveness of the proposed framework. Figure 8 illustrates the visualization results of our AE-Reorient interaction, where the visibility of the heavily occluded targets is enhanced to improve the success rate of subsequent manipulations.

5   Conclusion

In this paper, we have proposed AE-Reorient for the pick-and-place task in dense and cluttered scenes, which decreases the occlusion of target objects and improves the success rate of grasping and placing by active pushing. We applied a reinforcement learning framework to learn the push-generation strategy. The exploration of active interaction provides an effective success rate versus execution time tradeoff for grasping target objects in cluttered scenes. Extensive experiments demonstrate the effectiveness and efficiency of the proposed AE-Reorient. Our framework uses RGB-D image information to autonomously and interactively find targets in clutter, which made us see the possibility of robots being applied to more general scenarios. However, our work only validates the effectiveness of autonomous exploration in cluttered scenes and does not take into account more physical details, and there are broad prospects for the general scene operation of robots.

Acknowledgements. This work was supported in part by the National Natural Science Foundation of China under Grant 61976023 and Grant U22B2050.

References

1. Calli, B., Walsman, A., Singh, A., Srinivasa, S., Abbeel, P., Dollar, A.M.: Benchmarking in manipulation research: the ycb object and model set and benchmarking protocols. arXiv preprint arXiv:1502.03143 (2015)
2. Cheng, S., Mo, K., Shao, L.: Learning to regrasp by learning to place. arXiv preprint arXiv:2109.08817 (2021)
3. Coumans, E., Bai, Y.: Pybullet, a python module for physics simulation for games, robotics and machine learning (2016)
4. Huang, S., Wang, Z., Zhou, J., Jiwen, L.: Planning irregular object packing via hierarchical reinforcement learning. RAL **8**(1), 81–88 (2022)
5. Liu, Z., Wang, Z., Huang, S., Zhou, J., Lu, J.: Ge-grasp: efficient target-oriented grasping in dense clutter. In: IROS, pp. 1388–1395 (2022)
6. Novkovic, T., Pautrat, R., Furrer, F., Breyer, M., Siegwart, R., Nieto, J.: Object finding in cluttered scenes using interactive perception. In: ICRA, pp. 8338–8344 (2020)
7. Raessa, M., Wan, W., Harada, K.: Planning to repose long and heavy objects considering a combination of regrasp and constrained drooping. Assem. Autom. **41**(3), 324–332 (2021)
8. Tang, B., Sukhatme, G.S.: Selective object rearrangement in clutter. In: Conference on Robot Learning (2022)
9. Wada, K., James, S., Davison, A.J.: Reorientbot: learning object reorientation for specific-posed placement. In: ICRA, pp. 8252–8258 (2022)
10. Wang, Z., Jiwen, L., Ziyi, W., Zhou, J.: Learning efficient binarized object detectors with information compression. PAMI **44**(6), 3082–3095 (2021)
11. Wang, Z., Jiwen, L., Zhou, J.: Learning channel-wise interactions for binary convolutional neural networks. PAMI **43**(10), 3432–3445 (2020)
12. Wang, Z., Xiao, H., Duan, Y., Zhou, J., Lu, J.: Learning deep binary descriptors via bitwise interaction mining. PAMI **45**, 1919–1933 (2022)
13. Wermelinger, M., Johns, R., Gramazio, F., Kohler, M., Hutter, M.: Grasping and object reorientation for autonomous construction of stone structures. RAL **6**(3), 5105–5112 (2021)
14. Wu, Z., Wang, Z., Lu, J., Yan, H.: Category-level shape estimation for densely cluttered objects. arXiv preprint arXiv:2302.11983 (2023)
15. Wu, Z., Wang, Z., Wei, Z., Wei, Y., Yan, H.: Smart explorer: recognizing objects in dense clutter via interactive exploration. In: IROS, pp. 6600–6607 (2022)
16. Xu, P., Chen, Z., Wang, J., Meng, M.Q.H.: Planar manipulation via learning regrasping. arXiv preprint arXiv:2210.05349 (2022)

17. Xu, X., Wang, Z., Zhou, J., Lu, J.: Binarizing sparse convolutional networks for efficient point cloud analysis. arXiv preprint arXiv:2303.15493 (2023)
18. Ye, X., Yang, Y.: Efficient robotic object search via hiem: Hierarchical policy learning with intrinsic-extrinsic modeling. RAL **6**(3), 4425–4432 (2021)
19. Yuan, S., Shao, L., Yako, C.L., Gruebele, A., Salisbury, J.K.: Design and control of roller grasper v2 for in-hand manipulation. In: IROS, pp. 9151–9158 (2020)
20. Zeng, A., Song, S., Welker, S., Lee, J., Rodriguez, A., Funkhouser, T.: Learning synergies between pushing and grasping with self-supervised deep reinforcement learning. In: IROS, pp. 4238–4245 (2018)

A Novel Contactless Prediction Algorithm of Indoor Thermal Comfort Based on Posture Estimation

Shuchang Chu[1], Xiaogang Cheng[1(✉)], Yufeng Zhou[1], Xintao Hu[1], Caoxin Xu[1], Xiaolong Liu[1], Qing Wang[1], and Bin Yang[2]

[1] College of Telecommunications and Information Engineering, Nanjing University of Posts and Telecommunications, Nanjing, China
chengxg@njupt.edu.cn
[2] School of Energy and Safety Engineering, Tianjing Chengjian University, Tianjin, China

Abstract. Currently, with the rising energy consumption bringing about the greenhouse effect, the proposed "double carbon" strategy has significant value. Traditional building temperature control solutions have resulted in a certain amount of wasted energy, but the construction of real-time non-contact human thermal comfort detection can effectively alleviate this situation and realise a 'people-centred' intelligent building. Accurate and effective determination of human thermal comfort in intelligent buildings is significant. Human behavioral actions can provide important feedback signals to building heating, ventilation, and air conditioning systems. However, there is a lack of effective methods for real-time, low-cost, non-contact human thermal discomfort state detection. In this paper, a contactless thermal comfort prediction method based on skeletal keypoints was proposed, which is intended to avoid overcooling and overheating and to improve indoor human environmental satisfaction. The experiment used a questionnaire to select six actions with high confidence levels to produce a dataset on thermal discomfort. The concept of action sequences was proposed and corresponding dataset and pose recognition algorithms were produced. The final experimental results show that the method can improve the robustness of the model and effectively estimate thermal discomfort.

Keywords: Thermal Comfort · OpenPose · Skeletal Keypoints · Deep Learning · Action Sequences

1 Introduction

Health, intelligence, and low carbon are the current trends in the international building industry. Improving healthy environments and achieving energy savings has become a new demand and hot topic. Currently, heating, ventilation, and air conditioning (HVAC) systems is responsible for maintaining comfortable indoor temperature, humidity, and air quality, which also means a large number of building energy consumption. Studies

---

The original version of this chapter was revised: The name of the author Bin Yang has been corrected. The correction to this chapter is available at
https://doi.org/10.1007/978-3-031-46314-3_34

H. Lu et al. (Eds.): ICIG 2023, LNCS 14358, pp. 287–297, 2023.
https://doi.org/10.1007/978-3-031-46314-3_23

have shown that the HVAC system accounts for 40% of a building's energy consumption, which can be as high as 60%, especially for non-residential built environments [1, 2]. Moreover, home heating consumes almost 12% of the energy consumed [3]. Therefore, it is urgent to design a thermal comfort system,which could reduce the interaction with the user and autonomously turn on and off high-voltage AC to reduce system energy consumption[4].

Indoor thermal comfort is essential to people's lives and health issues. Research shows that most people spend 90% of their time indoors [5]. Among various elements of the indoor environment, indoor temperature is considered to be the main reference factor for human thermal comfort [6–8].

With the development of deep learning, HVAC systems based on computer vision and neural networks have attracted much attention [9–12]. Currently, computer vision technology has provided reliable technical support for non-contact detection of human core temperature and indoor air environment factors. Non-contact human thermal comfort prediction is mainly through the detection of skin temperature, heart rate, movement, etc. C. Song et al. [13] established the body temperature prediction model based on collected thermal camera facial skin images, which provides highly accurate body temperature under varying environmental conditions, such as hot, cold, and motion and comfort conditions.CHENG et al. [14] captured video of skin changes and skin temperature on the back of the subject's hand under thermal environmental stimulation via an RGB camera. Skin texture features were observed in combination with Eulerian video amplification, and a 315-layer deep neural network was constructed relying on skin feature data, such as fine movements and texture changes. The network constructs a relationship between skin features and skin temperature. Faridah F et al. [15] used a low-cost thermal imaging camera for the detection of seven types of thermal sensations by facial skin temperature. The facial skin temperature was determined by four measurement points: forehead, nose, cheek, and chin. And an artificial neural network was constructed based on the four facial measurement points.papers [16, 17] proposed to use heart rate variability (HRV) as an alternative indicator of thermal comfort status. And observed that HRV is distinctively different depending on the thermal environment and that it is possible to reliably predict each subject's thermal state.Guillaume Lopez et al. [18] proposed an automatic control system based on the Heart Rate Variability Index (HRVI) to detect the thermal comfort status of users and to quantify the differences between individual thermal comfort, thus increasing the satisfaction rate of all indoor users and saving energy.

In addition, with the rapid development of deep learning, OpenPose [19] was proposed as an open-source platform based on deep learning. Okugawa et al. [20] used OpenPose to extract key point data of soldiers' posture during the parade, and evaluated their synchronization level based on data such as their arms swing amplitude. Tanaka et al. [21] used deep learning to classify and identify preparatory actions for specific behaviors based on coordinate data extracted by OpenPose. T. Kitamura et al. [22] have improved OpenPose on the issue of inaccurate extreme posture detection in motion situations. This method is aimed to improve the training of extreme posture 2D posture estimators by using a new motion dataset and proposed data enhancement strategy.

OpenPose can generate keypoint coordinates for human bones and help estimate the human body's thermal comfort. Usually, human behavior can convey many information, including personal thermal comfort. When we feel hot, we roll up our sleeves, fan with our hands, and wipe sweat; When we feel cold, we usually rub our hands, cross our arms, and wear hats. Therefore, human behavioral actions can be used to extract human thermal sensation states, which provide important feedback signals for energy-saving control of building HVAC systems.

Yang et al. [23] defined 12 types of thermal discomfort actions and designed a posture recognition algorithm for each action. Combine the OpenPose platform to obtain human body key points, and input the key points into the established posture recognition network to output the thermal discomfort status and level of the human body. Cheng et al. [24] proposed a vision based thermal comfort detection method for human sleep, summarized 10 types of thermal comfort sleep postures, combined with OpenPose to construct a basic algorithm framework for detecting human sleep postures, and established corresponding weight models.

In this paper, a hot and cold pose recognition algorithm based on pose keypoints detection and a convolutional neural network is proposed. The main contributions of this paper are as follows:

1. This experiment used a questionnaire to collect the degree of hot and cold recognition of 17 candidate postures. Six postures related to human thermal discomfort were defined, and nine subjects were invited to collect the raw dataset of the six actions through OpenPose.
2. The concept of "action sequence" was proposed, large amounts of data on daily postures(1.6 million frames) were collected, and the action sequence dataset was pre-processed and produced.
3. The fundamental algorithm framework ASC(convolutional neural network for action sequence) for detecting postures was built, which validate the better robustness of the algorithm by two comparative tests.

The paper is organized into the following sections: In Sect. 2, we present the acquisition of the dataset, the definition of the action sequences, and the proposed two-channel cascade network ASC. In Sect. 3 the experiments and the analysis of the results are presented. Finally, in Sect. 4, conclusions and recommendations for future research are presented.

2   Research Methods

In order to construct an effective thermal comfort model, indoor human postures dataset was collected, from which six postures related to thermal discomfort were defined. With a normal RGB camera, large amounts of data on stand posture (1.6 million frames) were collected to create the static dataset. In this paper, pose estimation is achieved by correspondence between body keypoints, and we use OpenPose for keypoints detection.On the basis of this, the algorithm proposed was implemented.

2.1   Static Dataset Construction

In this experiment, a questionnaire survey was used to collect the degree of recognition of the 17 candidate poses by participants. The experiment selected six actions with high confidence in hot and cold, which can be used to represent the hot and cold state of the human body. These actions are numbered 1 to 6. These actions are numbered 1 to 6. The following Table 1 shows the detailed actions.

Table 1. Movement Posture and Its Meaning

Number	Pose	Thermal Sensation
1	Raise your hand to wipe sweat	hot
2	Roll up your sleeves	hot
3	Stretch your arms	hot
4	lift your arms	cold
5	Clasp hands and breathing in	cold
6	Contract your forearms	cold

This experiment used a common RGB camera and invited nine young Asian men to participate. Their hot and cold gestures were collected and numbered. Table 2 shows information about the subjects.

Table 2. Subject Information Table

Number	Sex	Age/year	Height/cm	Weight/kg
1	Man	24	183	70
2	Man	25	175	75
3	Man	24	181	83
4	Man	25	168	95
5	Man	23	175	65
6	Man	23	172	72
7	Man	25	160	58
8	Man	27	175	71
9	Man	25	176	65

2.2 Experimental Procedure

During the experiment, the subjects arrived at the designated area before the experiment began. They were asked to perform the previously designated six hot and cold movements in turn, each of which was a dynamic process, including the initial stage when the arm was just lifted and the movement state in the middle of the arm, and finally returned to the natural standing state. This is considered a movement cycle. Each action is required to be completed within two minutes, followed by the acquisition of the next action until all six postures have been collected.

OpenPose first detects the joint points of all the people in the image and then connects them to group them together, thus finding the joints of each person and constructing individual poses. The advantage of this method is that it is not affected by the number of people in the image.

In this paper, OpenPose is used to extract synchronously bone keypoints while the experiment starting.It is able to extract and process the captured video frames, detect the keypoints of the human posture skeleton, store the pixel coordinates of these keypoints in a dictionary format, and draw the bone lines between the keypoints on the original video frame map. Figure 1 is a schematic diagram of the posture skeleton corresponding to the posture key point data output by OpenPose.

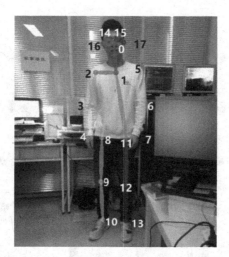

Fig. 1. Location Map of Eighteen Joint Points.

In the Fig. 1,0 for the nose, 1 for the neck, 2, 3 and 4 for the right shoulder, right elbow and right wrist respectively, 5, 6 and 7 for the left shoulder, left elbow and left wrist respectively, 8, 9 and 10 for the right hip, right knee and right ankle respectively, 11, 12 and 13 for the left hip, left knee and left ankle respectively, 14 and 15 for the right eye and left eye respectively, 16 and 17 for the right ear and left ear respectively.

The original frame size of the video is 640*480, where the coordinates of (0, 0) represent the pixel points in the top left corner of the image and (639, 479) represent the pixel coordinate values in the bottom right corner of the image. To improve the training performance of the network, the pixel coordinates (x, y) of the key points were experimentally normalized.

2.3 Definition of Action Sequences

Due to the existence of many similar or even identical data in static frame data, for example, at the beginning of these movements, the body is in a natural standing position, which produces many highly repetitive frames. This problem can lead to overfitting of the model. To solve overfitting, we can reduce the redundancy of the data by reducing it. For this purpose, action sequences are proposed.

Based on the continuous and dynamic nature of the action, one keyframe is selected from each of the three phases of the action process: beginning, middle, and end, and the three keyframes are combined into one sample. The selection of keyframes for each of the three phases is subjective, as each individual is different and the period of each action is different. Figure 2 visualizes the process of combining six action pose keypoints into a single sample.

Fig. 2. Schematic diagram of the synthesis of the six movements.

The samples obtained based on the synthesis of the three phases of the action sequence contain three frames of keypoints data, and the number of coordinates in the samples is 18*3, each sample contains 54 keypoints coordinates, each consisting of x and y. Each sample data then consists of 108 scalars.

2.4   Pose Recognition Algorithm Based on Action Sequence

The dataset contained 9 subjects, and the data from 7 of them were randomly selected as the training data and the other 2 as the test data. The sample size of the training set was 8130 and the sample size of the test set was 2405.

Network Metrics.
For classification models, the cross entropy loss function is used:

$$CE = -\sum_{k=1}^{n} t_k \log(SoftMax(y_k)) \tag{1}$$

k represents the category and n is the number of categories; t_k represents the true category label of the kth category, which has only two values of 0 or 1 in one-hot encoding and only the label of the correct solution is 1; y_k represents the raw output of the kth output neuron of the neural network;

SoftMax turns the original output values of multiple output neurons into probability values of the corresponding categories. The formula for SoftMax is as follows:

$$SoftMax(y_k) = \frac{e^{y_k}}{\sum_{i=1}^{n} e^{y_i}} \tag{2}$$

In the testing phase, the same metrics used have cross-entropy CE, evaluated along with the output category correctness Accuracy, which can be used to judge the accuracy of the network in recognizing actions. Accuracy is calculated as follows:

$$Accuracy = \frac{1}{N} \sum_{i=1}^{N} |Onehot(y_i) = t_i| \tag{3}$$

where y_i and t_i represent the original output values of the corresponding neurons of the neural network, the true labels respectively, and N represents the size of the entire data set involved in the test.

Network Structure.
In previous research, the keypoints coordinate data detected by OpenPose was inputed into a fully connected neural network(FCN) for training. However, FCN requires more model parameters than convolutional neural networks(CNN).In order to reduce the model parameters and increase the training speed, the CNN was adopted as the backbone network in this paper. In the following, we performed a two-step pre-processing of the input data.

In the first stage, the action sequences are concatenated together in the depth direction to obtain a sample with the shape of (18, 2, 3), which has three channels like the RGB image. Since the data is not uniform in length and width, it is reshaped into the "shape" of (6, 6, 3). The input to the network is the keypoints data feature matrix, which is passed through five layers of convolutional networks with similar parameters to obtain a feature vector of length 256, and then through two layers of fully connected networks to output the classification results.

In the second stage, the data are normalized based on the differences in individual positions. Due to the process of acquiring the raw data, the human body is required to be at a certain distance from the acquisition camera and within the standing area, so under such loose acquisition conditions, the relative position of the portraits in the image will vary, which means that deviation exist in the input data of the model. To overcome this defect, a new channel is added and the coordinates of the neck are used as the reference point for a further normalization process. That is, the coordinate at the neck is defined as (0, 0), while the other keypoints coordinates are the values after subtracting the neck keypoint coordinates. Network accepts two inputs, and after the feature extraction process of parallel structure, two feature vectors of 256 length are obtained, which are then fused with features, and after two layers of fully connected network, the classification results are obtained. The specific network structure is shown in Fig. 3.

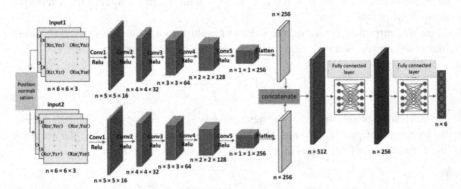

Fig. 3. Input1 is the original action sequence data, input2 is the data obtained after position normalization.

3   Results and Discussion

The construction of the neural network in this paper was based on Pytorch, and the model was built using the Pytorch framework for training and testing of prediction results, saving the model during training to ensure that the model parameters could be obtained. The training set is No. 2, 3, 5, 6, 7, 8, and 9, with a sample size of 8130 for 7 subjects, and the test set is No. 1 and 4, with a sample size of 2405 for 2 subjects. The number of training iterations (epoch) is 100, the batch-size is 64, and the learning rate is 0.0003. Figure 4 shows the accuracy graphs for training and validation based on action sequences. As shown in the figure, the convergence speed of the network is fast and there is almost no oscillation. The final loss value on the test set was 0.0000038, with a correct Accuracy of 100%. The accuracy of the dataset is high due to the small number of data sets as only six poses were collected.

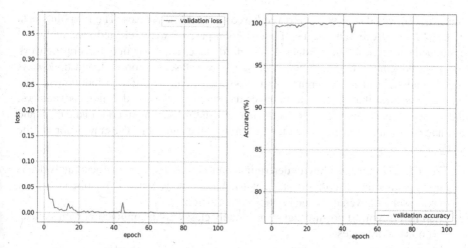

Fig. 4. ASC network: Loss, Accuracy curves for the convolution + dual input structure test set.

To verify the validity of ASC model, two comparison experiments were conducted. A fully connected network and a convolutional neural network without position normalisation were constructed for comparison respectively. The results are shown in the following Table 3.

Table 3. Comparison of experimental results

Network Model	Accuracy	Loss(CE)
FCN(Without position normalization)	94.7193%	0.1840
CNN(Without position normalization)	99.9168%	0.0042
ASC(With position normalization)	100%	0.0000038

The experimental results show that action sequences rather than complete videos were used as network input can effectively reduce data redundancy and does not lose the main feature information. Also, convolutional neural networks rather than fully connected neural networks were used as the backbone network can effectively perform feature extraction, reduce the parameters of the network and improve the training speed of the network. On top of this, data pre-processing through dual channels, eliminating position differences and increasing the normalised input can improve the robustness of the algorithm.

4 Conclusion

This study proposes a novel non-contact method for detecting human thermal comfort in indoor working conditions. In the first stage, from a macroscopic human hot and cold posture perspective, data was collected for six hot and cold postures.In the second stage, the collected data was improved based on action sequences. The keypoints data of the frames at different stages of each action process were selected separately and combined into a new sample data. In the third stage, a convolutional neural network for pose recognition based on an action sequence dataset is proposed, and the data is position normalised for differences in the positions held by different individuals. The final results show that the action sequence dataset is provided with unique advantages, the convolutional structure is more effective in handling key point coordinate data, and normalization can better improve the robustness of the algorithm The conclusions of the study are as follows:

1. The vision-based algorithm for determining hot and cold posture can accurately determine the thermal discomfort state of the human body when it is subconsciously making some movements due to body conditionin.;
2. Thermal discomfort posture can be accurately classified in conjunction with skeletal keypoints coordinates.

More work needs to be done in the future to improve the algorithm to classify and detect more poses, only 6 poses are defined in this paper, more poses can be collected for research in the future. A hot and cold gesture recognition algorithm based on skeletal keypoints and deep learning predicts how hot the human body is still from a macroscopic action gesture. The algorithm uses six representative hot and cold gestures, but in reality, people may have dozens or hundreds of movements to characterise their thermal comfort level, so these six gestures cannot characterise all hot and cold gestures.Also, this paper only predicts thermal comfort for a single person, for some densely populated places there is still a need to design thermal comfort y prediction models for multiple people.

References

1. Fayyaz, M., Farhan, A.A., Javed, A.R.: Thermal comfort model for hvac buildings using machine learning. Arabian J. Sci. Eng. 1–16 (2022)
2. Zhang, L., Sanake, S.: Thermal comfort aggregation modeling based on social science theory: Towards a comfort-driven cyber human system framework. In: Computing in Civil Engineering 2019: Data, Sensing, and Analytics, pp. 547–554. American Society of Civil Engineers Reston, VA (2019)
3. Auffenberg, F., Snow, S., Stein, S., Rogers, A.: A comfort-based approach to smart heating and air conditioning. ACM Trans. Intell. Sys. Technol. (TIST) 9(3), 1–20 (2017)
4. Ding, Z., Fu, Q., Chen, J., Wu, H., Lu, Y., Hu, F.: Multi-zone residential hvac control with satisfying occupants' thermal comfort requirements and saving energy via reinforcement learning. In: Parallel and Distributed Computing, Applications and Technologies: 22nd International Conference, PDCAT 2021, Guangzhou, China, December 17–19, 2021, Proceedings. pp. 441–451. Springer (2022)
5. Bratman, G.N., Hamilton, J.P., Daily, G.C.: The impacts of nature experience on human cognitive function and mental health. Ann. N. Y. Acad. Sci. 1249(1), 118–136 (2012)
6. Yang, B., et al.: Non-invasive (non-contact) measurements of human thermal physiology signals and thermal comfort/discomfort poses-a review. Energy and Buildings 224, 110261 (2020)
7. Morresi, N., et al.: Sensing physiological and environmental quantities to measure human thermal comfort through machine learning techniques. IEEE Sens. J. 21(10), 12322–12337 (2021)

8. Afzal, A., et al.: Human thermal comfort in passenger vehicles using an organic phase change material–an experimental investigation, neural network modelling, and optimization. Build. Environ. **180**, 107012 (2020)
9. Borodinecs, A., Zemitis, J., Palcikovskis, A.: Hvac system control solutions based on modern it technologies: A review article. Energies **15**(18), 6726 (2022)
10. Tien, P.W., Wei, S., Calautit, J.: A computer vision-based occupancy and equipment usage detection ápproach for reducing building energy demand. Energies **14**(1), 156 (2020)
11. Liu, Y., Yang, B., Lin, Z.: A pilot study of occupant centric control stratum ventilation based on computer vision. In: E3S Web of Conferences. vol. 356, p. 01029. EDP Sciences (2022)
12. hahramani, A., et al.: Infrared-fused vision-based thermoregulation performance estimation for personal thermal comfort-driven hvac system controls. Buildings **12**(8), 1241 (2022)
13. Song, C., Lee, S.: Accurate non-contact body temperature measurement with thermal camera under varying environment conditions. In: 2022 16th International Conference on Ubiquitous Information Management and Communication (IMCOM), pp. 1–6. IEEE (2022)
14. Cheng, X., Yang, B., Hedman, A., Olofsson, T., Li, H., Van Gool, L.: Nidl: A pilot study of contactless measurement of skin temperature for intelligent building. Energy and Buildings **198**, 340–352 (2019)
15. Faridah, F., et al.: Feasibility study to detect occupant thermal sensation using a low-cost thermal camera for indoor environments in indonesia. Build. Serv. Eng. Res. Technol. **42**(4), 389–404 (2021)
16. Nkurikiyeyezu, K.N., Suzuki, Y., Lopez, G.F.: Heart rate variability as a predictive biomarker of thermal comfort. J. Ambient. Intell. Humaniz. Comput. **9**, 1465–1477 (2018)
17. Wu, G., Liu, H., Wu, S., Liu, G., Liang, C.: Can heart rate variability (hrv) be used as a biomarker of thermal comfort for mine workers? Int. J. Environ. Res. Public Health **18**(14), 7615 (2021)
18. Lopez, G., Aoki, T., Nkurikiyeyezu, K., Yokokubo, A.: Model for thermal comfort and energy saving based on individual sensation estimation. arXiv preprint arXiv:2003.04311 (2020)
19. Cao, Z., Simon, T., Wei, S.E., Sheikh, Y.: Realtime multi-person 2d pose estimation using part affinity fields. In: Proceedings of the IEEE conference on computer vision and pattern recognition, pp. 7291–7299 (2017)
20. Okugawa, Y., Kubo, M., Sato, H., Viet, B.D.: Evaluation for the synchronization of the parade with openpose. J. Robotics Netw. Artif. Life **6**(3), 162–166 (2019)
21. Tanaka, R., Oshima, C., Nakayama, K.: Intention inference from 2d poses of preliminary action using openpose. In: Proceedings of the Genetic and Evolutionary Computation Conference Companion, pp. 1697–1700 (2019)
22. Kitamura, T., Teshima, H., Thomas, D., Kawasaki, H.: Refining openpose with a new sports dataset for robust 2d pose estimation. In: Proceedings of the IEEE/CVF Winter Conference on Applications of Computer Vision, pp. 672–681 (2022)
23. Yang, B., Cheng, X., Dai, D., Olofsson, T., Li, H., Meier, A.: Real-time and contactless measurements of thermal discomfort based on human poses for energy efficient control of buildings. Build. Environ. **162**, 106284 (2019)
24. Cheng, X., Hu, F., Yang, B., Wang, F., Olofsson, T.: Contactless sleep posture measurements for demand-controlled sleep thermal comfort: A pilot study. Indoor Air **32**(12), e13175 (2022)

A Real-Time Wind Turbine Blade Damage Detection Method Based on an Improved YOLOv5 Algorithm

Zhiming Zhang[1,2,3], Chaoyi Dong[1,2,3(✉)], Ze Wei[1,2,3], Weidong Zan[1,2,3],
Jianfei Zhao[4], Fu Hao[4], and Xiaoyan Chen[1,2,3]

[1] College of Electric Power, Inner Mongolia University of Technology, Hohhot 010080, China
dongchaoyi@imut.edu.cn
[2] Intelligent Energy Technology and Equipment Engineering Research Centre of Colleges and Universities in Inner Mongolia, Hohhot 010080, Inner Mongolia, China
[3] Engineering Research Center of Large Energy Storage Technology, Ministry of Education, Hohhot 010051, Inner Mongolia, China
[4] Inner Mongolia Electric Power Survey and Design Institute Co., Ltd., Hohhot 010020, Inner Mongolia, China

Abstract. In this paper, a lightweight wind turbine blade damage detection network MC-YOLO is proposed to overcome the problems of the current wind turbine blade defect detection algorithm, for examples, low accuracy, poor real-time performance, and difficult model deployment. Firstly, the backbone network of a YOLOv5s network is replaced with a MobileNetV3 network, which reduces the number of network parameters and computation and realizes the compression of feature extraction network. Then a CA attention mechanism has been introduced into the backbone network to enhance the attention to small-sized defects. Finally, the network structure of the neck network is optimized to enhance the utilization of shallow features and strengthen the discriminative ability of different-sized defects. A series of test experiments were conducted on a self-built dataset collected from real wind farms and the result shows that the proposed MC-YOLO network decreases the number of parameters by 95% compared to YOLOv5s; the model volume is only 3MB; the image detection speed in CPU mode can reach 25 frames/second, and the in the test set can reach 94.2%. Therefore, the proposed network can reduce the difficulty of deployment in edge computing devices and meet the real-time defect detection requirements.

Keywords: Wind turbine blade · YOLOv5 · Lightweight · Attentional mechanisms

1 Introduction

In the context of China's "double carbon" target, the scale of wind power generation is increasing, with a total installed capacity of 340 million kW by the end of 2021 [1]. As the core component of wind turbine, the health of wind turbine blade is crucial

H. Lu et al. (Eds.): ICIG 2023, LNCS 14358, pp. 298–309, 2023.
https://doi.org/10.1007/978-3-031-46314-3_24

to the whole wind power generation system. At present, most wind farms are built in remote areas, such as onshore, mountainous areas, offshore areas, desert areas, and other complex natural environments. There are many factors that can cause damage to the wind turbine blades, such as strong winds, sand and gravel, lightning strikes, ice cover, seawater erosion will intensify blade breakage and aging. These kinds of damage often superimposes on each other. If the damages cannot be timely repaired, they may make the blade surface aerodynamic efficiency changed, and eventually lead to the whole blade breakage. Therefore, efficient detection of wind turbine blade damages is important for safe production and extension of the life of blades.

Most of the detection methods at this stage rely on manual visual inspection using telescopes or various types of sensors, such as strain measurement, acoustic emission, ultrasonic, vibration, and thermal imaging [2]. The sensor installation location has a great impact on the detection accuracy, and the sensors are prone to fail with the damage of the wind turbine blade. These methods not only have poor robustness, but also are costly, and difficult to meet power energy production needs. With the rapid development of deep learning, machine vision-based target detection methods began to be gradually applied to wind turbine blade damage detection. The UAV technology is applied to obtaining high-definition images of wind turbine blade. Then the images are enhanced through segmentation. Finally the classification of damages are conducted using deep learning algorithms. These machine vision-based target detection methods can effectively improve the inspection efficiency and detection accuracy [3].

Researchers have done a great deal of work in this field. Peng Yang et al. proposed a DenseNet201-FF model, which improved the recognition ability of the network under complex background, and finally achieved a fault recognition accuracy of about 97.15% [4]. Jun Ying et al. optimized the SSD network by replacing VGG16 with ResNet-50d. A SPP layer was added in P5 stage, a BiFPN structure was added in Neck part, and IOU loss and positive example matching rules was supplemented. The mAP value of wind turbine blade defect detection was improved from 68.9% to 82.1% for the improved model [5]. Yuping Wu et al. proposed a spanning feature merged network structure based on YOLOv3-tiny to fuse and relearn feature information in different depths. An Inception module was also introduced, in which the input feature maps were combined and compressed by the multiple convolutional kernels of four parallel channels. The model was compressed to 1/4 of the original model and the mAP of the compressed model increased to 88.58% for a self-colllected dataset [6]. Yilun Li et al. improved the ResNet residual network and the CSPDarkNet network in the YOLOv4 backbone network, and then inserted the improved feature pyramid network. The final mAP value has been improved from 81.7% to 87.7% [7]. Rui Zhang et al. constructed a SOD-YOLO network based on the YOLOv5 network. A micro-scale detection layer was added to the original YOLOv5, the anchor points were re-clustered using the K-means algorithm, and a CBAM attention mechanism was supplemented to each feature fusion layer. All the three improvements reduced the loss of small target defect feature information. At the same time, a channel pruning algorithm is also used to reduce the size of the model. The network achieved 95.1% mAP on the self-built dataset, which is 7.82% higher than the original network, and 28.3% higher FPS [8].

The above studies have focused on recognition accuracy improvement and model lightweighting. However, the detection effect and real-time performance of these networks are still not good enough to balance detection accuracy and detection speed, and the large size of the models also poses a challenge for deployment to edge computing devices. In this paper, we propose MC-YOLO, a lightweight wind turbine blade defect detection network, which can show a better real-time performance than the previous networks. The following improvements were made in the paper: Firstly, a MobileNetV3 is used to replace the backbone network of YOLOv5s and thus the back of the YOLOv5s was rebuilt. While maintaining the accuracy, the computation and parameter number of the feature extraction network were greatly reduced. Secondly, we added a CA attention mechanism to enhance the attention to small-sized defects. The neck network was optimized to strengthen the fusion between different feature layers and made up for the precision loss caused by the lightweight feature extraction network. Finally, a series of experiments were carried out to fully verify the effectiveness of the proposed algorithm. The result showed that the proposed network can meet the requirements of low computation power edge computing device deployment.

2 Principle of MC-YOLO Network Algorithm

2.1 YOLOv5s Network Structure

YOLOv5 is the more mature algorithm in the YOLO series, which is divided into four versions of YOLOv5 (s, m, l, x) depending on the depth and width of the model. YOLOv5s has the best real-time performance, and this paper improves the network for this network. The network is mainly composed of three parts: Backbone, Neck and Prediction. The input side uses Mosaic data enhancement to enrich the data set, randomly draws 4 pictures for scaling, distribution and finally splicing, which not only enriches the test set, but also increases the robustness of the network by adding many extra small targets due to the picture scaling; adds the adaptive anchor frame calculation function to get the best initial anchor frame; also adds the picture adaptive scaling to fill the black edge after picture scaling, which increases the inference speed. The backbone network is designed with C3 module to replace the original CSP module, which uses the residual structure to solve the problem of large computation caused by the repetition of gradient information. And the neck network also adopts C3 module to reduce the computation. The main body still adopts FPN + PAN structure to aggregate the semantic information and location information of the backbone network. The prediction end performs the prediction frame regression as well as the final prediction using CIOU-NMS on the different size feature maps output from the neck network.

2.2 MobileNetV3 Network Structure

MobileNet network is a lightweight network proposed by Google [9], MobileNetV3 as the latest achievement of the series, it inherits the advantages of the previous two generations of networks, while the original use of Neural Architecture Search (NAS) algorithm to redesign the network structure, the time-consuming layer is optimized, while ensuring the accuracy of the detection time is significantly reduced, the network mainly has the following characteristics:

Depthwise Separable Convolution. MobileNetV3 continues to use depthwise separable convolution to achieve parameter compression. The main idea of this method is to split the regular convolution kernel into two parts: a depth convolution layer and a 1×1 point-by-point convolution layer. Assuming that the input feature map is with C channels, the conventional convolution kernel size is $K \times K \times C$, and the output feature map is M, the number of parameters required for conventional convolution is given by the following equation:

$$P_1 = K \times K \times C \times M \tag{1}$$

Now using depthwise separable convolution, the feature map passes through a depth convolution layer consisting of $C\ K \times K \times 1$ convolution kernels, and each channel feature map of the input is convolved and output, and then passes through a point convolution layer consisting of $M\ 1 \times 1 \times C$ convolution kernels, and each channel feature map is weighted and output M feature maps, at which point the parametric number of convolution operations is shown in the following equation:

$$P_2 = K \times K \times C + 1 \times 1 \times C \times M \tag{2}$$

The depthwise separable convolution is compared with the conventional convolutional covariance in the following equation. It can be seen that the number of parameters decreases significantly after using depthwise separable convolution and then maintaining the premise that the accuracy does not change much, which can effectively improve the model inference speed.

$$\frac{P_2}{P_1} = \frac{K \times K \times C + 1 \times 1 \times C \times M}{K \times K \times C \times M} = \frac{1}{M} + \frac{1}{K^2} \tag{3}$$

Improved Bottleneck Residual Structure. The bottleneck residual structure adopted by MobileNetV2 is retained in the network structure. Conventional residual structures first decrease dimension and then increase dimension, but after the depthwise separable convolution to compress the number of parameters and then downscaled will lead to the problem of less feature information retention, so here the 1×1 convolution kernel is first upscaled and then downscaled. The SE attention mechanism is also introduced to enhance the attention to different channels, and the improved bottleneck residual structure is shown in Fig. 1.

In the figure, GA pooling is a global average pooling operation and FC is a fully connected layer. By pooling the feature maps obtained after dimensioning and convolution, the vectors corresponding to the number of channels are obtained, and the weights of each channel feature map are finally obtained after the calculation of the two fully connected layers and multiplied with the feature maps to achieve the focus on different channel features.

Improved Activation Function. The more commonly used activation function part of the model is the swish activation function, but the activation function is complicated to calculate and derive, and it is not conducive to model quantification. Therefore, MobileNetV3 proposed h-sigmoid and h-swish activation functions to approximate sigmoid and activation functions by using the idea of approximation.

$$h - sigmoid[x] = \frac{ReLU6(X + 3)}{6} \tag{4}$$

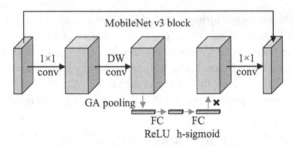

Fig. 1. Schematic diagram of the improved bottleneck residual structure.

$$h - swish[x] = x \cdot h - sigmoid(x) \tag{5}$$

The sigmoid activation function used in the SE attention mechanism in the previous subsection is replaced with h-sigmoid, while the activation function in the backbone network is replaced with h-swish. It can be seen from the above equation that the new proposed activation function elimination is simpler to compute and helps to reduce the computational complexity.

2.3 MC-YOLO Network Structure

As the fastest detection network among the four versions, YOLOv5s can balance precision and detection speed well in the task of defect detection. However, the current detection speed is still difficult to meet the real-time requirements. The MC-YOLO network proposed in this paper is based on the improvement of YOLOv5s network. The main improvement points are introduced below.

Backbone Network Optimization. The backbone network has a large number of convolutional layers, which can effectively extract the target features, but it is also the main reason for the decrease of detection speed. MobileNetV3 adopts a large number of depthwise separable convolution, and the number of network parameters is small, so we consider replacing the backbone network with the MobileNetV3 network to achieve more efficient extraction of image features and reduce the number of parameters and the amount of computation, and finally achieve the compression of the model size. The complete network structure is shown in Fig. 2.

The CBH module in the backbone network is to replace the activation function of the CBS module in the original network with h-swish, and the M-block is the basic module in the MobileNetV3 network. The number of backbone network parameters before improvement is about 26.6M. After improvement, the number of MC-YOLO backbone network parameters is about 0.65M. Compared with the original network parameters, the number of parameters is reduced by 97.5%, and the overall light weight of the model is achieved.

CA Attention Mechanism. Because defects such as sand holes and is small targets. As the focus and difficulty of the detection task, the accuracy rate of such defects is not high, and the loss of accuracy is inevitable after the light weight of the backbone network,

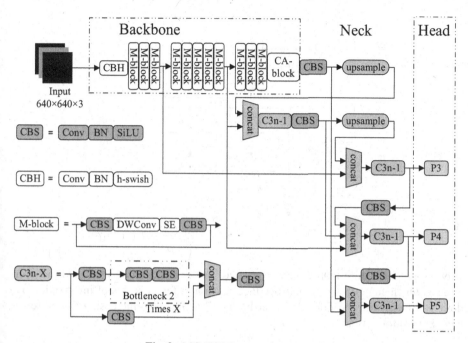

Fig. 2. MC-YOLO network structure.

so the CA attention mechanism is added to the last layer of the backbone network to improve the attention to small targets. The CA attention mechanism not only considers the information of different channels, but also pays attention to the location information [10], and the CA attention mechanism is implemented as shown in the Fig. 3.

In order to avoid the loss of location information, instead of global average pooling of the input feature map xc, the attention weight map is decomposed and pooled in X and Y directions separately to generate attention weight maps in both directions. The X-direction attention weight map is then dimensionally stitched with the Y-direction attention weight map and downscaled to the same number of channels as the original with a 1×1 convolution kernel to achieve the purpose of fusing the channel information. The spliced attention weight map needs to be normalized, and then the attention weight map f is obtained by Sigmoid activation function. f is the weight of the input feature map in X and Y directions, and the weight map is dimensionally partitioned by X and Y directions to obtain separate weight information in two dimensions, and finally the weight maps in two directions are up-dimensioned to the input feature map by 1×1 convolution. Finally, the weight maps in both directions are up-dimensioned to the dimension of the input feature map by 1×1 convolution, and then multiplied with the input feature map to obtain the output feature map focusing on the key regions.

Neck Network Optimization. The neck network is responsible for fusing the different layers of features output from the backbone network and further extracting the higher dimensional abstract features. The daily inspection of wind turbine blade focuses on medium area pockmark damage and small size holes and grit damage. The original

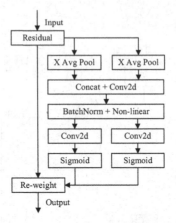

Fig. 3. CA attention mechanism.

network output feature map at layer 8 is used for the detection of small and medium targets, which can effectively improve the focus on different scales of information by directly fusing with the information at layers 17 and 21 and increasing the reuse of contextual information.

3 Experiment and Results

3.1 Dataset Production

The image dataset used in this paper is a self-built dataset, with images collected from the Guodian wind power plant in Hohhot, Inner Mongolia and the old Gongzhong wind farm in Baotou Brilliance. A DJI Phantom 4 PRO UAV was used to capture the wind turbine blade at close range and manually remove the blurred images. 1113 valid images were obtained. Labelimg, an open source annotation software, was used to annotate the images and expand the original data by means of panning and flipping to add noise, resulting in 4452 valid images. Finally, the training set, test set and validation set were divided in the ratio of 8:1:1.

According to the actual collection of data from the wind farm, four main defects are defined: holes, scratches, pockmarks and marks, with a number of approximately 2000 labels each. The mark category is due to the wind turbine blade itself has arrows and other marks will cause defects false alarm, so the surface of the wind turbine blade arrows and other marks for manual labeling to improve the detection effect.

3.2 Experimental Environment and Evaluation Indicators

The experimental hardware platform uses Intel Core i9-12900k CPU, Nvidia GeForce RTX4080 16G GPU and 32G running memory. The software platform used Windows 11 operating system, Python version 3.7, deep learning framework Pytorch version 1.13.0,

Table 1. Experiment parameter.

Experiment parameter	Value
Epoch	350
Batch size	8
Optimizer	SGD
Learning rate	0.01
Size	640 × 640
Momentum	0.932
Workers	12

Cuda version 11.6.2, and was trained using pre-trained weights based on the COCO dataset, and other basic experimental parameters are shown in Table 1.

In this paper, mAP@0.5 is used to evaluate the accuracy of the model, and Parameters, FLOPs, detection frame rate FPS in CPU mode, model size and other indicators are used to evaluate the real-time performance of the model. The accuracy index is defined as follows. Where, TP is defined as the number of labels predicted to be true and also actually true; FP is the number of labels predicted to be false but actually true; FN is the number of labels predicted as false but actually true. mAP@0.5 is the mAP for IOU = 0.5. Because embedded edge computing devices usually do not carry independent GPU, it is more practical to use the frame rate data of single CPU mode.

$$Precision = \frac{TP}{TP + FP} \tag{6}$$

$$AP = \int_0^1 precision(t)dt \tag{7}$$

$$mAP = \frac{\sum_{n=1}^N AP_n}{N} \tag{8}$$

3.3 Experimental Environment and Evaluation Indicators

This study first sets up a series of comparative experiments to verify the effectiveness of the algorithm, and the experimental results are shown in the following table. It can be seen from Table 2 that the accuracy of YOLOv5 can reach 94.8%, which is the highest among all algorithms. However, the frame rate is only 11.2 frames per second in CPU mode, which makes it difficult to detect the video stream returned by the UAV in real time. The frame rate of the backbone network optimized by ShuffleNetV2 and MobileNetV3 network is significantly improved, reaching 15.9 frames/s and 21.4 frames/s respectively. After replacing the backbone with ShuffleNetV2, the accuracy is greatly reduced. After replacing the backbone with MobileNetV3, the optimization is better than the former in accuracy and frame rate. Compared with the original network, the accuracy is slightly decreased, but the frame rate is almost doubled. However, after adding the SE attention mechanism, the detection frame rate decreases, and after adding the CA attention mechanism, the frame rate is further increased to 22 frames per second while maintaining a high accuracy. Finally, the MC-YOLO algorithm proposed in this paper, compared with YOLOv5, the accuracy is only reduced by 0.6% but the frame rate is doubled to 25.1 frames per second. At the same time, the number of parameters, calculation amount and model size are greatly reduced compared with the original network, and there is little difference with other experimental groups.

Table 2. Improvement process experimental results.

Model	mAP@0.5	Parameter $/ \times 10^6$	GFlops	FPS f/s	Size /MB
YOLOv5s	94.8%	26.6	16.0	11.2	13.7
YOLOv5s + ShuffleNetV2	90.6%	0.85	1.9	15.9	2.0
YOLOv5s + MobileNetV3	91.4%	1.38	2.2	21.4	3.0
YOLOv5s + MobileNetV3 + SE	93.3%	1.41	2.3	19.7	3.1
YOLOv5s + MobileNetV3 + CA	93.8%	1.38	2.3	22.0	3.0
MC-YOLO	94.2%	1.38	2.4	25.1	3.0

In order to further verify the effectiveness of MC-YOLO algorithm, it is also compared with classical algorithms such as YOLOv4-tiny, YOLOv3 and SSD, and the experimental results are shown in Table 3. It can be seen from the table that the size of SSD model is 118MB, the size of YOLOv3 and YOLOv4 model is 235MB and 244MB, respectively. The size of the model is dozens of times that of MC-YOLO, and the size of YOLOv5s model is also 4 times that of MC-YOLO. Moreover, the accuracy of SSD algorithm is only 79.5%. The accuracy of YOLOv3 is only 78.8% lower than that of SSD, but the detection speed is slightly faster. The detection accuracy and detection speed of YOLOv4 are improved, but the accuracy is still lower than that of YOLOv5s. While the accuracy of MC-YOLO is almost equal to that of YOLOv5, the model size and detection accuracy of MC-YOLO are comprehensively surpassed, which is more conducive to the deployment of mobile terminals with low computational power in UAV inspection system to realize real-time fault detection.

As can be seen from the above two groups of experiments, the detection frame rate of MC-YOLO network increased from 11.2 frames per second to 25.1 frames per second compared with YOLOv5. Model volume decreased 78.1% to only 3MB; Floating-point arithmetic fell by 85%. Figure 4 shows mAP@0.5 and loss curves after the training. The red line is MC-YOLO and the blue line is YOLOv5s. The loss curve indicates that the

Table 3. Experimental results of different algorithms.

Model	mAP@0.5	FPS f/s	Size /MB
SSD	79.5%	7.4	118
YOLOv3	78.8%	7.9	235
YOLOv4	83.2%	8.5	244
YOLOv5s	94.8%	11.2	13.7
MC-YOLO	94.2%	25.1	3.0

network converges after 350 training rounds. Although the lightweight network causes a certain loss of accuracy, the accuracy of the improved MC-YOLO network is close to that of the original network, and the accuracy curve is smoother, indicating that MC-YOLO network has stronger robustness than the original network.

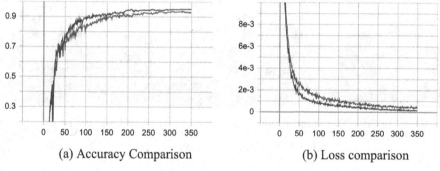

(a) Accuracy Comparison   (b) Loss comparison

Fig. 4. Training result

The accuracy of MC-YOLO network is almost the same as that of the original network, but the detection frame rate is doubled, which maintains a high accuracy while the model is lightweight. It can be seen that the algorithm proposed in this paper has more application potential. Figure 5 shows the actual detection effect, with the MC-YOLO detection effect on the left and YOLOv5s detection effect on the right.

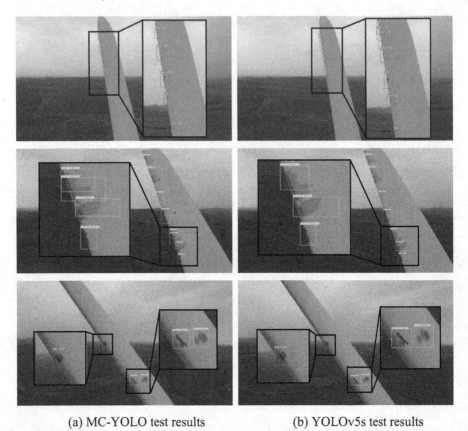

(a) MC-YOLO test results   (b) YOLOv5s test results

Fig. 5. Comparison of detection effect.

4 Conclusion

To overcome the problems of low accuracy, poor real-time performance, and difficult deployment of the current wind turbine blade defect detection algorithm, this paper proposes a lightweight MC-YOLO detection network to detect the typical wind turbine blade defects. Initially, a MobileNetV3 is used to replace the backbone network of YOLOv5s and reduce the network complexity. Then, a CA attention mechanism is introduced into the backbone network to increase the attention to small targets. Finally, the neck network structure was also changed and the low-level features were repeated by means of cross-layer connection. Consequently, the detection speed of 25.1 frame/second was achieved on the CPU, and the mAP@0.5 can still reach 94.2% while maintaining lightweight. The test results showed that the method has good detection effects on various types of defects, and also has a satisfactory detection speed. Thus, the lightweight detection network proposed in this paper greatly improves the detection speed while ensuring high accuracy. When using drones to inspect wind turbine blade defects, the model can be deployed to the ground station or airborne equipment to realize real-time offline detection. In the future research, a defect detection dataset with richer samples will be established, such as establishing defect grading or increasing the data set of categories to improve the practicability of the model.

Acknowledgments. This work was supported by the National Natural Science Foundation of China (61364018 and 61863029), Inner Mongolia Natural Science Foundation (2016JQ07, 2020MS06020, and 2021MS06017), Inner Mongolia Scientific and Technological Achievements Transformation Project (CGZH2018129), and Science and Technology Plan Project of the Inner Mongolia Autonomous Region (Key Technology Project).

References

1. Statistical report on wind power hoisting capacity in China in 2021. Wind Energy **147**(05), 38–52 (2022)
2. Du, Y., Zhou, S., Jing, X., et al.: Damage detection techniques for wind turbine blades: a review. Mech. Syst. Signal Process. **141**, 106445 (2020)
3. Tang, Z., Sun, D., Li, Y., et al.: Fan blade crack detection model based on improved FA optimized SVM. Renewable Energy **40**(9), 1189–1194 (2022)
4. Yang, P., Dong, C., Zhao, X., et al.: The surface damage identifications of wind turbine blades based on ResNet50 algorithm. In: 2020 39th Chinese Control Conference (CCC), pp. 6340–6344. IEEE (2020)
5. Ying, J., Liu, X., Zeng, G., et al.: Research and application of fan blade defect detection based on SSD algorithm optimization. Zhejiang Electric Power **40**(08), 47–52 (2021)
6. Wu, Y., Liu, H., Wu, J., et al.: Application of improved YOLOv3-Tiny network in wind blade damage detection. Hebei Indus. Technol. **38**(05), 401–408 (2021)
7. Li, Y., Cheng, H., Dong, L., et al.: Wind turbine blade defect detection algorithm based on improved Yolov4. Fan Technology **64**(01), 46–53 (2022)
8. Zhang, R., Wen, C.: SOD - YOLO: A small target defect detection algorithm for wind turbine blades based on improved YOLOv5. Adv. Theo. Simulat. **5**(7), 2100631 (2022)
9. Howard, A., Sandler, M., Chu, G., et al.: Searching for mobilenetv3. In: Proceedings of the IEEE/CVF international conference on computer vision, pp. 1314–1324. IEEE (2019)
10. Hou, Q., Zhou, D., Feng, J.: Coordinate attention for efficient mobile network design. In: Proceedings of the IEEE/CVF conference on computer vision and pattern recognition, pp. 13713–13722. IEEE (2021)

Intensify Perception Transformer Generative Adversarial Network for Image Super-Resolution

Yuzhen Chen[1,2,3], Gencheng Wang[1,2,3], Rong Chen[1,2,3(✉)], and Zi Hui[1,2,3]

[1] Xizang Minzu University, Xianyang 712000, Shaanxi, China
{wgc,cr2008}@xzmu.edu.cn
[2] Key Laboratory of Optical Information Processing and Visualization Technology of Tibet Autonomous Region, Xianyang 712000, Shaanxi, China
[3] Xizang Cyberspace Governance Research Center, Xianyang 712000, Shaanxi, China

Abstract. Generative adversarial networks (GANs) are widely used for image super-resolution (SR) and have recently attracted increasing attention due to their potential to generate rich details. However, generators are usually based on convolutional neural networks, which lack global modeling capacity and limit the performance of the network. To address this problem, we propose a hierarchical partitioned Transformer block to extract features at different scales, which alleviates the loss of information and helps global modelling. We then design a Transformer in residual block to reconstruct more natural structural textures in SR results. Finally, we integrate the intensify perception Transformer network with an existing discriminator network to form the intensify perception Transformer generative adversarial network (IPTGAN). We conducted experiments on several benchmark datasets, RealSR dataset and PIRM self-validation dataset to verify the generalization ability of our IPTGAN. The results show that our IPTGAN exhibits better visual quality and significantly less complexity compared to several state-of-the-art GAN-based image SR methods.

Keywords: Image super-resolution · GAN · Transformer · Moderated self-attention · Intensify perception

1 Introduction

Image super-resolution (SR), which aims to generate a high-resolution (HR) image from a given low-resolution (LR) image by attempting to recover the missing information, is a low-level computer vision (CV) task. Since the pioneering work of SRCNN [5], deep convolutional neural networks (CNNs) have brought prosperous development to the field of image SR. Peak signal-to-noise ratio (PSNR) has been used as a measure for various SR networks, but the PSNR metric fundamentally diverges from the subjective evaluation of human observers. As a result, PSNR-oriented methods tend to produce smoother results without

H. Lu et al. (Eds.): ICIG 2023, LNCS 14358, pp. 310–321, 2023.
https://doi.org/10.1007/978-3-031-46314-3_25

sufficient high-frequency details. To address this issue, several perceptual-driven methods have been proposed to improve the visual quality of SR results. For instance, the perceptual loss [9] is proposed to optimize SR methods in a feature space instead of a pixel space.

Generative adversarial network (GAN) consists of a generator network responsible for generating SR images and a discriminator network that tries to distinguish between SR images and real HR images. Through the competition of the generator and the discriminator, the GAN is encouraged to favor images that look more real. The original GAN [4, 7] used a fully-connected network and was limited to generating small images. One milestone in achieving visually pleasing results is SRGAN [12]. The basic block of SRGAN is built with residual blocks and optimized using perceptual loss. With these techniques, SRGAN significantly improves the overall visual quality of reconstructions compared to PSNR-oriented methods. DCGAN [19] was the first to scale up GAN using CNN, which allowed for stable training at higher resolutions and with deeper generator. ESRGAN [21], as a representative work, proposed a practical perceptual loss as well as a residual in residual dense block (RRDB) to produce SR images with convincing visual quality. Since then, using CNNs as GAN backbone in CV has become a common practice. However, CNNs have a limited receptive field, which makes it inefficient to process long-range dependencies without passing through sufficient layers. This can result in a loss of feature information and fine details, leading to high computational costs and optimization difficulties.

Recently, Transformers have demonstrated effectiveness in global modeling and have been applied to various CV tasks, such as image classification, object detection, semantic segmentation and SR. It is important to note that while Transformer-based networks generally have higher computational complexity compared to CNNs, the utilization of self-attention in Transformers greatly enhances the expressive power of the model. The self-attention enables network to model dependencies effectively, allowing it to focus on comprehensive information. Taking inspiration from the above, we propose a perceptual-driven Transformer-based GAN, called the intensify perception Transformer generative adversarial network (IPTGAN), to address the aforementioned limitations and drawbacks. First, we improve the network structure by introducing the Transformer and residual connections to enhance the information flow and better learn the features of the data. We further introduce hierarchization and partition into different size strategies to the Transformer, allowing for a flexible receptive field and enabling global modeling. Additionally, we propose a moderated self-attention (MSA) enabling the network to learn more information. The contributions of our work can be summarized as follows:

- We propose a Transformer in residual block (TRB) that enables the network to capture more pixel information, resulting in improved result quality. The TRB is efficient and extensible, it can be easy to integrate into SR networks.
- We propose a intensify perception Transformer network (IPTNet), which is a generator with excellent scalability. It can be combined with existing discriminators to form GANs, achieving excellent SR results.

- We propose IPTGAN, a perception-driven yet powerful GAN, to efficiently address the SISR problem. IPTGAN performs well not only on benchmark datasets but also on RealSR dataset and PIRM self-validation dataset, achieving superior visual results compared to several state-of-the-art GAN-based methods. Furthermore, IPTGAN requires significantly fewer parameters than ESRGAN, making it more practical in real-world applications.

2   Related Work

2.1   GAN-Based SR Methods

GANs are a class of generative models that are learned through a minimax optimization game between a generator network and a discriminator network. The GANs have been proven to be competitive in learning mappings among manifolds and thus improving local textures. SRGAN [12] was the first to introduce GAN into SR, where the generator was composed of residual blocks. To enhance the results, SRGAN employed perceptual and adversarial losses for training. EnhanceNet [20] and SRFeat [18] utilized multiple loss terms or discriminators to improve performance. ESRGAN [21] further improved the performance of SRGAN by proposing RRDB, removing batch normalization layers and employing the relativistic discriminator [10]. Although the RRDB has demonstrated effectiveness, it still has a significant number of parameters, resulting in considerable computational costs. BSRGAN [23] is a blind SR method that performs SR by designing a complex degradation process that mimics real-world conditions. BSRGAN incorporates a pixel alignment technique to correct spatial distortion and ensure pixel-level matching between the SR image and the HR image. However, it still faces the issue of over-smoothing in SR images.

2.2   Transformer-Based SR Methods

Transformer was initially developed for natural language processing, researchers have found that the self-attention in the Transformer effectively models dependencies among data. ViT [6] was the first to introduce the Transformer into CV by achieving highly competitive ImageNet classification results, treating an image as a sequence of 16×16 visual words. Swin Transformer [15] adopts a similar idea to ViT, introducing shifted window mechanism to enhance performance. However, it has a high computational complexity, especially for large input images. SwinIR [13] inherits the Swin Transformer for SR task and achieves impressive results. However, it also inherits many components that were designed for high-level CV task, making them redundant and fragmented for SR. Swin Transformer V2 [14] improves upon the Swin Transformer by using larger window sizes and a new data adaptive training strategy. However, it involves a more complex training process and requires additional time and computational costs. Although Swin Transformer and Swin Transformer V2 did not specifically introduce the Transformer into GANs and SR tasks, they are indeed representative works in CV.

3 Methods

As previously stated, our main aim is to enhance the overall perceptual quality of the SR images. The IPTGAN follows the same principle as the traditional GAN, where the competition between the two networks enables the generator to produce images that are more realistic and closer to the ground truths. The IPTNet is illustrated in Fig. 1.

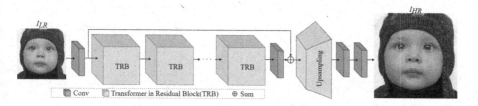

Fig. 1. The architecture of the proposed IPTNet for IPTGAN.

3.1 Generator

The IPTNet comprises three main components: a shallow feature extraction module, a deep feature extraction module and an image reconstruction module. The shallow feature extraction module includes a convolutional layer, while the deep feature extraction module consists of multiple TRBs and a convolutional layer. The reconstruction module consists of a upsampling layer and two convolutional layers.

Transformer in Residual Block. The design of the TRB is inspired by the RRDB, which has become a classical algorithm in this field by combining multiple convolutional layers with a dense connection to achieve a deep network structure. However, the limited receptive field of convolution makes it inefficient to process long-range dependencies without passing through sufficient layers. Additionally, training a deep enough network presents significant computational and time costs. As shown in Fig. 2(a), the TRB consists of three hierarchical partitioned Transformer blocks (HPTBs) and a residual connection. To avoid imposing unnecessary burdens on the TRB, we have removed the dense connection, as each HPTB already has two residual connections. By leveraging the strong modeling capabilities of the Transformer, we can achieve better results with significantly fewer parameters and layers.

Hierarchical Partitioned Transformer Block. HPTB adopts the classic Transformer framework. The input features will pass-through layer normalization (LayerNorm), hierarchical partitioned moderated self-attention (HPMS) shown in Fig. 2(b), LayerNorm and multi-layer perceptron (MLP) in sequence.

Convolutions and previous Transformers extract features at a fixed size. However, the fixed size is not directly related to the image contents, and it may lead to the loss of pixel information at the edges of the split blocks. To address this issue, we divide the input channels into k groups and then into blocks of different sizes for MSA calculation. Additionally, shifted window machine shifts the window in a diagonal direction, then extracting the shifted features. This approach further mitigates the loss of pixel information and facilitates communication among surrounding pixels, resulting in improved image generation.

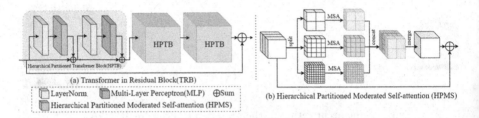

(a) Transformer in Residual Block(TRB)

☐ LayerNorm ☐ Multi-Layer Perceptron(MLP) ⊕ Sum
☐ Hierarchical Partitioned Moderated Self-attention (HPMS)

(b) Hierarchical Partitioned Moderated Self-attention (HPMS)

Fig. 2. The process of Transformer in residual block. (a) is the Transformer in residual block. (b) is the hierarchical partitioned moderated self-attention.

Moderated Self-attention. The conventional self-attention in the Transformer employs dot-product to measure the similarity between the query vector (q) and the key vector (k) of a pixel pair. However, this method often produces extreme values that will lead to attention being disproportionately focused on a few pixels, resulting in suboptimal reconstructions. In contrast, cosine similarity is naturally normalized. By leveraging cosine for self-attention, more eased values can be obtained, offering a more accurate measurement of similarity between vectors. Unlike the commonly used SoftMax, which is more suitable for classification tasks, our approach generates attention values that are better suited for SR tasks. The proposed MSA calculation can be expressed as follows:

$$f_{msa} = \frac{q \cdot k}{||q|| \times ||k||} \cdot v/\tau \tag{1}$$

In (1), where the τ is a learnable scalar and the v is the value vector. By this method, the values of MSA are distributed more evenly so that more information can be noticed and learned.

Self-attention can be time-consuming, especially when dealing with input feature of large size. To address this issue and enhance network training efficiency, HPTB incorporates the shared attention mechanism derived from ELAN. This approach enables network to calculate self-attention only for specific HPMSs, while the subsequent HPMSs at the same scale can directly reuse the precomputed attention values. Consequently, network eliminate two reshapes and one convolution operations for each self-attention calculation. Although this method results in a slight reduction in SR performance, the impact is negligible in light of the substantial reduction in computational costs and time required.

3.2   Discriminator

It is well-known that pixel-wise PSNR-oriented SR methods often result in over-smoothed results and fail to adequately recover high-frequency details. The discriminator is trained to discriminate between the generated SR image (I_{SR}) and the HR image (I_{HR}). We adopt the relativistic discriminator introduced in ESRGAN, which differs from the standard discriminator in SRGAN. Instead of estimating the probability of I_{SR} being real and natural like the standard discriminator, the relativistic discriminator aims to predict the relative realism between I_{SR} and I_{HR}. This utilization of the relativistic discriminator enables the generation of sharper edges and more realistic texture details.

3.3   Losses

In order to ensure consistency between the content of I_{SR} and I_{HR}, our IPTGAN is trained using a combination of multiple loss functions, which can be formulated as follows:

$$L_G = L_p + \lambda L_G^{Ra} + \eta L_1 \tag{2}$$

where $L_1 = E_{I_{LR}} \| I_{HR} - I_{SR} \|_1$ denotes the content loss, measuring the 1-norm distance between I_{HR} and I_{SR}. The L_p represents the perceptual loss proposed by ESRGAN, while the λ and the η are coefficients used to balance the different loss terms. In (2), L_G^{Ra} is defined as:

$$L_G^{Ra} = -E_{I_{HR}}[log(1 - D_{Ra}(I_{HR}, I_{SR}))] - E_{I_{SR}}[log(D_{Ra}(I_{HR}, I_{SR}))] \tag{3}$$

where D_{Ra} refers to the standard discriminator with the relativistic average discriminator [10]. The $E_{I_{HR}}[\cdot]$ and $E_{I_{SR}}[\cdot]$ represents the operation of averaging over all real and fake data within the mini-batch, respectively.

4   Experiments

4.1   Training Details

Following ESRGAN, all experiments are performed with a scaling factor of ×4 between I_{LR} and I_{HR}. We obtain the I_{LR} by bicubic the I_{HR}. For training data, we utilize the DIV2K dataset [1], which comprises 800 high-quality images. We train the IPTGAN in RGB channels and augment the training dataset with random horizontal flips and 90° rotations. We evaluate the IPTGAN on several benchmark datasets: Set14 [22], BSD100 [16], Urban100 [8] and Manga109 [17]. We further test our IPTGAN on RealSR dataset [3] and PIRM self-validation dataset [2].

The IPTNet is trained using the perceptual loss with $\lambda = 5 \times 10^{-3}$ and $\eta = 1 \times 10^{-2}$. The learning rate is set to 1×10^{-4} and halved at $[50k, 100k, 200k, 300k]$ iterations. The window sizes of HPMS are set to 4×4, 8×8 and 16×16. The shared attention is set to $n = 1$, i.e., only calculate the first HPMS. We use Adam [11] and alternately update the generator and discriminator networks until the model converges. The IPTGAN is implemented using PyTorch on NVIDIA 3080Ti GPU.

4.2 Quantitative Evaluation

As shown in Table 1, we compared our IPTGAN with three state-of-the-art GAN-based SR methods, namely SRGAN [12], BSRGAN [23] and ESRGAN [21], using several public benchmark datasets. Remarkably, despite having significantly fewer parameters, IPTGAN consistently outperformed all other methods in terms of PSNR, structure similarity index measure (SSIM) and perceptual index (PI). We further compared the IPTNet and IPTGAN on several benchmark datasets, the result is shown in Table 2.

Table 1. PSNR/SSIM/PI comparisons of IPTGAN and several state-of-the-art GAN-based SR methods on several benchmarks at ×4.

Model	Param (K)	FLOPs (G)	Set14 (PSNR/SSIM/PI)	BSD100 (PSNR/SSIM/PI)	Urban100 (PSNR/SSIM/PI)	Manga109 (PSNR/SSIM/PI)
SRGAN	1547	231	24.21/0.6349/1.31	23.68/0.5990/1.32	−/−	−/−
BSRGAN	16697	1835	23.60/0.6295/1.46	23.91/0.6084/1.50	21.55/0.6467/1.63	22.84/0.7529/1.43
ESRGAN	16697	1859	**24.17**/0.6440/1.25	23.45/0.5975/1.27	21.99/0.6707/1.40	24.93/0.7838/1.02
IPTGAN	8212	596	23.61/**0.6468**/1.23	**23.94**/**0.6263**/**1.20**	**22.52**/**0.6984**/**1.34**	**25.03**/**0.8061**/**0.95**

Table 2. PSNR/SSIM/PI comparisons of IPTGAN and IPTNet on several benchmarks at ×4.

Model	Set14 (PSNR/SSIM/PI)	BSD100 (PSNR/SSIM/PI)	Urban100 (PSNR/SSIM/PI)	Manga109 (PSNR/SSIM/PI)
IPTNet	**24.57**/0.6451/1.41	**24.98**/0.6237/1.45	**23.47**/0.6955/1.58	**26.21**/0.8012/1.29
IPTGAN	23.61/**0.6468**/**1.23**	23.94/**0.6263**/**1.20**	22.52/**0.6984**/**1.35**	25.03/**0.8061**/**0.95**

4.3 Qualitative Results

We compared our IPTGAN with SRGAN [12], BSRGAN [23] and ESRGAN [21] on several benchmark datasets. Since SRGAN was not evaluated on Urban100, we present the comparison graphs separately in Fig. 3 and Fig. 4. As shown in these figures, the IPTGAN generates more natural and realistic effects such as stairs, cactus and tiger stripes. The restored images of wolves, fences and holes exhibit better overall visual consistency with the ground truth. In contrast, other methods tend to produce images that are either too smooth or too sharp. Results demonstrate that IPTGAN achieves competitive performance under the same scaling factor. The PI values also show the SR images generated by IPTGAN outperform other methods. Noteworthy, the parameters of IPTGAN are significantly less and achieved SR results that are more consistent with the ground truth and human visual effects.

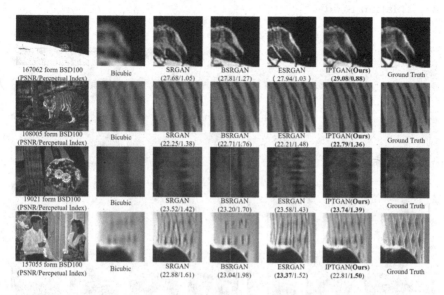

Fig. 3. Visual comparison of IPTGAN with other GAN-based SR methods at ×4. The best values are in **bold faces. Please zoom in for the best view.**

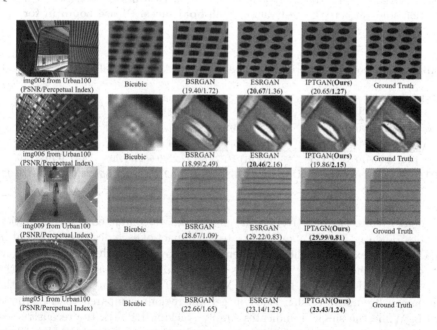

Fig. 4. Visual comparison of IPTGAN with other GAN-based SR methods on Urban100 dataset ×4. The best values are in **bold faces. Please zoom in for the best view.**

4.4   Ablation Study

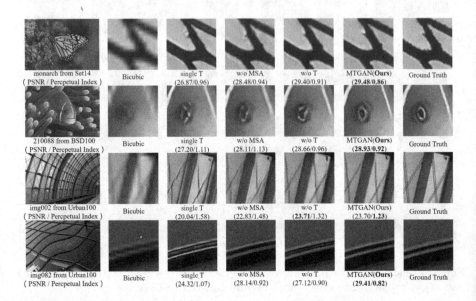

Fig. 5. Overall visual comparison of the effects of each design in IPTGAN in the ablation study at ×4. The best values are in **bold faces**. **Please zoom in for the best view**.

Table 3. The ablation experimental results of IPTGAN on several benchmarks at ×4.

Model	Set14 (PSNR/SSIM/PI)	BSD100 (PSNR/SSIM/PI)	Urban100 (PSNR/SSIM/PI)	Manga109 (PSNR/SSIM/PI)
single T	22.48/0.5934/1.37	22.67/0.5704/1.37	20.57/0.6193/1.66	22.84/0.7435/1.18
w/o MSA	23.40/0.6291/1.33	23.60/0.6076/1.32	21.74/0.6644/1.56	24.29/0.7861/ 1.07
w/o T	23.56/0.6349/1.27	23.78/0.6172/1.27	22.26/0.6821/1.49	24.77/0.7938/1.00
IPTGAN	**23.61/0.6468/1.23**	**23.94/0.6263/1.20**	**22.52/0.6984/1.35**	**25.03/0.8061/0.95**

To demonstrate the effectiveness of our design, we conducted several ablation studies. The Fig. 5 and Table 3 illustrate the impact of each design component in IPTGAN. As expected, when self-attention employs dot product for calculations (w/o MSA), the resulting SR images exhibit blurring and artifacts. Similarly, when the two LayerNorm layers and MLP of HPTB are removed (w/o T), the SR image becomes oversharpened in certain regions compared to the ground truth. While the single T indicates simply stacking HPTBs, the reconstructed results still lack naturalness. This is because the mere stacking of HPTBs fails to achieve the effect obtained by a set of three HPTBs and a residual connection. The SR images produced by IPTGAN are visually pleasing, displaying more natural textures and edges without noticeable artifacts.

Fig. 6. Visual comparison of IPTGAN with ESRGAN on RealSR dataset and PIRM self-validation dataset at ×4. The best values are in **bold faces. Please zoom in for the best view**.

4.5 Generalization Ability

We evaluated IPTGAN on RealSR dataset and PIRM self-validation dataset, which are used to evaluate the performance of SR methods in real-world scenarios [2]. These datasets consist of images from various scenes, including natural landscapes, urban buildings and portraits. Since ESRGAN is also tested on the

PIRM self-validation dataset, in this section we only show comparisons of the visual effects with ESRGAN as shown in Fig. 6. Our IPTGAN successfully reconstructs softer lines in wool, lake surfaces and textile, aligning with the subjective evaluation of human observers and exhibiting better consistency with the ground truth compared to ESRGAN. By demonstrating SR results of these challenging datasets, IPTGAN showcases its enhanced generalization ability and adaptability to process real-world images.

5   Conclusion

In this paper, we propose a Transformer-based SR generator that leverages both the hierarchization and partition into different size strategies, as well as the moderated self-attention, to enhance pixel-to-pixel communication and make more information available for learning. The proposed TRB further improves the performance of the IPTNet. Experimental results show that IPTGAN surpasses several state-of-the-art GAN-based SR methods in several benchmark datasets while utilizing significantly fewer parameters. The generalization ability test demonstrates the abilities of IPTGAN. Although IPTGAN exhibits promising results, we acknowledge a limitation where the SR image may lack sufficient high-frequent details in specific areas. Our future research will focus on enhancing the network's capability to generate high-frequent details.

References

1. Agustsson, E., Timofte, R.: NTIRE 2017 challenge on single image super-resolution: dataset and study. In: CVPRW (2017)
2. Blau, Y., Mechrez, R., Timofte, R., et al.: The 2018 PIRM challenge on perceptual image super-resolution. In: ECCV (2018)
3. Cai, J., Zeng, H., Yong, H., Cao, Z., Zhang, L.: Toward real-world single image super-resolution: a new benchmark and a new model. In: International Conference on Computer Vision, ICCV, pp. 3086–3095 (2019)
4. Denton, E.L., Chintala, S., Szlam, A., et al.: Deep generative image models using a laplacian pyramid of adversarial networks. In: NeurIPS (2015)
5. Dong, C., Loy, C.C., He, K., Tang, X.: Learning a deep convolutional network for image super-resolution. In: Fleet, D., Pajdla, T., Schiele, B., Tuytelaars, T. (eds.) ECCV 2014. LNCS, vol. 8692, pp. 184–199. Springer, Cham (2014). https://doi.org/10.1007/978-3-319-10593-2_13
6. Dosovitskiy, A., Beyer, L., Kolesnikov, A., et al.: An image is worth 16×16 words: transformers for image recognition at scale. In: ICLR (2021)
7. Goodfellow, I.J., Pouget-Abadie, J., Mirza, M., et al.: Generative adversarial nets. In: NeurIPS (2014)
8. Huang, J., Singh, A., Ahuja, N.: Single image super-resolution from transformed self-exemplars. In: CVPR (2015)
9. Johnson, J., Alahi, A., Fei-Fei, L.: Perceptual losses for real-time style transfer and super-resolution. In: Leibe, B., Matas, J., Sebe, N., Welling, M. (eds.) ECCV 2016. LNCS, vol. 9906, pp. 694–711. Springer, Cham (2016). https://doi.org/10.1007/978-3-319-46475-6_43

10. Jolicoeur-Martineau, A.: The relativistic discriminator: a key element missing from standard GAN. In: ICLR (2019)
11. Kingma, D.P., Ba, J.: Adam: a method for stochastic optimization. In: ICLR (2015)
12. Ledig, C., Theis, L., Huszar, F., et al.: Photo-realistic single image super-resolution using a generative adversarial network. In: CVPR (2017)
13. Liang, J., Cao, J., et al.: Swinir: image restoration using swin transformer. In: ICCVW (2021)
14. Liu, Z., Hu, H., Lin, Y., et al.: Swin transformer V2: scaling up capacity and resolution. In: CVPR (2022)
15. Liu, Z., Lin, Y., Cao, Y., et al.: Swin transformer: hierarchical vision transformer using shifted windows. In: ICCV (2021)
16. Martin, D.R., Fowlkes, C.C., Tal, D., et al.: A database of human segmented natural images and its application to evaluating segmentation algorithms and measuring ecological statistics. In: ICCV (2001)
17. Matsui, Y., et al.: Sketch-based manga retrieval using manga109 dataset. Multimedia Tools Appl. **76**, 21811–21838 (2017)
18. Park, S., Son, H., Cho, S., Hong, K., Lee, S.: Srfeat: single image super-resolution with feature discrimination. In: ECCV (2018)
19. Radford, A., Metz, L., Chintala, S.: Unsupervised representation learning with deep convolutional generative adversarial networks. In: ICLR (2016)
20. Sajjadi, M.S.M., Schölkopf, B., Hirsch, M.: Enhancenet: single image super-resolution through automated texture synthesis. In: ICCV (2017)
21. Wang, X., Yu, K., Wu, S., et al.: ESRGAN: enhanced super-resolution generative adversarial networks. In: ECCV (2018)
22. Zeyde, R., Elad, M., Protter, M.: On single image scale-up using sparse-representations. In: Curves and Surfaces (2010)
23. Zhang, K., Liang, J., Gool, L.V., et al.: Designing a practical degradation model for deep blind image super-resolution. In: ICCV (2021)

Referring Expression Comprehension Based on Cross Modal Feature Fusion and Iterative Reasoning

Chao Zhang, Wei Wu[✉], and Yu Zhao

Department of Computer Science, Inner Mongolia University, Huhhot 010021, China
cswuwei@imu.edu.cn

Abstract. The task of Referring Expression Comprehension is a multimodal task, which involves two different fields: Computer Vision and Natural Language Processing. Specifically, the task is to locate image region that correspond to the description provided in the given a image and a natural language expression. This paper aims to address the problem that the current task can not effectively fuse visual and textual features in the multimodal alignment stage and can not effectively utilize visual and textual formation in the prediction stage. Two improvement measures are proposed: multimodal feature fusion and iterative reasoning based on multimodal attention mechanism. In the multimodal feature fusion stage, three feature fusion modules are used to fuse visual and textual features from different perspectives to obtain rich visual and textual information; in the iterative reasoning stage, visual and textual features are accessed several times to gradually optimize the target prediction region. In order to verify the performance of the proposed method in this paper, a large number of experiments were conducted on three public datasets.

Keywords: Referring Expression Comprehension · Feature Fusion · Iterative Reasoning

1 Introduction

With the development of Artificial Intelligence in the fields of Computer Vision and Natural Language Processing, multimodal tasks involving these two fields have also received extensive attention, and Referring Expression Comprehension (REC) is one of the research focuses in this field. REC is to give a image and a natural language expression, and output the region of the object described by the language expression in the image. REC contains more natural language information than the target detection task, when positioning an object, it is necessary to first understand the input language information, fuse it with visual information, and finally use the fused feature representation for positioning prediction. Therefore, REC has regional and unique characteristics.

The current implementation methods for REC can be divided into three types: Two-stage method, One-stage method and Transformer method. The two-stage method [1–4] divides REC into two stages, In the first stage, candidate regions are generated, and in the second stage, the language expression are used to select the best matching region. The one-stage method [5–8] eliminates the process of generating candidate regions, inputs textual information as feature vectors into the network for fusion, and uses sliding windows for prediction. The Transformer method [9] inputs visual and textual information together into transformer encoding for feature fusion and prediction through linear regression. Through the analysis of the current REC, it is found that in the feature fusion stage, the two-stage method and the one-stage method overly focus on local information and lack global information. The transformer method, due to its attention mechanism, models global information better but pays less attention to local relationships. In the prediction stage, none of the three methods effectively utilized visual and textual information for prediction.

In response to the above issues, this paper proposes two improvement measures: Multi Module Feature Fusion Strategy based on Attention Mechanism and Iterative Reasoning Method based on Multimodal Attention Mechanism. In the feature fusion stage, this paper uses three feature fusion modules. The visual language matching module establishes associations between visual and textual information through a multi-head attention, providing global features for the model. The language guided encoding module and visual guided encoding module capture local information between modalities through multiple multi-head attention, providing rich contextual features for the model. In the target prediction phase, this paper uses iterative reasoning method, uses a learnable target query vector, obtains visual and textual features through attention mechanism, and updates the target query vector using residual structure and feedforward neural network. After multiple visits to visual and textual features, rich visual and textual information is obtained. Overall, the contributions of this paper are as follows:

1. In the feature fusion stage, this paper proposes a multi module feature fusion strategy based on attention mechanism to align visual and textual information. By using three feature fusion modules to fuse visual and textual features from different perspectives, the global and local contextual relationships of visual and textual are obtained. And fuse the output information of the three feature fusion modules for subsequent target prediction.
2. In the target prediction stage, this paper proposes an iterative reasoning method based on multimodal attention mechanism, which uses learnable query vectors to access visual and textual features multiple times to obtain rich visual information. Finally, the query vectors are input into the feedforward network to predict the target region through linear regression.
3. A large number of comparative experiments were conducted on three popular datasets to verify the performance of the proposed method, and the effectiveness of the proposed method was demonstrated through quantitative and qualitative experiments.

2   Related Work

2.1   Referring Expression Comprehension

REC was initially implemented using a two-stage method, which proposed a modular approach in MAttNet [1] to extract textual information (subjects, positions, relationships, etc.) and perform modular fusion with images. Later methods proposed fusion strategies such as graph attention mechanism [2] and neural module tree network [3] for improvement. Later, a one-stage method was used to implement REC. In FAOA [5], a Yolo network was proposed to implement REC, where textual features were fused with each anchor point as feature vectors. Subsequently, methods such as subquery inference [7] and feature pyramid network [8] were proposed for improvement. The latest method is implemented using the Transformer method, which encodes textual features and recognition features into one-dimensional vectors in TransVG [9] and inputs them into the transformer for feature fusion. The subsequent improvement TransVG ++ [10] removes the simple visual language transformer and performs visual language fusion by designing a language conditional Visual Transformer (LViT) in the visual feature encoder.

2.2 Transformer

Transformer in Natural Language Processing. In the field of Natural Language Processing (NLP), understanding and processing textual data is a major research challenge. With the introduction of transformer, the repetitive structure of RNN networks that relied solely on attention mechanisms was eliminated, and transformer were not affected by gradient vanishing or parallelization issues, which helped accelerate training for a wider network. The recent model structure adopts a self-supervised transformer, with BERT [11] and its variants [12, 13] based on transformer bidirectional encoding as the automatic encoding language model built on transformer encoding.

Transformer in Computer Vision. With the successful enlightenment of transformer in the field of Natural Language Processing and the rapid development of models based on visual attention, many recent studies have transplanted transformer to Computer Vision (CV) tasks and achieved some results. Cordonnier et al.[14] theoretically proved the equivalence between multi-head self attention and traditional CNN networks, and designed a pure transformer using patch downsampling and quadratic position encoding to verify its theory. Dosovitskiy et al.'s ViT[15] further extends this pure transformer to large-scale pre-training, and ViT's transformer structure can achieve excellent performance in image classification tasks. In addition, Visual Transformer has also achieved good performance in other CV tasks, such as detection [16], segmentation [14, 17], etc.

3 Method

The overall structure is shown in Fig. 1. The model can be divided into three parts, from left to right: feature extraction of images and texts, multi module feature fusion, and iterative reasoning. The model first inputs a image and a language expression into separate branches for feature extraction. For the image, visual features are obtained through convolutional operations and transformer encoding, and for the language expression, textual features are obtained through encoding input into the BERT [11]. Then, the extracted visual and textual features are fused using three feature fusion modules. Then the outputs of the three feature fusion modules are fused, and the fusion features and visual and textual features obtained are input into iterative reasoning. Through the iterative reasoning module based on multimodal attention mechanism, the visual and textual features are comprehensively considered, and the prediction target region is carried out through the FFN network (network composed of full connection layer with activation function).

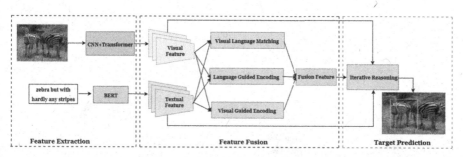

Fig. 1. Overall network structure.

3.1 Feature Extraction

For the input image, feature extraction is performed through convolution and transformer, the high-dimensional visual features are first obtained through the convolution operation, ResNet is used as the backbone network. After the convolution operation, the height and width of the feature map become 1/32 of the original image size, and the number of channels become 2048. Afterwards, through the convolution of 1 × 1 reduces the number of feature map channels to 256, and then the height and width of the feature map are flattened into one-dimensional vectors, and position encoding is added to input into the transformer. The transformer consists of 6 transformer encoding layers, each consisting of multi-head self attention and feedforward network. For the input language expression, convert each word ID into a one hot vector and mask it. Before inputting the transformer, convert the one hot vector into a language token, add [CLS] and [SEP] at the start and end positions, and add positional encoding information to input into the transformer. The transformer consists of 12 transformer encoding layers, each consisting of multi-head self attention and feedforward network. The channel numbers of the two fully connected layers in the feedforward network are 3072 and 768, respectively.

3.2 Multimodal Feature Fusion Based on Attention Mechanism

Visual Language Matching Module. The structure is shown in Fig. 2, visual features F_v are used as query, and textual features F_l are used as key and value to input into multi-head attention. Relevant semantic features F_s are collected for each visual feature vector in the feature map through the attention mechanism. Afterwards, F_v and F_s are projected onto the same spatial dimension through linear mapping represented by F'_v and F'_s. And the attention value S corresponding to each spatial position is calculated using dot product operation. The formula is as follows:

$$S(x, y) = \alpha * \exp(-\frac{(1 - F'_v(x, y)F'_s(x, y))^2}{2\sigma^2}) \tag{1}$$

where F'_v and F'_s represent the output of linear map, (x, y) represents the position of each point. Through this module, obtain attention value S for each position in the space. Multiplying F_v and S to obtain global features F. The formula is as follows:

$$F = F_v * S \tag{2}$$

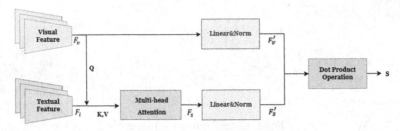

Fig. 2. Visual Language Matching Module.

Language Guided Encoding Module The structure is shown in Fig. 3, visual features F_v are used as query, and textual features F_l are used as key and value to input into multi-head attention, and output the feature map F_c with semantic information. Merge F'_v and F'_c into the second multi-head self attention using a residual structure, and the output is represented in F_{vc}.

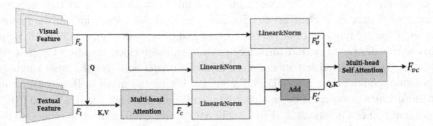

Fig. 3. Language Guided Encoding Module.

Visual Guided Encoding Module. The structure is shown in Fig. 4, textual features F_l are used as query, visual features F_v are used as key and value, input into the first multi-head attention, and output F_s. F'_l and F'_s are merged and input into the second multi-head attention using a residual structure, outputting F_t. Then merge F'_t and F'_v through a residual structure and input them into the third multi-head self attention, outputting F_{vl}. The next step involves computing the fusion features $\widehat{F_v}$, as described by the following formula:

$$\widehat{F_v} = (F + F_{vc} + F_{vl}) * S \tag{3}$$

where F represents global features(formula 2), F_{vc} and F_{vl} represent local features. To obtain the fusion features, the sum of F, F_{vc} and F_{vl} is multiplied by S.

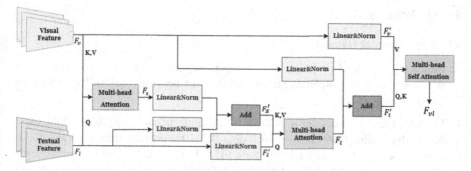

Fig. 4. Visual Guided Encoding Module.

3.3 Iterative Reasoning Based on Multimodal Attention Mechanism

The structure is shown in Fig. 5. In the target prediction stage, a multi-layer cross modal network is used to infer the target region, with each layer having the same network structure. In the first layer of the network, a learnable target query vector t_q^i is first initialized as the query, and textual features F_l are used as key and value to input into the first multi-head attention, the textual information is collected, and the output is represented in t_l. Afterwards, input t_l as the query, $\widehat{F_v}$ as the key, and F_v as the value into the second multi-head attention to collect visual information. Afterwards, the target query vector t_q^i is updated through residual structure and feedforward network. The formula is as follows:

$$t_q' = LN(t_q^i + t_v) \tag{4}$$

$$t_q^{i+1} = LN(t_q' + FFN(t_q')) \tag{5}$$

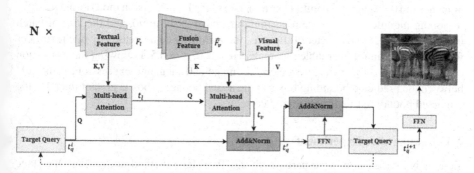

Fig. 5. Iterative Reasoning Based on Multimodal Attention Mechanism.

4 Experiments

4.1 Experimental Dataset

To evaluate the method proposed in this paper, we conducted extensive experiments on three commonly used Referring Expression Comprehension datasets, RefCOCO and RefCOCO+, RefCOCOg.

1. The RefCOCO [18] dataset is collected using ReferitGame [19] on the MSCOCO dataset. It contains 19994 images, including 142210 reference expressions and 50000 reference objects. It is divided into train (42404 objects), val (3811 objects), testA (1975 objects), and testB (1810 objects). Among them, testA only contains images of people in the category, while testB contains images of other categories.
2. The RefCOCO + [18] dataset is also collected using ReferitGame on the MSCOCO dataset.However, RefCOCO + added taboo words when collecting data, prohibiting the addition of positional information in reference expressions. RefCOCO + contains 19992 images, including 141564 reference expressions for 49856 reference objects. It is also divided into train (42278 objects), val (3805 objects), testA (1975 objects), and testB (1798 objects).
3. The RefCOCOg [20, 21] dataset was collected on the MSCOCO dataset following the Mechanical Turk task [20]. It contains 25799 images, including 95010 reference expressions for 49822 reference objects. There are two partitioning methods for the RefCOCOg dataset, one based on RefCOCOg-Google [20] partitioning, and the other based on RefCOCOg-umd [21] partitioning. In RefCOCOg-Google, it is divided into train (44822 objects) and val (5000 objects). In RefCOCOg-umd, it is divided into train (42226 objects), val (2573 objects), and test (5023 objects).

4.2 Implementation Details

In feature extraction, the input image size is set to 640×640, set the maximum length of the input language expression to 40. During the training process, the AdamW optimizer [22] is used to train the model. Set the initial learning rate of the visual and language branches to 10^{-5}, and set the initial learning rate of the feature fusion module and iterative reasoning module to 10^{-4}. The total training Epoch is set to 90, and the size of batch training data is set to 64. After 60 Epochs, the learning rate decreases by one tenth. For formula (1), set initial learnable parameters $\alpha = 1.0$, $\sigma = 0.5$. Following the evaluation criteria of previous work [7, 9], given the image and language expression, if the IoU between the predicted bounding box and the actual bounding box is greater than 0.5, the predicted bounding box is considered correct.

4.3 Comparative Experiment

Table 1 is divided into three parts, with the Two-stage method above, the One-stage method in the middle, and the Transformer method below. Through comparison, the method proposed in this paper shows significant improvement compared to the Two-stage and One-stage methods. In the Transformer method, there is also a significant improvement compared to the baseline TransVG, and there is a certain improvement compared to the new TransVG++.

Table 1. This paper proposes comparative experiments with other methods on RefCOCO, RefCOCO +, and RefCOCOg.

Models	RefCOCO			RefCOCO +			RefCOCOg		
	val	testA	testB	val	testA	testB	val-g	val-u	test-u
MAttNet [1]	76.65	81.44	69.99	65.33	71.62	56.02	-	66.58	67.27
LGRANs [2]	-	76.60	66.40	-	64.00	53.40	61.78	-	-
NMTree [3]	76.41	81.21	70.09	66.46	72.02	57.52	**64.62**	65.87	66.44
Ref-NMS [23]	**80.70**	**84.00**	**76.04**	**68.25**	**73.68**	**59.42**	-	**70.55**	**70.62**
FAOA [5]	72.54	74.35	68.50	56.81	60.23	49.60	56.12	61.33	60.36
ReSC-Large [7]	77.63	80.45	72.30	63.59	68.36	56.81	**63.12**	**67.30**	**67.20**
LBYL-Net [8]	79.67	**82.91**	74.15	**68.64**	**73.38**	**59.49**	62.70	-	-
TransVG [9]	80.32	82.67	78.12	63.50	68.15	55.63	66.56	67.66	67.44
TransVG++ [10]	82.93	85.45	77.67	69.17	74.46	59.59	70.60	70.98	71.83
Ours	**84.58**	**87.43**	**79.51**	**72.54**	**77.68**	**63.94**	**72.06**	**74.43**	**74.08**

4.4   Ablation Experiment

In Table 2, the first two lines correspond to two-stage methods, and the feature fusion strategy proposed in this paper is inspired by these methods. In the fourth and fifth lines, we present the performance of our proposed method. The fourth line represents the performance of using only the transformer, while the fifth line represents the performance of our proposed method, which demonstrates the effectiveness of our proposed multimodal feature fusion modules.

In Table 3, the first line is a one-stage method, and the iterative reasoning method proposed in this paper is inspired by it. The second line is the baseline TransVG, and the third line is without iterative reasoning, the fourth line uses iterative reasoning. The effectiveness of the iterative reasoning method proposed in this paper has been demonstrated through experiments.

In Table 4, VLMM represents visual language matching module, LGCM represents language guided encoding module, LGCM represents visual guided encoding module, MIR represents multimodal iterative reasoning. Comparing the Mean IoU and accuracy under different combinations, it can be seen that the performance of the modules proposed in this paper gradually improves.

Table 2. Conduct experiments on the attention mechanism based multimodal feature fusion proposed in this paper on RefCOCO and RefCOCOg.

Models	Backbone	RefCOCO			RefCOCOg	
		val	testA	testB	val-u	test-u
LGRANs [2]	VGG16	-	76.60	66.40	-	-
NMTree [3]	ResNet-101	76.41	81.21	70.09	65.87	66.44
TransVG[9]	ResNet-50	80.32	82.67	78.12	67.66	67.44
TransVG[9]	ResNet-101	81.02	82.72	78.35	68.67	67.33
TransVG++ [10]	ViT-tiny	82.93	85.45	77.67	70.98	71.83
Ours(w VLMM)	ResNet-50	82.96	86.74	78.41	73.88	73.01
Ours (w VLMM + LGCM + VGCM)	ResNet-50	**84.58**	**87.43**	**79.51**	**74.43**	**74.08**

Table 3. Iterative reasoning based on multimodal attention mechanism proposed in this paper is experimented on RefCOCO and RefCOCOg.

Models	Backbone	RefCOCO			RefCOCOg	
		val	testA	testB	val-u	test-u
ReSC-Large [7]	DarkNet-53	77.63	80.45	72.30	67.30	67.20
TransVG [9]	ResNet-50	80.32	82.67	78.12	67.66	67.44
Ours (w/o)	ResNet-50	83.56	87.20	79.14	72.99	72.65
Ours	ResNet-50	**84.58**	**87.43**	**79.51**	**74.43**	**74.08**

Table 4. Analyze the various components proposed in the paper on the val of RefCOCOg-umd.

VLMM	LGCM	VGCM	MIR	Mean IoU	Acc@0.5	Acc@0.6	Acc@0.7
				62.52	69.20	64.81	58.52
			√	64.06	70.75	66.93	60.93
√	√	√		64.55	72.99	68.78	62.89
√			√	66.49	73.88	69.53	63.91
√	√		√	65.87	73.33	69.32	63.28
√	√	√	√	**67.20**	**74.43**	**70.59**	**64.50**

4.5 Visualization Experiment

To verify the practicality of the proposed method, visualization experiments were conducted on RefCOCO, RefCOCO+ and RefCOCOg, and the results are shown in Figs. 6 and 7.

In Fig. 6, the first column represents the original image, the second and third columns represent the prediction boxes generated by the corresponding language expression, and the fourth column represents the real annotation boxes. By using the method proposed in this paper to train the model, it is possible to effectively locate the target region and achieve good results on all three datasets.

In Fig. 7, the first column represents the original image, and the following three columns are language expression written in RefCOCO, RefCOCO+, and RefCOCOg formats for prediction, RefCOCO, RefCOCO+ lean towards phrases, RefCOCOg lean towards complete sentences, and there are no positional words in RefCOCO+. In the figure, it can be seen that for simple images, the region described by the language expression can be well located. For multiple objects of the same type in the image, as shown in line 3 of Fig. 7, the language expression needs to use positional information and the relationship between surrounding objects to distinguish and eliminate the influence of interference.

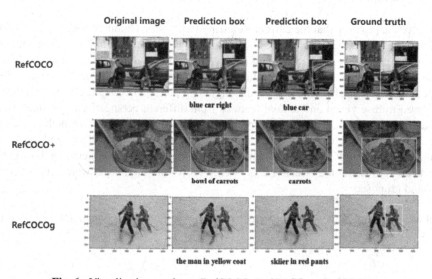

Fig. 6. Visualization results on RefCOCO, RefCOCO +, RefCOCOg.

Fig. 7. Visualization results on the three datasets.

5 Conclusion

To solve the problem that the current Referring Expression Comprehension task cannot effectively fuse visual and textual features in the phase of multimodal alignment, and unable to effectively utilize visual and textual information during the prediction phase. This paper proposes multimodal feature fusion and iterative reasoning based on multimodal attention mechanism. During the alignment phase, three feature fusion modules are used to fuse visual and textual features from different perspectives, obtaining rich visual and textual information. In the prediction stage, iterative reasoning method is used to access visual and textual features multiple times, gradually optimizing and reducing prediction ambiguity. And a large number of experiments were conducted on three public datasets to verify the effectiveness of each individual module as well as the overall method proposed.

Acknowledgment. This work is supported by the Inner Mongolia Science and Technology Project No. 2021GG0166.

References

1. Yu, L., Lin, Z., et al.: Mattnet: modular attention network for referring expression comprehension. In: CVPR, pp. 1307–1315 (2018)
2. Wang, P., Wu, Q., et al.: Neighbourhood watch: Referring expression comprehension via language-guided graph attention networks. In: CVPR, pp. 1960–1968 (2019)
3. Liu, D., Zhang, H., Wu, F., Zha, Z.-J.: Learning to assemble neural module tree networks for visual grounding. In: ICCV, pp. 4673–4682 (2019)
4. Yang, S., et al.: Dynamic graph attention for referring expression comprehension. In: ICCV, pp. 4644–4653 (2019)

5. Yang, Z., et al.: A fast and accurate one-stage approach to visual grounding. In: ICCV, pp. 4683–4693 (2019)

6. Luo, G., et al.: Multi-task collaborative network for joint referring expression comprehension and segmentation. In: Proceedings of the IEEE/CVF Conference on computer vision and pattern recognition, pp.10034–10043 (2020)

7. Yang, Z., Chen, T., Wang, L., Luo, J.: Improving one-stage visual grounding by recursive sub-query construction. In: Vedaldi, A., Bischof, H., Brox, T., Frahm, J.-M. (eds.) ECCV 2020. LNCS, vol. 12359, pp. 387–404. Springer, Cham (2020). https://doi.org/10.1007/978-3-030-58568-6_23

8. Huang, B., Lian, D., et al.: Look before you leap: Learning landmark features for one-stage visual grounding. In: Proceedings of the IEEE/CVF Conference on Computer Vision and Pattern Recognition, pp. 16888–16897 (2021)

9. Deng, J., et al.: Transvg: End-to-end visual grounding with transformers. In: Proceedings of the IEEE/CVF International Conference on Computer Vision, pp. 1769–1779 (2021)

10. Deng, J., Yang, Z., Liu, D., et al.:Transvg++: End-to-end visual grounding with language conditioned vision transformer. arXiv preprint arXiv:2206.06619 (2022)

11. Devlin, J., Chang, M.-W. Lee, K. Toutanova, K.: Bert: Pre-training of deep bidirectional transformers for language understanding. arXiv:1810.04805 (2018)

12. Liu, Y., et al.: Roberta: A robustly optimized bert pretraining approach. arXiv:1907.11692 (2019)

13. Lan, Z, et al.: Albert: A lite bert for self-supervised learning of language representations. In: ICLR (2020)

14. Cheng, B., et al.: Per-pixel classification is not all you need for semantic segmentation. In: NeurIPS, pp. 17864–17875 (2021)

15. Dosovitskiy, A., et al.: An image is worth 16×16 words: Transformers for image recognition at scale. In: ICLR (2021)

16. Carion, N., Massa, F., Synnaeve, G., Usunier, N., Kirillov, A., Zagoruyko, S.: End-to-end object detection with transformers. In: Vedaldi, A., Bischof, H., Brox, T., Frahm, J.-M. (eds.) ECCV 2020. LNCS, vol. 12346, pp. 213–229. Springer, Cham (2020). https://doi.org/10.1007/978-3-030-58452-8_13

17. Wang, H., et al.: Max-deeplab: End-to-end panoptic segmentation with mask transformers. In: CVPR, pp. 5463–5474 (2021)

18. Yu, L., Poirson, P., Yang, S., Berg, A.C., Berg, T.L.: Modeling context in referring expressions. In: Leibe, B., Matas, J., Sebe, N., Welling, M. (eds.) ECCV 2016. LNCS, vol. 9906, pp. 69–85. Springer, Cham (2016). https://doi.org/10.1007/978-3-319-46475-6_5

19. Kazemzadeh, S., Ordonez, V., Matten, M., et al.: Referitgame: Referring to objects in photographs of natural scenes. In: Proceedings of the 2014 Conference on Empirical Methods in Natural Language Processing (EMNLP), pp. 787–798 (2014)

20. Mao, J., et al.: Generation and comprehension of unambiguous object descriptions. In: Proceedings of the IEEE conference on computer vision and pattern recognition, pp. 11–20 (2016)

21. Nagaraja, V.K., Morariu, V.I., Davis, L.S.: Modeling context between objects for referring expression understanding. In: Leibe, B., Matas, J., Sebe, N., Welling, M. (eds.) ECCV 2016. LNCS, vol. 9908, pp. 792–807. Springer, Cham (2016). https://doi.org/10.1007/978-3-319-46493-0_48

22. Loshchilov, I., Hutter, F.: Decoupled weight decay regularization. In: International Conference on Learning Representations (2018)

23. Chen, L., et al.: Ref-nms: breaking proposal bottlenecks in two-stage referring expression grounding. Proc. AAAI Conf. Artif. Intell. **35**, 1036–1044 (2021)

ADS-B-Based Spatial-Temporal Multi-scale Object Detection Network for Airport Scenes

Lanjie Jiang[1,2], Xiang Zhang[1,2(✉)], Yudie Liu[1,2], and Tingyu Li[1,2]

[1] University of Electronic Science and Technology of China, Chengdu 611731, Sichuan, China
{202052012112,202152011924}@std.uestc.edu.cn
[2] Yangtze Delta Region Institute (Quzhou), University of Electronic Science and Technology of China, Quzhou 324000, Zhejiang, China
uestchero@uestc.edu.cn

Abstract. Aircraft detection is important for intelligent airport applications. This task is challenging due to some problems, e.g. the aircraft is usually small and the appearance varies dramatically with view angle. In this paper, we introduce the Automatic Dependent Surveillance-Broadcast (ADS-B) signal into the object detection framework. ADS-B is a kind of airport-specific data, which provides the aircraft location information in real-time. We use the ADS-B signal as prior information to guide aircraft detection. Firstly, from the spatial perspective, we construct an ADS-B-based saliency function, and use it to apply attention to certain spatial regions during feature extraction. Because the aircraft is likely to be in the area of attention, the detection accuracy can be improved, especially for small aircraft. Secondly, from the temporal perspective, we predict the motion direction of moving aircraft based on historical ADS-B data, and use it to generate real-time updated anchors. In addition, the shape and scale prior are also considered in the anchor generation process. The generated anchor is able to fit aircraft shape well, even in the case of drastic viewangle changes. Finally, experiments are conducted on the AGVS-T dataset to verify the effectiveness of the proposed method.

Keywords: ADS-B · Aircraft detection · Intelligent airport

1 Introduction

Modern airports are a complex system that makes it increasingly difficult for controllers to monitor airport activities, leading to increasingly serious safety issues. Therefore, the development of airport video surveillance systems is particularly important. Airport object detection aims to detect aircraft from images

Supported by the National Natural Science Foundation of China under grants U1733111 and U19A2052, and partly by the Project of Quzhou Municipal Government (2022D034).

H. Lu et al. (Eds.): ICIG 2023, LNCS 14358, pp. 334–345, 2023.
https://doi.org/10.1007/978-3-031-46314-3_27

and plays an important role in many airport monitoring applications. Although object detection has achieved great success in some public datasets, numerous experiments have shown that the performance of target recognition algorithms that perform well in basic theoretical research significantly decreases in airport environments. The particularity of aircraft targets and airport environments is the main reason for the performance degradation of basic research algorithms. An airplane is a complex target with different colors and exhibits completely different shapes at different angles, making recognition difficult. Unlike typical monitoring scenarios, the airport area is very extensive, with monitoring distances ranging from tens to hundreds or even thousands of meters, presenting a phenomenon of multi-scale coexistence. In addition, as a typical outdoor scene, airports are susceptible to various weather and lighting changes, as shown in Fig. 1.

Fig. 1. various weather and lighting changes in airport.

Due to the special nature of the airport environment mentioned above, ordinary traditional image detection algorithms are difficult to face such vast areas and complex meteorological changes, making it difficult to meet the needs of airport detection. We found that in the airport scene, not only image data but also other modal surveillance data can provide the information lacked by image data.

In this paper, the Automatic Dependent Surveillance-Broadcast (ADS-B), which is a kind of airport-specific data, is introduced in the object detection framework. ADS-B can provide four-dimensional position information of the aircraft (longitude, latitude, altitude and time), other possible additional information (conflict warning information, pilot input information, heading, turn point information, etc.), and aircraft identification and category information. In addition, it may include other additional information such as heading, airspeed, wind speed, wind direction, and aircraft external temperature. We propose an object detection algorithm called ASTNet, which is an ADS-B-based Spatial-Temporal multi-scale object detection algorithm. The algorithm is guided by spatial and temporal information for airport scene monitoring. At the spatial level, the ADS-B signal can be converted into the coordinate information of the activated vehicle in the form of a visual image. The converted image information of the ADS-B signal can be used as a reference to assist the model for better aircraft detection. With the ADS-B coordinates as the attention point to enhance the confidence capability in the ADS-B range, the model can be enhanced to determine the presence of aircraft in the ADS-B region. In terms of time-domain information, ADS-B provides various target trajectories, and the direction of the target's motion can be easily obtained through the trajectory tangential direction based on the target trajectory. The detection accuracy can be improved by modifying the aspect ratio of the target detection anchor box according to the motion direction.

In conclusion, the main contributions of this paper are: Firstly, the network provides an ADS-B information processing module, which is mainly responsible for processing the input ADS-B information. ASTNet can convert ADS-B into image coordinates based on the isotope mapping of the corresponding image to obtain ADS-B position attention, enhance the attention of the ADS-B signal area, and improve detection accuracy. After calibrating the input ADS-B information, ASTNet can obtain the target motion trajectory based on time-domain information. Trajectories can be used to predict the direction of target motion and obtain a target motion direction map, which is helpful for scaling correction of anchor boxes.

2   Related Work

2.1   Deep Learning Based Object Detection

Compared with traditional object detection algorithms, deep learning based object detection algorithms have great potential. They not only have the advantages of simple structure, fast operation, and high detection accuracy, but also can achieve various complex object detection tasks, greatly improving the accuracy, reliability, and operability of object detection, making them the preferred algorithm in the field of object detection today.

From the perspective of whether a prior anchor needs to be explicitly defined, it can be roughly divided into anchor based and anchor free. If an anchor needs to be defined, it is anchor based. Currently, most mainstream algorithms are of this type, such as Fast RCNN [5], RetinaNet [17], YOLO [3], and so on; Anchor free has gradually become popular since 2019. Its biggest advantage is that it does not require complex settings and can classify and locate points on each output feature map. It has fewer parameters, making it easier to understand. Typical algorithms are FCOS [21] and CenterNet [4], among others.

Early multi-scale detection has two ideas. One is to use convolution kernels of different sizes to obtain information at different scales by different receptive field sizes, and the other is to use image pyramids to detect objects at different scales by inputting images of different scales. However, both approaches are computationally expensive and suffer from a limited range of receptive fields.

Most of the classical networks in object detection such as Fast R-CNN [5], Faster R-CNN [2], and SPPNet [6] only use the last layer of the deep neural network for prediction. However, it is difficult to detect small targets in deep feature maps due to the loss of spatial and detailed feature information. Liu [1] proposed a multi-scale object detection algorithm Single shot multibox detector(SSD) to detect smaller targets using shallower feature maps and larger targets using deeper feature maps.

Later, in order to save computational resources and obtain better feature fusion, Lin [7] proposed the Feature Pyramid network(FPN) by combining the advantages of single feature mapping, pyramid feature hierarchy and integrated features. FPN uses feature maps of different stages to form a feature pyramid network to represent objects at different scales, and then performs object detection based on the feature pyramid. Since FPN [7] was proposed, several versions have been iterated one after another, from no fusion [1] to top-down unidirectional fusion [7–9], and gradually to bidirectional fusion [10,11].

2.2   Aircraft Detection

Due to the complexity and variability of airport scenes, the performance of the detection algorithm will also be affected to some extent, resulting in performance degradation. Therefore, some researchers have also conducted detection research for specific airport tasks.

In airport scenes, objects of the same type have large size variations, and the scale of the same object can differ by more than ten times between far and near views. Furthermore, there is a multi-scale coexistence phenomenon of aircraft in this scene, which is known as the multi-scale problem. Although multi-scale object detection algorithms currently have good performance, they are still difficult to adapt to airport object detection scenarios. Based on this, some scholars have conducted research at a more detailed level of the algorithm process, including the design of attention mechanisms, etc. For example, a multi-scale object detection method for simultaneous attention in complex scenes was proposed based on attention mechanisms.

Multi-modal object detection is also an effective method for airport object detection algorithms. Multi-modal object detection is an effective method for airport object detection algorithms. Laser radar can provide dense depth information with high density, precision, and 3D information. Several point cloud-based object detection algorithms have been developed, such as Frustum-PointNet [12] and RVNet [13], which use image detection and point cloud detection to locate objects. CRFNet [14] is another detection model that uses multi-level feature fusion and BlackIn to enhance the learning of radar information for object detection.

3   Methods

Based on the reliable information provided by ADS-B, we propose a new object detection algorithm ASTNet for airport scene monitoring based on spatio-temporal information guidance.

In terms of spatial information, the ADS-B signal can be converted to be image coordinate information as a reference to assist the model to better detect the aircraft. The ADS-B coordinates are used as the attention point to enhance the confidence capability in the ADS-B range. In terms of time domain information, ADS-B provides the trajectory of each target, and the motion direction of the target is obtained based on the tangential direction of the target trajectory, which can improve the detection accuracy by correcting the aspect ratio of the target anchor. The new idea is shown in Fig. 2

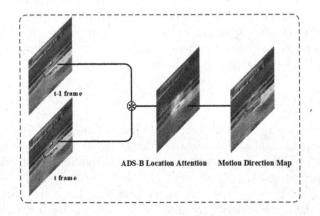

Fig. 2. The idea of our algorithm.

3.1   Architecture Overview

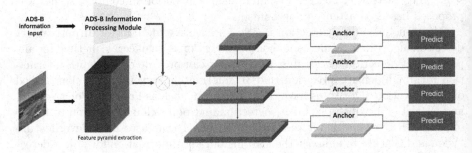

Fig. 3. An overview of our ADS-B-based Spatial-Temporal Network for aircraft detection (ASTNet).

The algorithm flowchart is shown in Fig. 3, which includes two parts: ADS-B information processing module and ADS-B-based image object detector.

In the ADS-B information processing module, the ADS-B information is converted into image coordinates by isotope mapping to get ADS-B Location Attention. After calibrating the input ADS-B message The corresponding Anchor is generated by combining the Location and Ratio information.

3.2   ADS-B

ADS-B (Automatic Dependent Surveillance-Broadcast) is a technology used in aviation to broadcast an aircraft's position, altitude, speed, and other information to air traffic control and other aircraft in the vicinity. This technology can also be utilized in object detection, particularly for detecting and tracking aircraft.

ADS-B can provide accurate and real-time information on an aircraft's location and movement, which can be used to create a comprehensive view of the airspace. This information can be integrated with other detection technologies, such as radar and cameras, to improve the accuracy and reliability of object detection.

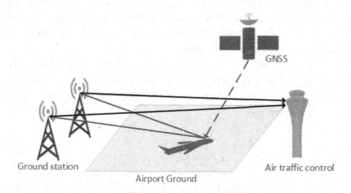

Fig. 4. The concept of ADS-B.

Figure 4 illustrates the concept of ADS-B. The aircraft obtains its geographic coordinates from the Global Navigation Satellite System (GNSS). The location information, as well as speed and call sign, are broadcasted in the form of ADS-B messages through the transponder installed in the front of the aircraft. The location information broadcasted by the aircraft is first received by ground stations and then sent to the control tower to be processed by airport controllers. The location information is given in the form of three-dimensional WGS84 coordinates. Since the movement of the aircraft on the airport surface can be considered as a movement on a plane, it can be transformed into image coordinates based on homography. The transformed image coordinates are mapped to the touchdown point of the front wheel of the aircraft, as shown in Fig. 5. Next, we introduce the proposed network under the assumption that the coordinate transformation has been completed.

3.3   ADS-B Location Attention

At the spatial level, the ADS-B signal is converted to present the coordinate information of the activated aircraft as a visual image. Since the position of the

Fig. 5. Coordinate conversion result.

ADS-B signal is on the front tire of the aircraft, the distance deviation from the center of the aircraft makes the coordinates only used as a reference. During training, to make the ADS-B signal assisted model for detecting the aircraft better. Taking the ADS-B coordinates as a point of attention, it is necessary to enhance the ability to classify within the ADS-B range, the model can determine that there is an aircraft in ADS-B area.

We define that the ADS-B signal in image coordinates of the aircraft i at t frame as (x_i^t, y_i^t). The position of the ADS-B signal in the feature map is calculated according to the proportion of the position occupied by the ADS-B signal in the original image:

$$\begin{cases} x_{n\_i}^t = x_i^t \cdot M_x, y_{n\_i}^t = y_i^t \cdot M_y \\ M_x = \frac{W_{image}}{W_n}, M_y = \frac{H_{image}}{H_n} \end{cases} \tag{1}$$

where $x_{n\_i}^t$, $y_{n\_i}^t$ are the coordinate where the signal is converted at the n feature map. While the W_{image}, H_{image} are the width and height of original image and the W_n, H_n are the width and height of the nth prediction head.

For each ADS-B signal, we can get a attention position provided by an signal in each scale of the feature map. Based on it, we propose the improvement.

The location prediction generated by anchor can be optimized for the attention position provided by each ADS-B signal. Then, we use $Y \in [0,1]^{\frac{W}{R} \times \frac{H}{R} \times C}$ to mark the position weight of the image, where R denotes the downsampling factor of each layer feature map. In the form of $Y \in [0,1]^{\frac{W}{R} \times \frac{H}{R} \times C}$, a Gaussian kernel is used to distribute the ADS-B points (M_x, M_y) on the feature graph in the sampled image. The Gaussian kernel is expressed as:

$$Y_{xyc} = \exp\left(-\frac{(x - \tilde{p}_x)^2 + (y - \tilde{p}_y)^2}{2\sigma_p^2}\right) \tag{2}$$

where σ_p is a standard deviation related to the size of the target. At this time, the weight diagram of anchor position generated represents the possibility of the existence of anchor at each point with probability. The greater the probability value, the greater the possibility of generating anchor at this point. The visualization of feature maps is shown in Fig. 6.

Input   Visualization without ADS-B   Visualization with ADS-B

Fig. 6. Visualization of feature map. The samples are divided into images with ADS-B signal and images without ADS-B signal.

3.4 Motion Direction Map

We found a clear correlation between the ratio of the aircraft object detection box and the direction of object motion in the airport scene image, as shown in Fig. 7. In terms of time-domain information, ADS-B provides the trajectories of various targets, and the direction of object motion can be easily obtained based on the tangential direction of the object trajectory. The aspect ratio of the object detection anchor box is modified according to the direction of motion to improve the detection accuracy.

The basic idea is to use (x, y) to represent the motion direction of the transformed ADS-B point positions on each layer of the feature map to obtain the motion direction map.

a) Correlation between the ratio of the box and the direction of object motion

b) More movement direction

Fig. 7. Movement direction diagram.

3.5   Anchor Generation Module

As shown in the Fig. 8, based on the feature map after feature pyramid, we use two branches to predict the location and ratio of the anchor respectively, and then combine the feature map scale information of each layer to get the anchors. The entire method can be end-to-end trained.

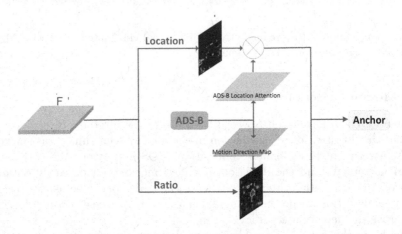

Fig. 8. The structure of Anchor Generation Module.

Location Prediction. Inspired by guiding Anchor [15], the location prediction branch is to predict which regions should come to generate anchor, which is a binary classification problem.

In particular, the ADS-B location attention map obtained from the ADS-B signal is weighted to obtain the output of $1 \times W \times H$, and then after a pixel-by-pixel Sigmod, the anchor confidence level of each position is obtained. Then a predefined threshold is used to exclude most of the pixel locations with low confidence. With the location prediction, we can filter out a small portion of the region as the candidate centroid position for anchor, making the number of anchors much lower. In inference, after predicting the position, only the anchors are computed, which can save computational resources.

Ratio Prediction. The goal of the ratio prediction branch is to predict the optimal aspect ratio for a given anchor position, which is a regression problem.

The motion direction map obtained based on the ADS-B signal is assigned a ratio to each point in the feature map by 1×1 convolution, with an output size of $1 \times W \times H$. The nearest ADS-B point is found for each feature mapping point as its ratio.

Generate Anchors. By combining the position prediction branch, ratio prediction branch, and scale information of each layer's feature map, we can generate anchors. Find the nearest ratio for each position, where the anchor is sparse and different for each position.

4   Experiments

We conduct experiments on the AGVS-T dataset [16]. Description of the reason of using this dataset, and the details of this dataset. In particular, we have to use such a video-based dataset, because there is a temporal module in our method. ADS-B information obtained through simulation

Fig. 9. The result of ASTNet.

4.1   Implementation Details and Main Results

Each of our experiments is based on MMDetection v2.0 [18]. By default, we train the networks for 12 epochs using NVIDIA 3060 TI (2 images per GPU). For the training process, the 1x schedule represents 12 epochs. The initial learning rate is 0.001. It respectively decreases by 0.1 at 9 and 12 epochs in the 1x schedule.

Table 1. Comparison of object detection performance on AVGS test-dev.

Network	Schedule	AP
RetinaNet [17]	1x	74.6
PANet [19]	1x	75.2
FSAF [22]	1x	79.6
FCOS [21]	1x	77.3
YOLOX [20]	1x	80.1
GA-RPN [15]	1x	80.8
DESTR [23]	1x	81.3
ours	1x	**83.6**

We exhibit re-implemented results of the corresponding baselines for fair comparisons. We have shown the results of our ASTNet on AGVS-T, as shown in Fig. 9. As can be observed, our method has the best detection integrity. We exhibit re-implemented results of the corresponding baselines for fair comparisons. Our method achieves 83.6 AP on AGVS-T test-dev, as demonstrated in Table 1.

4.2   Ablation Experiments

Table 2. Effect of each component on AGVS test-dev.

baseline	ALA	MDM	AGM	AP
✓				77.1
✓			✓	79.4
✓	✓		✓	80.9
✓		✓	✓	81.3
✓	✓	✓	✓	**83.6**

We also test the impact of each proposed ASTNet component on AGVS in Table 2. The training procedure runs on 1x schedule. For fair comparisons, ablation experiments are conducted under the same conditions. Experiments have proven the effectiveness of each module.

5   Conclusion

To address the challenge of insufficient object detection performance in airport scenes caused by factors such as target occlusion, scene changes, targets with a similar color to the scene, small targets, and motion blur. In this paper, we propose an ADS-B-based Spatial-Temporal multi-scale object detection network (ASTNet) for airport scenes, which integrates the processed ADS-B information into traditional deep learning image object detectors. The spatial and temporal information obtained from ADS-B can effectively guide airport object detection. Our experimental results show that the proposed algorithm achieves 83.6 AP on the AGVS dataset, significantly improving object detection performance in airport scenarios.

References

1. Liu, W., et al.: SSD: single shot multibox detector. In: European conference on computer vision, pp. 21–37 (2016)
2. Ren, S., He, K., Girshick, R., Sun, J.: Faster R-CNN: towards real-time object detection with region proposal networks. In: Advances in Neural Information Processing Systems, vol. 28 (2015)
3. Redmon, J., Divvala, S., Girshick, R., Farhadi, A.: You only look once: unified, real-time object detection. In: Proceedings of the IEEE Conference on Computer Vision and Pattern Recognition, pp. 779–788 (2016)
4. Zhou, X., Wang, D., Krähenbühl, P.: Objects as points. arXiv preprint arXiv:1904.07850 (2019)
5. Girshick, R.: Fast R-CNN. In: Proceedings of the IEEE International Conference on Computer Vision, pp. 1440–1448 (2015)

6. Purkait, P., Zhao, C., Zach, C.: SPP-Net: deep absolute pose regression with synthetic views. arXiv preprint arXiv:1712.03452 (2017)
7. Lin, T.Y., Dollár, P., Girshick, R., He, K., Hariharan, B., Belongie, S.: Feature pyramid networks for object detection. In: Proceedings of the IEEE Conference on Computer Vision and Pattern Recognition, pp. 2117–2125 (2017)
8. Liang, Z., Shao, J., Zhang, D., Gao, L.: Small object detection using deep feature pyramid networks. In: Pacific Rim Conference on Multimedia, pp. 554–564 (2018)
9. Pang, J., Chen, K., Shi, J., Feng, H., Ouyang, W., Lin, D.: Libra R-CNN: towards balanced learning for object detection. In: Proceedings of the IEEE/CVF Conference on Computer Vision and Pattern Recognition, pp. 821–830 (2019)
10. Liu, S., Qi, L., Qin, H., Shi, J., Jia, J.: Path aggregation network for instance segmentation. In: Proceedings of the IEEE Conference on Computer Vision and Pattern Recognition, pp. 8759–8768 (2018)
11. Liu, S., Huang, D., Wang, Y.: Learning spatial fusion for single-shot object detection. arXiv preprint arXiv:1911.09516 (2019)
12. Qi, C.R., Liu, W., Wu, C., Su, H., Guibas, L.J.: Frustum PointNets for 3D object detection from RGB-D data. In: Proceedings of the IEEE International Conference on Computer Vision, pp. 918–927 (2018)
13. Zhu, H., Zhang, C., Fang, Q., Cao, X., Liu, H.: RVNet: learning to reconstruct 3D visible objects with single-view depth and silhouette supervision. In: Proceedings of the IEEE/CVF Conference on Computer Vision and Pattern Recognition, pp. 14129–14138 (2020)
14. Yang, J., Yang, H., Yan, J.: CRFNet: conditional random fields network for semantic segmentation. In: Proceedings of the IEEE Conference on Computer Vision and Pattern Recognition, pp. 1465–1474 (2018)
15. Wang, J., Chen, K., Yang, S., Loy, C.C., Lin, D.: Guiding anchors for image segmentation. In: Proceedings of the IEEE International Conference on Computer Vision, pp. 4844–4853 (2019)
16. http://www.agvs-caac.com/
17. Lin, T.Y., Goyal, P., Girshick, R., He, K., Dollár, P.: Focal loss for dense object detection. In: Proceedings of the IEEE International Conference on Computer Vision, pp. 2980–2988 (2017)
18. Chen, K., et al.: MMDetection: open mmlab detection toolbox and benchmark. arXiv preprint arXiv:1906.07155 (2019)
19. Liu, S., Zhang, X., Wang, C., Liu, X.: PANet: path aggregation network for instance segmentation. In: Proceedings of the IEEE Conference on Computer Vision and Pattern Recognition, pp. 8759–8768 (2018)
20. Ge, Z., Liu, S., Wang, F., Li, Z., Sun, J.: YOLOX: exceeding YOLO series in 2021. In: Proceedings of the IEEE/CVF Conference on Computer Vision and Pattern Recognition, pp. 10296–10305 (2021)
21. Tian, Z., Shen, C., Chen, H., He, T.: FCOS: fully convolutional one-stage object detection. In: Proceedings of the IEEE/CVF International Conference on Computer Vision, pp. 9627–9636 (2019)
22. Tian, X., Shen, J., Chen, L.: FSAF: feature fusion single shot multibox detector. In: Proceedings of the IEEE Conference on Computer Vision and Pattern Recognition, pp. 12689–12698 (2019)
23. He, L., Todorovic, S.: DESTR: object detection with split transformer. In: Proceedings of the IEEE/CVF Conference on Computer Vision and Pattern Recognition, pp. 9377–9386 (2022)

Unsupervised Segmentation of Haze Regions as Hard Attention for Haze Classification

Jingyu Li[1], Haokai Ma[1], Xiangxian Li[1], Zhuang Qi[1], Xiangxu Meng[1], and Lei Meng[1,2(✉)]

[1] Shandong University, Jinan, Shandong, China
{jingyu_lee,mahaokai,xiangxian_lee,z_qi}@mail.sdu.edu.cn,
{mxx,lmeng}@sdu.edu.cn
[2] Shandong Research Institute of Industrial Technology, Jinan, China

Abstract. Haze classification plays a crucial role in air quality and visibility assessment. In contrast to traditional image classification, haze classification requires the classifier to capture the characteristics of different levels of haze. However, existing methods primarily focus on feature extraction while neglecting the interference of background information. To address this issue, this paper proposes a hard attention infused network (HAINet) for haze classification, consisting of an unsupervised segmentation module (USM) and a hybrid information fusion module (HIF). The USM is used to extract haze area information in an unsupervised manner, generating various forms of haze images. The HIA selects different various forms of haze images, as a hard attention mechanism, to reduce the impact of background and improve classification performance. We conduct experiments on two datasets, Hazel-level and Haze-Wild, in terms of performance comparison, ablation study, and case studies. The results show that our method effectively reduces the impact of background noise in haze images and consistently improves the classification performance.

Keywords: Haze classification · Hard attention · Unsupervised segmentation · Image classification

1 Introduction

In recent years, deep learning has witnessed remarkable advancements across various fields, including classification [6,16,17,20,29,38,40], recommendation [22–25,30], image generation [14,15,35,39] and federal learning [21,32]. Haze classification [7,37,43] has gained widespread employment in the field of air quality and visibility assessment [13,28], especially autonomous driving [8,9]. Unlike conventional image classification tasks, haze classification focuses on determining the level of haze in an image rather than identifying objects within the image. Previous research has primarily concentrated on feature extraction for haze classification [2,19,33,42]. However, even the state-of-the-art deep learning methods [19,41,44] face difficulties in accurately classifying images with heavy

H. Lu et al. (Eds.): ICIG 2023, LNCS 14358, pp. 346–359, 2023.
https://doi.org/10.1007/978-3-031-46314-3_28

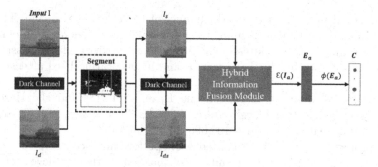

Fig. 1. Illustration to HAINet for haze classification. HAINet generates multiple haze images including the original image **I**, the dark channel of original image $\mathbf{I}_d$, the segmented image $\mathbf{I}_s$ and the dark channel of segmented image $\mathbf{I}_{ds}$, which contain multiple haze information from the input haze image via the dark channel and segmentation module. The final feature $\mathbf{E}_a$ is obtained by a fusion of the images from the selected images for haze classification $\mathbf{I}_o \oplus \mathbf{I}_s = \mathbf{I}_a \mapsto \mathbf{E}_a \mapsto C$.

haze, which can be attributed to the presence of complex backgrounds. Therefore, there is a need for a method can mitigate the influence of background on haze classification results.

The haze classification methods currently available can be broadly categorized into three groups: pixel value statistics methods, engineering methods and haze feature learning approaches. The pixel value statistics methods obtain haze levels by analyzing statistics of prior knowledge haze images, such as color [3,10,27,31] and dark channel prior [8,18], which are limited by their reliance on prior knowledge. Engineering methods [36,43,45] extract visible features like edges and colors from input images and use classifiers like SVM to classify haze levels, but their effectiveness is heavily dependent on the feature selection [2,33,42]. Haze feature learning approaches use deep learning methods [46,47] to classify haze images, leveraging techniques such as network ensembles [33,41], multi-branch training [26,42], and pre-training [2,7]. However, these approaches have lower performance when classifying heavy haze images, as the features of the background can interfere with the classification results.

We present a novel approach named HAINet to address the aforementioned challenges in haze classification, which comprises two main modules: the unsupervised segmentation module (USM) and the hybrid information fusion module (HIF). The USM module uses the dark channel prior and an unsupervised contrastive method to identify and segment the haze regions from the background scenes. It has two sub-modules: Dark Channel and Segment. The HIF module takes the original and segmented images from the pre-processed pool as inputs to the classifier. By concatenating both images and extracting an enhanced feature, HIF module creates a hard attention mechanism that combines information from different forms of haze images to improve the performance of the classifier. The overall framework of the proposed approach is illustrated in Fig. 1. The USM module pre-processes the input image and generates a pool of pre-processed images, including the original image, the dark channel of the original image, the segmented image and the dark channel of the segmented image. The HIF module fuses these images as input to the classifier and generates an enhanced image. Overall, HAINet addresses the limitations of existing haze classification methods by segmenting the haze regions and incorporating hard attention into models.

Experiments were conducted on the Hazel-level [18] and the Haze-Wild datasets, where the Hazel-level dataset contains 3024 images in 9 classes, and the Haze-Wild dataset contains 100,000 images in 10 classes. The performance of the proposed method is evaluated with performance comparison, ablation studies, and case studies. The results show that our method achieves consistent performance gains as compared with backbones.

To summarize, this paper includes two main contributions:

– A novel haze classification approach HAINet, is proposed to address the issue of background noise in haze classification tasks by focusing on the haze region in the image, which is achieved through the extraction of various forms of haze images, and effectively exclude the negative effects of background noise on the classification process.
– We explore the role of different haze image forms in the classification task and show that extracting haze region information can shift the model's attention from objects to haze. Experiments demonstrate that HAINet can integrate haze information of pre-processed images and continuously improve the classification results.

2   Related Works

2.1   Using Pixel Value Statistics as Haze Features

The pixel value statistics method involves counting the input haze image information, computing the haze value of the input image based on the statistical results, and comparing the haze value and the threshold value to determine the haze level [1]. The information comprises the lowest/highest pixel value of the original RGB image [10,27], dark channel priors [8], depth map [18], transmitted image [3], etc. These parameters undergo operations such as logarithmic, division, and pooling calculations to achieve transformation [18]. However, these methods are constrained by the construction of specific functions, which results in poor scalability.

2.2   Engineering Method

Engineering methods involve extracting features from images through manual feature engineering and training the model using machine learning methods. Typically, color histograms [36,43], color model parameters [45], regions of interest, and power spectral slopes [19] are extracted as features from raw RGB images, depth maps, and dark channel maps [44]. A regression model, such as a support vector regression, is then used to predict the level of haze and find

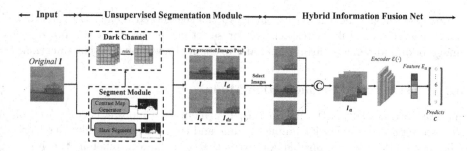

Fig. 2. Illustration of proposed methods HAINet. In forward propagation, the original image **I** goes through the USM module to get the pre-processed images pool including the original image **I**, the dark channel of the original image **I**$_d$, the segmented image **I**$_s$ and the dark channel of segmented image **I**$_{ds}$. The HIF module selects images from the pool and fuses them to generate the augmented image **I**$_a$.

the corresponding class from the index. Alternatively, multiple or cascaded support vector machines can be employed to directly classify images [44]. While this method enhances the classification robustness by fitting to a large amount of data, the selection of features limits the precision of model classification.

2.3 Haze Feature Learning Method

The deep learning approach in deep learning allows the model to learn autonomously by extracting features and outputting classification results. However, since it is difficult to train models using complete haze images, related works have improved the model training framework. For instance, model ensemble methods [33,41] achieve feature enhancement by training multiple basic models and adapting a meta-learner to learn to fuse the basic models' output. Similarly, the multi-branch method [26,42] proposes multiple classifiers in different training branches to obtain better predictions. Pre-training [2,7] and multi-task training [46,47] are also viable options. Although the deep learning method does not require feature engineering, most current works lack constraints on the background problem of haze classification.

Overall, deep learning method has made significant progress in haze classification, but effective methods for effectively addressing the issue of background noise in haze images, which could significantly enhance the performance of haze classification models, are still lacking.

3 Technique

3.1 Framework Overview

As depicted in Fig. 2, the proposed framework consists of two main modules: the USM module and the HIF module. The USM module serves as a pre-processing step for the input image and generates a processed image pool containing various versions of the original image, such as the dark channel of the original image, the segmented image, and the dark channel of the segmented image. On the other hand, the HIF module is responsible for selecting images from the processed image pool and concatenating them at the channel level for haze classification.

3.2   Unsupervised Segmentation Module

As illustrated in Fig. 2, the unsupervised segmentation module is comprised of two sub-modules: the Dark Channel module and the Segment module. The Dark Channel module is responsible for extracting the darkest pixel in the input image, while the Segment module utilizes the UCM [12] algorithm to extract haze information regions from the input image I. Unlike UCM, the Segment module focuses on the effect of different representations of haze images on the classification results. The output of this module is a pool of pre-processed images, including the original image I, the dark channel of the original image I_d, the segmented image I_s, and the dark channel of the segmented image I_{ds}.

Dark Channel Module. Existing work [8] has shown that the haze pixel values are stable across RGB channels and dark channels. Specifically, the dark channel image $\mathbf{I}_d$ is obtained by taking the minimum pixel value across the RGB channels at each pixel location in the original input image $\mathbf{I}$.

– **Calculate the Dark Channel Images.** This procedure aims to count the pixel information in the image $\mathbf{I}$. We use a filter $\mathbf{F}_d$ to get the channel map $\mathbf{I}_d$. The filter $\mathbf{F}_d$ uses the equation below:

$$\mathbf{F}_d(x) = \min_{y \in \Omega(x)} (\min_{c \in \{R,G,B\}} \mathbf{I}^c(y)), \tag{1}$$

where x represents a pixel, $\mathbf{I}^c(\cdot)$ denotes the c channel of image $\mathbf{I}$, $\Omega(x)$ means the neighboring pixels of x.

Segment Module. Due to the excellent performance of UCM in segmenting haze, we have chosen to use it as the main program for the Segment module. However, we have made some modifications to the original method to reduce the computational burden and improve the efficiency of the program without sacrificing performance. Specifically, we have changed the method of acquiring the haze region by removing the step of calculating the denoising map. These improvements have resulted in faster running times without compromising the quality of the output. The improved steps are as follows.

– **Get the Contrastive map.** We use two filters $\mathbf{F}_b$ and $\mathbf{F}_d$ to get the contrastive image $\mathbf{I}_c$. $\mathbf{F}_d$ is defined as Eq. 1. $\mathbf{F}_b$ and $\mathbf{I}_c$ is defined as the following.

$$\mathbf{F}_b(x) = \max_{y \in \Omega(x)} (\max_{c \in \{R,G,B\}} \mathbf{I}^c(y)), \tag{2}$$

$$\mathbf{I}_c(x) = \begin{cases} 255, & \text{if } x > v_{\text{threshold}} \text{ or img}_{\text{mean}} < \text{gray} \\ x, & \text{otherwise} \end{cases}, \tag{3}$$

where $v_{threshold} = \frac{1}{2}\left(mean(v_c) + median(v_c)\right)$, $v_c = I_b(x) - I_d(x)$, img_{mean} $= \frac{1}{3}\sum_{c\in\{R,G,B\}}(I^c)$ and $gray = 0.3I^R + 0.33I^G + 0.45I^B$.

- **Get the haze segmented map.** We use a filter $\mathbf{F}_p$ defined as Eqs 4 to get the position information of haze region. Then we can obtain the haze segmented map $\mathbf{I}_s$ according to the matrix $\mathbf{P}$ which get by the Eqs 5.

$$\mathbf{F}_p(x) = \max_{y\in\Omega(x)} \mathbf{I}_c(y), \tag{4}$$

$$\mathbf{P}(x) = \begin{cases} 0 & \text{if } \mathbf{F}_p(x) == 255 \\ 1 & \text{otherwise} \end{cases} \tag{5}$$

3.3 Hybrid Information Fusion Module

The HIF module is proposed to address the problem of the influence of background information. This module selects pre-processed images from the processed image pool and fuses them for classification. As shown in Fig. 2, the module outputs the haze level classification result.

Input Augmentation. The input to this module is a multi-channel hybrid map, which is created by concatenating the selected pre-processed images. An encoder ϵ_a is utilized to extract the feature. Then the feature $\mathbf{E}a$ is forwarded to the classifier for the purpose of classification. The multi-channel hybrid map $\mathbf{I}a$ is acquired by utilizing the equations outlined in Eq. 6.

$$\mathbf{I}_a = concat(\mathbf{I}, \mathbf{I}_p). \tag{6}$$

where $\mathbf{I}_p$ contains $[I_d, I_s, I_{ds}]$

Training Strategies. HIF is optimized by minimizing loss $\mathcal{L}_c$.

$$\mathcal{L}_c = CE(C, C'). \tag{7}$$

where C means the predicated label and C' means the groundtruth.

4 Experiments

4.1 Datasets

Experiments were conducted on two datasets to evaluate visual haze classification. One is Hazel-level, while the other is Haze-wild. Further details regarding the two datasets are provided below:

- **The Image Hazel-level Dataset (Hazel-level Dataset)**: The image Hazel-level dataset [18] contains 3024 synthetic images with 9 classes. These images are based on the algorithms and dataset provided by the FRIDA dataset.
- **Haze-Wild Dataset**: Source datasets contain 5000 sunny and 5000 cloudy images are used to generate 10 levels of fogging images with original images as level 0 through a monocular depth estimation model [5].

4.2 Implementation Details

We implemented the proposed methods and the algorithms in comparison by python. For proposed HAINet framework, the model details are as follows:

- As for unsupervised segmentation module, We set the parameters as the setting of the original paper [12]. For the HIF module, the parameter settings vary depending on the dataset used for experimentation. Specifically, on the Haze-level dataset, batch size of 16 and a learning rate of 5e-4 are utilized. On the Haze-wild dataset, batch size of 128 and a learning rate of 1e-3 are used. In both cases, the Adam optimizer is employed. Additionally, the decay is set to 0.1 or 0.5 for every N epoches. The base models used in the paper are ResNet18 and ResNet50 [9]. The original image, along with the pre-processed images, is resized to a size of 64 × 64.

4.3 Performance Comparison

This section presents a performance comparison between HAINet and existing haze classification methods, including three pixel value statistics methods: Saturation & RGB-correlation Detection [1], Filter-Based Fog Detection [10], HSV-Based Fog Detection [27], the engineering method SVM [45], and haze feature learning method CNN PAPLE [41], LeNet5 [11], ResNet18 [9], ResNet50 [9] and VIT [4]. For both algorithms, we fine-tune their hyper-parameters to obtain their best performance in the experiments. We can observe the followings as shown in the Table 1:

- Among all the methods evaluated, the precision of the Haze-Wild dataset was found to be lower than that of the Haze-level dataset. This phenomenon suggests that images with more complex backgrounds can negatively impact the precision of haze classification.
- The pixel value statistics methods were observed to perform poorly on both datasets, which could be attributed to the fact that haze levels cannot be accurately assessed solely based on numerical values. These methods are commonly used to identify the presence of haze in an input image, and the final haze value can be easily affected by background factors when measured in numerical terms.
- In comparison to the pixel value statistics methods, the engineering method has been observed to achieve a performance improvement of 46.21% on both datasets. However, the performance of this method is constrained by the selection of features utilized.
- Among the haze feature learning methods, the CNN method has been found to outperform the handcrafted feature extraction method, achieving a precision improvement of 64.07% on the Hazel-level dataset and 99.19% on the Haze-Wild dataset, which has a simpler background. This result highlights the advantages of data fitting.
- **ViT Performance Analysis.** Although ViT achieves competitive results, its performance is still inferior to that of ResNet on the Hazel-level dataset.

Table 1. Precision comparison of haze classification algorithms on Hazel-level and Haze-wild datasets.

Type	Model	Datasets	
		Hazel-level	Haze-Wild
Pixel Value Statistics Method	Saturation & RGB-correlation [1]	0.1529	0.1018
	Filter-Based [10]	0.2063	0.2121
	HSV-Based [27]	0.2431	0.1779
Engineering Method	SVM [45]	0.4532	0.2601
Haze Feature Learning Method	PAPLE [41]	0.7636	0.5181
	LeNet5 [11]	0.8745	0.6843
	ResNet18 [9]	0.8998	0.7650
	ResNet50 [9]	0.9031	0.7694
	ViT [4]	0.8459	0.7890
	HAINet(ResNet50)	**0.9372**	0.8102
	HAINet(ResNet18)	0.9328	**0.8320**

Table 2. Classification precision of different selections of pre-processed images on Hazel-level dataset and Haze-Wild dataset. O = the original image; D = the dark channel of original image; O/D(HRS) = the segmented image of O or D.

Model	Hazel-level		Haze-Wild	
	ResNet18	ResNet50	ResNet18	ResNet50
O	0.8998	0.9031	0.7650	0.7694
+O(HRS)	0.9251	0.9196	0.8170	0.7878
+D(HRS)	0.9196	0.9262	0.8179	0.8137
+O(HRS)+D	0.9240	0.9207	0.8274	0.7423
+D(HRS)+D	0.9284	0.9328	0.8287	**0.8236**
+O(HRS)+D(HRS)+D	**0.9328**	**0.9372**	**0.8320**	0.8102

This could be attributed to the synthetic backgrounds used in the hazel-level dataset, which may not fully represent real-life situations. Another reason for the disparity could be the challenge of transferring pre-trained knowledge from traditional image classification tasks to the haze classification task. On the other hand, ViT performs better than ResNet on the Haze-Wild dataset, suggesting its potential for handling real-life haze scenarios.

– The proposed method has been found to achieve a significant precision improvement over existing methods that use different backbones on both datasets. This demonstrates the effectiveness of removing background factors from haze images to enhance the performance of the network.

In summary, pixel value statistics and engineering methods have limited results due to information loss and assumptions that may not match the data. In contrast, the proposed HAINet achieves significantly better precision on both the

Hazel-level and Haze-wild datasets compared to existing methods with different backbones. This demonstrates the effectiveness of using haze images with background factors removed to improve network performance.

4.4   Ablation Study

In this section, we investigate the effect of the pre-processed images on the classification results under different methods.

Evaluation on the Input Augmentation with Segmented Images: As illustrated in Table 2, the "+O(HRS)"' and "+D(HRS)" rows indicate that using the original images with the augmentation of segmented images as input, both achieve better performance on two datasets and backbones. Notably, except for the case of using ResNet18 on the Hazel-level dataset, it was found that the augmentation of dark channel segmented images outperforms the augmentation of original segmented images alone. This suggests that the dark channel of segmented images contains more informative features about haze, which can be effectively captured by the model. Overall, these results demonstrate the importance of incorporating segmented images as an augmentation strategy for haze classification.

Evaluation on the Input Augmentation with Segmented Images and the Dark Channel of Original Images: As shown in the row "+O(HRS)+D" and "+D(HRS)+D" of the Table 2, the performance improvement achieved by these augmentations is significant compared to the previously mentioned. Specifically, the classification results obtained using the "+D(HRS)+D" augmentation outperform those obtained using the "+O(HRS)+D" augmentation, albeit only slightly. This finding further highlights the importance of removing background factors in haze classification. By reducing the impact of background information, the model is able to focus more on the informative features of the haze itself, leading to improved performance.

Evaluation on Input Augmentation with All Pre-processed Images: As shown in the row "+O(HRS)+D(HRS)+D" of Table 2, the model achieves the best performance on the Hazel-level dataset and the Haze-Wild dataset except using ResNet50. Even when using ResNet50 on the Haze-Wild dataset, the model still shows significant improvement compared to the base model. This finding suggests that by combining the respective advantages of segmented and dark channel images, the model can better capture informative features of haze and thus improve classification performance. Overall, the results indicate the importance of leveraging background factors and incorporating appropriate input augmentation techniques for haze classification.

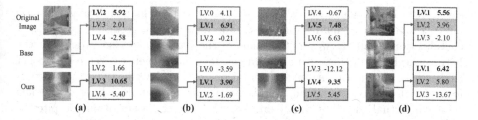

Fig. 3. Visualization of feature attentions and model predictions of Base model (the blue branch) and HAINet (the brown branch). We use GradCAM [34] to generate heatmaps and show outputs near the ground truth, the ground-truth level is emphasized by background color, while the predicted level is marked in bolded blue and bolded brown respectively. (Color figure online)

4.5 Case Study

In this section, we utilized GradCAM [34] to investigate the variation in model focus when using haze images with removed background information as an input enhancement method versus using direct input of the original images for haze classification. The displayed images were randomly chosen from the test set of the Haze-Wild dataset, and ResNet18 was utilized as the backbone.

As shown in Fig. 3 (a), when using the original input, the model predicts the wrong class, but after adding the input enhancement method, the model correctly predicts the haze class. The heat map generated by GradCAM reveals that the base model is more focused on identifying possible objects in the image rather than the haze region when the original haze image is input. In the specific example, the base model tends to focus on the lower right corner region, while the haze region is concentrated in the left rear view, leading the model to make an incorrect prediction. However, after incorporating the image with the background information removed, the model is able to focus better on the left region where the haze exists and extract more informative features about the haze, ultimately leading to a correct prediction of the haze class. This highlights the importance of input enhancement in improving model attention and performance in haze classification tasks.

As shown in Fig. 3 (b), both the base model using the original image as input and the HAINet model using input augmentation achieve correct prediction results. However, in the base model using the original image as input, the heat map shows that its focus is concentrated on the upper right corner and a small part of the lower left corner area, while the haze area is mainly concentrated in the upper left corner area, and the base model only focuses on a small part of the haze area, thus predicting the correct haze level. The heat map shows the model focuses on the entire haze area and concentrates on the haze concentration area to get the correct haze level.

In Fig. 3 (c) it can be seen the base model successfully predicts the correct haze level, while the model enhanced by the input augmentation incorrectly predicts the level. The haze in this image is mainly concentrated on the left side of the Ferris wheel and above the roof. The heat map indicates the base model's attention is mainly focused on the haze region, resulting in a correct classification result. However, the focus of the base model also extends to the Ferris wheel region, indicating the model may have been distracted by other elements in the image. After augmentation, the model effectively narrows its focus on the haze region, but in this particular case, it may have overlooked some contextual cues that were helpful for the correct classification. Despite the wrong prediction, the model's output is still informative. The predicted level is closely related to the true level and has much higher values than the other levels.

In Fig. 3 (d), the base model and HAINet model using input augmentation both predict the wrong haze level. The heat map illustrates that the base model concentrates on identifying objects in the picture, such as the vehicles in the lower right corner and the buildings in the upper left corner. However, after applying input enhancement, the HAINet model prioritizes the haze region in the upper right corner and neglects the objects in the picture, resulting in a different but still incorrect prediction. Notably, the predicted values of HAINet are closer to the actual values compared to those of the base model, indicating better performance.

Overall, the classification of haze images is negatively affected by the interference of background information. The approach presented in this study effectively eliminates this interference by removing the background information and using it as a hard attention mechanism to direct the model's focus toward the haze region. This method proves to be effective in improving the performance of haze classification tasks.

5   Conclusion

This paper introduces an approach named HAINet that effectively tackles the challenge of separating background information in haze images and improving haze classification performance. Conventional classification methods often prioritize object detection in images and disregard haze regions, which is not ideal for the haze classification task. In our proposed method, the unsupervised segmentation module separates the background information in input images and generates multiple images containing haze information. The HAINet model implements a hard attention mechanism, which focuses the model's attention on the haze region. Experimental results show that our method successfully shifts the model's attention from objects to the haze region, leading to a significant improvement in haze classification performance.

In future work, we will investigate more suitable image fusion mechanisms that can better integrate the information from multiple images with mainly haze information, further improving the model's ability to focus on the haze region. Additionally, we plan to further enhance the robustness of the background separation technique, making the hard attention mechanism applicable to a wider range of image classification tasks beyond haze classification.

Acknowledgements. This work is supported by TaiShan Scholars Program (Grant no. tsqn202211289) and Excellent Youth Scholars Program of Shandong Province (Grant no. 2022HWYQ-048).

References

1. Alami, S., Ezzine, A., Elhassouni, F.: Local fog detection based on saturation and RGB-correlation. In: 2016 13th International Conference on Computer Graphics, Imaging and Visualization (CGiV), pp. 1–5. IEEE (2016)
2. Chakma, A., Vizena, B., Cao, T., Lin, J., Zhang, J.: Image-based air quality analysis using deep convolutional neural network. In: IEEE ICIP, pp. 3949–3952 (2017)
3. Chen, Y., Wang, J., Li, S., Wang, W.: Multi-feature based foggy image classification. IOP Conf. Ser.: Earth Environ. Sci. **234**, 012089 (2019)
4. Dosovitskiy, A., Beyer, L., Kolesnikov, A., et al.: An image is worth 16x16 words: transformers for image recognition at scale. arXiv preprint arXiv:2010.11929
5. Godard, C., Mac Aodha, O., Firman, M., Brostow, G.J.: Digging into self-supervised monocular depth prediction (2019)
6. Guan, Q.L., Zheng, Y., Meng, L., Dong, L.Q., Hao, Q.: Improving the generalization of visual classification models across IoT cameras via cross-modal inference and fusion. IEEE Internet Things J. **PP**, 1 (2023)
7. Guo, L., et al.: Haze image classification method based on Alexnet network transfer model. J. Phys.: Conf. Ser. **1176**, 032011 (2019). IOP Publishing (2019)
8. He, K., Sun, J., Tang, X.: Single image haze removal using dark channel prior. IEEE Trans. Pattern Anal. Mach. Intell. **33**, 2341–2353 (2010)
9. He, K., Zhang, X., Ren, S., Sun, J.: Deep residual learning for image recognition. In: Proceedings of the CVPR, pp. 770–778 (2016)
10. Jeong, K., Choi, K., Kim, D., Song, B.C.: Fast fog detection for de-fogging of road driving images. IEICE Trans. Inf. Syst. **E101.D**, 473–480 (2018)
11. LeCun, Y., Bottou, L., Bengio, Y., Haffner, P.: Gradient-based learning applied to document recognition. Proc. IEEE **86**(11), 2278–2324 (1998)
12. Li, J., Ma, H., Li, X., Meng, L., Meng, X.: Unsupervised contrastive masking for visual haze classification. In: Proceedings of ICMR (2022)
13. Li, R., Liu, X., Li, X.: Estimation of the $PM_{2.5}$ pollution levels in Beijing based on nighttime light data from the defense meteorological satellite program-operational Linescan system. Atmosphere **6**(5), 607–622 (2015)
14. Li, X., Wu, L., Chen, X., Meng, L., Meng, X.: DSE-Net: artistic font image synthesis via disentangled style encoding. In: 2022 IEEE International Conference on Multimedia and Expo (ICME), pp. 1–6. IEEE (2022)
15. Li, X., Wu, L., Wang, C., Meng, L., Meng, X.: Compositional zero-shot artistic font synthesis. In: Proceedings of IJCAI (2023)
16. Li, X., Ma, H., Meng, L., Meng, X.: Comparative study of adversarial training methods for long-tailed classification. In: Proceedings of the 1st International Workshop on Adversarial Learning for Multimedia, pp. 1–7 (2021)
17. Li, X., Zheng, Y., Ma, H., Qi, Z., Meng, X., Meng, L.: Cross-modal learning using privileged information for long-tailed image classification. In: CVM (2023)
18. Li, Y., Huang, J., Luo, J.: Using user generated online photos to estimate and monitor air pollution in major cities. In: Proceedings of the 7th International Conference on Internet Multimedia Computing and Service, pp. 1–5 (2015)
19. Liu, C., Tsow, F., Zou, Y., Tao, N.: Particle pollution estimation based on image analysis. PLoS ONE **11**(2), e0145955 (2016)

20. Liu, J., et al.: Prompt learning with cross-modal feature alignment for visual domain adaptation. In: CAAI (2022)
21. Liu, T., Qi, Z., Chen, Z., Meng, X., Meng, L.: Cross-training with prototypical distillation for improving the generalization of federated learning. In: ICME (2023)
22. Ma, H., Li, X., Meng, L., Meng, X.: Comparative study of adversarial training methods for cold-start recommendation. In: Proceedings of ADVM (2021)
23. Ma, H., Qi, Z., Dong, X., Li, X., Zheng, Y., Meng, X.M.L.: Cross-modal content inference and feature enrichment for cold-start recommendation. In: IJCNN (2023)
24. Ma, H., et al.: Exploring false hard negative sample in cross-domain recommendation. In: RecSys (2023)
25. Ma, H., et al.: Triple sequence learning for cross-domain recommendation. arXiv preprint arXiv:2304.05027 (2023)
26. Ma, J., Li, K., Han, Y., Yang, J.: Image-based air pollution estimation using hybrid convolutional neural network. In: ICPR, pp. 471–476. IEEE (2018)
27. Mao, J., Phommasak, U., Watanabe, S., Shioya, H.: Detecting foggy images and estimating the haze degree factor. J. Comput. Sci. Syst. Biol. **7**(6), 226–228 (2014)
28. Mei, S., Li, H., Fan, J., Zhu, X., Dyer, C.R.: Inferring air pollution by sniffing social media. In: 2014 IEEE/ACM International Conference on Advances in Social Networks Analysis and Mining (ASONAM 2014), pp. 534–539. IEEE (2014)
29. Meng, L., et al.: Learning using privileged information for food recognition. In: Proceedings of the 27th ACM International Conference on Multimedia, pp. 557–565 (2019)
30. Meng, L., Feng, F., He, X., Gao, X., Chua, T.S.: Heterogeneous fusion of semantic and collaborative information for visually-aware food recommendation. In: Proceedings of MM (2020)
31. Qi, Z., Chen, X.: A novel density-based outlier detection method using key attributes. Intell. Data Anal. **26**(6), 1431–1449 (2022)
32. Qi, Z., Wang, Y., Chen, Z., Wang, R., Meng, X., Meng, L.: Clustering-based curriculum construction for sample-balanced federated learning. In: Fang, L., Povey, D., Zhai, G., Mei, T., Wang, R. (eds.) Artificial Intelligence. CICAI 2022. LNCS, vol. 13606. Springer, Cham (2022). https://doi.org/10.1007/978-3-031-20503-3_13
33. Rijal, N., Gutta, R.T., Cao, T., Lin, J., Bo, Q., Zhang, J.: Ensemble of deep neural networks for estimating particulate matter from images. In: ICIVC (2018)
34. Selvaraju, R.R., Cogswell, M., Das, A., Vedantam, R., Parikh, D., Batra, D.: Grad-CAM: visual explanations from deep networks via gradient-based localization. In: Proceedings of ICCV, pp. 618–626 (2017)
35. Sun, W., et al.: Sequential fusion of multi-view video frames for 3D scene generation. In: Fang, L., Povey, D., Zhai, G., Mei, T., Wang, R. (eds.) Artificial Intelligence. CICAI 2022. LNCS, vol. 13604. Springer, Cham (2022). https://doi.org/10.1007/978-3-031-20497-5_49
36. Wang, H., Yuan, X., Wang, X., Zhang, Y., Dai, Q.: Real-time air quality estimation based on color image processing. In: 2014 IEEE Visual Communications and Image Processing Conference, pp. 326–329. IEEE (2014)
37. Wang, X., et al.: Feature enhancement and fusion for image-based particle matter estimation with F-MSE loss. In: IEEE ICIP, pp. 768–772. IEEE (2020)
38. Wang, Y., Li, X., Ma, H., Qi, Z., Meng, X., Meng, L.: Causal inference with sample balancing for out-of-distribution detection in visual classification. In: Fang, L., Povey, D., Zhai, G., Mei, T., Wang, R. (eds.) Artificial Intelligence. CICAI 2022. LNCS, vol. 13604. Springer, Cham (2022). https://doi.org/10.1007/978-3-031-20497-5_47

39. Wang, Y., et al.: Meta-causal feature learning for out-of-distribution generalization. In: Karlinsky, L., Michaeli, T., Nishino, K. (eds.) Computer Vision – ECCV 2022 Workshops. ECCV 2022. LNCS, vol. 13806. Springer, Cham (2022). https://doi.org/10.1007/978-3-031-25075-0_36

40. Wang, Y., Qi, Z., Li, X., Liu, J., Meng, X., Meng, L.: Multi-channel attentive weighting of visual frames for multimodal video classification. In: IJCNN (2023)

41. Zhang, C., Yan, J., Li, C., Rui, X., Liu, L., Bie, R.: On estimating air pollution from photos using convolutional neural network. In: Proceedings of MM (2016)

42. Zhang, C., Yan, J., Li, C., Wu, H., Bie, R.: End-to-end learning for image-based air quality level estimation. Mach. Vis. Appl. **29**(4), 601–615 (2018)

43. Zhang, Y., Sun, G., Ren, Q., Zhao, D.: Foggy images classification based on features extraction and SVM. In: Proceeding of 2013 International Conference on Software Engineering and Computer Science, pp. 14–142 (2013)

44. Zhang, Z., Ma, H., Fu, H., Liu, L., Zhang, C.: Outdoor air quality level inference via surveillance cameras. Mobile Inf. Syst. **2016**, 1–10 (2016)

45. Zhang, Z., Ma, H., Fu, H., Wang, X.: Outdoor air quality inference from single image. In: International Conference on Multimedia Modeling (2015)

46. Zhao, X., Jiang, J., Feng, K., Wu, B., Luan, J., Ji, M.: The method of classifying fog level of outdoor video images based on convolutional neural networks. J. Indian Soc. Remote Sens. **49**(9), 2261–2271 (2021)

47. Zhao, X., Zhang, T., Chen, W., Wu, W.: Image dehazing based on haze degree classification. In: CAC, pp. 4186–4191. IEEE (2020)

Learning to Fuse Residual and Conditional Information for Video Compression and Reconstruction

Ran Wang[1], Zhuang Qi[1], Xiangxu Meng[1], and Lei Meng[1,2(✉)]

[1] Shandong University, Jinan, Shandong, China
{wr0702,z_qi}@mail.sdu.edu.cn, {mxx,lmeng}@sdu.edu.cn
[2] Shandong Research Institute of Industrial Technol, Jinan, China

Abstract. With the rapid development of the Internet, video compression and reconstruction have attracted more and more attention as the use and transmission frequency of video data have increased dramatically. Traditional methods rely on hand-crafted modules for inter-frame and intra-frame coding, but they often fail to fully exploit the redundant information of video frames. To address this problem, this paper proposes a deep learning video compression method which combines conditional context information and residual information to fully compress intra-frame and inter-frame redundancy. Specifically, the proposed algorithm uses conditional coding to provide rich context information for residual methods. At the same time, residual coding supports conditional coding in dealing with redundant information. By fusing the video frames generated by the two methods, information complementarity is achieved. Experimental results from two benchmark datasets show that our method can effectively remove redundancy between video frames and reconstruct video frames with low distortion to achieve better than state-of-the-art (SOTA) performance.

Keywords: Video compression · Residual coding · Conditional coding

1 Introduction

With the rapid development of digital media technology, a large amount of video content has been generated and contributes about 80% of the Internet traffic. However, the large-scale and high-redundancy properties prevent a large number of videos from being widely available. Therefore, it is very meaningful and critical to design an efficient video compression method to reduce the bandwidth required for video transmission and the storage space on the terminal device. Meanwhile, this may bring benefits for other vision tasks, such as video object detection [8,23] or tracking [9,40].

Traditional video compression methods [28,36] are implemented through hand-crafted modules, however, it has been observed that they cannot achieve end-to-end optimization and have limited compression efficiency. Recently, deep learning has found applications in areas such as recommendation [19–22,24],

H. Lu et al. (Eds.): ICIG 2023, LNCS 14358, pp. 360–372, 2023.
https://doi.org/10.1007/978-3-031-46314-3_29

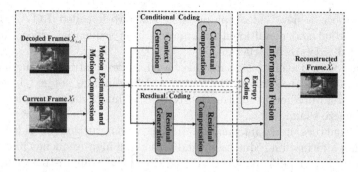

Fig. 1. Illustration of RCVC for Video compression with residual coding and conditional coding based on motion information.

classification [3,13,14,16,32,34], image generation [11,12,29,33] and federated learning [17,27]. Recently, deep learning has demonstrated superior capabilities in computer vision tasks and has also received increasing attention in video compression tasks [10,15,18,38]. Existing deep learning-based video compression frameworks mainly include: residual coding framework and conditional coding framework. Residual coding method [5,18,38] uses residual information to reduce redundancy between video frames, but the subtraction operation it uses is too simple to obtain enough effective information. Compared with residual coding, conditional coding [10] can obtain rich context information, which can help the model to learn high-frequency information in video frames and supplement the residual information obtained in residual coding, but conditional coding methods prone to artifacts.

To address these problems, this paper proposes a dual-channel video compression framework, named RCVC, which combines residual coding and conditional coding. Figure 1 shows the entire framework, which can achieve information complementation and mitigate the interference of redundant information. Specifically, RCVC first uses the motion estimation module to obtain the original optical flow information, and uses the relevant encoder to obtain the encoded optical flow information to mine the temporal redundancy between video frames. Second, RCVC uses the residual coding module to obtain residual information between video frames to reduce the interference of redundant information. Meanwhile, RCVC uses the conditional coding module to generate rich conditional information. This enables the compression of residual information and context information. Finally, RCVC fuses the residual reconstruction and conditionally reconstructed video frames based on the fusion module to complete the integration of video frame information. Throughout the process, the entropy encoding module compresses the potential representation losslessly to create a bitstream.

Experiments are conducted on the Vimeo90K and UVG datasets in terms of performance comparison and ablation study for the effectiveness of the proposed. The experimental results show that the proposed method is superior to the traditional methods and existing state-of-the-art method in PSNR and MS-SSIM evaluation indexes. In summary, the main contributions of this paper are as follows:

- We propose a new video compression framework called RCVC that can fuse residual and conditional information from sequential video frames for improved video reconstruction.
- We propose a feature fusion module based on residual reconstruction frame and conditional reconstruction frame, which combines context information and residual prediction information to achieve information complementarity and squeeze redundancy.
- Our framework adds information to the reconstruction of video frames, reducing information redundancy and preserving high-frequency information, achieving better performance than traditional and state-of-the-art methods.

2   Related Works

2.1   Image Compression

In the past few years, image compression based on deep learning [1,2,4,7,26,31] has developed rapidly. Image compression technology based on deep learning has achieved significant performance, surpassing traditional hand-designed lossy image encoders [30], which has greatly promoted the development of video compression technology. For example, the superprior model proposed by Balle et al. [1], which helps transform the marginal probability model of encoded symbols into a joint model by introducing additional latent variables as priors. This reduces redundancy and lowers the bit rate. It is also widely used in motion codecs and residual codecs for video compression. He et al. [4] proposed to use checkerboard convolution as a parallel alternative to the serial autoregressive context model, which has a better degree of parallelism under the same complexity. This provides an idea for us to further speed up the coding speed in conditional coding video compression framework.

2.2   Video Compression

Traditional video compression algorithms [28,36] mainly follow the prediction coding structure and rely on manually designed modules, such as discrete cosine transform (DCT) and block-based motion estimation, to reduce the spatiotemporal redundancy between video frames. Manual methods provide effective compression results under standards such as H.264 [36] and H.265 [28], however, due to splitting between modules, they are difficult to achieve overall joint optimization, and there are compression artifacts and other problems. Therefore, video compression technology based on deep learning [5,6,10,15,18,38,39] has received more and more attention. Lu et al. [18] proposed the first end-to-end rate-distortion optimization video compression framework, which replaced the key modules in traditional hybrid video codecs with deep neural networks. Hu et al. [5] proposed a resolution adaptive optical flow compression method, which considered rate-distortion optimization when encoding motion vectors (MV). Researchers at Microsoft Research [10] proposed a new coding paradigm called

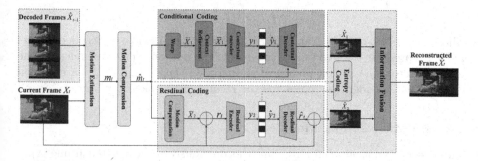

Fig. 2. Overview of our proposed video compression scheme. Motion Estimation and Motion Compression obtain motion information $\hat{m}_t$ from the current frame X_t and the previous reconstructed frame X_{t-1}, Conditional Coding extracts video contextual features based on the motion information $\hat{m}_t$, and Residual Coding evaluates the information quality of the reconstructed frame $\hat{X}_t$ to remove redundant video information.

conditional coding framework, which uses motion estimation and motion compensation modules to generate contexts as conditional guidance for codecs and entropy models. In this paper, we propose a video compression method (RCVC) which integrates the feature information obtained by the conditional encoding method and the residual encoding method, so as to achieve better compression effect.

3 Method

In this section, we will detail the motion estimation and motion compression module, residual coding module, conditional coding module, information fusion module and strategies to train the framework. An overview of our scheme is depicted in Fig. 2.

3.1 Motion Estimation and Compression Module

The process of video compression is as follows, first we feed the current frame X_t and the previously reconstructed frame $\hat{X}_{t-1}$ into a neural network-based motion estimation module to estimate the optical flow. Then we can get two-dimensional optical flow information, that is, the displacement deviation in adjacent video frames. In this paper, the motion estimation module is based on the pre-trained Spynet. The obtained motion vector m_t is compressed lossily by the motion encoder, and then the optical flow information is reconstructed at the decoding end to mine the time redundancy between the adjacent two frames. The reconstructed motion vector is denoted as $\hat{m}_t$. The motion estimation and motion compression process can be expressed as:

$$m_t = ME\left(X_t, \hat{X}_{t-1}\right) \tag{1}$$

$$\hat{m}_t = f_{Dn} \left(Q \left(f_{En} \left(m_t \right) \right) \right) \tag{2}$$

where X_t is the current frame. $\hat{X}_{t-1}$ refers to the previously decoded frame. $ME(\cdot)$ represents the function of generating the motion vector. m_t refers to the motion vector. $Q(\cdot)$ is the quantization operation. $f_{En}(\cdot)$ and $f_{Dn}(\cdot)$ are motion encoder and decoder. $\hat{m}_t$ represents the reconstructed motion vector.

3.2   Residual Coding Module

The decoded motion vector $\hat{m}_t$ and the previously reconstructed frame $\hat{X}_{t-1}$ are input into the motion compensation module, which can obtain the predicted frame $\bar{X}_2$ of the current frame. Subtracting the current frame and the predicted frame can obtain residual information r_t. The residual information enters the residual encoder, and the quantization operation is realized by adding random noise, and the quantized information is put into the entropy model to obtain the estimated potential rate. Finally, the quantified residual information $\hat{y}_2$ is entered into the residual decoder to obtain the reconstructed residual $\hat{r}_t$. The residual coding module can be expressed as:

$$\hat{X}_2 = f_{RD} \left(Q \left(f_{RE} \left(X_t - \bar{X}_2 \right) \right) \right) + \bar{X}_2 \tag{3}$$

where $\bar{X}_2$ refers to the predicted frame. $Q(\cdot)$ is the quantization operation. $f_{RE}(.)$ and $f_{RD}(\cdot)$ are residual encoder and decoder. $\hat{X}_2$ represents the reconstructed frames obtained by the residual method.

3.3   Conditional Coding Module

The purpose of the conditional coding module is to obtain context information and encode and decode context information. By distorting motion vector and previously decoded frames, conditional context information contains more dimensions than residual information, allowing information in video frames to be more fully exploited. The context information is compressed into its latent representation by the conditional encoder, and then the same quantization operation is performed, the context information knows the guidance of the conditional decoder decoding, and finally the reconstructed context information is obtained. The conditional coding module can be expressed as:

$$\hat{X}_1 = f_{CD} \left(Q \left(f_{CE} \left(X_t \mid \bar{X}_1 \right), \bar{X}_1 \right) \right) \tag{4}$$

where $\bar{X}_1$ refers to the context information. $Q(\cdot)$ is the quantization operation. $f_{CE}(\cdot)$ and $f_{CD}(\cdot)$ are conditional encoder and decoder. $\hat{X}_1$ represents the reconstructed frames obtained by the conditional method.

3.4   Information Fusion Module

To better eliminate redundancy, we combine residual information and confition information, which complement each other. With the residual coding framework, we can get a preliminary reconstruction of the original frame, however, due to the simple subtraction, there will be artifacts and noise. At this time, the context information provided by conditional coding can help us further refine the reconstruction frame, so the fusion module we propose is to input the context information and two reconstruction frames at the same time, and combine the reference features of multiple frames through the CNN network to achieve better frame reconstruction. The fusion module can be formulated as:

$$\hat{X}_t = FN\left(\hat{X}_1, \hat{X}_2\right) \tag{5}$$

where $\hat{X}_t$ refers to the decoded frame. $\hat{X}_1$ represents the reconstructed frames obtained by the conditional method. $\hat{X}_2$ represents the reconstructed frames obtained by the residual method. $FN(\cdot)$ represents the function for fusing the information from the two video frames.

3.5 Training Strategy

In our proposed framework, we optimize the following Rate Distortion (RD) trade-off realizing using least bitrate to get the best reconstruction quality:

$$L_t = \lambda \cdot D\left(X_t, \hat{X}_t\right) + R_t^{\hat{m}} + R_t^{\hat{y}_1} + R_t^{\hat{y}_2} \tag{6}$$

L_t is the loss function for the current time step t. λ controls the trade-off between the distortion D and the bitrate cost R. $D(X_t, \hat{X}_t)$ refers to the distortion between the input frame X_t and the reconstructed frame $\hat{X}_t$, where $D(\cdot)$ denotes MSE (mean squared error) or MS-SSIM (multiscale structural similarity) for different targets. In this paper we select MSE, where D consists of three parts. R is calculated as the cross-entropy between the true probability and the estimated probabilities of the latent code. $R_t^{\hat{m}}$ represents the bit rate used for encoding the quantized motion vector latent representation and the associated hyper prior. $R_t^{\hat{y}_1}$ represents the bit rate used for encoding the quantized residual latent representation and the associated hyper prior. $R_t^{\hat{y}_2}$ represents the bit rate used for encoding the quantized contextual latent representation and the associated hyper prior.

4 Experiments

4.1 Experimental Setup

Training Dataset. The training dataset is selected from the Vimeo90K dataset [37], which is 82G in size and contains 89,800 independent video clips with different contents downloaded from vimeo.com, which cover various scenes and actions, each with a sequence of 7 video frames and a resolution of 448×256 for the training images.

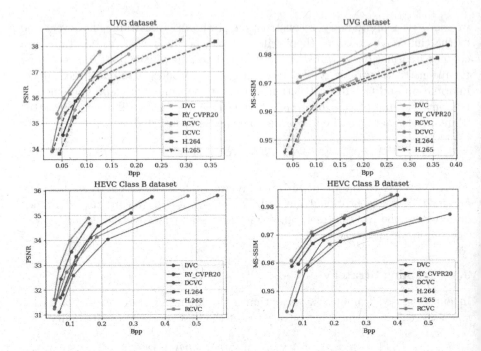

Fig. 3. Comparison between our proposed method with traditional video compression methods [28,36] and the deep learning-based video compression methods [10,18,38] on the UVG and HEVC ClassB datasets.

Test Datasets. To evaluate the performance of the proposed method, UVG [25] and HEVC [28] datasets are used for the evaluation. UVG dataset contains seven high frame rate videos. The resolution is 1920×1080, where the difference between adjacent frames is small. The HEVC dataset contains 16 Class B, C, D, and E videos ranging in resolution from 416×240 to 1920×1080.

Evaluation Metrics. To measure the distortion of reconstructed frames, two evaluation metrics are used in this paper: PSNR and MS-SSIM [35]. MS-SSIM can reflect the perception of distortion better than PSNR.

Implementation Details. Our learning rate is set to 1e-4 at the beginning and then decayed to 1e-5. The batch size was set to 16. For the λ, we set it to 256, 512, 1024, and 2048, respectively.

4.2   Performance Comparison

Figure 3 shows the rate-distortion performance of the traditional video compression methods [28,36] and the deep learning-based video compression methods [10,18,38] on the UVG and HEVC ClassB datasets. The horizontal coordinate is the bit rate. The higher the bit rate, the larger the volume occupied by

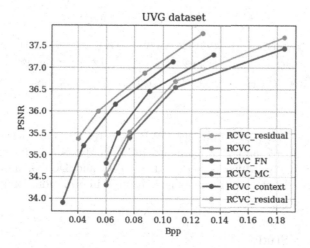

Fig. 4. Ablation Experiments. RCVC_residual verify the role of the residual coding module. RCVC_FN verify the role of the Feature Fusion Module. RCVC_MC verify the importance of motion compensation modules in video compression frameworks. RCVC_context validates the effect of context conditions on reconstructing video frames.

the compressed video, the vertical axis is the compressed mass PSNR, and the larger the PSNR, the higher the reconstructed video quality. Fixed the horizontal coordinates, look at the vertical coordinates, the curve means the compression quality of the image at the same bit rate, and the upper curve above means that we get better compression quality at the same bit rate. Fixed vertical coordinates, which means that in the bit rate case with the same compression mass, the curve on the left can get a higher compression rate and a smaller bit rate. We have made the following findings:

- The video compression method based on deep learning outperforms the traditional video compression method in both the PSNR and MS-SSIM metrics. Deep learning can realize the end-to-end joint optimization, which is more effective than the manually designed traditional video compression.
- From the PSNR evaluation index, the proposed video compression method (RCVC) for fusion residual encoding and conditional encoding is about 1 dB higher than the DVC, and about 0.2dB higher than the DCVC. Our method can obtain the sample compressed reconstruction quality while saving the code rate. It shows that by integrating the information of the two modules, we can greatly reduce the redundancy between frames and reduce the information loss in the compression reconstruction process.
- From the MS-SSIN evaluation metric, at the same bpp level, our RCVC method was 0.1 dB higher than the DVC method, slightly better compared with the DCVC method. It shows that we can get more video frames in line with our subjective visual perception by integrating information.

Table 1. The BD-Bitrate comparison.

Method	RCVC	DCVC	DVC	X265	X264
UVG	−28.8%	−25.3%	17.2%	0.0%	30.3%
HEVC ClassB	−29.3%	−26%	7.9%	0.0%	35%

Table 1 shows the corresponding BD-Bitrate results. Our proposed RCVC method saves 28.8% and 29.3% bitrate in UVG dataset and HEVC ClassB dataset, respectively, which is better than DVC and DCVC, indicating that we have obtained better bitrate savings through information complementarity (Fig. 4).

4.3 Ablation Study

In this section, ablation experiments were performed to validate the role of each module in our proposed RCVC framework.

The experimental results show that the PSNR at the same bpp level drops by about 1 dB, indicating that the motion compression module is crucial for us to obtain more accurate motion information. After the removal of the residual coding module, the PSNR decreased at the same bpp level by approximately 1 dB, indicating that the residual information can remove the temporal redundancy and thus put attention to the critical information. The PSNR decreased by about 2dB, indicating that conditional context information can be learned to high-frequency information in video compression. After removing the fusion module, the performance of video compression decreased by 1dB, indicating that our fusion information can assist us in video reconstruction.

4.4 Case Study

Figure 5 shows the reconstructed video frames of different video compression frameworks, which are from the residual coding framework DVC [18], the conditional coding framework DCVC [10], and the RCVC deep learning video compression framework we propose. The initial frame picks up one of the frames in the UVG dataset for a high frame rate video ReadySteadyGo.

From the figure, it can be found that the background color of the video frame reconstructed by the DVC method is quite different from the original picture, and the blur degree of the object is higher, indicating that its distortion degree is high. Moreover, from the details of the amplification, the DVC method has obvious compression artifacts, indicating that the image quality obtained by using only a simple subtraction operation is relatively rough and has noise interference. Overall, the image quality reconstructed by DCVC and RCVC methods is significantly better than that of DVC methods. However, in the recovery of high-frequency details, the RCVC method is better than the DCVC method. Specifically, we observed that the contours of distant houses in the images reconstructed

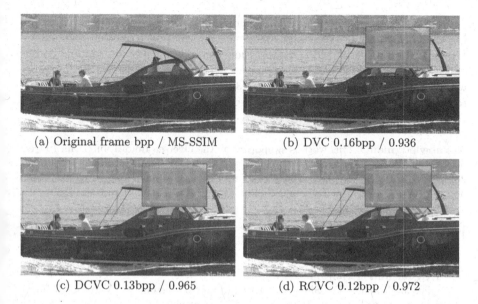

(a) Original frame bpp / MS-SSIM   (b) DVC 0.16bpp / 0.936

(c) DCVC 0.13bpp / 0.965   (d) RCVC 0.12bpp / 0.972

Fig. 5. Qualitative comparison. The reconstructed frames are from DVC, DCVC, and our RCVC method. Our method either achieves better visual quality or uses fewer bits.

by the RCVC method were more clearly visible, closer to the original picture, and their BPP was smaller. This indicates that RCVC obtains both the rebuild quality and a smaller proportion in memory. It shows that we can not only effectively remove noise by stitching context information and RGB prediction, but also achieve better detail restoration through information complementarity.

5   Conclusion

The goal of video compression is to obtain the best reconstruction quality at the cost of minimal bit rate. Traditional video compression method and compression method based on a priori deep learning mostly adopt residual coding framework, theoretically, the current to code pixels may be associated with all the previously reconstructed pixels, for the traditional encoder, due to the huge search space, it is difficult to use artificial rules to show the correlation between the pixels. Thus, the deep learning-based video compression method first generates the prediction frame from the prior decoded frame, and then calculates the residual difference between the current frame and the predicted frame. The residue is encoded into a stream, and the decoder decods the stream to obtain the reconstructed residual, and finally adds with the predicted frame to obtain the decoded frame. Given the prediction frame residual frame is a good way to denoising, but it is simple and effective, but not the optimal solution, because to find the residual operation is a simple manual design subtraction operation, can not completely remove the amount of redundancy of the whole frame.

In this paper, we combine residual coding and conditional coding, by obtaining the correlation between high frequency information to better redundancy. Experiments show that video compression methods integrating residual coding and conditional coding can achieve better performance. In the future, our work will combine advanced causal inference [39] technology to infer the invariant factors that affect video quality. Second, expand it to more challenging settings, such as federated learning [23].

Acknowledgment. This work is supported by the Oversea Innovation Team Project of the "20 Regulations for New Universities" funding program of Jinan (Grant no. 2021GXRC073), the Excellent Youth Scholars Program of Shandong Province (Grant no. 2022HWYQ-048), the TaiShan Scholars Program (Grant no. tsqn202211289).

References

1. Ballé, J., Laparra, V., Simoncelli, E.P.: End-to-end optimized image compression. arXiv preprint arXiv:1611.01704 (2016)
2. Ballé, J., Minnen, D., Singh, S., Hwang, S.J., Johnston, N.: Variational image compression with a scale hyperprior. arXiv preprint arXiv:1802.01436 (2018)
3. Guan, Q.L., Zheng, Y., Meng, L., Dong, L.Q., Hao, Q.: Improving the generalization of visual classification models across IoT cameras via cross-modal inference and fusion. IEEE Internet Things J. **10**, 15835–15846 (2023)
4. He, D., Zheng, Y., Sun, B., Wang, Y., Qin, H.: Checkerboard context model for efficient learned image compression. In: 2021 IEEE/CVF Conference on Computer Vision and Pattern Recognition (CVPR), pp. 14766–14775 (2021). https://doi.org/10.1109/CVPR46437.2021.01453
5. Hu, Z., Chen, Z., Xu, D., Lu, G., Ouyang, W., Gu, S.: Improving deep video compression by resolution-adaptive flow coding. In: Vedaldi, A., Bischof, H., Brox, T., Frahm, J.-M. (eds.) ECCV 2020. LNCS, vol. 12347, pp. 193–209. Springer, Cham (2020). https://doi.org/10.1007/978-3-030-58536-5_12
6. Hu, Z., Lu, G., Xu, D.: FVC: a new framework towards deep video compression in feature space. In: Proceedings of the IEEE/CVF Conference on Computer Vision and Pattern Recognition, pp. 1502–1511 (2021)
7. Johnston, N., et al.: Improved lossy image compression with priming and spatially adaptive bit rates for recurrent networks. In: Proceedings of the IEEE conference on computer vision and pattern recognition, pp. 4385–4393 (2018)
8. Lee, S.J., Lee, S., Cho, S.I., Kang, S.J.: Object detection-based video retargeting with spatial-temporal consistency. IEEE Trans. Circuits Syst. Video Technol. **30**(12), 4434–4439 (2020)
9. Li, C., Liu, X., Zhang, X., Qin, B.: Design of UAV single object tracking algorithm based on feature fusion. In: 2021 40th Chinese Control Conference (CCC), pp. 3088–3092. IEEE (2021)
10. Li, J., Li, B., Lu, Y.: Deep contextual video compression. Adv. Neural. Inf. Process. Syst. **34**, 18114–18125 (2021)
11. Li, X., Wu, L., Chen, X., Meng, L., Meng, X.: DSE-Net: artistic font image synthesis via disentangled style encoding. In: 2022 IEEE International Conference on Multimedia and Expo (ICME), pp. 1–6. IEEE (2022)
12. Li, X., Wu, L., Wang, C., Meng, L., Meng, X.: Compositional zero-shot artistic font synthesis. In: Proceedings of IJCAI (2023)

13. Li, X., Ma, H., Meng, L., Meng, X.: Comparative study of adversarial training methods for long-tailed classification. In: Proceedings of the 1st International Workshop on Adversarial Learning for Multimedia,

14. Li, X., Zheng, Y., Ma, H., Qi, Z., Meng, X., Meng, L.: Cross-modal learning using privileged information for long-tailed image classification. In: Proceedings of CVM (2023)

15. Lin, J., Liu, D., Li, H., Wu, F.: M-LVC: multiple frames prediction for learned video compression. In: Proceedings of the IEEE/CVF Conference on Computer Vision and Pattern Recognition, pp. 3546–3554 (2020)

16. Liu, J., et al.: Prompt learning with cross-modal feature alignment for visual domain adaptation. In: Proceedings of CAAI (2022)

17. Liu, T., Qi, Z., Chen, Z., Meng, X., Meng, L.: Cross-training with prototypical distillation for improving the generalization of federated learning. In: Proceedings of ICME (2023)

18. Lu, G., Ouyang, W., Xu, D., Zhang, X., Cai, C., Gao, Z.: DVC: an end-to-end deep video compression framework. In: Proceedings of the IEEE/CVF Conference on Computer Vision and Pattern Recognition, pp. 11006–11015 (2019)

19. Ma, H., Li, X., Meng, L., Meng, X.: Comparative study of adversarial training methods for cold-start recommendation. In: Proceedings of ADVM (2021)

20. Ma, H., Qi, Z., Dong, X., Li, X., Zheng, Y., Meng, X.M.L.: Cross-modal content inference and feature enrichment for cold-start recommendation. In: Proceedings of IJCNN (2023)

21. Ma, H., et al.: Exploring false hard negative sample in cross-domain recommendation. In: Proceedings of RecSys (2023)

22. Ma, H., et al.: Triple sequence learning for cross-domain recommendation. arXiv preprint arXiv:2304.05027 (2023)

23. McMahan, B., Moore, E., Ramage, D., Hampson, S., y Arcas, B.A.: Communication-efficient learning of deep networks from decentralized data. In: Artificial intelligence and statistics, pp. 1273–1282. PMLR (2017)

24. Meng, L., Feng, F., He, X., Gao, X., Chua, T.S.: Heterogeneous fusion of semantic and collaborative information for visually-aware food recommendation. In: Proceedings of MM (2020)

25. Mercat, A., Viitanen, M., Vanne, J.: UVG dataset: 50/120fps 4K sequences for video codec analysis and development. In: Proceedings of the 11th ACM Multimedia Systems Conference, pp. 297–302 (2020)

26. Minnen, D., Ballé, J., Toderici, G.D.: Joint autoregressive and hierarchical priors for learned image compression. In: Advances in Neural Information Processing Systems, vol. 31 (2018)

27. Qi, Z., Wang, Y., Chen, Z., Wang, R., Meng, X., Meng, L.: Clustering-based curriculum construction for sample-balanced federated learning. In: Fang, L., Povey, D., Zhai, G., Mei, T., Wang, R. (eds.) Artificial Intelligence. CICAI 2022. Lecture Notes in Computer Science, vol. 13606, pp. 155–166. Springer, Cham (2022). https://doi.org/10.1007/978-3-031-20503-3_13

28. Sullivan, G.J., Ohm, J.R., Han, W.J., Wiegand, T.: Overview of the high efficiency video coding (HEVC) standard. IEEE Trans. Circuits Syst. Video Technol. **22**(12), 1649–1668 (2012)

29. Sun, W., Li, X., Li, M., Wang, Y., Zheng, Y., Meng, X., Meng, L.: Sequential fusion of multi-view video frames for 3D scene generation. In: Fang, L., Povey, D., Zhai, G., Mei, T., Wang, R. (eds.) Artificial Intelligence. CICAI 2022. Lecture Notes in Computer Science, vol. 13604, pp. 597–608. Springer, Cham (2022). https://doi.org/10.1007/978-3-031-20497-5_49

30. Taubman, D., Marcellin, M.: JPEG 2000: standard for interactive imaging. Proc. IEEE **90**(8), 1336–1357 (2002). https://doi.org/10.1109/JPROC.2002.800725
31. Toderici, G., et al.: Variable rate image compression with recurrent neural networks. arXiv preprint arXiv:1511.06085 (2015)
32. Wang, Y., Li, X., Ma, H., Qi, Z., Meng, X., Meng, L.: Causal inference with sample balancing for out-of-distribution detection in visual classification. In: Fang, L., Povey, D., Zhai, G., Mei, T., Wang, R. (eds.) Artificial Intelligence. CICAI 2022. Lecture Notes in Computer Science, vol. 13604, pp. 572–583. Springer, Cham (2022). https://doi.org/10.1007/978-3-031-20497-5_47
33. Wang, Y., Li, X., Qi, Z., Li, J., Li, X., Meng, X., Meng, L.: Meta-causal feature learning for out-of-distribution generalization. In: Karlinsky, L., Michaeli, T., Nishino, K. (eds.) Computer Vision – ECCV 2022 Workshops. ECCV 2022. Lecture Notes in Computer Science, vol. 13806, pp. 530–545. Springer, Cham (2022). https://doi.org/10.1007/978-3-031-25075-0_36
34. Wang, Y., Qi, Z., Li, X., Liu, J., Meng, X., Meng, L.: Multi-channel attentive weighting of visual frames for multimodal video classification. In: Proceedings of IJCNN (2023)
35. Wang, Z., Simoncelli, E.P., Bovik, A.C.: Multiscale structural similarity for image quality assessment. In: The Thirty-Seventh Asilomar Conference on Signals, Systems and Computers, vol. 2, pp. 1398–1402. IEEE (2003)
36. Wiegand, T., Sullivan, G.J., Bjontegaard, G., Luthra, A.: Overview of the h. 264/AVC video coding standard. IEEE Trans. Circ. Syst. Video Technol. **13**(7), 560–576 (2003)
37. Xue, T., Chen, B., Wu, J., Wei, D., Freeman, W.T.: Video enhancement with task-oriented flow. Int. J. Comput. Vision **127**, 1106–1125 (2019)
38. Yang, R., Mentzer, F., Gool, L.V., Timofte, R.: Learning for video compression with hierarchical quality and recurrent enhancement. In: Proceedings of the IEEE/CVF Conference on Computer Vision and Pattern Recognition, pp. 6628–6637 (2020)
39. Yao, L., Chu, Z., Li, S., Li, Y., Gao, J., Zhang, A.: A survey on causal inference. ACM Trans. Knowl. Disc. Data (TKDD) **15**(5), 1–46 (2021)
40. Yao, R., Lin, G., Xia, S., Zhao, J., Zhou, Y.: Video object segmentation and tracking: a survey. ACM Trans. Intell. Syst. Technol. (TIST) **11**(4), 1–47 (2020)

A Two-Stage 3D Object Detection Algorithm Based on Deep Learning

Honggang Luan$^{(\boxtimes)}$ ⓘ, Yang Gao ⓘ, Zengfeng Song, and Chuanxi Zhang

Chang'an University, Xi'an Shaanxi 710000, China
1728095876@qq.com

Abstract. Object detection in point clouds is an important fundamental problem for many applications such as autonomous driving. The cutting-edge methods generally apply an end-to-end frame to detect the objects from the point clouds, while the traditional methods generally apply a multistep frame that clusters the points before detecting it. The end-to-end frame has been proven to be much better in many aspects, but the good detection effect is supported by a large amount of training data. As is well known, the difficulty of creating point clouds datasets is much greater than that of images datasets. Moreover, when the scenes undergo significant changes, the detection effect of end-to-end frame often decreases significantly. Therefore, on the basis of traditional detection algorithms, we propose a flexible and highly transferable two-stage algorithm AF3D where the point clouds is firstly clustered into clusters which were then detected by a classification network based on deep learning. We verify the algorithm on both the KITTI dataset and our own dataset, and compared it with Pointpillars. The conclusion indicates that AF3D has better robustness than Pointpillars in unfamiliar scenes.

Keywords: 3D object detection · deep learning · autonomous vehicles · point clouds

1 Introduction

The development of autonomous vehicles is expected to greatly improve the safety and the efficiency of our traffic system. Among many related technologies, environmental perception plays a very important and fundamental role for autonomous vehicles. Benefit from its strong environmental adaptability and the capability to acquire accurate depth information, LiDAR has become one of the most popular sensors for the perception task [1, 2]. Quite different from camera, which is arguably the most popular sensor in this field, LiDAR provides 3D point clouds rather than 2D image [3]. So, detecting objects from a 3D point clouds without color and texture character is becoming an important challenge.

Traditional approaches for the detection task in 3D point clouds generally refer to a two-stage frame, which clusters the points and then detects the clusters. In this paper, we apply deep learning technology to cluster detection and propose an accurate and flexible two-stage 3D point clouds object detection algorithm AF3D (Accurate and Flexible 3D

ⓒ The Author(s), under exclusive license to Springer Nature Switzerland AG 2023
I. Lu et al. (Eds.): ICIG 2023, LNCS 14358, pp. 373–384, 2023.
https://doi.org/10.1007/978-3-031-46314-3_30

Object Detection Algorithm) where points were clustered and then detected by a neural network.

The main contributions of this work can be summarized as follows:

1. Based on deep learning methods, we construct an effective classification network.
2. We propose a flexible two-stage 3D object detection algorithm AF3D.
3. We verify the effectiveness of this method based on our own dataset.

2 Related Work

Two-stage frames generally include a points extraction or cluster step before the detection.

2.1 Clustering Methods

Common clustering methods include five categories, that are partition clustering, distance clustering, density clustering, hierarchical clustering and grid clustering [4]. K-means clustering algorithm may be one of the most typical partition clustering algorithms which iteratively find the centers of different clusters and the points nearest to the centers respectively [5]. However, K-means algorithm requires too many manually adjusted parameters and performs poor regarding complex shape objects. Recent progress of the partition clustering algorithm may be found in [6]. Euclidean clustering may be one of the most typical distance clustering algorithms, which clusters the nearest points in to one class [7]. As a very typical density cluster algorithm, DBSCAN (Density-Based Spatial Clustering of Applications with Noise) treats the closely linked points as one cluster [8]. Some recent progress of this category may be found in [9, 10]. In recent years, hybrid clustering algorithms, which combine several different cluster algorithms, have gradually attracted more attention. Wang et al. [11] proposed the SPSO-FCM algorithm which combines the improved particle swarm optimization algorithm with the fuzzy C-means algorithm to cluster the points. The algorithm has fast convergence speed and clear boundary region segmentation, especially for scenes with complex profile and large number of point clouds, it can get better segmentation results. We think there will be more hybrid clustering algorithms in the future.

2.2 Detection Methods

For detection, traditional methods have developed various algorithms based on the 3D geometric features of the points. In 2019, S. Shi et al. [12] migrated the image segmentation network RCNN to point clouds data and proposed a two-stage 3D object detection network called Point RCNN. The author has further proposed an improved version called PV-RCNN [13] which uses efficient 3D voxel convolution and point clouds convolution to estimate the confidence and spatial location of objects. In 2021, Z. Li [14] proposed an efficient two-stage detection network LiDAR-RCNN. This method uses a voxelization method to remove background points, and then builds a Pointnet-based network to extract features, classify the object and locate it. In addition, the Voxel-RCNN[15] proposed in 2021 further demonstrates that applying deep learning technology to point clouds based object detection is the current mainstream trend.

3   Methodology

We combined traditional object detection algorithms and built a PFC-Net network based on Pointnet [16], proposing a flexible and accurate 3D object detection algorithm AF3D. The AF3D algorithm framework is shown in Fig. 1. The entire algorithm framework mainly consists of two stages. In the first stage, ground segmentation is performed first, and then cluster the remaining point clouds to obtain point clusters $\{C_1, C_2, C_3......C_{k-1}, C_k\}$. In the second stage, the point clouds classification network PFC-Net is first built. Secondly, clusters are input into the trained classification network PFC-Net to classify the clusters. Then we can obtain the semantic information of each cluster class, perform bounding box fitting on the classified objects, and obtain network inference results.

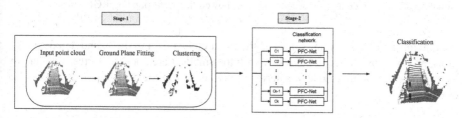

Fig. 1. AF3D network overview

3.1   Stage 1: Ground Point Clouds Segmentation and Non-ground Point Clouds Clustering

To improve the search efficiency of point clouds data, we use three-dimensional KD-Tree to establish topological relationship for point clouds data. It is because compared with Octree, KD-tree can bring better computational efficiency [17, 18].

In addition, we used the segmentation fitting algorithm proposed by Dimitris Zermas et al. [19] to achieve ground segmentation, the algorithms outperform similar approaches in running time, while producing similar results. After removing the ground point clouds, the non-ground point clouds need to be segmented and divided into several clusters. Comprehensively comparing the commonly clustering algorithms, the DBSCAN algorithm can effectively deal with noise points, obtain clusters of any shape from the noisy spatial database by segmentation, and connect adjacent regions with sufficient density, and does not need to specify the number of clusters in advance. Therefore, the non-ground point clouds clustering is performed by the DBSCAN algorithm. We set the clustering neighborhood radius of the DBSCAN algorithm to 0.45m and the MinPts value is set to 10. The non-ground point clouds clustering effect using DBSCAN is shown in Fig. 2. The first column is the point clouds clustering effect, and the second is the original images accordingly. It can be found that all the point clouds are properly clustered.

Bounding box fitting operation is required after clustering. We obtain the 3D bounding box by using the bounding box fitting method based on the minimum enclosing rectangle with less computation. This method obtains the outer rectangle according to

Fig. 2. Point clouds clustering results based on DBSCAN algorithm. The first column is the point clouds clustering effect, and the second column showed the corresponding RGB image.

the maximum and minimum values of the point clouds data in the X and Y axis directions, and obtains the rectangular box with the smallest area or the shortest side length by continuous rotation. Finally, a series of parameters of the 3D bounding box can be obtained.

3.2 Stage 2: Classification Network PFC-Net

To classify the clusters generated by the clustering algorithm and detect objects from the clusters we built the PFC-Net network. The network structure of PFC-Net is shown in Fig. 3. The network accepts cluster input as a tensor $(N, 3)$, where N represents the number of points input and 3 represents the channel information of the points. It should be noted that the points mentioned here refer to the points contained in each cluster. Feature extraction is performed by multiple weight-shared MLP modules. So that feature map F1 represented by a tensor of size $(N, 1024)$ is obtained. After that the global feature, whose size is $(1,1024)$, is obtained by a Max-Pooling layer. By concatenating both the global feature and the feature map F1, feature map F2 is obtained. F_2 represented by a tensor of size $(N, 2048)$, contains both multi-dimensional features and the global features of the all the points of cluster. Then the feature map F2 would be passed through two weight-shared MLPs and a Max-Pooling layer for further feature extraction and finally gets a new feature map F3 represented by a tensor whose size is $(1,1024)$. After that F3 is sent to three fully connected layers to obtain the classification result.

3.3 PFC-Net network training

KITTI 3D Object Dataset. The KITTI dataset was jointly established by Karlsruhe Institute of Technology in Germany and Toyota American Institute of Technology in 2012 [20]. It is one of the most commonly used public datasets for research on autonomous driving environment perception algorithms. The KITTI 3D Object dataset for the 3D object detection task consists of 7481 training samples and 7518 testing samples, mainly including various types of cars, pedestrians, and cyclists. The KITTI 3D Object dataset covers multiple scenes such as highways, suburbs, and urban roads. Each frame of data

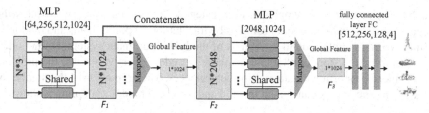

Fig. 3. The structure of the point clouds classification network PFC-Net. It takes N points as input, and output the classification scores for 4 classes. The four classes are pedestrian, car, cyclist and other object.

includes point clouds and their corresponding RGB images, label files, etc. According to the cutoff value and occlusion scale, the dataset samples can be divided into easy, medium and difficult.

Data Reconstruction. The KITTI 3D Object dataset cannot be directly used for the training of PFC-Net. Therefore, we reconstructed the KITTI 3D Object dataset. First, using the relationship between the raw point clouds data and its corresponding label files, the point clouds data belonging to three categories of cars, cyclists, and pedestrians are extracted and assigned corresponding category labels. Secondly, we use the data augmentation method to balance the number of samples in each category, aiming at the problem of poor generalization ability of the model due to the unbalanced number of samples in each category. The reconstruction of the KITTI 3D Object dataset mainly includes two parts: object point clouds extraction and data enhancement. The specific steps are as follows.

Object point clouds extraction: For each frame of point clouds in the KITTI training set, the label categories of "Van", "Car", "Truck", and "Tram" are unified into "Car". Only "Car", "Pedestrian", "Cyclist" are kept. Since the KITTI 3D Object dataset only labels the point clouds from the camera perspective, we only process the point clouds from the camera perspective. According to the conversion relationship between the camera coordinate system and the lidar coordinate system, the point clouds in the three-dimensional bounding box with categories "Car", "Pedestrian" and "Cyclist" are save to folders one by one and assign category labels. Remove the ground points of the remaining point clouds after extracting the object, and perform DBSCAN clustering. Save the resulting other object clusters and name the category "Otherobjects". So far, we have extracted four categories of datasets, "Car", "Pedestrian", "Cyclist", and "Otherobjects" from the KITTI 3D Object dataset to train the point clouds classification network.

Data augmentation: We reconstructed the training set of 7481 frames and obtained a total of 27346 training samples, of which the number of "Car" categories is 12564, the number of "Pedestrian" categories is 3272, the number of "Cyclist" categories is 1526, and the number of "Otherobjects" categories is 9984. The proportions of the four types of samples in the KITTI 3D Object reconstruction data set are quite different. The imbalance of the number of samples will cause the network model to focus on learning the categories with a large number of samples during the training process, and despise the categories with a small number of samples, which will affect the classification effect and generalization ability of the network model. Therefore, in response to the problem of unbalanced number of samples in each category, on the one hand, we expand the categories with a small number of samples by translating the point clouds and randomly rotating a certain angle around the Z-axis of the lidar coordinate system. On the other hand, the Weighted Random Sampler method is used to effectively solve the problem of unbalanced proportion of samples in each category. The proportion of the number of samples after the data enhancement method and weighted random sampling is shown in Table 1.

Table 1. The proportion of each category before and after data enhancement (%)

Category	Car	Pedestrian	Cyclist	Other objects
Before data augmentation	46.92	13.41	5.24	44.91
After data augmentation	37.45	23.67	18.33	20.55
After weighted random sampling	25.46	24.67	24.36	25.51

Verification of PFC-Net. The verification was running on a workstation whose CPU is Inter i7 10700KF, GPU is NVIDIA RTX3080, video memory is 8G, and memory is 12G. The software environment includes Unbutu18.04 LTS, Cuda11.1, Cudnn8.0.5 and Python3.7.

Due to the difference in the number of point clouds of various categories extracted, the point clouds data needs to be preprocessed uniformly before being input into the network. If the number of object cluster point clouds is less than 1024, it will be supplemented to 1024 by zero padding. If the number of point clouds of the object cluster is more than 1024, downsample the number of point clouds to 1024. We use the farthest points sampling to downsample the point clouds.

PFC-Net is trained on the reconstructed KITTI 3D Object dataset. The reconstructed KITTI 3D Object dataset is divided into training set and test set according to the ratio of 8:2. The point clouds classification network PFC-Net adopts the cross-entropy loss function shown as (1).

$$L = \frac{1}{N}\sum_i L_i = -\frac{1}{N}\sum_i \sum_{c=1}^{M} y_{ic} \log(p_{ic}) \tag{1}$$

Here M represents the number of categories, i is the sample index, c is the category index and y_{ic} represents a sign function where y_{ic} equal to 1 only if the predicted category of the network is consistent with the label, otherwise y_{ic} equal to 0. P_{ic} represents the predicted probability value of the sample i belonging to the category c.

The reconstructed KITTI 3D Object dataset is standardized as the network input. The ground-truth category information is used as the label, using the Adam optimizer with an initial learning rate of $1*10^{--3}$, the maximum number of iterations Epoch is 150, and the batch size is 128.

The training loss curve of PFC-Net is shown in Fig. 4. The vertical axis represents the loss function value, and the horizontal axis represents the number of training cycles. At the 80th training cycle, the network model training basically fits.

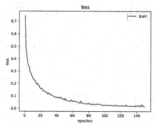

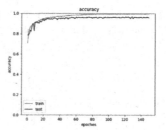

Fig. 4. PFC-Net training Loss curve. The vertical axis represents the loss function value, and the horizontal axis represents the number of training cycles.

Fig. 5. PFC-Net classification average accuracy curve. The vertical axis represents the overall accuracy, and the horizontal axis represents the number of training cycles.

We quantitatively analyze the performance of PFC-Net using the average accuracy of all categories as the evaluation metric. The average accuracy curve is shown in Fig. 5. The vertical axis represents the overall accuracy, and the horizontal axis represents the number of training cycles. The average accuracy of point clouds classification on the training set is as high as 99.21%, and the average accuracy of point clouds classification on the test set is as high as 95.78%. After training, PFC-Net has a good performance in point clouds classification tasks, and can accurately complete the classification task of point clouds clusters.

3.4 Verification of AF3D

The process of using AF3D algorithm for 3D object detection in this paper is as follows. First, the point clouds within the camera view are extracted, then ground points are removed and non-ground points are clustered, and the processed clusters are used as input to the PFC-Net network for classification. Then we can obtain the semantic information of each cluster, perform bounding box fitting on the classified objects, and obtain preliminary network inference results. In the next step, we further filter according to the actual size of objects such as cars, pedestrians, and cyclists. For the car category the maximum height is set to 2.5 m, the maximum length is set to 8 m, and the minimum height threshold is 1.5 m. Due to the severe occlusion of some cars in the dataset, the minimum length threshold for car size is not specified. When the height and length of the cluster is greater than the maximum height and length threshold of the car category or when the height of the cluster is less than the minimum height threshold, we discard it. For the cyclist category the maximum height threshold is set to 2 m, the maximum length threshold is 2.5 m, and the minimum height threshold is 1.25 m. For the pedestrian category the maximum height threshold is set to 2 m and the minimum height threshold is 1.2 5m.

The experimental results of AF3D and Pointpillars based on the KITTI 3D Object are shown in Table 2.

The visualization results of AF3D based on the KITTI 3D Object dataset are shown in Fig. 6. The first column of images represents the extraction of ground points (green is the ground, gray is the non-ground point clouds). The second column of images is a

Table 2. Detection accuracy (%) of AF3D algorithm on KITTI 3D Object dataset. E represents easy, M represents medium and D represents difficult.

Methods	Cars			Pedestrians			Cyclists		
	E	M	D	E	M	D	E	M	D
Pointpillars	83.60	74.58	71.55	50.31	44.08	40.97	79.76	59.35	56.38
AF3D	73.92	70.87	62.41	43.21	41.52	38.83	68.32	61.76	51.42

visualization of the clustering effect. The third column of images is a classification of the clusters (red for cars, blue for cyclists, and green for pedestrians). The fourth column of images is the RGB image corresponding to the point clouds.

Fig. 6. The visualization results of AF3D on KITTI 3D Object dataset.

4   Vehicle experiment

In this section, we run the algorithm on our own vehicle to conduct an experimental comparison between the Pointpillars and AF3D algorithms based on our dataset.

4.1 Experiment Platform

The hardware equipment on the car includes lidar mounting bracket, HESAI Technology Pandar 64-line lidar, monocular camera, differential GPS and a laptop. Among them, the lidar is installed on the lidar bracket at the center axis of the car, at a height of about 1.90 m from the ground.

4.2 Experiment Data

We establish communication between PC and lidar based on ROS (Robot Operating System). The operating frequency of lidar is 10Hz by default. We drove the experimental car along the main road of the school. Part of the scene is shown in Fig. 7. The laser point clouds data and camera data can be visualized by Rviz during the driving process. We store the point clouds data in Pcd format. Because the speed of the data collection vehicle is relatively low, a frame of point clouds data is selected every 2 s, and a total of 200 frames of point clouds data are selected. We use 3D bounding boxes to annotate cars, cyclists, and pedestrians within each frame of the point clouds.

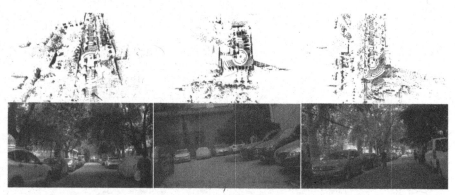

Fig. 7. Examples of some scenarios of our vehicle data collection. The first row showed 3 laser point clouds, and the second row showed the corresponding RGB image.

4.3 Data Preprocessing and Annotation

In the process of collecting data, the lidar will generate a small number of NaN (Not a Number) points, noise points, and outliers due to the material of obstacles and its own accuracy. Therefore, it is necessary to preprocess each frame of the lidar point clouds to remove the NaN value in the laser point clouds data, and then intercept the region of interest through through-pass filtering. The threshold is shown in eq. (2). Secondly, the point clouds in the region of interest is filtered through statistical filtering to filter out noise points and outliers to complete the preprocessing process.

$$\begin{cases} -40 \le x \le 40 \\ -20 \le y \le 20 \end{cases} \tag{2}$$

We use the open-source software PCAT to label the selected 200 frames of point clouds data in turn. It includes three categories: "Car", "Pedestrian" and "Cyclist".

4.4 Comparison of Two Methods on the Experiment dataset

THE Pointpillars and AF3D are tested based on our own vehicle dataset without retraining, and the detection accuracy is shown in Table 3.

Table 3. The detection accuracy (%) of the two algorithms on our experiment data set

Methods	Cars	Pedestrians	Cyclists
Pointpillars (recurrence)	52.24	31.73	39.46
AF3D	69.74	41.25	54.33

The detection results obtained by AF3D and Pointpillars are shown in Fig. 8. The first column shows the detection result of the AF3D network, and the second column shows the detection result of Pointpillars network. The third column is the label result.

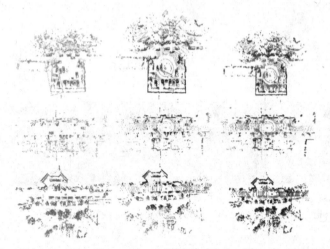

Fig. 8. Visualization of detection results of AF3D and Pointpillars on experiment dataset.

4.5 Analyze

From the verification results on the KITTI 3D Object dataset in Table 2, it can be seen that the detection accuracy of cars is higher, followed by the accuracy of cyclists. Pedestrians have obtained the lowest detection accuracy. This is because of two reasons. Firstly, these different categories of objects generally appear different number of points, Secondly the proportion of the categories are different in the original dataset.

Our experiment is a unfamiliar scene for both Pointpillars and AF3D algorithms. It can be found that the detection accuracy of AF3D algorithm is better than Pointpillars. The detection accuracy of AF3D of cars, pedestrians and cyclists is 17.5%, 9.52% and 14.87% higher than that of Pointpillars, respectively. This is because AF3D firstly clustering the point clouds and then PFC-Net detects the clusters in turn. Here the character of the cluster would only slightly change in different scenes so the performance of AF3D would be impacted less. In contrast, the context information used by Pointpillars would be quite different in different scenes. So, the two-stage structure adopted by AF3D can reserve more detection capability in unfamiliar scenes.

5   Conclusion

This paper has proposed a 3D point clouds detection method AF3D based on deep learning. AF3D is a combination of Deep learning technology and traditional two-stage frame. By comparing the performance of Pointpillars in unfamiliar scenes, we found that the traditional two-stage frame can help on reducing the computation resource request and enhance the adaptability of unfamiliar scenes.

As the performance of the two-stage frame algorithm greatly relies on the clustering accuracy, improving the clustering algorithm may be of our future interest.

References

1. Zamanakos, G., Tsochatzidis, L., Amanatiadis, A., Pratikakis, I.: A comprehensive survey of LIDAR-based 3D object detection methods with deep learning for autonomous driving. Comput. Graph. **99**, 153–181 (2021)
2. Ghasemieh, A., Kashef, R.: 3D object detection for autonomous driving: methods, models, sensors, data, and challenges. Transport. Eng **8**, 100115 (2022)
3. Gupta, A., Anpalagan, A., Guan, L., Khwaja, A.S.: Deep learning for object detection and scene perception in self-driving cars: survey, challenges, and open issues. Array **10**, 100057 (2021)
4. Wang, Z., Li, Q., Zhang, Z., Wang, K., Yang, J.: Research progress of unmanned vehicle point cloud clustering algorithm. World Sci.-Tech. R & D **43**, 274–285 (2021)
5. Wang, S., Liu, C., Xing, S.: Review on k-means clustering algorithm. J. East China Jiaotong Univ. **39**, 119–126 (2022)
6. Ikotun, A.M., Almutari, M.S., Ezugwu, A.E.: K-Means-based nature-inspired metaheuristic algorithms for automatic data clustering problems: recent advances and future directions. Appl. Sci. **11**, 11246 (2021)
7. Xue, L., Qi, C., Zhang, B., Zhang, X., Wu, C.: Object size and orientation recognition based on 3d points cloud Euclideam clustering and RANSAC boundary fitting. Machine Des. Res. **34**, 44–48+53 (2018)
8. Chen, W., Shi, H.: Improved DBSCAN clustering algorithm based on KD tree. Comput. Syst. Appl. **31**, 305–310 (2022)
9. Fan, X., Xu, G., Li, W., Wang, Q., Chang, L.: Target segmentation method for three-dimensional LiDAR point cloud based on depth image. Chin. J. Lasers **46**, 292–299 (2019)
10. Zhang, C., Huang, W., Niu, T., Liu, Z., Li, G., Cao, D.: Review of clustering technology and its application in coordinating vehicle subsystems. Automot. Innov. **6**, 89–115 (2023)
11. Wang, X., Wu, L., Chen, H., Shi, H.: Region segmentation of point cloud data based on improved particle swarm optimization fuzzy clustering. Opt. Precis. Eng. **25**, 563–573 (2017)
12. Shi, S., Wang, X., Li, H.: PointRCNN: 3D object proposal generation and detection from point cloud. In: 2019 IEEE/CVF Conference on Computer Vision and Pattern Recognition (CVPR 2019). pp. 770–779. IEEE Computer Society, Los Alamitos (2019)
13. Shi, S., et al.: PV-RCNN: Point-voxel feature set abstraction for 3D object detection. In: 2020 IEEE/CVF Conference on Computer Vision and Pattern Recognition (CVPR). pp. 10526–10535. IEEE, Seattle, WA, USA (2020)
14. Li, Z., Wang, F., Wang, N.: LiDAR R-CNN: an efficient and universal 3D object detector. In: 2021 IEEE/CVF Conference on Computer Vision and Pattern Recognition, CVPR 2021, pp. 7542–7551. IEEE Computer Society, Los Alamitos (2021)
15. Deng, J., Shi, S., Li, P., Zhou, W., Zhang, Y., Li, H.: Voxel R-CNN: towards high performance voxel-based 3d object detection. In: Thirty-Fifth Aaai Conference on Artificial Intelligence, Thirty-Third Conference on Innovative Applications of Artificial Intelligence and the Eleventh Symposium on Educational Advances in Artificial Intelligence, pp. 1201–1209. Assoc. Advancement Artificial Intelligence, Palo Alto (2021)
16. Qi, C.R., Su, H., Mo, K., Guibas, L.J.: PointNet: deep learning on point sets for 3D classification and segmentation. In: 30th IEEE Conference on Computer Vision and Pattern Recognition (CVPR 2017), pp. 77–85. IEEE, New York (2017)
17. Zhang, H.: Organization and visualization of points cloud data based on octree. J. Taiyuan Normal Univ. Nat. Sci. Edition **10**, 128–132 (2011)
18. Fu, C., Li, G., Song, R., Gao, W., Liu, S.: OctAttention: octree-based large-scale contexts model for point cloud compression. Proc. AAAI Conf. Artif. Intell. **36**(1), 625–633 (2022). https://doi.org/10.1609/aaai.v36i1.19942

19. Zermas, D., Izzat, I., Papanikolopoulos, N.: Fast segmentation of 3D point clouds: a paradigm on LiDAR data for autonomous vehicle applications. In: 2017 IEEE International Conference on Robotics and Automation. ICRA 2017, 29 May 2017–3 June 2017, pp. 5067–5073. Institute of Electrical and Electronics Engineers Inc., Singapore, Singapore (2017)
20. Geiger, A., Lenz, P., Urtasun, R.: Are we ready for autonomous driving? the KITTI vision benchmark suite. In: 2012 IEEE Conference on Computer Vision and Pattern Recognition (CVPR), pp. 3354–3361. IEEE, New York (2012)

Dual Temporal Memory Network for Video Salient Object Detection

Ziyang Wang, Jinpan Li, and Junxia Li[✉]

CICAEET, School of Computer, Nanjing University of Information Science and Technology, Nanjing 210044, China
20211249425@nuist.edu.cn, junxiali99@163.com

Abstract. Video salient object detection (VSOD) aims at distinguishing the salient objects from the complex background and highlighting them uniformly in the spatiotemporal domain. One of the fundamental challenges in VSOD is how to make the most use of the temporal information to boost the performance. We propose a dual temporal memory network (DTMNet) which stores short- and long-term video sequence information preceding the current frame as the temporal memories to address the temporal modeling in VSOD. The proposed network consists of two temporal modules including a short-term co-inference learning (SCL) sub-module and a long-range memory learning (LML) sub-module. The SCL is designed for inferencing spatiotemporal interactions between neighboring frames of the current input video clip. The LML aims to satisfy the logical reasoning sequence in timeline and learn the long-time range information between current clip and the previous video clips. Comprehensive evaluations well demonstrate the effectiveness and robustness of our proposed architecture.

Keywords: Video saliency detection · Spatiotemporal information · Co-inference · Memory learning

1 Introduction

Video salient object detection (VSOD) is a fundamental task in computer vision community, where the most visually distinctive object that mostly attracts human attention is discovered in a video sequence automatically. It has various applications such as video object segmentation, video compression, object tracking, scene rendering, and autonomous driving, to name a few [1–4].

Different from the static image saliency detection over spatial domain only, the incursion of temporal information in video data is a critical factor that makes VSOD challenging. Deep learning based VSOD methods usually exploit some classic techniques (*e.g.*, optical flow [6], 3D convolution [7] and ConvLSTM [8]) to capture the temporal information. Compared to traditional VSOD methods, these deep models typically achieve better performance due to the strong learning ability of neural network. However, these methods only consider the short-term temporal information between

© The Author(s), under exclusive license to Springer Nature Switzerland AG 2023
Y. Lu et al. (Eds.): ICIG 2023, LNCS 14358, pp. 385–396, 2023.
https://doi.org/10.1007/978-3-031-46314-3_31

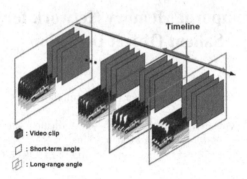

Fig. 1. Time-based analysis of our proposed dual temporal memory network. The red box corresponds to the short-term co-inference learning (SCL) module, and the orange box corresponds to the long-range memory learning (LML) module. (Color figure online)

adjacent video frames, or the relationship between consecutive four input images, lacking the characterization of long-term information.

To address the above issue, we design a dual temporal memory network (DTMNet) to infer inner spatiotemporal information in few images and long-range spatiotemporal information for images up to the current frame. In detail, in order to learn spatial information and find co-salient objects in consecutive frames, we introduce a short-term co-inference learning (SCL) module in the middle layer of the encoder. For compensating spatiotemporal information learned in consecutive frames and studying long-term spatiotemporal information, we propose a long-range memory learning (LML) module, which consists of two simplified, pre-information guided convolutional GRUs and dilated 3D convolution. Figure 1 shows the length of time for SCL module and LML module to learn time-space information in the time dimension respectively. It is note that each video group has effects in both SCL and LML. Our proposed network contributes to a powerful and fast (20–22 fps) deep video object detection model. We consider that the proposed method is a robust network that can learn spatiotemporal information in an appropriate manner between short-term co-inference and long-range angle. Overall, the contributions of this paper can be summarized as follows.

- From a short-term perspective, we establish a novel short-term co-inference learning (SCL) module for co-inferencing salient objects and learning local spatiotemporal information in short video clips.
- Considering that the spatiotemporal information learned by consecutive short video clips is far from sufficient, we design a long-range memory learning (LML) module through a long-range perspective. By aggregating the current clip and previous memory information, LML can obtain better global logical content and make frame representation more robust.
- The proposed DTMNet achieves comparable results in the VSOD task.

2 Related Work

Wang *et al.* [12] present a novel spatiotemporal saliency detection method to estimate salient regions in videos based on the gradient flow field and energy optimization, which incorporates intra-frame boundary information and inter-frame motion information together. Chen *et al.* [13] propose a spatial-temporal saliency fusion and low-rank coherency guided saliency diffusion method to fuse the color saliency based on global motion clues in a batch-wise fashion. In [14], pixel-level temporal and spatial saliency maps are adaptively fused by integrating motion distinctiveness of superpixels with a scheme of temporal saliency prediction and adjustment. Liu *et al.* [15] utilize superpixel-level motion, color histograms as well as global motion histogram to extract features for saliency measurement, and a superpixel-level graph with the addition of a virtual background node is exploited reasonably to generate the motion saliency maps. Fang *et al.* [16] design a video saliency model based on feature contrast in compressed domain, in which the static saliency map is calculated on the basis of luminance, color, and texture features, and the motion saliency map is computed by motion features. Xi *et al.* [17] discuss how to identify the background priors for a video and then design a saliency model by utilizing background priors.

With the success of deep learning, more and more effective VSOD models exploit deep neural networks to extract features and use some mechanisms such as ConvLSTM, optical flow, and self-attention to explore spatiotemporal information. More specifically, Le and Sugimoto [18] present an end-to-end 3D fully convolutional network that uses 3D filters to learn spatial and temporal information and transfer 3D deep features to pixel-level saliency prediction, outputting saliency voxels. Wang *et al.* [19] firstly propose a deep learning model to efficiently detect salient regions in videos and design a novel dynamic saliency information coding scheme, which can learn diverse saliency information and avoid overfitting. Song *et al.* [5] introduce a recurrent network architecture called pyramid dilated bidirectional ConvLSTM and adopt forward and backward ConvLSTM units to extract multi-scale spatiotemporal information. Li *et al.* [20] develop a multi-task motion guided video salient object detection network to detect the most distinctive spatiotemporal information in the video. During the training process, the network learns to use two sub-networks to accommodate two sub-tasks and to make them adapt to each other. Yan *et al.* [9] attempt to learn spatial and temporal cues for both contrast inference and coherence enhancement by utilizing pseudo-labels and some annotations.

Although these methods are efficient for the VSOD task, most of them are short of consideration for long-range spatiotemporal information or only consideration of short-term spatiotemporal information. In this paper, we propose a network that combines short- and long-term analysis, which can learn robust short and long-term spatiotemporal information.

3 The Proposed Architecture

Our goal is to design a network with better extraction capabilities that can extract rich spatiotemporal information from different dimensions. Therefore, we hope to make full

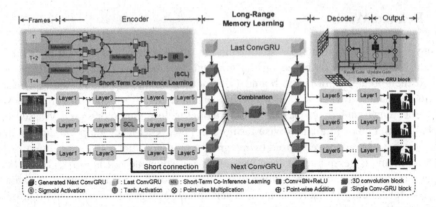

Fig. 2. The overall architecture of our proposed model. The network is composed by two components: short-term co-inference learning (SCL) module and long-range memory learning (LML) module. A video clip with T frames (here we set T=5) is fed into the encoder to extract features.

use of multiple frames features of different lengths in the timeline as a supplement to existing methods and then propose our DTMNet. In this section, two main modules will be introduced in detail: short-term con-inference learning (SCL) module (upper left corner in Fig. 2) and the long-term memory learning (LML) module (the middle part in Fig. 2).

3.1   Short-Term Co-inference Learning

The SCL module consists of two blocks: co-inference feature aggregation (CIFA) and inference reinforcement (IR). CIFA is used to infer the salient object correlations between consecutive frames and learn spatiotemporal information from the current video clip, while IR is designed to emphasize feature representation capabilities by co-inferring each subsequent layer with global features learned from CIFA.

Co-inference Feature Aggregation. We have learned that the feature aggregation process in the middle layers is more effective and can generate accurate and detailed salient feature maps. Based on this, CIFA extracts short-term spatiotemporal information through several "Inference" blocks in the third layer of the encoder (purple blocks in SCL module in Fig. 2). Considering each "Inference" block can only infer spatiotemporal information in two different images, and the dynamic change of consecutive frames is very small, we first use two "Inference" blocks to learn the inherent spatiotemporal information between multiple frames by skipping frames (e.g., 1 and 3 or 3 and 5), and then repeat this operation twice to generate global co-inference feature maps. It should be noted that our video dataset collection is frame skipping, so the true distance for each "Inference" is about 10 frames. Specifically, we define the generated two feature maps as D_1 and D_2, which are 3D-tensors corresponding to width W, height H and channel C. The affinity matrix S between T_1 and T_2 can be computed as:

$$S = D_1^T P^{-1} W P D_2, \tag{1}$$

where P is an invertible matrix and W is a diagonal matrix. Then, we use the softmax function to normalize the rows and columns of the similarity matrix S. In order to emphasis the foreground of the video group and the short-term inherent spatiotemporal information, we first multiply the learned affinity matrix S with it's original tensor D_i and then concate the feature maps corresponding to the two frames. After the combination process, we use convolution blocks to compress the channels of the newly generated feature maps to their original size:

$$Z = Conv.(concat(D_1 * \Gamma(S), D_2 * \Gamma(S^T))), \qquad (2)$$

Here, Γ is the softmax activation function, and *concat* means the concatenation operation. $Conv.$ denotes the convolution kernel.

Finally, we generate short-term inferenced feature maps by combining the two generated blocks Z_i with same process "Inference" in the mid layer of the encoder.

Inference Reinforcement. After obtaining the global co-inference feature maps from co-inference feature aggregation block, we propose an inference reinforcement block to enhance the effectiveness of the initial saliency map in the third layer, and then perform collaborative inference with each block in the next two layers. As shown in Fig. 2 (red line after CIFA), the newly generated global co-inference feature maps Z is passed to the fourth and fifth layers for each frame. We first use the standard deviation of Gaussian kernel k and maximum function to increase the weight coefficient of salient regions. In detail, each newly generated attention map Z_{i-new} is defined as follows:

$$Z_{i-new} = Max(f_{min,max}(Convg(Z_i, k)), Z_i), \qquad (3)$$

where $Convg$ is a convolution operation with a Gaussian kernel k and zero bias, and $f_{min,max}$ is used to normalize feature map and to make the range of the feature map between $[0, 1]$. Max represents the maximum function. It is designed to enhance the weight of salient regions of the original feature map S. It is worth noting that Z_i is generated from Z via up-sampling of the same size with original.

The above operation filters out unimportant edge information of salient objects though the initial saliency map. In this way, we obtained three new blocks with effective single channel feature maps, which enhanced the initial saliency map while maintaining the same size as the original last three layers in the encoder. Then, we multiply each refined feature map Z_{i-new} by its corresponding layer to obtain the total video group. Unlike other methods that are most independent in encoder process, we propose block co-inferencing for short-term spatiotemporal information and transmit it to the deeper layers. The ith feature map is formulated as:

$$f_*^i = f_i \odot Z_i, \qquad (4)$$

where f_i is the current encoder layer. Z_i is the ith refined feature map and i is between three and five.

3.2 Long-Range Memory Learning

Due to the recent VSOD methods only considering short-term correlations between consecutive frames or treating them as static saliency task, we consider that the spatiotemporal information inferred from SCL is limited and mostly based on the current video group. However, there is still semantic correlation information between long-distance video clips. In order to generate saliency map as accurate as possible, we jointly infer long-range semantic correlation information from two perspectives: temporal information in the current video group and the information from previous video memories.

Stacked Co-inference ConvGRU. As a convolutional counterpart of conventional fully connected LSTM, ConvLSTM has been applied to many video based tasks, such as video super-resolution and video object segmentation. ConvLSTM converts spatial information from this frame to the next, while preserving the temporal dependency of modeling. ConvLSTM consists of one memory cell and three gates: input gate, output gate and forgetting gate. Similar to ConvLSTM, the structure and efficiency of ConvGRU (shown in the upper right corner of Fig. 2) are basically the same as ConvLSTM. ConvGRU is popular in video saliency detection tasks because ConvLSTM is rather time-consuming. Specifically, ConvGRU only has two gates and has fewer activation actions and fewer parameters than ConvLSTM.

For each ConvGRU unit, it consists of a reset gate R_t, an update gate Z_t, a new memory cell $\tilde{H}_t$ and the output H_t. As an accumulator of state information, the memory cell $\tilde{H}_t$ is refreshed through actions between reset gate R_t and an update gate Z_t with current input blocks X_t in this frame and last historical state H_{t-1}. When the input arrives, the reset gate R_t and update gate Z_t will be selectively activated ,and then finally transmitted to the memory cell $\tilde{H}_t$. Specifically, the reset gate R_t is designed to select appropriate information from historical state H_{t-1} and current input X_t for long-term memory. Then, the update gate Z_t is used to select long-term memory and forgetting a certain part of the historical memory. According to the above definitions, a single ConvGRU can be formulated as follows:

$$
\begin{aligned}
Z_t &= \sigma(w_{xz} * X_t + w_{hz} * H_{t-1}), \\
R_t &= \sigma(w_{xr} * X_t + w_{hr} * H_{t-1}), \\
\tilde{H}_t &= f(w_{xh} * X_t + R_t \circ (w_{hh} * H_{t-1})), \\
H_t &= (1 - Z_t) \circ \tilde{H}_t + Z_t \circ H_{t-1},
\end{aligned}
\tag{5}
$$

where σ and f correspond to the sigmoid activation and tanh activation function, respectively. ' $*$ ' denotes the convolution operator and ' $\circ$ ' denotes the Hadamard product. It is note that all the gates (R_t and Z_t), memory cells ($\tilde{H}_t$ and H_{t-1}) and weights (w) are 3D-tensors.

Different from the common stacked convGRU that copies the current frame information as another input into the first ConvGRU block, we design a new co-inference ConvGRU based on the stacked ConGRU for co-inferring spatiotemporal information over a long range time. We adopt a circular method to generate the required information for the next group of ConvGRU in the current group and store it (the dark blue cube in Fig. 2). In the next group, we fuse the memory information from the previous group (the light blue cube in Fig. 2) with the information learned at the front end of the current group, and obtain long-term spatiotemporal information through co-inference. In this way, our new designed co-inference ConvGRU can not only transmit information between the current video group frames, but also transmit the information from multiple previous video groups in chronological order, which can serve as supplementary information for the current video group.

Representation Combination. Considering that the previous modules have parallel relationships on the timeline and only enhance representations of the w and h dimensions, which is effective for SOD tasks, we propose a novel time-dimensional representation combination structure based on 3D convolution. Specifically, we first concate the T feature maps generated by stacked co-inference ConvGRU, and then use 3D convolution block to learn more global spatiotemporal correlation information in the short-term time dimension. Finally, we re-distribute the combined feature maps in the order of stacked co-inference ConvGRU, and generate feature maps with enhanced temporal representation.

4 Experiments

4.1 Experimental Setup

Datasets and Metrics. We train and evaluate the performance of our proposed method on several extensively used video object detection public benchmark datasets: DUTS [21], DAVIS2016 [22], FBMS [23], ViSal [12] and DAVSOD [24], all of which are available online. We adopted maximum F-measure (max$\mathcal{F}$), the structure measure ($\mathcal{S}$) and the mean absolute error (MAE) to evaluate the accuracy of the detected saliency.

Training Sets. The proposed DTMNet is employed on PyTorch-1.0, which is a flexible deep learning platform. We first utilize the DUTS-TR [21] dataset to pre-train backbone: ResNet50 with dilated convolution blocks for singe image saliency learning. After pre-training process, we add the proposed SCL module and LML module to the backbone, and utilize Adam optimizer [25] with learning rate of $5e - 5$ and weight decay of $1e - 5$ to train our network until it converges. In this setting, we take DAVSOD [24], FBMS [23], DAVIS [22] and DUTS [21] as training process and reshape the input images or video groups to 448×448 randomly. It is note that the pre-training process takes approximately 10 hours with 24 epochs and the second training process takes about 15 hours for 15 epochs on a PC with operating system Ubuntu 16.04 and NVIDIA 2080Ti GPU.

Table 1. Effect of each module in terms of max$\mathcal{F}$, $\mathcal{S}$ and MAE on DAVIS2016 and FBMS datasets. "LML", "SC" and "SCL" denote the long-range memory learning module, the stacked co-inference ConvGRU module and the short-term co-inference learning module, respectively. "Final Saliency" corresponds to the DTMNet. The best results are shown in **bold**.

Methods	DAVIS2016			FBMS		
	max$\mathcal{F}$	$\mathcal{S}$	MAE	max$\mathcal{F}$	$\mathcal{S}$	MAE
Backbone	0.709	0.797	0.050	0.708	0.767	0.092
w/ LML	0.880	0.902	0.024	0.871	0.888	0.040
w/ SC	0.869	0.896	0.026	0.871	0.889	0.040
w/ SCL	0.863	0.896	0.024	0.861	0.884	0.040
Final Saliency	**0.887**	**0.910**	**0.021**	**0.877**	**0.896**	**0.036**

4.2 Ablation Analysis

In this section, we will discuss the effectiveness of each main component of the proposed DTMNet on the DAVIS2016 and FBMS datasets, and present overall comparison results in Table 1.

Effectiveness of Different Modules. In this part, we verify the effectiveness of our proposed short-term co-inference learning (SCL) module, long-range memory learning (LML) module and some details in LML module. In Table 1, "w/ LML" and "w/ SCL" denote adding LML and SCL with backbone respectively, and "Final Saliency" means the proposed DTMNet. Obviously, "w/ LML" and "w/ SCL" outperform the backbone in terms of all the evaluation metrics, and the performance of "Final Saliency" outperforms "w/ LML" and "w/ SCL", which proves the effectiveness of the SCL module and the LML module.

Besides, in order to prove the effectiveness of the LML module, we compare the versions of "w/ SC" and "w/ LML", where "w/ SC" means ignoring the long-range information and only considering the short-term spatiotemporal information between the current video clips. "SC" is the stacked co-inference ConvGRU module. From Table 1, we can see that "w/ LML" obtains a performance improvement of 1.1% for the max F-measure, 0.6% for the S-measure and 0.2% for MAE in the DAVIS2016 dataset compared to "w/ SC". Overall, the performance gradually improves through the different modules in our method. It is worth noting that the performance of "w/ SC" and "w/ LML" on the DAVIS2016 is obviously different, while the performance on the FBMS dataset is similar, because the DAVIS2016 frames are continuous, while FBMS frames are skip (20 frames at a time). That is to say, a video clip (5 frames) in FBMS may exceed 100 frames on the timeline, which will make our LML module useless.

4.3 Comparison with the State-of-the-Art Methods

Quantitative Comparison. We compare our video saliency network with other state-of-the-art image/video saliency models for quantitative comparison, including two

Table 2. Quantitative evaluation in terms of max$\mathcal{F}$, $\mathcal{S}$ and MAE scores in four popular datasets. ↑ indicates higher scores on the metric are better and ↓ presents lower scores on the metric are better. "-" indicates no reported. The top three performances are shown in red, green and blue respectively.

	DAVIS2016			FBMS			ViSal			DAVSOD		
	max$\mathcal{F}$↑	$\mathcal{S}$↑	MAE↓	max$\mathcal{F}$↑	$\mathcal{S}$↑	MAE↓	max$\mathcal{F}$↑	$\mathcal{S}$↑	MAE↓	max$\mathcal{F}$↑	$\mathcal{S}$↑	MAE↓
DSS	0.720	0.791	0.059	0.760	0.831	0.080	0.917	0.925	0.024	0.545	0.630	0.112
BMPM	0.769	0.834	0.046	0.791	0.844	0.056	0.925	0.930	0.022	0.599	0.704	0.089
SCOM	0.783	0.832	0.048	0.797	0.794	0.079	0.831	0.762	0.122	0.464	0.599	0.220
SCNN	0.714	0.783	0.064	0.762	0.794	0.095	0.831	0.847	0.071	0.532	0.674	0.128
DLVS	0.708	0.794	0.061	0.759	0.794	0.091	0.852	0.881	0.048	0.521	0.657	0.129
FGRN	0.783	0.838	0.043	0.767	0.809	0.088	0.848	0.861	0.045	0.573	0.693	0.098
MBNM	0.861	0.887	0.031	0.816	0.857	0.047	0.883	0.898	0.020	0.520	0.637	0.159
PDBM	0.855	0.882	0.028	0.821	0.851	0.064	0.888	0.907	0.032	0.572	0.698	0.116
RCR	0.848	0.886	0.027	0.859	0.872	0.053	0.906	0.922	0.026	0.653	0.741	0.087
SSAV	0.860	0.892	0.028	0.865	0.879	0.040	0.938	0.943	0.021	0.603	0.724	0.092
LSTI	0.880	0.827	0.031	0.795	0.816	0.084	0.909	0.922	0.027	-	-	-
PSCA	0.880	0.902	0.022	0.837	0.868	0.040	0.940	0.946	0.017	0.655	0.741	0.086
Ours	0.887	0.910	0.021	0.877	0.896	0.036	0.948	0.949	0.014	0.670	0.764	0.079

image salient object detection methods (DSS [27], BMPM [28]) and ten deep learning methods (SCOM [29], SCNN [30], DLVS [19], FGRN [11], PDBM [5], MBNM [31], RCRNet [9], SSAV [24], LSTI [32] and PSCA [10]). By utilizing the same code provided by Fan et al. [24] to compute metrics, Table 2 shows the quantitative evaluation of maximum F-measure, S-measure, and mean absolute error with existing methods. As can be seen, our proposed methods outperforms all state-of-the-art image/video saliency models in terms of all the evaluation metrics, which demonstrates the effectiveness of the proposed DTMNet, even on the challenging datasets DAVSOD. For image salient detection methods (e.g., DSS [27], BMPM [28]), they perform better than some traditional non-deep learning methods in video salient datasets, especially for salient objects that are obvious in each video group (e.g., ViSal). However, for some challenging datasets containing multiple salient objects (e.g., FBMS and DAVSOD), where moving objects are different from these salient objects in a single image, image saliency detection methods cannot distinguish continuous salient objects in moving videos.

Visual Comparison. We list 11 recent state-of-the-art methods including MST [26], SCOM [29], SCNN [30], DLVSD [19], FGRN [11], MBNM [31], PDBM [5], RCR [9], SSAV [24], LSTI [32], PSCA [10] for visual comparison with our method (some methods don't show their saliency maps). It is worth noting that due to the different or incomplete datasets given by some methods, we have not given a comparison of all methods and only select examples in ViSal, FBMS and DAVIS2016 datasets. As shown in Fig. 3, the proposed method not only accurately distinguishes salient objects in videos, but also obtains accurate and continuous salient images in different challenging application

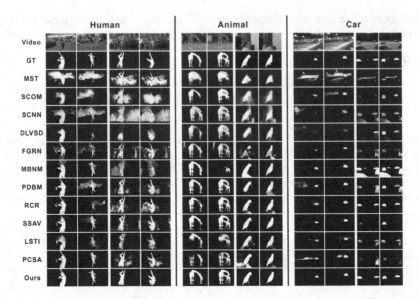

Fig. 3. The visual comparison examples of saliency maps produced by our proposed method and several state-of-the-art saliency methods. The 1–13th rows show the input frames, ground truth, and the results of state-of-the-art methods. The last row is our saliency maps.

scenarios. For the human category in Fig. 3, there is a lot of interference between the people in the background and the people in the foreground, which leads to many algorithms recognizing the background as a prominent object. For the car category which has a rapid displacement in Fig. 3, the non-salient objects with dynamic changes can also cause a certain degree of interference with salient objects. However, our proposed DTMNet can well recognize the salient objects in these video scenes, indicating that our network can utilize short-term and long-term spatiotemporal information to discover continuous dynamic movement changes and effectively solve the aforementioned problems.

5   Conclusions

In this paper, we focus on video saliency object detection by emphasizing the short- and long-term spatiotemporal information, and propose a dual temporal memory network (DTMNet). The DTMNet is mainly composed of two modules: a short-term co-inference learning (SCL) sub-module and a long-range memory learning (LML) sub-module. Experimental evaluations on four datasets indicate that the proposed method provides more accurate video saliency maps compared to the state-of-the-art video saliency detection methods. In further work, we will focus on replacing the backbone with a lightweight networks to improve the detection speed while maintain the accuracy.

Acknowledgments. This work was supported in part by the National Key Research and Development Program of China under Grant 2018AAA0100400, and in part by the National Science Fund of China under Grant 62272235 and Grand U21B2044.

References

1. Wei, Y., et al.: STC: A simple to complex framework for weakly-supervised semantic segmentation. IEEE Trans. Pattern Anal. Mach. Intell. **39**(11), 2314–2320 (2017)
2. Itti, L.: Automatic foveation for video compression using a neurobiological model of visual attention. IEEE Trans. Image Process. **13**(10), 1304–1318 (2004)
3. Wu, H., Li, G., Luo, X.: Weighted attentional blocks for probabilistic object tracking. Vis. Comput. **30**(2), 229–243 (2014)
4. Zhang, Z., Fidler, S., Urtasun, R.: Instance-level segmentation for autonomous driving with deep densely connected MRFs. In: IEEE International Conference on Computer Vision and Pattern Recognition, pp. 669–677 (2016)
5. Song, H., et al.: Pyramid dilated deeper ConvLSTM for video salient object detection. In: Ferrari, V., Hebert, M., Sminchisescu, C., Weiss, Y. (eds.) ECCV 2018. LNCS, vol. 11215, pp. 744–760. Springer, Cham (2018). https://doi.org/10.1007/978-3-030-01252-6_44
6. Dosovitskiy, et al.: FlowNet: learning optical flow with convolutional networks. In: IEEE International Conference on Computer Vision, pp. 2758–2766 (2015)
7. Liang, M., Yang, B., Wang, S., Urtasun, R.: Deep continuous fusion for multi-sensor 3D object detection. In: Ferrari, V., Hebert, M., Sminchisescu, C., Weiss, Y. (eds.) ECCV 2018. LNCS, vol. 11220, pp. 663–678. Springer, Cham (2018). https://doi.org/10.1007/978-3-030-01270-0_39
8. Shi, X., Chen, Z., Wang, H., Yeung, D.Y., Wong, W.K., Woo, W.C.: Convolutional LSTM network: a machine learning approach for precipitation nowcasting. In: Advances in Neural Information Processing Systems, pp. 802–810 (2015)
9. Yan, P., et al.: Semi-supervised video salient object detection using pseudo-labels. In: IEEE International Conference on Computer Vision, pp. 7284–7293 (2019)
10. Gu, Y., Wang, L., Wang, Z., Qin, H.: Pyramid constrained self-attention network for fast video salient object detection. In: Association for the Advance of Artificial Intelligence, pp. 10869–10876 (2020)
11. Li, G., et al.: Flow guided recurrent neural encoder for video salient object detection. In: IEEE International Conference on Computer Vision and Pattern Recognition, pp. 3243–3252 (2018)
12. Wang, W., Shen, J., Shao, L.: Consistent video saliency using local gradient flow optimization and global refinement. IEEE Trans. Image Process. **24**, 4185–4196 (2015)
13. Chen, C., Li, S., Wang, Y., Qin, H., Hao, A.: Video saliency detection via spatial-temporal fusion and low-rank coherency diffusion. IEEE Trans. Image Process. **26**, 3156–3170 (2017)
14. Liu, Z., Zhang, X., Luo, S., Le Meur, O.: Superpixel-based spatiotemporal saliency detection. IEEE Trans. Circ. Syst. Video Technol. **24**, 1522–1540 (2014)
15. Liu, Z., Li, J., Ye, L., Sun, G., Shen, L.: Saliency detection for unconstrained videos using superpixel-level graph and spatiotemporal propagation. IEEE Trans. Circ. Syst. Video Technol. **27**, 2527–2542 (2017)
16. Fang, Y., Lin, W., Chen, Z., Tsai, C., Lin, C.: A video saliency detection model in compressed domain. IEEE Trans. Circuits Syst. Video Technol. **24**(1), 27–38 (2014)
17. Xi, T., Zhao, W., Wang, H., Lin, W.: Salient object detection with spatiotemporal background priors for video. IEEE Trans. Image Process. **26**(7), 3425–3436 (2017)
18. Le, T.-N., Sugimoto, A.: Deeply supervised 3D recurrent FCN for salient object detection in videos. In: The 28th British Machine Vision Conference, pp. 1–13 (2017)

19. Wang, W., Shen, J., Shao, L.: Video salient object detection via fully convolutional networks. IEEE Trans. Image Process. **27**, 38–49 (2018)
20. Li, H., Chen, G., Li, G., Yu, Y.: Motion guided attention for video salient object detection. In: IEEE International Conference on Computer Vision, pp. 7274–7283 (2019)
21. Wang, L., et al.: Learning to detect salient objects with image-level supervision. In: IEEE International Conference on Computer Vision and Pattern Recognition, pp. 136–145 (2017)
22. Perazzi, F., Pont-Tuset, J., McWilliams, B., Van Gool, L., Gross, M., Sorkine-Hornung, A.: A benchmark dataset and evaluation methodology for video object segmentation. In: IEEE Conference on Computer Vision and Pattern Recognition, pp. 724–732 (2017)
23. Brox, T., Malik, J.: Object segmentation by long term analysis of point trajectories. In: Daniilidis, K., Maragos, P., Paragios, N. (eds.) ECCV 2010. LNCS, vol. 6315, pp. 282–295. Springer, Heidelberg (2010). https://doi.org/10.1007/978-3-642-15555-0_21
24. Fan, D., Wang, W., Cheng, M., Shen, J.: Shifting more attention to video salient object detection. In: IEEE Conference on Computer Vision and Pattern Recognition, pp. 8554–8564 (2019)
25. Kingma, D.P., Ba, J.: Adam: a method for stochastic optimization. Comput. Sci (2014)
26. Tu, W., He, S., Yang, Q., Chien, S.: Real-time salient object detection with a minimum spanning tree. In: IEEE International Conference on Computer Vision and Pattern Recognition, pp. 2334–2342 (2016)
27. Hou, Q., Cheng, M., Hu, X., Borji, A., Torr, P.: Deeply supervised salient object detection with short connections. In: IEEE Conference on Computer Vision and Pattern Recognition (2017)
28. Zhang, L., Dai, J., Lu, H., Gang, W.: A Bi-directional message passing model for salient object detection. In: IEEE Conference on Computer Vision and Pattern Recognition (2018)
29. Chen, Y., Zou, W., Tang, Y., Li, X., Xu, C., Komodakis, N.: SCOM: spatiotemporal constrained optimization for salient object detection. IEEE Trans. Image Process. **27**, 3345–3357 (2018)
30. Tang, Y., Zou, W., Jin, Z., Chen, Y., Hua, Y., Li, X.: Weakly supervised salient object detection with spatiotemporal cascade neural networks. In: IEEE Transactions on Circuits and Systems for Video Technology, pp. 1973–1984 (2019)
31. Li, S., Seybold, B., Vorobyov, A., Lei, X., Kuo, C.-C.J.: Unsupervised video object segmentation with motion-based bilateral networks. In: Ferrari, V., Hebert, M., Sminchisescu, C., Weiss, Y. (eds.) ECCV 2018. LNCS, vol. 11207, pp. 215–231. Springer, Cham (2018). https://doi.org/10.1007/978-3-030-01219-9_13
32. Chen, C., Wang, G., Peng, C., Zhang, X., Qin, H.: Improved robust video saliency detection based on long-term spatial-temporal information. IEEE Trans. Image Process. **29**, 1090–1100 (2020)

Cross-Modality Fused Graph Convolutional Network for Image-Text Sentiment Analysis

Qianhui Tan, Xinyang Shen, Zhiyuan Bai, and Yunbao Sun$^{(\boxtimes)}$

The Engineering Research Center of Digital, Forensics, Ministry of Education and Collaborative Innovation Center of Atmospheric Environment and Equipment Technology, Nanjing University of Information Science and Technology, Nanjing 210000, China
tanqianhui@aliyun.com, sunyb@nuist.edu.cn

Abstract. Image-text sentiment analysis aims to mine the emotional semantics conveyed by image and text information. Psychological research shows that the conveyed sentiment depends on the long-range correlation and interaction of sentiment contextual features within and between the modalities of text and image. However, most of the previous works use the feature stitching strategy based on gating and attention mechanism to fuse image-text data, and do not fully exploit the relationship within and between modalities. In this paper, we propose a cross-modality fused graph convolutional network for image-text sentiment classification. The proposed network reasons on intra-modal and inter-modal graphs to realizes the fusion between text and image. In addition, the huge intra class variability of multimodal data affects the accuracy of sentiment analysis. Therefore, we design a sample sentiment similarity loss function to help the model learn sentiment-related similar features from image and text data. Extensive experiments on image-text sentiment datasets show that the proposed network outperforms the existing sentiment analysis models.

Keywords: Image-text Sentiment Analysis · Graph Convolutional Network · Sentiment Similarity

1 Introduction

Personal sentiment is an important attribute of human society. In recent years, with the rapid development of mobile internet technology, people are more and more prone to express their emotions through posting images and words through social media, such as webchat, Facebook, et.al. Figure 1 shows some examples of social media posts with text and images. It can be seen that text and the corresponding image content complement each other in emotional expression. Efficient and correct extraction and analysis of emotions from social media data have a wide range of applications in advertising recommendation, user behavior prediction and many other fields. Therefore, the task

This work was supported in part by National Key Research and Development Program under Grant 2022YFC2405600, in part by the National Natural Science Foundation of China under Grant 62276139 and Grant U2001211.

of image-text sentiment analysis has attracted extensive attention from both academia and industry. However, emotion semantics are more abstract and complex. Due to the correlation between the image and the corresponding text description in social media, compared with the single modal image sentiment analysis task, the joint information of the image-text two modalities can make full use of the complementary advantages between the image and the text information, so as to achieve more accurate sentiment analysis.

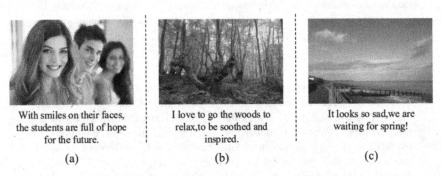

With smiles on their faces, the students are full of hope for the future.	I love to go the woods to relax, to be soothed and inspired.	It looks so sad, we are waiting for spring!
(a)	(b)	(c)

Fig. 1. Examples of text and images in social media.

Psychological research shows that the joint contextual expression of emotional elements in images and texts plays the key role in stimulating human emotion [1, 2]. To be specific, related content in images and texts and their associated emotional content in their respective modalities evoke emotions [3]. Hence, the key of image-text sentiment analysis is how to efficiently capture the sentiment correlation between the two modalities and fully integrate them. Existing image-text sentiment analysis methods mainly use gated attention mechanism to simply fuse the two modalities and concatenate the weighted feature for sentiment classification. Although these methods can achieve better results than single-modal sentiment analysis models, the simple attention mechanism cannot well capture the complex emotional interactions between two modal features. Graph convolutional networks can model unstructured sentiment connections between modal features through the edge link between nodes [4, 5] it has practical applications in cross-modality tasks like image caption [6] and sarcasm detection [7]. The huge intra-class differences and inter-class similarities among multimodal sentiment data has a great negative impact on sentiment analysis. Therefore, we not only need to learn the emotional connection between the features of a single sample, but also need to mine the emotional connection between several image-text samples, so as to assist the model to learn emotional features more efficiently. Inspired by the above discussion, firstly, we proposed cross-modality fused graph convolutional module to establish emotional associations within a single modality and between modality features, thereby enhancing the overall emotional contextual representation of image-text features. Concretely, we construct modal graphs and cross-modal interaction graphs to explicitly connect visual information and corresponding text content, and assign weights to edges of graph by computing the sentiment similarity of node features. Through graph convolution operations, our model can dynamically aggregate target sentiment information in modal features efficiently. Then, in order to mitigate the impact of intra-class differences in affective features, we designed a sample sentiment similarity loss function. Based on the labels of batch samples, we compare the global sentiment similarity of samples belong to the same class in a batch to help model learn the key features of similar emotional expression from complex image-text features.

The main contributions of our work are summarized as follows:

(1) We propose a cross-modality fused graph convolutional network for image-text sentiment analysis based on cross-modality fused graph convolutional module which can help model aggregate single-modal emotional context features and learn the emotional connection between two modalities. Experiments show that the proposed architecture can efficiently align and fuse features of image and text.

(2) We propose a sample sentiment similarity loss function is proposed to assist the network learn common features related to the target sentiment category from multimodal data by comparing the global sentiment similarity of positive samples. Compared with the previous single image-text emotion representation model, our model can capture the global co-occurrence characteristics of the dataset which improve the performance of the sentiment classification.

2 Related Work

2.1 Image-text Sentiment Analysis

Compared with traditional single-modal sentiment data, multi-modal data provides richer features for sentiment analysis tasks. How to realize the alignment and fusion of the two modal features is the key to realize the image-text sentiment analysis. You et al. [8] proposed a cross-modality consistency regression (CCR) method to jointly learn text and sentiment features by applying consistency constraints on related but different modality features. Chen et al. [9] considered emojis in Twitter as additional semantics for sentiment analysis by learning an amalgam emoji embedding. Hu et al. [10] proposed a multi-modal sentiment analysis model to study the potential emotions of users through a comprehensive study of text, images and tags on social media. Xu et al. [11] rely on visual features of objects and scenes to identify important sentence words through attention mechanism. Aiming at the interaction between different modalities, Xu et al. [12] proposed a co-memory network for multi-modal sentiment prediction, which iteratively explores the mutual relationship between images and texts. Huang et al. [13] combined an attention module with a mode-gated LSTM to study the complementary cross-modal information of a given image-text pair. In order to predict people's emotions after reading news articles, Guo et al. [14] introduced two multimodal news datasets and proposed a layout-driven network. Considering the connection between social images, Xu et al. [15] proposed a Hierarchical Deep Fusion (HDF) network to study the cross-modal correlation at different levels. Huang et al. [16] used a hybrid fusion strategy to combine single-modal features with internal cross-modal interactions to predict image-text sentiment. Most of the above methods use gating or attention mechanism to eliminate redundant information in multi-modal data, and only concatenate the global sentiment feature vectors of text and image, and then send them to the multi-layer perceptron for fusion to predict the sentiment category, without making full use of the sentiment correlation between the two modalities, which leads to suboptimal performance of the model. In addition, it is not enough to only consider the information interaction between modalities, and the data between modalities also have a certain sentiment correlation. Obtaining the relationship dependence of the data between modalities can obtain a more accurate single-modal sentiment representation, thereby improving the overall performance of the image-text sentiment analysis model.

2.2 Graph Neural Networks

Models based on graph neural networks (GNN), including graph convolutional network (GCN) [5] and graph attention network (GAT) [4] have achieved promising performance in many recent research studies, such as visual representation learning [17], text representation learning [18], and recommendation systems. Further, there are also some research studies explored graph models to deal with the multimodal tasks, such as multimodal sentiment detection, multimodal named entity recognition, cross-modal video moment retrieval, multimodal neural machine translation. In the task of image-text sentiment analysis, Yang et al. first proposed MGNN [19], a graph representation learning based sentiment classification network.

3 Methodology

This section will introduce the proposed cross-modality fused graph convolutional network in detail. Figure 2 shows the overall architecture of the sentiment analysis model in this paper, which consists of three parts: image-text feature extraction module (FEM), cross-modality fused graph convolutional module (CMFGCM), and global fusion module (GFM). In the graph and text feature extraction module, the pre-trained Bert-base model and ResNet50 model are used as feature extractors to obtain the initial image and text features which are expanded into node vector representations in modality graphs. Secondly, the cross-modality fused graph convolutional module is designed. The modal graph and multi-modal interaction graph of node features are constructed by calculating the emotional similarity between nodes. The intra-modal and inter-modal emotional context features are aggregated by dynamic reasoning on the graph to enhance the expression level of emotional semantics. Then, a global fusion module is used to calculate the attention coefficients of each node vector and fuse them with weights to obtain the global representation of the image-text sentiment. Finally, the network learning is guided by the sentiment classification loss function and the sample sentiment similarity loss function.

3.1 Feature Extraction Module (FEM)

For text processing, given a sequence of words $s = \{w_i\}_{i=1}^n$, where n is the length of text s. We first use the pre-trained Bert model to map each word w_i into a text sentiment feature $T = \{t_C, t_1, t_2, ..., t_S\}$, $T \in R^{n_t \times d_t}$ with dimension d_t, where each sentiment vector can be regarded as a node representation in the subsequent modal graph of cross-modality fused graph convolutional module.

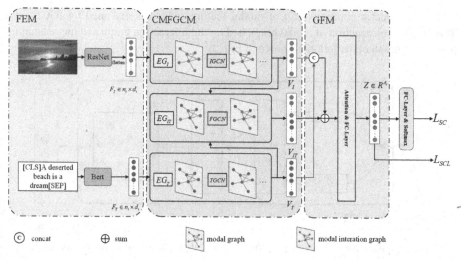

Fig. 2. The framework of the model proposed. Note that EG_m denotes the edge generator for modality, and $IGCN$, $TGCN$, $FGCN$ respectively represent graph convolution of image, text and multimodal fusion modality, L_{SC} represents loss function of sentiment classification and L_{SCL} represents sample sentiment similarity comparison loss function.

For image features, given an image corresponding to a text feature T, the image data is first input into the pre-trained ResNet, and the image sentiment features $I_c' \in R^{p_i \times p_i \times d_i}$ output by the last convolution layer of ResNet are taken, where $p_i \times p_i$ is the size of the feature map and d_i is the number of channels of the image feature. Due to the subsequent use of emotion semantics to enhance the graph convolution module for multimodal feature interaction, it is necessary to make the dimension of the embedding vector of the image feature node correspond to the embedding vector of the text feature node. We use the fully connected layer to change the dimension of I_c' and arrange it according to the spatial grid, and expand the image emotion features into the final image node features $I' = \{i_1', i_2', ..., i_{n_i}'\}, I' \in R^{n_i \times d_t}$, where $n_i = p_i \times p_i$ and $I' = flatten(I_c'W_I + b_I)$ with *flatten* represents the expansion of the spatial dimension of the feature map into one dimension.

3.2 Cross-Modality Fused Graph Convolutional Module (CMFGCM)

There are unstructured connections between different elements in the modal data, and there are certain emotional associations between the data of different modalities. Using the emotional connection between data for reasoning can enhance the emotional semantic expression of single-modal and multi-modal fusion data. In addition, graph models have natural advantages in relation modeling. Therefore, we design an cross-modality fused graph convolutional module. In order to achieve multi-modal feature interaction while enhancing the emotional semantic expression of single-modal node features, we construct modal graphs and modal interaction graph for single-modal emotional features and initial fusion emotional features, and use IGCN, TGCN, and FGCN for inference, aggregating node features related to the target emotion. In particular, the initial fusion feature is a vector concatenation of modal features which is reasoned by IGCN and TGCN. The construction of modal graph and modal interaction graph and the reasoning process of graph convolution is shown in Fig. 3.

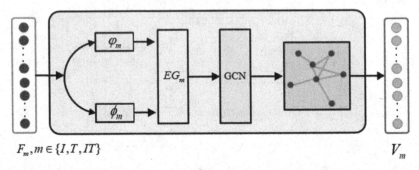

$$F_m, m \in \{I, T, IT\} \qquad\qquad\qquad\qquad\qquad V_m$$

Fig. 3. Construction and reasoning process of modal graph and modal interaction graph.

Given specific modal characteristics of emotional node V_m, $m \in \{T, I, F\}$, m represents the type of modalities, T, I, F, respectively, on behalf of the text, images and fusion sentiment data. Firstly, V_m is embedded into the new feature space by linear transformation functions φ_m and ϕ_m, then transformed feature vector $\varphi_m(v_m)$ and $\phi_m(v_m)$ is fed into the edge generation unit EG_m, and the emotional connection between node features are captured by calculating the similarity between node features. Calculation process is as follows:

$$\varphi_m(v_m^i) = W_{\varphi_m} v_m^i \tag{1}$$

$$\phi_m(v_m^i) = W_{\varphi_m} v_m^i \tag{2}$$

$$R_m(v_m^i, v_m^j) = \frac{\left\langle \varphi_m(v_m^i), \phi_m(v_m^j) \right\rangle}{\left\| \varphi_m(v_m^i) \right\| \left\| \phi_m(v_m^j) \right\|} \tag{3}$$

where, the formula (1) (2) represents the sentiment feature embedding, $R_m(,,)$ represents the similarity calculation function between nodes, W_{φ_m} and W_{φ_m} are linear transformation parameters that can be learned by backpropagation, and i, j represent the third and fourth node features. Then, the emotional association graph is constructed by using the calculated node similarity coefficient, which focuses on the design of the adjacency matrix. The adjacency matrix is computed as follows:

$$A_m^{i,j} = \frac{\exp(R_m(v_m^i, v_m^j))}{\sum_{k=1}^{L} \exp(R_m(v_m^i, v_m^k))} \tag{4}$$

$$\tilde{A}_m = A_m + I \tag{5}$$

where, L represents the number of nodes and I is the diagonal unit moment added to alleviate the problem of vanishing gradient and degradation. Through adjacency matrix $\tilde{A}_m$, the information interaction between two nodes with high emotional semantic similarity is enhanced, and the emotion expression of irrelevant node features is suppressed.

Finally, we aggregate node features with strong sentiment expression in single-modal data by graph convolution:

$$V_m^{(l+1)} = \sigma(\tilde{A}_m^{(l)} V_m^{(l)} \theta_m^{(l)}) \tag{6}$$

where, $\theta_m^{(l)}$ is the learnable parameter matrix of layer l graph convolution and $\sigma(\cdot)$ is the ReLU activation function. To prevent over smoothing caused by a large number of layers, we set the number of graph convolution layers to 2.

Note that when $m = IT$, F_{IT} is the concatenation of $V_I^{(M)}$ and $V_T^{(M)}$, M represents number of graph convolution layers.

3.3 Global Fusion Module (GFM)

In Sect. 3.2, the fusion node feature $V_{IT} \in R^{(n_t+n_i) \times d_t}$ of text and image is obtained through single-modal feature aggregation and multi-modal emotional interaction learning. Obviously, the sentiment feature vector with dimension $(n_t + n_i) \times d_t$ cannot be directly used for sentiment classification tasks. Thus, the fusion modal features related to the emotion display of labels in the fusion features are retrieved, and the attention weight is calculated as follows:

$$\tilde{q}_i = GELU(f_i W + b_1)W_2 + b_2 \tag{7}$$

$$q_i = \exp(\frac{\tilde{q}_i}{\sum_{j=1}^{n_t+n_i} \tilde{q}_j}) \tag{8}$$

The global features $Z \in R^{d_t}$ based on attention enhancement can be obtained by weighting and adding the attention weights of the computing stations and the features of the fusion nodes:

$$\tilde{Z} = \sum_{i=1}^{n_t+n_i} q_i f_i \tag{9}$$

$$Z = GELU(\tilde{Z} W_Z + b_Z) \tag{10}$$

3.4 Loss Function

The loss function of sentiment classification network in this paper is divided into two parts: sentiment classification loss function and sample sentiment similarity comparison loss function. Among them, the sentiment classification loss function helps the network to learn the embedded representation of single-modal and cross-modal fusion emotional features from the end to end. Due to the abstraction and complexity of emotional semantics, the single sentiment classification loss function has limited emotion recognition performance for some difficult samples. By learning similar sentiment features in the same batch of samples, the auxiliary network can obtain more accurate sentiment classification performance. The final loss function is calculated as follows:

$$L_{all} = L_{SC} + L_{SCL} \tag{11}$$

where, L_{SC} is the loss function of sentiment classification, L_{SCL} is the loss function of sample sentiment similarity comparison. The specific design and calculation of L_{SC} and L_{SCL} are as follows:

Sentiment Classification Loss Function: In Sect. 3.3, the initial fused emotional features are fed into the attention emotional feature fusion module to obtain the global emotional feature vector $Z \in R^{d_t}$ after adaptive fusion, as shown in Fig. 2. In this paper, $Z \in R^{d_t}$ is fed into the fully connected layer and the softmax function is used to highlight the response of the target emotional features to realize the automatic classification of image and text emotions. For the sentiment classification task in this chapter, we will use the cross-entropy loss function. The sentiment classification loss function is calculated as follows:

$$L_{sc} = Cross-Entropy(GELU(ZW_{sc} + b_{sc})) \tag{12}$$

Sample Sentiment Similarity Comparison Loss Function: A batch of M training samples is input into the sentiment classification network in this chapter, and the sentiment feature library $S = [Z_1, Z_2..., Z_M]$, $S \in R^{M \times d_t}$ consisting of M fused sentiment feature vectors $Z \in R^{d_t}$ is obtained, where each sentiment feature vector $Z \in R^{d_t}$ is the global representation of the current sample image-text sentiment. To assist the network to learn the sentiment differences between different samples, firstly, the similarity between each pair of M global sentiment fusion features is calculated:

$$sim(Z_i, Z_j) = \frac{\langle Z_i, Z_j \rangle}{\|Z_i\| \|Z_j\|} \tag{13}$$

Z_i, Z_j represent the global sentiment fusion features of the i th and j th samples in the same training batch, respectively. Then, based on the logsoftmax function, the similarity between the node and other global emotional features is normalized without considering the node itself, and the similar global features in the sample are highlighted. The calculation formula is as shown in Eq. 1, where, τ is the contrastive learning coefficient.

$$l_{i,j} = -\log \frac{\exp(sim(Z_i, Z_j)/\tau)}{\sum_{k=1}^{M} 1_{[k \neq i]} \exp(sim(Z_i, Z_k)/\tau)} \tag{14}$$

For each sample i, in order to ensure that the network can achieve accurate sentiment prediction, it is necessary to reduce the intra-class difference between it and similar positive samples. Therefore, in this paper, the sample sequence number consistent with the sentiment label of sample i in the same training batch is put into the positive sample set P_i. The contrastive learning loss function in this chapter is obtained by summing the sentiment similarity between sample i and all positive samples in P_i. The formula is as follows:

$$L_{SCL} = \sum_{i=1}^{M} \sum_{j=1}^{M} 1_{[j \in P_i]} l_{i,j} \tag{15}$$

4 Experiments

4.1 Dataset

This paper demonstrates the effectiveness of the proposed method on MVSA-Single and MVSA-Multiple dataset [20]. The samples in both datasets are collected from the social media website Twitter, where each image-text pair has a corresponding sentiment label. The samples in MVSA-Single and MVSA-Multiple have three sentiment labels, which are positive, negative and neutral. The sample labels of MVSA-Single are annotated by one annotator, and there are 4511 samples in total. Each sample in MVSA-Single is annotated by three annotators, and the total logarithm of image-text in the dataset is 17024. In this paper, the three data sets are divided into training set, validation set and test set according to the ratio of 8:1:1. The total number of images in the data set and the number of samples in each subset are compared in Table 1.

Table 1. Statistics of the sentiment datasets

Dataset	Train	Val	Test	Total
MVSA-Single	3608	451	452	4511
MVSA-Multiple	13618	1703	1703	17024

4.2 Experimental Settings

Firstly, considering the parameters and computation of the network, in terms of text and image feature extraction, this chapter selects Bert-base [21] and ResNet50 [22] as the encoders of the initial text and image features, respectively. For the training process of the model in MVSA-Single and MVSA-Multiple, the batch size is set to 32,64 respectively, and Adam optimizer is used for network learning to assist the network convergence, where the weight decay of the optimizer is set to 1e-5. The learning rate is initialized to 0.001, and every 10 epochs during training, the learning rate is reduced to the original 0.1.

4.3 Experimental Results and Analysis

In this paper, our model is compared with five existing image-text fusion sentiment analysis algorithms: MultiSentiNet [11], HSAN [23], CoMN [12], MVAN [24], and MGNN [19]. Among them, MultiSentiNet performs image-text fusion sentiment analysis by fusing object feature vectors, scene feature vectors and text feature vectors. HSAN uses cascaded semantic attention network to predict image-text sentiment based on image description. CoMN iteratively performs image-text feature interactions with a co-memory network. MVAN introduces a multi-view attention mechanism into the memory network for sentiment classification. From the perspective of data, MGNN uses graph neural network to discover the co-occurrence features between samples of the dataset. The detailed experimental results are shown in Table 2.

In order to illustrate the advantages of multi-modal data in the richness of sentiment information expression, this chapter also compares the experimental results of single-modal sentiment analysis models on MVSA-Single and MVSA-Multiple. For text and image analysis models, only text and image data in MVSA-Single and MVSA-Multiple are used for training, respectively. As can be seen from Table 2, Bert benefits from the advantage of long sequence relationship modeling brought by the self-attention mechanism, and its accuracy in sentiment classification of single text data is significantly higher than that of CNN and BiLSTM. Therefore, the pre-trained Bert model is used in the selection of feature extractor in this chapter.

It can be seen from the table data that compared with the single modal sentiment analysis model, MultiSentiNet can achieve better results on the task of image-text fusion sentiment analysis. This is because MultiSentiNet extracts two kinds of visual semantic features that can express emotion, scene and target. Furthermore, an attention mechanism guided by visual features is used to highlight important image-text features. Compared with the late multi-modal fusion with MultiSentiNet, CoMN uses the mid-term fusion method, through a common memory network, to gradually let the network perform multi-modal interaction in the process of image and text feature extraction.

Table 2. Experimental results of different models on MVSA-Single, MVSA-Multiple

Modality	Model	MVSA-Single		MVSA-Multiple	
		Acc	F1	Acc	F1
Text	CNN [25]	0.6819	0.5590	0.6564	0.5766
	BiLSTM [26]	0.7012	0.6506	0.6790	0.6643
	Bert [21]	**0.7111**	**0.6970**	0.6759	0.6624
Image	ResNet50 [22]	0.6467	0.6155	0.6188	0.6098
	ResNet101 [22]	0.6534	0.6213	0.6277	0.6139
Image + Text	MultiSentiNet [11]	0.6984	0.6963	0.6886	0.6811
	HSAN [23]	0.6988	0.6690	0.6796	0.6776
	CoMN [12]	0.7051	0.7001	0.6992	0.6983
	MVAN [24]	0.7298	0.7298	0.7236	0.7230
	MGNN [19]	0.7377	0.7270	0.7249	0.6934
	Ours	**0.7436**	**0.7411**	**0.7287**	**0.7245**

Although it can achieve better classification results, but due to the introduction of more noise in the fusion process. Its sentiment classification accuracy still has room for improvement. MVAN improves MultiSentiNet to realize the information interaction among scene, text and target features, so the accuracy of sentiment classification is significantly improved. MGNN starts to use GNN to explore the emotion-related co-occurrence features between samples in the dataset, and the effect of the model is also better than that of the previous models. However, the influence of emotion-related features in a single sample on the construction of the scene and object association graph is not fully considered. Compared with MGNN, the model in this chapter obtains an accuracy improvement of 0.59% and 0.38% on MVSA-Single and MVSA-Multiple datasets, respectively, which benefits from the advantages of the proposed algorithm in two aspects: Firstly, the semantic-enhanced graph convolution module was used to model the relationship between single-modal node features and graph convolution reasoning calculation by constructing a single-modal image spatial graph and a text graph, so as to remove the noise interference within the modal data and obtain more accurate visual and text emotion representation. Secondly, a multi-modal emotional interaction graph was constructed, and the multi-modal emotional features were fully integrated based on the emotional correlation between node features. In addition, the label contrast learning loss function proposed in this paper can also assist the model to more accurately identify the emotion expressed by the image and text data. In Sect. 4.4 of this chapter, detailed ablation experiments are set up to verify the effectiveness of the graph convolution module and loss function proposed in this chapter.

Table 3. Comparison of classification results between the single-modal model and ours

Image				
Text	RT@laurencekinlan I met my hero in cork last night. My bloody Ronnie looks very shameful?	Former youth team member Leo Zuta (right) looks dejected as @ Orlando City SC celebrates the goal	The dark and beautiful Seine in Paris	How to focus on species and have fun killing animals - their lives are vital to them! Selfish, soulless and degenerate Hunter
Label	Postive	Neutral	Postive	Negative
Bert	Negative	Neutral	Postive	Negative
ResNet50	Postive	Postive	Neutral	Postive
Ours	Postive	Neutral	Postive	Negative

As shown in Table 3, this paper provides the actual classification results of different modal optimal models on MVSA-Single and MVSA-Multiple datasets. It can be found that the algorithm in this chapter can accurately predict the emotion category of the image-text data, while the prediction results of the sentiment prediction model based on single modality are often biased. For example, the picture and text example in the first column of the table synthetically expresses the positive emotion of seeing the idol, but if we consider only the text modality, Bert mistakenly classifies this sample as negative emotion because of "shameful", while the smiling face of the figure in the picture clearly expresses the joy of the visual subject. Although the visual information of the image is more intuitive and the content is richer, the emotion category of the sample is not always clear. For example, the scene of the picture shown in the third column of the table lacks visual elements that can accurately express the emotion. The algorithm in this chapter can combine image and text information to obtain the correct classification results. In summary, the sentiment analysis of image and text based on ResNet can effectively alleviate the fuzzy problem of emotional expression of visual semantics.

4.4 Ablation Experiments

In order to verify the improvement effect of semantic enhanced graph convolution and label contrastive learning loss function proposed in this paper on the final classification accuracy of the network, this paper takes the network without semantic enhanced graph convolution module and contrastive learning loss function as baseline. Experiments are carried out on MVSA-Single and MVSA-Multiple datasets by successively adding semantic enhanced graph convolution modules for image, text and multi-modal data and contrastive learning loss functions. The experimental results are shown in Table 4, where IG, TG and FG respectively represent the image modality graph convolution module, the text modality graph convolution module and the fusion feature modality graph convolution module in ITMGCM, and SCL represents the sample emotional similarity comparison loss function.

By comparing the data in the table, it can be found that for the single-modal features extracted by pre-trained Bert and ResNet, IG and TG can improve the performance of baseline to a certain extent. Among them, IG betters than TG in enhancing sentiment representation of unimodal data, Because Bert itself can use the self-attention mechanism to realize the reasoning of the relationship between word vectors, but the high-level emotional features extracted by ResNet are difficult to perceive the overall association between image elements due to the limitation of the receptive field. The experimental results in the fifth row of the Table 4 show that the introduction of cross-modal emotional interaction graph convolution on the basis of emotional semantic enhancement of single-modal features can further enhance the overall emotional context expression of the network. On MVSA-Single and MVSA-Muliple dataset, the accuracy is improved by 1.09% and 2.09%, respectively. In the fifth row of the table, the label contraband learning loss function is introduced on the basis of the model "IG + TG + FG". The classification accuracy of the model can reach 74.36% and 72.87%, and its emotion recognition performance is significantly enhanced, which verifies the auxiliary effect of the label contraband learning loss function proposed in this paper on emotion classification tasks.

4.5 Visualization

In order to intuitively show the role of the semantic-enhanced graph convolution module in the modeling of the graph-text feature relationship, this chapter visualizes the image features output by the last layer of graph convolution in the process of multimodal emotional interaction, highlighting the emotional regions perceived by the network after multimodal feature fusion. The visualization results are shown in Fig. 4, and it can be

Table 4. Comparison of sentiment classification accuracy in ablation experiments

Model	MVSA-Single		MVSA-Multiple	
	Acc	F1	Acc	F1
Baseline	0.7132	0.6938	0.6832	0.6729
IG	0.7141	0.6987	0.6854	0.6735
TG	0.7137	0.6936	0.6871	0.6766
IG + TG	0.7186	0.7073	0.6894	0.6786
IG + TG + FG	0.7295	0.7232	0.7103	0.7189
IG + TG + FG + SCL	0.7436	0.7411	0.7287	0.7245

seen that the model can perceive the visual content corresponding to the semantics of "sky", "snow", "face", and "men" in the text, and give more attention to this part of the image content.

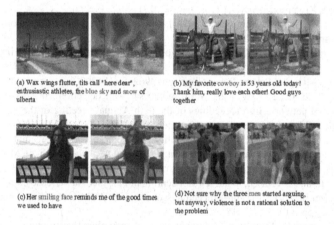

(a) Wax wings flutter, tits call "here dear", enthusiastic athletes, the blue sky and snow of ulberta

(b) My favorite cowboy is 53 years old today! Thank him, really love each other! Good guys together

(c) Her smiling face reminds me of the good times we used to have

(d) Not sure why the three men started arguing, but anyway, violence is not a rational solution to the problem

Fig. 4. Visualization of the sentiment regions that our network focuses on

5   Conclusions

In this paper, a cross-modality fused graph convolutional network based on cross-modality fused graph convolutional module is proposed to fill the defects of single-nodal image sentiment classification in emotional expression. In order to enhance the sentiment representation of single-modal features and utilize the sentiment correlation between modal features for fusion, this paper proposes an cross-modality fused graph convolutional module, which constructs sentiment correlation graphs for single-modal node features and multi-modal fusion node features respectively, and learns the sentiment contextual correlation between node data end-to-end, so as to highlight the contextual features with strong sentiment expression. Finally, due to the diversity and complexity of emotional factors, the model cannot accurately identify as traditional vision tasks. This paper proposes a sample similarity comparison loss function to help the model learn similar features related to emotion by comparing the emotional similarity between positive samples in the same batch, and alleviate the degradation of network recognition performance caused by the huge intra-class differences between similar samples. The experimental results on multi-modal emotion datasets MVAS-Single and MVSA-Multiple also prove the effectiveness of our model.

References

1. Lang, P.J., Bradley, M.M., Cuthbert, B.N.: Emotion, motivation, and anxiety: brain mechanisms and psychophysiology. Biol. Psychiat. **44**(12), 1248–1263 (1998)
2. Houwer, J.D., Hermans, D.: Differences in the affective processing of words and pictures. Cogn. Emot. **8**(1), 1–20 (1994)
3. Brosch, T.: The perception and categorization of emotional stimuli: a review. Cogn. Emot. **24**(3), 377–400 (2010)
4. Veličković, P., Cucurull, G., Casanova, A., Romero, A., Liò, P., Bengio, Y.: Graph attention networks. arXiv preprint arXiv:1710.10903 (2017)
5. Kipf, T.N., Welling, M.: Semi-supervised classification with graph convolutional networks. arXiv preprint arXiv:1609.02907 (2016)
6. Chen, S., Jin. Q., Wang, P., et al.: Say as you wish: Fine-grained control of image caption generation with abstract scene graphs. In: Proceedings of the IEEE/CVF Conference on Computer Vision and Pattern Recognition, pp. 9962–9971 (2020)
7. Liang, B., Lou, C., Li, X., et al.: Multi-modal sarcasm detection via cross-modal graph convolutional network. In: Proceedings of the 60th Annual Meeting of the Association for Computational Linguistics, vol. 1: Long Papers, pp. 1767–1777 (2022)
8. You, Q., Luo, J., Jin, H., et al.: Cross-modality consistent regression for joint visual-textual sentiment analysis of social multimedia. In: Proceedings of the Ninth ACM international conference on Web search and data mining, pp. 13–22 (2016)
9. Chen, Y., Yuan, J., You, Q., et al.: Twitter sentiment analysis via bi-sense emoji embedding and attention-based LSTM. In: Proceedings of the 26th ACM international conference on Multimedia, pp. 117–125 (2018)
10. Hu, A., Flaxman, S.: Multimodal sentiment analysis to explore the structure of emotions. In: Proceedings of the 24th ACM SIGKDD International Conference on Knowledge Discovery & Data Mining, pp. 350–358 (2018)
11. Xu, N., Mao, W.: Multisentinet: A deep semantic network for multimodal sentiment analysis. In: Proceedings of the 2017 ACM on Conference on Information and Knowledge Management, pp. 2399-2402 (2017)
12. Xu, N., Mao, W., Chen, G.: A co-memory network for multimodal sentiment analysis. In: The 41st International ACM SIGIR Conference on Research & Development in Information Retrieval, pp. 929–932 (2018)
13. Huang, F., Wei, K., Weng, J., Li, Z.: Attention-based modality-gated networks for image-text sentiment analysis. ACM Trans. Multimed. Comput. Commun. Appl. **16**(3), 1–19 (2020). https://doi.org/10.1145/3388861
14. Guo, W., Zhang, Y., Cai, X., et al.: LD-MAN: Layout-driven multimodal attention network for online news sentiment recognition. IEEE Trans. Multimed. **23**, 1785–1798 (2020)
15. Xu, J., Huang, F., Zhang, X., et al.: Sentiment analysis of social images via hierarchical deep fusion of content and links. Appl. Soft Comput. **80**, 387–399 (2019)

16. Huang, F., Zhang, X., Zhao, Z., et al.: Image–text sentiment analysis via deep multimodal attentive fusion. Knowl.-Based Syst. **167**, 26–37 (2019)
17. Zhang, J., Chen, M., Sun, H., et al.: Object semantics sentiment correlation analysis enhanced image sentiment classification. Knowl.-Based Syst. **191**, 105245 (2020)
18. Wang, B., Shen, T., Long, G., et al.: Structure-augmented text representation learning for efficient knowledge graph completion. In: Proceedings of the Web Conference 2021, pp. 1737–1748 (2021)
19. Yang, X., Feng, S., Zhang, Y., et al.: Multimodal sentiment detection based on multi-channel graph neural networks: In: Proceedings of the 59th Annual Meeting of the Association for Computational Linguistics and the 11th International Joint Conference on Natural Language Processing, vol. 1: Long Papers, pp. 328–339 (2021)
20. Niu, T., Zhu, S., Pang, L, et al.: Sentiment analysis on multi-view social data. In: MultiMedia Modeling: 22nd International Conference, MMM 2016, Miami, FL, USA, 4–6 Jan 2016, Proceedings, Part II 22. Springer International Publishing, pp. 15–27 (2016)
21. Devlin, J., Chang, M.W., Lee, K., et al.: Bert: Pre-training of deep bidirectional transformers for language understanding. arXiv preprint arXiv:1810.04805 (2018)
22. He, K., Zhang, X., Ren, S., et al.: Deep residual learning for image recognition. In: Proceedings of the IEEE Conference on Computer Vision and Pattern Recognition, pp. 770–778 (2016)
23. Dashtipour, K., Gogate, M., Li, J., et al.: A hybrid Persian sentiment analysis framework: integrating dependency grammar-based rules and deep neural networks. Neurocomputing **380**, 1–10 (2020)
24. Yang, X., Feng, S., Wang, D., et al.: Image-text multimodal emotion classification via multi-view attentional network. IEEE Trans. Multimedia **23**, 4014–4026 (2020)
25. Liu, S., Lee, I.: Sequence encoding incorporated CNN model for Email document sentiment classification. Appl. Soft Comput. **102**, 107104 (2021)
26. Xu, G., Meng, Y., Qiu, X., et al.: Sentiment analysis of comment texts based on BiLSTM. IEEE Access **7**, 51522–51532 (2019)

Local and Global Feature Interaction Network for Endoscope Image Classification

Zhengqi Dong[1], Benzhu Xu[2], Jun Shi[2(✉)], and Liping Zheng[2]

[1] School of Computer Science and Information Engineering, Hefei University of Technology, Hefei, China
[2] School of Software, Hefei University of Technology, Hefei, China
juns@hfut.edu.cn

Abstract. Convolutional Neural Network (CNN) shows great performance in the field of endoscopic image classification in past few years. It can capture local features of endoscopic images, but it fails to exploit global semantic information. Recently transformer is proposed and successfully applied in computer vision, which can model global long-range dependencies based on the self-attention mechanism. Considering the advantages of CNN and transformer, we propose a novel local and global feature interaction network for endoscope image classification. Different from the existed methods fusing CNN and transformer features, our method achieves these two kinds of features interaction during feature learning and further enhances the feature discrimination ability of CNN and transformer features. Specifically, our backbone consists of multiple CNN-FIB-Transformer (CFT) modules which includes CNN block, feature interaction block (FIB) and transformer encoder. Features extracted from CNN block and transformer encoder are fed into our proposed FIB in parallel, which can interact local and global features of endoscopic images through cross-attention mechanism and further improve their own feature representation capability. Furthermore, we also introduce the loss function of prediction alignment to guarantee the prediction consistency of CNN and transformer features, in addition of conventional cross-entropy loss functions for their own features. Experiments on two public endoscope image datasets (Kvasir2 and HyperKvasir) have demonstrated the feasibility and effectiveness of the proposed method for endoscope image classification.

Keywords: Vision Transformer · CNN · Endoscopic image classification · Feature Interaction · Prediction alignment

1 Introduction

Five of the top ten new cancer cases in the world are digestive tract diseases. Early screening and timely clinical intervention are the most reasonable treatment options. As the most commonly used screening method, endoscopy helps surgeons investigate abnormal lesions in the digestive tract and then diagnose them to determine whether they are at risk for cancer. However, surgeons need to check the large number of video frames during the endoscopic screening process, which is time-consuming. Besides, it is

H. Lu et al. (Eds.): ICIG 2023, LNCS 14358, pp. 412–424, 2023.
https://doi.org/10.1007/978-3-031-46314-3_33

prone to high false-positive results due to subjective experience differences of surgeons. Therefore, computer aided diagnosis (CAD) methods which can automatically classify endoscopic images are given more attention.

In the past decades, many automated endoscope image classification methods have been developed. Krishnan et al. [1] extract image contours corresponding to haustra creases in the colon and obtain the curvature of each contour to identify polyps and tumors. Dhandra et al. [2] apply morphological watershed segmentation method to recognize possible anomalies in endoscopic images. Magoulas et al. [3] classify endoscopic images into normal and malignant samples by second-order statistics and discrete wavelet transform-based methodologies. Song et al. [4] integrate multi-scale Gabor transform and local binarized histograms to classify normal and abnormal endoscopic images. However, they essentially use low-level features and thus the performance is limited by the way to design the features and classifier selection.

Convolutional neural network (CNN) [5–9] have been proposed and widely used in endoscope image classification over the past few years. The goal of CNN is to automatically learn deep and high-level features through hierarchical network architecture. Ahmed et al. [10] use AlexNet [5] to achieve gastrointestinal image classification. Ezzat et al. [11] apply multilayer convolution operation to extract high-level features of endoscopic images. Agrawal et al. [12] integrate multiple CNN to enhance the feature representation power. CNN has achieved the satisfactory results for endoscope image classification, which uses the convolution operation to discover the local features. However, it fails to capture global semantic information within the endoscope images which is likely to contribute for classification. Transformer [13] has attracted more attention in recent years, which focuses more on global semantic information through its multi-head self-attention (MHSA) mechanism. As the most representative transformer model in the computer vision community, vision transformer (ViT) [14] splits the image into fixed-size non-overlapping patches, and then converts them into token sequences through a fully connected layer. Finally, the tokens are fed into the transformer encoders which apply MHSA to learn the global semantics. Swin transformer (SwinT) [15] divides input feature maps into different fix-sized local windows, and carries out MHSA computation within each window. Therefore, the computation cost is reduced and SwinT can be scalable to large image scales with linear complexity. In the field of endoscope image classification, Hifuse [16] design a parallel framework of local and global feature blocks to efficiently capture local spatial contextual features and global semantic information representation of features at different scales, respectively. Essentially Hifuse uses the fused local-global features for classification. However, the inconsistency between these two kinds of features is likely to influence the classification performance.

Motivated by the above discussion, we propose a local and global feature interaction network for endoscope image classification. It is composed of multiple CNN-FIB-Transformer (CFT) modules which includes CNN block, feature interaction block (FIB) and transformer encoder. CNN block is designed to extract local features of endoscopy images according to the ResNet [8] architecture, and transformer encoder uses MHSA to explore global semantic information hidden under the endoscopic images. FIB receives the features extracted from CNN block and transformer encoder simultaneously, interacts the local and global features of endoscopic images through cross-attention mechanism and further improves feature representation capability of CNN block and transformer encoder. Finally, two standard cross-entropy loss functions are used to train the two branches of CNN block and transformer encoder, respectively. Furthermore, the loss function of prediction alignment is introduced to guarantee the prediction consistency of CNN-based and transformer-based features and thus strengthen the discrimination performance of features.

The contributions of this paper include:

1) We propose a local and global feature interaction network for endoscopic image classification. It uses CNN to extract the local features, applies the transformer encoder to obtain the global semantic information, and incorporates these two kinds of features through our proposed Feature Interaction Block (FIB), which uses cross-attention to fuse CNN-based local features and transformer-based global features in an interactive fashion.

2) Similar to the class token in ViT, we add an alignment token and introduce a new loss function for prediction alignment which calculates cross-entropy loss based on local features and global features to guarantee the prediction consistency of CNN-based and transformer-based features.

3) We conduct the proposed method on the public endoscope image datasets (Kvasir2 and HyperKvasir). Experimental results demonstrate our method has better classification results and ablation experiment indicates our proposed components have a crucial role in endoscope image classification.

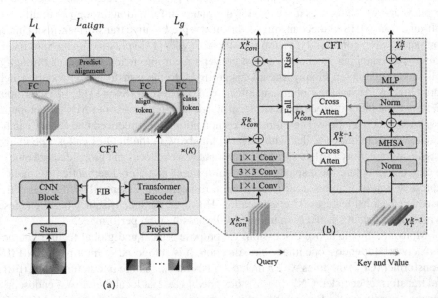

Fig. 1. (a) The Overall Architecture of Our Proposed Network. (b) Expansion Details of CFT Module

2 Methodology

2.1 Overview

The overall architecture of our proposed model is presented in Fig. 1. The backbone of our model contains K CNN-FIB-Transformer (CFT) modules which consist of three parts: CNN block, feature interaction block (FIB), transformer encoder. Stem block is used to extract initial local features of endoscope images, which are then fed to CNN block in first CFT module. On the other hand, we spilt the image into patches, and then, employ Project module to convert the image patches into patch tokens which are fed into transformer encoder in first CFT module. FIB is used to interact with the intermediate layer features of the CNN blocks and transformer encoder, and then return the interaction features to their respective blocks. Then, the augmented features from the CNN block and transformer encoder are fed into the feature extractor of the next CFT module. Finally, CNN-based feature and the class token generated by transformer are input into the fully connection (FC) layer respectively and the corresponding cross entropy loss is calculated. In particular, we introduce alignment token to calculate loss of prediction alignment with CNN feature after FC layer. And three loss functions will be employed to optimize our model.

2.2 Preprocessing

Assuming that original image is $X \in R^{C \times H \times W}$ with image height H, image width W and number of channels C, X is fed to Stem block which consist of a 7×7 convolution layer with a stride of 2, a 3×3 max pooling layer with stride of 2, batch normalization and RELU activation function. In this way, the original image X is preprocessed into X_{con}^0, which is used as input to the CNN block in the first CFT module. The stem operation can be formulated as follows:

$$X_{con}^0 = MaxPool(ReLU(BN(Conv^{7 \times 7}(X))))\qquad(1)$$

On the other hand, following ViT [14], original image X is converted into the patches with fixed-size and then these patches are inputted into Project block which converts the patches into sequence of tokens $(x_1, x_2, \ldots, x_E, \ldots x_M)$ by tokenizing and flattening. $x_i \in R^{D \times 1}(i = 1, \cdots, M)$ is the i-th token and D is the dimension of each token. Then, a class token and an alignment token are appended to the sequence of tokens for classification and prediction alignment. The generated token sequence can be described as $X_T^0 = (x_1, x_2, \ldots, x_E, \ldots x_M, x_{align}, x_{cls}) \in R^{D \times (M+2)}$, which is fed into transformer encoder in the first CFT module. Note that different from original ViT [14], we introduce the alignment token $x_{align} \in R^{D \times 1}$ which aims to guarantee the prediction consistency of CNN-based and transformer-based features and thus narrows down the gap between different kinds of features and image semantics.

2.3 CFT Module

As the core module of our method, the CFT structure is shown in Fig. 1(b). It contains three key components: CNN block, FIB and transformer encoder. CNN block and transformer encoder are able to capture local features and global semantic features of endoscopic images. Meanwhile, FIB is introduced to interact local and global features and further enhance their own feature representational ability.

Our proposed network contains K CFT modules where K equal to 12. The 12 CFT modules are divided into four stages, each of which contains 2, 2, 6 and 2 CFT modules. The specific parameters are shown in Table 1.

Table 1. Four Stages Specific Parameters Details of CFT Module.

Stage	Output Size	CNN Block	CFT FIB	Transformer encoder
1	56×56	$\begin{bmatrix} 1 \times 1, 64 \\ 3 \times 3, 64 \\ 1 \times 1, 256 \end{bmatrix} \times 2$	Cross Attention	$\begin{bmatrix} MHSA-6, 384 \\ 1 \times 1, 1536 \\ 1 \times 1, 384 \end{bmatrix} \times 2$
2	28×28	$\begin{bmatrix} 1 \times 1, 128 \\ 3 \times 3, 128 \\ 1 \times 1, 512 \end{bmatrix} \times 2$	Cross Attention	$\begin{bmatrix} MHSA-6, 384 \\ 1 \times 1, 1536 \\ 1 \times 1, 384 \end{bmatrix} \times 2$
3	14×14	$\begin{bmatrix} 1 \times 1, 256 \\ 3 \times 3, 256 \\ 1 \times 1, 1024 \end{bmatrix} \times 6$	Cross Attention	$\begin{bmatrix} MHSA-6, 384 \\ 1 \times 1, 1536 \\ 1 \times 1, 384 \end{bmatrix} \times 6$
4	7×7	$\begin{bmatrix} 1 \times 1, 256 \\ 3 \times 3, 256 \\ 1 \times 1, 1024 \end{bmatrix} \times 2$	Cross Attention	$\begin{bmatrix} MHSA-6, 384 \\ 1 \times 1, 1536 \\ 1 \times 1, 384 \end{bmatrix} \times 2$

CNN Block. As shown in Fig. 1(b), CNN block adopts traditional bottlenecks architecture which contains a 1×1 down-sampled convolution, a 3×3 spatial convolution, a 1×1 up-sampled convolution, a residual connection between the input and output of the bottleneck and multiple normalization functions and activation functions. The operations can be described:

$$\tilde{X}_{con}^k = f^{1 \times 1}(f^{3 \times 3}(f^{1 \times 1}(X_{con}^{k-1}))) + X_{con}^{k-1} \tag{2}$$

where $f^{1 \times 1}(\cdot)$ and $f^{3 \times 3}(\cdot)$ represent a combination of convolution operation, batch normalization and $ReLU$ activation function. k represents the k-th CFT module. The obtained CNN feature $\tilde{X}_{con}^k$ are inputted into the FIB block. X_{con}^{k-1} represents the output of the CNN block in the previous CFT module.

FIB Block. As shown in Fig. 1(b), the CNN features $\tilde{X}_{con}^k$ and the sequence of tokens X_T^{k-1} from the transformer encoder are fed into FIB. We use a cross-attention approach to blend these two kinds of features.

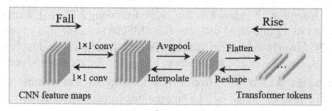

Fig. 2. Fall and Rise for Spatial Alignment of Feature Maps and Sequence of Tokens

Firstly, there is a significant dimensional difference between feature maps and sequence of tokens where the dimension of $\tilde{X}_{con}^k$ is $R^{C \times H \times W}$ but the dimension of X_T^{k-1} is $R^{D \times (M+2)}$. Therefore, A Fall/Rise operation (Fig. 2) is used to implement the spatial dimension alignment:

$$\overline{X}_{con}^k = Fall(\tilde{X}_{con}^k) \tag{2}$$

$$Fall(\cdot) = Flatten(AvgPool(Conv^{1 \times 1}())) \tag{3}$$

where $Flatten(\cdot)$ and $AvgPool(\cdot)$ represent flattening operation and average pooling operation, respectively.

Secondly, we take Q_{con} and Q_T as Query, respectively, the rest as Key and Value for cross-attention, so we setup two sets of trainable parameter matrices $(W_{con}^Q, W_{con}^K, W_{con}^V)$, (W_T^Q, W_T^K, W_T^V) to derive them. The above operators can be expressed as:

$$Q_{con} = \overline{X}_{con}^k \cdot W_{con}^Q, K_{con} = \overline{X}_{con}^k \cdot W_{con}^K, V_{con} = \overline{X}_{con}^k \cdot W_{con}^V$$

$$Q_T = X_T^{k-1} \cdot W_T^Q, K_T = X_T^{k-1} \cdot W_T^K, V_T = X_T^{k-1} \cdot W_T^V \tag{4}$$

where $Q_{con}, K_{con}, V_{con}, Q_T, K_T, V_T \in R^{D \times (M+2)}$.

Finally, after the two sets of query, key, and value are fed into cross-attention modules, we get two kinds of enhanced feature representation. For CNN block, we perform Rise operation on the enhanced image representation to complete the spatial dimension alignment, and then add $\tilde{X}_{con}^k$ to get X_{con}^k, which is used as the input of CNN block in the next layer of CFT module. For transformer encoder, we input the enhanced feature representation $\overline{X}_T^{k-1}$ into transformer encoder for the next step of calculation. The feature interaction uses the following formula:

$$X_{con}^k = (Rise(softmax\left(\frac{Q_{con}K_T^T}{\sqrt{d_k}}\right) \times V_T)) + \tilde{X}_{con}^k \tag{5}$$

$$Rise(\cdot) = interpolate(reshape()) \tag{6}$$

$$\overline{X}_T^{k-1} = softmax\left(\frac{Q_T K_{con}^T}{\sqrt{d_k}}\right) \times V_{con} \tag{7}$$

where $interpolate(\cdot)$ is interpolation operation and $reshape(\cdot)$ denotes dimension conversion operation.

Transformer Encoder. As shown in Fig. 1(b), following ViT [14], each transformer encoder consists of a multi-head self-attention (MHSA) module and a multi-layer perceptron (MLP). LayerNorm are applied before each layer and residual connections in both the self-attention layer and MLP block. Moreover, we receive the enhanced endoscope image representation $\overline{X}_T^{k-1}$ from FIB before transformer feature is fed into the MLP block. The final result X_T^k will be entered into transformer encoder of the CFT at the next level. The above calculation process can be expressed as:

$$X^M = MHSA(LN(X_T^{k-1})) + \overline{X}_T^{k-1} + X_T^{k-1} \tag{8}$$

$$X_T^k = MLP(LN(X^M)) + X^M \tag{9}$$

where $MHSA(\cdot)$, $LN(\cdot)$ and $MLP(\cdot)$ represent multi-head self-attention, Layer Normalization and multi-layer perceptron.

2.4 Endoscope Image Classification

As shown in Fig. 1(b), the full connection layer receives the output X_T^K and X_{con}^K from the last CFT module. After X_{con}^K is processed by the FC layer, we use softmax and the cross-entropy loss function to calculate the loss value:

$$\hat{Y}_i = softmax(FC\left(X_{con}^K\right) \tag{10}$$

$$L_l = \sum_{i=1}^{N} Y_i log\hat{Y}_i \tag{11}$$

where N represents the total number of images, $\hat{Y}_i$ is the predicted label, Y_i is ground truth, $FC(\cdot)$ denotes FC layer, and L_l represents cross-entropy loss function.

The class token x_{cls} is inputed into the FC layer to obtain the classification result, and we also take the cross-entropy loss function here:

$$\tilde{Y}_i = softmax(FC(x_{cls})) \tag{12}$$

$$L_g = \sum_{i=1}^{N} Y_i log\tilde{Y}_i \tag{13}$$

where $\tilde{Y}_i$ is the predicted label and L_g is also cross-entropy loss function.

In order to guarantee the prediction consistency of CNN and transformer features, we intend to use the alignment token x_{align} to align the label predicted by X_{con}^K.Loss function of prediction alignment is applied to make their predictions tend to be consistent, which can be described as follows:

$$\overline{Y}_i = softmax(FC(x_{dis})) \tag{14}$$

$$L_{align} = \sum_{i=1}^{N} argmax(\overline{Y}_i)log\hat{Y}_i \tag{15}$$

where $\overline{Y}_i$ is the predicted label, L_{align} represents cross-entropy loss function, $argmax(\cdot)$ is arguments of the maxima.

Finally, we combine L_l, L_g, and L_{align} as the final loss function.

$$L_{total} = \alpha L_l + \beta L_g + \gamma L_{align} \tag{16}$$

where α, β, γ are hyperparameters.

3 Experiments

3.1 Dataset

The two public endoscope image datasets Kvasir2 [17] and HyperKvasir [18] are used to evaluate our proposed network.

Kvasir2: This dataset contains 8000 endoscope images and 8 categories (z-line, pylorus, cecum, esophagitis, polyps, ulcerative colitis, dyed-lifted-polyps and dyed-resection-margins) as shown in Fig. 3. Each category has 1000 images. The image resolution ranges from 720×576 to 1920×1072 pixels. Following the practice [10, 11, 16], 80% of the images for each category are used as the training set, and the remaining 20% are used as the test set.

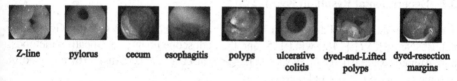

| Z-line | pylorus | cecum | esophagitis | polyps | ulcerative colitis | dyed-and-Lifted polyps | dyed-resection margins |

Fig. 3. Examples of Each Category in Kvasir2 Dataset

HyperKvasir: The dataset contains 10662 images depicting 23 different findings of the gastrointestinal (GI) tract (the findings in the dataset contain anatomical landmarks, pathological findings in the lumen, colon polyps, Barrett's esophagus, ulcerative colitis, etc.). Figure 4 shows sample for each category and their number. The image resolution ranges from 720×576 to 1920×1072 pixels. And the ratio of training-test is set to 8:2.

3.2 Implementation Details

Due to differences in the original image resolution, and to ensure the rigor of the controlled experiment, we first down-sampled the image to 224×244 resolution, and then carry out some image enhancement operations, such as rotation and normalization.

The number of CFT module K is set to 12 and hyperparameters α, β, γ are set to 0.45, 0.45 and 0.1. Adam optimizer is employed to train our model with the initial learning rate 0.0001, the batch size is set to 32, and training epoch is set to 100. Accuracy (ACC) and F1-score (F1) are taken as the evaluation metrics. In our experiment, we implement our framework with PyTorch on a single NVIDIA GeForce RTX 2080Ti GPU card with 11 GB memory.

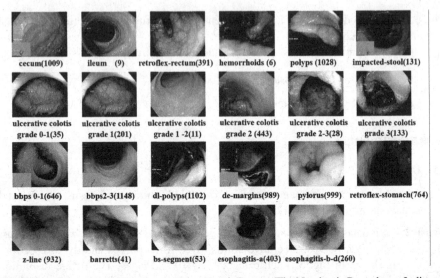

Fig. 4. Examples of Each Category in HyperKvasir Dataset(The Number in Parentheses Indicates the Number of Images)

3.3 Experimental Result on Kvasir2

The representative CNN and transformer methods, AlexNet [5], VGG [6], GoogleNet [7], ResNet [8], ViT [14], SwinT [15] and the endoscope image classification methods, e.g. Ahmed et al.[10], Dalia et al. [11], Agrawal et al. [12], Hifuse [16] are used to compared with our proposed method.

The experimental results on the Kvasir2 dataset are shown in Table 2. The CNN-based approach performs better than the transformer-based approach indicating that CNN has a better ability to capture image features on small datasets. It is worth noting that Hifuse achieves a third-place ranking. It demonstrates that combining local features based on CNN and global features based on transformer can yield more discriminative feature representation. Our method achieves the best results with ACC 90.6% and F1-Score 90.7%. It can be explained that local and global feature interaction through cross attention enhances the representational ability of CNN-based and transformer-based features.

3.4 Experimental Result on HyperKvasir

Compared with Kvasir2 dataset, HyperKvasir dataset is a large-scale endoscope image dataset and few researches are conducted on all the categories. We select 8 categories(cecum, polyps, ulcerative colitis, cleanliness of digestive tract, dyed- lifted-polyps, dyed-resection-margins, Z-line, pylorus) and total 7958 images for experiment, which are the main concerns of the surgeon to assess the performance of our method and. The results are shown in Table 3. The CNN-based and transformer-based method achieve relatively weak effects. Hifuse is better than the CNN-based and transformer-based methods and it can be demonstrated that CNN-based and transformer-based feature

Table 2. The Experimental Result on Kvasir2. (%)

Method	ACC	F1
AlexNet [5]	88.3	88.3
VGG [6]	88.4	88.5
GoogleNet [7]	85.6	85.9
ResNet [8]	89.4	89.5
ViT [14]	73.9	74.0
SwinT [15]	75.1	75.3
Ahmed et al. [10]	87.0	-
Dalia et al. [11]	88.0	-
Agrawal et al. [12]	83.8	-
Hifuse [16]	88.8	88.9
Ours	**90.6**	**90.7**

fusion is conductive to endoscope image classification. In our approach, ACC and F1-scorehave reach 95.9% and 95.8%, respectively. It is worth noting that unlike Kvasir2, there exists uneven distribution of samples and thus poses a great challenge for endoscope image classification. Our results demonstrate that the proposed method can obtain more discriminative feature representation by modeling local context features and global semantic information of endoscope images.

Table 3. The Experimental Result on HyperKvasir. (%)

Method	ACC	F1
AlexNet [5]	94.3	94.1
VGG [6]	94.1	94.1
GoogleNet [7]	90.9	90.8
ResNet [8]	94.9	94.8
ViT [14]	86.1	86.0
SwinT [15]	87.5	87.3
Hifuse [16]	95.3	95.4
Ours	**95.9**	**95.8**

3.5 Ablation Experiment

We evaluate the impact of each component of our model on the Kvasir2 and HyperKvasir dataset. 'CNN block + transformer encoder' refers to the decision integration of the predicted results of CNN block and transformer encoder, which serves as our inference. '+FIB' represents feature interaction in a cross-attention manner for CNN and transformer features. '+Alignment token' means that the alignment token is introduced in the training to guarantee the prediction consistency of CNN-based and transformer-based features.

As shown in Table 4, on the basis of network backbone only CNN block and transformer encoder, with the addition of FIB module, the classification result is more superior than without FIB on two datasets, it implies that the FIB module plays an active role in improving network performance. If alignment token is added on this basis, further improvement is achieved. Summarily, FIB makes features more distinctive by feature interaction. Alignment token guarantee the prediction consistency of CNN and transformer features. All of these make our method acquires better endoscope image classification ability.

Table 4. Ablation Experimental Results on Kvasir2 and HyperKvasir. (%)

Dataset	Kvasir2		HyperKvasir	
Metrics	ACC	F1	ACC	F1
CNN block + Transformer encoder	88.8	89.1	94.4	94.5
+FIB	89.6	89.7	94.8	94.7
+Alignment token	90.6	90.7	95.9	95.8

4 Conclusion

In this paper, we propose a novel local and global feature interaction network for endoscope image classification. To begin with, we extract the local feature and global feature of the endoscope image. Then, we interact these two features through the method of cross-attention. Finally, the feature representational ability of endoscope image is enhanced. Moreover, the loss function of prediction alignment is designed to guarantee the prediction consistency of CNN and transformer features. Experiments on the public datasets Kvasir2 and HyperKvasir demonstrate our method has better endoscope image classification performance.

Acknowledgment. This work was partly supported by the National Natural Science Foundation of China (grant no. 61906058, 61972128), partly supported by the Anhui Provincial Natural Science Foundation (grant no. 1908085MF210), and partly supported by the Fundamental Research Funds for the Central Universities of China (grant no. JZ2022HGTB0285).

References

1. Krishnan, S., Yang, X., Chan, K., Kumar, S., Goh, P.: Intestinal abnormality detection from endoscopic images. In: Proceedings of the 20th Annual International Conference of the IEEE Engineering in Medicine and Biology Society, vol. 20 Biomedical Engineering Towards the Year 2000 and Beyond (Cat. No. 98CH36286). vol. 2, pp. 895–898. IEEE (1998)
2. Dhandra, B., Hegadi, R.: Classification of abnormal endoscopic images using morphological watershed segmentation. In: Proceedings of International Conference on Cognition and Recognition (ICCR-2005). Mysore, India (2005)
3. Magoulas, G.D.: Neuronal networks and textural descriptors for automated tissue classification in endoscopy. Oncol. Rep. **15**(4), 997–1000 (2006)
4. Kodogiannis, V., Lygouras, J.N.: Neuro-fuzzy classification system for wireless-capsule endoscopic images. Int. J. Electr. Comput. Syst. Eng. **2**(1), 55–63 (2008)
5. Krizhevsky, A., Sutskever, I., Hinton, G.E.: Imagenet classification with deep convolutional neural networks. Commun. ACM **60**(6), 84–90 (2017)
6. Simonyan, K., Zisserman, A.: Very deep convolutional networks for large-scale image recognition. arXiv preprint arXiv:1409.1556 (2014)
7. Szegedy, C., et al.: Going deeper with convolutions. In: Proceedings of the IEEE Conference on Computer Vision and Pattern Recognition, pp. 1–9 (2015)
8. He, K., Zhang, X., Ren, S., Sun, J.: Deep residual learning for image recognition. In: Proceedings of the IEEE Conference on Computer Vision and Pattern Recognition, pp. 770–778 (2016)
9. Huang, G., Liu, Z., Van Der Maaten, L., Weinberger, K.Q.: Densely connected convolutional networks. In: Proceedings of the IEEE Conference on Computer Vision and Pattern Recognition, pp. 4700–4708 (2017)
10. Ahmed, A.: Classification of gastrointestinal images based on transfer learning and denoising convolutional neural networks. In: Saraswat, M., Roy, S., Chowdhury, C., Gandomi, A.H. (eds.) Proceedings of International Conference on Data Science and Applications. LNNS, vol. 288, pp. 631–639. Springer, Singapore (2022). https://doi.org/10.1007/978-981-16-5120-5_48
11. Ezzat, D., Afify, H.M., Taha, M.H.N., Hassanien, A.E.: Convolutional neural network with batch normalization for classification of endoscopic gastrointestinal diseases. In: Hassanien, A.E., Darwish, A. (eds.) Machine Learning and Big Data Analytics Paradigms: Analysis, Applications and Challenges. SBD, vol. 77, pp. 113–128. Springer, Cham (2021). https://doi.org/10.1007/978-3-030-59338-4_7
12. Agrawal, T., Gupta, R., Narayanan, S.: On evaluating CNN representations for low resource medical image classification. In: ICASSP 2019–2019 IEEE International Conference on Acoustics, Speech and Signal Processing (ICASSP), pp. 1363–1367. IEEE (2019)
13. Vaswani, A., et al.: Attention is all you need. In: Advances in Neural Information Processing Systems, vol. 30 (2017)
14. Dosovitskiy, A., et al.: An image is worth 16 × 16 words: Transformers for image recognition at scale. arXiv preprint arXiv:2010.11929 (2020)
15. Liu, Z., et al.: Swin transformer: Hierarchical vision transformer using shifted windows. In: Proceedings of the IEEE/CVF International Conference on Computer Vision, pp. 10012–10022 (2021)
16. Huo, X., et al.: Hifuse: Hierarchical multi-scale feature fusion network for medical image classification. arXiv preprint arXiv:2209.10218 (2022)

17. Pogorelov, K., et al.: Kvasir: a multi-class image dataset for computer aided gastrointestinal disease detection. In: Proceedings of the 8th ACM on Multimedia Systems Conference, pp. 164–169 (2017)
18. Borgli, H., et al.: Hyperkvasir, a comprehensive muti-class image and video dataset for gastrointestinal endoscopy. Sci. Data **7**(1), 283 (2020)

Correction to: A Novel Contactless Prediction Algorithm of Indoor Thermal Comfort Based on Posture Estimation

Shuchang Chu, Xiaogang Cheng, Yufeng Zhou, Xintao Hu,
Caoxin Xu, Xiaolong Liu, Qing Wang, and Bin Yang

Correction to:
Chapter 23 in: H. Lu et al. (Eds.): *Image and Graphics*,
LNCS 14358, https://doi.org/10.1007/978-3-031-46314-3_23

In the originally published version of chapter 23, the author name Bin Yang was incorrectly written as Bing Yang. This has been corrected.

The updated original version of this chapter can be found at
ttps://doi.org/10.1007/978-3-031-46314-3_23

© The Author(s), under exclusive license to Springer Nature Switzerland AG 2023
H. Lu et al. (Eds.): ICIG 2023, LNCS 14358, p. C1, 2023.
ttps://doi.org/10.1007/978-3-031-46314-3_34

Author Index

© The Editor(s) (if applicable) and The Author(s), under exclusive license
to Springer Nature Switzerland AG 2023
H. Lu et al. (Eds.): ICIG 2023, LNCS 14358, pp. 425–426, 2023.
https://doi.org/10.1007/978-3-031-46314-3

Printed in the United States
by Baker & Taylor Publisher Services